The Military History
of Late Rome
AD 395–425

For my wife Sini, and children Ari and Nanna

The Military History of Late Rome AD 395–425

Dr. Ilkka Syvänne

As Plato observed, the military is like a dog, who fights loyally for the master he knows. Addressing soldiers of all ranks by name especially inspires them. Homer voices this excellent advice through Agamemnon. Finally, war is the king's craft and his soldiers his tools. He must know them to use them well. ... Naturally, his own people best provide this soldiery. ... The military must be kin with them it defends, or it will prey upon them.

Synesius, *de Regno*, tr. by Alan Cameron

Pen & Sword
MILITARY

First published in Great Britain in 2020 by
Pen & Sword Military
an imprint of
Pen & Sword Books Ltd
47 Church Street
Barnsley
South Yorkshire
S70 2AS

ISBN 978 1 84884 854 2

A CIP catalogue record for this book is available from the British Library

Typeset in Ehrhardt by
Mac Style
Printed and bound in the UK by TJ Books Ltd, Padstow, Cornwall

Pen & Sword Books Limited incorporates the imprints of Atlas,
Archaeology, Aviation, Discovery, Family History, Fiction, History,
Maritime, Military, Military Classics, Politics, Select, Transport,
True Crime, Air World, Frontline Publishing, Leo Cooper,
Remember When, Seaforth Publishing, The Praetorian Press,
Wharncliffe Local History, Wharncliffe Transport,
Wharncliffe True Crime and White Owl.

For a complete list of Pen & Sword titles please contact
PEN & SWORD BOOKS LIMITED
47 Church Street, Barnsley, South Yorkshire, S70 2AS, England
E-mail: enquiries@pen-and-sword.co.uk
Website: www.pen-and-sword.co.uk

Contents

Acknowledgements

Acknowledgments are due to the very same persons that I mentioned in the first book. I thank both Professor Geoffrey Greatrex for his recommendation and the Commissioning Editor Philip Sidnell for accepting my book proposal. Similarly, I owe a big thanks to Matt Jones and others in the Pen & Sword for their stellar work.

I also thank my family Sini, Ari and Nanna for their patience.

Thanks are also due to my father and late mother who unknowingly also contributed to this volume by bringing back books and photos from Sicily in May 2005. The principal results of that trip, however, shall be seen in the MHLR Volume 4.

Professor Geoffrey Greatrex, Lucas MacMahon and Perry Gray also read a chapter or two each, and I thank them for the insightful comments they gave, but none of them is responsible for any remaining mistakes or omissions – for these I am the only one to blame.

I also want to thank in particular Jyrki Halme, a fellow Finn and re-enactor of the Late Roman era, for his outstanding contribution and support. Without his efforts this monograph like the other books of mine would be a lot less colourful. He has not only contributed his photos, but also provided his insight into the period equipment. The Polish re-enactor group Vicus Ultimus also deserves very great thanks for the photos that they have contributed. Anyone who sees these photos immediately understands why I praise them.

None of those who have contributed to this monograph is responsible for any of the mistakes or omissions that remain. Those are the sole responsibility of the author.

List of Plates

List of Maps

Preface

The intention of this book, the third in a series of seven, is to present an overview of all the principal aspects of Roman military history during the years 395–425. It was then that the Empire started its slow decline. The structure of the book follows the reigns of the emperors in chronological order, and the events and wars are also usually presented in chronological order. However, for the sake of ease of reading some events that took place in one particular sector of the empire are grouped together. This uneven survival of evidence means that there are huge gaps in our knowledge and that some of my conclusions are only my best-educated guesses.

The text follows the same principles as the first book and includes direct references to the sources only when my conclusions can be considered controversial or new. I have also not included descriptions or analyses of the sources used and their problems, because there exists expert literature devoted to this subject. Some general comments, however, are in order. All of the period sources had their limitations. The narrative histories were restricted to dealing with only certain types of information (mainly politics and wars) and followed the literary models set before them. The ecclesiastical histories concentrated mainly on religious events. The panegyrics and orations were also naturally restricted by the genre. All the authors writing within the Roman Empire had to take into account the fact that they wrote under dictators who had power over life and death. We should also not forget the personal goals of the authors, which naturally varied. The quality of the Armenian, Georgian, Arabic and Persian histories etc. vary greatly, and in contrast to the Roman material also present legendary material that has to be sifted through carefully. Regardless, in places these sources allow one to shed light on the otherwise murky events and should be treated simply with the same scepticism as the Roman sources.

The content is once again full of terms and expressions that describe the situation with warts and all. It is all too common for historians to fall in love with the subject of their study, so that this results in the whitewash of history. The current trend of following the politically-correct approach reinforces this very unfortunate trend. My approach to history is to attempt to describe the events and persons as accurately and objectively as possible for a historian. I acknowledge, however, that every study is subjective, but that does not remove the responsibility to seek the truth, however ugly it is – and ugly it is. If one wants to understand today's world, one has to understand the past.

In this study when I refer to Spain I mean the whole of the Iberian Peninsula including Lusitania (modern Portugal). However, when I refer to Britain, I mean only the portion under Roman control. This solution has been adopted solely for the sake of making referrals easier.

As far as the language, transliteration, and titles are concerned I have usually adopted the easiest solution. I have used the transliterations most commonly used except in the case of Greek military terms, which I have generally transliterated so that I have maintained the original F of the Greek instead of using the PH. I have also adopted the practice of Oxford University Press and used capital letters for all offices which could be held by only one person at a time. I have also used capital letters for all specific types of troops and military units. However, when I have referred to several office holders simultaneously (e.g. *comites*/counts, *duces*/dukes) I have used small letters.

All illustrations, drawings, maps and diagrams etc. have been drawn and prepared by the author unless stated otherwise. I have used the Barrington Atlas as the principal source for the Maps.

Abbreviations

Cav.	Cavalry
CGall. 452	Chronica Gallica 452 (Chron. Min., Mommsen, Berlin 1892)
CGall. 511	Chronica Gallica 511 (Chron. Min., Mommsen, Berlin 1892)
Com. Dom.	Comes Domesticorum (Count of Domestics)
CRP	Comes Rei Privatae (Count of the Privy Purse)
CSL	Comes Sacrarum Largitionum (Count of the Sacred Largesse)
GC	Georgian Chronicles
Hydat.	Hydatius
Inf.	Infantry
Isid. HRGVS	Isidorus of Seville, *Historia de regibus Gothorum, Vandalorum et Suevorum*
LHF	Anon. *Liber Historiae Francorum*
LI	Light infantry
Mag. Eq.	Magister Equitum (Master of Horse)
Mag. Ped.	Magister Peditum (Master of Foot)
Mag. Eq. et Ped.	Magister Equitum et Peditum (Master of Horse and Foot)
MVM	Magister Utriusque Militiae (Master of All Arms of Service)
MVM Praes.	Magister Utriusque Militiae Praesentales (Praesental MVM)
Mag. Mil.	Magister Militum (Master of Soldiers)
Mag.Off.	Magister Officiorum (Master of Office)
Marc. Com. or Marc.	Marcellinus Comes
Or.	Orations
PKA.	Peri katastaseôs aplêktou also known as De castrametatione and Campaign Organization
PLRE1	See Bibliography
PLRE2	See Bibliography
PP	Praefectus Praetorio (Praetorian Prefect)
PPI	Praefectus Praetorio Italiae et Africae (PP of Italy and Africa)
PPIL	Praefectus Praetorio Illyrici
PPG	Praefectus Praetorio Galliarum
PPO	Praefectus Praetorio Orientis
PSC	Praepositus Sacri Cubiculi (Leader of Sacred Bedroom)
PVC	Praefectus Urbis Constantiopolitanae (Urban Prefect of Constantinople)
PVR	Praefectus Urbis Romae
QSP	Quaestor Sacri Palatii (Questor of the Sacred Palace)
REF1	See Bibliography
REF2	See Bibliography

strategos = dux maior?
hypostrategos = dux minor?

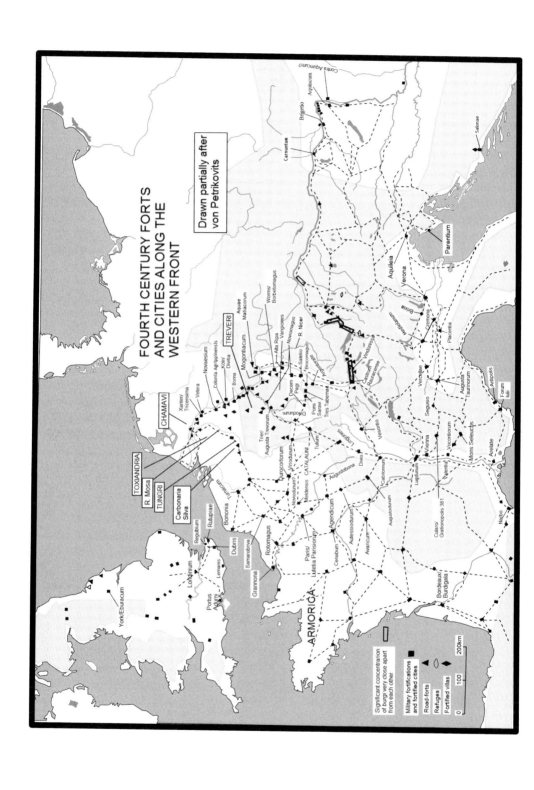

FOURTH CENTURY FORTS
AND CITIES ALONG THE
WESTERN FRONT

Drawn partially after
von Petrikovits

CHAMAVI

TOXIANDRIA

R. Mosa

TUNGRI

Carbonaria
Silva

TREVERI

Aquae
Mattiacorum

Worms/
Borbetomagus

Mogontiacum

Vangiones

Alta Ripa

Noviomagus

R. Nicer

Colonia Agrippinensis

Köln/
Divitia

Bonna

Saletio

Decem
Pagi

Brocomagus

Argentorate

Tres Tabernae

Pons
Saravi

Vindonissa

Castrum
Rauracense

Vetera

Xanten/
Tricensima

Novaesium

Divodurum

Trier/
Augusta Trevorum

Turicortorum

Virodunum

Tullum

Langones

Mediensis CATALAUNI

Noviodunum

Augustobona

Dibio

Cabillonum

Augustodunum

Culars/
Grationopolis 381

Valentia

Lugdunum

Vienna

Voccortorum

Mons Seleucis

Arelate

Narbo

Bordeaux/
Burdigala

Avaricum

Augustodunum

Cenabum

Autessiodorum

Agendicum

Paris/
Lutetia Parisiorum

Rotomagus

Grannona

Samarobriva

Dubris

Rutupiae

Bononia

Regulbium

Lemanis

Londinium

Portus
Adurni

York/Eburacum

ARMORICA

Vesontio

Cremona

Placentia

Vindonissa

Mediolanum

Brixia

Verona

Aquileia

Parentium

Antipolis

Forum
Iulii

Segusio

Vercellae

Augusta
Taurinorum

Salonae

Carnuntum

Brigetio

Aquincum

Contra Aquincum?

Significant concentration
of burgi very close apart
from each other

■ Military fortifications
and fortified cities

◀ Road-forts

◆ Refuges

◆ Fortified villas

0   100   200km

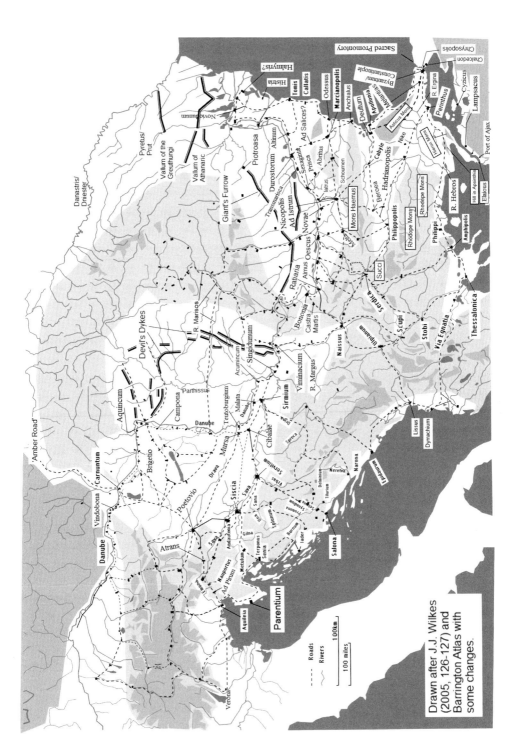

Drawn after J.J. Wilkes (2005, 126-127) and Barrington Atlas with some changes.

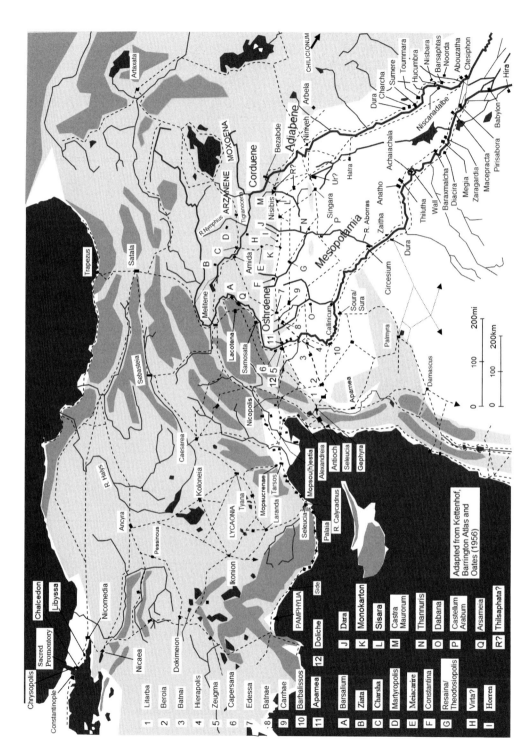

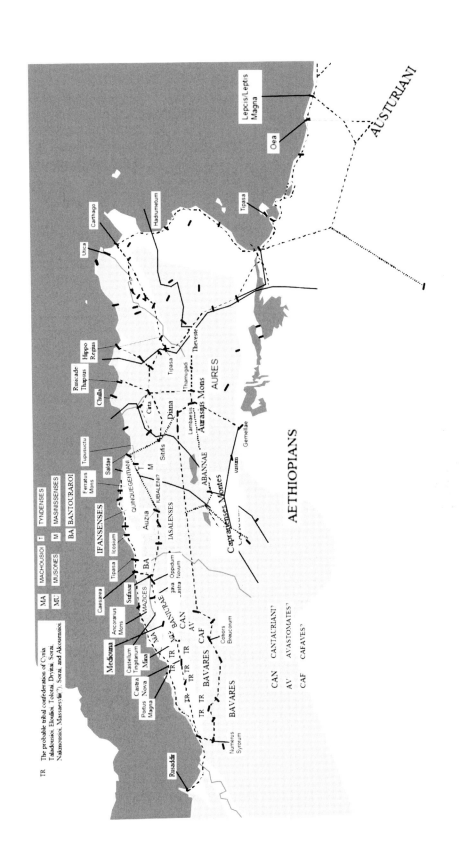

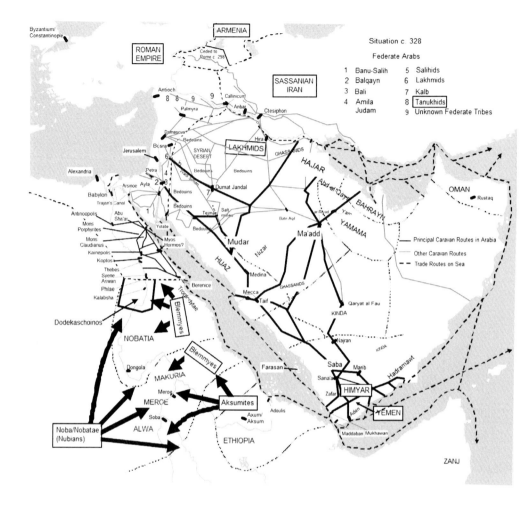

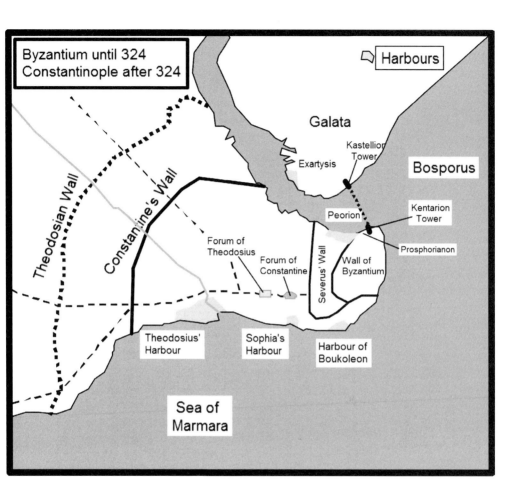

Byzantium until 324
Constantinople after 324

Harbours

Galata

Bosporus

Theodosian Wall

Constantine's Wall

Kastellion Tower

Exartysis

Peorion

Kentarion Tower

Prosphorianon

Forum of Theodosius

Forum of Constantine

Severus' Wall

Wall of Byzantium

Theodosius' Harbour

Sophia's Harbour

Harbour of Boukoleon

Sea of Marmara

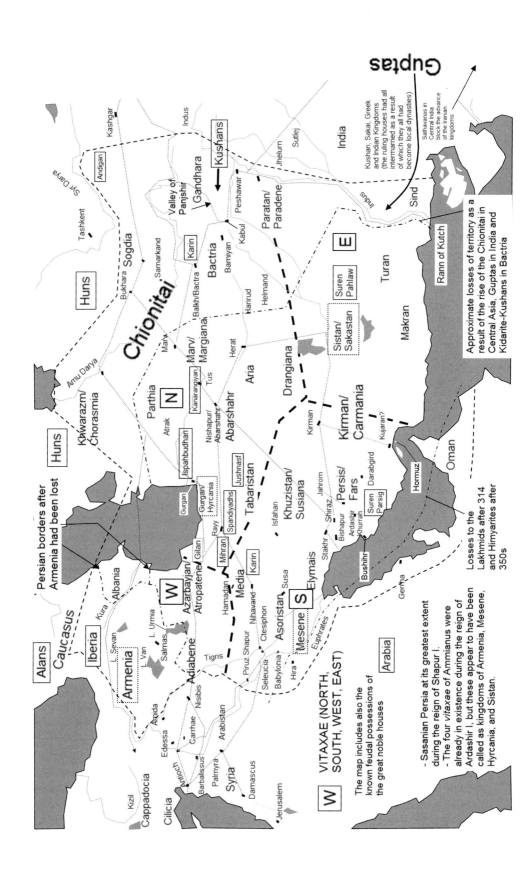

Guptas

Kushan, Sakai, Greek and Indian Kingdoms (the ruling houses had all intermarried as a result of which they all had become local dynasties)

Sathavanas in Central India block the advance of the Iranian kingdoms

India

Kushans

Gandhara

Valley of Panjshir

Karin

Bactria

Bamiyan

Kabul

Peshawar

Paratan/ Paradene

E

Suren Pahlaw

Sistan/ Sakastan

Turan

Makran

Rann of Kutch

Sind

Indus

Approximate losses of territory as a result of the rise of the Chionitai in Central Asia, Guptas in India and Kidarite-Kushans in Bactria

Kashgar

Andigan

Indus

Syr Darya

Tashkent

Huns

Sogdia

Bukhara

Samarkand

Chionitai

Marv/ Margiana

Balkh/Bactra

Herat

Aria

Harirud

Helmand

Drangiana

Kirman/ Carmania

Kirman

Kujaran?

Oman

Hormuz

Amu Darya

Khwarazm/ Chorasmia

Huns

Parthia

Atrak

N

Nishapur/ Abarshahr

Kanaranqiyan

Tus

Abarshahr

Isfahan

Persis/ Fars

Shiraz

Jahrom

Darabgird

Bishapur

Ardashir Khurrah

Stakhr

Suren Parsig

Bushihr

Germa

Losses to the Lakhnids after 314 and Himyarites after 350s

Persian borders after Armenia had been lost

Gurgan

Ispahbudhan

Jushnasf

Gurgan/ Hyrcania

Tabaristan

Rayy

Spandiyadhs

Mihran

Karin

Gilan

Azarbaijan/ Atropatene

W

Media

Hamadan

Nihavand

Asoristan

Susa

Elymais

Mesene

S

Euphrates

Alans

Caucasus

Iberia

Albania

Kura

L. Sevan

L. Urmia

Salmas

L. Van

Armenia

Adiabene

Nisibis

Arqida

Carrhae

Tigris

Piruz Shapur

Ctesiphon

Seleucia

Babylonia

Hira

Arabistan

Arabia

Edessa

Barbalissus

Palmyra

Antioch

Syria

Damascus

Jerusalem

Cappadocia

Cilicia

Kizil

W VITAXAE (NORTH, SOUTH, WEST, EAST)

The map includes also the known feudal possessions of the great noble houses.

- Sasanian Persia at its greatest extent during the reign of Shapur I.
- The four vitaxae of Ammianus were already in existence during the reign of Ardashir I, but these appear to have been called as kingdoms of Armenia, Mesene, Hyrcania, and Sistan.

Jhelum

Sutlej

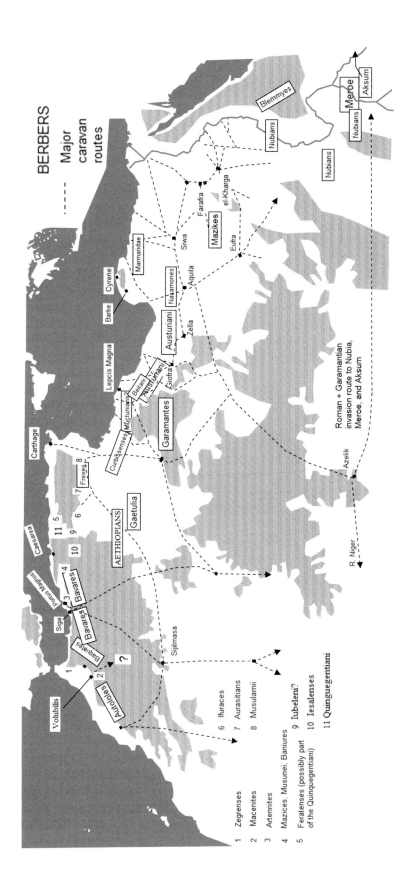

BERBERS

----- Major caravan routes

Volubilis
Siga
Portus Magnus
Caesarea
Carthage
Lepcis Magna
Barke
Cyrene
Marmaridae
Siwa
Farafra
el-Kharga
Blemmyes
Nubians
Meroe
Aksum
Nubians
Nubians
Mazikes
Eufra
Aquila
Nasamones
Austuriani
Zella
Giofra
Beitani
Xustuniani
Garamantes
Curbissenses
Micturiani?
Frexes
AETHIOPIANS
Gaetulia
Bavares
Bavares
Baquates
Autololes
Sijilmasa
Azelik
R. Niger

Roman + Garamantian invasion route to Nubia, Meroe, and Aksum

1   Zegrenses
2   Macenites
3   Artennites
4   Mazices, Musunei, Baniures
5   Feratenses (possibly part of the Quinquegentiani)
6   Ifuraces
7   Aurasitians
8   Musulamii
9   **Iubeleni?**
10 **Iesalenses**
11 **Quinguegentiani**

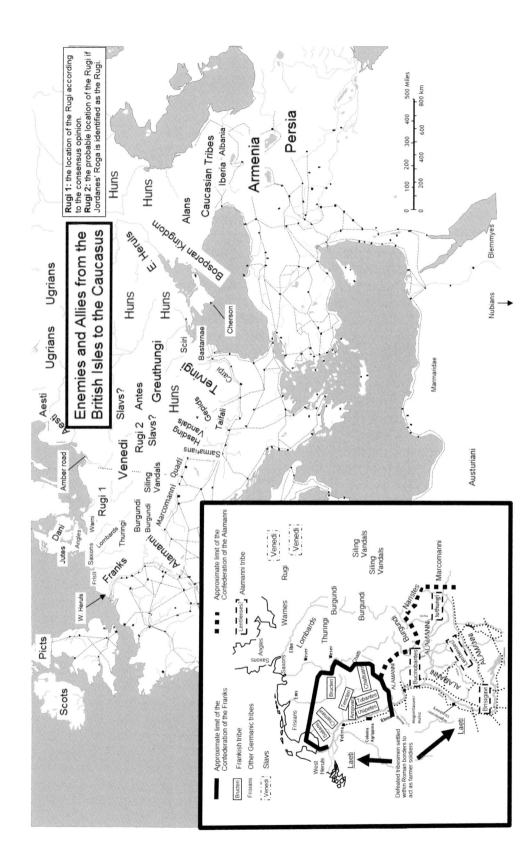

Enemies and Allies from the British Isles to the Caucasus

Rugi 1: the location of the Rugi according to the consensus opinion.
Rugi 2: the probable location of the Rugi if Jordanes' Roga is identified as the Rugi.

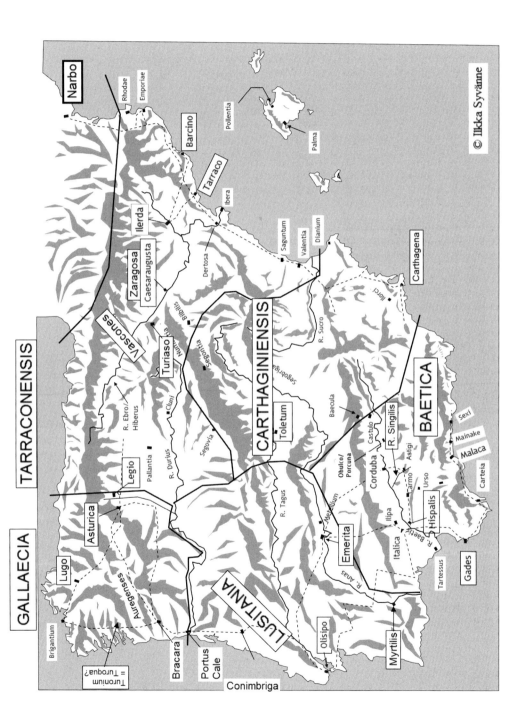

GALLAECIA

TARRACONENSIS

Narbo

Rhodae
Emporiae

Barcino

Tarraco

Ibera

Ilerda

Zaragosa
Caesaraugusta

Dertosa

Saguntum
Valentia
Dianium

Carthagena

Vascones

Turiaso

bilbilis

Segontia

R. Sucro

Segobriga

CARTHAGINIENSIS

BAETICA

R. Ebro/
Hiberus

Cluni

Numantia

Toletum

Baecula

Castulo
R. Singilis

Sexi

Mainake

Malaca

Carteia

Pallantia

Segovia

R. Durius

Ohulco/
Porcuna

Corduba
Astigi
Carmo
Urso

Ilorci

Legio

Asturica

Lugo

R. Tagus

Metellinum

Ilipa

Hispalis

R. Baetis

Auregenses

R. Anas

Emerita

Italica

Tartessus

Gades

Brigantium

Turonium
= Turoqua?

Bracara

Portus
Cale

Conimbriga

LUSITANIA

Olisipo

Myrtilis

© Ilkka Syvänne

Fifth Century Athens

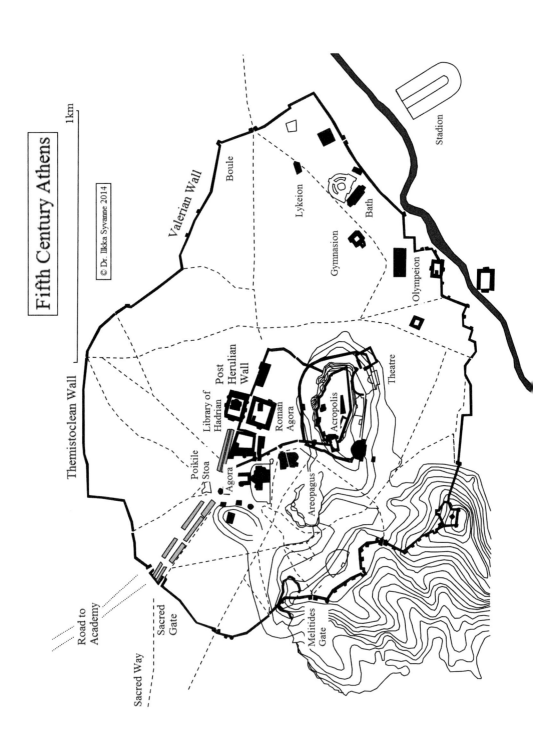

1km

© Dr. Ilkka Syvänne 2014

Themistoclean Wall

Valerian Wall

Road to Academy

Sacred Way

Sacred Gate

Poikile Stoa

Agora

Library of Hadrian

Post Herulian Wall

Roman Agora

Areopagus

Melitides Gate

Acropolis

Theatre

Boule

Lykeion

Gymnasion

Bath

Olympeion

Stadion

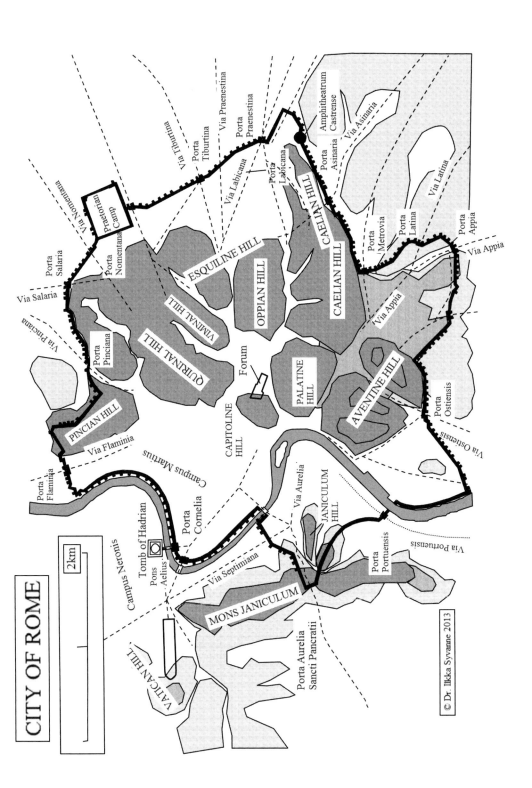

CITY OF ROME

2km

VATICAN HILL

Porta Flaminia
Via Flaminia
PINCIAN HILL
Porta Pinciana
Via Pinciana
Via Salaria
Porta Salaria
Porta Nomentana
Via Nomentana
Praetorian Camp

Via Tiburtina
Porta Tiburtina
Via Praenestina
Porta Praenestina
Via Labicana
Porta Labicana

Amphitheatrum Castrense
Via Asinaria
Porta Asinaria
Via Latina
Porta Appia
Via Appia
Porta Latina
Porta Metrovia
Via Appia

QUIRINAL HILL
VIMINAL HILL
ESQUILINE HILL
OPPIAN HILL
CAELIAN HILL

Forum
CAPITOLINE HILL
PALATINE HILL
AVENTINE HILL

Porta Ostiensis
Via Ostiensis

Campus Martius
Tomb of Hadrian
Campus Neronis
Pons Aelius
Porta Cornelia
Via Septimiana
Via Aurelia
JANICULUM HILL
Via Portuensis
Porta Portuensis

MONS JANICULUM
Porta Aurelia Sancti Pancratii

© Dr. Ilkka Syvänne 2013

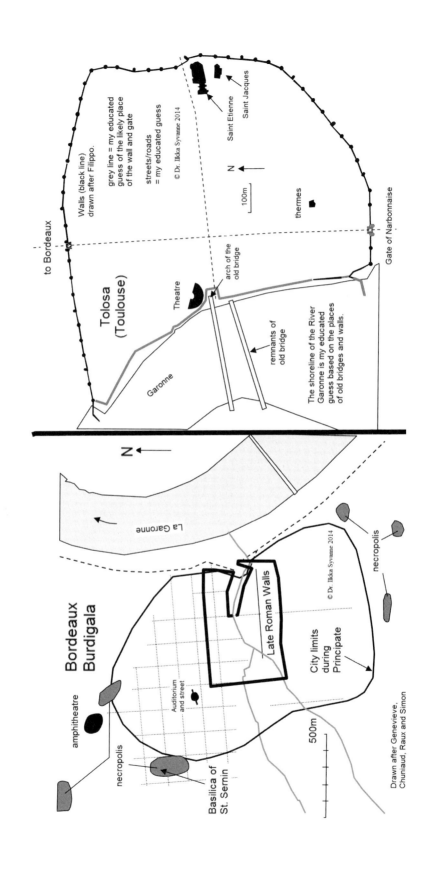

Tolosa (Toulouse)

to Bordeaux

Walls (black line) drawn after Filippo.

grey line = my educated guess of the likely place of the wall and gate

streets/roads = my educated guess

© Dr. Ilkka Syvänne 2014

N

100m

Saint Etienne

Saint Jacques

thermes

Gate of Narbonnaise

Theatre

arch of the old bridge

Garonne

remnants of old bridge

The shoreline of the River Garonne is my educated guess based on the places of old bridges and walls.

N

La Garonne

Bordeaux Burdigala

amphitheatre

necropolis

Auditorium and street

Basilica of St. Sernin

Late Roman Walls

City limits during Principate

necropolis

© Dr. Ilkka Syvänne 2014

500m

Drawn after Genevieve, Chuniaud, Raux and Simon

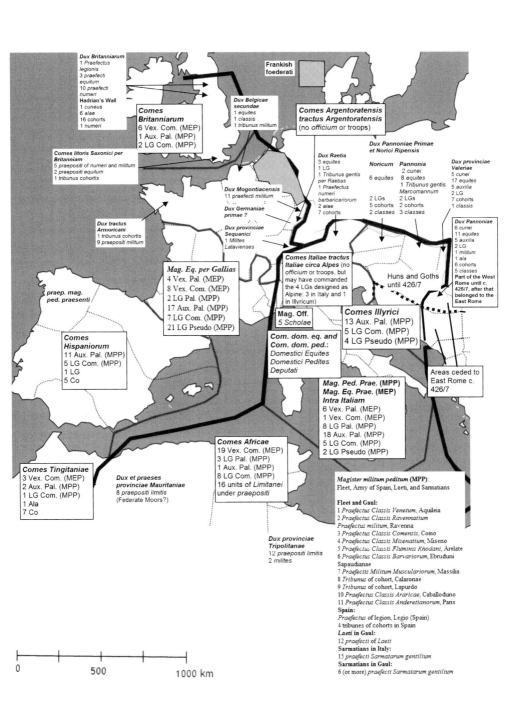

Dux Britanniarum
1 Praefectus
legionis
3 praefecti
equitum
10 praefecti
numeri
Hadrian's Wall
1 cuneus
6 alae
16 cohorts
1 numeri

Comes Britanniarum
6 Vex. Com. (MEP)
1 Aux. Pal. (MPP)
2 LG Com. (MPP)

Frankish
foederati

Comes Argentoratensis tractus Argentoratensis (no officium or troops)

Comes litoris Saxonici per Britanniam
5 praepositi of numeri and militum
2 praepositi equitum
1 tribunus cohortis

Dux Belgicae secundae
1 equites
1 classis
1 tribunus militum

Dux Pannoniae Primae et Norici Ripensis

	Noricum	Pannonia
	6 equites	2 cunei
		8 equites
		1 Tribunus gentis Marcomannum
	2 LGs	2 LGs
	5 cohorts	2 cohorts
	2 classes	3 classes

Dux Raetia
3 equites
1 LG
1 Tribunus gentis per Raetias
1 Praefectus numeri barbaricariorum
2 alae
7 cohorts

Dux provinciae Valeriae
5 cunei
17 equites
5 auxilia
2 LG
7 cohorts
1 classis

Dux Mogontiacensis
11 praefecti militum

Dux Germaniae primae ?

Dux tractus Armoricani
1 tribunus cohortis
9 praepositi militum

Dux provinciae Sequanici
1 Milites Latavienses

Dux Pannoniae
6 cunei
11 equites
5 auxilia
2 LG
1 militum
1 ala
6 cohorts
5 classes
Part of the West Rome until c. 426/7, after that belonged to the East Rome

Comes Italiae tractus Italiae circa Alpes (no officium or troops, but may have commanded the 4 LGs designed as Alpine: 3 in Italy and 1 in Illyricum)

Huns and Goths until 426/7

Mag. Eq. per Gallias
4 Vex. Pal. (MEP)
8 Vex. Com. (MEP)
2 LG Pal. (MPP)
17 Aux. Pal. (MPP)
7 LG Com. (MPP)
21 LG Pseudo (MPP)

Mag. Off.
5 Scholae

Comes Illyrici
13 Aux. Pal. (MPP)
5 LG Com. (MPP)
4 LG Pseudo (MPP)

Com. dom. eq. and Com. dom. ped.:
Domestici Equites
Domestici Pedites
Deputati

praep. mag. ped. praesenti

Comes Hispaniorum
11 Aux. Pal. (MPP)
5 LG Com. (MPP)
1 LG
5 Co

Areas ceded to East Rome c. 426/7

Mag. Ped. Prae. (MPP)
Mag. Eq. Prae. (MEP)
Intra Italiam
6 Vex. Pal. (MEP)
1 Vex. Com. (MEP)
8 LG Pal. (MPP)
18 Aux. Pal. (MPP)
5 LG Com. (MPP)
2 LG Pseudo (MPP)

Comes Africae
19 Vex. Com. (MEP)
3 LG Pal. (MPP)
1 Aux. Pal. (MPP)
8 LG Com. (MPP)
16 units of Limitanei under praepositi

Comes Tingitaniae
3 Vex. Com. (MEP)
2 Aux. Pal. (MPP)
1 LG Com. (MPP)
1 Ala
7 Co

Dux et praeses provinciae Mauritaniae
8 praepositi limitis
(Federate Moors?)

Dux provinciae Tripolitanae
12 praepositi limitis
2 milites

Magister militum peditum (MPP):
Fleet, Army of Spain, Laeti, and Sarmatians

Fleet and Gaul:
1 Praefectus Classis Venetum, Aquileia
2 Praefectus Classis Ravennatium
Praefectus militum, Ravenna
3 Praefectus Classis Comensis, Como
4 Praefectus Classis Misenatium, Miseno
5 Praefectus Classis Fluminis Rhodani, Arelate
6 Praefectus Classis Barvariorum, Ebruduni Sapaudianae
7 Praefectis Militum Muscularionum, Massilia
8 Tribunus of cohort, Calaronae
9 Tribunus of cohort, Lapurdo
10 Praefectus Classis Araricas, Caballoduno
11 Praefectus Classis Anderetianorum, Paris
Spain:
Praefectus of legion, Legio (Spain)
4 tribunes of cohorts in Spain
Laeti in Gaul:
12 praefecti of Laeti
Sarmatians in Italy:
15 praefecti Sarmatarum gentilium
Sarmatians in Gaul:
6 (or more) praefecti Sarmatarum gentilium

0   500   1000 km

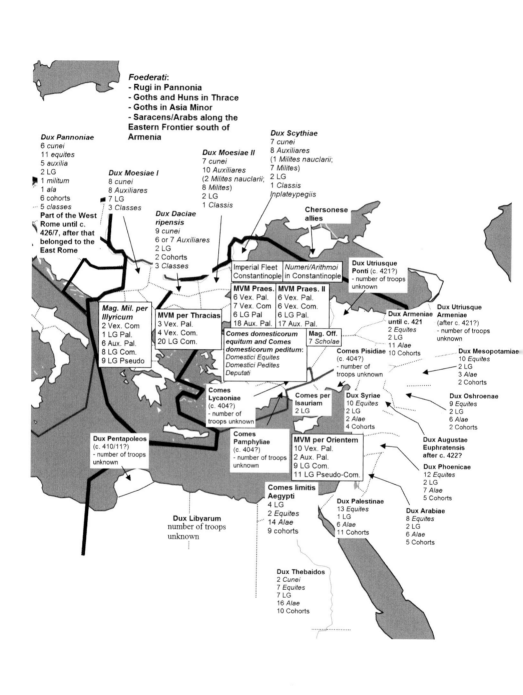

Chapter One

Introduction

1.1: Roman Society and Administration in 395

At the time of Theodosius the Great's death in 395 the Roman Empire was not only divided administratively into two halves, East and West Rome, but it was also a society which was deeply divided within. It was divided by religion, class, and race.

The weakness of the emperors vis-à-vis their generals after the year 363 had resulted in the permanent division of the Empire so that each half possessed its own Emperor, administration and armed forces. The administrators and soldiers of each half had their own vested interests to uphold, which meant that the two halves could cooperate effectively only for short periods of time – typically, cooperation in the fifth century ended when some Western individual (emperor or *magister*) reasserted his own power vis-à-vis the easterners by resorting to the use of foreign tribesmen against the easterners. The widespread corruption of the high-ranking military and of civil servants had alienated both the common soldiers and civilians from society, so that both could see their own ruling classes as their real enemies and the barbarians as their saviours.

Some sections of the population, which included a very significant portion of the senatorial class, had also grown tired of the presence of barbarian federates on their soil and had started to yearn for the old glory days of the ancient Roman Empire. These persons had formed a false image of the past so that they thought that it had been the native Romans who had forged the Empire without any help from the allies. These same persons also considered the high ranking military officers of barbarian or half-barbarian descent to be obstacles to their own careers and had therefore developed highly-racist attitudes towards the barbarians living in their midst. These men accused the foreigners of disloyalty and thought that the top positions within the Empire should be the preserve of native, cultured Romans.

At the very top of the Roman administration was naturally the Emperor, with the title of Augustus, who usually designated his successor with the title Caesar, but in 395 there were no Caesars and neither of the *augusti* ruled in practice because both were young and inexperienced. In the West the de facto ruler was *Mag.Ped.* Stilicho and in the East the *PPO* Rufinus. The Emperor was advised in all important matters by the Consistory, which acted as a Council of the State. In practice, however, the Emperor (or the power behind the throne) could make whatever decisions were necessary without consulting this body of advisors, let alone the Senate, which was also supposed to act in this advisory role. Indeed, there still existed senates in Rome and Constantinople which could be included in the decision making process as a rubber stamp when the Emperor (or the power behind the throne) wanted to court the goodwill of the moneyed senators, but this was not usually necessary and could not be done when it was important to make decisions fast.

The imperial administration was divided into three sections: 1) Military; 2) Palatine; and 3) Imperial and Fiscal Administration. In the West the *Mag.Ped.* acted as a supreme commander of all armed forces thanks to the power wielded by the *Mag.Ped.* Stilicho. In the East the Military Command was hierarchially divided among the *magistri* (masters) so that the two praesental *magistri* had a superior position. The division of the uppermost command into two commands in the East weakened the relative position of the military vis-à-vis the Emperor and other members of the administration, with the result that the de facto power in the East was in the hands of the *PPO* Rufinus in 395. The morale of the armed forces was low thanks to the widespread corruption of the top brass. (See Vol. 2.) The top brass acted as a sort of godfathers for criminal gangs who extorted the salaries of the soldiers. The men who stole the money and gave their higher-ups their share of the loot were naturally the officers directly in contact with the rank-and-file. The military mafia also offered protection to those civilians who paid bribes so that they would not have to pay taxes. The officers also kept 'dead souls' in the books so that they could pocket their salaries. The relationship between the armed forces and civilians was also very low thanks to this very same fact. The officers in general can be considered to have been greedy criminals.

The Palatine Administration was divided into two halves. The Palace and its staff were controlled by the *Praepositus Sacri Cubiculi* (First/Chamberlain of the Sacred Bedchamber), who was usually a eunuch. The *spatharii* (sword-bearers) who served under the *PSC* were also used as bodyguards of the Emperor and Empress. The other half of the Palatine Administration consisted of the imperial bodyguards proper, who served under the *Magister Officiorum* (Master of Offices) under whom served the *Comes Domesticorum* or *comites domesticorum* and the actual bodyguards.

The actual administrators of the Empire served under the *Magister Officiorum*. In this capacity the *Magister Officiorum* acted as a sort of Prime and Foreign Minister. In addition to this, he was the Spy Master of the Empire who commanded the professional spies, bodyguard units, the *agentes in rebus*, and the *notarii*. The actual military intelligence was primarily conducted by the armed forces under the guidance of the *protectores domestici*, dispatched to the staffs of generals for this purpose. The imperial *Quaestor* prepared legislation and wrote responses to the petitions and letters sent to the emperor.

The provinces and collection of taxes were under three parallel administrations (the Praetorian Prefecture, the *Comes* of the Sacred Largesse, and the *Comes res privatae*). The *annona* (taxes in kind paid to the soldiers) and other regular taxes were collected by the local city councils under the guidance of the praetorian prefects and their personnel. The so-called donatives (money and bullion given to soldiers on special occasions, paid by the middle class and the rich) were collected by the *Comes* of the Sacred Largesse through his workforce. The *Comes res privatae* was in charge of collecting the taxes/profits/rents from imperial lands and businesses. In practice, the soldiers, *agentes in rebus*, *curiosi* and *notarii* infringed upon this system so that they extorted money from the city councils, taxpayers and civil servants. This was too easy for all of these organizations to do. The civil servants needed detachments of soldiers to protect them during the collection of taxes, which meant that the soldiers stole part of the taxes. The other officials in their turn could extort part of the taxes/profit thanks to their position as spies and inspectors.

The diagram below gives a general overview of the administrative system of the Roman Empire in 395. It is based on the diagrams of Syvänne (Vols. 1–2), Haldon and Delmaire. It gives only a general glimpse of the system and may contain some features which were not in force in 395, the reason for this being the fact that emperors changed the system as required by the situation so that the administrative system was not the same throughout the Late-Roman period. For example, it is well known that the *PPO* Rufinus had control of the imperial arms factories, which were then taken away from the prefecture and placed under the *Magister Officiorum* when he fell from power.

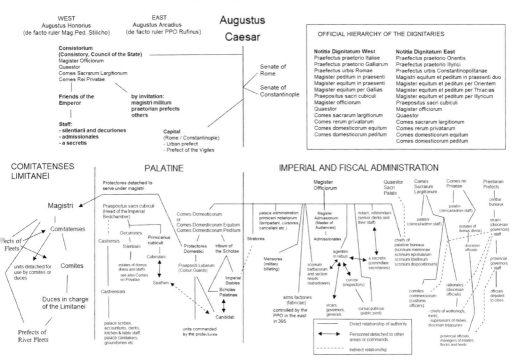

ROMAN ADMINISTRATION IN 395

Intelligence Gathering

The Late-Roman intelligence gathering network consisted of the following basic components: 1) the Emperor's special operatives; 2) the units of bodyguards and their detached personnel (esp. the *Protectores Domestici*); 3) professional spies operated by the military leadership with the help of the *Protectores* on their staff; 4) regular military forces; 5) *Agentes in Rebus* and *Notarii*; 6) civilian policemen and paramilitary forces; 7) religious control wielded by the emperor through priests; and 8) informers. The first seven organizations were used for both internal and external security functions, while number eight served only internal security needs. The following diagram gives a summary of the organization. At the turn of the fifth century the effectiveness of the organization suffered from the effects of the massive corruption of the military forces. For further details, see Syvänne MHLR Vols. 1–2 and Syvänne 2015 ASMEA.[1]

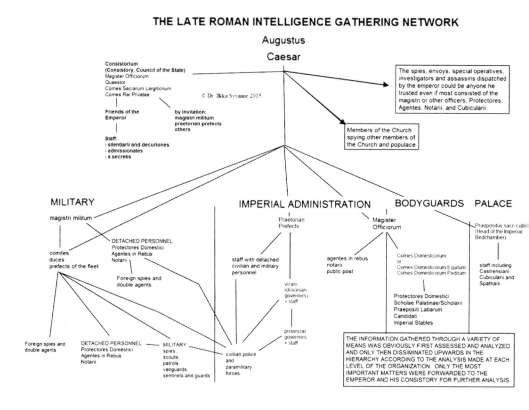

1.2: The Military in 395[2]

Strategy

The era from 395 until about 491 saw a massive increase in the size of a typical field army. This process had already started during the period under discussion (395–425). There were several reasons for this sudden massing together of the manpower to form massive field armies that had been previously distributed around the various frontiers and cities. Firstly, the migrating peoples increased the sheer scale of the problems facing the Romans. Secondly, the frontier- and field-armies were less effective than previously thanks to the poor motivation and morale among the rank-and-file caused by corruption, which made it necessary to gather together resources. Thirdly, fifth-century military commanders preferred on a conceptual level quantity over the quality, which was criticized by Vegetius (see below). It was largely thanks to the vast resources, wealth and the sophisticated administrative structures of the Roman Empire that the Roman marshals could adopt this ultimately self-destructive course.

Vegetius' treatise includes scathing criticisms of this approach:

> However, in every battle it is not so much numbers and untrained force as it is skill and training that are accustomed to bring victory.
>
> Preface, tr. by Stelten p.3

An army is referred to as a multitude, not only of legions, but also of auxiliaries [*i.e. foederati*] and even of cavalrymen, brought together for waging war. The extent of this is determined by the teachers of warfare. For when the examples are reread of Xerxes, Darius, Mithridates and other kings, who equipped innumerable peoples for battle it appears evident that exceedingly large armies were suppressed more because of their own multitude than because of the courage of the enemy [*i.e. Vegetius criticizes the contemporary use of huge armies which consisted of numerous different peoples and compares this with the Persian practice*]. For too great a multitude is subject to very many misfortunes; it is always slower on the marches in proportion to its own mass of men: indeed, on longer lines of march it is liable to suffer sudden attack even from a few men; moreover, in crossing difficult places of rivers, it is often caught off guard on account of the delay caused by the baggage; furthermore, food for numerous animals and horses is gathered with great effort. Also the problems involving the grain supply, which in every expedition must be avoided, quickly wear out larger armies; for no matter with what diligence the grain supply is prepared, it fails that much sooner in proportion to the greater number of whom it is sought. And finally the water itself is sometimes barely sufficient for an excessive multitude. But if by accident the battle line should retreat, it is inevitable that many from a large number fall and those who have fled, once they have been terrified, afterwards fear battle [*with this statement Vegetius notes that when the army is larger the casualties and demoralization of the survivors are proportionally greater after a defeat, which in turn made it more difficult for the Romans to mount a new attack against the enemy*]. The ancients, however, who had learned the remedies for these difficulties by experience, wished to have an army not so large in number as skilled in arms. Therefore, in less serious wars they believed that one legion with mixed auxiliaries, that is 10,000 foot soldiers and 2,000 cavalrymen, was able to be sufficient; which unit, praetores, as lesser leaders, often led into the military operations [*in a late Roman context this would represent a ducal frontier army*]. But if the force of the enemy was said to be great, a consular power, as a major official, was sent out with 20,000 foot soldiers and 4,000 cavalrymen [*in a late Roman context this would represent a field army under a single magister militum*]. But if an infinite multitude from most savage nations rose up in arms [*i.e. a migrating horde of the fifth century AD, which was like the invasion of the Teutons and Cimbri of the late Republic, or any of the subsequent mass migrations*], then with extreme necessity compelling, two leaders and two armies were sent out with a command of this type [*in a late Roman context this would represent two field/praesental armies*]. … Finally, although in diverse regions against diverse enemies war was fought almost every year by the Roman people, the supply of soldiers was sufficient because they judged it more useful not to have such large armies [*unlike the commanders of Vegetius' lifetime*] but rather to have more armies [*the amassing of resources into a single massive field army in the fifth century made it impossible to engage several enemies simultaneously on other fronts, but it obviously enabled the massing of forces for a pitched battle against a single enemy, while with the use of several smaller armies it was not possible to fight decisive pitched battle, but allowed the engagement of the enemy in a protracted guerrilla war to starve the enemy out*]; nevertheless, with this rule being preserved, that there never would be a greater multitude of allied auxiliaries [*i.e. Gothic foederati in a late Roman context*] than of Roman citizens in a camp.

Vegetius 3.1. tr. b y Stelten 123–5 with parentheses and comments added.

Contrary to the period narrative evidence, far too many historians have claimed that the Late Romans lacked the ability to put massive armies into the field. This does not take into account the fact that the Romans produced such a surplus of agricultural produce that they could support cities with myriads and even hundreds of thousands of inhabitants, the best examples of the latter being Rome, Milan, Alexandria, Antioch and Constantinople. If the administrative organs could provide food for these cities, then these were certainly able to transport similar amounts of food supplies for armies to locales that possessed good roads or rivers or were located close to the coasts. In fact, it took until the 19th century for most of the European cities to attain again the size of cities during Roman times. As far as the infrastructure of the cities is concerned, it took until the latter half of the 19th century for the same cities to obtain amenities like running water and draining/plumbing considered normal signs of civilization in Roman times. One has to take these things into consideration when considering the population sizes and potential military manpower of the Roman Empire.

When one remembers this, the army sizes of the Roman era are not that far-fetched in comparison to the armies of the turn of the 19th century. Rothenberg (25ff.) states that it was the change from subsistence to surplus farming [the existence of the large cities proves that Romans produced a similar surplus!] that enabled the population roughly to double in the 18th century, and that made it possible for Revolutionary France, Napoleon and their enemies to collect armies consisting of hundreds of thousands of men. In short, if the size of the urban population is a reflection of the efficiency of farming practices and of the size of the male population able to bear arms, the Romans clearly possessed at least equal chances to collect large armies as the European states at the end of the 18th century. It should also be stressed that the Romans, just like the Germanic and nomadic tribal confederacies, could march through even sparsely populated areas when they possessed enough oxen-drawn carts and wagons to carry the necessary supplies. The best Napoleonic example of this is Napoleon's Russian campaign, with 614,000 men travelling across vast expenses of sparsely populated areas. It was only thanks to the very skilful use of scorched earth tactics that the Russians were able to defeat the invaders at Moscow. The French ran out of supplies simply because they advanced to Moscow and not to St. Petersburg, which could have been supplied by sea. This option of using scorched earth tactics against wagon-bound enemies was also available to the Romans, but it was not always successful (see Vol.1 and the Persian invasion of 359). As regards the effects of corruption, it should be kept in mind that Napoleon's logistical services were corrupt to the bone and still able to feed the huge armies fielded by him.[3] The same was true of the corrupt Romans.

Vegetius' text also includes another very valuable referral:

> The name of the legions still remains in the army today, but through carelessness of previous generations its strength has been broken, since the desire for honour has replaced the reward of virtue, and soldiers, who had been accustomed to be promoted because of effort, are now promoted through favour [*i.e. the progression in ranks was no longer based on ability but on favour, the result of the widespread corruption after 365*]. Furthermore, after veterans are dismissed through discharge papers ... no others have been recruited. Furthermore, it happens that some are weakened through sickness and are discharged, that some desert or perish ... so that, unless a crowd of young men every year, perhaps every month, takes place of those who withdraw, the army is soon depleted no matter how large it is [*note that Vegetius considered the paper strength to be large and it is in fact possible that he implies that the paper strength of the legion was still 6,000 men and that the reason for the depletion of the strength lay in corruption; i.e. the officers pocketed the salaries of the missing men*]. There is also another reason why the legions are decreasing in number: there is more work in serving in them, the arms are too heavy, the duties too numerous, and the training too severe. Avoiding these, very many hurry to take their oath of military service in the auxiliaries [*i.e. in the foederati*], where both the sweat is less and the rewards come sooner [*this phenomenon can be attested to the reigns of Arcadius and Honorius*].
>
> Vegetius 2.3. tr. by Stelten p.69 with one change and additions inside parentheses.

The above suggests several different things. Firstly, the Romans still possessed large forces on paper, but thanks to the fact that the actual legions (still considered to have been 6,000 strong if Vegetius' referrals to this number are correct) had been depleted through corruption and the officers were no longer capable men (it is therefore no wonder that there were so many barbarian generals), the Roman army was a paper tiger. The second phenomenon was the enrolment of *foederati* among the regular army during the reign of Honorius and the enrolment of the natives among the *foederati* and *bucellarii*, as this was very lucrative for the natives as confirmed by Orosius (7.40ff., esp. 7.40.7, 7.41.7; Olymp. frg. 7.4). It should not be forgotten that at least in the East the enrolment of natives into the *foederati* and *bucellarii* was actually encouraged, at least by the 'anti-barbarian' party if Synesius' thoughts reflected those of Aurelianus, as seems very probable. The goal of this group was to dilute the existing barbarian units with natives so that it would be more difficult for them to revolt. In fact, this policy appears to have been a success in the East and resulted in the creation of a separate commander for all the *foederati*, attested for the first time for the year 422.

The two maps of the troop dispositions in the Map Section show the known locations of the armed forces in the early fifth century. It is based on the *Notitia Dignitatum* and other sources and shows some later developments. (For these, see this volume and Volumes 4–5.) For example, it is quite probable that there were still regular units along the lower Rhine in 395 which are no longer present in the *Notitia Dignitatum*. It is also clear that the separate commands (shown in the second map) which are mentioned for the first time for the reign of Leo in the East actually date from the reigns of Arcadius and Theodosius II, but were still not in existence at the beginning of our period in 395. It is probable that the paper strength of the armed forces remained close to the 645,000. Note that these figures do not include the *bucellarii*, citizen militia, and allies located outside the borders. The *Notitia Dignitatum* also appears to have left out the Gothic and other Federates, which I have added to the maps. The naval strategy of the Empire will be dealt with separately later.

Equipment[4]
The military equipment used by the Romans remained essentially the same as before, but with the difference that the vast majority of the forces appear to have worn lighter armour than previously, as suggested by Vegetius. The best proofs of this are the period works of art which corroborate Vegetius' statement. The standard piece of armour worn by the Roman army appears to have been the muscle armour made out of leather. It should be noted, however, that this does not preclude the use of other types of armour by some selected units. Once again the best proof of this comes from the period works of art which show the Romans using segmented plate, metal muscle, mail, lamellar, and scale armours, and various types of shields. (See Volume 2 along with the illustrations included in this volume.)

The type of equipment worn by the soldiers depended on the type of force and type of mission. The horsemen of the cataphract cavalry and *clibanarii* were fully armoured and meant to break up enemy formations. The horses of the former appear to have carried only frontal armour, while the horses of the latter were more fully protected, but the sources could use the terms *catafractarii* and *clibanarii* interchangeably, which makes the distinction less clear than it probably was officially. It was also typical for them to carry some sort of spear, composite bows, javelins, swords, helmets and shields, but the *clibanarii* proper appear to have not used shields. The equipment used by the regular cavalry was the same with the exception that their horses were usually not armoured or wore only frontal armour. There were also special units of more lightly-equipped horsemen, javelin-throwers, lancers and mounted archers.

The heavy infantry consisted of two main variants: 1) heavy infantry who wore some sort of armour (leather, padded coats, metal armour of mail, scale, plate or lamellar), helmets, swords and used either spears or javelins with different types of shields, depending upon the opponent (against cavalry usually spears and against infantry usually javelins); and 2) multipurpose heavy infantry who carried also composite bows and arrows besides their other equipment. This is not surprising because a quarter to a third of the Roman regular infantry had always been taught how to use the composite bow. These same men could be used as multipurpose troops and light infantry as needed, even if the regulars employed

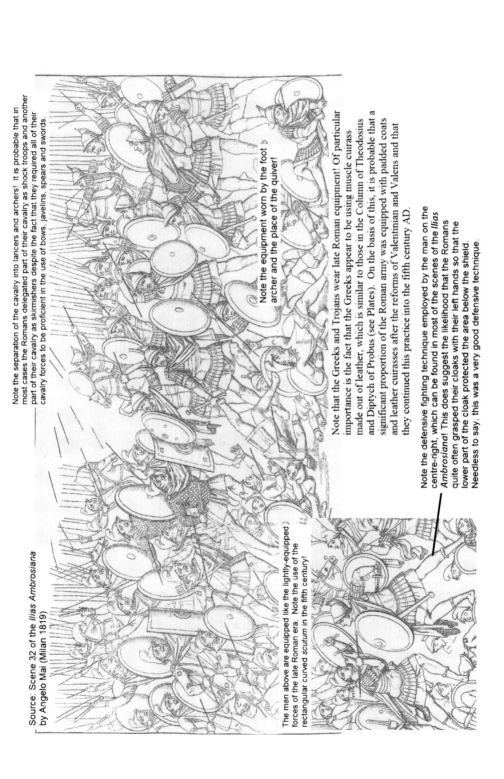

Source: Scene 32 of the *Ilias Ambrosiana* by Angelo Mai (Milan 1819)

Note the separation of the cavalry into lancers and archers! It is probable that in most cases the Romans delegated part of their cavalry as shock troops and another part of their cavalry as skirmishers despite the fact that they required all of their cavalry forces to be proficient in the use of bows, javelins, spears and swords.

Note the equipment worn by the foot archer and the place of the quiver!

Note that the Greeks and Trojans wear late Roman equipment! Of particular importance is the fact that the Greeks appear to be using muscle cuirass made out of leather, which is similar to those in the Column of Theodosius and Diptych of Probus (see Plates). On the basis of this, it is probable that a significant proportion of the Roman army was equipped with padded coats and leather cuirasses after the reforms of Valentinian and Valens and that they continued this practice into the fifth century AD.

Note the defensive fighting technique employed by the man on the centre-right, which can be found in most of the scenes of the *Ilias Ambrosiana!* This does suggest the likelihood that the Romans quite often grasped their cloaks with their left hands so that the lower part of the cloak protected the area below the shield. Needless to say, this was a very good defensive technique.

The men above are equipped like the lightly-equipped forces of the late Roman era. Note the use of the rectangular curved *scutum* in the fifth century!

these usually only in sieges. All soldiers were also taught how to use slings and throw stones and were thus employed whenever needed.

The light infantry proper consisted of three main variants; 1) javelin-throwers equipped with javelins, swords, shields, and helmets or hats (they could wear armour or be without it); 2) slingers who were equipped with slings/staff-slings, swords and helmets or hats (and could carry also shields); and 3) archers who were equipped with bows, arrows, swords and helmets or hats (and could also use armour and shields). When needed the heavy infantry could also be equipped with lighter equipment for use in difficult terrain.

In addition to this, there were specialist units that could use clubs or maces against enemy heavy cavalry or some other pieces of equipment like crossbows or torsion crossbows for other uses. The artillerymen, engineers and other specialists were obviously equipped with their own pieces of equipment so that they could perform their own duties as expected.

The tribal units, such as the various units of Huns, Arabs and Moors, were naturally equipped with their native equipment in addition to which they could use some pieces of Roman equipment.

The illustrations included in this book and Plates Section show the main variants of troops used by the Romans at this time.

According to Menestrier, these five mounted men are likely to be the highest ranking Roman *duces* (generals). It is quite possible that he was right because the typology of the helmets does suggest that each man could have commanded the other men with similar helmets, but it is also possible that these mounted men simply represent the cavalry portion of each similarly helmeted group of soldiers. If four of these men are commanders of the *Scholae* and one *Magister Militum*, then it would be possible to think that the three Gothic commanders (identified here below as Federates) would have been the remaining commanders of the *Scholae* (2 units of *gentile* plus one unknown). Note the rectangular shield for the *dux* on the top centre. Source: Drawing of the Column of Theodosius by Menestrier (1765).

Menestrier identifies this rider as a *Praefectus Excubitorum Imperatoris*, but since the term is anachronistic it is perhaps best to identify him as *Comes Domesticorum*. He would have been in charge of the men wearing helmets of similar style. If this is the case there still remains the problem of how many *Domestici Equites* and *Peditum* there were under Theodosius I. Source: Drawing of the Column of Theodosius by Menestrier (1765).

Three commanders of Gothic origin shown by their fur cloaks (Federate commanders?). It is possible that the leading commander is Fravitta. The second and third ones may represent Gainas and Alaric. Source: Drawing of the Column of Theodosius by Menestrier (1765).

Imperial Bodyguards and Other Bodyguards
In 395 the de facto Imperial Bodyguard of the Emperor consisted of his entire household:
1) *Domestici* (or *Protectores Domestici*) *Pedites* and *Equites* (the elite/officers of the military bodyguards); 2) *Scholae* (including presumably the *Candidati* and *Labarum* Guard) who formed the main military branch of the bodyguards; 3) Personnel under the *Comes* or *Tribunus Stabuli* (Count or Tribune of the Stables or Sacred Stables); 4) Personnel under the *Cura Palatii* (*Kouropalates*; Curator of the Palace); and 5) Eunuchs of the bedchamber.

The reason why I include numbers 3 and 4 among the Imperial Bodyguards is that the Edict issued at Constantinople on 21 March 413 (CTh 6.13) states that: 1) if the *Praepositus* (means acting commander) and tribunes of the *Scholae*, the Tribune of the Sacred Stables and the *Cura Palatii* should obtain the rank of *Comes* together with the *Praepositus* and not attain any higher rank, they were to be numbered equal in rank to the *comites* (counts) of Egypt and of the Diocese of Pontus when they retired from service; 2) if any of these were to obtain the position of *Praepositus* of the *Scholae* without the rank of *Comes*, they were to be ranked equal to the *duces* of the provinces when they retired from service.

This piece of legislation is important for several reasons. Firstly, it proves that the *Scholae* could be commanded by the tribune of the *Scholae*, the tribune of the Sacred Stables, or the *Cura Palatii* without the rank of *Comes* so that these men were considered to be acting commanders (*praepositi*). Secondly, this also suggests that the Tribune of the Stables was sometimes the highest ranking man in the Stables without the rank of *Comes* and one may presume that when he had the rank of *Comes* he was usually also the acting commander of the *Scholae*. Thirdly, it suggests that when the *Comes* or *Tribunus* of the Stables or the *Cura Palatii* exercised command over the *Scholae* that we should include their staffs also among the Imperial Bodyguards. Notably, Aureolus, the famous general of Gallienus, had served in the Stables before becoming *Hipparchos*. Therefore, the inclusion of the staff of the Stables among the Imperial Bodyguards must date from the third century, which is also proven by the presence of the *stratores* (equerries) among the Emperor's cavalry bodyguards and in his presence (see *Caracalla: A Military Biography*). The fact that the *Equites Stablesiani* cavalry units were distributed all over the Empire by the time of the *Notitia Dignitatum* proves that these units (presumably named as *Stablesiani* because these units were commanded by members of the Sacred Stables) were probably formed during the reign of Gallienus or before, and were subsequently separated for security reasons, as happened to many former bodyguard units when rulers changed. Fourthly, this legislation proves that the acting commander of the *Scholae* was not always the *Comes Domesticorum*, as usually presumed. This also brings forth the question of whether we should consider the *Comes Domesticorum* to have been simultaneously the commander of the *Stablesiani* as *Comes Stabuli* and commander of the staff of the *Cura Palatii* when he held the title of *Comes [Stabuli?] et Cura Palatii* or whether this should be the other way around? The fact that Flavius Aetius (formerly *Cura Palatii*) bore the title of *Comes Domesticorum et Sacrorum Stabulorum* in 451 suggests strongly that the *Comes Domesticorum* could act simultaneously as *Comes*/Commander of the *Domestici*, *Stablesiani*, *Curae Palatiorum* and *Scholae*. It is probable that in such cases only one of their commanders held the rank of *Comes* and was therefore superior to all others.

There is also the problem concerning the relationship between the very high ranking *Cura Palatii* and the ordinary, lowly *curae palatiorum* who ranked below the *castrensis* (in charge of the materials of the Imperial Palace). We know that Aetius served as *Cura Palatii* for the usurper John in 423–425 and we know that at least one *Cura Palatii* had the title of *Patricius* in the East during the fifth century (Bury, 1911, 33–34) and that from the reign of Justinian I onwards the title of *Kouropalates* was usually granted only to a designated successor of the Emperor (e.g. Justin II) or to a member of the imperial family (Bury, 1911, 34–35). In fact, Philostorgius (12.14) already calls Aetius, the *Cura Palatii*, 'hypostrategos Iôannou tou Tyrannou' (second-in-command/under/lieutenant general of John the Tyrant). The four men known to have the title of *Cura Palatii* or *Tribunus et Cura Palatii* from the fourth century (see PLRE1) also appear to have belonged to the imperial bodyguards. This means that *Cura Palatii* may have already become a very important rank during the fourth century and definitely was so by the fifth century, and it cannot be identified with the lowly ranking *curae palatiorum*. One possibility is that the *Cura Palatii* was the man in charge of all materials and supplies of the Imperial Palace, including the Imperial Bodyguards. This would have enabled him to exercise great influence over many matters and which would then have helped him to obtain the command of the other units belonging to the Imperial Household.

It is also very likely that Arcadius created new personal bodyguard units for political reasons. According to Theophanes (AM5891) and Malalas (13.47), the Emperor Arcadius created his own military forces known as the *Arcadiaci* at Constantinople in AD 398/9. This was a wise decision. I would actually go so far as to claim, contrary to the consensus opinion among historians, that Arcadius was not quite as ineffectual a ruler as the ancient sources make him to be. (See the narrative for further details.)

In addition to the *Arcadiaci* mentioned by Theophanes, Arcadius also appears to have created an equal number of units called *Honoriani* so that each Arcadiaci unit was paralleled with a unit called *Honoriani*. I would suggest that it is probable that this was also a policy statement on the part of Arcadius and his government, and he must have taken this decision at the time when he was seeking reconciliation with his brother, possibly by renaming some of the units. The *ND Oriens* includes the following, into which I have emended the probably missing units inside parentheses with a question mark.

EAST:

Cavalry:		Infantry	
Palatini and *Comitatenses*			
Vex. Pal.		Aux. Pal.	
Equites Arcades (i.e. Arcadiani)	(Or. 5)	Felices Honoriani iuniores	(Or.5)
[Equites Honoriani?]		Felices Arcadiani iuniores	(Or. 6)
Comites Arcadiaci	(Or. 8)	Felices Arcadiani seniores	(Or. 7)
Comites Honoriaci	(Or. 8)	Felices Honoriani seniores	(Or. 7)

Limitanei

Ala Arcadiana nuper constituta (Or. 28)
[Ala Honoariani?]
Equites Felices Honoriani, Asfynis (Or. 31)
[Equites Felices Arcadiani?]
Equites Felices Honoriani Illyriciani, Constantia (Or. 36)
[Equites Felices Arcadiani Illyriciani?]

The fact that these units are no longer posted in the capital but are spread out according to the *ND*, some even into the *Limitanei*, suggests strongly that after their creation the *Arcadiani/Honoriani* were considered too powerful a concentration of military power by someone in the capital, the most likely candidate for that being the caretaker government that reigned in the name of Theodosius II after the death of Arcadius in 408. The fact that some of the units were demoted to the *Limitanei* suggests that these units may have taken part in some sort of plot against the rulers. The missing units would simply have been disbanded or were sent to the West to support Honorius. It also seems probable that at the time of their creation the *Arcadiaci/Arcadiani/Honoriani* units were grouped together, so that all served under the personal command of the Emperor or his trusted man. The extant cavalry units in the ND suggest a force of over 3,000 horsemen and if one adds the probably-missing units the total is over 5,000 horsemen, which would make the new cavalry bodyguard units even stronger than the *Scholae*. The extant infantry would have had more than 2,000 (if 500+ per unit) or 4,000 (if 1,000+ per unit) men, which would make the infantry component approximately equal in size to the cavalry. However, on the basis of Zosimus' numbers it is also possible that we are talking about considerably more sizable forces than this. It is possible that the cavalry units had 1,600 men apiece and that the infantry contingent would also have been larger. (See below and later.)

As regards the dating of the creation of similar units in the West we are on less certain ground. What is certain is that at the time of the creation of these units the Western government saw no reason to seek the approval of the Eastern government because it did not create any *Arcadiaci* units, but only *Honoriani* units. Similarly, we do not know the reason why and where these units were created. Since all *Honoriani* units (all of which are *palatine* units) in the ND remain subjected to the *Mag.Ped.* and *Mag. Eq.* it appears probable that the *Honoriani* were also created by the Emperor or someone in his court for the protection of the Emperor's person. What is certain is that the *Honoriani* units had been created before the year 407 and that they had been originally Federates who had been enrolled into the regular army and that they had been spread out to different theatres of operation prior to 407. The reason for this is that Orosius (7.40.7) states that the usurper Constantine sent *Honoriaci*, which had previously been *foederati*, against Honorius' cousins in Spain in 407 or 408. The original *foederati* were quite probably created by Stilicho when he campaigned in Gaul in 396, or in 397 by Honorius' advisors (see the narrative), or had been sent from the east, but when these became regular units with the title *Honoriani/Honoriaci* is less certain. It is quite probable that Constantine got his units of *Honoriaci* as a result of the failed campaign of Sarus against him in 407. The rest would still have remained in Italy. It seems probable that the dispositions visible in the ND resulted from a later safety measure by Constantius III, who would have wanted to weaken Honorius' position by spreading the *Honoriani* to different theatres.

In contrast to the East, the Western *Honoriani* had considerably more infantry than cavalry, which may be a reflection of the greater ease of collecting Germans from the Rhine frontier. The size of the cavalry contingent was either 1,500 or 2,000 horsemen while the infantry contingent consisted of 6,500 infantry (if 500+ men *auxilia*) or 7,500 (if 1000+ men *auxilia*) with missing units. It is actually probable that the actual strength would have been close to the 5,000-footmen and 1,600-horsemen *tagma* of Zosimus. The following list once again gives the extant units and adds the probable missing units in parentheses. Considering the use of *tagmata* to denote an ancient legion by Zosimus for this date, it is possible that the *Honoriani auxilia* units consisted of about 1,000 men apiece, the legions of 5,000 apiece and each *equites* of 1,600 men apiece, who were then grouped together into *arithmoi/numeri/legiones* so that there would have been altogether about 6,400 cavalry and 22,000 infantry.[5]

WEST

Cavalry:		Infantry	
Palatini and *Comitatenses*			
Vex. Pal.		Aux. Pal.	
[Equites Honoriani Taifali seniores]		Honoriani Atecotti seniores	(Occ. 5)
Equites Honoriani Taifali iuniores	(Occ. 6)	Honoriani Atecotti iuniores	(Occ. 5)
Equites Honoriani seniores	(Occ. 6)	Honoriani Marcomanni seniores	(Occ. 5)
Equites Honoriani iuniores	(Occ. 6)	Honoriani Marcomanni iuniores	(Occ. 5)
		Honoriani Mauri seniores	(Occ. 5)
		Honoriani Mauri iuniores	(Occ. 5)
		Honoriani Victores iuniores	(Occ. 5)
		[Honoriani Victores seniores]	
		Honoriani Ascarii seniores	(Occ. 5)
		[Honoriani Ascarii iuniores]	
		Honoriani Gallicani	(Occ.5)
[Honoriani Gallicani iuniores?]			
Leg. Comitatenses			
Lanciarii Gallicani Honoriani	(Occ. 5)		
		Honoriani felices Gallicani	(Occ. 5)

As noted in the previous volume, at the turn of the fifth century there also existed unofficial units of private bodyguards which were called collectively *bucellarii* (the eaters of hardtack *bucellatum*). Not only did wealthy individuals like Stilicho and Rufinus have these, but the emperors had theirs too. This development was dangerous because the magnates could use these forces for their private purposes and it is therefore not at all surprising that Stilicho and Rufinus both employed such large numbers of these forces that one can call those real private armies. The mercenary *bucellarii* consisted of both barbarians and Romans and were naturally considered to be elite forces loyal only to their employer.[6]

Regular Army and Foederati

The regular army consisted of four separate forces: 1) *Palatini*; 2) *Comitatenses*; 2) *Limitanei*; and 3) *Foederati*.[7] The *Palatini* units were mobile reserve units that served under praesental *magistri*, but which could also be detached to serve under other officers. They received the highest salaries right after the imperial bodyguard units. The *Comitatenses* consisted of the mobile forces billeted in the cities, which could be used as reserve forces wherever needed. The *Comitatenses* were usually commanded by the *magistri* (masters), but some units were also detached to the frontiers to bolster the forces serving under the local *duces* (dukes) or *comites*. The *Limitanei* served under the *duces* or *comites* along the frontiers. The *Limitanei* were usually expected to protect only the section of the frontier where they were billeted, but when needed they or detachments from these units could still be transferred elsewehere. The *Comitatenses* were considered to consist of higher-grade troops so that they received higher salaries than the *Limitanei*. The so-called *Pseudo-Comitatenses* consisted of former *Limitanei* units which had been promoted to the *Comitatenses*.

Roman Military Doctrine and Campaigns

The standard Roman military doctrine expected: 1) commanders to be skilled professionals; 2) soldiers to possess superior training and equipment; 3) the intelligence gathering to be perfect so that commanders always knew what their enemies were up to; 4) the logistical network to perform so well that it was possible for the Romans to operate without any supply problems in order that they could avoid fighting a pitched battle with the enemy if necessary; 5) that the generals and officers always followed all the standard safety protocols so that the enemy could not learn Roman intentions in advance and so that Roman armies were always protected by layers of spies, scouts and patrols and that the armies were always encamped inside fortifications (either in cities or fortified camps) with access to plentiful supplies of water, fodder and food; 6) their generals to use the best possible strategy and tactics to defeat their enemies; 7) that their soldiers had good morale and fighting spirit (i.e. that they received their salaries regularly and were not subject to abuse by their superiors); 8) that the soldiers were disciplined; and 9) that the Roman civilian population supported their military forces.

During the latter half of the fourth century the Roman military fell well short of this ideal thanks to the fact that the top brass was thoroughly corrupt. There were still elite units close to the imperial court that did perform as expected thanks to the fact that it was less easy to fleece the men close to the prying eyes of the Emperor, but the vast majority of the forces suffered from the results of this corruption. The men were not so well equipped and trained as the military doctrine, expected thanks to the fact that their officers stole their salaries and the roster books were filled up with vast numbers of non-

Two variants of lateral phalanx with reserves not in scale (there were also other variants depending upon the size of the army, the placing of the reserves, and deployment of the light infantry)

left: over 24,000 footmen deployed as double phalanx when the baggage train did not accompany the army. Light infantry shown by the boxes without lines. Light infantry in irregular groups could also be posted on the flanks to make the formation a square.
right: Lateral phalanx with less than 24,000 footmen with the baggage line and artillery carts (the black line). The light infantry posted on the flanks between the heavy infantry and cavalry. This tactic enabled the Romans to use their light infantry against enemy cavalry and infantry simultaneously and also lengthened the line.

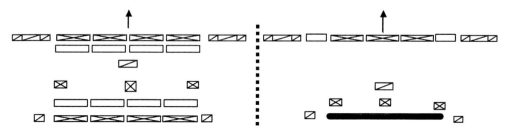

simplified versions of the standard infantry battle formations

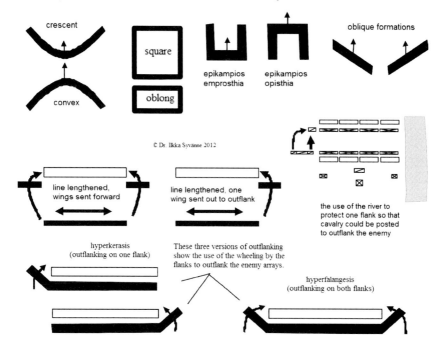

© Dr. Ilkka Syvänne 2012

crescent

convex

square

oblong

epikampios emprosthia

epikampios opisthia

oblique formations

line lengthened, wings sent forward

line lengthened, one wing sent out to outflank

the use of the river to protect one flank so that cavalry could be posted to outflank the enemy

hyperkerasis (outflanking on one flank)

These three versions of outflanking show the use of the wheeling by the flanks to outflank the enemy arrays.

hyperfalangesis (outflanking on both flanks)

HOLLOW SQUARE

Squares with not enough horsemen to form five *parataxeis* per side were to be formed as four *mere/taxeis/parataxeis* per side which does correspond with the number of gates in the 12 taxiarchy formation. (PKA 6, 8.24ff.). It was also possible to place several smaller infantry squares/oblongs side by side so that cavalry was deployed behind and on the flanks.

HOLLOW SQUARE

16 taxiarchies with 8,200 horseman divided into 24 units/*taxeis* (six per side) on addition to which were the imperial reserves (1,000 men) with the emperor. If there were more cavalry, as there were expected to be, these were to be distributed to the sides according to this model (*PKA* 1, 81.-21). According to the *Praecepta Militaria* (2.15), one was to place 12 *parataxeis* into the 12 intervals, but in addition to this figure there appears to have been the reserves and scouts (2.3-8, 2.11). Essentially the same info can also be found from Ouranos' *Taktika*. It should be noted that unlike the *PKA*, these treatises consider each of the corners to be one taxiarchy with the result that the previous researchers have not noted the variant with 12 taxiarchies. It was also possible to place several smaller infantry squares/oblongs side by side so that cavalry was deployed behind and on the flanks

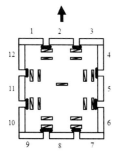

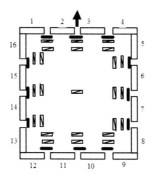

existent soldiers so that the officers could pocket their salaries. On top of that the officers had started to employ mercenaries (*bucellarii*) as their own favourite forces so that they could run their own criminal organizations that fleeced the soldiers and civilians without any of the problems that could have resulted from the use of regulars. Unsurprisingly, the rank-and-file of the armed forces was thoroughly demoralized. It was thanks to this and thanks to the corrupt practices of the tax officials that the civilian population was similarly demoralized and considered their army and imperial administrators to be their enemies. (See Volume 2.)

The standard combat doctrine of the armed forces remained the same as before, for which see Vols. 1 and 2 with Syvänne (2004, 2011). The commander was expected to be ready to use assassinations, political ploys, ruses, ambushes, surprise attacks, pitched battles and siege operations as necessary. The standard mixed formation was still the phalanx with its many variants and the standard cavalry array was the Italian Drill array with two battle lines. The officers expected their men to be able to perform all

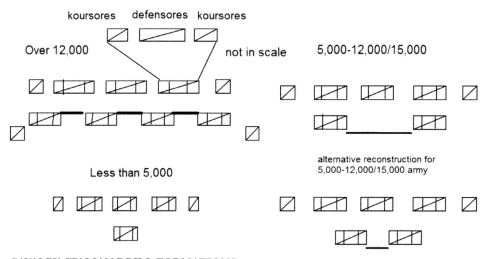

CAVALRY: ITALIAN DRILL FORMATIONS

These arrays were usually preceded by a separate vanguard. Each of the divisions in the array consisted of two elements: *koursores* (runners) and *defensores* (defenders). The former could be used for skirmishing and pursuit of the enemy in irregular order at the gallop while the *defensores* defended them by maintaining their close order at a canter/trot. Alternatively, the whole array could attack without any skirmishing either at the gallop or at the trot in close order. The second support line was usually used as a reserve force while the fill-up units between their divisions ensured that their intervals remained wide enough for the first line to retreat through. The outflankers on the right and the flank guards on the left of the first line were used either to prevent outflanking or were used to outflank the enemy. The third line in the largest variant was used to protect the rear. It was also possible to use separate ambushers outside the array, if the terrain permitted this. If the Romans outnumbered the enemy significantly, they outflanked the enemy on both flanks. If they had approximately the same number of men, they tried to outflank the enemy with their right wing. If they had fewer men than the enemy, they held back their flanks and tried to break the enemy's centre. The cavalry units in this array usually consisted of multi-purpose forces so that the middle ranks of each unit used bows or javelins while the front ranks with armoured horses spearheaded the attack. If this was not possible, then the lighter units were simply placed on both sides of the heavier units to act as *koursores*.

the standard combat manoeuvres associated with the various variations of the phalanx or cavalry formations so that they could face threats from the front, rear and flanks as necessary, deepen or thin the array, and so that they could outflank the enemy array or break through it at a chosen point. The diagrams show the standard variations of the phalanx array in use. After the year 365 the principal array in use was the hollow square/oblong or several hollow oblongs placed side by side. The standard cavalry arrays are shown after the infantry ones.

The Roman Navy

Ships and Combat[8]

Roman naval strategy and tactics were based on their superior ship designs and professional seamen, which gave them an absolute tactical superiority over all of their enemies. This superiority dominated the Roman strategic, operational and tactical thinking until around the 460s. The Roman fleets always sought to engage their enemies in battle so that they would retain complete control over the waterways.

The Roman navy superiority was not limited to a single class of ships, because they employed a far greater variety of specialist ships than any of their enemies could hope to match. The Roman navy used: seagoing war galleys; river galleys and boats; various

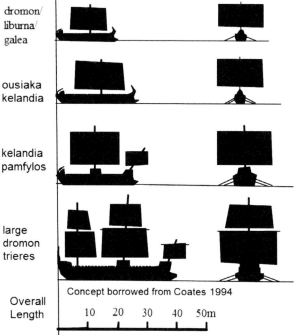

dromon/liburna, a single *ordines* (rank) of oarsmen (30 or 50 oared; 1 or 2 rowers per oar; this version 30 oared/1 rower per oar); 1 mast.

ousiaka kelandia, bireme (each side 2 x 25 oars; one rower per oar); a crew of rowers/marines one *ousia* (108/110 men) plus sailors; 1 mast.

kelandia pamfylos bireme (two rowers per oar in the upper deck and one rower per oar in the lower deck; or two rowers per oar on both decks); a crew of 120-160 rowers/marines plus marines/sailors; 2 masts possibly with several sails.

dromon trieres, bireme, different size variants; upper deck always 3 rowers/marines per oar ('trireme'), lower deck one to two per oar; 220/230 rowers/marines plus other crew including 70 marines/soldiers; masts 2-3 possibly with several sails several per mast; towers 1-3.

dromon/liburna/galea

ousiaka kelandia

kelandia pamfylos

large dromon trieres

Concept borrowed from Coates 1994

Overall Length 10 20 30 40 50m

The number of masts, the number of sails per mast, (some works of art have several sails per mast) and the type of sails (lateen vs. oblong) are all issues of which the historians have so far failed to reach a consensus opinion. It is possible or even probable that there existed several different solutions in simultaneous use during the late Roman period.

© Ilkka Syvänne 2013

types of scouting and patrolling vessels; special transport ships (e.g. horse transports and landing craft); and rafts. These resources were supplemented by corvéed or hired civilian transport/merchant ships.

The principal ship of war was the so-called *liburna/dromon*, which came in various shapes and sizes. This was an era of experimentation. Some of the ships were still using the traditional bronze-ram or the hybrid ram-spur while some of the ships were fitted the newer spur/spike, and in addition some of the ships had several sails or lateen sails instead of the square ones, while some ships may even have had real rudders or were powered by oxen. The sewn ships (dhows), the Germanic longboats, and the Irish curraghs were too weakly constructed to engage the true Roman war galleys in naval combat. All *liburnae/dromones* were bireme galleys which were classed as shown in the illustration (Syvänne, 2004, 2011, 2013–16).

The illustrations show some of the experimental ship types in use at this time.

large transport ships carrying wheat from Africa and Egypt representative of the largest transports used in logistical role (source: Notitia Dignitatum)

Column of Arcadius (ca. 400-408) (no longer extant, drawn after a 16th century illustration)

Illustration in the 5th Century Iliad (Drawn after Pitassi)

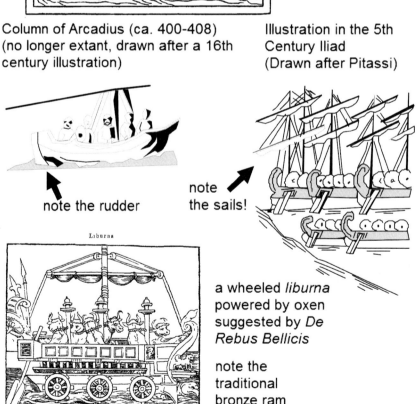

note the rudder

note the sails!

a wheeled *liburna* powered by oxen suggested by *De Rebus Bellicis*

note the traditional bronze ram

The narrative sources suggest that the Romans still used their ships for ramming, but the adoption of the spurs suggest that the nature of naval combat was slowly changing so that the use of missiles (stone throwers, arrow/spear shooters, crossbows, bows, slings, darts, javelins, fire bombs, fire-darts) and boarding actions gained greater importance. The spur could also be used as a spike to puncture the enemy hull above the waterline. The largest dromons could also be equipped with defensive bulwarks and towers and a beam/ram (attached to the mast like a sail-yard) used like a ram against the enemy's deck and personnel.

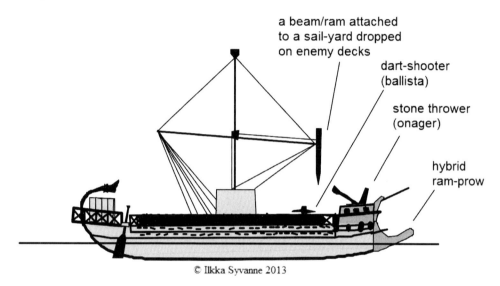

© Ilkka Syvanne 2013

It is also quite clear that the Romans wanted to retain their naval supremacy, hence the stress put on the secrecy aspect of ship construction (CTh 9.40.24 dated 24 Sept. 419, tr. by Pharr, p.258):

> The same Augustuses to Monaxius, Praetorian Prefect. Those persons who have betrayed to the barbarians the art of building ships, that was hitherto unknown to them, shall be freed from imminent punishment and imprisonment because of the petition of the Most Revered Asclepiades, Bishop of the City of Chersonesus, but We degree that capital punishment shall be inflicted both upon these men and upon any others if they should perpetrate anything similar in the future.

The superior ship designs, highly professional seamen and naval officers, and the availability of high quality intelligence of enemy activities formed the basis of Roman naval combat doctrine. The Romans employed joint- and combined-operations, ambushes and surprise attacks, blockades, economic warfare, and battles in battle formation (crescent, convex, phalanx possibly with ships in reserve behind the flanks, double phalanx, circle). The standard combat doctrine was to fight only in fair-weather summers, but when necessary, the Romans did conduct naval operations during winter or in poor weather conditions. See Syvänne (2004, 2011, 2013–16).

The diagram shows the main stages of a naval battle.

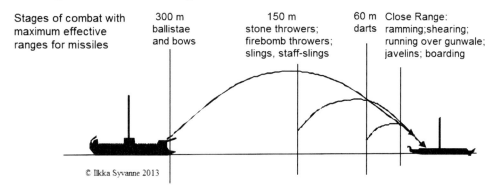

Naval Strategy: Grand Strategy and Strategy.

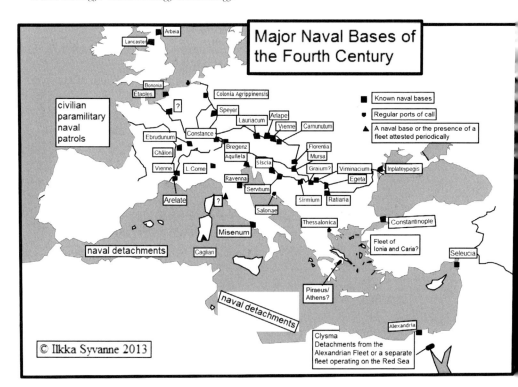

The Romans considered their naval forces and army to be mutually dependent. The mutual dependence is best exemplified by the fact that the Romans almost always employed the two services simultaneously in joint operations. The deployment pattern of the Roman fleets reflected the perceived levels of opposition. The imperial fleets (usually based at Ravenna, Misenum, Aquileia, and Constantinople) with their larger ships formed the strategic reserve and principal naval striking forces of the Empire. Most of the provincial fleets were deployed to oppose enemy raiders and to protect the frontiers. The other areas were protected either by naval detachments, civilian paramilitary forces, or by allies (mainly the Red Sea, Persian Gulf, Arabic Sea, and Indian Ocean). The Roman fleets and their allies could expect to be able to overcome any enemy either through combat, or show of force, or promise of access to Roman markets, or their combination, except when the Romans were undergoing civil wars. The accompanying map shows the principal naval bases of the fourth century.

Even if the naval bases remained the same for most of the time, the ways in which the naval forces were used depended on the needs and goals set up by each Emperor for each particular period of time. This meant that the use of the naval assets usually formed only one aspect of the whole so that the Emperor could attempt to use simultaneously for example a combination of trade embargoes, diplomacy, alliances, threats of military action, and actual military action to achieve a particular objective. Regardless of this some general conclusions can be made. Depending on the type of fleet and the size and type of the vessel used, the fleets were typically used for five major missions: 1) to control the seas, rivers and lakes (enemy fleets were either defeated in combat and/or forced to remain inactive); 2) to project power ashore with amphibious operations, blockades, and active siege operations; 3) to raid enemy coasts and shipping: 4) to protect shipments and trade routes; 5) to protect the cities, coastal areas and other frontiers.

Roman military doctrine also recognized the projection of power from land to sea, which essentially consisted of the capture of ports and harbours by land forces to make it impossible for an enemy fleet to operate. However, during this era the Romans were usually in possession of the harbours, which meant that the same concept was employed against them by their land-based barbarian enemies. The Romans also used far-shooting mural artillery, able to outdistance any ship-mounted artillery, to keep the enemy away from the harbours, which can be considered to belong to the same category of projection of power from the land to the sea.

The coastal defence can be divided into passive/defensive and active/offensive measures taken by the fleets. The former consisted of the forts and towers along the coasts and rivers and of the fortified towns and cities. The duties of the passive/defensive operations (control of harbours, collection of tolls/taxes, prevention of smuggling and wrecking, guarding of the coasts against piratical attacks) were performed mainly by the civilian police/paramilitary forces (probably under a *custodes litorum*) with the support of military forces detached for this duty. The active/offensive measures were mainly performed by the fleets, but corvéed civilian ships could also perform active anti-piratical duties. In extreme emergencies, such as when Stilicho closed the Italian coastline to the East Romans, the Romans corvéed masses of civilian paramilitary forces to support the regular forces in guarding the coasts.

Siege Warfare
This chapter presents only a short analysis of the main features of siege warfare and a summary of the new developments that took place during 395–425. Those who are interested in reading more should consult Volume 1 and my monograph *Age of Hippotoxotai*. Both also include longer bibiliographies that should enable the reader to conduct further research.

Offensive siege techniques consisted of the following: 1) Offer of terms; 2) Surprise attacks; 3) Betrayal of the city by a traitor; 4) Assault with minimum equipment;

5) Assault with siege engines; and 6) Starving the defenders. Defensive siege techniques consisted of the following: 1) Building of sophisticated fortificatations and the storaging of adequate supplies to withstand a siege; 2) Use of walls and siege engines to negate the attack; 3) Use of a relief army against the besiegers; 4) Use of diversionary invasion; 5) Use of guerrilla warfare against the besiegers to starve them into leaving the area; and 6) Offer of terms.

In the first two volumes we have seen that the Romans had inherited a rich tradition of siege engines from the Greeks that they had improved. These included *sambuca*, various kinds of siege towers, various kinds of battering rams (from the simple rams all the way up to the city-taker '*helepolis*'), borers, drills, flails, a 'fire hose' to spread liquids, mining equipment, various types of sheds, fire bombs, cranes, and various types of artillery (small to large ballistae, steel-spring powered artillery, repeating ballista, *onagers* and possibly also mangonels/trebuchets etc.).[9] Some of these are illustrated. (See also Vol. 1.)

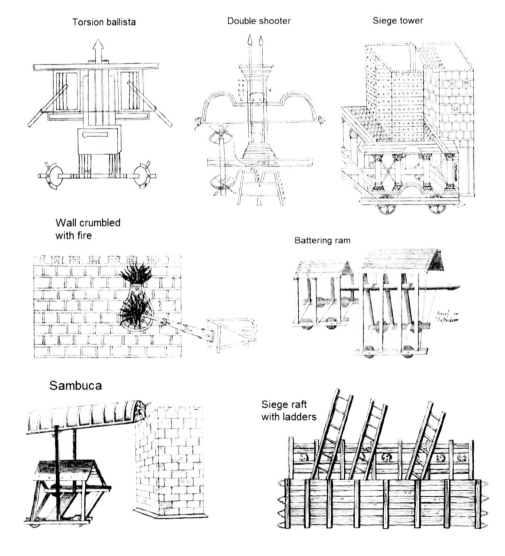

Torsion ballista

Double shooter

Siege tower

Wall crumbled with fire

Battering ram

Sambuca

Siege raft with ladders

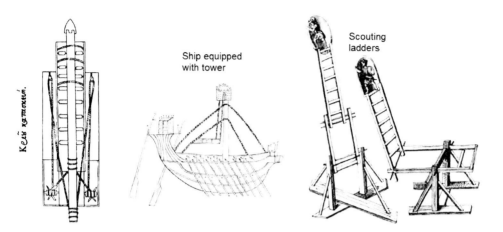

Ship equipped
with tower

Scouting
ladders

The Romans may also have added a new and more-destructive variant of siege artillery to the siege arsenal by the fourth century, which was the trebuchet. The best circumstantial evidence for this are two facts: 1) the Romans had adopted the onager as their standard stone thrower instead of the old extra-large ballista; 2) since the onager could not throw stones/rocks as large as the extra-large ballista, it is probable that the Romans had started to use trebuchets when the intention was to throw heavier objects to crush walls or siege engines; and 3) the sources state that the Roman stone throwers were shooting stones that weighed as much as 181 kg. Regardless of this, it is quite possible that the East Romans continued to employ also the largest ballista variant because the sources constantly demonstrate them using various kinds of ancient devices even in the 11th and 12th centuries.

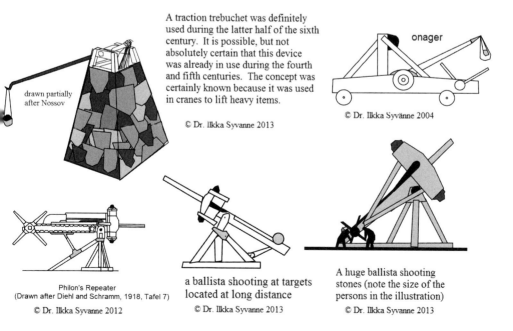

A traction trebuchet was definitely used during the latter half of the sixth century. It is possible, but not absolutely certain that this device was already in use during the fourth and fifth centuries. The concept was certainly known because it was used in cranes to lift heavy items.

© Dr. Ilkka Syvanne 2013

drawn partially after Nossov

onager

© Dr. Ilkka Syvänne 2004

Philon's Repeater
(Drawn after Diehl and Schramm, 1918, Tafel 7)
© Dr. Ilkka Syvanne 2012

a ballista shooting at targets located at long distance
© Dr. Ilkka Syvanne 2013

A huge ballista shooting stones (note the size of the persons in the illustration)
© Dr. Ilkka Syvanne 2013

What is certain is that the Romans were using trebuchets by the sixth century because the *Strategikon* describes an artillery piece in which the beam revolved on both ends which suggests either the use of the counterweight-type or the traction-trebuchet in which the pullers were unprotected. The *Miracula St. Demetrii* describes the Avars (or rather the Slavs in their service using a device that a Roman deserter had taught them to use) using a tower-like trebuchet in which the pullers were inside the protective cover of the tower. This latter variant did not have a beam revolving at both ends like the example shown by the *Strategikon*, which has caused the above-mentioned educated guess on my part. On the basis of this, I would suggest that the East Romans may have already started to use some sort of counterweight trebuchet or alternatively a hybrid trebuchet (counterweight beam with men pulling ropes) by the fourth century. The only problem with this is that Chevedden has shown that the first certain piece of evidence for the hybrid version comes later than this and that the first definite evidence for the use of the counterweight trebuchet comes from the reign of Alexios Komnenos (who may have invented the device). This is actually not conclusive, because it is possible that Alexios Komnenos improved an existing counterweight device, for example by making the counterweight free-moving whereas the older would have had a fixed weight, or that the East Romans had just stopped using the already-invented device just like they had not continued to use the crossbow – the crossbows used by the Normans clearly surprised the East Romans during the eleventh century. The evidence of course is not conclusive and I have included the examples of the various kinds of artillery pieces only to show what types of devices I have described – the only thing that is certain is that the East Romans were able to shoot heavy objects at the enemy. Note, however, that the illustrations do not include the mobile artillery wagons, but these were one of the standard pieces of equipment used. These were also used in set piece battles and during marching to protect the marching column(s), half-square, square or squares.

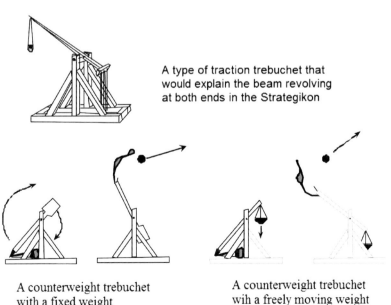

A type of traction trebuchet that would explain the beam revolving at both ends in the Strategikon

A counterweight trebuchet with a fixed weight (drawn after Nossov)

A counterweight trebuchet with a freely moving weight (drawn after Nossov)

The Romans were inheritors of two defensive siege traditions, their own and the Hellenistic siege theory. The former formed the basis upon which the late-fourth-century and early-fifth-century Romans added features borrowed from the Hellenistic theory as presented by Philo of Byzantium (who wrote his treatise probably before ca. 225 BC). The third- to fourth-century Roman fortifications were usually square in shape, but could also follow the lay of the land. The principal building materials for the walls were stone, brick and rubble. The typical shapes for the towers were square, round, u-shaped, octagonal and fan (see Vol. 1). The first extant evidence for the re-introduction of the Hellenistic hexagonal, pentagonal and triangular towers comes from the fort of Alta Ripa which was built by Valentinian I who was clearly very interested in engineering,

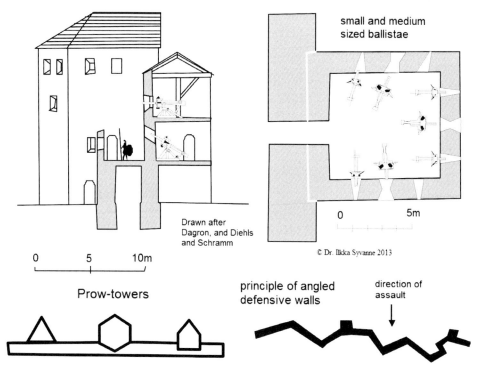

small and medium sized ballistae

Drawn after Dagron, and Diehls and Schramm

© Dr. Ilkka Syvänne 2013

0   5   10m

Prow-towers

principle of angled defensive walls

direction of assault

The accompanying illustrations show some of the principles promoted by Philo of Byzantium in his treatise *Mechanike Syntaxis* Book 5. These included the use of triangular, pentagonal, and hexagonal towers (see the chapters dealing with the cities of Constantinople, Erzurum/Theodosiopolis, Antioch); the use of double walls and the use of angled walls to create cheap substitutes for towers. Of these the use of the angled defences was well-known as, for example, the walls of Dura Europos show, but the East Romans started to add this feature to other walls to make these stronger (note for example the Walls of Thessalonica). As we shall see, the East Romans also resumed the use of the pentagonal prow-tower in their major fortifications during the fifth and sixth centuries. In addition to this, they also started to add a second outer wall to their fortifications, as suggested by Philon (A45ff.), but with the difference that the space between the inner and outer wall was greater. In the case of the Theodosian Walls of the city of Constantinople both walls also had towers. This proves that the East Romans were not mere imitators but also adapted the old theory to new circumstances. The use of Philonian concepts (as well as the continued copying of old treatises) proves that the Romans also used these military treatises, as I have repeatedly stated throughout my career as a historian and military historian!

architecture and military engines. On the basis of this, it is possible that he started the fad of adding prow-towers to the fortifications that becomes ever more evident as the fifth century progressed, so that from the sixth century onwards the prow-towers can be found in most Byzantine walls. The cities and forts with prow-towers datable to this period include: Sergiopolis, Erzurum/Theodosiopolis (see the narrative), Antioch (see the narrative), and Saranda Kolonnes at Paphos in Cyprus. The other new phenomenon for the fifth century is the emergence of double walls of the type that can be evidenced in Constantinople. Taken together, all of these additions made the walls more defensible and stronger than before which suggests that the siege skills of the enemies of Rome had improved. The angled defences provided by the prow-towers were particularly useful against artillery, which suggests that enemies had improved that arm of service in particular. (For a fuller discussion, see the narrative in Vol.4.[10]) On the basis of the many fortification projects around the Empire, especially during the reign of Theodosius II, it would be easy to fall into the perception that the Romans had entirely adopted a defensive 'Maginot' mentality – this is false. The Romans always assumed the offensive whenever they possessed enough military strength, for example against the Persians in 421–422, against the Huns in 426/7 and after 450, and against the Vandals (See Vol. 4). Regardless, it is still clear that the fifth century can be characterized as the century during which the Romans resorted to the use of fortifications more than in previous centuries to even out the odds – in the case of East Rome quite successfully.

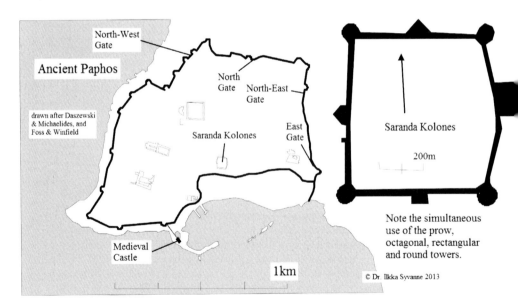

Ancient Paphos

North-West Gate

North Gate

North-East Gate

East Gate

Saranda Kolones

Medieval Castle

drawn after Daszewski & Michaelides, and Foss & Winfield

1km

Saranda Kolones

200m

Note the simultaneous use of the prow, octagonal, rectangular and round towers.

© Dr. Ilkka Syvänne 2013

Roman defensive systems varied according to region, but in general consisted of the following elements: 1) Spies inside enemy territory; 2) Forward-posted guard towers, small forts, patrols (foot, horse, boats); 3) Fortified manors, villas and villages; 4) Defensive lines (roads with forts and fortifications and fortified cities, or actual linear walls such as Hadrian's Wall, or seas/rivers with forces to guard those) guarded by frontier forces and allied barbarians; 5) Fortified cities, and blocking walls (e.g. at Chersonesus, Thermopylae) to block a route with mobile reserves; 6) Strategically important cities relatively close to the border that possessed sizable garrisons and which could be used as forward staging posts for invasions, such as York, London, Boulogne, Cologne, Treves (Trier), Mogontiacum (Mainz), Argentorate (Strasbourg), Vindonissa, Carnuntum, Aquincum, Mursa, Sirmium, Singidunum, Viminacium, Naissus, Oescus, Novae, Marcianopolis, Noviodunum, Satala, Trapezus, Theodosiopolis (Erzurum), Samosata, Melitene, Amida, Edessa, Theodosiopolis (Resaina), Callinicum, Palmyra, and Damascus; 7) Small, less-important cities located at strategic crossroads or important river crossings such as Paris, Tours, Orleans, Poetovio, Callinicum, Barbalissus, or the capitals of the provinces; 8) Psychologically and strategically important cities further inland or further along the coast such as Lugdunum (Lyons), Valentia (Valence), Arelate (Arles), Marseilles, Burdigala (Bordeaux), Tolosa (Toulouse), Narbo (Narbonne), Carthagena, Carthage, Naples, Rome, Ravenna, Milan, Aquileia, Siscia, Serdica, Philippopolis, Hadrianopolis (Adrianople), Constantinople, Thessalonica, and Alexandria; 9) Major logistical hubs and military bases such as Arelate, Ticinum (Pavia), Bononia (Bologna), Ravenna, Aquileia, Carthage, Salona, Thessalonica, Constantinople, and Antioch/Seleucia.

The drawing of the city of Bologna by Ovidio Montalbani (1601) is included here as an example of a major logistical hub and military base. It demonstrates well the concept of having an outer wall for the core city, which would have been used to house the troops in transit. When the government decided to assemble a major army, the space between the walls was used as safe camping grounds for the army.[11] These cities were usually

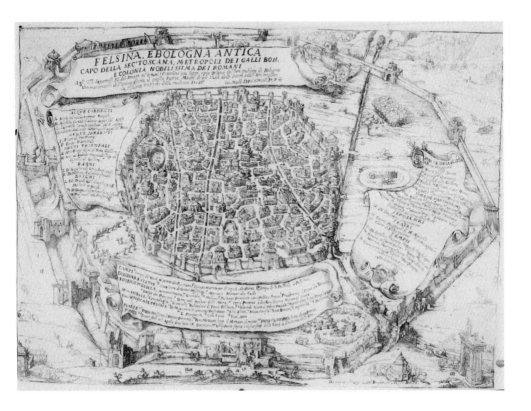

better fortified than the rest and possessed sizable garrisons to form the core force of the field armies due to be assembled there. The same concept can also be found in the wall system of the city of Constantinople after the building of the Theodosian Walls, however eventually both cities grew up to the new walls. Additional examples of all types of cities can be found in the body of the text.

At the beginning of the period under discussion the Romans and Sasanians were the most sophisticated practitioners of siege warfare. The Romans had two advantages over the Persians, which were their more sophisticated fortifications and artillery, while the Persians usually had the advantage of superior numbers of men that they were ready to waste if necessary to obtain their goal. However, during this era it was more typical that they cooperated rather than fought against each other, because both faced the same enemy – the Huns – and both adopted the same solution, which was to build fortifications against them. The building of the Derbend Wall and Theodosian Wall of Constantinople proved great successes, but still did not prevent the Huns from ravaging other regions. Unfortunately for the Romans, Roman turncoats, traitors and prisoners helped the Huns to overcome Roman defensive systems based on fortifications. The Germanic peoples were equally inept besiegers as the Huns, but they managed to overcome the defences by their numbers, as a result of which they were given land within the Roman Empire – which effectively negated all the previous defensive systems along the frontiers.

Corruption and the Armed Forces

One of the principal problems facing the Roman Empire was the corruption of the military from the top to the bottom. The problem had already been recognized by Theodosius I, who introduced a series of Edicts against this in the early 390s. These measure included for example: CTh 7.4.18 (29 July 393), in which no person was allowed to demand money instead of *annona*; CTh 7.4.19 (30 July 393), in which no military man was to demand money instead of their *annona*; CTh 7.1.14 (29 April 394, in which infants were not to be enrolled above the lowest military grade; and CTh 7.9.3 (29 July 393), in which soldiers were not allowed to collect 'extras' ('pickles') from their hosts.

However, a real rash of legislation against various forms of military corruption followed after the death of Theodosius I, which proves that the situation had become desperate. The problem caused by the new class of soldiers called *bucellarii* ('private retainers') becomes visible for the first time in this legislation. The state attempted to prevent officers from employing soldiers as their own private servants and retainers.

The Western Government's legislation against military corruption included: CTh 7.12.3 (4/6 July 395), in which soldiers who engaged in business by extending their leave of absence without permission were to be reduced in rank; CTh 7.1.18 (19 March 400), in which counts and dukes were to be fined if they promoted/transferred men from one class of soldiers to another in return for bribes; CTh 7.4.22, in which the soldiers were not allowed to extort more supplies/taxes than their warrants allowed, and were ordered to buy produce at market prices; and CTh 7.4.26 (31 March 401), in which military tax collectors were not allowed to have any dealings with the taxed provincials, but the taxes were to be collected by governors and their staff (i.e. this prevented military men from abusing the provincials).

The corresponding legislation of the Eastern Government included: CTh 7.1.15 (19 February 396), in which the Duke of Armenia Remistheus was ordered to prevent the men from keeping soldiers in their private employ (i.e. as *bucellarii* or as feudal forces); CTh 7.1.16 (28 January 398), in which all soldiers who wandered about in Asia without proper permission were to be apprehended; CTh 7.1.17 (1 Feb 398), in which if any praesental soldiers or any other soldiers were found either in private employment or engaged in their own pursuits, they and their accomplices were to be fined; CTh 7.4.21 (17 April 396), in which the provincials were instructed to appeal to the judge (usually the governor) if the soldiers caused any losses because they would not accept the supplies brought to them, and if the governor did not act he and his staff were to be fined severely; CTh 7.4.24 (25 March 398), in which if paymasters or military accountants were in possession of more supplies than listed, they were to be punished with heavy fines; and CTh 7.4.26 (23 May 398), in which citizens of the city of Epiphania would be allowed to pay their wine *annona* with cheaper, 'young' wine (presumably soldiers had demanded the older variant).

The following narrative proves that both governments were at least temporarily able to alleviate the problem with these legislative measures. It is quite clear that the real collapse of the Western system occurred only after Stilicho's downfall.

Paramilitary Forces

© Dr. Ilkka Syvänne 2014

The funerary monument of Markos Aurelios Diodoros (Marcus Aurelius Diodorus) from Hierapolis of Phyrgia shows the police forces of Asia Minor and their equipment. The equipment consisted of leather banded *lorica* and a thick *subarmalis* underneath, spears, clubs and fustis (?). From other sources we known that they could also use swords and shields. Some of the men were mounted while others were on foot. The dogs were used to track down the bandits and criminals. (drawn after: D'Amato)

As has been noted in the previous volumes, the Romans also maintained significant numbers of police forces and paramilitary forces which performed very significant security functions under the guidance provided by the governors and their staff, and under the guidance of the members of the military establishment detached for this duty – it was this latter function that enabled soldiers to abuse their positions in the above-mentioned manner. The paramilitary forces were used to: suppress brigandage and piracy; collect taxes and customs; control movements of people and goods; guard roads and borders; and defend their own territories and cities. The existence of these paramilitary forces made it possible for the military forces to concentrate their efforts on winning wars. The accompanying illustration shows what type of equipment the paramilitary police forces used when operating against bandits.

The civilian defensive structures (villas, manors and fortified villages) could also have very important defensive function against invaders, which on occasion frustrated all enemy attempts to capture them or to take booty. The following illustrations give a good indication of how massive these defences could be. In the course of the fifth century the inhabitants and owners of these establishments started to seek accommodation with the barbarians in their midst so that these structures lost their defensive functions, quite often peacefully. The reason for this was that the barbarians of Germanic origin were offered good career prospects and were less corrupt in every sense of the word than the imperial officials and officers.

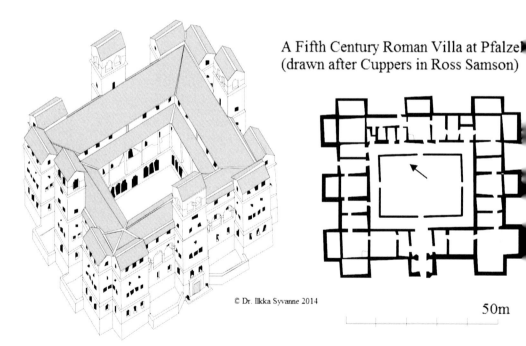

A Fifth Century Roman Villa at Pfalzel
(drawn after Cuppers in Ross Samson)

© Dr. Ilkka Syvanne 2014

50m

Chapter Two

Enemies and Allies

The following overview of the enemies and allies of Rome is a summary of the information presented in Volumes 1 and 2. Those who want to know more of the enemies and their fighting methods or of the sources used are advised to consult these.

Extreme West

The Irish and the Picts

The Romans faced five types of threats in Britain: 1) usurpations; 2) local mutinies, 3) Picts; 4) Irish (Scotti and Attescotti); and 5) Saxons. The Picts, Irish and Saxons could pose a serious threat to the Romans only when they cooperated or when the Romans were distracted by civil war or enemy invasion in Gaul. The Picts occupied what is today known by the name Scotland, after the Irish 'Scotti' who settled there later. Pictland consisted of seven kingdoms, each of which was ruled by a 'king'. Each of the kingdoms was divided into clans and sub-clans. The seven kingdoms in their turn consisted of two separate 'peoples', called Verturiones and Dicalydones (northern and southern Picts), each of which was ruled by a High King. The Dicalydones appear to have been the senior branch so that its king occasionally served as the sole High King of the Picts.

The so-called 'higher men' formed the core of warriors, which could be reinforced by the levy of free farmers. The commoners (subjects?) and slaves were forbidden to carry weapons. My own estimate is that the military potential of the Picts consisted of a minimum of 20,000 young warriors and 10,000 older ones. The Pictish fleet was divided into northern and southern fleets, each of which consisted of 150 longboats and curraghs, each with a minimum crew of 14 rowers and one steersman. The fleet formed the principal threat to the Roman defences because it enabled the Picts to bypass Hadrian's Wall.

The vast majority of the Picts did not use armour or helmets, and even their name 'Picti' meant 'the painted' or 'tattooed ones'. Their only form of protection was the shield. Most of the warriors were equipped with spears, javelins, pikes or axes, while the warrior elite also carried short swords or seaxes. The rest were equipped with the crossbow, or the simple wooden bow. Their battle tactics were quite basic, being based on the use of the infantry phalanx and cavalry wings. The standard way of waging war was the use of raids and guerrilla tactics behind the Roman lines. The Picts could accomplish this either by forcing their way through Hadrian's Wall at one location or by bypassing it and the coastal forts south of it in ships and boats.

The Irish (Scotti, Attescotti, and others) did not pose any serious threat thanks to the fact that Ancient Ireland was very fragmented. It appears to have consisted of about 150 tribal kingdoms, which were grouped together into 5–7 provinces called Fifths. Each of these kingdoms had its own tribal army called a *Tuath* that consisted of the noble families and their clients. The kings were divided into four ranks: king of one *Tuath*; king of several *Tuaths* (including his own); king of a Fifth, and a High King when there existed a person who had managed to unite several the Fifths under his rule. The average strength of one *Tuath* appears to have been about 700 men. Most of the warriors were lightly-equipped javelin-throwers. The Romans were lucky that the Irish were so divided and that some of them cooperated with the Romans (see the forthcoming Syvänne, *Britain in the Age of Arthur*). The Irish raiders targeted primarily the coastal lowlands of Wales, which they probably attacked using the seagoing currachs/curraghs. It is probable that the largest of these had crews of about 30–50 men.

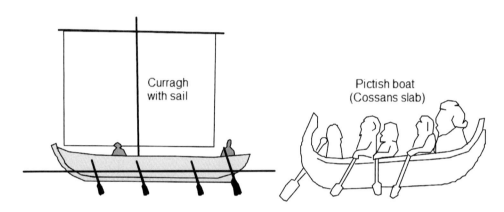

Thanks to their divisions and small numbers, the Picts and Irish did not pose any serious threat to the Romans when the Roman garrisons were at their full strength, but when the garrison was withdrawn to the continent as a result of civil wars or as a result of some major invasion, their united forces proved too powerful for the remaining Roman forces to resist. For examples of typical Picts and Irish warriors, see the Plates.

From the English Channel to the Caucasus

The Germanic Peoples: General Description
The Germanic peoples consisted of three major groupings: 1) the Scandinavian tribes (Angles, Jutes, Danes, etc.); 2) western Germanic tribes/confederacies who spoke a western dialect (Saxons, Franks, Alamanni, Suevi/Suebi, Marcomanni, Thuringians, Lombards, western branch of the Heruls, etc.); and 3) eastern Germanic tribes/confederacies who spoke an eastern dialect (Goths, eastern branch of the Heruls, Burgundi, Vandals, Gepids, Taifali, Rugi, Sciri, Bastarni, etc.). The first mentioned group concern us here only in the context of their inclusion among the so-called Saxons.

All of the Germanic peoples demonstrated some similarities. All Germans were known to be bold and fearless in combat so that they were particularly to be feared in hand-to-hand combat either on horseback or on foot. It is not a coincidence that the Germanic peoples were known for their berserks. There were some differences, however, between the so-called 'west' and 'east' Germans and between tribes (for example the

Franks were known for their *francisca* throwing axe and the Saxons for their *seax* sword). The most important of these was that the east German tribes had been influenced by the steppe peoples so that all of them fielded significant numbers of cavalry, and in some cases the cavalry actually formed their principal arm of service. Even if all Germanic peoples possessed some innate abilities as sailors, for some unknown reason, the second important factor was that the peoples who lived by the sea also had navies. This was particularly true of the so-called Saxon confederacy with its allied tribes of the Angles, Danes and Jutes who raided the coasts of Britain, Gaul and Spain with relative frequency.

On board a ship the equipment of the Saxon raiders appears to have consisted of bows, thrown stones, spears, shields and *seaxes/scramasaxes*. On land the Saxons employed typical Germanic battle tactics based on the use of shieldwalls and infantry wedges. Their ships appear to have resembled closely the clinker-built ships of the Vikings. These ships were powered by both sails and oars, and their crews consisted of about 30 to 60 men, while the largest ships would probably have had about 100 to 120 men on board. The Saxons were a particularly difficult enemy to counter thanks to the fact that their homeland was located far away from the Roman borders.

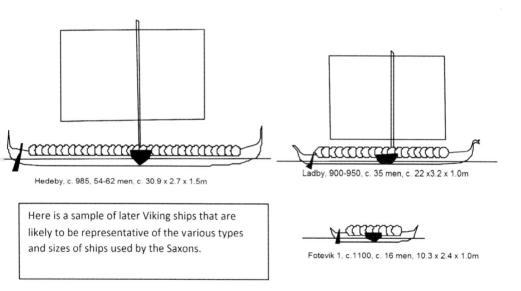

Hedeby, c. 985, 54-62 men, c. 30.9 x 2.7 x 1.5m

Ladby, 900-950, c. 35 men, c. 22 x3.2 x 1.0m

Here is a sample of later Viking ships that are likely to be representative of the various types and sizes of ships used by the Saxons.

Fotevik 1, c.1100, c. 16 men, 10.3 x 2.4 x 1.0m

Most of the Germanic societies also resembled each other in that there were: 1) tribal confederacies ruled by a single high-king or by temporary war-leaders or by high-kings; 2) large tribes ruled by single kings, below whom there were lesser kings/princes' (*reguli*) in charge of smaller tribes or sub-tribes and nobles (*optimates*); and 3) tribal quasi-democracies which were ruled by a judge/president with the help of a council of elders.

The principal striking force of all Germanic tribes consisted of the wealthier nobles (*optimates*) and their retinues, but the entire free male population was still obliged to serve as a tribal levy so that each 'hundred' was required to contribute a hundred warriors for the army. The entire male population was also divided into age-groupings so that the young warriors could prove their manhood in combat or hunting before being considered eligible to marry a woman and seed children. The older men, the fathers, usually stayed back home and formed the reserve force while the 'young-ones', and the nobles and their retinues fought the wars. It was only in emergencies that the 'older-ones' were required to fight. The tribes could bolster their numbers by hiring mercenaries or by forming alliances. The Germans expected their warriors to bring their own supplies, which could then be supplemented by provisions handed over by the rulers or allies or by living off the land. This meant that all Germanic armies were vulnerable to the denial of supplies.

The military equipment of the Germanic tribes had some common chacteristics. The common warriors were usually equipped with a spear and/or javelin(s), shield, and some sort of sword or knife, while the poorest were equipped only with a bow and knife or sword. In the west most of these men consisted of footmen, but among the 'East Germans' these men could consist of both infantry and cavalry. The noblemen and their retinues fought usually as horsemen. The cavalry retinues were typically equipped with the full panoply of equipment (a long-sword, short-sword, knife, spear, javelin(s), armour, shield, and helmet), but there were tribal variations. The Frankish and Herul nobility and their retinues were usually unarmoured, while the Goths and other Germans (e.g. Scandinavians) favoured the use of heavy armour. The East Germanic cavalry also usually included mounted archers and multi-purpose troops equally adept at fighting with bows and melee weapons, some of which were drawn from the ranks of allied tribes or mercenaries of Huns, Sarmatians and Alans. All Germanic peoples used wagon fortresses when they travelled as tribes or in large numbers. The Germanic peoples were also known for their poor siege skills, which resulted from their lack of engineering skills associated with the building of cities of stone.

Even if the Germanic peoples were particularly known for their Germanic fury in pitched battles, their military methods were not limited to this. The Germans were quite adept users of surprise attacks, guerrilla warfare, raids, scorched earth, alliances and ruses and so forth. Therefore, the Roman commanders had to be prepared to wage various types of war when they faced the Germans. On top of it all, the Germans were truly fearsome enemies to face in pitched battle thanks to their formidable fighting spirit, which they combined with the use of close order formations. The Germanic battle formations were formed on the basis of tribe, kinship, and common interest so that the entire battle line was usually divided into three commands, left, centre and right, but it was rare for the Germans to use reserves.

The Germanic infantry could fight equally well in difficult and open terrain thanks to the fact that they used all the same basic fighting orders (irregular, open, close, *foulkon*/tortoise) as the Romans. The principal infantry battle formations were the phalanx/shield wall, the hollow-square, circle, and the wedge. The cavalry was usually placed on the wings. When the Germans reached the range of missiles, they usually attacked wildly. If only part of the line had taken part in the attack, the Germans usually repeated the attack with another part of their line, but if their entire line had attacked then the lack of reserves ensured that the battle was usually lost after the first failed attack. The use of infantry armies was more typical for the 'West Germans' while the 'East Germans' usually placed their infantry behind their cavalry line as a defensive bulwark behind which to regroup. It was also typical for the 'East Germanic peoples' to use the wagon laager (*carrago*) as their last defensive base.

Germanic cavalry units employed both close and irregular (*droungos, globus*) orders in combat, as a result of which they were equally usable for pitched battles, skirmishing and for ambushes. The principal cavalry formations were a single line without reserves or a single line with reserves/ambushers. The use of cavalry armies was more typical for the 'East Germanic peoples' than for their western cousins because the latter usually lacked adequate numbers of horsemen for anything but raiding. The Germans usually avoided any complicated manoeuvres eand simply charged at a gallop straight at the enemy and repeated that if the enemy did not flee. This wild, undisciplined and impetuous cavalry attack at the gallop exploited the psychological impact of the sight of such attack would make on the enemy.[1]

During the fourth century the Romans almost always sought to engage the Germans in pitched battles, because their armies still consisted predominantly of infantry which was better suited to conventional warfare. This made also strategic sense, because the defeating of the enemy enabled the Romans to pillage enemy territory which in its turn usually forced the Germans to negotiate a treaty on Roman terms. It was also typical for the Romans to use the divide-and-rule approach with their dealings so that they would not face overwhelming numbers of enemy forces along their European frontiers. It was only with overwhelming numerical superiority that the Germans could hope to defeat the Romans.

At the turn of the fifth century, the Roman world was in a state of turmoil resulting from the appearance of the Huns in Eastern Europe after about 370. The Huns had crushed the Alanic and Gothic confederacies before they themselves were broken up into smaller confederacies after the death of their supreme leader. Their onslaught had forced vast numbers of Goths, Alans and mercenary Huns to seek safety within Roman territory. After some fighting these were settled in Roman territory. There were now large settlements of Goths, Alans and Huns in Roman Pannonia, Thrace and Asia Minor. In addition to this, there were vast numbers of Hunnic *bucellarii* serving under Stilicho and Rufinus. At the time of the death of Theodosius I in 395, part of these forces and other allied forces from across the Danubian border were located in Italy as a result of the civil war. In addition to this, there were Gothic forces with their allies on the barbarian side of the Danube, some of which were loyal to the Huns (those who were led by the Amals and others in the Crimean region) and some of which were fleeing from the Huns, for example under Radagaisus, into Roman territory. The movement of the Huns towards the West had also created a domino effect, so that Germanic tribes (Vandals, Burgundians, Alamanni, Goths) and remnants of the Alan and Sarmatian confederacies were moving towards the West and the Rhine frontier. The mouth of the Rhine up to Mainz was protected by the Frankish *Laeti* and Federates so that there were Franks on both sides of the Rhine. These forces stayed loyal to the Romans. The Rhine frontier south of Mainz was protected by the Alamannic *Laeti* and Federates, and again there were Alamanni on both sides of the river, but in this case the loyalty of the Alamanni on the other side of the Rhine was suspect.

The Greek Cities of the Black Sea

The Romans managed to retain control of the Greek colonies/cities of the Black Sea like Cherson (Chersonesus) and Olbia despite the Hunnish onslaught, but the Bosporan Kingdom fell to the Huns as a result of a Roman military victory in about 382–383 (see Vol. 2). Consequently, the Bosporan Kingdom is here considered to be part of the Hunnish Confederacy. The Greek cities probably retained their autonomy and their previous military organization to a certain extent so that they maintained their paramilitary forces for self-defence. Therefore, the armies of Olbia and Cherson continued to consist of the levy of the male populace (Greeks, Sarmatians and Goths) and of mercenaries, plus detachments of Roman forces posted in the area to bolster their defences. It is probable, even though the sources do not mention this, that the cavalry began to incorporate Hunnish influences so that from the late fourth century onwards the Crimean cavalry consisted of two types of cavalry: 1) Sarmatian/Gothic heavy lancers and multipurpose cavalry; 2) Hun-style light cavalry. It is also probable that the Chersonese continued to use war-chariots/wagons armed with torsion-powered crossbows or ballistae to counter the nomadic cavalry. These cities also possessed fleets, as well as Roman naval detachments. Both of these cities were located in highly vulnerable positions and it was this that ensured their willigness to stay loyal to the Romans.

The Huns[2]

According to Ammianus (31.2), the Huns were terrible nomads who inhabited the areas beyond the Maeotic Sea near the Glacial Ocean. The Huns were ugly nomads who scarred their faces so that they would not get beards. They lived in wagons and spent their lives on the backs of their horses. Their horses (steppe ponies) were ugly but hardy, i.e. just like the other steppe horses. According to Ammianus, the Huns were not

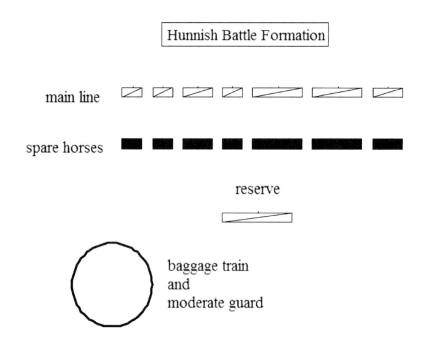

Hunnish Battle Formation

main line

spare horses

reserve

baggage train
and
moderate guard

controlled by royalty, but were ruled in a disorderly fashion by their nobility. The other sources, however, make it clear that they could choose a king to act as their supreme leader. Consequently, it is clear that Ammianus' referral was valid only for the time period after 378 when he was writing. Just like the other nomads, the Huns were greedy, faithless, unreliable and prone to follow their impulses.

The Huns fought as light cavalry and possessed unprecedented rapidity of movement, enabling them to surprise their enemies. In pitched battles, the Huns arrayed first together and then spread out in scattered wedges to pepper foes with arrows from all directions. The Huns were particularly fearsome warriors because they not only fought at a distance, but also fought with swords at close quarters fearlessly, and, when their enemies were protecting themselves against sword cuts, others threw lassoes and entangled their limbs, regardless of whether they were on foot or on horseback. The Romans had not faced these kinds of highly-mobile tactics based on the use of mounted archery after the demise of the Parthians, but as we shall see these did not pose any significant problems for the fourth century army, even if the Romans clearly appreciated the military qualities of the Huns. The best evidence of this is their large-scale employment as auxiliaries and mercenaries as well as the copying of their mobile cavalry tactics.

The best evidence for Hun tactics comes from a late source, the sixth-century *Strategikon* (11.2). According to this treatise the Huns did not divide their battle array in three divisions, but into several units of irregular size that were arrayed side by side to form the battleline. In addition to this, the Huns posted a separate reserve behind that could be used to ambush the enemy or as support troops for the first line. They posted their spare horses close behind the main line and their baggage train with a guard on the right or left, two to three miles behind. The preferred battle tactics were to fight at long range in scattered wedges and the use of ambushes, feigned retreats, and outflanking to defeat the enemy.

According to the *Strategikon*, the Hunnish peoples were equipped with mail armour, swords, spears, and bows. The horses of the tribal nobility also wore frontal armour of felt or iron. The Huns used spears (slung over the shoulder) and bows as required by the situation. For the early period this needs some qualifications. Ammianus (31.2.1ff.) states in no uncertain terms that the fourth-century Huns were lightly-equipped and in fact most appear not to have worn armour at all. However, this doesn't preclude the use of armour by the nobility and it is practically certain that they did. It is in light of the above and below that one has to consider the recent truly-inspiring debate by Roy Boss and Simon MacDowall in Slingshot 285. Both are right and wrong at the same time. It is certain that the Huns obtained an ever-increasing amount of armour after c. 376, but this doesn't mean that they would have become 'heavy cavalry'. In fact, the Huns had always acted as both light and heavy cavalry as required by the situation. The Huns attacked immediately to close quarters if they deemed this advantageous and skirmished when this seemed better. Just like in eighteenth- or nineteenth-century Europe, it was not necessary to possess armour to fight like heavy cavalry. Similarly, the heavy armour worn by the front rankers didn't make the cavalry unit heavy cavalry, as the example of Mongols so well proves (Syvänne, 2012). The standard tactic appears to have been to array the units in ranks and files just like the Romans, Alans and Mongols so that the armoured troops were placed in front to protect the lightly equipped. The attack would then begin with a charge while shooting arrows. If the enemy showed signs of disorder, the attack was immediately pressed home, but if the enemy withstood the volleys of arrows and the frightening sight of the madly shouting Huns, the Hun units retreated in irregular *droungos* (wedge) arrays. If the latter happened and the enemy pursued, the Huns could attempt to ambush them or outflank them. Otherwise the charge was repeated again and again until either arrows ran out, or enemy resistance collapsed, or the enemy pursued carelessly. (For examples of typical Huns, see the Plates.)

According to the Scythic Drill of the Strategikon (6.1), the Scythian units were all formed in the same manner (no *koursores* or *defensores*) in one line so that it was divided into two *moirai* (instead of three). In combat these units were used so that the two flanks advanced as if to encircle and then moved towards each other so that they continued in a circle so that the right wing was on the outside and the left on the inside until their reached the opposite part of the line previously occupied by the other left. Contrary to my previous interpretation, I have interpreted this so that the left wing galloped in front of the enemy line to the right while the right wing galloped around the enemy to the left. This interpretation has been inspired by Roy Boss' recent analysis of Hun tactics. This makes more sense than placing the left wing inside a circle where they would not have been able to shoot towards their enemy on the right.

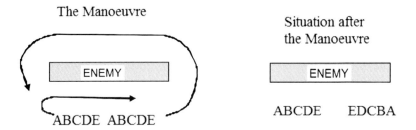

The Manoeuvre

Situation after the Manoeuvre

ENEMY

ABCDE ABCDE

ENEMY

ABCDE   EDCBA

When the Romans used cavalry, for example in the vanguard, the best tactic was to charge the Hun battle formation before it could scatter, but not to follow too far if they fled because the Huns often placed an ambush behind their line. Unfortunately, we do not know whether the Romans used this tactic during the fourth century thanks to the scanty evidence, but they definitely did use this approach in the sixth. The use of a similar tactical approach against the Persians does suggest that the Romans had always been aware of the best tactics against cavalry. When facing cavalry the standard procedure for any army was also to attempt to force the enemy against an obstacle so that it could be annihilated. This was particularly important when the army consisted mainly of infantry, as the Roman army did. The Hun cavalry could not really make any impact on the Roman infantry as long as there were enough footmen who maintained their order. However, the same was also true the other way around. The infantry could not catch the mobile Huns unless there was an obstacle (ditch, valley, mountain, river, lake, sea, etc.) behind the Hun lines. If Roman infantry fought Hun armies in open terrain, the side that had more supplies to outlast the enemy won, but the Romans did not face any serious difficulties in dealing with the Huns before the reign of Attila. (See Vols. 2–4.)

Caucasus, Colchis, Tzanica, Iberia and Albania

The small mountain peoples of the Caucasus were important because they occupied the strategically important passes of the Caucasus Mountains. From west to east these consisted of the proto-Adyghes (Adyghes, Tcherkesses), Zikhes, Saniges, Abasgis, Apsilis, Svanes, Dvales, Gogours, Lekhs and Massagetae.

All of these tribes fielded light infantry well-suited to the mountaineous terrain and small numbers of cavalry, with the exception of the so-called Massagetae, who were nomadic horsemen, and the proto-Adyghes, who were pirates besides being mountaineers. The latter used slender and light boats with crews of 25 to 30 men, which the Greeks called '*kamares*'. These formed only a localized nuisance for the Romans, which they dealt with by posting garrisons along the coasts and naval patrols to police the sea. The Romans did not raid their territories in revenge, because it lacked suitable mooring places, but used land campaigns along the coast and bribery to convince the tribal leadership to follow their wishes. Therefore, in normal circumstances the proto-Adyghes were Roman clients, just like the Saniges (from the area around modern Sotchi), Zikhes (around Sebastopolis), Abasgi, Apsili and Lazi. All of these possessed small Roman forts, garrisons and veteran settlements in their respective areas. The Romans used these tribes to protect the coastal trade network and the westernmost passes of the Caucasus.

In short, Roman strategy in the area was to control the coastline (Saniges to Colchis/Lazica) with a fleet, forts, garrisons, veteran settlements, and diplomacy (the threat of force combined with bribery). The rest of the Caucasus the Romans attempted to control through diplomacy. In other words, by keeping Iberia friendly, it was possible to prevent the northerners from attacking Asia Minor or Syria directly through the Darial Pass, but this solution was insufficient without Persian cooperation as they could let the nomads through the Derbend Pass. The Tzani were a mountain tribe which occupied the area just south of Lazica, along the border with Persarmenia. The Romans did not attempt to occupy the area permanently before the reign of Justinian thanks to the cost involved and were satisfied with the nominal subjection of the tribe. Only when the status quo was upset to the degree that the Tzani conducted major raids did the Romans conduct punishing expeditions until the tribal leadership adopted a more conciliatory tone in their dealings. The Romans did not attempt to prevent banditry, but only the occurrence of major operations.

The central portion of the Caucasus was controlled by the Svanes and Dvales. They occupied the strategically-important Darial Pass, the Caucasian Gate, or the Gate of the Alans. These tribes were usually controlled by the Iberian Kingdom. The Gogours and Lekhs were sedentary tribes that occupied what is today called Dagesthan. Their neighbours, the Alans, Massagetae, Huns(?) and Sarmates, were semi-nomads. These tribes did not control any major passes. The easternmost neighbours, the semi-nomadic Massagetae 'Huns' (Maskouts) controlled the strategically-important Daruband Pass. The Maskouts were unreliable clients of Persia, which was problematic when the Huns were pressing from the north. The Persian solution to the problem was to fortify the Derbend/Daruband Pass, as we shall see.

At the turn of the fifth century Iberia retained a fair amount of independence thanks to its betrayal of the Persians in 382/3 (see Vol. 2). It clearly retained good relationship with Persia, but in such a manner that in practice it sided with the Romans, as we shall see (see the events of 421–422). The adoption of the Christian faith during the first half of the fourth century played an important role in this. Iberia was too small to resist either of the superpowers, but still managed to maintain some autonomy of action in the right circumstances.

Iberian society was based on the Iranian class/caste system, just like the Armenian and Albanian societies. Most of the upper classes had either intermarried with Iranian (mainly Parthian or Saka) noble houses or were members of Iranian noble houses. Consequently, it is not surprising to find Iberia being ruled by an Arsacid king below whom served a hierarchy of officials, the names and functions of which had been borrowed from Persia. The most important of these was the supreme judge of the land, who was also the chief of the army (*Spaspet*) and presumably also the principal spy master of the realm. The military forces consisted of the magnates/aristocrats and their retinues of petty nobles who formed the feudal cavalry of the realm. The petty people performed their military duties as infantry. The semi-dependent agriculturalists/peasants (i.e. tenants) formed the fourth state, with no military obligations. The feudal cavalry forces consisted of about 20,000 horsemen and 5,000–7,000 royal cavalry, commanded by the *Spaspet*. These forces could be bolstered by at least 30,000 foot and by allied contigents. The cavalry consisted of multi-purpose troops equipped for both long and short range combat and the wealthiest were equipped as cataphracts. The footmen consisted of spearmen, javelineers and archers. The horsemen fought like their neighbours the Albanians, Armenians and Persians and their infantry used phalanx arrays and light infantry tactics as required by the situation. Hence it can be said that the Iberian armies were qualitatively not weaker than those of their neighbours – their only significant problem was that they did not have as many men as the Alans, Huns, Armenians, Romans and Persians.

Albania consisted of a multitude of peoples who spoke 26 languages or dialects, which had one ruler that had been superimposed on them by the Arsacids. The Albanians consisted therefore of nomads, shepherds, agriculturalists and urbanized peoples and of the Iranian/Parthian/Persian warriors settled in the area. The military potential of the Albanian Kingdom was roughly about 60,000–70,000 infantry and 30,000–35,000 cavalry, in addition to which would have come the levy of the masses called into service only in emergencies. The cataphracts formed the crème de la crème of the armed forces so that the bulk of the army consisted of the usual multi-purpose cavalry, infantry spearmen, and foot archers. Thanks to its geographic position, Albania belonged quite securely to the Persian sphere of influence and it was only rarely that the Romans could challenge this. The strategic position of Albania was very significant because it occupied the area just south of the Derbend Pass.

The Sasanian Empire

Society

Sasanian Persia was a hierarchial caste society which consisted of the *Shahanshah*, four ranks of nobles (kings and sons of the Shahanshah; other members of the Sasanian royal family; heads of the seven magnate houses; regular nobility, the *azadan*. The lesser nobles, the *dehkan*, were not yet considered as part of the nobility), four estates of the realm (clergy, warriors, commoners, merchants), and finally the non-Iranians under the satraps. The first three classes of nobles held all the higher ranking offices and military commands, while the lesser ranks were reserved for the *azadan*. There were altogether some 600 different ranks of dignitary positions. All major office holders and officers of the realm were simultaneously priests or high priests. Sasanian society and its laws were entirely based on the doctrines of Zoroastrian religion, which meant that the position of the 'magi' (clergy) was paramount. The priests acted as councillors to the ruler as officials, judges, religious police, internal security apparatus etc. The importance of religion and the magi to the Sasanians meant that the enemies always targeted members of the clergy and the temples to undermine the standing of the Sasanian rulers.

Agriculture formed the basis of the Sasanian economy, as in most ancient empires, which meant that one of the principal objectives of the Sasanian military system was to defend their breadbaskets (Iraq and Khuzistan). Unfortunately for the Sasanians, the former was vulnerable to Roman raids and invasions. The control exercised by the Sasanians over the trade with India, Central Asia, Rome and Africa formed the second pillar of the Sasanian economy. Unfortunately for them, the Romans possessed superior naval capabilities which they could employ to control the trade routes of the Red Sea and Indian Ocean, and the eastern sections of the trade network were constantly threatened by the Central Asian nomads or by the various Indian powers.

Sasanian Military

The Sasanian military organization was hierarchial: at the top was the *Shahanshah* (king of kings), then the *Iran-spahbadh* (Supreme Commander of Iran), the *Hazarbed/Chiliarch* (Commander of the 'Thousands', 'Prime Minister' with military duties), the *Sparapet* (Commander of Cavalry, hereditary in the Ispahbudhan family), the *Pushtigban-salar* (Commander of the Royal Guard), the four *vitaxae*, *Kanarang* (hereditary position in the Kanarangiya Family) and 30 other local kings, the *Paygan-salar* (Commander of the Infantry), the *spahbadhs* (generals), the *marzbans* (governors), the lesser officers (commanders of forts, elite cavalry, foot archers etc.) the special functionaries (senior vet, supply officers etc.), and finally the regulars. This well-organized administrative and military system made the Persians the most dangerous of the foes the Romans faced.

The Sasanian armed forces consisted of different arms of service: the bodyguard units (the most important being the 10,000 Immortals and the *pushtighban* Guard, the latter of which may have been the equivalent of the Achaemenid Kinsmen Guard), the heavy cavalry (*asvaran/savaran*), the light cavalry provided by mercenaries and tribal forces, the elephants of the royal house, the foot soldiers (*paygan*), the navy, and the logistical services, all of which had their own role to play in the overall strategy. The Sasanians also produced a series of military manuals to enable their officers and soldiers to perform as expected.

The Sasanians organized their armies according to the decimal system, but in such a way that these figures included the recruits and servants just like the Roman figures. These units consisted of the 100 men 'company' (*washt*), 1,000 men 'regiment'(*drafsh*), and of the 10,000 men 'division'(*gund*). The narrative sources prove that the Persian division consisted in actuality of 6,000 fighting men (*caterva*/legion) grouped together into armies of 12,000 men plus auxiliaries. Thanks to their well organized administration and large population the Sasanians were able to put into the field larger and better-equipped and -organized armies than any of Rome's other enemies. The Sasanian field armies could regularly put in the field about 50,000–60,000 men, and in exceptional cases even 90,000 to 120,000 men, without including servants and workmen in the figures. In short, the Sasanians were able to put in the field more men than the Romans, but with the cost that they left the other fronts thinly defended.

The principal striking force of the Persian army was its 'knightly' cataphract cavalry, which consisted of the *aswaran* and *azadan*. These super-heavies were equipped both for long (bow) and short distance combat (*contus*, sword, short sword, axe, mace, etc.) and were fully armoured (variously with mail, plate, scale or lamellar) from head to toe. Towards the end of our period the Persian cavalry underwent an important change: they adopted the use of the shield to improve their ability to withstand enemy arrows, and started to pay more attention to the power of their archery over the sheer quantity of arrows shot. Their horses were armoured either with chain-mail, or scale, or lamellar, or leather, or leather armour with metal plates. Most of the Armenians in Persian service also belonged to this category and often formed the elite lancers of the Persian army. In contrast to the regular cavalry forces consisting of the Persians and Parthians, most of the allied cavalry (mainly Sagestani, Albanians, Kushans, Arabs, and Kadiseni) wore only light equipment and fought as light cavalry. (See the Plates.)

The Persians also possessed infantry forces drawn from the ranks of the peasants, which were divided into the heavy infantry and light infantry categories. They served primarily as servants to the knights and as 'cannon-fodder' in sieges. The standard infantry tactic was to place wattle mantlets or huge shields in front as protective cover for the light infantry archers behind. The heavy infantry as such usually fought as a phalanx of spearmen, but there also existed close quarters elite infantry that fought either with swords like the gladiator *Murmillones* or as javelinmen like the allied mercenary Dailamite/Dilemnite/Daylami tribesmen. (See the Plates.)

The Sasanian elephant corps was divided for different uses according to the amount of training they had received. The elephants were used as: 1) beasts of burden; 2) a construction force; 3) a combat force as 'tanks' to create openings in the enemy line; 4) moving siege towers/rams; and 5) as a commander's mount. Only the most highly-trained beasts were usable in sieges and battles and could carry towers. When deployed as part of the battle line the pachyderms could be placed in front, or behind, or on the flanks of the army as required by the situation. The war elephants were basically weapons of terror, but as such their effectivess against the Romans was limited because the Romans knew how to counter them.

We do know that the Sasanian naval forces consisted of dhows able to carry 100 passangers, but unfortunately we do not know how their navy was organized. The Sasanians may have had a small permanent navy, but we do not know this for sure. What is certain is that it was not large. This made it possible for the allies of Rome – the Lakhmids, Himyarites and Aksumites – to exercise periodical control of the Persian Gulf even without Roman help. The Persian navy could pose a problem for the Romans only when the Romans could not detach any naval forces to the Red Sea or Indian Ocean for flag-waving missions. The Persian dhows were too weakly built to face the Roman galleys in combat. (See the Plates.)

The Sasanian military methods were just as sophisticated as the Roman ones. The Sasanians rarely made any policy moves against the Romans without making calculations of what would serve their interest best. The Persian military operations were based on information obtained from a network of spies and their military campaigns were orderly and disciplined and supported by relatively well-functioning administrative apparatus. The Persians were equally adept in the use of unorthodox and orthodox warfare.

The principal Persian tactic was to force their enemies to face a devastating barrage of arrows before the armies would lock in hand-to-hand combat, but if deemed necessary the Persians were also ready to charge immediately or retreat to avoid unfavourable situation.

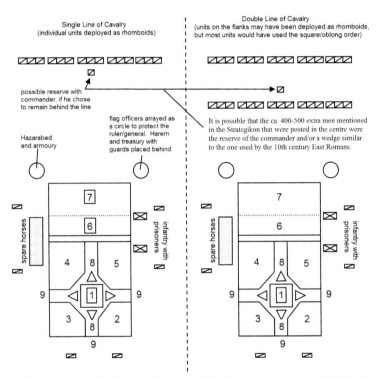

The two standard Persian cavalry formations with infantry and camp placed behind (not in scale)

- the probable structure of a Persian marching camp based on the supposition that later Muslim practices mirrored those of old Persia: 1) King or general, his entourage, guards, war chest etc. 2-5) Officers, officials, doctors, elephant keeper, entourages, guards, servants etc. 6) Cavalry. 7) Infantry. 8) Roads. 9) Gates. The Persians also posted a strong guard unit on one side of the camp to act as ambushing and guarding forces against any army trying to surprise them in their camp.

- the rear half with the ruler's entourage (1-5, 8-9) was the camp proper, and the front half (7) with infantry and wagons, hospital (could also include a trench and caltrops) was the portion facing the enemy (with no gates) that served as bulwark against attackers. The cavalry advanced from the camp proper and from (6) against the enemy to form the cavalry battle array. When the camp was built behind the battle line to protect the army in battle, it could include separate cavalry detachments to protect the flanks and rear, which I have added to the illustration on the basis of the later practices. The reason for this reconstruction is that the Tafrij, which includes these detachments, includes several borrowings from the earlier Persian treatises as a result of which it is possible that these were also used by the Sasanians.

After Syvänne (2004, 2009) based on the Strategikon (11.1), Tarfij (The 5-lines formation), Gotha (Square formation), and illustration of the ancient Persian battle array by Fakhr-i Mudabbir.

The Persian cavalry battle-line had two basic formations (single line and double line) and several variants (as portrayed in the accompanying image). The use of allies could also cause the array to consist of specialized sections with differing equipment so that the left-handed mounted archers were deployed on the left wing and the lancers on the right wing. The double line formation had two variants: 1) first line of light cavalry and second line of cataphracts; or 2) both lines consisting of cataphracts. In both cases the standard tactic was to soften up the enemy first with a barrage of arrows launched by the first line so that it could replenish its ammunition by withdrawing behind the second, while the second line moved forward to either continue to pepper the enemy with arrows or to charge. If infantry and servants accompanied the army, the Sasanians usually placed them in the rear, in front of the camp, but on occasion the Sasanians also deployed their infantry just behind the cavalry or in the centre. If the army included elephants, these were deployed as required by the tactics used. The Sasanians always sought to outflank the enemy on one or both flanks, if possible, or used the terrain to negate enemy advantages or attempted to break the enemy centre with a desperate charge. In emergencies, the Persians formed a defensive circle on the spot to deter enemy attacks from all directions.

The Sasanian siege techniques mirrored those of Rome, but with the difference that they possessed a more powerful archery arm, were more formidable in defence, and were more ready to assault enemy fortresses, regardless of the cost in expendable peasants.

In sum, the Sasanians were by far the most sophisticated and dangerous of the enemies the Romans faced.

Deserts from Mesopotamia to Egypt: the Arabs

The Arab/Saracen tribes from Mesopotamia to Arabia consisted of a great variety of tribes, some of which lived in Roman territory, or in Persian territory, or in the areas between, or travelled from one area to another. Some of the tribes were urbanized and/ or sedentary while others were semi-nomadic or entirely nomadic. Consequently, the Romans were forced to adopt different approaches towards each of these groups. The Romanized sedentary tribes were considered Romans, but those tribes that had retained their tribal structures and cultures were treated as barbarian federate tribes. The same was also true of the federate or non-federate tribes who lived inside the Roman territory or travelled from one area to another or were located outside Roman direct influence. The last two mentioned formed a buffer zone against the tribes that lived further away, but the Romans almost always sought to control all tribes regardless of their location, either directly or indirectly, in order to protect their own territory and the trade routes in the most efficient manner possible.

The principal threats to the Romans were the tribes that retained their tribal traditions, which not only included the Bedouins but also the sedentary populations that exploited the desert terrain in the same manner and tended to be against the Romans. The Romans sought to counter this with garrisons, forts, diplomacy and alliances. All the Arabs, including the Federates, sedentary populations as well as the Bedouins, exploited camels to transport men and supplies, and used horses for fighting. The use of camels as mounts in combat was very rare. The camels enabled their users to move in the deserts from one oasis to another unless this was blocked by the enemy. This meant that the Arabs could suddenly emerge from the desert to raid villages and cities and then retreat back to the desert. However, even if the typical Saracen threat consisted solely of this type of banditry, the Arabs still posed a formidable threat on the battlefield when they chose to fight.

Most of the Arabic cavalry forces consisted of light cavalry lancers (spears, javelins, sword, shield, and possibly armour) and to a lesser extent of mounted archers, but some of the men were equipped with both. The wealthier warriors could also equip themselves as cataphracts, but after the fall of Palmyra their numbers remained very small. In contrast to the rest, the tribes of central Arabia preferred to use a mix of camel-mounted infantry and cavalry lancers in combat. The Arabic lancers typically attacked at gallop in loose and irregular formation, which was followed up, if successful, by a pursuit, or, if unsuccessful, by a retreat. However, thanks to Roman and Persian influence some of the Arabic tribes had learnt to deploy their cavalry in tight and well-ordered formations, which made their charge quite formidable. In open terrain the Arabs deployed their infantry as tightly-arrayed phalanxes, and in difficult terrain in irregular loose formation. Those tribes that lived along the coasts of the Red Sea engaged in piracy, but their sewn ships (dhows) posed no serious naval threat to the Romans. The Himyarites of Yemen were a special case, because they formed a regional power which competed periodically with the Arabs of Hira and Ethiopians of Aksum. The Himyarites were important because they controlled the best ports for the trade with India. Therefore the Romans sought to control them either through their allies the Aksumites or through flag-waving missions that forced the Himyarites to stay clients of Rome. (See Plates.)

By Roman standards the Himyarite forces were small, and the Himyarite armies rarely had more than 4,000 to 6,000 men. The Himyarite soldiers (heavy and light infantry, heavy regular cavalry and Bedouins) were disciplined and were able to perform complex battlefield manoeuvres, but there were just too few of them to offer any serious resistance for the Romans when the Romans decided to put pressure on the rulers of the region. The Himyarite ships, the dhows, were also too weak to offer serious resistance against the Roman war galleys. It was thanks to this that the Romans could exercise control over the region with relative little effort.

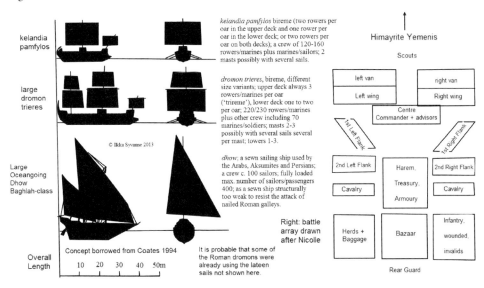

kelandia pamfylos

kelandia pamfylos bireme (two rowers per oar in the upper deck and one rower per oar in the lower deck; or two rowers per oar on both decks); a crew of 120-160 rowers/marines plus marines/sailors; 2 masts possibly with several sails.

large dromon trieres

dromon trieres, bireme, different size variants; upper deck always 3 rowers/marines per oar ('trireme'), lower deck one to two per oar; 220/230 rowers/marines plus other crew including 70 marines/soldiers; masts 2-3 possibly with several sails several per mast; towers 1-3.

© Ilkka Syvanne 2013

Large Oceangoing Dhow Baghlah-class

dhow; a sewn sailing ship used by the Arabs, Aksumites and Persians; a crew c. 100 sailors; fully loaded max. number of sailors/passengers 400; as a sewn ship structurally too weak to resist the attack of nailed Roman galleys.

Concept borrowed from Coates 1994

Overall Length   10   20   30   40   50m

It is probable that some of the Roman dromons were already using the lateen sails not shown here.

Himayrite Yemenis

Scouts

left van		right van
Left wing		Right wing
	Centre Commander + advisors	

1st Left Flank   1st Right Flank

2nd Left Flank	Harem,	2nd Right Flank
Cavalry	Treasury, Armoury	Cavalry
		Infantry,
Herds + Baggage	Bazaar	wounded,
		invalids

Rear Guard

Right: battle array drawn after Nicolle

Egyptian Frontier (see also Appendix 3)

From the point of view of strategy, Egypt was probably the most significant frontier area. It was the most important breadbasket of the empire. It provided surplus foodstuff for Thrace, Constantinople and the armies of the East, and in addition to this it lay between two important commercial routes: 1) the Nile route through which the merchants brought merchandise from Africa and the Red Sea (through Myos Hormos and Berenice); and 2) the Red Sea route through Trajan's Canal that brought merchandise from Arabia, Africa, India, and China. Furthermore, Egypt also possessed some very important gold and emerald mines in the eastern desert (between the Nile and the Red Sea) as well as quarries of building stone. In short, it was largely thanks to the great wealth of Egypt that the Eastern emperors could feed and pay their court and army without having to resort to the heavy taxing of the rest of the populace.

The principal threats to this wealth were: 1) urban unrest in the city of Alexandria and elsewhere; 2) the nomadic and semi-nomadic tribes of the south (mainly the Blemmyes and Nubians), west (the Berbers) and east (the Arabs); and 3) the well-organized Aksumite Kingdom of Ethiopia. The Roman response to the first problem was to station garrisons near Alexandria and other important locales, as well as to use more civilian police forces than anywhere else. The Romans sought to counter the second problem by placing small garrisons in strategic locales, but the events of the turn of the fifth century prove that these were insufficient when the tribes united their forces. The third threat was solved by concluding an alliance with the Aksumites.

The Blemmyes (modern Beja) of the eastern desert formed the principal threat to Roman territories and trade in Egypt, but their forces were neither sophisticated nor large enough to pose a really serious threat. On land the Blemmyes employed camel-mounted infantry armies and circular camel ramparts so that their dismounted footmen fought as a phalanx, behind which was placed the circular camp, and at sea they used a 'pirate' navy which consisted of sewn ships and boats (dhows). Most of the Blemmye warriors were unarmoured and equipped only with spears and bows (for which they used poisoned arrows). The Blemmyes lacked siege skills, which enabled the Romans to contain the Blemmye threat with some strategically-placed small fortifications and garrisons.

The nomadic Nubians (ancient Noba/Nobatae) lived to the west and south of the Blemmyes. They consisted of three kingdoms, which in turn consisted of several tribes and sub-groups. The northernmost of the kingdoms was the Kingdom of Nobadia (also known as the X-Culture), which was allied with Rome. To the south of them were the Kingdoms of Makuria and Alwa. The Nubians possessed superb foot archers, some heavy infantry (equipped with spears, halberds, small spears or javelins, single-edged swords, and leather shields) and small numbers of cavalry. Makuria possessed better cavalry than the rest because it possessed an excellent breed of horse called Dongolawi. The Romans sought to exercise control over the Nubians through a combination of alliances and military force, resulting in them forming alliances with some of the Nubians against others and cooperating with the Aksumites when deemed wise.

The Berbers did not pose any serious threat to Egypt after the reign of Diocletian (see Vol.1) and their renewed military action in the 390s appears to have come as a nasty surprise because the Roman response was initially too weak to contain it. The Arabs had threatened Egypt during the revolt of Mavia, but the secure alliance structure with the Arabs after that secured the Sinai frontier against similar occurences.

The Christian Ethiopian Kingdom of Aksum (Ethiopia) served as the principal ally of Rome from the 320s until 390, but appears to have lost its preferred status after that so that the Romans allowed it to lose its control of the surrounding regions. The probable reason for this was the state of peace between Rome and Persia after 384. (See Vols. 1 and 2, with Appendix 3.) We do not know enough to make any certain conclusions regarding the treaty status between the Romans and the Aksumites from about 390 until 440 beyond the probability that the relationship may have soured at some point in time before being restored to its former standing by 437 – a date when the Aksumites are known to have been a client kingdom of Rome. (See Appendix 3.) The Aksumites were important for the Romans for three reasons: 1) it had a sizeable Christian population; 2) it was strategically located so that it controlled the Red Sea and Nile trade routes; and 3) it was a source of gold bullion because it traded with the peoples of the interior of Africa. Consequently, the Aksumites mattered.

The Aksumite Empire was a loose structure in which the core area consisted of the Kingdom of Aksum and its outlying areas of subjected tribes that paid tribute to the Aksumite King of Kings. This loose structure strengthened the Roman position vis-à-vis the Aksumite ruler. It was easy for the Romans to either prop up the position of the Aksumite ruler or weaken him by supporting outlying areas against him. The Romans did not even need any major military effort to achieve this. The Aksumite armed forces were small by Roman standards (a typical major expeditionary army consisted usually only of 3,000–4,000 men) and poorly equipped (most of the army consisted of light infantry javelineers), and their dhows were no match for the Roman war galleys. It was only by committing their entire army (ca. 50,000 men) against the Romans that the Aksumites could hope to resist them and if they did this they lost control of their own subject kingdoms.

From Libya to Mauritania Tingitana: The Berbers (See also the Maps Section, with Appendix 3)

There was no ethnic unity among the inhabitants of Roman north Africa from Libya to Mauritania Tingitana. There were the 'natives' of the coast (descendants of the Punic population), Moors/Berbers, Greeks, Jews, Blacks, Roman colonists and others. With the exceptions of the Moors/Berbers the others had largely been 'Romanized'. In fact this was also reflected in their status. The Berbers had retained their tribal traditions and were therefore considered barbarians and had not been granted Roman citizenship. The only Berbers who had been granted the citizenship were those persons whom the Romans had installed as chieftains and primates of their tribes. The Berbers also posed another problem due to there being Berber tribes both inside and outside the Roman borders, plus there were also tribes that spent part of the year inside and part of the year outside the borders. Consequently, the Romans and the local populace faced several potentially hostile Berber tribes both within and outside the borders of the provinces. And we should not forget that North Africa was one of the principal breadbaskets of the Empire, and following the creation of Constantinople the city of Rome had become entirely dependent upon its supply of corn.

The provinces of Mauritania were a special case, because the archaeological and documentary evidence proves that the Romans placed responsibilty for part of the defence on the local Berber tribes, which were granted the Federate status: the famous *foedus* with the Goths in 382 was not an unprecedented experiment.

The fighting methods of the different Berber tribes mirrored their place of habitation and mode of living. The mountain tribes tilled the land, fought mainly on foot, and used fortified towers as places of refuge, while the 'desert' nomads or semi-nomads lived mainly off their livestocks and fought as light cavalry. The basic unit of Berber society was the *ikh* (people). The village of the sedentary Berbers consisted of two to three *ikhs*, and the tribe of several such villages. The basic unit of the nomadic tribes was a wagon, which were united to form a camel-caravan of people, several of which in combination would form a tribe. The large tribes were ruled by kings and the small tribes by tribal elders, and the confederation of tribes by a temporary military chief.

The typical form of military activity in the area was banditry, but when the Berbers managed to form a confederation or one tribe achieved supremacy over its neighbours, the Berbers could pose a serious threat. In such cases it was possible for the Berbers to achieve a very significant numerical superiority over the local Romans, because the Romans did not usually post significant forces in the area. The typically confederate army consisted of about 20,000–30,000 men, but could also reach the figure of 100,000 men in very exceptional circumstances. However, even then the lightly-equipped Berbers usually favoured the use of raids, ambushes, feigned retreats, and surprise attacks against the Romans over pitched battles. The Romans had several significant advantages over the Berbers, which were: 1) Berber confederacies were liable to break up, as a result of which it was possible to obtain deserters; 2) Berber tribes possessed poor siege skills, as a result of which even small garrisons, forts and even earth walls could hold them in check; 3) it was possible for the Romans to force the Berbers to the negotiating table simply by denying them access to agricultural produce; 4) Roman field armies possessed tactical superiority over their enemies thanks to their better training and discipline; and 5) the divisions within the tribes enabled the Romans to maintain a network of tribal spies.

The light infantry and cavalry of the nomadic or semi-nomadic Moors/Berbers had won great renown in the ancient world. Their principal pieces of martial equipment consisted simply of two or three short, light javelins/spears and of small circular shields of reed, which they used to great effect. The light cavalry was also famous for their use of unbridled horses and very aggressive irregular way of fighting. In fact, the Romans both recruited Berbers and adopted Berber light cavalry tactics as their own, and even incorporated Berbers into their elite Imperial bodyguard cavalry.

The typical Berber way of fighting consisted of the exploitation of the terrain, which included the use of deserts and mountains as places of refuge and combat. The camels were used as beasts of burden and as emergency bulwarks for their camps. Besides the rings of camels, the camps could also include similar barriers of oxen/cattle, donkeys, sheep, and goats, all of which were hobbled together to form a significant obstacle. The standard tactic was to use camels only as beasts of burden and horses for the actual combat, and to attack with cavalry or to ambush a careless foe. The light infantry could also be used like heavy infantry when needed so that it assumed the phalanx formation.

However, even if the above is a good general description of the Berber tactics, there was still a great deal of variety resulting from their habitat and mode of living. The best evidence for this comes from Corippus' pen, who states (1.85ff.) that the Marmaridan (Austurian/Laguatan) tribes consisted of: 1) the Frexes who employed both infantry and cavalry; 2) the Austur who used their circular camp as a base of operations; 3) the bloodthirsty Llaguas who employed cavalry lancers; 4) the sword-wielding Ifuraces who carried shields and attacked by leaping up and down for dramatic effect; 5) the Muctunians from the wastes of Libya who preferred to fight in the vanguard; 6) the lake tribes that employed boats; and 7) the Barcaei (probably neo-Berbers/inhabitants close to the Barca/Barke) who tied their shields to their left hand and their swords to their right with bracelets. In addition to these there were the other Berber tribes, most of whom consisted of ploughmen or of mountaineers like the Aurasitians (tribes of the Aures) who employed only cavalry armed with a two-ended sharp bladed weapon and a shield. Some tribes also used poisoned arrows. The Garamantes in their turn were famous for their light cavalry, but as far as we know it is probable that they still employed infantry armed with spears and shields, and bow-armed infantry as well as war-chariots. Their two-wheeled chariots could be assembled and taken apart for transport as needed. As far as we know, the Berber tribes of Mauretania (e.g. Quinquegentani, Bavares, Baquates, etc.) fought like the typical nomadic Berbers and employed light infantry and cavalry as well as circular camps with camels. In contrast to the other Berbers, the Mauritanian tribes also appear to have employed small numbers of pirates. Unfortunately, we do not know what types of vessels they used, but it seems probable that these were unable to meet Roman war galleys one-to-one so that their principal strategy was to avoid contact with warships. There is no reliable period evidence for the way in which the Autololes fought, but on the basis of earlier referrals it is possible that they employed highly-mobile light infantry.

It is quite obvious why the mobile nomadic tribes posed a greater threat to the Roman interests than the mountain tribes or sedentary tribes. The latter had dwellings and fields that made them static targets. In contrast, the only ways for the Romans to defeat the former was to crush them decisively in a pitched battle and/or to isolate them in the desert so that they would be forced to eat their herds of domesticated animals. This latter method would either force the nomads to negotiate or to march north where they could be destroyed by the Romans.

The standard Berber offensive strategy was to raid Roman territories. The standard defensive strategy was to avoid pitched battles with the Romans and either to retreat into their mountain holdouts or to the desert. If the Romans managed to surprise the nomadic Moors in the open, the Berbers formed a defensive circular palisaded camp by tying together their camels and other domesticated animals and scattered caltrops or placed stakes. The tribesmen (spearmen, slingers, archers) took defensive positions both along the openings in the barricades and within the barricades. The women, children, and baggage were placed in the middle, and were used in defence only in emergencies. If the terrain allowed, the Berbers also often placed ambushers outside the camp to attack any careless foe in the rear when they approached. If the Berbers decided to fight a pitched battle, they usually employed their light infantry in the front as a phalanx, behind which they placed their light cavalry which was used for harassment and pursuit. It was also possible that sometimes the Berbers employed only cavalry.

Internal Threats

Contrary to what one would expect, the principal threats facing the Romans even during the age of mass migrations were not the barbarians, but internal enemies. The most important of these were naturally usurpers who could use the Roman resources against the other Romans. The above information suffices to describe their forces. However, there were also other internal forces threatening the Roman Empire. The most important of these were the internal divisions within the state, which consisted of the alienation of the population caused by widespread corruption. The religious quarrels and racist reaction against the barbarians were not unimportant either. When all of these centrifugal forces were combined at a time when the Empire was threatened by outside and inside forces, as happened at the turn of the fifth century, the Romans were in real trouble.

The least important sources of internal trouble were the peoples and tribes who lived inside the Empire, but who were not assimilated. These consisted of the Jews, Samaritans, Tzani, Isaurians and Berbers. Their revolts could lead to a full-scale war that required the intervention of the army, but in comparison with the above they did not pose a real existential threat to the Roman state. They were just too poorly- and lightly-equipped by Roman standards to oppose the Roman army. Furthermore, the problems with the Jews and Samaritans were actually usually caused by persecution. In other words, the foolish Roman policies were the principal cause for these. In short, these problems could have been easily avoided. The situation was about to change when the Romans allowed the masses of armed Germanic peoples to settle inside the Empire. Their presence weakened the Roman ability to control other dissidents inside the Empire. Most importantly, the intensification of the persecution of religious minorities intensified under the bigoted Catholic-Orthodox rulers, which led to an ever-deepening sense of discontent among these minorities – to put it simply, the persecution of the minorities caused them to lose their loyalty towards the Empire.

Chapter Three

The Year 395:[1] Stilicho vs. Rufinus
The Puppet Masters: Stilicho and Rufinus
The Puppets: Honorius and Arcadius

Stilicho's and Rufinus' Moves to Secure Their Power

After his death Theodosius was succeeded by his two sons Honorius and Arcadius who were not only young (Honorius 10 yrs and Arcadius 17 or 18), but also lacked a suitable military education. Thanks to this, both had been given tutors who were the actual rulers. Rufinus acted as unofficial vice-regent for Arcadius and Stilicho for Honorius. The first thing both of these men did after the death of Theodosius was to secure their own position by acting as patrons while also amassing money from all possible sources. They needed this money so that they could bribe the army, the high command and other power brokers. The patronage in this case meant that both were ready to accept bribes, so that those who sought office could buy those from them, both were ready to accept bribes from defendants or from others who wanted a favourable ruling. As noted by several historians, as an Easterner Stilicho lacked a solid power base in the West which meant that he was more reliant on the support of the wealthy senatorial families than his predecessors.[2] The influential pagan senator Symmachus served as Stilicho's guide in these matters. Stilicho adopted the policy of tolerance towards pagans, for example by allowing the senators to return the statue of Victory to the Senate House, and he was also tolerant towards the Christian heretics among them. He demonstrated this by appointing several such persons to important positions. It is therefore not surprising to find that there were several pagans in the top brass under Stilicho. However, this concerned only the persons who were politically, economically or militarily important. Stilicho was himself staunchly Catholic and was the prime motor behind Honorius' legislation against pagans and heretics, but this was directed towards the commoners. The purpose of this legislation was obviously to keep the Catholic clergy happy.[3] This was not a new phenomenon, because even Theodosius I had felt it necessary to buy the support of the House of the Anicii/Auchenii by nominating two of its members, the brothers Probinus and Olybrius, as consuls for the year 395. It was wise even for emperors to show proper respect to the most influential families in the West.

Since the 'regents' controlled access to the court, both emperors were quite unaware of what was going on, and even if they were they could have done very little about it. The simple reason for the amassing of wealth through corruption by both Stilicho and Rufinus was that ever since the corruption among the upper hierarchies of the imperial administration and military had been allowed to run rampant after 365 the person who had the most wealth to spread had the most power. It should be noted, however, that Zosimus changes his view of Stilicho from the corrupt person of Eunapius, who is his source for the above, into that of an upright person by the time Stilicho dies. It is possible that the difference reflects the use of different sources as is usually assumed, but in my opinion an even likelier answer is that once Stilicho had secured his position he did indeed change his policies so that his goal was then to make the imperial administration as free from corruption as possible. Stilicho was also quite prepared to strengthen his own position by courting the Senate, treating it and its members courteously and showing tolerance towards paganism. The destruction of temples was stopped and the statue of Victory was returned to the Senate House.

At the time of Theodosius' death at Milan on 17 January 395 Stilicho was de facto commander of the Western armies as *magister peditum* or (*comes et*) *magister utriusque militiae* (*praesentalis*), and of the bulk of the Eastern field armies (probably the two Eastern praesental armies). This made him the most powerful military commander in the Empire. In addition to this, Stilicho claimed that on his deathbed Theodosius had made him the guardian of both his sons. We do not know the truth of the claim was because Stilicho in a position to fabricate such a claim, but in light of the fact that Theodosius knew the

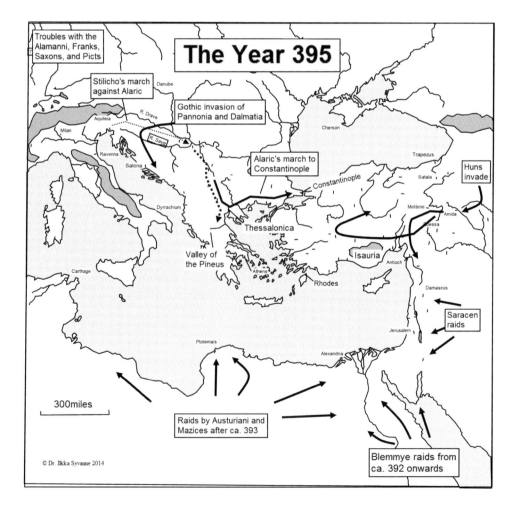

The Year 395

Troubles with the Alamanni, Franks, Saxons, and Picts

Stilicho's march against Alaric

Danube

R. Drave

Aquileia

Milan

R. Save

Ravenna

Gothic invasion of Pannonia and Dalmatia

Salona

Cherson

Trapezus

Huns invade

Alaric's march to Constantinople

Dyrrachium

Constantinople

Satala

Melitene

Amida

Edessa

Thessalonica

Valley of the Pineus

Carthage

Athens

Isauria

Antioch

Rhodes

Damascus

Ptolemais

Jerusalem

Saracen raids

Alexandria

300miles

Raids by Austuriani and Mazices after ca. 393

© Dr. Ilkka Syvänne 2014

Blemmye raids from ca. 392 onwards

true character of Rufinus, it is by no means impossible that he would have wanted his relative Stilicho to hold the reins of power and to protect his sons. Theodosius also knew that the teenage Arcadius was not really suited to rule an empire and therefore in need of guidance. Stilicho was the best candidate for that job. He was related to the family through marriage, he had extensive military experience, and, most importantly, he was a half-barbarian (his father was a Vandal who had served as a cavalry commander under Valens), as a result of which he could not hope to gain the throne(s) for himself. What is certain, however, is that neither Stilicho nor Rufinus could act as official guardian/vice-regent for Arcadius because he was 17 or 18 years old and therefore regarded as an adult. It was just that Arcadius was an inexperienced, comfort-loving young person whose views could be influenced by those near him. However, as we shall see, it was still Arcadius who called the final shots. In addition, as time passed he also assumed a much greater role in the governing of the Empire than is usually assumed.

What is important about the above is (regardless of the fact whether Stilicho's claim was true) that by claiming to be the guardian of Arcadius, Stilicho was also claiming to be the de facto ruler of the East. Rufinus, not unnaturally, would not accept this claim. His position in the East was quite secure because he had been ruling in the name of Arcadius for some time and because he had either managed to bribe the key players or had placed his appointees in the key offices. He was also a Catholic and native Roman. However, his position was weakened by two things: 1) he had made many enemies in the course of his rise to power; and most importantly 2) because the Eastern praesental armies were in the West under the command of Stilicho. The presence of the disillusioned Alaric (a member of the Tervingian royal house, the Baltha-braves) and his mostly Gothic *foederati* in the Balkans (they had been sent back in the middle of winter) was also a double-edged sword. According to Zosimus, the reason for Alaric's hostility was that Theodosius had given him only the command of the barbarians but not command of the regular army. In other words, he wanted a higher military rank than he had been given.

The two competitors also sought to tie themselves more closely to the imperial families through marriage contracts, but only Stilicho succeeded in this. Stilicho betrothed his daughter Maria to Honorius in 395. The couple were then united in about 397/398 (Zos. 5.3, 5.4.1, 5.12.1, 5.28; dated to 397 by Cameron). By contrast, Rufinus failed in his attempts to have his daughter marry Arcadius thanks to very skilful plotting by the eunuch and *Praepositus Sacri Cubicularii* Eutropius, who managed to have Arcadius marry the daughter of Bauto, who had been raised in the household of one of the sons of Promotus (the mortal enemy of Rufinus). Arcadius' marriage with Aelia Eudoxia naturally weakened Rufinus' hold on him quite decisively.

The Invasions and Revolts of 395[4]

After Theodosius and Stilicho had defeated Arbogastes and Eugenius, they pacified Italy and the 'Alpine tribes' between September 394 and January 395 (Claudian Ruf. 2.1ff.). This appears to mean that Stilicho and other generals did the pacifying while Theodosius visited Rome to court the powerbrokers, the senators and especially the House of Anicii. In consequence of this West Rome was peaceful. In contrast, the situation in the East was quite unsettled. Alaric and his mostly Gothic *foederati* revolted in Macedonia, probably at the instigation of Rufinus, from where they then advanced to Thrace opposite Constantinople.[5] Alaric's forces consisted mostly of the Tervingi Goths and their allies the Huns and Alans, together with a mixed group of others who had joined the warband. In my opinion, however, the Gothic element was dominant.[6] This is proven by the sources that refer to the forces solely as Goths and which subsequently call their leaders kings of Goths. The Greuthungi Goths, Alans and Huns who had been settled in Pannonia by Gratian in 380 appear to have been equally dissatisfied with the situation, because we learn from Claudian that other Goths had crossed the frozen Danube into Pannonia in 395, from whence they advanced into the borders of Dalmatia. It is probable that the Federates of Pannonia had actually invited their brethren across the frontier because no fighting is reported to have taken place at the border. The likely reason for the arrival of these Goths in the area and their invasion of Pannonia and Dalmatia is that they were fleeing from the Huns of Uldin. The fact that there were Gothic invaders in Dalmatia/Pannonia (Claudian, Ruf. 2.36–48) while Alaric was in Thrace or Macedonia or Thessaly proves that these invaders were a separate group of Goths, most likely already under the leadership of Radagaisus – who was certainly their commander later.

The invaders also included the Marcomanni and Quadi. The archaeological record shows clear signs of the destruction brought about by the invaders. The Gothic invaders reached Salona, and although this city and the other fortified cities along the coast were spared destruction, they inflicted such massive damage to the north of the province of Dalmatia that most of the cities were abandoned in favour of old hillforts. The imperial textile factory at Bassiana in Pannonia Inferior was also transferred to the more secure Salona at this time. The people also fled from Pannonia and north Dalmatia to the protection of the fortified cities of the Adriatic coast and its islands. At a later date, when Alaric was devastating Italy, many Italians did the same and fled to the relative safety provided by the Dalmatian coastal areas.[7]

The situation was made worse by the fact that the Huns invaded during the winter of 394/5 through the Darial Pass into Iberia, Armenia and from there to Persian and Roman territory. According to Claudian, the Huns reached the Halys River, Cilicia, the Orontes River, and Syria. This invasion meant that forces posted in the East could not be transferred to the Balkans, and what was even worse was that the forces posted in the East were too few in number to offer effective resistance against the Huns.

Ancient sources claim that it was Rufinus who had invited these invaders and who had instigated the revolt of Alaric to preoccupy Stilicho. It is usually thought that this was propaganda spread by Rufinus' enemies, but in my opinion the situation was more complex than that. The reason for the belief that Rufinus had invited the Huns to invade Asia Minor, Mesopotamia and Syria is that the people were quite aware that Rufinus possessed a sizable private guard of Huns and that he had previously been very accommodating towards the barbarians. It is probable that modern historians are correct about this aspect. The accusation that Rufinus would have called the Huns to invade the East is indeed likely to be untrue. However, the accusation that Rufinus had asked Alaric to revolt is actually likely to be true. Firstly, Rufinus lacked military experience and prestige, as a result of which he needed to prove his usefulness to the state. Secondly, in the absence of the praesental armies Rufinus needed to obtain forces that would be loyal to him. By instigating Alaric to revolt, Rufinus would have demonstrated to the people, nobility and emperor in Constantinople that the Gothic Federates posed a serious risk that only an experience statesman like he could handle, and then by diffusing the danger in person Rufinus proved that his services were indispensable to the state.[8] As a result of Rufinus' devious move Alaric and his followers were also in personal debt to him. Unfortunately for Rufinus, his plots actually contributed to his own downfall.

Stilicho and Alaric's First Attempt to Secure a Military Command[9]

Alaric and his mainly Gothic *foederati* felt that Theodosius and the Roman high command had purposefully sent the Gothic vanguard against overwhelming odds at the Battle of the Frigidus River in order to cause casualties (supposedly 10,000 Goths out of 20,000 lost their lives) among the former rebels. Consequently, Alaric and his men wanted to be rewarded for their bravery at the Battle of Frigidus. As noted above, Alaric was also not satisfied with only the command of the *foederati*, but wanted a regular command. The minimum requirement for Alaric personally appears to have been to be rewarded with the office of *magister militum*. Theodosius had failed to do that, but now Rufinus offered him his best chance if he would just follow Rufinus' wishes. Alaric was quite prepared to comply and he incited his Gothic followers to start a rebellion. In order to secure his own position Alaric had himself crowned as king of the Goths, which means that he became the first king of the Tervingi since they had replaced kings with judges at the beginning of the fourth century.

Alaric pillaged Macedonia and Thrace, but left Rufinus' estates (undoubtedly including the Huns billeted there) unharmed, and then advanced against Constantinople, which he put under siege. The leaving of someone's estates unharmed was a standard stratagem in antiquity to compromise the person in question, but in this case there is actually every reason to believe that Alaric and Rufinus were indeed cooperating and that it was because of this that Alaric did what he did.

Therefore, when the Goths were at the gates of Constantinople Rufinus dressed himself as a Goth and went out of the city in person to meet Alaric. As a result of their conference Alaric abandoned the siege and marched to Thessaly. I agree with Liebeschuetz (1990, p.58) that the evidence points to the conclusion that Rufinus bought Alaric and his *foederati* with a promise that entailed some form of billeting arrangement in Thessaly, because it is quite clear that the Goths were not in revolt after the meeting. It is also quite probable that Rufinus had agreed to obtain the position of *MVM per Illyricum* for Alaric in return for his services. The murder of Rufinus changed the situation. It was then clear that the government would not keep its promises and Alaric and his *foederati* had to restart their revolt to put pressure on the Eastern government to keep its promises. (See later.)

In the meanwhile, when the news of the invasion of Pannonia and Dalmatia and the revolt of Alaric was brought to the ears of Stilicho, he acted like a good commander was expected. After the snow had melted, he assembled the Western and Eastern forces and marched across the Julian Alps against the enemy. Claudian (Ruf. 2.100ff.) states that when Stilicho had crossed the Alps the barbarian hordes immediately stopped their ravages and assembled together in a plain in Thessaly. The barbarians built a fortification which consisted of a double moat, planted stakes at intervals, and formed their ox-hide rigged wagons all around like a wall. In other words, the Goths formed their traditional *carrago* (wagon laager) somewhere in the Valley of Pineus in Thessaly.

It is unfortunate that Claudian fails to tell us how Stilicho dealt with the Gothic invaders of Pannonia and Dalmatia, because the army inside the *carrago* clearly belonged to Alaric and not to the other army, unless Alaric had somehow managed to obtain their support as well, which is unlikely in light of future events. The likely reason for this is that Stilicho had done something that was considered dishonourable, such as buying peace from the invaders, and this was therefore something that needed to be suppressed in a panegyric. Since we know that Stilicho reached Thessaly only in September/October (the date can be counted backwards from the date of the death of Rufinus), it is clear that the pacification of the Goths of Pannonia would have taken at least two to three months, if Stilicho did indeed march to the Balkans immediately after the snows had melted. It is probable that Stilicho settled the invaders (probably under Radagaisus) where they had invaded, namely in Dalmatia, because there were also Federates settled in Pannonia. The border between East and West Rome was located at Epidamnus (Procopius, *Wars* 3.1.16), which means that Dalmatia was under Stilicho's jurisdiction to give to the settlers. Since we also know that the allies of Alaric for the years 400–402 consisted of those settled in Illyria, it is very likely that the new invaders were indeed settled in Dalmatia, which could be considered to be part of Illyricum/Illyria (see later).

Stilicho (Claud., Ruf. 2171ff.) marched his army close to the enemy *carrago* and deployed his 'cohorts' for battle. The Armenian cavalry was posted on the left wing and the Gallic cavalry to the right wing. The infantry was presumably deployed between these wings. Claudian (Ruf. 2.171ff.) claims that the precipices and deep rivers would not have been able to stop the charge of these cavalry forces and he claims that the Goths would have been destroyed if Stilicho would have just given the order. However, this was not to be because it was not in Rufinus' interest to allow this. In fact, he had already pleaded his case successfully with the emperor Arcadius, who had agreed to order Stilicho to leave Alaric unmolested and return the Eastern armies to Constantinople.

I agree with O'Flynn (pp.32–33) and Hughes (pp.80–87) that it is very likely that Stilicho had considerable difficulties in controlling his Western forces that he had previously defeated, the *foederati* enrolled into the Eastern field army, and the other Eastern field armies, and that it was these difficulties that contributed to Stilicho's willigness to obey Arcadius' command to abandon the campaign and send the Eastern forces to Constantinople. In my opinion, however, it is still clear that Claudian is correct in stating that Stilicho was also eager to obey because he saw a chance to use Gainas and the Eastern forces to assassinate Rufinus. In this he had collaborators in Constantinople who included at least the eunuch *Praepositus Sacri Cubicularii* Eutropius. It is quite clear that Stilicho ordered Gainas to take the Eastern armies into Constantinople with orders to assassinate Rufinus. Stilicho and Gainas had large numbers of willing collaborators. The Eastern field armies would have by then learnt of the pillage of Thrace by Alaric's forces and of the treaty between Rufinus and Alaric. We should not forget that most of the Eastern field armies had families and possessions in Thrace and they were more than eager to march home and take revenge against Rufinus.

It is also quite obvious that Stilicho had to abandon his campaign against Alaric after he had dispatched Gainas to Constantinople and return to Italy, because most of his forces now consisted of the Westerners who did not feel any particular loyalty towards him. Stilicho needed to strengthen his own standing among these men and to fill up the West's depleted ranks with new recruits. He also needed a successful military campaign before he would dare to challenge Alaric and the Eastern Empire again. (See PLRE Stilicho, Claud. in Ruf. 2.101ff, 2.202ff., Zos 5.7, Joh. Ant. fr. 190, Philost 11.3.) It is therefore not surprising that Stilicho's next campaign in the winter/spring of 395/396 was directed against the peoples of the Danube and Rhine.

In the meanwhile, Gainas led his forces via Thessalonica to Constantinople, where the army was paraded in the Campus Martius just outside the city in honour of Arcadius. This appears to have been done in collusion with Arcadius and Eutropius so that Rufinus was separated from his bodyguards, because he had to accompany the emperor to meet the army outside the city (Zos. 5.7.4–5). According to Claudian's narrative (Ruf. 2.348ff.), the army was deployed so that the infantry was arrayed on the left and cavalry on the right. The horsemen wore helmets and scale armour (*lamina*), and the heads of their horses were encased in iron and their forequarters with iron plates so that they looked like moving iron statues. In short, Claudian claims that the Roman cavalry consisted primarily of cataphracts. On 27 November 395, when the emperor and Rufinus arrived, the soldiers duly surrounded Rufinus and drew their swords. Then one of the men burst forward and thrust his sword into the man while stating that he was acting as the hand of Stilicho. After this, the rest followed his example and hacked Rufinus to pieces, and these pieces were then transfixed on the spears to demonstrate their deed to the rest of the army and populace. The populace showed their support by rushing to the scene to hurl stones at Rufinus' head, which had been transfixed on a spear. So ended the illustrious career of Rufinus, and Eutropius became the principal advisor of Arcadius. Rufinus' wife and daughter fled to a church, but were spared and then sent to Jerusalem.

Thanks to the fact that the young emperor had come to trust Eutropius, the killing of Rufinus meant the rise of Eutropius to power. Eutropius' first move was to confiscate most of Rufinus' estates for himself and let others take the rest, and the assumption of the powers previously held by Rufinus. His next move was to remove all those from office who had supported Rufinus or who could challenge his position. Eutropius used the former sausage-seller, now an officer, Bargus to level false accusations against Timasius, who was duly convicted into exile on an Egyptian oasis by the court presided over by Saturninus and Procopius. En route there, Timasius disappeared. According to one story, Timasius' son Syagrius rescued him with the help of some robbers, but the truth was not known. The only thing that was certain is that both Timasius and Syagrius were never seen again. Bargus was initially rewarded with a promotion, but soon after this it was his turn to be convicted with the help of his estranged wife. Another important person to fall from power was Abundantius who was first exiled to Sidon and then to Pityus. Eutropius owed his position to Abundantius and he repaid him with ingratitude. But this was not the entire extent of the purge. According to Claudian, the prisons were filled with nobles, and places of exile in the deserts of 'Meroe' and 'Ethiopia' were filled with weeping exiles.[10]

Eutropius replaced these men with supporters of his own. Some of these were men of lowly origins. The principal reason for this was that as a eunuch Eutropius' own background was filled with inglorious details. He may have served as a eunuch-prostitute and as a panderer/pimp to his slave masters before he was granted his freedom. Consequently, he felt himself secure only when surrounded by men of similar lowly origins and who owed their rise to power to him. These included the new *Magister Officiorum* Hosius, who was a former slave and cook of Spanish origins, and the *comes* (?) Leo, who was a former weaver by profession. He was also a drunkard and womanizer. Both belonged to the advisory council of Eutropius. The role of Hosius, in particular, was instrumental in the securing of power for Eutropius. Some of the powers previously held by the praetorian prefects were now handed over to the *Magister Officiorum*, but this was not the most important of the functions performed by the *Mag.Off.* Zosimus states that Eutropius had spies in almost every province to spy upon the populace and to enquire whether there would be any chance for the confiscation of property on some excuse. These spies would have been controlled by Hosius in his capacity as *Magister Officiorum*. The young *Comes Domesticorum* Subarmachius, an excellent archer who belonged to the royal house of Colchis, was not only a hopeless drunkard, but even more importantly completely loyal to Eutropius. This means that Eutropius had an absolute hold on all intelligence and security services and the units of imperial bodyguards in and around the capital. Arcadius had no other alternative than to follow the wishes of his eunuch advisor.[11]

The second class of administrators used by Eutropius consisted of career men who did not have aspirations to overthrow Eutropius. He found two such career men: Caesarius (395–397) and Eutychianus (397–399). The former was rewarded with a consulship in 397 and the latter in 398. Eutychianus was the Typhos of Synesius' *de Providentia*, the wicked son of Taurus, leader of the pro-German party and brother of Aurelianus (the Osiris of Synesius).[12] In truth, Eutychianus, just like his master Eutropius, was not pro-German but rather a pragmatist who followed the policy that he and his patron considered the wisest in the circumstances, which was to appease some barbarians in order to keep them divided. Eutropius also made certain that the security apparatus of the court and the central administration was securely in his hands by making Hosius, a former cook, *Mag. Off.* Eutropius also knew that he had two serious weaknesses that he needed to overcome: 1) he lacked military experience; and 2) as a eunuch he also lacked the respect of military men. Consequently, as I noted above, the *MVM per Illyricum* Abundantius and *MVM Praesentalis* Timasius were exiled and their offices were apparently kept vacant (no office holders are known for the period), and Gainas was not given any new high command as a reward for the killing of Rufinus.[13] In spite of this, Gainas still managed to improve his own position for the future through patronage because, according to Sozomen (8.4), Gainas promoted several of his friends to *tagmatarches* (tribunes?). This proves that Gainas did have some influence within the court, even if he probably failed to obtain the position and respect he yearned for.

The initial consequence of the murder of Rufinus and the rise of Eutropius was a peace between East and West Rome, but this situation did not last because Stilicho had his own plans regarding the East, which was to serve as its de facto ruler in the name of Arcadius. Eutropius would have none of this. He was adamant that the only person suited to rule the East was none other than him. It was only a matter of time before the egos of these two puppet masters would collide. In other words, I see no reason to oppose the picture painted by the ancient sources regarding the ambitions of these two men.

The Huns Invade the East in 395[14]

In late 394 the Huns appear to have noted that it was possible to use the Darial Pass[15] instead of the usual Darbend Pass. It must have been lightly defended. In addition to this, the peoples south of it appear not to have expected any invasion through it. Since Claudian states that the invaders marched over the Armenian snows, it is also clear that the Huns launched their invasion so early in the year (probably still in winter or late-winter) that it was totally unexpected. It was a rude awakening for the unsuspecting peoples south of the Caucasus. This was not the only problem facing the East at this time, for Philostorgius (11.8) states that at the same time as this happened the Mazices and

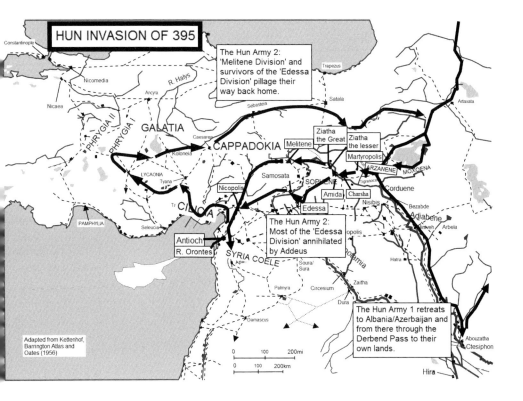

Austuriani devastated Libya and a significant portion of Egypt, and in addition to this they also attacked the Africans (presumably Tripolitania) to their west.

The Huns crossed the Don near its mouth, after which they turned southeast and broke through the Darial Pass into Iberia and from thence Armenia and Arzanene where they appear to have divided their forces into two armies, each of which in the course of the campaign divided themselves in two so that there were altogether four separate divisions.

The army consisting of two divisions, one under Basich and the other under Kursich advanced along the Tigris valley all the way up to Ctesiphon. The invasion had clearly taken the Persians by surprise, because it was only there that the Huns faced the first serious obstacle in the form of a major field army. It must have consisted of the bodyguard units posted in the capital and of the forces of the neighbouring provinces and probably also of the Arabs of the neighbouring Hira. On the basis of Priscus' account the Persians appear to have managed to surprise one of the Hun divisions while it was spread out in plundering. The Persians managed to gain the higher ground (as their military doctrine called for), from which they started to pepper the Huns with volleys of arrows. The surprised Huns did not attempt to resist but fled immediately and left behind most of their loot, but were overtaken by the pursuers. The Persians released 18,000 Roman male captives that the Huns had captured whilst still in the Roman territory. The Persians sent most of the survivors back, but some chose to remain in the Persian territory because they feared the Huns too much.

The next Persian ruler Yazdgert I (399–421) attempted to send the rest back, but about 800 still chose to stay. See later. These gestures of goodwill strengthened the Perso-Roman alliance which existed at the time. The figure of 18,000 males suggests that the fast-moving four divisions of the Hun army could easily take 72,000 male captives and at the same time inflict many more casualties through outright killing. This gives a good indication of how destructive ancient military campaigns could be for the losing side in terms of economic damage and lives lost.

The surviving Huns, most of which must have consisted of the division that was not surprised, managed to escape with only a small portion of their loot. According to Priscus' account Basich and Kursich took a different route than they had taken previously because this allowed them to defend themselves better than along the other. The reason that they had also pillaged the supplies along the route they had taken previously was not unimportant either. They marched to a place where the flame rose from the stone under the sea, which I take to refer to modern Azerbaijan (ancient Albania). This would indicate that they retreated through the Derband Pass. Maenchen-Helfen notes that the homes of the Huns of Basich and Kursich were not in the north of the Caucasus, but in Europe because these two leaders offered their services to the West Romans later.

The second army appears to have separated from the army in Arzanene, from where it advanced to Martyropolis and from there via Batnai to Amida (John of Ephesus/Pseudo-Dionysius[16]) where the army seems to have divided into two. One division advanced to Melitene and from there to Coelosyria (Philostorgius) while the other advanced towards Edessa (John of Ephesus/Pseudo-Dionysius), the base of the *magister militum per Orientem* Addeus. The division that advanced towards Melitene stopped to besiege the fortress of Ziatha. There were two fortresses called Ziatha, the great and the lesser. It was Ziatha the Great that the Huns besieged, because the local populace had taken refuge there. The circuit length of the walls of the fort itself was ten stades, and it was located on a mountain between the Tigris and the Deba so that it could be approached only from the north through one gate, in addition to which there were two aqueducts which went down to the rivers. The Huns somehow managed to gain possession of the one gate and the aqueducts with the result that they were able to subdue the defenders through thirst. Is this one of the instances in which some of the Romans wilfully deserted to the Huns with the result that they gained possession of the strategic approaches to the fort? After thirst had taken its toll, the remaining defenders surrendered, but were ruthlessly butchered and the fort burned. Just like the Mongols later, the Hunnic strategy was to terrorize all around with the speed of their invasion, combined with a ruthless policy of butchering all those who dared to resist them. It was an effective strategy, as their later notoriety well attests.

According to Euphemia and the Goth, the *stratelates* Addai (Addeus) did not allow the Federates to charge out of the city of Edessa against the Huns supposedly because there was 'treason' amongst them. The same story is also confirmed by Joshua the Stylite. It was generally believed that Rufinus, who had Hunnic bodyguards and who was staunchly Catholic, had invited the Huns to destroy the Arian Federate Goths. It is quite obvious that this was just hostile innuendo. John of Ephesus' account makes clear what the real reason was. According to him, when the Huns had crossed the Euphrates opposite Samosata, the bridge was cut off and the Romans assembled their forces and annihilated the entire Hun force so that there were no survivors. Since we know that the other division that had advanced to Melitene was on the western side of the Euphrates and were able to advance to Coelosyria and from there to Asia Minor (see below), it is clear that the Huns that were annihilated were on the eastern side where the Roman field army was assembled at Edessa. Consequently, Addeus, who was most likely heavily outnumbered, used a ruse (this was the real 'treason' and not Rufinus' or Goths' plans) and let part of the Hunnic force across and then cut off the bridge by some technical device (the Romans had either weakened the structures, or used fire-ships and/or fire-bombs) so that he was able to cut the remaining Huns to pieces. The Huns in their turn must have been destroyed by cavalry forces, mainly by the Gothic Federates, because it would have been impossible to catch the fleeing cavalry with infantry even when the bulk of the Hun force were against the river. This was a textbook case on how to force a nomadic foe to fight a pitched battle. Addeus must have been an able tactician, even if it is clear that he must have been one of those officers whom Libanius criticized for their corrupt practices.

The survivors of the 'Edessa Division' probably joined the 'Melitene Division' somewhere near Nicopolis and advanced past Antioch and over the River Orontes into Coelosyria (Syria Coele). After they had pillaged their hearts out, the Huns retreated past Antioch and then invaded Cilicia, Phrygia (Provinces Phrygia I-II), Galatia (where they reached the Halys River) and from there Cappadocia, after which they appear to have retreated through Armenia. Unfortunately, the sources do not state their route of retreat. They may have then used the Darial Pass for retreat, which would have taken them through Iberia once again, or alternatively they may have advanced into Albania (they had not yet pillaged it, which speaks for this alternative) where they would have met the First Army.

Overall, despite the loss of perhaps 25 to 30 per cent of their force (losses: the First Army defeated before Ctesiphon and chased away; most of the Edessa Division destroyed by the Romans; and the other losses incurred) and despite the fact that the Romans had lost no major cities to the invaders, the Huns seem to have considered the invasion a success for they attempted it again soon after this. The principal reason for this must have been that, according to Theodoret, there were many locals who willingly joined the invaders and fought in their ranks. The corruption of the top brass and the billeting of regular troops and Federates in the cities and villages had made the local civilian population quite ready to join the Huns. Joining the Huns promised freedom from oppression and arbitrary taxation, and who can blame the locals for yearning for freedom. The Huns must have thought the Empire ripe for taking. However, the inhabitants who initially welcomed the Huns soon learnt to fear them. The Huns were unlike the Goths and other Germans in the West, who were settled peoples with less harsh habits. The Huns were a predatory band of nomads who had less respect for life and property. It was not without reason that far larger numbers of Roman prisoners were quite eager to flee away from the Huns than there were deserters ready to join the Huns for the sake of freedom. The Huns did not settle in Roman lands but pillaged and looted it for financial gain. In contrast, the Germans settled on Roman lands and let the people live as before except that they extorted less tax than the corrupt imperial authorities. The principal difference between East and West Rome was that the latter faced such enemies that were psychologically less threatening to the populace at large than were the Huns and Persians to the Easterners. (See Syvänne: ASMEA 2014–2015).

Theodosius I
(source: Cohen)

Arcadius
(source: Beger 1696)

Honorius
(source: Cohen)

Chapter Four

The Years 395–399: Stilicho vs. Eutropius
The Puppet Masters: Stilicho and Eutropius
The Puppets: Honorius and Arcadius

West: Stilicho's Blitzkrieg along the Rhine in 396

The chaos resulting from the untimely death of Theodosius I did not lead to troubles only in the East, but also in the West. Stilicho's first objective was to secure the Rhine frontier with a lightning campaign. Stilicho was back in Milan by early 396 (PLRE1; Paulin V. Amb. 34), after which he conducted a campaign of intimidation along the Rhine (PLRE1; Claud. de cons. Stil. 1.189–245, de IV cons. Hon. 439–59).

According to Claudian, the reason for Stilicho's lighting campaign along the Rhine was that the Frankish kings (kings of the Cauci = Chauci) Marcomer (Marcomeres) and Sunno were attempting to raise a revolt in 396(?). The Suebi (also called occasionally Sygambri), who must be the Alamanni, were also planning to join the revolt. He further claims that the enemies included the Bastarnae, the Salii [Franks], the Bructeri from the Hercynian forests [Franks], the Cimbri, and the tall Cherusci from the Elbe. The inclusion of the Bastarnae presumably means that some parts of that nation had travelled west, possibly in conjunction with the Cherusci, where they would have joined the Frankish Confederacy. The Cimbri may have consisted of the remnants of that tribe that had been forced to flee their homes to join the Franks. Stilicho launched a lightning campaign to prevent this union of nations and also to obtain new recruits for his badly depleted army. Stilicho advanced through the Raetian Alps and forced the Suebi (Alamanni) to submit, which meant that Stilicho had nipped the forming of the grand alliance in the bud. When Stilicho's army then marched along the Rhine and reached the Frankish territories, the Franks decided to seek peace by handing over Marcomer. He was exiled to Etruria. Sunno attempted to avenge this, but was duly killed by his own men. I would date this latter event to the year 398 because Stilicho and Honorius received envoys seeking peace from both the Franks and Suebi (Alamanni) in late 398. According to Claudian, Stilicho appointed a new ruler for the Franks after the death of Sunno. I would interpret this to mean that Stilicho either raised Genobaudes to the throne of all the Franks or he raised some other unknown person to this same position.

East: Alaric's Second Attempt to Obtain Official Recognition 395–397[1]

One of the consequences of the rise of Eutropius was renewed hostilities between Alaric and the East Roman Empire. Zosimus (5.5.1 ff.) mistakenly thinks that these took place while Rufinus still held the reins of power. Eutropius felt unable to honour Rufinus's agreement with Alaric, which left the latter no other alternative than to put pressure on the government by raiding Greece, which also enabled him to feed and maintain his army and civilian followers. His efforts were helped by the fact that the proconsul of Achaiae, Antiochus, and the commander of the garrison of Thermopylae (rank unknown), Gerontius, were both appointees of Rufinus. The subsequent details (Zos. 5.6.3–4) prove that Gerontius was also in charge of the defences of the Isthmus of Corinth, which means that he had far greater military command than would be immediately apparent. In fact, it is clear that these two men controlled all the defensive structures of Greece including their citizen militias, which means that their position in the defensive structures of the Empire has not received appropriate attention in previous research. In my opinion, these two offices with their military forces were in all probability created during the reign of Gallienus. In this case the most important point, however, is that these two men were not motivated to support Eutropius. It was in their interest to undermine Eutropius' position by showing him to be incapable of defending the Empire.

According to Zosimus, when Alaric left Thrace (this would have taken place after the meeting with Rufinus mentioned above), he marched to Macedonia and Thessaly. It was in Thessaly where Alaric encountered Stilicho's army as discussed above and where he would have stayed until the news of the death of Rufinus with its consequences reached him. It was after this that he rebelled again and sent envoys to Antiochus and Gerontius to ask their support for his march south. These men complied and Gerontius withdrew his garrison away from Thermopylae and allowed Alaric to continue his march into Boeotia, which Alaric proceeded to sack without mercy. The only place which he left untouched was the city of Thebes because of its strong defences and because he was in a hurry to reach Athens.

According to Zosimus, Alaric hoped to take the city of Athens easily because it possessed too small a population to defend its long walls successfully and because its harbour Piraeus was short of provisions, but his hopes were not fulfilled. According to Zosimus' version, the reasons were the apparitions of the goddess Athena on the wall and after that the hero Achilles. He claims that these apparitions proved too much for Alaric to bear, so he sent heralds to negotiate a peace settlement with the Athenians. A more likely version would be that Alaric saw the people (and possibly also some professional soldiers) on the walls and came to the conclusion that it would be too costly to attempt to take the city. The terms were that Alaric was allowed to enter the city in the company of a few followers. When he did this, he was welcomed with open arms, and after he had bathed and had been entertained by the citizens and had received gifts, he left the city and the whole of Attica unharmed. In other words, the Athenians bought the peace and this was enough to satisfy the needs of Alaric and his followers.

After this Alaric advanced on the double against Megara, which his forces captured with a sudden attack. From there he proceeded through the undefended Isthmus, because Gerontius had withdrawn its defenders, against Corinth. Corinth and the surrounding villages were captured and pillaged. The next object was the city of Argos, which was also duly taken. Then the Goths proceeded to pillage the land between Argos and Sparta. According to Zosimus, Alaric also captured the city of Sparta because of Roman greed, as a result of which it was not defended by brave defenders. The rulers of Sparta were treacherous and followed the wishes of their superiors. These superiors must mean

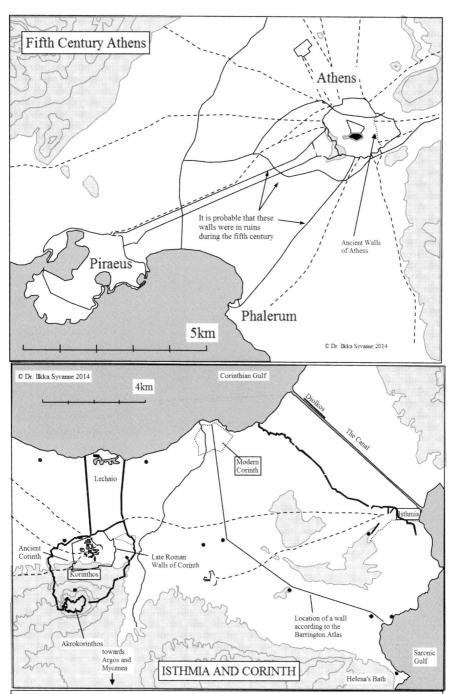

The above map of Isthmia and Corinth shows how easy it would have been for the Romans to block the route, if they would have wanted, hence the ancient accusations of collaboration between the man in charge of the defence and Alaric. It is practically certain that the accusations have a basis in truth. Alaric's Visigoths were numerous enough to occupy the entire width of the Isthmus, but it is still probable the army was still marched along the roads. The landing beach of Stilicho's army was obviously located in the Corinthian Gulf, probably in Lechaio.

Antiochus and Gerontius. In other words, these two men allowed Alaric and his Goths to pillage the Peloponnese at their will. According to Claudian (Gothic 191–193), the Goths encircled the city of Amyclae (Amyklai) south of Sparta by posting their cavalry on the heights of the Taygetos Mountains. On the basis of this it is probable that they took Amyklai as well, and one may make the educated guess that the Goths would also have pillaged all the other places close by.

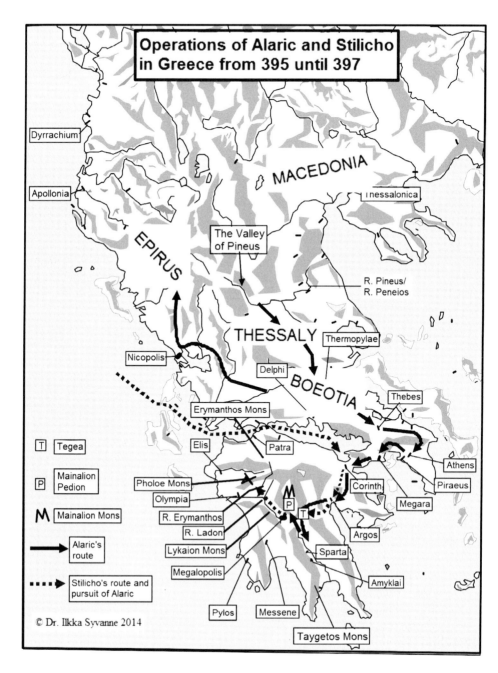

Operations of Alaric and Stilicho in Greece from 395 until 397

© Dr. Ilkka Syvänne 2014

When this was brought to Stilicho's attention, he decided to put a stop to it by leading an army against Alaric. Some historians think that Stilicho was attempting to wrest control of Greece away from East Rome, while some other historians like Ian Hughes (2010, p.95 with notes) think that Stilicho was acting out of concern for the welfare of the Roman people. In my opinion, both views are false. Stilicho was just exploiting an opportunity to interfere in Eastern politics to undermine Eutropius' position and to demonstrate that Arcadius needed his help. It is also probable that he wanted to eliminate Alaric and his Goths before Eutropius' government would wise up and use these forces against him. When the news of this invasion of the Peloponnese by Stilicho was brought to the ears of Eutropius, he manoeuvred to have Stilicho declared an enemy of the state by Arcadius so that Stilicho could not hope to obtain any support from any East Roman officials and officers. This also meant the confiscation of all property owned by Stilicho in the East.

After the preparations had been accomplished, Stilicho assembled his forces and fleet and sailed to the devastated Corinth where he landed his troops. Claudian (Claudian *IV Hon* Hawkins ed. and tr. vol.1, 4.559ff. with very slight changes; Platnauer ed. 4.461ff.): describes the campaign as follows:

When Gaul's extent to order was restored, Greece tottering, for support you arms implored: Ionia's waves a numerous fleet beheld, And winds with labour on the canvass dwelled. [*Stilicho had assembled a massive fleet and army to deal with Alaric.*] The ships their course by Neptune's favour bore along the liquid plain to Corinth's shore. At length Plaemon, who had left his home, an exile from the isthmus forced to roam in safety with his mother now returned to greet the port for which their bosoms burned. In floods of gore the wheels of warriors moved; The fur-clad youth no longer powerful proved; By dire disease had some been swept away, while other victims of the battle lay. [*This refers to the entire length of the campaign and proves that there were several battles and skirmishes all of which ended in Roman victory so that the Goths had been forced to seek refuge from behind their wagons and/or on mountains.*] Not all Lycaeus' branches [*the Lykaion Mountians just NW of Megalopolis*], brought in aid, not plenteous stores from Erymanthus' shade [*This can mean either the Erymanthos Mons or the river Erymanthos, but the information in Zosimus suggests the latter.*]. When heaped the lofty funeral piles to raise were found sufficient for the holy blaze; And Maenalus [*Mainalion Mons or Mainalion Pedion, the latter being likelier; on the basis of geography it is probable that Lycaeus, Maenalus and Erymanthus are in the wrong order in the text.*], with pleasure wood supplied to burn the relics of the havoc wide. Let Ephyre [*Corinth*] scatter ashes to the air; Let Sparta and Arcadia freed from care. On slaughtered heaps of lifeless bodies tread; And weary Greece take breath, relieved from dread! [*This suggests that the fighting between Stilicho and Alaric took place near Megalopolis and that the Romans first forced the Goths to seek safety in Lykaion Mons and then in the Mainalion Pedion, from which the Goths retreated to the River Erymanthus and from there to Mt. Phoebus as mentioned by Zosimus.*] A nation which overspread wide Scythia's snows: Fierce hordes that Athos' brow could not enclose, and even too narrow proved the extent of Thrace to give the savages sufficient space [*this refers to the massive numbers of Goths*], now breathless by your blows and generals fell; [*Claudian includes additional information*] about a battle on the River Ladon in Stilicho 1.183–4, which is left out here.] And those the world of late scarcely bound contracted on a single hill were found. [*This refers to the last place of refuge on Mt. Phoebus mentioned by Zosimus.*] Athirst and hemmed with thirst tormented as entrenched they lay. They sought for water turned another way which Stilicho at first by means expert with wondrous skill had managed to diver through vales unknown where he contrived a course in which the river from the foe to force. [*This refers to the turning of the course of the River Erymanthos so that the Goths who were occupying a place close to Mt. Phoebus were denied access to water. It was thanks to this engineering feat that Stilicho decided to play a waiting game and not force the issue.*] What cause for wonder then is this defeat, when you to serve barbarians now entreat? The cross Sarmatian with you ensigns moves [*There were settlements of Sarmatians in Italy.*]; The Gelon stripped of furs a soldier proves and for you makes war [*These are probably Goths serving under Stilicho*]; the Alani even seek to adopt the ways that Latin manners speak? [*There were large numbers of Alans settled in Italy.*] You choose for war brave men and for peace friends of justice and keep them in their positions. [*The above refers to the very large numbers of Federates serving under Stilicho*]

In short, my reconstruction of events is as follows. Stilicho took with him a truly large expeditionary force in which most of the cavalry consisted probably of the Sarmatians, Goths and Alans. Most of the soldiers, however, would still have consisted of infantry because these were easier to ship in sufficient numbers than the horsemen with their mounts. After having disembarked his army, Stilicho led his forces from Corinth via Argos and Mantineia to Tegea, while the Goths apparently withdrew towards Megalopolis possibly to the area between Megalopolis and Tegea known as Mainalion Pedion (or just south of it on Borreion Mons) or on the highland plain just west of Tegea. Stilicho duly pursued the retreating Goths and inflicted a defeat on them which forced the Goths to seek shelter on the slopes of Mainalion Pedion. After this, the Goths manoeuvred towards Megalopolis, but were once again defeated by Stilicho and forced to seek shelter on the slopes of Lykaion Mons. The Goths then managed to retreat towards the north-west. Stilicho pursued and attacked their forces close to the River Ladon and inflicted such a defeat that the river was filled up with corpses (Claudian Stilicho 1. 183–184). The Goths fled to the slopes of the Pholoe Mons, which the Romans then besieged, hoping to starve the Goths out after Stilicho had diverted the River Erymanthos from its course so that the Goths no longer received any water to drink.

What happened next is described by Zosimus (5.7.2–3, pp.136-7, 1814 translator unknown with additions inside parentheses):

Arriving in the Peloponnesus, he [*Stilicho*] compelled the Barbarians to fly to Pholoe where he might with ease have destroyed them all through the want of provisions had he not yielded himself up to luxury and licentiousness. [*Even though this was meant as a derogatory remark, this still refers to the standard practice among the period soldiers and generals, which were followed even the men were married.*] He likewise permitted his soldiers to plunder what the Barbarians had left; thus giving the enemy an opportunity to depart from Peloponnesus, to carry their spoils with them to Epirus, and to pillage all the towns in that country. When Stilicho heard of these transactions, he sailed back to Italy without having effected anything except bringing on the Greeks much greater and more grievous calamities by means of the soldiers whom he had taken with him. [*This refers to the living off the land and pillaging of the locals by Stilicho's forces.*]

The reason for the ability of the Goths to escape from the cordon of Roman troops appears to have been that they bribed some of the soldiers (their fellow Goths?) with gold. Zosimus' account suggests that the retreat of the Goths after this was so speedy that Stilicho was unable to catch them and, consequently, when Stilicho learnt of it he allowed his soldiers to pillage whatever the Goths had left behind, after which he decided to retreat to Italy.[2] This was the only wise course to take in the circumstances, because Honorius and his advisors were at loss what to do with the situation they were facing. Gildo had revolted and had cut off the grain supply to the city of Rome, and the Scots and Picts had invaded Roman Britain. Had Stilicho pursued Alaric north, it is possible that Honorius' government would have collapsed in the meanwhile. On top of which Stilicho faced the unwelcome prospect of forcing the East Romans to make a deal with Alaric so that they could unite their forces against Stilicho. Contrary to Hughes (2010, 99), I do not believe that Stilicho was forced to stop his campaign because he faced supply problems. He clearly had had enough supplies to besiege the Goths on a mountain, which proves that he had enough supplies! The real reasons for Stilicho's decision to retreat consisted solely of the strategic problems he would have faced had he decided to continue his campaign in Greece. He could have forced the East Romans and Alaric to unite their forces, while in the west Honorius faced the revolt of Gildo and the invasion of Britain. In fact, this is precisely what happened. Eutropius and Alaric found each other and concluded a peace. Alaric was appointed *MVM per Illyricum*, probably in 398, as a result of which he obtained full control of the tax-gathering and arms-production facilities in the area under his jurisdiction so that he could support his people (PLRE1). In addition to this, Alaric naturally gained control of the local regular Roman force. It was this that angered Gainas and Tribigild, who were not similarly rewarded despite being completely loyal to the Empire.

Despite the way in which it ended, Stilicho's campaign still had positive consequences for the Peleponnese. It had still freed the population of the Peloponnese from the hostile yoke and enabled them to start rebuilding their lives. These efforts are visible in the archaeological record. A good example of this is the refortification of Sparta, which was done hastily and unprofessionally after Alaric had sacked it in 396.[3]

It seems probable that the break between the administrations of Stilicho and Eutropius caused Stilicho to resort to the unprecedented practice of placing numerous guards to guard the coasts and harbours. There are four pieces of evidence to support this. Firstly, there is the claim of Eunapius (fr. 66.2) that during the time of the eunuch Eutropius he was unable to learn what happened in the West. According to Eunapius, those officials or soldiers who had access to information on political activity distorted it to their own advantage. The merchants were equally useless as sources because they too distorted the truth in order to obtain profit. This clearly implies a sudden stop to the normal traffic of information between the two halves of the Empire. Edict 7.16.1 of the Theodosian Code addressed by Honorius and Theodosius II to the *PP* Theodorus on 10 December 408 clarifies what had happened.

According to this Edict, the then-public-enemy Stilicho had some time in the past (before his downfall in August 408) created a new practice of posting numerous guards to the shores and harbours to prevent Easterners having access to the West. The fact that some merchants had managed to get through, as clearly stated by Eunapius, doesn't mean that Stilicho had not instituted the embargo already in 397–398, because smugglers would always find ways to bypass the obstacles.[4] It is clear that these restrictions on travel and commerce were immediately removed after the two halves were reconciled in 400, only to be reconstituted immediately after the two halves became hostile once again in about 405. It is possible that the guards placed on duty in 396 were retained, even if traffic was allowed. On the other hand, it is possible that the guards were not kept on duty during those periods in which there was no need for it. The Code cannot be used as evidence for either alternative, because it no longer includes the edicts regarding this matter.

The guarding of the coasts and harbours naturally led to the stopping of traffic of people and goods between the two halves of the Empire, which was detrimental to the economy and imperial tax yield, which brings to the forefront two other edicts contained in the Code. According to these (CTh 7.13.13 and 14, issued at Padua on 24 September and 12 November 397), Honorius granted to the senators and to those who had leased their land from the Privy Purse the privilege of being able to commute their quota of recruits with a money payment of 25 *solidi* per recruit, plus the money needed for clothing and food. These edicts had undoubtedly two purposes. The most important of these was that the state of war and halting of all commerce between the two halves of the Empire had created a situation in which the tax yield had fallen below what was needed, thanks to the fact that Honorius no longer received any income from the tolls on commercial traffic between East and West. In short, the purpose of these measures was to fill up the imperial coffers. The second purpose was of course to please the rich senators with this measure.

The Revolt of Gildo against Stilicho in 397–398[5]

The revolt of the *MVM per Africam* Gildo against Stilicho and his change of allegiance to the Eastern government took place in the autumn of 397. Claudian (Gildo 56ff., esp. 66–67) describes the event so that Gildo conquered the Province of Africa with Carthage close to the end of autumn in 397, and thereby obtained full control over the corn deliveries from North Africa to Rome. If Claudian is correct, then Gildo actually did not have control of Carthage before this, but after this Gildo controlled all land from the coast of Egypt up to Tingi (Tingitana).

In his Panegyric on Stilicho's first consulship (Hawkins ed. and tr. vol.2, Stilicho 1.371ff.; Platnauer ed. 1.244ff. with additions inside parentheses) Claudian provides important details of the forces employed by Gildo and the extent of his operations:

> By Gildo's furies had the Moors been led, A people placed beneath high Atlas' head, whose regions SOL overpowers with burning ray. The Cinyps passes in his winding way [*A small river on the N. coast of Africa formed the eastern boundary of Tripolis.*

It is also used in a general sense to denote the whole of Libya or Africa.]; The Triton [*the great salt lake el-Sibkah south of Tunis*] with rolling waters leaves as near the Hesperian gardens [*Hesperides were guardians of the golden apples near Mt. Atlas or meant in the general sense Libya.*] glide his waves. The Gir waters, the most renowned river of Ethiopian climes [*North-African Ethiopia in modern Algeria*], which like the Nile overflows the neighbouring ground. With him the Nubians, bearing arrows in their head-dress [*Note their presence in the Arch of Constantine the Great. The Nubians were famous for their archery skills.*], moved; The swift Garamantians his confederates proved; Nor Ammon [*Ammon was the main god of the Austuriani/ Laguatani*] though with answers of dismay the lively Nasamonians could delay. [*The Garamantes and Nasamonians were part of the Austurian Confederacy.*] In crowds the warriors through Numidia sped; Thick dust Gaetulian Syrtes covered [*see the Maps section*]; The numerous flights of arrows, seen arise, appeared to darken Carthagian skies [*implies that Gildo was forced to conquer Carthage*]. Here some with rods their rapid coursers guide; There others wear the lion's tawny hide, and skins of monsters huge with labour brought from Meroe in arid deserts caught [*implies once again the presence of Nubians who may have strengthened their numbers with the native Meroitic forces.*]. The heads of serpent with gaping jaws they as helmets bear [*could mean the heads of crocodiles or giant constrictor snakes*], and vipers' scales upon their quivers glare… Gildo left the Libyan climes to the rule of the Eastern Empire… From East edicts passed to subvert the loyalty of governors. No longer corn-supplies the other gave; These stores denied fell famine reared her head, and through the trembling city of Rome horror spread.

As noted, Gildo showed his support for the Eastern government by cutting off the corn supply to Rome, which eventually forced Stilicho to evacuate Greece when the war became prolonged and led to the severe shortage of corn in Rome. It was fortunate for the Romans that the corn-supplies were delivered during summer (Claudian, Gildo 54), which enabled the Western authorities to re-organize their supply network so that they shipped grain from Gaul and Spain to Portus and then along the Tiber to the city of Rome, despite the referrals of Claudian to the extremes of hunger caused by Gildo and Eutropius for the Romans (Claudian, Eutr. 1.399ff.). It is of course possible or even probable in light of what Claudian states that this is indeed what happened when Stilicho was away in Greece. Claudian appears to imply that the entire administration in Italy and Rome was paralyzed when it was not directed by Stilicho in person. And, in fact, the information given by Claudian regarding the preparations made for the re-conquest of Africa from Gildo lends support for this conclusion.

According to Claudian (Gildo 349ff.), Honorius and his staff had already formed a plan to conduct a military campaign in person against Gildo before Stilicho returned from Greece. He claims that Honorius had already prepared and manned the ships, and had already ordered all his barbarian subjects (Germani and Sygambri) to bring their allied fleets before Stilicho arrived. In light of this, it is quite easy to see why Stilicho hurried back from Greece. He needed to organize the corn supply of the city of Rome and to prevent Honorius from making very dangerous strategic mistakes. Another statement of Claudian (Eutr. 1.371ff.) may prove that Honorius had indeed been planning to ask the Germans to contribute their forces for the campaign as he claimed. Claudian claims that Stilicho received envoys from the Cauci (Franks) and Suebi (Alamanni) (collectively called Germani/Sygambri) with offers of peace with hostages in the fall of 398 and with the request to appoint new rulers without having conducted military campaigns against them in 398. Stilicho and Honorius duly accepted these peace proposals and appointed new rulers and gave both nations laws to follow. This does suggest the probability that Honorius and his advisors had thought it advisable to order the Germans to send their allied fleets against North Africa in 398. If the Germans had agreed to send their fleets, this would have been a dangerous move because it would have given them control over one of the breadbaskets of the Empire, and if they did not because the orders were contrary to their treaties of alliance (which are unlikely to have included clauses for the sending of fleets to assist the Romans), the orders endangered the existing treaty relationships. The fact that the Franks and Alamanni considered it necessary to offer peace in 398 suggests that there had been some sort of break in the relationship after Stilicho's campaign in 396, the likeliest reason for this being the above-mentioned request of Honorius as described by Claudian and probably also the planned revolt of Sunno.

We do not possess any definite information regarding the date of the creation of the units called *Honoriani/Honoriaci*, which had previously consisted of the *Foederati*. My own tentative suggestion is that Honorius and his advisors created these units for the African campaign that he planned to lead in person. This is by far the likeliest explanation for the creation of the new force for the campaign alluded to by Claudian. Most of the men consisted of Germans, as subsequent events make clear, with the implication that these men were those that Honorius had asked the Germans to contribute to his campaign. The creation of this army and its concentration close to the court with leaders loyal to Honorius would have spelled trouble for Stilicho. It is no wonder that Stilicho ensured that the planned campaign did not take place and that the troops in question were distributed throughout the Empire and not concentrated in Milan.

Claudian appears to preserve two versions of what happened next. According to Claudian's *Gildo*, Stilicho managed to convince Honorius to abandon his plans. He stated that imperial presence worked better from a distance. Closeness would diminish its awe. It was wiser for the Romans to employ Mascezel, the brother of Gildo, because he would be able to bring about defections in the enemy camp. Stilicho knew this, because Mascezel had arrived from Africa only recently with accurate information regarding Gildo's position in the area. There was no need for the sending of massive forces into North Africa. The reign of terror that Gildo had instituted would make his subjects eager to desert him at the very first opportunity once his brother arrived on the scene. Consequently, Stilicho chose the most famous elite units of the army to accompany Mascezel, and prepared a fleet in the harbours of Etruria to ship these to their destination. There was also no doubt that Mascezel would seek to kill his brother Gildo. Gildo had attempted to murder him and had then killed Mascezel's children.

According to Claudian's *On Stilicho's First Consulship* (325ff.), Stilicho re-established the custom of having the Senate declare war on the enemy, which had not been used in ages. This may imply that Honorius was not so easily convinced to abandon his campaign and that Stilicho had to employ the Senate in order to force Honorius to abandon his plans. Whatever the truth, it is still clear that Stilicho's position was not strong and that he needed to seek the support of the Senate for his decisions, as has been suggested by John Matthews (e.g. 268–273) and Ian Hughes. It is quite possible that one of the reasons for the marriage of Honorius with Stilicho's daughter Maria in late 397 or in early 398 was to console Honorius for the disappointment of not being allowed to lead the campaign in person.

Claudian (*Stilicho's 1st Consulship*, free translation based on Hawkins ed. and tr. volume 2, Stilicho 2.449ff and Platnauer ed. 1.333ff.) gives a good description of the strategy adopted by Stilicho in this case:

The veteran cohorts you strengthen and new prepare, and two fleets provide, one to carry corn for the purpose of alleviating hunger of the populace, and one for war... You could have filled the Tyrrhene Sea with your standards, the Syrtes with your fleet and Libya with your maniples, but your anger was calmed by the prudent fear that this might cause Gildo to think that you would advance against him with overwhelming force so that he would retreat into the hot desert and torrid lands [*See Syvänne 2004 with the M.A. Thesis 2000 on the same topic for the tactical choices available to the Roman commander when the Romans faced this prospect.*], or cause him to flee to east so that he would destroy the cities with fire. It is marvellous to tell that you feared to be feared and prevented his despair in the face of your vengeance. How greatly this increased his confidence of victory! The towers of hostile Carthage were now safe and the Phoenician fields rejoiced with numbers of unarmed husbandmen whose fields might have been laid waste by the fleeing Gildo. He was deluded in his vain hopes by sparing what was ours while not escaping his due punishment... He advanced as if he could ride them all down with his fast moving cavalry, and boasted that he would move down to the dust the Gauls who were enervated by the heat of the sun. But soon he learnt that in vain were the wounds caused by the venomous darts of Ethiopia [*note the presence of North African Ethiopians and/ or real Ethiopians from the east*] and so were the thick hails of javelins and round clouds of horsemen. They could not withstand the Latin pila [*heavy javelins*]. The cowardly Nasamonians are scattered in flight. The Garamantians throw shafts, but beg for mercy. The Autololes flee to their native deserts [*as I suspected in Vol.1 the Autololes had migrated west where they had also retained there original fighting style.*]. The panicked Mazaces throws aside his arms [*a part of the Austurian Confederation*]. The Moors urge their labouring horses in vain. The brigand is conveyed on a small boat from the shore, but is thrown by the winds to the fatal harbour of Tabraca. He discovered that no element offered a place of refuge from Stilicho.

In short, by employing Mascezel with a small number of elite forces it was possible to avoid having to fight a prolonged guerrilla war in which the cities and fields of North Africa would have been destroyed even before the fight would have started in earnest in the deserts. Claudian's account implies that the Roman leadership expected Gildo to learn in advance who commanded the invasion force, what its strength was and when it would arrive. This is actually not surprising because it was a question of civil war. It should be noted, however, that Stilicho had two fleets built, while he also strengthened the army with new recruits from Gaul: a fleet of warships and a fleet of corn transports

(Claudian, Stilicho 1.305ff.). The former was employed by Mascezel while the latter was used for the transporting of victuals from Gaul and Spain to Rome and could also be used if necessary to transport a large army to North Africa and/or to transport corn from Africa to Rome, even if this is not specifically stated by Claudian. This is something that can be read between the lines. Despite the fact that the Scots and Picts were threatening Britain, Stilicho clearly made no move to leave Italy before Mascezel had accomplished his mission. The reason for this must have been that he was prepared to go there in person if he needed – Britain was not as important as North Africa.

The elite units dispatched by Stilicho consisted of cohorts drawn from the Palatine legions Ioviani Seniores and Herculiani Seniores, and of the Nervii (*Sagittarii Nervii, Auxilia Palatina*), *Felices* (*Felices Iuniores Auxilia Palatina*, or *Equites Constantiani Felices Vexillationes Comitatenses*), *Legio Augusti* (*VIII Augusta or Octaviani?*) and *Leones Iuniores* (*Auxilia Palatina*). This information has usually been compared with Orosius's account, according to which Mascezel had 5,000 men against Gildo in the last decisive battle, but this is a mistake. Ian Hughes suspects that it is possible that Claudian did not include any low ranking forces in his list so that Mascezel may have had more men in the beginning of his campaign than he appears to have. Bury (after Seeck) suggests that Mascezel had about 10,000 men. This is possible, but necessarily so, because Mascezel's purpose was to win through diplomacy. In this context it is important to understand that the number of troops with Mascezel at the last battle cannot be used as evidence for the number of troops he had at the beginning of his campaign. The principal reason for this conclusion is that Mascezel would have needed to leave garrisons at Carthage and other important locations when he advanced to meet his brother on the battlefield. However, one may make the educated guess that each of the units would have had roughly about 1,000 men so that the entire force would have consisted of about 6,000 men, the equivalent of one old legion. If one interprets the *Nervii* of Claudian as the *Sagittarii Nervii* and the *Felices* as the *Equites Constantiani Felices*, then the purpose was to dispatch what would have been the equivalent of one old legion, but which in this case would have been composed of separate units of heavily armoured legionaries, medium infantry auxiliaries, light infantry auxiliaries and heavy cavalry. Zosimus (5.11.3) calls the size of this force large, but this is an overstatement in light of the details provided by Orosius and Claudian, even if one adds to the figures Berber auxiliaries and marines.

The expedition sailed from Pisa to the island Capraria, where Mascezel encouraged his followers by taking on board monks with whom he prayed and fasted day and night. With this gesture Mascezel associated himself and his expedition with the righteous Christian cause. He essentially promised to salvage the Christians of North Africa from the clutches of his pagan brother. From Capraria Mascezel continued his journey to Cagliari in Sardinia and from there to North Africa.[6]

According to Orosius (7.36), the decisive battle between Mascezel and Gildo was fought in the valley of the River Ardalius between Ammaedara and Theveste. He also states that the war and vengeance was ended without bloodshed, which is an overstatement but still indicative of the probable tactic adopted by Gildo. It seems probable that Gildo let his brother disembark the army without opposition while he with the regular forces withdrew to the interior (probably to Theveste), where he collected his tribal allies. Gildo's strategy appears to have been to abandon the unreliable coastal regions immediately and concentrate his army in the interior, where it would be easier to assemble the Berber allies from the various regions. This means that Mascezel probably disembarked his forces at Carthage, and, after having secured his position and having left a suitable-sized garrison (ca. 1,000 men plus the marines of the fleet?) to secure the city of Carthage, he advanced with the rest of his forces against Gildo. Mascezel was undoubtedly aware that he would be heavily outnumbered, which means that he was relying on being able to cause desertions among the enemy forces – he undoubtedly had a better reputation among the Africans and Berbers than his brother, plus he was also the wronged party. Mascezel was also more acceptable to the local urban and sedentary populations of the coastal regions because he was acting as the defender of the Christians against the pagan Gildo. In light of what Claudian and Orosius state this is even very probable.

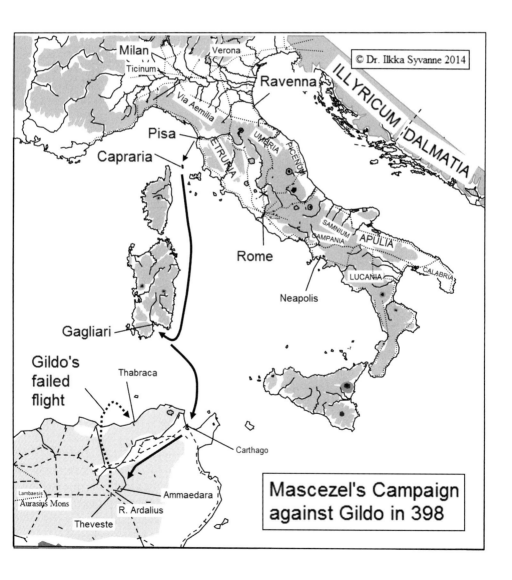

Claudian (Gildo 162ff.) claims that Gildo was a womaniser and a rapist, who executed those with any wealth or beautiful wives with trumped-up charges, and who was a known user of poisons and deadly herbs. When Gildo then got bored with the women he had forcibly taken, he always handed these over to his barbarian soldiers to mate. This same account is confirmed by other sources (e.g. by Orosius 7.36), which also point out how greedy and corrupt Gildo was and how he followed the heathen ways with every form of licentiousness. It would be easy to dismiss these accusations as baseless innuendo levelled against a foreign enemy but for the fact that Gildo was indeed forced to retreat into the interior without any attempt at holding the fortified cities of the coast. This does suggest that he had every reason to fear that the local citizens would betray him and open the gates, hence his readiness to retreat into the interior where he had the support of the local Berber tribesmen.

Orosius (and Marcellinus a.398.4) goes on to claim that Mascezel had encamped his small 5,000-strong army by the River Ardalius/Ardalio when the news was brought to him that 70,000 enemy soldiers had taken position in front of him. At first Mascezel was at a loss what to do, but after a delay he finally decided to leave his current position and march through the narrow river valley to Theveste, but then Orosius claims that on the following night he had a dream in which St. Ambrose instructed him to stay where he was and continue his march only after the third day. It is not impossible that a religious man would have had such a dream that would have appeared as a sort of revelation based on the real situation (the human brain does solve problems during the sleep), but one cannot entirely rule out the possibility that Mascezel would have invented such a dream to improve the morale of his soldiers. Consequently, Mascezel stayed where he was in an effort to lure the enemy into the valley where its overwhelmingly superior numbers would be useless. The enemy foolishly complied and when on the third day the enemy had advanced into the valley, Mascezel led his army forward. Orosius claims that by then Gildo's army had surrounded Mascezel's army in the valley. It is possible that this did indeed happen, but the sequence of events rather suggests that the enemy was advancing as a column spearheaded by the regular Roman troops (*militia*) under Gildo, and that Mascezel's forces were by no means surrounded, but let us still assume that Orosius is correct because Mascezel's purpose was to win through negotiation and not through fighting. When the regulars came into sight Mascezel met them in person and entreated them with words to change sides. When one of the standard-bearers (*signifer*) urged his men to attack, Mascezel struck his arm with a *gladius*-sword with the result that his *vexillum*-standard fell. The other regular cohorts interpreted this as a sign of surrender with the result that their standard-bearers reversed their standards towards Gildo. When the Berbers saw this, they thought that the regulars had deserted them, with the result that they panicked and fled in all directions. Gildo fled to some coastal city where he seized a ship and put out to sea, probably in an effort to reach the Eastern Empire. However, thanks to contrary winds his ship was forced back to the shore at Tabraca (it is possible that the sailors did this on purpose) where Gildo was captured and then strangled on 31 July 398.

Gildo had used his long tenure 'well' from the point of view of his own wealth. His estates, which were confiscated after his death, were so extensive that a new official called the *Comes Gildoniaci Patrimonii* had to be created to manage them (see PLRE1). This proves that Gildo was corrupt to the bone and had basically ruined the provinces under his control. It is no surprise that Mascezel was able to achieve his miraculous victory.

Contrary to the Catholic religious policy followed by the emperors in the West and East after 379, Gildo had also favoured the heretics, namely the Donatists who were even called '*Gildonis satellites*'. This is not surprising in light of the fact that Gildo appears to have been a pagan (see PLRE1 with Orosius 7.36). Gildo's intention must have been to secure a loyal base of followers (both heretics and corrupt officials/officers) in Africa who knew that their standing depended solely on their master Gildo. This created a situation in which, after the defeat of Gildo, the new administration was unable to follow the orthodox religious policy of the emperors. We know that the new officials in charge of the African provinces did not re-establish the Catholic Faith in Africa immediately, because Orosius states that this happened only after 413 (see later). Consequently, as regards Christian heretics Africa remained a special case within the Empire. It was preferable to maintain peace in Africa through religious tolerance, because North Africa was the breadbasket of Rome. One can say with good reason that the West-Roman economy was entirely reliant on the corn and taxes it got from North Africa. It was not unimportant either that West Rome also obtained a significant proportion of the gold needed for the minting of gold coins from West Africa via the caravan routes passing through the territory of Garamantes to Tripolitania.

However, religious tolerance was not enlarged to encompass the pagans. They were to be eradicated from Africa. In order to perform this mission, the Western government appointed Iovius as a special *Comes* for this task. On 19 March 399, he and the *Comes Africae* Gaudentius destroyed pagan temples in Carthage, after which they moved on to destroy temples in other parts of Africa.[7] The operation was a great success. It is possible that intolerance towards pagans was one of the causes contributing to the serious troubles the Romans were facing at Berber hands.

What is known is that the Berbers who had previously supported Gildo fled east and west and became bandits who threatened both halves of the Empire. This is not surprising in light of the composition of Gildo's forces mentioned above by Claudian and needlessly suspected by some modern researchers. The problem, however, became acute only later when the adverse weather caused other people to join the bandits (see Appendix 3). Denis Roques (1987, 220ff.) suggests that the fall of Gildo caused the East Roman government to dispatch a *comes et magister utriusque militiae per Orientem* to *Libya Superioris* (=*Pentapolis*) to reorganize its defensive structures, with the result that both Libyas were separated from Egypt and placed under a separate single commander who had the title *dux Libyarum*. This is the likeliest scenario, but it is also possible that the change took place earlier or later, or that both Libyas actually received separate *duces*. The idea was to secure the border against West Rome in a situation in which the East Roman general Gildo had been defeated. It is also possible that some reinforcements were sent there to bolster the defences at the same time.[8]

After his mission had been accomplished, Mascezel returned in triumph to Italy. He expected to be rewarded, but Stilicho had other ideas. He did not want any competitors around him. Consequently, Stilicho at first flattered Mascezel, but then had his bodyguards throw Mascezel into the river when they were crossing a bridge. Mascezel did not know how to swim and he was drowned in the currents while Stilicho watched and laughed.

The Troubled Rhine and Stilicho's British Campaign in 397–398

On the basis of Claudian's account (Eutr. 1.371ff.; Stilicho 1.191ff.) the Rhine frontier was suffering from some sort of troubles in early 398, which were possibly caused by Honorius's policies mentioned above. It is probable that this was the instance in which the Frankish king Sunno had attempted to rebel and was then killed by his own men, with the result that the Franks and Alamanni asked the Romans to nominate new kings. What is certain is that their envoys were present at the court in Milan in the autumn of 398. It is probable that it was then that the Romans gave to the Franks a single ruler who was to become the ancestor of the Merovingian house. As discussed above, it is also possible that one of the reasons for the renewal of troubles along the Rhine were the demands made by Honorius regarding his planned African campaign.

In light of Claudian's referrals to Stilicho's military successes against the Irish, Scots and Saxons in Britain in 398 it has often been suggested that he conducted a military campaign there in that year. This event is usually connected with Gildas' second Pictish war, after which the Romans withdrew the *legio* in 401 or 402. (See for example Salway (311ff.) with Miller).

Miller has usefully collected the extant evidence in Claudian and Gildas for the campaign, but has made one serious mistake regarding the timing of the campaign, because he does not include the referral to the time in his quote of Claudian's *Against Eutropius* 1 (391ff.), which I quote from Hawkins ed. and tr. volume 2 (1.565ff.; p.19ff; Platnauer ed. 1.391ff.) with some changes.

> However, the voice of truth proclaimed the crime to all the world that stained the Orient clime; The ears of Rome received at length the sound [*of the nomination of Eutropius as consul for the year 399, the news would have reached Rome before the year 398 so that Miller's dating January 399 is wrong in this context.*]… This having said, the powerful goddess [*Rome*] bore, her rapid course beyond the Po's famed shore, through airy regions towards the camp she flew, where soon the imperial ruler [*Honorius*] met her view [*This would have been in Milan*]. Honorius then with Stilicho was seen and Germans near who with humble mien for peace which he with bounteous heart bestowed. The Cauci were given laws. The flaxen-haired Suevi were given constitution. He sets a king over these and signs a treaty when hostages had been given. Others he took as allies for war so that the Sycambrians cut their flowing flocks of hair and serve under Roman standards. Rome [*the goddess*] felt pride and joy… Rome removed her veil of encircling cloud and spoke these words: 'O Prince! Success in distant countries shows how much to thee my powerful sceptres owes. The Saxons are subdued and the seas are safe. And Britain is safe from the Picts. And at my feet are the humbled Franks and Suevi. The Rhine I now own my Germanicus. But what Alas! The Orient realm envies with jealous eyes our success… Of Gildo's perfidy I ought not to relate… the guilty wretch got a well-deserved death at Tabraca and whosoever take up arms against you shall perish in like manner.'

In short, it is clear that the campaign against the Saxons and Picts took place before the fall of 398 for it to reach the ears of the rulers in Milan before the arrival of the German envoys. The other references to this event, usefully collected by Miller, show that the Romans had defeated the invading Saxons and the legion that Stilicho had apparently dispatched to Britain had defeated the invading Picts and Scots (Irish). This legion was later withdrawn to the continent to face Alaric in 401. Stilicho had also built forts in Britain that protected it against the Saxons and Scots. It is not known whether these campaigns included naval expeditions against Ireland, Caledonia and the Orkneys, as had

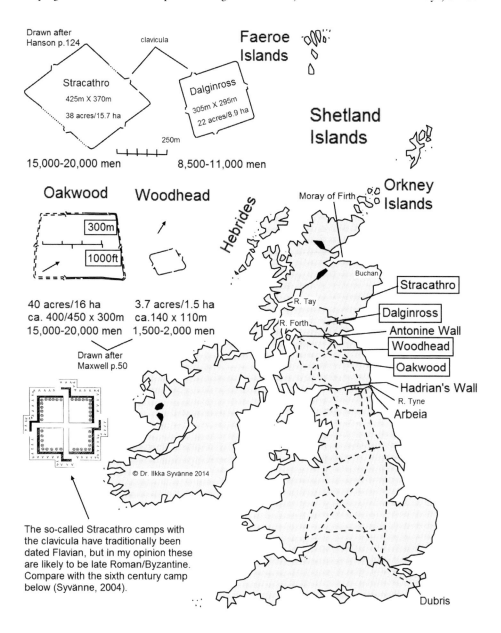

Drawn after Hanson p.124

clavicula

Stracathro
425m X 370m
38 acres/15.7 ha
250m
15,000-20,000 men

Dalginross
305m X 295m
22 acres/8.9 ha
8,500-11,000 men

Faeroe Islands

Shetland Islands

Oakwood
300m
1000ft
40 acres/16 ha
ca. 400/450 x 300m
15,000-20,000 men

Woodhead
3.7 acres/1.5 ha
ca.140 x 110m
1,500-2,000 men

Drawn after Maxwell p.50

© Dr. Ilkka Syvänne 2014

Hebrides

Moray of Firth

Orkney Islands

Buchan

Stracathro

R. Tay

Dalginross

R. Forth

Antonine Wall

Woodhead

Oakwood

Hadrian's Wall

R. Tyne

Arbeia

Dubris

The so-called Stracathro camps with the clavicula have traditionally been dated Flavian, but in my opinion these are likely to be late Roman/Byzantine. Compare with the sixth century camp below (Syvänne, 2004).

been the case during the reign of Theodosius I, but one cannot exclude this possibility in its entirety merely on the grounds that Claudian fails to state this directly. It is possible that he implied it with the statements that the enemies had been defeated.

As regards the size of the legion dispatched, it is impossible to be absolutely certain about its size, but a force of 1,000–2,000 men would seem quite a small figure if the intention was to protect as large an area as the whole of Britain. Consequently, I would suggest that Claudian meant the generic old legion of 5,000–6,000 men with ca. 500–600 cavalry, consisting of several units grouped together known as a *meros* or *legio*.

We do not know any details of this campaign, but the map which shows some probable late Roman marching camps in Britain gives an indication of where the Romans may have operated. The map is based on my own interpretation of the archaeological finds. It is usually suggested that the small numbers of so-called Stracathro camps with *clavicula* would date from the Flavian period, but in my opinion this is a mistake because this type of camp was particularly typical for the late-Roman period and less typical for earlier periods (see the accompanying map). It should be noted that it is impossible to date any of the camps to any particular reign. The Late Romans campaigned in the areas in question for example under Constantius I, Constantine the Great, Valentinian, Theodosius I and Honorius. It might be theoretically possible to connect the small Woodhead camp with the single Late-Roman legion if Stilicho did indeed dispatch so small a force, but this is far from certain, because there would have been enough local forces present in Britain to collect armies of about 15,000–20,000 men and there exist two camps of this size as well.

The Troubles of the Desert Frontier from Libya to Palestine in ca. 390–412

According to an important article by Denis Roques, at about this time began an eastward migration of the Austuriani which eventually created a domino effect all the way to Egypt and beyond. The reason for this conclusion is that many saints' lives and Jerome's letter 136 (in PL 22 col. 1086; and also in the Preface to the Commentary of Ezekiel, Book 3 PL 25 col 75) suggests that Berbers raided Egypt, Palestine, Phoenicia and Syria in about 410. Roques has speculated (see also above) that this was caused by the imperial persecution of Gildo's former supporters, because the Theodosian Code (CTh 7.19, dated 20 July 399) includes an Edict dealing with the problem of the Saturiani and Subafrenses that had revolted. Roques is undoubtedly correct to identify the Saturiani with the Austuriani. The Subafrenses escape easy identification, but may have been the Frexes or Fretenses. Roques suggests that these tribes moved east and were united with the Mazikes (Maziques) after which they marched to Cyrenaica and Egypt. However, in my opinion he has erred both in the timing of the troubles and in the cause-effect relationship, even if it is very probable that the presecution of Gildo's followers contributed to the phenomenon. Regardless, the fact remains that the troubles originated in Tripolitania and not in North Africa and the troubles also started before the revolt of Gildo, because Silvanus (Silvanus 5 PLRE1) had received the title of *Dux et Corrector Limitis Tripolitanae* by 27 March 393 and his successor Flavius Macedonius (Macedonius 8 PLRE1) had received an even grander title of *Comes et Dux Tripolitanae* with the honour *Patricius*, all of which imply serious troubles in Tripolitania, the neighbour of Cyrene. In addition to this, Roques has not taken into account the referral to the Ishmaelites in the same letter of Jerome, which makes it likely that some Arabic tribes were responsible for most of the devastation in Palestine, Phoenicia and Syria. In contrast, Irfan Shahid (BAFOC 22–23) claims that the Arabs were responsible for all the devastation, but she has failed to take into account the referrals to the Barcaei and Africa. It is clear that the Arabs and Berbers were both on the warpath.

Consequently, one can say that the tribes of Tripolitania were in an almost constant state of revolt from the early 390s onwards, and since the problem then spread east in the form of migration, it is probable that the cause of the revolt and migration was drought or rain (temporary climate change) and/or the emergence of locusts after good years that had caused tribes to attempt to seek a livelihood elsewhere. In fact there exists convincing evidence for a climate change for the turn of the fifth century from various places, all of which contributed to the mass migration of peoples from the 390s until 410s. This did not concern only the peoples of the desert, because either the Sea of Marmara was frozen for 20 days (Chronicon Paschale) or mountainous icebergs floated through the Sea of Marmara for 30 days (Marcellinus Comes) in 401. Procopius (3.3.1) states that the Vandals left Pannonia because of hunger, which means that one of the contributing factors in the mass migrations that brought Rome to its knees was indeed climate change – the cooling of the climate in Eurasia, North Africa and Arabia.[9] For the Romans the problems with the nomadic or semi-nomadic peoples of Africa and Arabia obviously meant that the trade contacts with Central Africa were cut off and that their own agricultural areas outside the fortified cities were pillaged and burned, and this was not even the whole extent of their troubles in the area. The Blemmyes defeated the Federate Nubians of the Dodekachoinos and forced them to evacuate the area in about 392/394. It is possible that the Blemmyes did this at the behest of the Romans, but we do not have enough details to make any certain conclusions. The Nubians reconquered the area at some point in time before 410/420 only to lose these areas once again to the Blemmyes by 423. It is very unfortunate that we do not know what the Roman role was in these tribal wars. For a fuller discussion, see the subsequent chapters with the Appendix 3.

The Bosporan Invasion in 397–398 and Eutropius' Fleeting Day of Glory in 399

The sources for the invasion of Asia Minor and Syria in 397–398 are very scanty, but on the basis of Claudian's *Against Eutropius* it is clear that the Bosporans and Alans invaded Asia Minor in about 397/398 and were then defeated by Eutropius, as a result of which Eutropius had himself nominated as consul for the year 399. The usual mistake is to identify the invaders with the Huns, but Claudian's text leaves no other alternative than to conclude that the invading forces consisted of the Goths of the Bosporus and of the Caucasian Alans. It should be remembered that the reason for Eutropius' ability to concentrate his forces against the invaders resulted from his very wise diplomacy. The alliances with Alaric and Gildo secured his western frontier against possible attacks by Stilicho.

The sources are as follows:

1) Claudian tr. by Hawkins Volume 2 (1.347ff.; p.12ff; Platnauer ed. 1.231ff.) with some changes:

An eunuch [*Eutropius*] judge!... The consul's actions prodigies reveal... What age or country has ever had eunuchs as judges?... Oh what a profanation. He even bears arms... Bellona scorn upon her face, beheld the Orient sinking in disgrace. When this old Amazon [*Eutropius. However, it is also possible that this had the double significance or reminding the audience that the Alans who had 'Amazon' warriors had let the enemy through the Darial Pass.*] the Getae [*the Getae means usually the Goths in Claudian and it is probable that the meaning is the same also in this case.*] spied with bow in hand and quiver well supplied, our enemies rejoiced at the sight and thought that men of the realm already failed. Flames spread, walls fell and dread havoc filled the plain, and hope found safety solely beyond the Phasis, mothers in dismay from Cappadocian domes were dragged away. The captive flocks from homes were forces to go and sip on Caucasus the flaky snow; For Scythian forests change the smiling fields and verdant pastures that Mount Argaeus yields [*a mountain in Cappadocia*]. Beyond Cimmerian fens [*beyond the Sea of Azov*], the defence of Tauric tribes [*this area, the Gothia, was under the Gothic rule at this time.*], the Syrian youth in servitude were found [*implies that one of the enemy divisions reached Syria.*]. So much spoil there were that the savage horde turned to slaughter [*there were too many prisoners to take north and in order to speed up the flight the slowest were killed.*]. However, Eutropius (can an effeminate slave feel shame?...) with conqueror's look returned in triumph. The infantry their floating flags displayed [*peditum vexilla*], cavalry squadrons like their chief in arms arrayed [*turmae similes meaning that the cavalry was armed as mounted archers like Eutropius*], and maniples of eunuchs thought worth of legions meet him and embrace their saviour... Eutropius was himself quite elated. His hollow cheeks he laboured to inflate... with broken tone, his voice appeared to fail; He seemed to struggle with the coming tear; Detailed his battle to a sister dear; To her expressed how vain his efforts proved to serve the state; that malice round him moved, that envy... Old sexless lump! What – try the sword to wield?... To perfect men resign the use of arms; Why fill two palaces with dire alarms and brothers [*Honorius and Arcadius*] joined by nature into hatred rise?... For such exploits Eutropius asked the year [*consulship for the year 399*].

2) Claudian tr. by Hawkins (Eutr. 2, Praef.; Platnauer ed. Praef 55–6.) with some changes.

Your bow and spear no longer fills the Armenian bosoms with fear nor do you proudly mounted on your fleet courser scour the plain. [*This suggests the likelihood that Eutropius had first defeated the invaders and had then pursued them at least up to Persarmenia, where he probably inflicted a new defeat on them; The arrival of the Roman army in Persarmenia would have been a breach of the peace treaty between the two powers*].

3) Claudian tr. by Hawkins (Eutr. 2. 114-16, p.36; Platnauer ed. 2.81-3) with some changes:

What should the soldiers hear that he won great battles single-handed? Should Constantine and Byzas be told that this wretch is the third founder of the city?

4) Claudian tr. by Hawkins (Eutr. 2. 133ff, p.37; Platnauer ed. 2.95-102) with some changes.

The frost more mild [*spring 399*], now gentle Zephyrus' breezes cheered [*a westerly wind*] and the flowers bursting buds appeared. A journey full of pomp while in the lap of peace, the court to the walls of Ancyra its annual journey was preparing. Eutropius all arranged, sea-toils to avoid, and move at pleasure during summer's sun [*Eutropius probably took Arcadius with him to Ancyra*]; The splendid train returned as if they'd brought the Medes in chains or Indus' waves had sought. [*I would suggest that Eutropius was conducting diplomatic negotiations with the Armenian king Khosrov for the purpose of beginning operations against Persia for which there exists circumstantial evidence in Moses Khorenatsi's history; the revolts of Tribigild and Gainas put a stop to these plans.*]

5) Claudian tr. by Hawkins (Eutr. 2.539ff., p.50; Platnauer ed. 2.365ff.) with some changes:

Eutropius cried: 'Away such sights as these! This time for other cares you arms should seize [*Eutropius chided the members of his council including Hosius and Leo*]; Enough for me Armenia to defend, not singly with so many to contend. [*It is possible that he secured the Armenian frontier during the war against Tribigild or that this meant the previous war which had tired the old man, but the former is likelier.*] To silver hairs, I pray, indulgence yield, and let youth take charge of the war [*against Tribigild as will be made clear later*].'

The above account makes it quite clear that contrary to the popular view among the historians, the invaders consisted of the Bosporan Goths and other peoples inhabiting the area (included Greeks, Roman settlers, Sarmatians, Alans, Huns and others), and of the Alans (modern Ossetians) occupying the area just north of the Darial Pass (the Gate of the Alans). There are two reasons for this: Firstly, Claudian calls the invaders Amazons, who are to be identified with the Sarmatians and Alans, and Getae, who are the Goths; Secondly, we know that the eastern half of the Crimea and the Bosporan Kingdom were at this time ruled by the Goths. It appears probable that the casualties suffered by the Huns in 395 had enabled the Bosporan Goths to overthrow the Hun yoke once more, as they had already done at least once in the 380s (see Vol.2).[10]

Consequently, it is probable that the invaders passed through the Darial Pass (The Gate of the Alans) and then divided themselves into two divisions (Bosporans and Alans?). One of these divisions reached Cappadocia and then retreated across the Phasis into Colchis and Iberia and then through the Darial Pass back into Scythia. The second of these divisions apparently reached Syria, from whence they took prisoners also into Scythia. It is possible that elements from both of these divisions reached the Mediterranean coast.

It is unfortunate that we are not given any details of these campaigns and of the very effective counter-attack led by Eutropius in person. All that is clear is that Eutropius fought several battles with a combined force of infantry and cavalry against the invaders in which he defeated them, and that he pursued the fleeing invaders at least up to Persarmenia. It is also probable that some of the invaders killed some of their prisoners in order to be able to flee faster. The use of the combined-arms concept makes it probable that Eutropius used the standard tactics employed at this time, which was to use several hollow infantry squares/oblongs together with cavalry. It is not at all surprising that the invading cavalry forces could not cope with this tactic. Eutropius had achieved a great success, worthy of a triumph and a consulship, but the fact that he was a eunuch made this unacceptable in the eyes of the traditionalists and also in the Federate Gothic eyes. It was an affront to the Federate Gothic generals that their efforts were not appreciated as high as the efforts of the effeminate eunuch. On top of that, it is also possible that they considered the killing of their distant relatives similarly distasteful and not something worthy of a consulship. It is also very probable that both Gainas (presumably in charge of his Goths and the Army of Thrace, but he may also have held control of some praesental forces) and Tribigild (whose Ostrogothic and Greuthungi followers were billeted in Phrygia) had played an important role in the defeat of their fellow Goths and Alans. Eutropius failed to reward them properly, and added to the insult by appointing himself (through Arcadius) as a consul for the year 399 – and this at a time when Eutropius had rewarded Alaric with office even after he had devastated Greece. It was mostly because of this that the Federate Gothic forces started their revolt in 399.

It is similarly very unfortunate that the Georgian and Armenian sources fail to give us any further details, but it is still possible to connect the events of the year 398–400 in Moses Khorenatsi (pp. 311ff.) with the general scheme of things. The reason for the silence in these sources is simple: both appear to have been in the habit of hiding all embarrassing details. According to Moses, at some point in time during Arcadius' reign the Armenian nobles had first asked Khosrov, the King of Persarmenia, to negotiate on their behalf so that Arcadius would allow them to become subjects of Khosrov. According to Moses, Khosrov agreed to this and gave a promise to Arcadius that he would continue to pay the tribute from the Greek sector if he would allow its feudal lords to rejoin Armenia. Arcadius (or rather Eutropius) agreed because he feared that the feudal lords would revolt otherwise. Khosrov sealed the alliance with Rome by nominating Sahak the Great as Archbishop of Armenia. This account has been needlessly suspected by Thomson (p.313, n.1) on the ground that it is not included in Lazar's history and because Moses previously stated that the Romans appointed a *comes* to take charge of Armenia. This account of the years 398 and 399 does fit the sequence of events described as far as the Roman rulers and events are concerned, but there are two significant problems, which are that the names of the Persian rulers in Moses are wrong, and that his account is contradicted by Lazar. This means that the sections concerning Armenia in the following reconstruction should only be seen as tentative. It is by no means impossible that the Romans changed their policy temporarily, especially as the alliance with Khosrov was far more advantageous to them than possessing a smaller portion of Armenia, if they did not care to respect the treaties made with Persia.

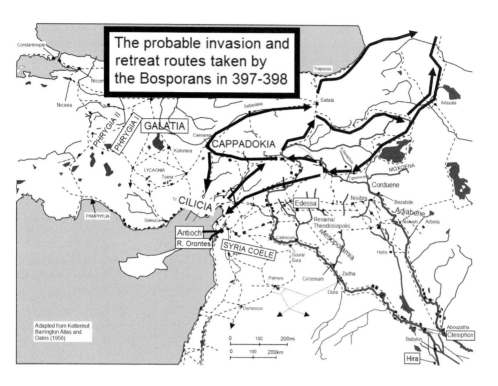

According to Moses (314ff.), Shapuh [this should be Bahram IV 388–399, if his counterpart was Arcadius] was angry with Khosrov for his friendly relationship with Arcadius and for the appointment of Sahak. He sent messengers to Armenia, with the result that Khosrov burst into anger and dispatched envoys of his own to Arcadius' court suggesting an alliance againt the Persians. Shapuh, however, launched a pre-emptive attack and sent his son Artashir (Ardashir) with a large army to Armenia. When Arcadius refused to assist Khosrov, he surrendered to Artashir, who duly imprisoned him and set up Artashir's brother Vramshapuh as King of Armenia. Khosrov was imprisoned in the fortress called Anush. According to Lazar's version, the Armenian princes requested that the Persians replace Khosrov with Vramshapuh and Khosrov was summoned to the court and deposed. These accounts can of course be reconciled if one assumes that Lazar has left out the use of the force in these events, but the problem of timing them remains.

As noted the best fit would be the years 397–400. The reason for this is the friendly relationship between Khosrov and Arcadius, which could easily have resulted from the Roman operations against the invading Bosporans and Alans in Persarmenian territory. If the rulers were not on friendly terms, it is difficult to see how the Roman intervention in Armenia would not have resulted in hostilities. The friendly relations between these two nations in their turn would explain why the Persians intervened in Armenia and deposed Khosrov, while the revolt of Tribigild and Gainas explains why the Romans were unwilling to commit their army in the defence of their ally. The other alternative is that the deposition of Khosrov took place at another time and that Eutropius' operations in Persarmenia were the reason for the murder of Bahram IV and for the hostilities that took place in 399–400.

What is known with certainty is that the Persians murdered their ruler Bahram IV and replaced him with his son Yazdgerd I, who started a war against East Rome. We also know that the *MVM per Orientem* Fravitta protected the frontier at that time (see later) and that it is probable that Eutropius protected the Armenian section of the frontier zone while Tribigild rebelled in Asia Minor in 399.

Claudian tr. by Hawkins (Eutr. 2.709, p.56; Platnauer ed. 2.474ff.) with some changes.

Amid these rumours of distress and shame [*the revolt of Tribigild*] intelligence of worse disasters came. Again the Babylonians [*Persians*] spread alarms. Another sovereign [*Yazdgerd I, 399–421*] led their troops in arms. The Parthians viewing peace with hateful eyes desired at once to break the peace imposed by the Romans [*means the peace of 384; see Vol.2*]. Among the Medes respect to kings is shown and shedding blood of princes rarely known because the culprit's entire family is killed in punishment [*the punishment is correct, but in practice the magnates and magi murdered several rulers*]... But what would not happen when Eutropius' name marks the year! The friendly Sapor's throne was overturned [*the Shapuh of Moses, but whose real name was Bahram IV*]... that the flaming torches of the Furies were born across the Euphrates [*Fravitta was in charge of this portion of the frontier while Eutropius defended the Armenian frontier.*] to kindle rebellion so that nothing could escape carnage.

In sum, the events described by Moses do fit the circumstances of the year 399. The Persians started hostilities against the Romans under their new ruler Yazdgerd I, but these did not result in any major operations against each other. The Romans were unable to assist the Armenians, which sealed their fate. The resulting deposition of Khosrov and the handing over of the 'Greek' portion of Armenia back to the Romans and the deposition of Eutropius (the likely architect of the Eastern policy) would have been the kind of result that would have restored the previous status quo, which in turn would have been the most satisfactory result to both.

Chapter Five

Gainas' Revolt and the Rise of Arcadius in 399–400[1]

Gainas' Play: Tribigild Revolts

In the spring of 399 Gainas instructed his relative Tribigild to begin a revolt with his Greuthungi Goths at Nacoleia in Phrygia. According to Zosimus, Gainas was unsatisfied with his own position. He thought that as *magister militum* he would have been entitled to receive greater honours and more financial support than he did. It was thanks to this that he was unable to satisfy the needs of his barbarian supporters with gifts, while Eutropius was looting everything that he could lay his hands on. Secondly, and equally importantly, he was envious that the eunuch Eutropius had been nominated as *patricius* and had received the consulship for the year 399 as a reward for his military successes in 398. This was an affront to his manhood as well. Tribigild was similarly unsatisfied with the rewards he had received in return for his military services. According to Claudian (Eutr. 2.153ff.), Tribigild/Tarbigildus was the commander of the Ostrogoths and Greuthungi in Phrygia. This separation of Ostrogoths and Greuthungi is curious and suggests that we should not necessarily consider them to be the same tribe. It is possible that this revolt had been encouraged and supported by Stilicho who was clearly opposed to Eutropius. Claudian even urged him to make a military intervention in the East to prevent the consulship of Eutropius.[2]

Despite the fact that none of the ancient sources even hints at this, I would suggest that it is very probable that the whole Gothic revolt had been orchestrated by Arcadius in conjunction with Gainas for the sole purpose of overthrowing Eutropius, just like they had previously cooperated in the overthrow of Rufinus. It is also possible or even probable that they had the full backing of Stilicho for their plot to destroy Eutropius. In addition, it seems probable that Arcadius had no intention of replacing Eutropius with Gainas. On the contrary, it is quite evident that his plan was to gain full control of his own realm. The reason for this conclusion is that Arcadius had started to raise new forces, the *Arcadiaci/Arcadiani* and *Honoriaci/Honoriani* (see introduction), just prior to the beginning of the revolt, which were then used against Gainas when the right opportunity arose (Theophanes AM5891; Malalas 13.47). Arcadius clearly understood that he needed new forces that were loyal only to him and which he could use against anyone who threatened him. Arcadius could not put any trust in the existing forces posted close to the capital which were either under Gainas or under Eutropius's trusted servants Hosius, Subarmachius and Leo.

When Tribigild reached Phrygia, he collected his followers and attacked Lydia. In a short while he had captured large numbers of men, women and children with the result that slaves and outcasts flocked to his colours. All those who could fled to the coast and then sailed to the islands. When the news of the Gothic revolt reached the West, Stilicho tried to use it as an excuse to take over the East from Eutropius, but in vain.[3] Honorius and his advisors did not see any advantage in making Stilicho too powerful. It was Gainas who took advantage of the situation. Note that the Roman ability to react to these problems was hindered by the troubles in Cyrenaica, Egypt and the East. The reason for the subsequent inactivity of the Eastern field army was that the Persians had started to prosecute Christians and were assembling their army for an invasion of Roman territory.

In the midst of the chaos prevailing in the Eastern Empire, the Persian *Shahanshah* Bahram IV had been murdered by his nobles in 399. He was succeeded by his son Yazdgerd I (Tabari i.847; Claud. Eutr. 2.474ff.). Yazdgerd was for some unknown reason unhappy with the current relationship with Rome, which spelled trouble for the Romans and Christians in Persia. One possible reason for this is that the nobles and magi had been unhappy with the peace with Rome and that they demanded war. The second possible reason is that the situation was just too good for an opportunistic invasion: the Romans were fighting a civil war. The third possible reason could be that when the Bosporans invaded Roman territory in 397/8, Eutropius and the Roman commanders had pursued them into Persarmenia. Fourthly, it is possible that the reason was the proposed alliance between Khosrov and Rome as suggested above. Whatever the reason, Yazdgerd started to persecute the Christians and threatened Rome with a war at the same time as Tribigild was roaming free in Asia Minor (Claud. In Eutr. 2.474ff.).

According to Moses (2.52), the Romans and Persians fought each other when the Romans were engaged in civil war (it is possible that this refers to the year 408). Blockley (1992, 195) suggests that Fravitta achieved some successes against the Persians while Tribigild and Gainas were roaming free in Asia Minor, but it is probable that these operations amounted to nothing more than skirmishes. I would suggest that whatever took place in the east, Eutropius did not take part but retreated to the capital with Arcadius at the latest after Leo's army had been crushed so that someone else took charge of the Armenian theatre. It is not surprising that in this situation the Romans wanted to reaffirm the peace on the eastern frontier as soon as possible and immediately dispatched an embassy to Persia.[4] It was thanks to the combined efforts of this embassy and the efforts of the Bishop of Sophanene, Marutha, who also visited Ctesiphon, that the relationship improved significantly. The key figure in the improved relationship was Marutha, who was as a result of this called 'mediator of peace and concord between East and West'. Yazdgerd's son was ill and the Persian magi healers were powerless to help. Marutha had medical training. He not only healed the son, but also the headache from which the king-of-kings was suffering. As a sign of his goodwill Yazdgerd I gave to Marutha the relics of Christian martyrs (who had been martyred during Shapur II's reign). The relics were deposited in a new frontier town which received the name of Martyropolis (the City of the Martyrs). In addition to this, Yazdgerd returned the remaining Roman captives that the fleeing Huns had abandoned in Persian territory in 395 when the Huns had been forced to flee. The peace between Rome and Persia enabled Yazdgerd to move against the nobles and magi who had murdered his father and were threatening his own life.[5] Arcadius was also happy with the result. As long as his Eastern army under Fravitta was tied up in the east, he was at the mercy of Gainas, but now it was free. (See below.)

The peace between Rome and Persia enabled Yazdgerd to secure his own position vis-à-vis nobility and magi, because when the Empire was not in a state of war, the ruler was not dependent on the military support of his nobility. In the words of Tabari, when

Yazdgerd achieved power he at first appointed the Suren Mihr-Narses as *Hazarbed/ Hazarabed* (roughly Prime Minister) and ruled wisely, but after Yazdgerd had established his position, his contempt for the nobles and magi became visible and intense. Yazdgerd's aim was nothing less than to centralize all power into his own hands and force the nobility to follow feudal principles. The nobility was angry over the centralizing of power and over the taxation of their lands (they paid taxes when their armies were not required in the field) while the magi were angry over the religious tolerance shown by the ruler towards the Christians and Jews.

Eutropius' Response

Gainas' aim was probably to force Arcadius to appoint him as *MVM Praesentalis* so that he would be able to wrest power from Eutropius. According to Zosimus (5.14), Arcadius lost his composure in this situation and granted all his powers to Eutropius so that he could save the Empire. In my opinion it is probable that Arcadius' intention was to make Eutropius bear all the blame for the subsequent failure so that it would be easier to get rid of him. One of his goals must have been to remove those forces from the capital that were loyal to Eutropius so that it would be easier to apprehend Eutropius when the right moment came. According to Claudian (Eutr. 2), Eutropius' first reaction was to attempt to negotiate with Tribigild and bribe him with offices and money, but when this failed he convened his council of advisors. It was in the meeting of this council that Leo promised to defeat the rebel without any assistance and he was indeed tasked with this mission. The wily eunuch feared Gainas and therefore purposefully divided the command of the war between the two men, Gainas and Leo, so that neither could pose any threat, but still made the mistake of making Gainas the superior of the two so that Gainas was the *strategos* and Leo the *hypostrategos*. Eutropius sent Leo against Tribigild and kept Gainas in Thrace to safeguard the capital. This division of duties suggests that Leo had been given one of the Praesental armies and Gainas the other. In this situation, Gainas ordered Tribigild to proceed to the Hellespont, but the latter refused because Leo had placed his army in between. Consequently, Tribigild turned his army towards Pisidia. Gainas' aim was probably to destroy Leo's army with Tribigild's army, but Tribigild apparently considered his army too weak to accomplish that. According to Zosimus (5.16.4), Tribigild's decision to march to Pisidia was a grave mistake, because if Tribigild had marched straight to the coast of Lydia, he could have captured Ionia from where he could have obtained as large a navy as he liked with which he could then have plundered the whole of the East all the way up to Egypt without any fear of having to face an army. This suggests two things. Firstly, there was clearly a navy posted in Ionia that Tribigild could have captured for his own use. Secondly, Zosimus' account suggests that at the time the fleets of Syria and Egypt were either not combat ready or were too small to oppose this fleet.

While Tribigild moved eastwards Leo did nothing, because he feared that Tribigild would be able to bypass him if he were to leave the neighbourhood of the Hellespont. Consequently, Tribigild was able to pillage every city in Pisidia, because the barbarians posted there joined his ranks. Gainas crossed with his army into Asia while maintaining his pretence of fighting against Tribigild. He led his army to Pisidia and then started to shadow Tribigild. The subsequent events make it clear that Leo must also have marched his army close to the scene of operations. According to Zosimus, Gainas now secretly sent additional forces to Tribigild. Even though not mentioned by Zosimus, it was possible to represent these reinforcements as deserters.

After this, Tribigild made the mistake of leading his cavalry army into Pamphylia, which was completely unsuited for his army. On top of this, a local noble called Valentinus of Selga took charge of the defensive operations in the area. He collected the local paramilitary forces, which consisted of slaves and farmers, and placed these on the higher ground beside the road leading into Selga. According to Zosimus, the spot was ideally suited for an ambush, because on the other side of the road lay marsh and on the other lay a narrow pass which in its narrowest point allowed only two men abreast. If my hypothesis regarding the location of the battle site is correct (see the accompanying map), Zosimus' description is slightly inaccurate in that the pass was actually behind the marsh. Valentinus had placed the local military commander Florentius with his men in this pass to block the way of escape. What is notable about this is that a local noble, who was also quite probably the local police chief, was able to take command of military forces posted in the area thanks to the influence he wielded locally.

According to Zosimus, once Tribigild's forces arrived below Selga (inaccurate, see the map) when it was still dark, the local paramilitary forces started to bombard them with stone slingshots. Most of the barbarians died under the hail of stones, because the only two avenues of escape were blocked. Regardless, some still tried to flee into the marsh with the result that they were drowned. However, Tribigild with 300 of his followers managed

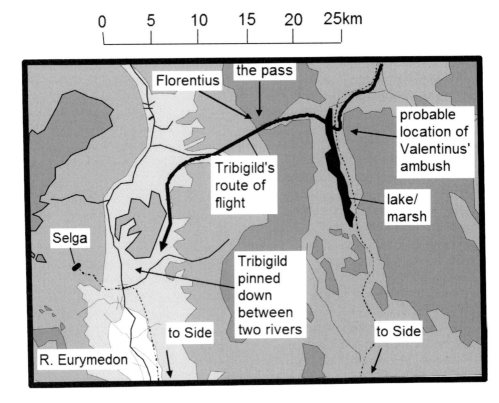

to reach the pass. He bribed Florentius to let them through only to find himself trapped by the rest of the city dwellers, who forced Tribigild and his followers between the Rivers Melas (on the eastern side of the city) and Eurymedon (passing through Aspendus). Tribigild managed to send a plea of help to Gainas, who was naturally distressed by the situation. However, then Gainas came up with a great idea. He could exploit the situation to his own advantage. Gainas sent an order to Leo to march his army to Pamphylia to assist Valentinus. At the same time, he sent barbarian *lochoi* (units) to all Roman camps in the area to corrupt them so that Tribigild would get a chance to escape. The barbarians that Gainas had dispatched to Leo attacked him and wiped out his army and killed its leader. This suggests that the other barbarian detachments sent by Gainas did the same to other Roman forces at about the same time. It should be noted that this version is slightly at variance with what Claudian states, but both accounts can be reconciled if one makes the assumption that the Goths inside Leo's camp simply cooperated with the Goths of Tribigild.

Claudian (Eutr. 2.603ff., p.52ff.; Platnauer ed. 2.409ff.) presents the events as follows (tr. by Hawkins). It is improbable that he would have known the exact circumstances of the death of Leo, but it is still probable that his colourful description is close to what must have happened to a flabby, panicking unsoldierly commander.

Troops proud of graces, fond of city ease and gaming, leisure and baths, not suffering of scorching sun nor chilling rain, and how different it is to the army which toiled under the leadership Stilicho, that which under arms braved the frosts of Thrace and passed the winters in the open air and broke with their axes the frozen waters of Hebrus to quell thirst [*refers to the Balkan wars of the early 390s; see Vol.2.*]. But when command was taken by another leader [*Leo*], they forsook their former general. The luxury of Byzantium and Ancyra's pomp [*these forces had clearly accompanied Eutrupius to Ancyra*] enervated their vigour. To advance before the foot, no cavalry was brought. No suitable ground was sought for camps. No sentries were placed to make entrenchments secure. No roads were explored by scouts… The wings devoid of order passed the ground. Confusion appeared around everywhere. The crowd moved on through forests overgrown, crossways and narrow paths and vales unknown. So wander coursers when without a guide… Tarbigilus [*Tribigild*] feigned flight and raised presumptuous hoped in vain Leo… Soon to the camp, where sleep profoundly reigned among the winc-sodden army… the enemy unseen attacked with speed. Some as they left their couch were doomed to bleed, while others who in slumber drew their breath were suddenly despatched to the realms of death. A neighbouring fen received crowds that fled and the marsh was heaped with floods of dead bodies. In terror, Leo on a horse withdrew, more swift than a deer or antelope, his sweating and foaming courser in flight, and it tumbled under the weight of Leo and sank into the mire… Puffed, sighed and panted like a swine, which was destined to become a feast, squealing when Hosius armed him with a shining knife, and robe tucked up… However, behind his back among the trees, the foliage quivered with the passing breeze, which seemed to Leo's ear like missile weapons [*note the association of mounted archery with the Goths*], and his fancied wounds were realized by fear; Imagination felt the piercing dart … He pictured to his mind approaching death and hurt and by fright alone reigned his breath [*this suggests a heart failure resulting from fear*]. Wretch who the comb advised thee exchange for the sword.

Once again it was possible to present the hostilities committed by the Gothic troops in support of Tribigild as desertion/revolt with which Gainas had nothing to do. In fact, Cameron and Long (e.g. 324ff.), and Liebeschuetz go so far as to claim that the cooperation between Gainas and Tribigild was Zosimus' invention, which bears no relation to truth. According to their interpretation, Tribigild's revolt was genuine and Gainas just exploited it to his own advantage, which would mean that the desertions that caused the destruction of the Roman armies were genuine as well. I do not accept this interpretation, because there is nothing inherently implausible in the picture that Zosimus presents. It was entirely possible to present the desertion of Goths so that Gainas was not held responsible and even if someone suspected the truth, and it is certain that Gainas' motives were suspected, there was little that the emperor could do before being able to assemble enough men to oppose Gainas.

When the surrounding Roman armies had been destroyed, Tribigild was free to march to Phrygia. One may presume that Tribigild's 300 men were now bolstered by the barbarians Gainas had sent to reinforce Leo and the other Roman garrisons. According to Claudian (Eutr. 2.471ff.), the death of Leo caused panic in Constantinople, so that some claimed that Tribigild was advancing against Galatia, while others claimed that he planned to attack Bithynia, and still others claimed that Tribigild possessed a fleet and was advancing by land and sea. It is in fact possible that Tribigild may have captured some ships because he and Gainas were later able to pose a credible threat to the capital across the straits.

The Fall of Eutropius

In this situation Gainas claimed that he was unable to defeat Tribigild and that it was better to come to some kind of agreement with him. Tribigild's terms were that Eutropius should be deposed. Unfortunately for Eutropius, this demand came at the worst possible moment, because just previously he had quarrelled with the empress and had been forced to seek asylum in a church, despite his own legislation against such (Soz. 8.7). This in fact proves that the emperor had the last word and was in a position to remove Eutropius from power – at least after the armies that had been loyal to Eutropius had been transferred to Asia Minor. It was very unwise for Eutropius to treat the empress high-handedly and he paid dearly for his mistake. According to Eutropius' own legislation, the seeking of shelter in a church did not protect that person against the law, and indeed it did not provide him with a sanctuary. It only caused Eutropius' enemies to admonish him for his own lack of respect for the laws he had enacted. Consequently, the emperor was quite prepared to accept the terms proposed. Eutropius was exiled to Cyprus. Not unnaturally, at the same time as Eutropius fell, fell his supporters Eutychianus and Hosius. However, contrary to the wishes of Gainas, Arcadius appointed the head of the anti-Gothic party Aurelianus as the next *PPO*. Gainas had clearly not taken into account this possibility. No new *Mag. Off.* is recorded, but it is still possible that there existed one because it is difficult to imagine that the different departments of the administration would not have had a head. It is probable that whoever this person was, he belonged to the same party as Aurelianus – perhaps he was the commander of the *Arcadiaci* and *Honoriani* created at about this time (see above and below). The fall of Eutropius also strengthened Eudoxia's position so that on 9 January 400 she was proclaimed *Augusta*. She was to wield great influence on her husband's policies.

As noted above, according to Theophanes (AM5891), the emperor Arcadius had created his own military forces called the *Arcadiaci* in Constantinople in AD 398/9. This was a wise decision and would probably have taken place roughly at the same time as Gainas threatened the capital. I would actually go so far as to claim that, contrary to the common opinion among historians, it is quite clear that Arcadius was not quite as ineffectual a ruler as the ancient sources make him out to be. Several instances make it clear that Arcadius always made the final decisions (see e.g. 'Chapter East 400–408'). The creation of personal units of bodyguards who would be loyal only to Arcadius can be seen as a wise decision as the events of the year 400 prove. It was also Arcadius who went in person to meet Gainas when the situation so demanded in August 399 (see below). The way in which Arcadius secured the throne for his underage son Theodosius II also shows novel and ingenious thinking, as we shall see. In short, there are strong reasons to believe that Arcadius was acting dishonestly when he dealt with Gainas. His intention was solely to buy time for the creation and training of the new personal bodyguard units that would be solely loyal to him.

Synesius (*De Providentia* 1.15) claims that Aurelianus began to recruit native Romans to replace the barbarian troops. It would therefore be easy to connect this with the recruitment of the *Arcadiaci/Arcadiani* and credit should be given to Aurelianus with the raising of these, but the existence of barbarian units, the *auxilia palatinae*, among the *Arcadiaci* make this problematic. One possible answer is that the *auxilia palatinae* units were just added to the corps despite the wishes of Aurelianus and possibly after his dismissal. It is therefore quite possible that it had been Aurelianus who had given Arcadius the idea of creating a corps of his own.

Gainas Supreme

Gainas was not satisfied with the exile of Eutropius and demanded that he be executed. Arcadius ordered Aurelianus to recall Eutropius, which the new *PPO* duly did and then executed the unfortunate eunuch at Chalcedon. This did not satisfy Gainas, and the policies of the intensely anti-Gothic Aurelianus even less so. Regardless of this, Gainas still kept up the presence and took an oath of loyalty to the emperor in his own and in Tribigild's name. After this, Gainas marched his army through Phrygia and Lydia while Tribigild followed through upper Lydia and bypassed the city of Sardis. Gainas and Tribigild met each other at Thyateira (Zos. 5.18.5), where they discussed their future plans. Gainas had decided to abandon all pretences of loyalty towards Arcadius in order to achieve his goal of becoming the de facto ruler of the Empire, as Eutropius had been. It was then that Tribigild expressed his regret that he had not sacked the city of Sardis. Consequently, the united armies turned around to pillage the city of Sardis, but to no avail because the storms had flooded the land and had made the rivers impassable.

Consequently, the armies divided once again so that Gainas led his army to the city of Chalcedon in Bithynia opposite the city of Constantinople, while Tribigild led his army to the city of Lampsacus in the Hellespont. Both armies pillaged everything en route to their destinities.

Gainas reached Chalchedon in April 399 and sent a demand to meet Arcadius face-to-face. Arcadius assembled his Sacred Consistory (Soz. 8.4). All councillors were unanimous that it was not yet possible to confront Gainas and that it was best to agree to whatever terms he demanded. They needed time to prepare a trap for the wily Goth. In light of this, it seems probable that Gainas and Tribigild possessed some sort of fleet with which they could threaten the capital. Consequently, Arcadius went to meet the rebel at the shrine of the Martyr St. Euphemia near Chalcedon. Arcadius was clearly not a coward. The ancient sources are in the habit of calling Arcadius lethargic because he did not lead his armies in person. This approach has unfortunately misled most modern historians to think that Arcadius was indeed lethargic, but this is utterly false. If we were to adopt a similar approach today, we would have to call all of our modern leaders lethargic solely because they do not lead armies in person! Please note, however, that if Arcadius was party to the plot to destroy Eutropius, as I have suggested above as one possibility, it is likely that the meeting of the leaders was just meant as a show. On the other hand, it is possible that even if Arcadius and Gainas had cooperated in the beginning of Tribigild's revolt, that the appetite of Gainas had grown when he had managed to remove his enemies so that the negotiations were really what they appeared to be and that Arcadius was really attempting to buy time through concessions. The latter is likelier.

Gainas demanded that Aurelianus, Saturninus (an experienced veteran commander) and John (a *Comes* who was rumoured to be the lover of the empress and father of Theodosius II) all were to be handed over to him. All of these were close friends of the empress and Arcadius' advisors. Gainas also demanded that he and Tribigild were to be allowed to cross into Europe unhindered. Arcadius was forced to agree. The three men named faced execution, but somehow Arcadius managed to convince Gainas to change the sentence to exile. The Goths were shipped across to Europe either in late 399 or early 400, and the three men were exiled to Cyprus in early 400. In response, Arcadius elevated his wife Aelia Eudoxia as *Augusta* on 9 January 400. The intention was probably to calm his wife and to signal to all that Arcadius was still in power and that Arcadius' trusted advisors and Eudoxia's friends John, Aurelianus and Saturninus would be rewarded when the time was right. Their exile would be only temporary.

According to Cameron and Long, Arcadius now re-appointed Caesarius as *PPO* and made Gainas *MVM* and consul for the year 400. Their interpretation is that Caesarius was the Typhos of Synesius' *De Providentia*, the elder brother Aurelianus (the Osiris of Synesius' *De Providentia*). This interpretation is opposed by those, for example Liebeschuetz (1990, 114–5) and Holum (1982/89, 63ff.), who accept A.H.M. Jones' interpretation that Synesius' Typhos was Eutychianus. They therefore suggest that Aurelianus' successor as *PPO* was his elder brother Eutychianus. I am inclined to follow this latter interpretation because it seems to better fit the circumstances. However, the evidence is so uncertain that both interpretations can still be considered plausible.

Gainas Rides into a Trap

After Gainas had got what he wanted, he crossed to Constantinople and then sent an order for Tribigild to cross over to the Chersonese (Zos. 5.18.9–10). He billeted his troops in Constantinople so that the court troops were forced to hand over their houses (one third of the houses of their host) to the newcomers. In addition to this, Gainas demanded and got one church inside the city for the Arians. According to Zosimus (5.18.10), Gainas gave his Goths an order to conquer the city immediately after they witnessed the last of the soldiers leaving the city.[6] This plan proved useless because instead of soldiers leaving the city, Arcadius brought inside the city his new Corps of *Arcadiaci*, which was now placed to guard the palace together with the court troops that had lost their housing (these are the 'heavenly forces'). In addition to this, Arcadius had ordered the *MVM per Orientem* Fravitta to bring assistance to the capital, which proves that the Romans had managed to negotiate a peace settlement with Yazdgerd by then. In this situation the hotheaded John Chrysostom, the Patriarch of Constantinople, also could not remain silent. He reproached both Arcadius and Gainas publicly for the handing of the church to the Arians, and thereby incited the populace against the Goths just in time for what was to follow. It is quite possible, or even probable, that John acted as instructed by the imperial authorities when he incited the populace to anger.

At first Gainas attempted to rob the moneylenders/banks, but to no avail because the owners had been warned in advance by the imperial security organs to take their money to some safe place. Next Gainas ordered his Goths to set the palace on fire, probably with the idea that he could then bring his forces to the palace to assist the palace staff in extinguishing the fire. This came to naught because when the men approached the palace they saw a multitude of tall armed men standing guard. When the Goths returned and informed Gainas that fresh troops (these would be the *Arcadiaci* and Eastern Field Army) had arrived to guard the palace, Gainas did not believe them. He was sure that no new troops had entered the city. When the persons who Gainas had sent to the palace next night brought back the same news, Gainas went in person to check the situation. It was then that he became convinced that Arcadius had managed to bring into the city reinforcements from other cities.

Gainas realized that his days would be numbered if he were to remain in the city and with this in mind he pretended to be in poor health which would require him to go outside the city to pray at the Church erected in honour of John the Baptist at Hebdomon on 12 July 400. Zosimus claims that Gainas went outside the city to obtain forces (undoubtedly Tribigild's forces that would have been billeted somewhere in Thrace) with which to attack the city with the help of those still inside. It is possible that this was Gainas' emergency plan in a situation in which his plans had been foiled, but it was all in vain. At the same time as Gainas left the city, he sent orders for all the Goths to place their arms inside chariots and leave the city in secret during the following night. The soldiers who guarded the walls stopped the chariots when it was discovered that arms were hidden in them and ordered the Goths to hand over their weapons. The Goths responded by killing the guards and by forcing their way through. The resulting commotion caused panic in the city, but order was soon restored when the emperor Arcadius declared Gainas a public enemy and ordered all the Goths inside the city to be killed. The soldiers rushed after the Goths everywhere and a massacre ensued. The civilians joined the soldiers in killing men, women and children. Even those who had sought refuge in the Arian Church were killed after Arcadius gave the order to set the church on fire.[7] Liebeschuetz (1990, 118ff.) is undoubtedly correct in noting that the killing of the Goths was done in an orderly manner, so that the emperor's troops ensured that only those Goths who belonged to Gainas' forces were killed, because it is clear that not all Goths inside the city were killed. It is indeed quite probable that some Gothic troops, especially those belonging to the Imperial Guards, fought on Arcadius' side against Gainas' Goths. Aurelianus, John and Saturninus were duly recalled back to the capital on 12 July 400 (PLRE).

The expulsion of Gainas' Goths from Constantinople, together with the massacre of the remaining Goths of Gainas inside the city, enabled the government to move against those who were suspected of colluding with Gainas. These men included the *PPO* Eutychianus, who was replaced by Caesarius in the summer of 400. The emperor set up an inquiry, but apparently it found no reason to suspect Eutychianus of any real wrongdoing because he was reappointed as *PPO* in 404. However, this doesn't mean that the investigators would not have found persons who had collaborated with Gainas, because there exist Edicts (CTh 9.42.17; 10.10.23) from 19 January 401 that state that it would be possible for proscribed persons to plea for the restoration of their property if done within two years. Liebeschuetz rightly suggests that the Edicts prove that some men had lost their property as a result of an investigation. The emperor was clearly prepared to show clemency towards his subjects in order to achieve internal peace.[8]

Goth vs. Goth: Fravitta vs. Gainas

When Gainas' plans had been foiled through the foresight of Arcadius and his advisors, Gainas attempted to pillage the cities of Thrace, but to no avail because all of the walled cities were vigilantly guarded by their magistrates and inhabitants. The previous fighting in the area had made the cities well-prepared for such an eventuality and everyone was ready to fight to the death. In other words, the imperial government had prepared the cities well for the probability that the Goths might attempt to ravage Thrace. When Gainas realized that the inhabitants had not left anything for him to rob outside the walls, he decided to march to the Chersonese, from where he would be able to cross to Asia where the pickings would be easier. Since Zosimus (5.21.1) states that Gainas was forced to fight his way through the Long Wall of the Chersonese, it is probable that Tribigild had meanwhile marched north to Thrace. Gainas deployed his army on the heights from opposite Parium down to Lampsacus, Abydus and the Straits.

In this context, Socrates (6.6) states that when Gainas marched to the Chersonese with the idea that he would cross to the Asian side at Lampsacus, Arcadius dispatched forces in pursuit both by land and by sea. He also states that: 'For while the barbarians, destitute of ships, were attempting to cross on rafts, and in vessels hastily put together, suddenly the Roman fleet appeared and the west wind began to blow hard. This afforded easy passage to the Romans.'[9] I would suggest that this did not refer to the actual naval battle, as the following sentence after the quote states, but rather to the fact that the Imperial Fleet which was dispatched from Constantinople was able to reach the Asian shore faster than the Goths were able to obtain ships from the Chersonese thanks to the west wind.

Socrates' statement that Arcadius also dispatched another army by land in pursuit is also of greatest importance for the interpretation of subsequent events. Socrates' account has to be taken seriously for the reason that he has preserved a condensed eyewitness account of Eusebius Scholasticus (auditor of Troilus the Sophist, see later) and the poem of Ammonius presented to Theodosius II in 439.

According to Zosimus' version, when Gainas had left the city of Constantinople, the Emperor and the Senate unanimously voted Fravitta as the *Strategos/Magister* of the war against Gainas. Fravitta was given a joint and combined army consisting of infantry, cavalry, navy (presumably consisting of the Imperial Navy of Constantinople and Ionia), and of the still loyal *foederati*. The core of this army consisted of the Eastern Field Army, which was bolstered by reinforcements from the *Limitanei*, Federates and Imperial Bodyguards (including probably some *Arcadiaci* and *Scholae* units). According to Zosimus, Fravitta reviewed and trained his army and fleet night and day for the eventual battle on the Asian side of the straits, but as the above-mentioned account of Socrates proves, this was only one half of the Roman armed forces. The other land-based army had been dispatched to isolate Gainas in the Chersonese. It is unfortunate that we do not know the name of the commander of this second force. Was he the elderly Saturninus (PLRE1 Saturninus 10; personal enemy of Gainas) or was he the *Comes* John (PLRE2 Ioannes 1), both of whom had already returned from exile, or was he someone else, for example Simplicius (PLRE2 Simplicius 2) or Pulcher (PLRE2), both of whom are attested as holding the office of *MVM* at about this time? What is certain is that the commander of this land army was a staunch Christian, because otherwise the pagan authors (Eunapius, Zosimus, Eusebius) would have not have hidden his identity. We know that the former *PPO* Aurelian, who had been exiled alongside with John and Saturninus, was rewarded with the patriciate and was allowed to renew his consular festivities in about September/October 400,[10] so it is possible that the other exiles were also rewarded – which in the case of Saturninus and John could easily have meant a military command against Gainas.

In order to prevent the enemy from crossing, Fravitta sailed up and down the Asian coast night and day to guard the approaches and to observe enemy activities. It did not take long for Gainas to run out of supplies, which made his situation desperate. Since there were not enough ships to carry the men and horses across, Gainas ordered the men to build boats suited to carrying both men and horses. After these had been built, the men and horses were embarked on the boats, but when the boats were launched they found that the boats could not be steered effectively with oars and were unresponsive to the pilots' attempts to steer them.

The Gothic rafts were presumably launched from the shore opposite the city of Lampsacus on 23 December 400 (date in the Chron. Pasch.), because Socrates states that this city was Gainas' objective. Gainas himself remained on shore, where he awaited the outcome of the naval battle. Fravitta had placed his ships a short distance from the shore (this probably means that the fleet was deployed as one line of galleys) and when he saw the rafts of the enemy fighting against the currents, he launched his fleet forward, evidently in a line abreast formation spearheaded by his flagship. If Fravitta followed the standard combat doctrine, he would also have had two smaller vessels (used for transmitting orders) following his ship so that both of his flanks would be protected by one vessel. Fravitta rammed his bronze-prowed flagship into the first enemy line ('*kata prôtên*

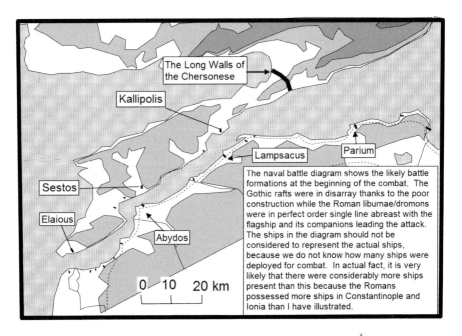

The naval battle diagram shows the likely battle formations at the beginning of the combat. The Gothic rafts were in disarray thanks to the poor construction while the Roman liburnae/dromons were in perfect order single line abreast with the flagship and its companions leading the attack. The ships in the diagram should not be considered to represent the actual ships, because we do not know how many ships were deployed for combat. In actual fact, it is very likely that there were considerably more ships present than this because the Romans possessed more ships in Constantinople and Ionia than I have illustrated.

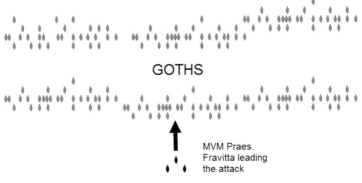

GOTHS

MVM Praes.
Fravitta leading
the attack

ROMANS

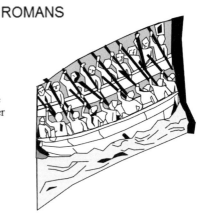

A scene of naval combat in the
Column of Arcadius (no longer
extant). Drawn after a 16th
century copy of the Column.

taxin') while the marines and soldiers onboard launched a hail of weapons at the enemy. The enemy vessel was sunk with all hands. The rest of the Roman fleet followed their commander's example. Most of the men and horses that had embarked on the Gothic vessels met their end that day. The deployment of the Gothic rafts in at least two lines was of no use against real warships.

Gainas led the remnants of his forces back to Thrace. Fravitta did not follow, but regrouped his forces in the Chersonese. He followed the ancient principle of not attempting to prevent the flight of a desperate enemy, because had he done that the enemy could have turned their defeat into victory. The majority of people, and certainly all those who were envious of Fravitta's success, claimed that 'he knew how to win, but not how to use it',[11] or alternatively accused him of purposefully allowing his fellow Goth to flee. According to Zosimus, Fravitta ignored the accusations and returned to Constantinople, expecting to be rewarded for his great success. Arcadius asked how Fravitta wanted to be rewarded. Fravitta, who was pagan, asked that he would be allowed to worship God in the ancestral manner. The emperor granted this and in addition made Fravitta consul for the year 401.[12]

It should be noted that the fact that Fravitta failed to pursue the Goths does not preclude the existence of a Roman army in Thrace that would have engaged the Goths. In fact, the criticism of Fravitta's actions becomes even more understandable when one takes into account the probability that Fravitta could have placed the fleeing Goths between two armies (his own and the one that had pursued Gainas by land) had he pursued vigorously.

In the meanwhile, before Fravitta was able to reach Constantinople, Gainas had continued his flight. He could not find any sustenance in Thrace because the area had previously been ravaged and the remaining provisions had been safely stored inside the cities. In addition to this, Gainas was afraid that the Romans accompanying him might betray him if another Roman army attacked him. Consequently, Gainas massacred the Romans in his army by surprise and then continued his retreat. On the basis of Arcadius' Column (two cavalry battles depicted after the naval battle, see the illustration) and the accounts of Sozomen (8.4) and Socrates (6.6), it is indeed probable that Gainas encountered another Roman army and was forced to fight two cavalry battles, with Romans pursuing him in Thrace before he reached the Danube. Sozomen and Socrates claim that the Roman detachment that encountered Gainas annihilated his army and killed him. It is probable that this is a mistake, either resulting from the fact that the panegyric for Fravitta written by Eusebius really claimed that Gainas had been killed by the Romans, or alternatively that it resulted from the condensing of the sources so that the Huns Gainas subsequently faced would also have been considered to have been Romans.

Indeed, according to Zosimus, Gainas was able to take his army across the Danube, but only to face the Huns. Uldin did not accept the presence of the Gothic army on his side of the Danube. In addition to this, he also thought that he could obtain the emperor's goodwill if he were to destroy the emperor's enemy. Consequently, Uldin assembled his army and led them against Gainas. Gainas in his turn had no other alternative than to fight the enemy. The armies engaged each other many times in combat, but in the end Gainas together with many of his followers died fighting in about December/January 400/401. Uldin dispatched Gainas' head to Constantinople. According to Zosimus

Roman cavalry pursuing and destroying Gainas' forces
Drawn after Melchior Lorich's (1527-1583/1588) drawing of
the Column of Arcadius. The Column is no longer extant.

(5.22.3), Arcadius rewarded Uldin with peace, but then adds that Thrace was in chaos because it was impossible to formulate any coherent policy as a result of the emperor's stupidity. It was thanks to this that the fugitive slaves and other deserters who called themselves Huns ravaged and pillaged the countryside in Thrace. It is impossible to know what Zosimus meant by this statement. Had Arcadius broken the peace with the Huns immediately (the Huns invaded Thrace in 404/5), or had he failed to promise pardon for the Roman deserters (e.g. men of Hunnish descent) who had deserted from Gainas' army, or had he failed to give a tax relief for Thrace, or was there some other reason for the troubles? What is notable about the situation is that the people ravaging Thrace called themselves Huns. The Huns clearly represented the promise of freedom, just as the Germanic invaders of Gaul and Spain subsequently represented to many Romans in the West, and it was because of this that the people in revolt called themselves Huns. Arcadius' solution to the social problem was to dispatch Fravitta with an army to solve the issue. Fravitta performed his mission admirably, if the butchery of people seeking liberty can be considered such. He killed all he could find and pacified Thrace.

In this context it is important to note that the Huns of Uldin were an independent group of Huns that lived north of the Danube opposite Moesia and Scythia (roughly in the area of modern Romania) and that these should not be confused with the Huns who lived alongside the Goths and Alans in Pannonia under Western control and who were Federates.

Arcadius' well-staged coup against Gainas brought with it another very important political change, which was the conclusion of a political concord between East and West, which existed from about mid-400 until late-403. The best evidence for this is that the Western government recognized Eastern consuls from 401 until 403. This thaw in relations coincided with Caesarius' tenure as *PPO* in the East (attested for the period from 8 December 400 until 11 June 403), but may still have been initiated under Eutychianus, who held the office from 11 December 399 until 12 July 400.[13] I would suggest that the reason for the sudden change in policy was Arcadius' purposeful attempt to seek a reconciliation with his brother amidst all the troubles. The earliest sign of this change of policy can be considered to have been the creation of the *Honoriani* units alongside with the *Arcadiaci*. The other possibility is of course that some of the *Arcadiaci* units changed their names to *Honoriani/Honoriaci* only after the reconciliation. Arcadius and his advisors wanted to secure their position by ending the conflict between East and West. It is possible that they also abandoned the *MVM per Illyricum* Alaric to his own devices, but there is no definite evidence for this and it is possible that the actions of Alaric actually contributed to the warming of relations.

It should be stressed, however, that the East did not adopt any anti-Germanic policy. Firstly, Arcadius's wife Eudoxia was the daughter of the Frankish general Bauto. Secondly, Fravitta and many other men of Germanic origins retained their positions. It was only a sign of pragmatism. In fact, it is usually suggested that Arcadius fell under the influence of his wife Eudoxia, which naturally precludes any possibility of a racist anti-Germanic policy by the government, even if there existed strong anti-Germanic sentiments among the traditionalists – the best proof of which are the poems of Synesius. The government was simply moving against those Goths whom it considered disloyal and not against all Goths or Germans.

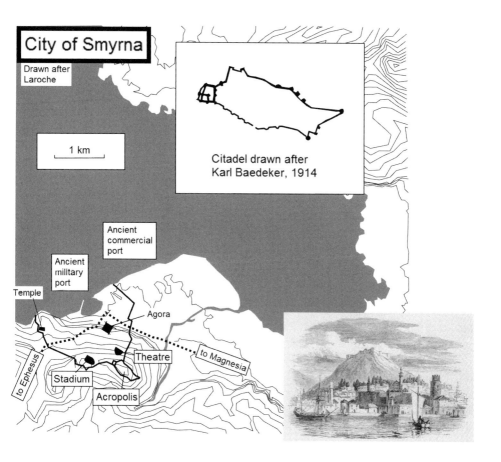

The Eastern Government spent the next years in rebuilding its strength, which included the fortification or refortification of strategic locales. This was a wise policy after years of ravages caused by wars. There exists an inscription that proves that the *Proconsul Asiae* Anatolius built walls at Smyrna and renamed the city after Arcadius (PLRE 2; Foss and Winfield, 130). It is unfortunate that the text doesn't date the construction more accurately. It states only that this took place during the reign of Arcadius, but in my opinion the likeliest date for the addition of walls for Smyrna would be in the immediate aftermath of the revolt of Gainas, which had proved that such walls could be needed. PLRE2 suggests that this Anatolius was not the *MVM per Orientem* Anatolius, who later built the city of Erzurum/Theodosiopolis, but in my opinion it is actually very likely that the *Proconsul Asiae* Anatolius was the same man, and that Anatolius was put in charge of the construction of the fortifications at Erzurum precisely because he had experience of such operations (see later). In this context it should also be noted that the construction of the city of Erzurum was not the only construction work that the PLRE2 notes for the *MVM* Anatolius 10. Even the PLRE2 acknowledges the building work at Heliopolis in Phoenecia in 440, the rebuilding of the city walls at Geraza in Arabia in 440, and that he also built the so-called Basilica of Anatolius at Antioch when he became the *MVM per Orientem* (Mal. 14.13), the last of which I would therefore suggest can be dated roughly to the year 420. All these details suggest that Anatalius became an expert in building projects. The walls of Smyrna are no longer extant but two travellers, Tournefort and van Egmont (noted by Foss and Winfield, 130), saw them in the eighteenth century. According to van Egmont, the circuit of the wall was ca. 12 miles, but Tournefort doesn't include any reference to the wall in question.

I have included Tournefort's information regarding the city (French 1717 and English tr. 1718) in Appendix I for consultation. On the previous page is my redrawing of Didier Laroche's modern reconstruction of the city of Smyrna (walls included), but it should be noted that the modern reconstruction is not in agreement with the information provided by Tournefort regarding the extent of the ancient city. Tournefort's text is also very valuable because he provides an evaluation of the strategic significance of the city. He thought that the city of Smyrna was 'the finest Port at which one can enter into the *Levant*, built at the bottom of a Bay, capable of holding the biggest Navy in the World'. According to Tournefort, the city of Smyrna was ideally located both as a commercial harbour and as a military harbour. It should be noted that the eighteenth-century port referred to was the Roman port, which was destroyed in the nineteenth century. On the basis of this, it is easy to make the educated guess that the principal purpose of fortifying the city was to secure this port from land-based

Aelia Eudoxia Augusta
Wife of the Emperor Arcadius
(source: E.A. Grosvenor)

enemies. It is also very probable that the Romans would have posted a naval detachment there, which must have been sizable, even if the sources fail to mention this. At the time Tournefort visited the city, the size of the garrison was 2,000 Janissaries, which must be considered the absolute minimum figure for the size of the late Roman garrison. In fact, since the city is likely to have been considerably more populous during late antiquity,[14] it is clear that the garrison would have also been significantly larger. The fortifying of Smyrna was an important decision. It secured the best harbour in the area against enemy forces and thereby protected the approaches along the coast of Asia Minor to the city of Constantinople.

It is probable that the *Arcadiaci/Arcadiani* were broken as a unified corps (as can be seen in the ND) very soon after Arcadius had managed to nominate his own men to all important military positions in order that its commander would not have obtained too much power in relation to the other commanders. The events prove that Arcadius' aim was to retain the final say in all matters of importance and not to fall under the undue influence of any powerful man or half-man as had happened under Rufinus and Eutropius.

The West 399–400

For the first time since 395 Stilicho was able to devote the entire year of 399 for the consolidation of his position and for the rebuilding of the armed forces. The confiscation of Gildo's estates brought in money which could be used for filling the ranks of the army. Since Stilicho needed the support of the senators, he could not force them to bear the cost of raising new forces. This meant that most of the recruiting/conscription was directed towards the barbarians living inside the Empire or at the sons of veterans. This is well proven by CTh 7.20.12 (January 400) which required sons of *laeti*, Alamanni, Sarmatians, and veterans together with vagrants and other people subject to conscription to join the armed forces. This obviously means that the barbarians played an ever-increasing role in the regular army as well.[15]

It is unlikely that Stilicho would have planned to interfere in Eastern affairs in 399 or 400 despite his efforts to rebuild his army and despite the urgings of Claudian's poetry to do so. The simple reasons for this are: 1) Stilicho's forces had been unable to defeat Alaric decisively on previous occasions, and it is unlikely that Stilicho would have liked to take the risk of facing the *MVM per Illyricum* Alaric and some other eastern commander working together; and 2) the revolt of Tribigild and Gainas had led to the overthrow of Eutropius, the mortal enemy of Stilicho, so there was no need to interfere.

Stilicho and the West could look forward to the peaceful year of 400, as is well proven by Claudian's Panegyric on Stilicho's Consulship, but this was not to be.

Chapter Six

Stilicho vs. Barbarians 400–406

Radagaisus Invades Raetia and Noricum in 400–401

According to Prosper (a.400), Cassiodorus (a. 400) and Jordanes (Get. 147), Alaric and Radagaisus invaded Italy in 400. From Claudian (see later) we learn that Stilicho was fighting in Raetia and Noricum at the time when Alaric invaded Italy, which makes it obvious that the invasions of Raetia and Noricum took place before Alaric's invasion. The other sources date the beginning of Alaric's invasion of Italy to the year 401 so that it took place either on 18 November 401 (Chron. Min. I.299) or on 22 November 401 (*Annales Ravennatenses*). Both versions are actually possible, but I have here accepted the usual interpretation that Alaric invaded in November 401 with the assumption that Stilicho's winter campaign against the barbarians in Raetia and Noricum during the winter of 401/402 was just as short as claimed by Claudian.

It is very unfortunate that the sources fail to state who the invaders of Raetia and Noricum were. The usual solution among historians has been to suggest that the invaders consisted either of the men (Vandals and others) led by Radagaisus, or of Vandals and

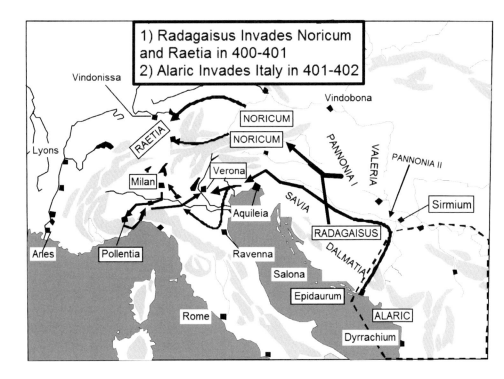

Alans. These versions are not mutually exclusive, so that it is possible that Radagaisus' Gothic army would also have included Vandals and Alans – in fact it is probable that his army included not only these but also Huns and various other groups of people on the move.[1] I would suggest that Radagaisus' forces consisted of a mix of tribes that included sections from all those tribes that accompanied him to Italy in 405 (see later). In other words, it is probable that he had at least about 350,000 men, women and children who consisted mostly of the Greuthungi Goths, Alans, and Huns settled in Pannonia, Savia and Dalmatia, and probably to a lesser extent of the Vandals settled in Pannonia by Constantine the Great and possibly even of the Vandals settled in Roman territory by Probus (see Vols. 1 and 2).[2] All of these various groupings of Federates lived right next to each other and it is very probable that they also cooperated with each other and with their fellow tribesmen across the Danube. The fighting component would have consisted of about 80,000–120,000 warriors or more.

The speech which Claudian puts into the mouth of Alaric allows one to clarify the situation further. According to Claudian, Alaric stated that: 'Our nation [the Goths] was strong even when we had no allies to rely on. Now that the Illyrians have put their government in my hands and made me their leader, I have acquired, thanks to Thracian labour, a vast quantity of missiles, swords, and helmets, and for my purposes I have forced Roman towns to turn over revenues, to which I am fully entitled, in the form of iron.'[3] As noted by Ian Hughes, the access to Roman state factories enabled Alaric to equip his men better than ever before, on top of which he now also had at least some Roman regulars in his army.

Alaric's Plans

It is very probable that Alaric started to make plans for future campaign or defence immediately after the reconciliation of the Western and Eastern governments in about mid-400. He knew that his own position was precarious if the two halves of the Empire cooperated against him. The other possibility is that the reconciliation of the two governments resulted from the treachery of Alaric, if he did indeed invade Italy in late 400 as claimed by Cassiodorus and Prosper. Another possibility is that the Eastern government incited Alaric covertly, but it should be noted that there is no evidence for this. It is unfortunate that we do not know the reason for Alaric's treachery or the order of events, but at least we know that Alaric was officially the first to break the treaty with the Romans and exploit the absence of Roman troops from Italy.

It is also uncertain what Alaric's exact objectives were. The best guess that modern research has come up with is that Alaric sought to extort a better deal for his followers from the Western Emperor. Jordanes (Get. 152) claims that Alaric sought land for his followers in Italy, which is quite possible because the Romans had already settled Sarmatians and Alans in the north of Italy and he could therefore expect a similar position, but what he did not understand was that the former had been settled there as refugees while he was seeking a similar opportunity through extortion. Whatever the timing, Alaric made meticulous plans for his forthcoming campaign. He formed an alliance with Radagaisus and proceeded to invade Italy after Stilicho had marched to the north. It is probable that Alaric had about the same number of men as Radagaisus.

The following quotes summarize the planning stage well. Claudian (Gothic tr. by Hawkins, 659ff., p.150ff. with some changes; Platnauer ed. 479ff. Italics) describes a fictitious scene in which Alaric asks the advice from the elders (the senate) of his tribes after Stilicho had broken through into Milan in the winter of 401/402 and in which the elders stated:

> Then arose one older than the rest… Away have passed almost thirty winters since we swam across the rapid Ister [*Danube*]… Who warned thee faith of treaties to maintain [*i.e. Claudian claims that Alaric broke the treaty against the advice of tribal elders. The veracity of this claim is confirmed by the fact that Stilicho was surprised.*] and in Emathia securely remain [*a district in Macedonia*]. Alaric upon him kept infuriated eyes. At length the rage that swelled his bosom… he spoke: 'Age has made you devoid of manly vigour and sense… Our strength was strong even when unsupported by allies, but now Illyricum my laws maintains [*This would also have included the Roman troops, and federate Goths, Alans and Huns that had been settled there previously. It is probable that these would also have included the forces under Radagaisus in Dalmatia.*]… for me the Thracians forge spears, helmets, swords… and the Roman towns now controlled by me contribute iron for my own uses [*This means that the East Romans equipped Alaric's forces.*]. To me thus destiny has favour shown… The gods too me impel [*Alaric was Christian. This is just an example of Claudian's literary tools.*]… O Alaric! no more delay; This very year now Latium's Alps give way even to the city of Rome penetrate shalt thou…

Stilicho's Response to the Invasions of Noricum and Raetia in 400–401

Claudian's text (Gothic 278ff.) makes it clear that Stilicho was still in Raetia when Alaric invaded Italy. He also appears to have taken with him most of the troops previously posted in Italy and to have left Saul in charge of the defence of north of Italy. Saul had been the commander of the Alans at the Battle of the Frigidus River in 394, which means that he was an old acquaintance of Stilicho who Stilicho had taken with him to the West. It is therefore also clear that Saul belonged to the 300,000 Sarmatians/Alans settled in Thrace, Scythia, and Macedonia by Constantine the Great in about 334. The rest of the Sarmatians/Alans had been settled in northern Italy, which means that Stilicho had made Saul the commander of his fellow tribesmen in Italy. It is important to note that the Sarmatians and Alans had retained their tribal traditions despite being settled in the Balkans or in Italy for about 70 years. It is probable that the central government had purposefully discouraged the assimilation of these tribes in order to retain their martial qualities for military service.[4]

This was a major war involving large numbers of soldiers and warriors. On the basis of Radagaisus' invading forces of the year 405, we can estimate that his forces consisted of about 350,000 men, women and children so that he would have had about 80,000–120,000 warriors. According to the ND, the Praesental Army posted in Italy consisted of 6 *Vexillationes Palalatinae* (ca. 3,000 men); 1 *Vexillationes Comitatenses* (500); 8 *Legiones Palatinae* (16,000); 18 *Auxilia Palatinae* (18,000); 5 *Legiones Comitatenses* (10,000); 2 *Legiones Pseudocomitatenses* (4,000), for a total of 3,500 horsemen and 48,000 infantry.

Let us assume that Stilicho took 4/5 of the infantry and all the cavalry forces. This would have given him a regular field army of about 3,500 horse and 40,000 foot (rounded up from 38,400). Stilicho probably left the *Scholae* behind to protect the imperial family. We should add to these figures the *bucellarii* of Stilicho (perhaps about 10,000 Huns), part of the Sarmatian settlers (ca. 20,000?) and the armies of the Alps, Raetia, Valeria, and Noricum/Pannonia. According to the ND, Raetia had 3 *equites* (ca. 1,500 horseman), 1 *Legio* (ca. 3,000 men), 1 *Tribunus gentis per Raetias* (ca. 6,000 infantry?), 1 *Praefectus numeri barbaricariorum* (ca. 10,000 cavalry?), 2 *alae* (ca. 1,000 cavalry), 7 cohorts (ca. 3,500 infantry), for a total of 12,500 horse and 12,500 foot. The same treatise gives Noricum and Pannonia 2 *cunei* (ca. 1,000 cavalry), 14 *equites* (7,000 cavalry), 1 *Tribunus gentis Marcomannum* (ca. 1,000 cavalry and 1,000 infantry?), 2 legions (ca. 6,000), 7 cohorts (ca. 3,500), and 5 *classes* (perhaps ca. 100 *lusoriae*, therefore possibly 2,500 marines), for a total of 9,000 horse and 13,000 foot. Valeria had 5 *cunei* (ca. 3,000 cavalry), 17 *equites* (8,500 cavalry), 5 *auxilia* (ca. 2,500 infantry), 2 legions (ca. 6,000 infantry), 7 cohorts (ca. 2,500 infantry), and 1 *classis* (perhaps 20 *lusoriae* with 500 marines), for a total of 11,500 horse and 11,500 foot. The Alpine forces consisted of four legions, but those are listed for other armies in the ND.

Consequently, Stilicho could augment his forces with 33,000 cavalry and 37,000 infantry. However, since these forces had already suffered serious damage and were also needed for the protection of the cities and forts, and because Stilicho would not have been able to assemble all of those together thanks to the presence of the enemy, it is probable that Stilicho could add only a third of these (ca. 11,000 cavalry and 12,000 infantry) to his field forces that he used to engage the invaders in combat. Therefore, my best educated guess for the size of Stilicho's field army is 44,500 cavalry and 52,000 infantry. Considering the fact that these consisted of regulars who were veterans of several wars, it is clear that this number was more than enough to face Radagaisus' tribesmen. It is therefore not surprising that Stilicho had managed to force the enemy to surrender before the end of the year 401 so that he was ready to return to Italy. True to his style, Stilicho did not attempt to crush and annihilate the invaders but concluded treaties with them that allowed them to settle in Raetia and Noricum. This naturally eased the making of the peace treaties, but did not secure peace for long (see below).

It is also quite possible that it was then that Stilicho made the deal with the Vandals mentioned by Jordanes (Get. 115). Jordanes states that Stilicho summoned the Vandals from Pannonia, after which they took possession of Gaul. This clearly refers to the year 406, but it is possible that the migration of the Vandals was performed in stages so that Stilicho directed the Vandals first to Noricum against Radagaisus and the Vandals were given land and food there in return for their help, and that their later movements coincided with movements of Radagaisus, who managed to form an alliance with them and then with the needs of Stilicho in 406. It would be easier to understand their subsequent march to Gaul, if they had already been given new homes closer to Gaul before that. But it should be kept in mind that there is no firm evidence for this.

Alaric Invades Italy on 18 November 401 or on 22 November 401 and the Battle of Timavus

Alaric exploited the alliance he had concluded with Radagaisus and invaded Italy when Stilicho was fighting against Radagaisus in Raetia and Noricum. Alaric would have had in all probability at least the same number of men, women and children as Radagaisus, but with the difference that his fighting forces (perhaps about 80,000–120,000 men) were better equipped. Jordanes (Get. 147ff.) is the only source that gives us the route taken by Alaric at the beginning of the campaign. According to him, Alaric marched his army through Pannonia, with Sirmium on his right side, to Italy in 400. Excepting the year, this is likely to be true because the route would have taken Alaric from the border town of Epidaurum along the road to Sirmium, from there along the road to Poetovio, and from there through the Julian Alps to Emona and the Frigidus River, a route with which he was quite familiar, as was also noted by Claudian (Gothic 281–288).

Jordanes goes on to claim that Alaric marched to the bridge over the River Candidianus at the third milestone from the city of Ravenna without meeting any resistance. This part of the story is clearly incorrect. We know from other sources that Alaric fought a battle at the River Timavus, which is close to the city of Aquileia, and then besieged the city in question. However, I do agree with Thomas Hodgkin (Vol. 1.2, pp. 710–711) that it is possible that Alaric advanced against Ravenna after the failed siege of Aquileia, as suggested by Jordanes' confused account. It is also quite possible that Alaric's initial plan was to advance straight to the city of Rome and that he changed his mind only after having learnt that a more lucrative prize, the Emperor Honorius, was located at the city of Milan and not in Rome. It is quite easy to understand how Jordanes could have confused the subsequent negotiations with Honorius at Milan if Alaric advanced to Milan via the city of Ravenna.

Regardless, it is quite clear that the passes of the Julian Alps were not defended against Alaric. It is possible or even probable that Stilicho may have taken its defenders with him when he marched against the invaders in Raetia and Noricum. The Goths appear to have outnumbered the remaining Roman defenders quite significantly because the Romans, or rather the Alans and Sarmatians settled in Italy under their leader Saul, attempted to stop the invaders by posting their forces behind the River Timavus. This is not specifically stated by the sources, but it is still probable that the defenders used the river as a line of defence when the battle was fought on its banks.

It is also probable that Saul commanded at least the Alans and other Federates that he had brought from the East together with significant numbers of the Alan and Sarmatian settlers of Italy. It is very likely that the reason for the false accusations of treachery made towards Saul resulted from the defeat he suffered at the Battle of the Timavus in November 401. It is very difficult to form any firm estimate for the size of the force under Saul, because we do not know how many of the 300,000 Sarmatian settlers of the year 334 (see Vol.1) were settled in Italy and how many in the Balkans. On top of this we do not know how many men Saul had brought with him from the East and we do not know how many men Stilicho had taken from Italy against Radagaisus. My own very rough guess is that Saul would have had about 30,000–40,000 men, which would naturally have been far too few to face the Visigothic nation on the march. Saul's defeat at the Timavus led to charges of treachery because the Visigothic host included Alans. The victory at the

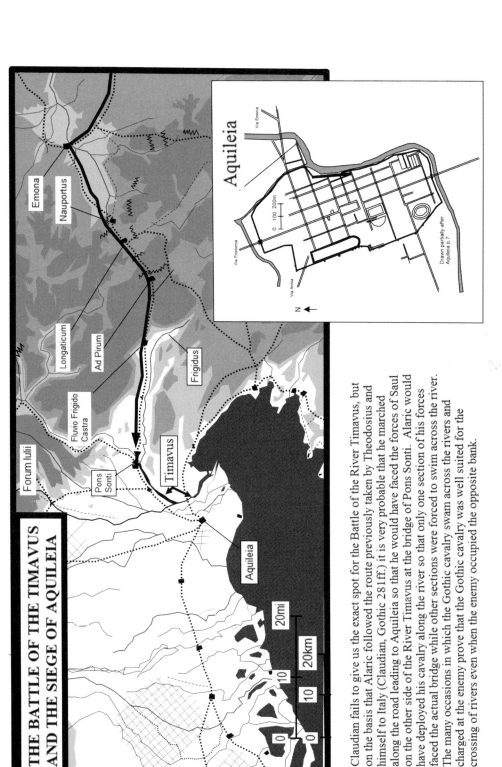

THE BATTLE OF THE TIMAVUS
AND THE SIEGE OF AQUILEIA

Claudian fails to give us the exact spot for the Battle of the River Timavus, but on the basis that Alaric followed the route previously taken by Theodosius and himself to Italy (Claudian, Gothic 281ff.) it is very probable that he marched along the road leading to Aquileia so that he would have faced the forces of Saul on the other side of the River Timavus at the bridge of Pons Sonti. Alaric would have deployed his cavalry along the river so that only one section of his forces faced the actual bridge while other sections were forced to swim across the river. The many occasions in which the Gothic cavalry swam across the rivers and charged at the enemy prove that the Gothic cavalry was well suited for the crossing of rivers even when the enemy occupied the opposite bank.

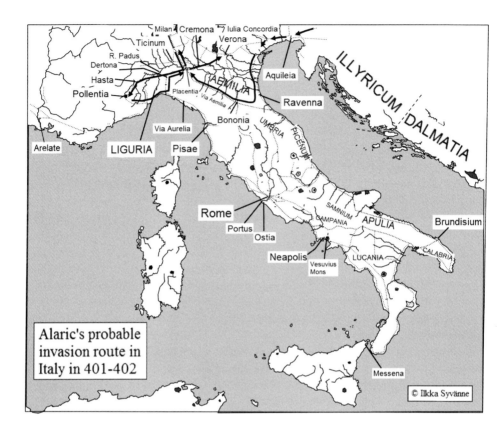

Timavus enabled Alaric to put Aquileia under siege, but it soon became apparent that the place was quite unassailable, with the result that the Goths marched to Ravenna (if we are to believe Jordanes) apparently with the intention of continuing the march to Rome, but when Alaric learnt that Honorius was in Milan, he decided to march there to compel Honorius to grant his Visigoths land and subsistence.[5]

The news of the Gothic invasion led to widespread panic in Italy. According to Claudian (Gothic, 213ff.), it seemed as if the Gothic cavalry could conquer all ramparts and cities, and some even thought that the Goths would embark their cavalry on ships and take Sardinia, Corsica and Sicily as well. The rich were fleeing and the people were turning to paganism to save themselves. All kinds of natural phenomena were seen as portents of something. These same superstitious fools also thought that the Thessalian witches accompanied the Goths to do them harm. Claudian's poem on the sixth consulship of Honorius (531ff.) proves that the inhabitants of the city of Rome also panicked when they learnt of the Gothic approach, with the result that they hastily built new walls for the city or renovated the old walls. These are the so-called Walls of Honorius.

As noted by Nick Fields, it is probable that the so-called Honorian restoration of the walls of Rome was the last major work done by a Roman emperor. Despite the apparent urgency of the situation, the builders paid attention to the appearance of the defences and not only to their defensive capabilities. This proves how vainglorious the inhabitants of the city had become. Regardless, it is still clear that the hasty changes made were practical and improved the defences considerably.

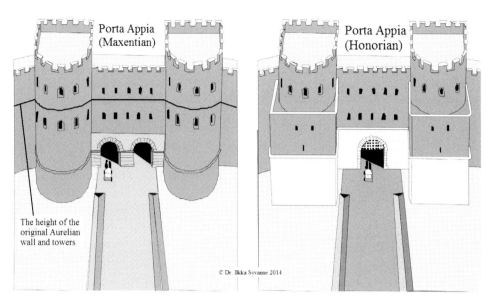

Porta Appia (Maxentian)

Porta Appia (Honorian)

The height of the original Aurelian wall and towers

© Dr. Ilkka Syvänne 2014

Most of the work done to the walls and towers consisted only of restoration and repair, because they were in relatively good condition. The only major change was that windows were replaced with loopholes on those towers where this could be done easily. The gateways, however, saw some major changes. With the exception of the Porta Portuensis, the other three great gateways (Flaminia, Appia, Ostiensis East) were now reduced to a single entranceway of ca. 4m in width and equipped with a portcullis, and new rectangular bases were added to the associated round towers (see the illustration, which is drawn after the one included in Fields). The rest of the gateways were also changed, the entranceway of the Porta Tiburtina being reduced to a width of 4m, whereas the Porta Asinaria and the Porta Chiusa were blocked by brickwork and never re-opened. The single-portal gateways were strengthened with curtains. There were therefore now 16 gates (originally 18) and 27 (originally 29) entrances (with postern gates) altogether. The length of the wall remained 19 km and it had 381 towers and possessed well over 700 ballistae, as Nick Fields puts it.[6]

In the absence of the Italian Field army, the government resorted to the hasty levying of recruits from whatever source was possible in Italy (Claudian, *Gothic*, tr. by Hawkins, 629ff., p.149.; Platnauer ed. 463ff. with some changes):

No wretched impressed levies ['*dilectus miseri*' *referring to the situation immediately after Stilicho had relieved the city of Milan in early 402*] these from mowing fields, whose novice hand the javelin feebly wields… nor Ceres from the harrow armed in haste who tries with awkward air the shield raise which fierce Bellona with derision views.

In short, the Italian farmers were pressed into service as levies immediately after the defeat at the Timavus. These were not sufficient to defeat the Goths, but they were quite sufficient to defend the cities against the invaders until the arrival of Stilicho's professional forces. Claudian continues:

...But when the Goths saw all our glorious youth, quickly levied footmen, *alae* of cavalry, a countryside protected by so many rivers and fortified cities, they were caught up in a snare on every part [*means the situation after the relief of Milan by Stilicho*], their hearts were seized by trouble they dared not voice and they grieved that they had invaded Italy...

The Goths were quite inept as besiegers – they could use only the blockade – and it was thanks to this that even the raw recruits and women were enough to defend the cities.

Historians have not recognized the fact that the levying of new forces in 401 meant a very significant increase in the size of the Roman army in Italy, which caused financial troubles as these forces were kept in arms. The subsequent Edict dealing with deserters (see the events after the war) prove that the men were kept in arms. The reason for the need to keep the men in arms was that the magnitude of the task of defending the West Roman Empire was deemed so daunting that it was felt to be necessary. The Romans faced simultaneously several large tribes migrating en masse. These were no longer the raids or invasions conducted by tribal youth, but real mass movements of entire peoples, tribes and confederacies of tribes.

And what would have been the likely size of the levy of the Italians? On the basis of the yearly levies of the Republican era it is quite easy to see that the minimum size for the levy would have been about 33,600–40,000 footmen and 2,400 cavalry. The maximum size would have been about 67,200–80,000 infantry and 4,800 cavalry. The reason for this is that the Republican-era Romans raised each year four legions (4,200–5,000 infantry and 300 cavalry per legion) and in emergencies even eight legions (33,600–40,000 foot and 2,400 horse) or even more. In addition to this, they required their Italian allies to contribute similar number of forces, with the exception that the allies were forced to contribute slightly more cavalry. However, when making calculations I have here purposefully lowered the cavalry figure of the allies to follow the Roman practise because it would have been more difficult to raise cavalry than infantry on a moment's notice.

The typical mediocre Classicist/Medievalist (or historian of the ancient period) would attempt to counter this with the claim that it was always difficult to raise armies during the Late Roman period, with the implication that they would not have been able to raise similar numbers of men as their Republican-era counterparts. This was undoubtedly true for normal times, but this was an emergency and it is quite clear that the Roman authorities pressed men into service with more than usual determination. Regardless, thanks to the probable opposition of the senators against this form of taxation and the reluctance of their tenants to join the army, I am still inclined to think that the actual number of new recruits was closer to the minimum figure rather than to the maximum, so that one can think that the state was able to raise something like 40,000–50,000 footmen and 2,400–3,500 horsemen. Even this number would have been enough to upset the balance of power in Italy, because it undoubtedly turned many of the senators against Stilicho and thereby nullified his previous attempts to woo the senatorial class. We should not forget, however, that this was not the entire force at the disposal of the authorities in the absence of Stilicho. There were still the remnants of Saul's forces and other forces left behind, including the marines of the fleets, and the citizen militias defending the cities. Taken together these were sufficient to defend the cities and fortresses.

The Siege of Milan in the winter of 401–402 (see the map of Milan on page 119): The Renewal of Troubles in Raetia and Noricum in 401/402

At some point in time during the campaign Alaric learned that Honorius and the court were still in Milan. As a result of this, he abandoned all other plans and besieged Honorius in Milan, presumably in the winter of 401/402. Honorius naturally learnt of this well in advance because the Gothic marching column moved very slowly as it was slowed down by the wagons carrying the families and all the loot the Goths had taken after the Battle of Adrianople in 378. Honorius and his court panicked and planned to flee to Gaul. When this news was brought to Stilicho, he appears to have returned from Raetia in the middle of winter 401/402 to convince Honorius to stay so that the defence of Italy would not collapse. Stilicho pointed out that his entire family was with Honorius and that this was not the first time that Italy had faced invaders. The presence of the Emperor on Italian soil was necessary for the maintenance of morale. It is quite clear that Stilicho was correct. The vast numbers of fresh recruits would have lost their morale had Honorius fled, and the defence of Italy was now entirely in their hands. Indeed, help was not long in coming. The only thing delaying it was the revolt of the already-pacified Raetia (the glades of Vindelicia) and Noricum, which required the attention of Stilicho and the Field Army. Consequently, Stilicho had to leave Honorius and his family behind in Milan and return to the north.[7] Claudian (*Gothic* tr. by Hawkins, 425ff., p.142ff.; Platnauer ed. 314ff. with some changes) describes the subsequent events as follows:

> These words [*of Stilicho*] relieved the people [*of the city of Milan*] from dismay, and calmed the court which was prepared to flee [*Stilicho convinced Honorius to remain at Milan*]. Then darkness fled and Italy raised her head because Caesar was ready to share her perils. Straight where Larius [*Larius/Comacinus Lacus/Lake of Como*] has verdant olive-trees winding its shores and waters fresh like Nereus motion make, a boat conveyed the hero [*Stilicho*] over the lake [*i.e. after Stilicho had left Milan he hastened north and crossed the lake Como on a boat with his horse. It is probable that he used the Classis Comensis for the transport of his retinue and supplies.*]. Then in spite of winter and inclement sky, he climbed the rugged sides of mountains high. Thus from the fasting young through deepest snows in silent night the furious lion goes; His neck by frost made rough, and yellow mane in ties congealed which icicles retain… Towards northern realms, the Hyrcanian forest lies, confining tracts where Rhaetia's summits rise. The Rhine and Danube hence derive their waves and both the rivers Latium's empire protect… Both fit for oars; their frozen face for wheels; And each, to Mars [*god of war*] and Boreas [*north-wind*] partial feels. But where Rhaetia marches with Italy mountains bounds with craggy apex and strike the sky, and offer dreadful narrow path, which is barely passable by human feet even in summer. With ice quite stiff [*dead*] have many there been found… many have closed their eyes beneath vast masses of snow, and often oxen and carts have been plunged into the white depths of ravine [*this is presumably an allusion to the difficulty of Stilicho's journey with the implication that it was equally difficult to bring supplies and soldiers through the Alps.*]. Sometimes the icy mountain suddenly falls downwards in an avalanche of ice…

These places Stilicho passed in mid-winter's cold. Stranger here was the god of rosy wine… The heroic chief content with humble fare in haste eaten with sword in hand, and cloak by moisture made heavy, urged his half-frozen horse to move on… his weary limbs obtained no soft bed. In caves of some dreadful beasts of prey or in some shepherd's hut he lay his shield… In forests the beds were on rugged soil, this sleep in snow. His cares and watchful toil brought peace for the world… The nations broke their treaties and encouraged by Latium's slaughters had overran the woods of Vindelici and oppressed the fields of Noricum. So slaves by false communication led to think… their master dead… The rebels thus perceived with great surprise the hero… again before their eyes…

… 'Has Getic war your courage raised and idly filled each breast with silly pride?' He [*Stilicho*] cried… 'Rome despite of fate will power sufficient find to punish those in rebellion…' With these warnings Stilicho checked the threatened rebellion and obtained new allies for war [*This implies that Stilicho had pacified the invaders before the winter and now pacified those again with his appearance and threats.*]. The hero enrolled the number required as allies so that these would not become a burden for Italy or a terror for their master [*i.e. Stilicho did not take so many barbarians with him that these could have posed a threat*]… the news of his return caused the cohorts to raise their standards in haste. The sight of Stilicho revived their courage… The first hastened the neighbouring troops of Rhaetia… with spoils from Vindelici to defend Ausonia [*This can mean that Stilicho marched first to Noricum and waited there for the arrival of other troops including those from the neighbouring Rhaetia, or that he advanced first to Rhaetia where the direct route from Lake Como would have taken him and assembled his army there and marched from there to Noricum to pacify it.*]. The legion came from the British confines where they had restrained the fierce Scots… and viewed the dying Pict… even agmina [*legions and other units*] that had put fear into the flaxen-haired Sycambri and those which had subjected the Chatti and wild Cherusci left the Rhine and turned their footsteps hither… Will you the fact believe… that Stilicho with steady hand maintains peace with the fear of his fame even when the territory is exposed to attack by the removal of garrisons [*i.e. the enemy did not exploit the absence of Roman garrisons because they feared Stilicho. However, there is also another explanation which is that the enemies simply did not have the necessary supplies to begin a campaign in the middle of winter.*]…

By you the course of Alaric was stopped… O fortune changed! How blessed our lot appears since thy return… Fresh vigour now to every quarter flows and hope in all the afflicted cities glows and by Hercules's superior hand… from the dreary shades of death to life was led… a voice unknown proclaimed to Rome the arrival of the leader famed… But who can paint the joy Honorius knew… [*when*] from the summits of lofty towers our eyes perceived a cloud of arising dust but yet uncertain if the dust meant allies in arms or dreadful foes. Then through the dusty cloud emerged the apex of Stilicho, glittering like a star with rays, and we recognized his gleaming white hair. Shouts were suddenly heard on every side: 'He comes, he comes, see Stilicho!'… wide the gates were thrown. Forth rushed a crowd with pride troops to own. These were no impressed levies…

Before this happened, however, the defenders were quite worried. At some point during the siege, presumably soon after Stilicho's return to the north, the Goths attempted to demoralize Honorius and the defenders of Milan with cavalry exercises in front of the city (Claudian Gothic 250–251). The fact that Alaric held these suggests that he possessed vast numbers of very well-equipped and drilled cavalry, which he could expect to demoralize the enemy. According to Claudian, in the middle of this exercise two wolves attacked Alaric's own escort with the result that the wolves were killed by missiles. Claudian claimed that both wolves had eaten humans previously so that their killing was to be seen as portent of the destruction of the enemies in front of Honorius' eyes. This is a good example of the kind of superstition prevailing at the time. What is important with this event is the fact the defenders did not lose their morale when the Gothic cavalry killed the wolves – the symbols of the city of Rome. Perhaps someone came up with the above-mentioned portent to calm down the nerves of the soldiers.

Claudian's Panegyric of Honorius' Sixth Consulship gives us further details of how Stilicho proceeded to relieve Milan after his lightning campaign in Raetia and Noricum. It is probable that Stilicho marched to Italy via the route across the Alps to Verona, or to Aquileia, the former route being likelier. Claudian (tr. Hawkins, Hon VI 625ff., p.181ff.; Platnauer ed. 441ff, with some changes):

> Alaric had overrun Greece and Thrace and had grown insolent by battles often won. He burst through the Alps with frantic fury and his troops round the trembling cities of Liguria drew with winter as his ally… Convinced the general would be soon in sight… The shades of night had overspread the skies and barbarian fires like stars I [*Honorius*] saw arise. The bugle had already sounded the first relief of the watch of soldiers when Stilicho arrived from the frozen north. The foe, however, lay between us. His interposing army shut the way and held the bridge which divided the banks of Addua with rapid foaming waves. How to act? – Delay, should Latium's leader try? – Honorius' peril forbade any delay. Should he break through the enemy's line? The force attending Stilicho was too small for this because he had left behind auxiliaries and brave cohorts to march faster to save us from danger. Thus placed in doubt, he thought his army too slow to wait [*Stilicho's own position was entirely dependent on the safety of the emperor*] and inflamed by virtue and affection true, disdaining life while dangers rose to view, with sword in hand he cut through the barbarian band and burst through the barbarian camp like a lightning bolt [*this implies a cavalry attack with his vanguard*]… See a man who did not attack the enemy with fraud in the midst of sleep, but opened up a passage for himself by his sword in the open light of day and arrived with blood besprinkled… Alaric's position was a stronger one on the bank of the river,… but neither the darts nor the river obstacle could move our her from his course… So was the swift Addua by my father traversed over.

Alaric knew that his negotiating position had weakened considerably after Stilicho had reached Milan. He knew that he would be forced to abandon the siege, because if he did not do so, he would face trouble: the Roman field army approaching Milan would be the hammer and the forces inside Milan would be the anvil. Consequently, he convened a council of war, which Claudian (tr. by Hawkins, Gothic, 651ff., p.149ff. already partially quoted above; Platnauer ed. 479ff, with some changes) describes as follows (we do not know how accurate the description is, but the Romans were certainly in a position to know what had been discussed after the war):

> …Alaric… a council called of elders great in arms. There sat long-haired senate of elders in furry skins. The scars of honour on each brow remained. The spear in hand their feeble steps sustained on lofty weapons as a staff applied. Then arose one older than the rest… Away have passed almost thirty winters since we swam across the rapid Ister [*Danube*]… Believe an ancient friend whose length of age has passed in field amid the battle's rage, who often in your tender years… and on your boyish back small quivers tied [*note the location of the quiver. It is the same as in most of the Roman works of art.*] and was wont parental kindness to show and to thy shoulders fit a little bow [*note the location of the bow*]… O hear my prayer to avoid dangers dire… with rapid movement quit Italy's soil so that you would not loose thy booty by seeking further spoils… [*this discussion took place before Pollentia*]… [*Alaric answered*]: 'Age has made you devoid of manly vigour and sense… To me thus destiny has favour shown… The gods too impel me [*see also Sozomen 9.6*]… This said, his troops he cheered with prospects bright and prepared to march… A stream the City [*Pollentia*] called… upon Liguria's furthest limits lies. The Getic chieftain reached… the place.'

After Alaric had abandoned the siege of Milan, he apparently decided to march to Gaul, because he advanced to Hasta. The Visigoths assaulted the city walls with disastrous consequences. The reason for this conclusion is that Claudian (Hon VI 201–209) considers the avenging walls of Hasta to be one the three defeats suffered by Alaric in Italy. Jordanes (Get. 152–155), however, claims that Honorius and the Senate finally decided to grant Alaric and his race land in Gaul and Spain, which Stilicho then exploited by treacherously attacking the Goths at Pollentia. This would explain why the Goths were subsequently so easily surprised at Pollentia, but the problem is that Jordanes associates this with the situation prevailing in 410. Regardless, I am still inclined to believe that Jordanes has just confused two separate events and promises, and that the Romans really promised Alaric land in Gaul after the failed assault of Hasta to lull him into false sense of security. This sort of treachery would naturally have been covered up by Claudian when discussing events. The route taken by Alaric after Hasta would have led him along the coastal route to Arelate/Arles and Gaul, which supports the version given by Jordanes.

Stilicho appears to have started a pursuit of Alaric's army once his main army reached Milan, but before this happened the Visigoths did have enough time to attempt to take the city of Hasta as noted above. It is unfortunate that Claudian fails to tell us the size of Stilicho's field army. All that we know is that these forces were enough to frighten and defeat the Visigoths, and we know that these included most of the praesental forces of Italy and Gaul, a British legion, Stilicho's *bucellarii*, Alans and Sarmatians, and barbarians from Raetia and Noricum. It is probable that Stilicho would have left the remnants of the frontier garrisons in their own bases to keep watch over the recently defeated barbarians.

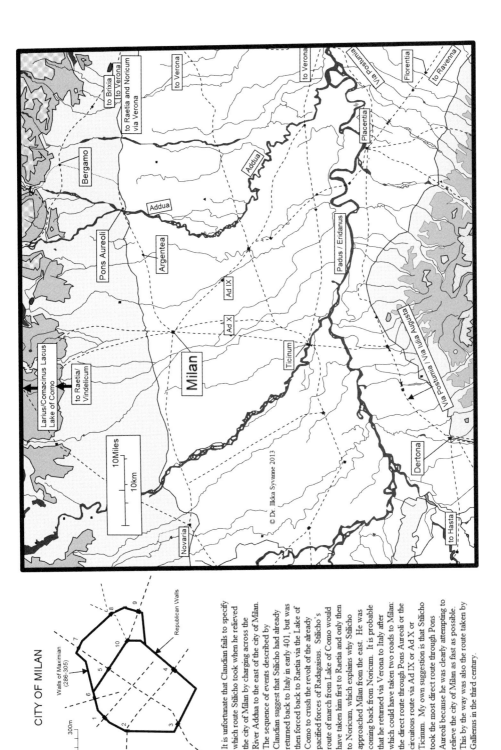

CITY OF MILAN

Walls of Maximian
(286-305)

Republican Walls

0   300m

GATES
1. Jovia
2. Vercellina
3. Ticiensis
4. Romana
5. ?
6. Comacina
7. Aurea
8. Argentea
9. Herculea
10 ?

It is unfortunate that Claudian fails to specify which route Stilicho took when he relieved the city of Milan by charging across the River Addua to the east of the city of Milan. The sequence of events described by Claudian suggest that Stilicho had already returned back to Italy in early 401, but was then forced back to Raetia via the Lake of Como to crush the revolt of the already pacified forces of Radagaisus. Stilicho´s route of march from Lake of Como would have taken him first to Raetia and only then to Noricum, which explains why Stilicho approached Milan from the east. He was coming back from Noricum. It is probable that he returned via Verona to Italy after which could have taken two roads to Milan: the direct route through Pons Aureoli or the circuitous route via Ad IX or Ad X or Ticinum. My own suggestion is that Stilicho took the most direct route through Pons Aureoli because he was clearly attempting to relieve the city of Milan as fast as possible. This by the way was also the route taken by Gallienus in the third century.

Let us therefore assume that Stilicho took with him back to Italy only the remnants of the forces he had taken to the north and that he would have lost about a third of his forces due to action, accidents and diseases, but into which he then added the reinforcements. I am assuming that Stilicho filled the ranks of his own *bucellarii* immediately from the barbarian captives so that it is the only figure that was not lower than before. The remnants of his field army would therefore have consisted of about 16,450 horse, 28,000 foot, and 10,000 *bucellarii*. The army of the *Magister Equitum per Gallias* consisted of 6,000 cavalry, 60,000 legionaries, and 17,000 auxiliaries. Since it is unlikely that Stilicho would have taken all of the forces (despite what Claudian states), I am making the educated guess that he took about two thirds, which would add up to about 4,000 horse, 40,000 legionaries, and 12,000 auxiliaries. This would give Stilicho an army of 30,450 cavalry and 80,000 infantry. However, since it is probable that Stilicho reinforced the garrisons of Raetia and Noricum, I am assuming that he left 20,000 footmen there, which leaves 60,000 foot for Stilicho. We should add to this figure at least the British legion and possibly also some units that had remained in Italy so that Stilicho probably had about 70,000–75,000 foot. On the basis of the width of the battlefield at Pollentia (see the map), it is probable that Stilicho's cavalry consisted of about 40,000 men too when one adds about 12,000 barbarians from Raetia and Noricum, and another 12,000 Alans and Sarmatians from Italy. This was a sizable army and probably outnumbered the Visigothic army, even if the Visigoths probably had more cavalry that the Romans.

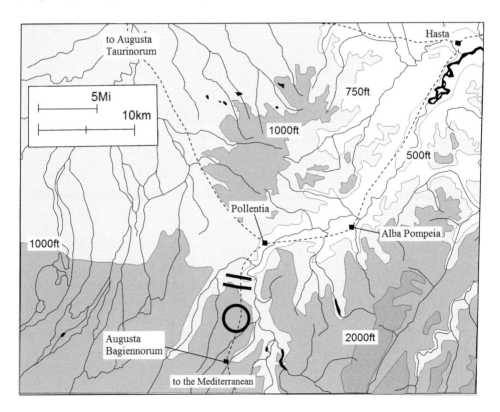

The Battle of Pollentia, Easter Day on 6 April 402

When the Goths had encamped just south of Pollentia and prepared to celebrate the Easter, Stilicho struck. It is quite probable that the Goths had been lulled into a false sense of security with the previous promise of land in Gaul so that the surprise was even greater than that caused by an attack being launched during Easter. Orosius (7.37, tr. by Raymond, Orosius, p.383–384 with additions inside parentheses with italics; similar account in Paulus Diaconus/Paul the Deacon, Historia Romana 12.13) describes the resulting battle as follows:

Stilicho, desiring it for his son [*the throne*], gave them [*barbarians*] so that the needs of the state in the sudden crisis might veil his wicked aim. I say nothing of King Alaric and his Goths, often defeated, often surrounded, but always allowed to escape. I say nothing of those unhappy doings at Pollentia when the chief command was entrusted to the barbarian and pagan general Saul who wickedly profaned the most solemn days and holy Eastertide and who compelled the enemy, then withdrawing on account of religious scruples, to fight. The judgement of God soon disclosed not only the power of His favour but also the demands of His vengeance, for although we conquered by fighting we were defeated in conquering. I say nothing of the intercine conflicts between the barbarians themselves, when two divisions of the Goths, and then the Alans and Huns, destroyed one another in mutual slaughter [*refers to the situation after the Italian, Raetian and Norican campaigns had failed*].

Claudian (tr. by Hawkins, Gothic, 765ff., p.158ff.; Platnauer ed. 558ff., already partially quoted above with some changes) gives us further details:

However, Stilicho for fight prepared; his ardour equally the army [*castra, i.e. forts which may be a simile for the use of hollow squares in combat*] shared; with rapid steps their march they forward pressed and he addressed them: 'O' allies [*o socii, the following, however, makes it clear that these socii were actually regulars*] take vengeance on behalf of the outraged Italy. Relieve the royal dome besieged [*Milan*]. Wipe out with arms the shame which the passage of Alps and the defeat at Timavus has caused. Behold that this is the enemy you put to flight so often in the fields of Greece [*the regulars, especially the infantry, would have had fresh memories of these*]… Be confident that nations far and wide, the fierce Britons, those from the Rhine and Ister, all stand prepared… Stop future contests by winning a victory now… a single victory will restore peace to the world… Such were the words of Stilicho to foot and horse. Their ardour raised, he sent commands to the auxiliary troops. Obedient to the state the Alani proved; wherever our trumpets called, they freely moved; Their chief renowned [*Saul*], who led this bold nation, thought that death for Latium was glorious. Though small was his limbs, yet nature gave him fire, high mind and eyes that flamed with furious ire. No part without hideous wound was seen and more proud was his visage by the scar that some spear-thrust had left… When Stilicho his services required,… he hastened as desired to bite the solid of Italy in death, happy warrior worthy of the Elysian fields who burned to prove false unjust suspicions with his blood [*the suspicions resulting from the defeat at Timavus*]. The horsemen, when their leader fell, turned their reins and exposed a flank. The whole army would have fled had not Stilicho with a legion brought help and rallied cavalry with infantry support, and so was the battle renewed. [*The ability of the legion to march forward independently suggests the use of the hollow square/oblong formation, which was the standard combat formation ever since the reforms of Valentinian and which was also used with such great success by Theodosius I at Poetovio in 388; see Vol.2*]... With a thirst of odious enemy blood, the soldiers passed by costly garments, carts laden with gold, heaps of silver, and eager only for the enemy's destruction trampled on the riches. They considered the blood more glorious than the gold. [*This proves that Stilicho's army was exceptionally disciplined and followed up the combat doctrine to the letter. The soldiers either passed the carrago or marched through it and did not begin looting before the enemy was defeated. This proves that Stilicho was a true disciplinarian and that the field army under his command was a first-rate fighting machine not weakened by corruption. Therefore, there is every reason to believe that after Stilicho had managed to secure his position in 395 he turned against all forms of corruption.*]... The foe with wily aim three before the troops the spoils taken from Valens which included his purple cloak torn from the flames... The people lately doomed to bear the chains were freed and so were all the nations that the Getae had led away captive... O Alaric! What sorrows rack thy breast, those treasures lost,... the fruits of plunder gained... with howling loud thy wife laments [*the capture of Alaric's wife and the families of the other warriors proved very valuable bargaining chips*]... The glory of the battle of Pollentia shall live forever.

My educated guess is that Stilicho deployed his forces in at least two lines so that he posted the cavalry in front for the purpose of making a surprise attack against the enemy *carrago* when they were least expecting it. It is probable that the cavalry was deployed as a single line, because it needed infantry support. If my calculations regarding the respective size of the cavalry forces on each side are correct, then this was to be expected if the Romans intended to match the length of the enemy cavalry line – the infantry would have acted as a reserve.

We do not possess any definite evidence for the infantry array, except that it is very probable that each of the generic legions (4,000–7,000 men per *meros/legio*) was deployed as a hollow square/oblong. It is possible that Stilicho used only a single line of 10–14 hollow squares/oblongs, or that he posted perhaps something like nine (left, centre and right each consisting of three legions) legions in the front and three behind as reserves for the wings and centre (and possibly one to guard the camp) – we just do not know. I have adopted here the former alternative with ca. 7,000-man legions for the reconstruction because this would have enabled Stilicho to cover the entire length of the field between the two rivers, but the other possibilty is equally plausible. Since the battle was fought on the plain, it is likely that the legions adopted the hollow oblong formation to widen the frontage (each of the flanks ca. 1,000 men and front/rear ca. 2,000 men with depths of 8 heavies and 4 light-armed, and extra men to act as reserves) it is also probable that there were wide intervals between them to allow the cavalry room to retreat when required. Similarly, I have also made the educated guess that Stilicho would have left his

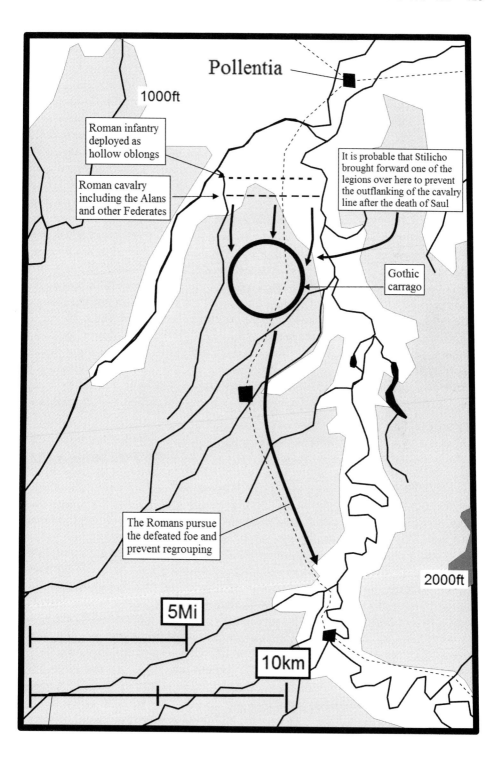

baggage train inside the city of Pollentia or just outside it in a fortified camp and that he would have left a strong guard behind to guard the baggage and city. The Roman combat doctrine required this and it is very likely that Stilicho followed it to the letter.

The accounts of Orosius and Claudian make it clear that the initial cavalry charge under Saul against the Visigothic *carrago* took the Goths by surprise. It is also quite clear that the Goths would have seen the approach of the enemy force from their vantage point so that they would have been able to form some sort of defensive line before the enemy reached the *carrago*. These forces and the wagon-fortress negated the impetus of the cavalry attack and enabled the Goths to regroup. When this happened a Goth or Goths managed to kill Saul. This occurred on one of the flanks, but we do not know which one. Both flanks are equally possible, even if the left flank would be slightly more probable (see the map) because this would explain better why Stilicho marched only a single legion forward and separated it from the rest of the infantry forces – it was on this side that the cavalry line would have been spread out thanks to the open terrain and the round shape of the *carrago*. It is also clear that this incident took place just outside the *carrago* because it was only after Stilicho had brought his legion forward that the Romans faced the Gothic carts laden with spoils. The arrival of the infantry tilted the balance in favour of the Romans. The Romans pursued, but the vast majority of the Gothic warriors still managed to flee thanks to the swiftness of their horses. The Romans captured the Visigothic families and possessions, the former of which they were able to use as hostages. This was not as great a success as Claudian makes it to be, because Alaric's Visigoths still remained a force to be reckoned with. Regardless, it is still clear that the strength of the Visigothic host had been greatly diminished at minimal cost, which Stilicho could easily replace from the garrisons of Italy.

Retreat from Pollentia and the Battle of Verona in July/August 402

Claudian (tr. by Hawkins, Gothic, 185ff., p.167ff.; Platnauer ed. 127ff, with some changes):

Alaric's hopes were crushed by the bloody defeat at Pollentia's field, though necessity demanded that his life was spared. His allies deserted him and his riches were lost. Compelled the will of fortune to obey and leave Latium, he traced back his way in shame. [*Claudian conflates two separate instances here. The actual desertion of the allies took place only after the battle of Verona. However, Claudian's text still makes it clear that Stilicho favoured a negotiated settlement with Alaric so that he would have to avoid fighting with a desperate enemy, and also because Stilicho sought to employ Alaric and his Goths as Federates.*]... So Alaric fled from Ausonia... When he approached the paths were open laid; Now difficulties every turn displayed. Each pass closed up was pictured to his mind, and streams of late scorned when left behind, now filled him with alarm during the return. Eridanus [*river personified here as god*] within his watery home beneath the glossy groves... he called, while raised above his wave, Liguarian streams, and those that Venetia have. The clear Ticinus and the Addua blue, swift Athesis, slow Mincius, and Timavus with his nine mouths lift their dripping heads from among their leafy banks and all mock the fugitive... [*This means that Alaric feared that Stilicho would not honour his word and allow his Goths retreat away from Italy unmolested. The crossing of the flooding rivers in the spring was particularly dangerous if Stilicho would decide to attack when the Goths were crossing.*]Verona too, contributed to Latium's victory over the Getae. Not even the ramparts of the avenging Hasta [*hasta means also spear*] and Pollentia did as much for the glory of Ausonia. Before those walls no treaties sacred proved, the savage chieftain… tried to change his fate [*Alaric broke his treaty and attempted to retreat to Rhaetia*]. In vain his fury… the destinies denied whatever he sought. On carcasses of numerous soldiers dead, voracious birds with eager hunger fed. The Athesis [*the river beside Verona*] unfriendly bodies bore and changed the waters of the Ionian Sea into human gore. The treaty broken Stilicho with haste took the field and in order his forces placed. Away from Rome now danger too was far, the Po with flowing stream divided war [*Stilicho's plan had also been to prevent Alaric from marching towards Rome*]. The hero received the news of the treachery with joyful eagerness [*the treachery gave Stilicho the rightful cause which he had lacked previously*]… with firm example he led the troops forward despite burning heat and clouds of dust. [*Stilicho presumably rushed to the scene to prevent Alaric's march towards Rhaetia and Gaul.*]

With sword in hand he flew from one part of the field to another wherever required and stationed troops at every point even on such points where the enemy did not expect them, and if the soldiers gave way, he brought auxiliaries without delay and secured the front [*Stilicho first arrayed his army for combat and then reinforced in person those sections that needed assistance. The agmine miles in the context of soldiers giving way suggests that the front of the battle array consisted of the regular legions each of which was probably arrayed as a hollow square/oblong and that the auxiliaries that he brought forward consisted primarily of the federate cavalry forces. In other words, Stilicho received the Gothic cavalry charge with his infantry and used his cavalry as reserves.*] Cunningly Ister [*Danube*] was overpowered with its kindred strength. The battle thus producing double gain, since by barbarians the savage hordes were slain. [*This suggests that after the Gothic attack had been halted with the Roman infantry, the federate forces pursued the Goths of Alaric. The terms used here suggest that a significant number of the Roman federates consisted of the forces obtained from the defeated Radagaisus, but the subsequent details also make it clear that the term barbarian auxiliary also included the regular Roman federates.*] He would also have captured and killed Alaric, had not the hasty speed of the Alan chief ruined Stilicho's carefully laid plans. Almost made prisoner, but the whip of Alaric was applied with force to make good the escape. Go, show how few have escaped from dire havoc and what numbers survive of Danube's race. Proclaim our triumph by thy own disgrace. [*This seems to be out of place here because it fits better the battle of Pollentia, but it is of course possible that the Alans once again charged with such an abandon that the plans were upset.*] However, the frightful slaughter had not dismayed his savage nature. Some secret path over the mountains he sought through which his vanquished forced might be brought to across the craggy rocks… and enter Rhaetia and Gaul, but Stilicho's prudent vigilance prevented his plans. Who could ever hope to deceive his vigilance in guarding the realm? The hero's plans were always thoroughly concealed [*He clearly kept tight control over information*] but the enemy had no power to conceal his own. The plans of the Getae were known to Stilicho before the enemy knew those… [*This implies that Stilicho either guessed what the enemy attempted or had very good spies and scouts.*] Alaric, unable to fulfil any of his aims, camped in trembling fear on a small hill. The horses fed on bitter leaves gnawed the bark of trees, and putrescent meats and summer's heat brought dire diseases and haughty soldiers taunted their leader and reminded him of their fettered children [*captured at Pollentia*]; Nor pestilence, nor famine, nor grief of lost plunder, nor shame, nor insolent words could dare him to take to the field of hand-to-hand combat, which he had tried so often before with poor results. And now desertions numerous every hour left bare the camp and diminished his power. Nor was sedition in concealment held, but openly whole wedges [*cunei*] and squadrons [*turmae*] defected.

Their general followed full of rage and war against his troops and with angry curses and prayers sought to hold them back… soldiers were deaf to all his commands and his power melted away… Which slaughter first, which last, shall I [*Alaric*] bewail? Not though alone Pollentia gives me pain, nor the loss of plundered treasures… Still around me cavalry and foot remained. With these conjoined the Apennines I gained… The inhabitants told me that the high hills ran from Liguria as far as Pelorus in Sicily and comprised the entire Italian race and divided the two seas… If I had followed up my first intention prompted by despair and had continued my march along those heights what lay beyond?… I might have expired in the field and involved the Roman realm in one dread fire… Yet in their hands were not spoils alone but my children and wives held captive… The fatal enemy Stilicho ensnared me with cunning stratagems and skill. He pretended to show mercy and he disarmed my people without a blow and moved me and war beyond the Po. Oh! worse than slavery these treaties prove! The fearless strength of the Getae was undone. [*This means that, after his defeat at Pollentia, Alaric was planning to march along the Apennines to Rome, but was convinced by Stilicho to agree to an armistice in return for hostages. However, Stilicho did this only to fool the Goths because his plan was to return the hostages only after the Goths had left Italian soil. The Goths felt duped and decided to break their treaty when they reached Verona.*]… I cannot rely on my comrades and my friends have turned against me… This said and Rome's dreaded eagles just in sight the trembling Alaric continued his flight… [*The referral to the Aquila-standards of the legions stands as still another good example of outstanding combat performance of the legions under Stilicho at Pollentia and Verona. It was their steadiness that had nulled the Gothic cavalry charges.*]

Since the Athesis (modern Adige) River features only as a conduit of bodies, and Claudian's description does not include any crossing of the river, and it was the Visigoths who charged at the Romans and Alaric's object was to march to Raetia, it is clear that the battle took place east of the Athesis and that the Visigoths did not attempt to hold the riverline against Stilicho. Taken together this means that the Visigoths had suddenly turned left to march to Raetia, which Stilicho anticipated. Since it is very improbable that Stilicho would have allowed the Goths to use the bridges inside the city of Verona (see the map), it is probable that he had built them a pontoon bridge somewhere south

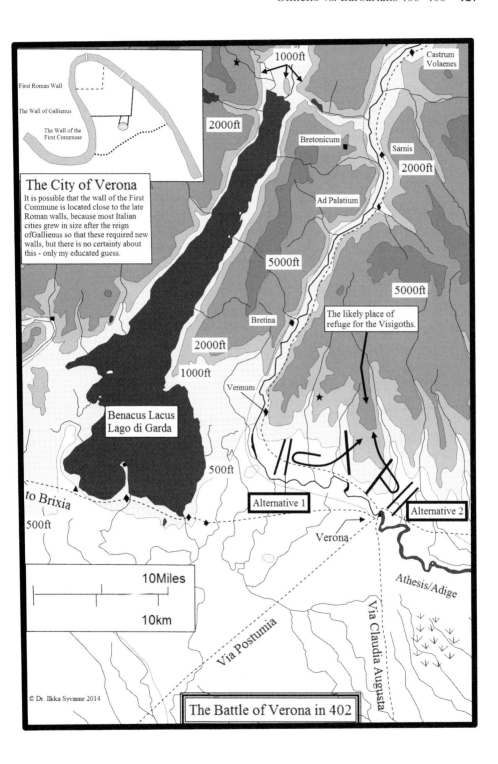

First Roman Wall

The Wall of Gallienus

The Wall of the
First Commune

The City of Verona

It is possible that the wall of the First
Commune is located close to the late
Roman walls, because most Italian
cities grew in size after the reign
ofGallienus so that these required new
walls, but there is no certainty about
this - only my educated guess.

1000ft

Castrum
Volaenes

2000ft

Bretonicum

Sarnis

2000ft

Ad Palatium

5000ft

5000ft

Bretina

The likely place of
refuge for the Visigoths.

2000ft

1000ft

Vennum

Benacus Lacus
Lago di Garda

500ft

Alternative 1

Alternative 2

to Brixia

500ft

Verona

Athesis/Adige

10Miles

10km

Via Postumia

Via Claudia Augusta

© Dr. Ilkka Syvänne 2014

The Battle of Verona in 402

of the city. This in turn means that Stilicho would have been quite aware of every move that the Goths made.

There are two alternative explanations for what happened after Stilicho learnt that Alaric was attempting to march to Raetia. The first and likelier alternative on the basis of Claudian's text (Alternative 1 on the map) is that he anticipated this as stated by Claudian and crossed the Athesis upstream by using a pontoon bridge (the cavalry would have swum across while the infantry used the bridge) and thereby blocked the route, forcing the Visigoths to charge. The second alternative (Alternative 2 on the map) is that Stilicho just followed the Visigoths and crossed the river by using the bridges of Verona (its ballistae would have protected the crossing) with infantry forming up as a column of hollow oblongs which then marched obliquely to protect the cavalry that would have crossed the river by swimming. In this case the unexpected speed of Stilicho's arrival would have forced the Visigoths to retrace their steps and attack Stilicho's army, which was all of a sudden threatening their rear.

Regardless of which alternative is correct, the width of the open terrain would have been exactly suited to the size of the army accompanying Stilicho. The principal difference between Pollentia and Verona is that this time Stilicho placed his infantry in the front to bear the brunt of the enemy charge, which it did successfully with the help of the cavalry reserves that Stilicho used to bring help whenever there was a need for this. When the Gothic charge had been brought to a halt, Stilicho sent his barbarian cavalry forward to the attack. This probably means that Stilicho kept his Roman cavalry in reserve this time. It is in fact possible that he could have increased the size of his cavalry force from the Sarmatian settlements of the north of Italy to enable him to do this – a thing which he was apparently unable to do before the Battle of Pollentia. The pursuit of the fleeing foe was performed so effectively that the Romans managed to isolate the Visigoths on a hill.

It is probable, even if Claudian fails to mention this, that after the Visigoths had fled to the hill that the Romans placed separate forces of infantry at least near Ad Palatium and Castrum Volaenes (see the map), because by doing so they would have cut off all routes leading to Raetia from the hills south and south-east of them, even in those cases where the Goths could have somehow managed to get through or bypass the obstacles of nature and the other guards posted around them. The corpses floating on the Athesis in Claudian would have consisted of those Goths who had tried to flee to the river rather than to the mountains.

The End of the War and Stilicho's Future Plans

Despite the fact that Stilicho had managed to isolate Alaric on a hill, he remained true to his cautious and devious nature. Stilicho decided that it was wiser to save Alaric with his forces for future use rather than attempt to destroy him. This approach was very cost effective and was also recommended in the military treatises: it was not considered wise to engage a desperate foe in a fight to the death. The saving of the foe who had just attacked Italy, however, was a very unpopular decision and Claudian (Gothic e.g.77ff., tr. by Platnaeur with comments added inside parentheses) attempted to represent this in the best possible light:

He [*Alaric*] who destined the women of Rome as victims of his lust has seen his own wives and children led away captive: he who in imagination had drained the countless wealth of our city became himself his victor's easy prey; he who once sought to corrupt the loyalty of our troops has been deserted by his own people and has returned to his country beggared of men and arms. ... But our clemency was in part due to another cause, ... to offer a way of escape ... lest, with the fear of death before their eyes, their rage should grow more terrible for being confined ... He [*Stilicho*] has conquered... a mighty people ... In the case of our latest foe Stilicho succeeded in combining in himself the diverse skill of all these three [*Fabius, Marcellus, Scipio*]; he broke their frenzy by delaying, vanquishing them in battle and drove the vanquished host from Italy. And all this in so short a time. ... he saw to it that the winter of our distress should last but one winter but that spring in its earliest months should bring back fair weather.

After Alaric had evacuated Italy Stilicho appears to have returned the captured families to the Visigoths as part of the treaty that he negotiated with him. This is clear from two facts: Alaric's descendants became rulers later and the Romans and Goths exchanged hostages in 405. There would not have been any reason for such if the Romans still held the Visigothic families as hostage. Notably, one of the hostages that the Romans handed to Alaric was Flavius Aetius (Gregory of Tours 2.8 with PLRE2 Alaricus) who was held by Alaric for three years. It is no wonder why Alaric stayed loyal to Stilicho later. Stilicho had shown remarkable clemency and had not harmed the hostages.

Zosimus' account (5.26.1–27.3, with 5.29) gives us the main reasons for Stilicho's decision to pardon Alaric. According to him, Stilicho made an agreement with Alaric for the purpose of detaching a number of Illyrian cities from Arcadius and it was only thanks to the invasion of Italy by Radagaisus in 405 that the plan was postponed. It appears probable that this means the conquest of the Balkans up to Thrace and then possibly the conquest of the entire East, because Alaric's subsequent advance into Epirus and Greece in 407 would have hardly been sufficient for the operation. It is also clear that Alaric was eventually settled in Dalmatia after Radagaisus defeated him following his flight from Italy, because Alaric advanced into Epirus, which was East Roman territory, only in 407. On the basis of the cooperation between Stilicho and Alaric, it is clear that Stilicho still entertained the thought of subjecting the East to his rule, probably so that his son Eucherius could act as his figurehead ruler. It is no wonder that Honorius started to turn against his benefactor. Every move Stilicho made appeared to prove that he had imperial ambitions of his own, even if he acted through figurehead rulers.

The Respite in Hostilities and the Triumph at Rome, 403–404

The ending of the invasion of Italy allowed the West Romans to breathe a sigh of relief, but the peace did not last long. The short respite resulted from intercine conflict among the barbarians and from the West-Roman need to rebuild their armies and defences. The former is proven by Orosius' referral (7.37.3) to the conflict between two armies ('*cunei*') of Goths on the one hand and between the Alans and Huns on the other just prior to Radagaisus' invasion of Italy. It was as a result of this that: 1) Radagaisus gained control of the area opposing the Julian Alps, as we shall see; 2) Alaric was forced to retreat to Dalmatia, which was part of West Rome and Radagaisus' former territory (Alaric advanced to Epirus only in 407, see Zos. 5.29); and 3) the Huns became allies of Rome. It is easy to see why Radagaisus was able to achieve this. The defeats suffered by Alaric previously would have weakened his position sufficiently for Radagaisus to be able to regain his ascendancy among the Goths of Pannonia. It is in fact probable that Stilicho actually wanted the former comrades to turn against each other and had probably made such peace treaties with them that put them at odds with each other. As regards the intercine war between the Huns and Alans, we are on more uncertain terms. It is probable that this referred to some section of the Alans liberating themselves from Hun oppression and offering their services to Radagaisus. Since we find the Huns cooperating with Stilicho in the coming conflict it is probable that most of the Huns had previously remained loyal to their Federate agreement while the Alans preferred to join Radagaisus.

In the meanwhile, the Italians started rebuilding their own lives. The harshness of the situation is quite apparent, as is the general unwillingness of the hastily-corvéed civilians to continue to serve in the army after the invaders had left. The best proof of the latter is the rash of Edicts in 403 (CTh 7.18.11–14) against deserters and harbourers of deserters given to the *PPI* Hadrianus (24 Feb, 25 July, and twice on 2 Oct.). These bespeak of the difficult situation prevailing in Italy in the immediate aftermath of three years of continuous invasion by the Goths and others.

The war also resulted in the change of strategy regarding the defence of the Empire. The Gothic siege of Honorius at Milan had demonstrated to Stilicho the vulnerability of his own position. He needed to secure the figurehead ruler better in order to safeguard his own position. Claudian's account (Hon. VI 494ff.) proves that Stilicho transferred Honorius to the more secure city of Ravenna in the immediate aftermath of the war, because it was from Ravenna that Honorius and Stilicho marched to Rome to celebrate the triumph over the invaders in 404 and Honorius to take the consular fasces in 404. This is also confirmed by extant legislation, which proves that Honorius was at Ravenna by December 402 (Matthews, 274). Honorius and Stilicho rode in the same triumphal chariot, while Stilicho's son Eucherius and wife Serena walked in front of the chariot. Claudian claims that the senators were dishonoured by not being allowed to march before the chariot.

The same triumphal procession proves that the West-Roman cavalry bodyguards were similarly heavily equipped with gilded golden armour as their Eastern counterparts. Claudian (Hon VI. 569ff., tr. by Platnaeur) states:

> When she sees the mail-clad knights and brazen-armoured horses she would fain know whence that iron race of men is sprung and what land it is gives birth to steeds of bronze. 'Has the god of Lemnos', she would ask, 'bestowed on metal the power to neigh, and forged living statues for the fight?' … how Juno's bird decks the gay crests upon their helmets, or how, beneath the golden armour on their horses' backs, the red silk waves and ripples over the strong shoulders.

The performance in the Circus shows how well-drilled the elite soldiers were. The widespread corruption of the top brass did not effect the quality of the equipment and training of the elite forces guarding the Emperor or Stilicho. Claudian (Hon VI 612ff. tr. by Platnauer with slight changes):

What majesty bows to majesty as the prince, clad in imperial scarlet returns the salutations of the people that crowd the tiers of the Circus! … Nor does the Circus display only horse-races; its floor, whereon chariots were wont to drive, is surrounded by a palisade, and in this new amphitheatre … Libyan lions shed their blood. This is the scene, too, of a military display; here we often see armed bands advancing and retiring in mazed movements that are nevertheless executed according to a fixed plan; we watch them wheel in perfect order, extent with disciplined precision, affording us the pleasing spectacle of mimic warfare. The leader cracks his whip and all execute in unison their new movements; now they clap their bucklers to their sides, now they brandish them above their heads; deeply sound the clashing shields, sharply ring the engaging swords, and, to the rhythm of beaten targes, the echoing song of steel is punctuated by the interclash of weapons. Suddenly the whole phalanx falls on its knees before thee and helmets bow down in reverence. Then the companies [*catervae*] separate, wheeling and counter-wheeling with ordered skill. … Then wheeling apart they form with circular masses [*orbes agmina*].

The reason why the show in question was performed at the Circus rather than in the amphitheatre is that it was located right next to the imperial residence on the Palatine Hill. The ruler could in practice walk straight from his palace to his auditorium above the Circus. The drill performed on the Circus shows well how the Romans expected their legions to fight, and their performance under Stilicho proves that these great expectations were met, at least when he was in charge of the discipline and training.

For some unknown reason on 22 April 404 Honorius delivered an Edict to the *PPI* Romulianus to remove all Jews and Samaritans from the School of *Agentes in Rebus* (CTh 16.8.16). We do not know whether there was some specific reason, such as a case of proven disloyalty, for this removal of Jews and Samaritans beyond the usual racist suspicions, or whether the loyalty of these religious groups was considered suspect in general – a concern or prejudice that is shared even by some modern intelligence organizations. It should be noted that the last mentioned fear does seem quite out of place in the West, because it was in the East that there were very real fears of the Jews and Samaritans joining the Persian invaders. No such thing could be expected to happen in the West. I would actually go so far as to claim that this specific Edict can be seen as an early example of Honorius' own prejudices, as exemplified by his later similar legislation. Honorius was certainly not alone in his anti-Semitic views, because these views were held by most of the Catholic clergy and it is also very probable that Stilicho shared these views. The reason for this conclusion is that it is well-known that Stilicho was himself a Christian zealot and was behind the penal laws of Honorius against pagans and heretics according to Augustinus (PLR1 with Augustinus Ep.97). However, the legislation and actions of Honorius after the death of Stilicho prove that Stilicho was still a moderate when compared with the arch-racist Honorius – which is not a great wonder considering Stilicho's Vandal background.

Radagaisus' Invasion 404–406[8]

Stilicho celebrated his second consulship in 405, but the year was not a good one for him. The Irish were so bold as to sail their fleet into the English Channel. According to the *Irish Annals* a.405, Niall of the Nine Hostages was killed by Eochaidh, son of Enna Ceinnseallach, at Muir n-Icht (Portus Iccius/Boulogne). He was succeeded by Dathi, who served as a loyal ally of Rome. (See also *Britain in the Age of Arthur* with the MHLR Vol. 4.) The location suggests that Niall had either sailed to Boulogne as an ally and was then killed there by his subjects, or that he had raided the port and was then defeated by the Roman Fleet, as a result of which one of his subjects assassinated him.

However, the principal event of the year 405 was the invasion of Italy by king Radagaisus and his Goths probably in the autumn. The *Annales Ravennatenses* (a. 404) dates the invasion of Italy by Radagaisus to the year 404, which is probably false as far as Italy is concerned, but it is possible that Radagaisus' invasion of West Roman territory began with a revolt in 404, so that he conquered the routes leading into Italy before actually marching into Italy in 405. The timing of Radagaisus' invasion of Italy was so beneficial for Arcadius that one wonders whether he had any role in it. It prevented the joint invasion of the east by Stilicho and Alaric.

The Invaders
According to Zosimus 5.26, Radagaisus had assembled an army of 400,000 Gauls and Germans from the Danube and the Rhine with which he invaded Italy. As is clear, Zosimus has here confused his sources. If Radagaisus' army consisted primarily of Goths, then his forces could not have come from two directions simultaneously, even when one attempts to rescue the story by suggesting invasion from Raetia through the Brenner Pass. This would have been plausible only if Radagaisus was an Alamannic king. However, since Radagaisus and his followers are said to have consisted of Goths, it is clear that we should see Radagaisus' invasion as progressing from Illyricum (where he had collected allies from across the Danube) through the Julian Alps into Italy, as in my reconstruction. Contrary to the consensus opinion among modern historians, Zosimus' figure of 400,000 warriors is quite credible as a total force because the invasion forces quite evidently consisted of several separate large tribes [the Vandal Federates of Pannonia and Noricum, the Siling and Hasding Vandals from across the Danube, and the Alans, Goths and Huns settled formerly by Gratian] which were migrating en masse with their families, even if the other sources put the strength of the invading force at 200,000 men. The latter figure refers to the invading force consisting solely of Goths under Radagaisus. However, I would suggest that Radagaisus' 200,000 Goths actually included also the women and children, so that that each of the three groups would have had over 100,000 warriors, in addition to which one would have to add the women and children. It is otherwise difficult to see the need for Stilicho and the imperial administration to resort to such desperate measures as they did.

The size of the allied forces coming to help the Romans gives a good clue of the magnitude of the problem. On the basis of the later nomadic forces in the area occupied by Uldin's Huns, Uldin alone must have had at least about 40,000–60,000 Huns at his disposal and on the basis of the size of the Alan and Sarmatian settlements in Italy and on the basis of the information referring to the situation in 408–409, the Federate force under Sarus must have had at least 30,000–40,000 men (because at the time of his revolt, after having suffered a number of casualties, he had still enough men to oppose the combined force of 30,000 Federates and Alaric's army – see later).

Stilicho's Reaction

As noted above, Stilicho considered the forces at his disposal too small to engage the migrating masses, as a result of which he resorted to desperate measures. He formed an alliance with Uldin and ordered Sarus to assemble his Federate forces (Goths in Orosius and Alans in Zosimus) and started to assemble the regulars at Ticinum. In the meanwhile, Stilicho avoided combat with the enemy. It should also be noted that if Stilicho and Alaric had not yet concluded the alliance (it is probable that they had done that already in 402), they definitely did so after Radagaisus' revolt against Alaric. What is clear is that at the time of Radagaisus' invasion of Italy Stilicho and Alaric were allies and therefore the Romans had nothing to fear from Alaric's direction.

The likely reason for Uldin's willigness to come to the assistance of Stilicho was that the Alans who were accompanying Radagaisus were fugitives from Uldin's Empire. It is also possible that Radagaisus and his Goths plus the Vandals had also fled from the Huns. It is probable that Sarus was the commander of the Federate Goths, Huns (the sources do not mention them, but there were subsequently Huns among the Federates and *bucellarii* in Italy) and Alans that had been settled in Pannonia and who had suffered from the ravages inflicted by Radagaisus' troops. Lebedynsky (2012, 14–5) notes that Sarus may actually have had an Alan name (*Sar** head, chieftain) even if his forces appear to have consisted of Goths. However, this is not accepted by all historians. For example, the PLRE2 considers Sarus' name to be Germanic and several of the sources call Sarus either *rex* or *dux Gothorum*. Thanks to the fact that groups of Alans and Goths had been united ever since the third century, it is impossible to be certain. It is quite probable that Sarus commanded a heterogenous force consisting of both peoples (and others like the Huns that had joined them). Since Zosimus includes Alans among the allies, it is quite clear that there were also Alans present. However, it is probable that these Alans belonged to two different groupings: 1) those who had previously been settled in Italy as Federates who were now ordered to obey Saru; and 2) those who had been settled in Pannonia in 380 and served now under Sarus.

We learn from Zosimus that Stilicho's main army which assembled at Ticinum consisted of 30 *arithmoi* (i.e. *numeri*), but it took about a year for Stilicho to assemble this army, and he considered even this number of troops to be inadequate. He waited for the arrival of the Huns, Goths and Alans before he would make his move. This means that Stilicho allowed the invaders to ravage the North-East of Italy unhindered. On the basis of the information that we have, it is impossible to make any certain estimation regarding the size of the Roman army. The *arithmos/numerus* could signify any generic unit. There are two possible ways to estimate the size of the regular force under Stilicho, which can then be compared with the size of the invading force. Firstly, it is possible to use Zosimus' own figures to form an estimate of what he meant with 30 *arithmoi*. Secondly, it is possible to use the information provided by the *Notitia Dignitatum*.

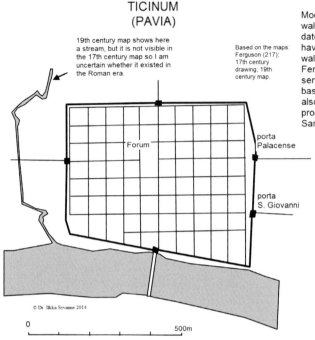

TICINUM
(PAVIA)

19th century map shows here
a stream, but it is not visible in
the 17th century map so I am
uncertain whether it existed in
the Roman era.

Based on the maps:
Ferguson (217);
17th century
drawing; 19th
century map.

Forum

porta
Palacense

porta
S. Giovanni

© Dr Ilkka Syvänne 2014

0   500m

Modern archaeologists attribute the
walls to the 6th century, but the precise
date is not known and these walls may
have actually consisted of older restored
walls (Ferguson, 215). In my opinion
Ferguson is right because Ticinum
served as one of the principal military
bases north of Italy. Notably, the city
also possessed a *fabrica* which
produced bows undoubtedly for the
Sarmatian Federates settled nearby.

The size of the city implies a
military garrison of about
17,500-20,000 men, but at
times of war this force could
have been bolstered by
additional troops that would
have been encamped outside
the walls if the location was
used as an assembly point as
happened in 405.

If one were to take Zosimus' own figures as a clue to the size of the *arithmos* he meant (Zos. 5.45.1: five Dalmatian elite *tagmata* comprising 6,000 men vs. Zos. 6.8.2: six *tagmata* comprising 40,000 men, i.e. a *tagma* = c.6,666 men = c.5,000 infantry and 1,600 cavalry or 6,000 infantry and 600 cavalry = an old legion)[9] then one can conclude that Stilicho would have had from 36,000 to 198,000 men, in addition to which came the Alans and Huns. Furthermore, it is actually possible that in 5.45.1 Zosimus actually meant that each *tagma* had 6,000 men (the size of the traditional legion without cavalry) rather than the total force. On the other hand there appears to be a difference in the way in which Zosimus uses the word *tagma*. In the Dalmatian instance he referred to particular legions of the *Comitatenses* (*Tertiani Italica, Tertia Herculea, Pacatienses, Mauri Cetrati* and *Propugnati Iuniores*), which may actually have been smaller than the traditional legions, while in the case of Stilicho's forces Zosimus may have referred to a 'generic' *arithmos*, the equivalent of a *legion/meros* consisting of several real units, which is clearly the meaning in the case of the *tagmata* referred to above. When one interprets the material so that the *arithmoi* would have meant the 6,000 to 6,600-man generic legions, Stilicho's Roman contingent would have consisted of 180,000 to 198,000 men (150,000 inf. plus 30,000 to 48,000 cav.), but this seems far too large a figure, even with the additions made previously as emergency measures in 400–402, because the sources make it clear that there were also other forces in Italy and because Stilicho would not have waited for reinforcements if he had so many men.

The second way to estimate the size of the *arithmoi* is to use the *Notitia Dignitatum* with conservative strength estimates. According to this text, the *Magister Peditum* had 8

Palatine legions (ca. 16,000 men), 18 *auxilia palatinae* (ca. 18,000 men), 5 *Comitatenses* legions (ca. 10,000) and 2 *Pseudo-Comitatenses* legions (ca. 4,000) in Italy. These would add up to 33 units, which is very close to the 30 *arithmoi* given by Zosimus. On the basis of this, it seems very probable that Zosimus meant the regular units stationed in Italy. The extra three *arithmoi* and the recent recruits would simply have been left to protect some important cities. This would suggest that at this time Stilicho had at his disposal only the army of Italy, which he bolstered with the addition of new forces.

In sum, it is likely that Stilicho had about 45,000 infantry (estimation based on 15 legions and 15 *auxilia palatinae*) at his disposal. We should add to these figures the cavalry units stationed in Italy under the *Magister Equitum*, which consisted of 7 cavalry *vexillationes* (ca. 3,500 horsemen), the *bucellarii* of Stilicho (ca. 10,000 cav.?), and the Germanic auxiliaries previously recruited by Stilicho (ca. 12,000 cavalry?), and at least 15 *praefecti Sarmatorum* in Italy (ca. 30,000 men) for a total of 55,500 horsemen.

The higher figures are actually not as farfetched as is usually assumed. It would have been very dangerous to call into Italy barbarian allies who would have had more than twice the number of troops possessed by the Romans. If the invaders had as many troops as the sources attest, it is clear that these would have to have been opposed with a similarly-huge army. In fact, given that Napoleon routinely fielded armies of similar size in pre-industrial Europe, especially in the thinly inhabited roadless vast tracts of Russia, it is quite plausible that the Romans and barbarians (who lived off the land like the French of Napoleon's day) could have used armies of similar size in the urbanized and thickly populated portions of northern Italy or Gaul. Of note is that Zosimus' text does refer to armies of similar size on several occasions, in which the emperors had amassed most of their resources for a decisive encounter (e.g. by Licinius and Constantine the Great). We should not forget that, for example Augustus and Trajan, had similarly amassed truly huge armies for their campaigns, especially when one takes into account the numbers of rowers in their fleets and supporting fleets. It is also quite possible that the lowered effectiveness of the regular Roman army that had resulted from the corruption of the officer cadre had made it necessary to collect even larger armies than was the case before. It is also not a coincidence that the later revolutionary France needed larger armies than the Bourbons had – the new conscipts/recruits were not as efficient as the regular army had been, which is also true of poorly motivated and equipped regulars. However, as discussed above, it is still probable that Stilicho relied mainly on his veteran infantry forces which were now bolstered with barbarian cavalry forces. He seems to have left the less-reliable green recruits of the years 400–402 behind to guard the cities.

The Progress of the War

Radagaisus divided his army into three corps so that it would be easier to live off the land (Chron. Gal. 452.52). One possibility is that this division of forces occurred at Verona, so that the northern division advanced towards Milan, the middle division towards Ticinum and the southern division towards Bononia, Florentia and Rome. The sources do not state what happened to the separate divisions beyond the fact that Radagaisus' division was destroyed by Stilicho and that another third of the force was destroyed by the Huns. This

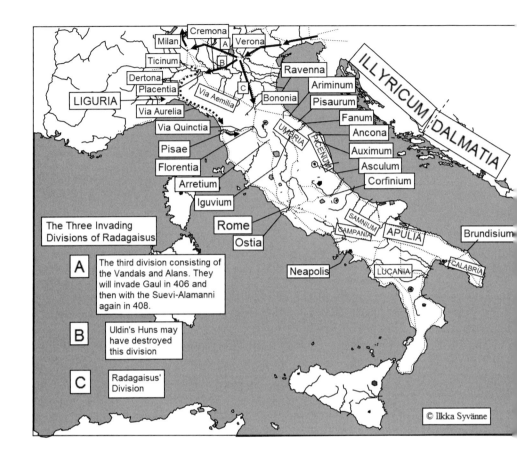

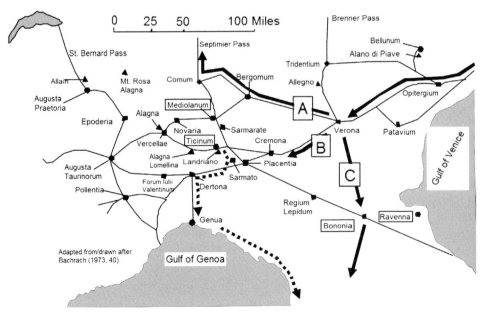

leaves one third of the invasion force unaccounted for. It is quite probable that this formed the barbarian invasion force consisting of the Vandals, Alans and Suevi that crossed the Rhine close to Mogontiacum (Mainz) on 31 December 406 (as regards the date, see below) as suggested by most modern historians. This is not accepted by all, but it is still the likeliest explanation of what happened. I suggest that the route taken by the northern division would have been to turn north near Milan, after which they would have marched to Raetia, after which they would have continued north until they invaded Gaul and were defeated by the army of Constantine III. (See also *Britain in the Age of Arthur*.) Readers should be aware that there were actually three invasions of Gaul in 406, 408 and 411 that have been conflated by both the ancient and even by modern historians (see later).

As regards the middle division, it probably attempted to rejoin Radagaisus after it had learnt that Stilicho's main army lay ahead, but with the result that the Huns, who were en route to join Stilicho at Ticinum, destroyed it. This is the likeliest explanation for its destruction. It is inherently less likely that the middle division would have been destroyed by the Huns only after the defeat of Radagaisus.

My educated guess is that Stilicho had assembled his army at Ticinum, probably in the expectation that Radagaisus would attempt to march to Gaul as Alaric had previously done. In fact, it is quite possible that this was the plan and that only a third of the enemy force managed to accomplish their objective (the northern enemy division). It is also evident that Stilicho was initially unwilling to engage the enemy in combat because he was so badly outnumbered (especially in cavalry) that he felt unable to engage even a third of the huge enemy army without first having called to his assistance reinforcements from whichever corner possible, and this included regular units from elsewhere, new recruits (see below), *foederati* and even Huns from across the Danube. It was only after Stilicho had assembled enough men (especially cavalry), noted that the Goths were not attempting to advance straight into Gaul, and was informed that the northern division had turned north and that the middle division had been annihilated by the Huns, that he advanced against those enemy forces that were then besieging Florentia. Indeed, Stilicho was lucky in that the Goths were not good besiegers. It was thanks to this that their progress had been halted in front of Florentia (Florence), which guarded the bridge over the River Arno.[10] However, Stilicho had not been entirely idle, because before this he had dispatched a delaying force under Arrianus to Rome to protect the Emperor and the capital. We do not know the composition of this force, but it is possible that it included part of the army assembled at Ticinum, because its commander appears to have been the former *consularis Liguriae* (PLRE2 *consularis Liguriae* in 397) where the city of Ticinum was located.

It should also be noted that there is no reason to criticize Stilicho for the fact that he did not attempt to defeat the invaders piecemeal one at a time by taking advantage of his inner lines of communication. This resulted from the fact that the vast majority of the enemy forces consisted of huge numbers of cavalry, while his own forces consisted mainly of infantry. The enemy simply possessed greater strategic mobility than he. The enemy were in a position to send their cavalry forces to the assistance of any threatened division before Stilicho could have engaged it.[11] It was thanks to this that Stilicho had formed the alliance with the Huns and had called the Federates under Sarus to his assistance. He not only needed more men, but he needed additional cavalry even more urgently.

Radagaisus was a savage pagan whose reputation preceded him. When his army approached Rome unopposed up to Florentia, because Stilicho had assembled his army at Ticinum, the Roman populace panicked and the pagans started to accuse the Christians of having brought about the crisis. Unsurprisingly, the irredeemable pagans started to offer sacrifices to the gods in public. According to the *Gallic Chronicle* (452.51), Arrianus retreated before the invaders into the city of Rome and then organized its defence. This Arrianus is otherwise unknown unless he is the *Consularis Liguriae* of the year 397 in the PLRE2. My educated guess is that he had since then been promoted into some sort of military command (and/or that he was in charge of the recently-recruited Italian forces in that capacity) and was now responsible for the defensive delaying action against the invaders and for the defence of the city of Rome. It is not known whether he was a pagan or whether it was one of his duties to stamp out the resurgence of paganism in Rome.

The extent of the crisis is evident from several facts. Firstly, the size of the invading force, even after it had been divided into three armies by Radagaisus for reasons of supply, was such that Stilicho lacked enough regulars and *foederati* to engage even one of those without first calling to his assistance Uldin and Sarus. As a result of this, the invaders were able to pillage cities far and wide (Chron. Gal. 452.52). Secondly, the collection of forces took almost a year to accomplish. Thirdly, the government saw it necessary to reiterate the need to punish deserters and those who turned to brigandage with the full severity of law (Edict to *PP* Longinianus in CTh 7.18.5, 24 March 406). Fourthly, the need to obtain recruits from any corner was such that Honorius, or rather his administration, issued two edicts (CTh 7.13.16, 17 April 406; CTh 7.13.17, 19 April 406) in which they called for all the freeborn of the country, for the love of their country, to join the military, which they were to do together with the slaves of the soldiers, *foederati* and the conquered peoples. The freeborn were promised 10 *solidi*, with 3 *solidi* given immediately. The slaves were promised equipment, freedom and 2 *solidi* of travel money. The desperation is evident from two things: 1) the freeborn were promised a generous payment in gold; and 2) slaves, who were usually exempted from service, were not only encouraged to join, but were also promised a generous payment. The Romans clearly faced a massive enemy force on their own soil.

The Battle of Florentia and Siege of Fiesole in the Spring of 406

Unfortunately we lack any detailed decription of the campaign, battle formations used, and of the decisive battle itself. All we have are the brief statements of Zosimus, Orosius and Augustinus. Zosimus claims that Stilicho crossed the Danube (probably a mistake for the River Arnus/Arno) and then with his whole army fell on the barbarians without warning (i.e. he surprised them) and destroyed their entire force. This can actually imply that Stilicho marched first along the Via Aurelia and then turned east along the Via Quinctia before crossing the river to the enemy's side and surprising them. The enemy had probably expected that Stilicho would use the same route as they had and may even have stationed their 'third' division to guard that route if it had not yet been destroyed. It is also possible that the surprise was caused by the timing of Stilicho's attack, which may have come so early in the spring as to be totally unexpected. Regardless, the attack was still so late in the spring that Florentia was on the point of surrender due to hunger before the attack took place. Orosius states that Stilicho struck Radagaisus with supernatural terror and drove him and his followers up into the mountains of Fiesole, where Stilicho besieged them. Augustine claims that the Goths were crushed without any Roman casualties in a battle that lasted only one day in which 100,000 Goths lost their lives. This would imply that the victory had been achieved by the allied cavalries, consisting of the Huns, Alans and Goths, but it is quite possible that Augustine has exaggerated the lack of casualties among the Roman side.

The 'supernatural terror' and lack of Roman casualties also suggest that it was a lightning attack that was performed by the Federate and Hun cavalries well in advance of the Roman infantry. The strength of the Federate corps (Goths, Alans and Huns) under Sarus at Bononia in 408 was at least 30,000 men strong, which means that the minimum strength for the 'Roman' cavalry forces was well over 60,000 horsemen, and with the Huns probably well over 100,000 horsemen. The width of the 'Roman' battle line cannot have been more than 4 km, because on the left were the mountains and on the right the River Arno and the city of Florentia. This means that the 'Roman' cavalry must have adopted a three-line formation for the attack. It would have been possible to use the two-line array with about 30,000 men per battle line, but the instructions in the *Strategikon* suggest the use of three lines for armies in excess of 42,000/49,000 men and it is also very probable that there were actually considerably more than 60,000 horsemen present, even if part of the cavalry force had been left to guard the rear of the main army.

According to Orosius, the lowest estimate for the number of men who had taken refuge on the rough and barren ridge was 200,000 men. The figure is credible only if it included the families too. This suggests that the Romans estimated that there were about 100,000 persons encamped on each of the three sides of the city of Florentia so that one third of that force had been annihilated in the attack. Now the position of the Goths was desperate. The Romans cut off supplies and it did not take long for the Goths to start to suffer from hunger. It did not take long either for the desertions to begin, and when Radagaisus realized that the situation was hopeless he tried to flee, but was captured and then executed outside the gates of Florentia on 23 August 406. The rest of the Goths surrendered on terms. The Romans enrolled 12,000 *optimates* (noblemen) into the federate corps, but most of the survivors were sold as slaves, in such quantities that the price of a slave dropped to a single piece of gold/'*aureus*' (Olymp. fr.9; Oros. 7.39.10). The fact that there were 12,000 *optimates* left after the battle to join the Roman army suggests that the minimum figure for Radagaisus' cavalry force was 24,000 horsemen, because each nobleman/knight was expected to have at least one squire. However, since it is clear that some of the men had more than one and that there had also been a very significant number of casualties resulting from the Roman surprise attack, the pursuit up to the mountain and from hunger, it is clear that there must have originally been at least 50,000 horsemen on the basis of the number of *optimates*, so that with the addition of regulars the number would have probably reached at least 100,000 'Gothic' horsemen. In sum, the figures given for the overall strength of the invading force are not as farfetched as usually thought.

As noted above, according to the *Gallic Chronicle* (452.52), the third part of the invading army was annihilated by the Huns, which does suggest the likelihood that at least one of the enemy divisions (if the Huns destroyed one division and Stilicho Radagaisus' force) managed to flee. It is also possible that Uldin's help did not take place in Italy, but

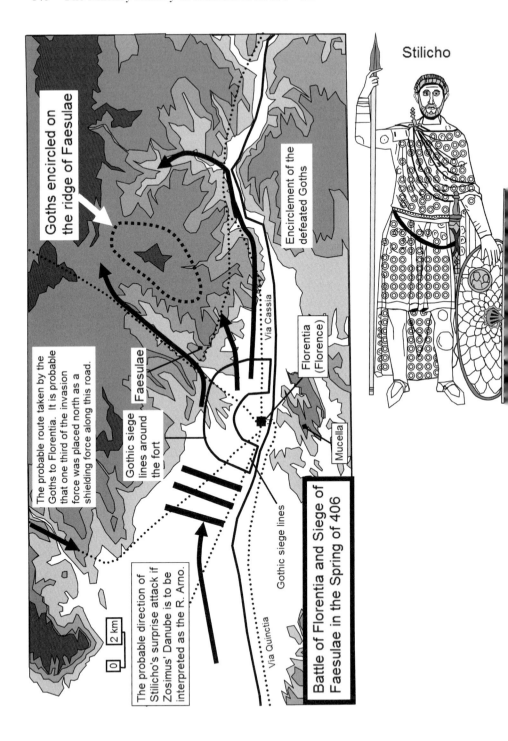

Stilicho

Goths encircled on the ridge of Faesulae

Encirclement of the defeated Goths

The probable route taken by the Goths to Florentia. It is probable that one third of the invasion force was placed north as a shielding force along this road.

Gothic siege lines around the fort

Faesulae

Via Cassia

Florentia (Florence)

Mucella

The probable direction of Stilicho's surprise attack if Zosimus' Danube is to be interpreted as the R. Arno.

0   2 km

Via Quinctia

Gothic siege lines

Battle of Florentia and Siege of Faesulae in the Spring of 406 rather somewhere near the Danube. However, since the sources are unanimous regarding the fact that Stilicho's army included Huns, it is safest to assume that the Huns either annihilated one of the divisions en route to Ticinum, or that Stilicho sent the Huns in pursuit of the fleeing enemy division (possibly placed as a rearguard for Radagaisus' army somewhere to the north) right after the battle of Florence, or that the third of the invading force meant Radagaisus' division which would then have been destroyed by the Huns in Stilicho's service.

As a result of his great victory Stilicho was the man of the hour. In recognition of his great services to the state a triumphal arch was built in Stilicho's honour at Rome.

Chapter Seven

The East 400–408: Arcadius, Eudoxia and the *Consistorium* in Charge

Contrary to common opinion among ancient and modern historians, the instances mentioned by the ancient sources actually prove that Arcadius was the man who made the final decisions and that he could do so at his will. He was not a person who just followed his wife's opinions or the opinions of his advisors. The best example of this is the following, which is commonly used to prove that Arcadius usually followed his wife's wishes. In late 400 Porphyry and Mark the Deacon travelled to Constantinople to ask the government to take action against paganism in Gaza and to destroy the temple of Zeus Marnas (Marneum). A *Castrensis* (eunuch of Eudoxia) and a man of God, Amantius helped the men to obtain an audience with the empress. The pregnant and religious Eudoxia agreed, and the holy men duly blessed her and promised a male child (Theodosius II). The emperor, however, refused to follow his wife's wishes. The people of Gaza paid their taxes and Arcadius did not want to endanger that flow of taxes. On 10 April 401 Arcadius and his wife were blessed with a son, the future emperor Theodosius II, which naturally strengthened Eudoxia's hold on her husband, and the hold of the holy men on Eudoxia. Eudoxia was a clever woman and came up with a ruse that would force her reluctant husband to follow her wishes. The child was baptized on the Epiphany feast, 6 January 402. In preparation for this Eudoxia gave instructions to Porphyry and his friends on how to act and to the man carrying the child. When the imperial retinue left the church, Porphyry and his associates brought a petition to Theodosius. The man who carried the child raised the child's head and proclaimed that Theodosius would decree whatever was in the petition. The men congratulated Arcadius for his son's decree. Theodosius was proclaimed *Augustus* on 10 January 402 and the petition became lawful.

Arcadius had in the meantime learnt what was in the petition, but agreed to grant the request because his wife nagged about it constantly. The other obvious reason for his decision is that Arcadius wanted to maintain the appearance that the imperial house was united to the general public. Eudoxia then sent the holy men to the *quaestor sacri palatii* who then drafted the petition into law, after which she instructed Amantius to seek a man to implement the law. Amantius chose Cynegius, a *clarissimus* and member of the *Consistorium*, to carry out the orders. Cynegius then took enough soldiers with him to intimidate the pagans of Gaza and carried out the orders with the help of the Christian holy men who had brought the petition.[1] It is quite clear from this that Arcadius had a mind of his own, even if in the end he agreed to carry out the wishes of his wife. The pagans of Gaza were expendables in comparison with a peace in the bedroom.

The birth of Theodosius II was a happy event, but it also brought a problem: how to secure Theodosius' position as crown-prince? Arcadius came up with a clever stratagem which effectively secured the throne both for himself and for his son. Arcadius was acutely aware that his position was not secure. On top of this, the new 'crown prince' Theodosius was a 'half-breed' because his mother was the daughter of the Frank Bauto. The political climate at the turn of the fifth century was not good for 'half-breeds'. Arcadius asked the Persian *Shahanshah* Yazdgerd I to become guardian of the newly-born Theodosius II. We do not know how Arcadius came up with the idea, but it is possible that one or several of his advisors suggested this. The possible candidates include the unknown Urban Prefect of Constantinople between 399–401, who had the nickname 'the Persian', and/or the *Comes* John (the favourite of the empress and the rumoured father of Theodosius), who was known for his hostility towards the West.[2]

After the idea had been formulated, Arcadius dispatched envoys bearing gifts (1,000 lbs of gold) to Persia to ask Yazdgerd to become guardian/tutor for his son. Yazdgerd accepted the proposal and sent Antiochus to become Theodosius' tutor. Arcadius was satisfied with the results and wrote a will in which he declared his son *Augustus* and Yazdgerd as Theodosius' guardian. We know the approximate date for this decision because it is known that Theodosius was declared *Augustus* on 10 January 402, which means that it must have happened after that. Greatrex dates Antiochus' arrival to have happened in around 404. Antiochus was staunchly Christian and raised Theodosius as a Christian, with the full backing of Arcadius. The thaw in the relationship between Rome and Persia also signified further cooperation between the empires the most important aspects of which were the peace and the mutually adopted policy of religious tolerance. It was thanks to this that Christians were able to convert people into their religion openly in Persia with the full backing of Yazdgerd and that Persian Fire-Worshippers were able to practice their religion openly in East Rome.

It is unfortunate that we do not know when the *Shahanshah* Yazdgerd I placed his son in the care of the Lakhmid King of Hira al-Mundhir, because that would be decisive for our understanding of who was the first (Arcadius or Yazdgerd) to use foreigners to protect their offspring. There exist two versions. According to one version, Yazdgerd's son Bahram was born in the seventh year of his reign (i.e. in about 405/406), which would mean that Yazdgerd imitated the solution adopted by Arcadius. However, according to another version Bahram was 20 years old in 420, which would imply that Arcadius had got the idea of using Yazdgerd as guardian from Yazdgerd's own solution. If the former is true, then Bahram would have been only 15–16 years old when he became ruler in 420. This makes the latter likelier, but it is still possible that the former could be true. Still another version states that Yazdgerd nominated al-Numan as ruler of Hira in about 404/5[3] and then made him guardian of his son Bahram, but this version doesn't give any date of birth for Bahram. Most of the extant evidence supports the alternative that al-Mundhir became ruler of Hira in 404/5, with the implication that Bahram would indeed have been only 15–16 when he became ruler. In light of the fact that both monarchs were threatened by their magnates, it is not at all surprising that they trusted each other more than their own people. According to Tabari (i.848), only the envoys from other monarchs could speak freely in the presence of Yazdgerd, which is highly suggestive of the situation. Yazdgerd did not trust any of his own subjects (Tab. i.848).

The peace between Rome and Persia gave the latter the chance of consolidating their grip on Hira. In around 405 Yazdgerd nominated the Lakhmid al-Mundhir al-Numan as king of al-Hira and gave him two units of soldiers, the *Dawsar*, consisting of 1,000

Tanukhids, and the *al-Shahba* (the Brightly Gleaming) consisting of 1,000 Persian cataphracts (Savarans). These two foreign units secured al-Mundhir's position against the natives. Persian support and these forces also ensured that Numan was able to subject all the Arab tribes bordering the Roman and Persian empires under his rule. According to Tabari, al-Numan (i.e. al-Mundhir) conducted deep raids into enemy territories, which included Syria. The referral to the invasion of Syria may have actually happened during the Romano-Persian War in 421–422 so that it would not have constituted a breach of the peace between Rome and Persia.

After Numan had secured his position, his standing army, which was posted near the capital Hira, consisted of seven tribal Arabic divisions and of the 1,000 Sasanian heavy cavalry. The close bond between the ruler of Hira and the Sasanians was sealed by the fact that Yazdgerd I sent his son Bahram to the court of Hira to be raised. As we shall see, the ruler of Hira had at least 40,000 horsemen at his disposal. As noted, Yazdgerd considered the Arab monarch more trustworthy than the Persian magnates and not without reason, as we shall see. The tie between Bahram and the Lakhmids was of the greatest importance for the events that ensued after 420.

The change in the relative strength of the various Arabic tribal groupings in between Rome and Persia brought about a change in Roman policies towards their Saracen Federates. As the presence of the *Dawsar* in the court of the Lakhmid king proves, the Romans had not only lost control over the Lakhmids, but also control over a section of the Tanukhid tribe. As a result of this, the loyalty of the Tanukhids still in Roman territory could also be considered suspect. This meant that the Romans had to find some other tribe to perform the same functions as previously performed either by the Lakhmids or by the Tanukhids. The solution was to promote the Salihids into the dominant position among the Arabic Federates after their phylarch Zokomos had converted into Christianity. The date of the conversion is not known with certainty, but Irfan Shahid has demonstrated that the likeliest date would be the reign of Arcadius in around 400.[4]

The core areas of this tribe ranged from the Wadi Sirhan to *Provincia Arabia*, and from *Phoenice Libanensis* to *Palestina Tertia*. However, it is possible that as the leading federate group, they also controlled tribes further north up to Chalcis ad Belum (Qinnasrin). It is unfortunate that we know very little about the military forces possessed by the Salihids. On the basis that the Federate Arabs usually consisted of cavalry lancers it appears probable that the Salihids used similar forces. On the other hand there is a reference in a poem to a unit known as the Zokomids that assisted the tribe of Udra against the Ghassanids. According to Shahid's translation of this poem, the unit in question was 'a magnificent division from the House of the Zokomids, that bristles with armour, thrusts with its spears, wards off the enemies from us, and fights ferociously'. Shahid interprets this to mean a unit of spearmen (i.e. infantry), but I would not preclude the possibility that the unit would have been a typical Arabic unit of spearmen, but better equipped as it was clearly an armoured unit. The other tribes that can be securely attested to have been included among the Federates in the fifth century are the Iyad (near Emesa), the Udra (Hijaz to Ayla), the Kalb (Dumat Jandal), the Bahra (location unknown), and the Tanukhids (north near Antioch), but it is probable there were also other tribes. The Salihids, Kalb and Udra protected primarily the Arabian frontier, while the rest protected the Mesopotamian and Syrian fronts.[5]

Arcadius' decision to use Persia to prop up his own position also meant the rise of the pro-Persian party into prominence at court. The leading lights among this group were unsurprisingly Antiochus (Greatrex and Bardill) and the *Comes* John (PLRE2 Ioannes 1). This group, under the guidance of Antiochus, gradually increased its power so that the *PPI* Caesarius, who had promoted concord between East and West, was replaced by Eutychianus in 403.[6] It was probably then that Fravitta accused the *Comes* John of destroying the unity between the emperors. According to Eunapius (fr.71.3), the audience agreed with the words of Fravitta, but since all were fearful of John, they made John their leader and murdered Fravitta. We do not know John's official position at the time, but we do know that he was definitely a *Comes* in 401 and that he was *Comes Sacrarum Largitionum* in 404. Regardless of what his official position was, he was among the most influential persons in the court during the period 399–404. The murder of Fravitta must have taken place in 403–404, because John's favourite Hierax was nominated as governor of Pamphylia at the same time as the Isaurians ravaged it and other neighbouring regions, and this war took place in about 404 but may have already started in the previous year.

The government appointed Arbazacius, who was a native of Isauria born in Armenia, to take charge of the crushing of the Isaurian revolt in 404. This suggests that the Isaurians were once again suffering from their periodic bouts of poor harvests that had forced them to descend from their mountains to ravage and pillage the neighbouring provinces. The Isaurians had been unable to take any of the walled cities, but they had more than made up for this by overrunning all the unwalled villages around. As a result of this, they had managed to amass a considerable amount of booty. Arbazacius achieved considerable success in the initial stages of the conflict, captured part of their booty and forced the bandits back into the mountains – all in 404. However, he did not pursue his advantage, but allowed the Isaurians to flee to safety in return for hefty bribes. After this, he surrendered himself to luxurious living and lust amongst his harem of mistresses and prostitutes. When this was brought to the attention of the court, he was recalled to face trial. Arbazacius was able to avoid this by bribing the empress with a sizable sum of money so that he was able to spend the rest of his days in the lap of luxury in the city of Constantinople.

The Isaurian war continued unabated for two more years. The Isaurians pillaged Caria, Pisidia, Lycaonia, Cilicia, Cappadocia, Coele-Syria, Syria, Phoenicia and even pillaged the island of Cyprus (Soz. 8.25; Philostorgius 11.8). Caria, Pisidia, Lycaonia, Cilicia, and Cappadocia appear to have already suffered in 404, because these areas received new armies and commanders in 404, but we do not know the dates when the Isaurians turned their attention towards the south and south-east. The very wide extent of the ravages caused by the relatively small numbers of Isaurians probably reflects the number of casualties suffered by the Roman army during the 'Gainas War', which in all probability meant that when the Huns invaded Thrace in 404–405 and Alaric Greece in 403–405, the government chose to transfer and keep most of the available field forces near the capital for its protection. The fact that the Isaurians were able to raid and pillage Cyprus also bespeaks of the weakness of the Syrian Fleet at this time, which has already been postulated in the context of Tribigild's revolt. We do not know how and who ended the Isaurian Revolt, but one may hazard a guess that after East and West reached an accord in 407, the Eastern government transferred some of the forces it had kept in the

Balkans to the East and that these forces then finally crushed the Isaurians in 407. It was probably then that the government appointed three new counts with armies to protect the provinces of Lycaonia, Pamphylia and Pisidia (CJ 12.59.10 or 12.60.10, depending on edition).

The governor of Pamphylia, the Alexandrian Hierax, was similarly a man corrupt to the bone. Despite the fact that the Isaurians had already plundered his province, he proceeded to extort money with even greater efficiency. However, when his superior, the local *vicarius* Herennianus became aware of this, he arrested Hierax and forced him to pay to the exchequer more money than he had stolen from the province in return for not being flogged. According to Eunapius (72.1), the empress (mistakenly named Pulcheria, even though she was Eudoxia) followed this policy in all cases involving governors. First the empress allowed the noblemen to buy governorships in return for money and when they were then caught looting their subjects, the governors were forced to pay more money in return for not being flogged. This was obviously a very efficient way to fill up the state coffers, but could not be continued for long. In fact, it is possible that this policy was really followed only when the *Comes* John was all powerful in court, and when he clearly lost his position after the murder of Fravitta (John disappears from the sources after 404), all his equally-corrupt supporters were punished with confiscations.

In the meanwhile, during the years 403–404 the East was also facing a series of other troubles. Honorius' letter to Arcadius, dated to shortly after 20 June 404, lists a number of grievances that Honorius had against the Eastern government, which include Eudoxia's proclamation as *Augusta* (Eudoxia was the daughter of the Frank Bauto and therefore not 'suitable' to be empress), the hiding of Alaric's pillage of Illyricum, and the treatment of John Chrysostom.[7] All of these were meant to serve as reasons for possible intervention by Stilicho in 405. The fact that Alaric had been ravaging Illyricum after the treaty he had made with Stilicho following his defeat in 402/3 makes it certain that Stilicho had instructed Alaric to invade Illyricum to put pressure on the Eastern government. Zosimus' text (5.26) clarifies the area which Alaric ravaged. It was Greece (part of the Prefecture of Illyricum), and, after the Eastern Government had failed to address the Western grievances appropriately, Stilicho opted to make the break public so that Honorius was able to appoint Alaric as *MVM per Illyricum* in 405, after which Alaric marched to Epirus to wait for the arrival of Stilicho (Sozomen 8.25).

Alaric, however, was not the only enemy ravaging the Balkans at this time. The Huns of Uldin crossed the Danube and invaded Thrace during the winter of 404/5 (see Maenchen-Helfen, 62–3). Consequently, while Alaric was ravaging Greece, Uldin was ravaging Thrace. In light of the fact that in 405 Stilicho was able to ask Uldin's help against Radagaisus, it is possible that Stilicho may have already concluded a treaty with Uldin in 404 for the very same purpose as he had concluded with Alaric, which was the taking of the Prefecture of Illyricum from the Eastern government.

The first extant piece of evidence which proves that the Huns were in possession of the northern bank of the Danube between Viminacium and Oescus dates from the year 408/9 when Uldin captured Castra Martis. However, it is probable that the Huns had already arrived there by 404. We can actually trace the progress of the Hunnic advance from Jordanes' (Get. 246–252) description of the advance of the Ostrogoths. He states that the Ostrogoths under Vinitharius the Amali sought to free themselves from the Huns by advancing against the Antae. Vinitharius lost the first encounter, but then managed to defeat the Antae. The King of the Antae Boz, his sons and 70 nobles were executed. It seems probable that the Heruls accompanied the Ostrogoths on their eastward trek, but the Ostrogoths were unable to enjoy their newly found freedom for longer than one year. The Hunnic King Balamber and his subjects, the Ostrogoths of Gesimund, combined their forces and attacked Vinitharius. Vinitharius won two battles, but then lost his life and battle at the third battle by the River Erac when Balamber shot an arrow into his head. Thereafter the Ostrogoths were united under Hunimund, who then attacked the Suevi [formerly known as Iuthungi[8]] – clearly on behalf of the Huns. It is not known whether he succeeded, because Jordanes then states that he died and was then succeeded by his son Thorismund. However, since we know that the Alamanni, Marcomanni and Quadi were among the subjects of Attila it appears possible that the initial conquest may have already been performed by Vinitharius. Thorismund in his turn fought against the Gepids in the second year of his reign, which once again must have been done on behalf of or in conjunction with the Huns. Thorismund won a great victory over the enemy, but then died because he fell from his horse. According to Jordanes, the Ostrogoths mourned the loss of the king so much that they were not ruled by any king for 40 years. A more prosaic reason would of course be that the Ostrogoths were ruled by the Huns and the decision would have rested with their ruler.

On the basis of there being a 40-year interval between the death of Thorismund and the enthroning of Valamir as the King of the Ostrogoths in about 443/4, the above-mentioned events would have taken place between the years 396/7 and 403/4. The sequence would also represent the enlargement of the Hun Empire to the areas previously

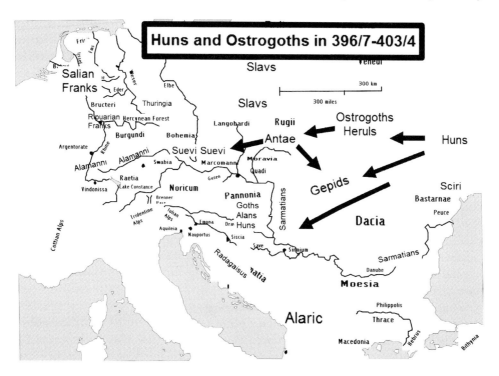

dominated by the Antae, Suevi and Gepids. This enlargement of the Hunnic Empire was also accompanied by the movement/dislocation of tribes: the Eastern Heruls ended up next to the Lombards and Gepids, so that the Lombards eventually became subjects of the Heruls; the Sciri (part of the Hunnic army in 408/9) and Rugii (served as Roman Federates in this area during the 430s) ended up north of the Danube approximately between Sirmium and Novae. It is also probable that the Bastarnae, the neighbours of the Sciri in Scythia, accompanied the Sciri to this area because they are later mentioned as subjects of Attila together with the Sciri. The defeated Antae in their turn appear to have migrated to the area vacated by the Sciri and Bastarnae, because this is the area where we find them in the sixth century. The Ostrogoths in their turn appear to have settled in the area vacated by the Antae just North-East of the Suevi-Iuthungi. This means that the East Romans now faced an entirely new set of enemies north of the Danube.

As stated in the letter of Honorius, there were also religious troubles closer to home at the very heart of the Eastern Empire. The relationship between the empress Eudoxia and John Chrysostom worsened, mainly because John would not accept the luxurious lifestyle of the empress and her female friends. John's situation was also complicated by the fact that he had unlawfully deposed several bishops in Asia Minor and he was opposed by the Patriarch of Alexandria, Theophilus. In June 403 Theophilus was summoned to appear before an ecclesiastical tribunal in Constantinople. His plan was to turn the tables so that he would be able to accuse John, and, thanks to poor judgement on John's part, this succeeded. It was then that John gave a sermon against women, which was interpreted in such a way that he had called the empress Eudoxia 'Jezebel'. When this was brought to Eudoxia's attention she was infuriated. Under the influence of his wife, the emperor was ready to listen to the enemies of John who had drawn up a list of accusations. The authorities transferred the synod to Chalcedon because John was too popular in Constantinople. John refused to attend the synod, with the result that the members of the synod asked the emperor to decide whether the Archbishop had spoken treasonably of the empress. Arcadius ordered John to be exiled, but the authorities could not fulfil the order because the populace gathered around St. Sophia and John's palace to protect their Archbishop. After this John delivered two speeches in which he called Eudoxia 'Jezebel' or 'Herodias', but he then surrendered himself to the authorities. When the populace learnt that Chrysostom had left they raised a riot. After this there was an earthquake, which the populace interpreted as a sign of heavenly anger. The empress was also frightened, either because she was afraid of the popular violence or because she was also superstitious. Eudoxia asked John to return and he graciously agreed. Chrysostom thanked the empress with a eulogy.

However, when the *PVC* Simplicius erected a porphyry column with a silver image of the empress close to St. Sophia in the autumn of 403, and the inauguration included dancing and music as in pagan ceremonies, the hot-headed Archbishop could not restrain himself. He once again called the empress 'Herodias' in a sermon. This was a grave mistake. Eudoxia and Arcadius now made certain that a Church Council would be packed with opponents of John, but there were still so many of his supporters present when the Council convened in early 404 that nothing could be achieved. In the end, the emperor gave the order that John was to be removed from office and put under house arrest. On Easter Eve the populace attempted to assemble at St. Sophia, but were dispersed by soldiers, and when they attempted to assemble in the Baths of Constantine, the soldiers dispersed them once again. John was kept in his palace for two months, after which Arcadius ordered him exiled. On the same night as John was banished, St.Sophia was set on fire. The fire spread from there to the Senate House, which was burned to the ground with its irreplaceable art treasures. The judicial inquiry accused either John or his friends for the fire with the result that his supporters were harshly persecuted. The banishment of John led immediately to trouble with the Western Church, which declared John's treatment illegal. Honorius also wrote to Arcadius three times, but to no avail. John died in exile in 407.

In 405 Arcadius nominated the Egyptian Anthemius as *PPO*. He proved to be one of the best Praetorian Prefects of the East the Roman Empire was ever blessed with. His greatest achievement was the building of the so-called Theodosian Walls during his tenure (10 July 405 – 18 April 414). The Walls were completed by 4 April 413. The building of these new walls enlarged the city significantly and thereby protected the inhabitants better than the previous walls. The decision to build the walls was based on an accurate analysis of the defensive needs of the Empire in the aftermath of the Hunnic invasion of 404. The Walls were to prove their defensive value again and again, until they were finally breached for the last time in 1453. The walls frustrated all attempts made by successive generations of nomads and Arabs.[9] Regardless of the generally-good evaluation of Anthemius' government, we should still not make the mistake that he would have been above promoting his friends and members of his family to the highest offices. It is quite clear that Anthemius must have been behind the promotion of his son Flavius Anthemius Isidorus to the office of *Proconsul Asiae*, which the latter held at some point in time between 405 and 410. We should not condemn him for this, because in order to succeed in ancient Rome one had to act as patron for friends and family. Basically, Anthemius had to promote his friends and family to important positions in the administration if he wanted to succeed in the power struggle.

The East Roman government was threatened by Stilicho and Alaric in 405, but the attack was postponed when Radagaisus invaded Italy. The year 405 is also important for another reason. It was then that the Huns of Uldin changed their allegiance to the Western Government. It is probable that this had already taken place before Radagaisus' invasion, because Uldin fought on behalf of Stilicho against Radagaisus. Stilicho was once again preparing to invade the East in 407, possibly with the help of Uldin, but the project was postponed because of the successful invasion of Gaul by the usurper Constantine III. In these circumstances, it is not surprising that the Eastern and Western governments chose to bury the hatchet and form alliance against the usurper. Arcadius and Anthemius promised to send help to the West while Stilicho was alive, which means that the policy change occurred at latest in the spring or early summer of 408. These forces did not reach the West until later because the death of Arcadius on 1 May 408 led to renewed troubles with the Persians and Huns.

Arcadius the Emperor, the Unsung Success Story 395–408

Contrary to the common view, and despite the handicap of not having a military education and not leading his armies in person, Arcadius' reign can be characterized as a great success. He was not the lethargic ruler of Synesius, but a man of great personal courage and a man ready to innovate when necessary. Arcadius revived the fortunes of the East while the fortunes of his less fortunate brother sunk to ever-spiralling lows. Both brothers were schemers, but it was Arcadius who had more common sense and who was more prepared to think outside the box. It is clear that Arcadius was blessed with older age at the time his father died and that his main enemies in the East were civilians rather than a single military ruler like Stilicho, but he was still able to crush decisively the military threat posed by Gainas and his mainly Gothic forces and he was also able to stymie Stilicho's plots against him. This was no mean feat. Arcadius ovethrew first Rufinus, with the help of Gainas, Eutropius and Stilicho, and then he played Gainas against Eutropius so that he was then able to get rid of Eutropius before crushing Gainas and his Goths. Arcadius was able to do the latter because he was ready to use the services of another Goth, Fravitta, who was also a pagan, and because he was wise enough to create the *Arcadiaci* to serve as his personal forces against the regular army and Federates.

And this was not all! Arcadius showed unprecedented foresight by concluding a de facto alliance with Yazgerd I by making the latter the guardian of his underage son Theodosius II. This decision ensured peace between the two superpowers and the security of Theodosius II against possible usurpers. Arcadius was married to a daughter of the Frankish general Bauto and he knew that his 'half-breed' son needed outside support to survive. The marriage with Eudoxia proves that Arcadius was not a racist like his brother, and he was certainly not an impotent sexually-deviant person like Honorius as his many children with Eudoxia prove. He did not hold similar insane racist hatred towards the Germanic peoples as Honorius did.

In the field of religious policies Arcadius and his wife Eudoxia were also innovators as is so well proven by Holum's (1982/1989) study of Eudoxia. They both claimed that their right to rule was divine and that their military successes resulted from the support of God. Their prayers to God brought victories, and they also advertised this in public on every opportunity. Regardless of this, it is still clear that the emperor was quite prepared to turn against the Church when he considered this necessary. He admitted pagans or closet pagans into every possible position within the Empire as long as the men in question were competent. He also demonstrated the imperial power over the Church when the very popular Archbishop John Chrysostom turned against the empress – a policy which was also opposed by Honorius and Stilicho. Arcadius' readiness to act, when necessary, naturally weakened the power of the Church.

Arcadius also demonstrated his skills as a ruler during the years 405–408. He changed his favourites in 405 when they had become too powerful and appointed the very gifted Anthemius in charge of the administration. The building of the so-called Theodosian Walls of Constantinople was probably started by Anthemius when Arcadius was still alive (which means that the building was begun with Arcadius' approval), probably in response to the Gainas crisis, and one should perhaps call these walls the Arcadian walls. It was these walls which were to save East Rome from most of the subsequent invaders. It was also Arcadius who apparently initiated the rapprochement between himself and Honorius, presumably with the purpose of stymieing Stilicho's objectives against Arcadius in 407–408. It was this rapprochement that led to the downfall of Stilicho and which then enabled Arcadius' successor to save Honorius in Ravenna.

Chapter Eight

The British Usurpers and Barbarian Invasions in 406–408: the Downfall of Stilicho

The Prefecture of Gaul in 406–407[1]

Either in late 406 or very early in 407 a man named Marcus usurped the throne in Britain. We do not know what the reasons were, but one may hazard a guess that the Britons felt that Honorius' government had neglected the defence of the island when it too had threats of its own – it is quite possible that there could have been invasions by any of the following which we know nothing about because the sources were not interested in the events of the periphery: the Irish (Scotti), Picts and Saxons. Marcus appears to have been a low-ranking soldier. The fact that he belonged to the lower stratum of society suggests that the Britons were also fed up with the corruption of the imperial authorities. Marcus appears not to have been able to fulfil the hopes placed on him, as a result of which he was killed and replaced by a man named Gratian, who was a local townsman. This was a sign of the times. The civilians (the city councils, city dwellers and peasants) and the lower ranks of the military were utterly fed up with the rampant corruption of the imperial authorities and the officer cadre. Gratian's rule lasted for only four months after which the troops became tired of him – i.e. he didn't land his troops on the continent and oust Honorius – consequently the Britons, in association with the local soldiers, elevated Constantine (Flavius Claudius Constantinus), an ordinary soldier, to the throne in very early 407, mainly because his name was auspicious.

Zosimus (6.3.1) claims that the reason for the rising of the usurpers Marcus, Gratian and Constantine in Britain was the invasion by the Vandals, Alans and Suevi of Gaul in 406. There also exist opposing traditions, according to which it was Stilicho who invited these barbarians (Alans, Suebi/Alamanni, Vandals, Burgundians) to attack Gaul (Jord. Get. 115; Orosius 7.38). Orosius claims that Stilicho's goal was to cause troubles in Gaul that would enable him to enthrone his son as ruler instead of Honorius, but it is clear that this is not the case (see later). I would rather suggest that these stories have a basis in truth. It is probable that Stilicho had indeed invited these barbarians to attack Gaul, but only for the purpose of attacking the usurpers of Britain who must have gained control of the armies posted in the north of Gaul by the time Stilicho made the request. It is also probable that Stilicho repeated his request to the barbarians in 408 after Sarus had failed.

As regards Britain, I would propose that we should see in this sequence of events the first signs of the love of freedom shown by the Roman Britons, the vestiges of which are still visible in the legends of King Arthur and the Round Table (see my monograph dealing with this). As is well known, the round shape was an expression of equality among the people seated, even if one of them was considered as the first among the equals (*Princeps*). The nomination of the city-councillor Gratianus as Emperor is the principal proof for my conjecture that the revolt must have been organized by the British nobility – the *posessores* of the city councils – who had become fed up with the rampant corruption and sought to rectify this through traditional means, which was the setting up of a usurper to overthrow the existing Emperor. The locals, presumably the city councillors and the lower ranks of the military, had clearly formed a Council (*consilium*) consisting of Councillors (*consiliarii*), which is mentioned as being in existence for the first time by Gildas (22–23) for the reign of King Vortigern. It seems probable that the British Council was used as a model for the Gallic Council at Arles in 407. It is therefore probable that this Council had first chosen Marcus to represent their rights, and after he had not fulfilled their expectations they had chosen one of their own, Gratianus, for the same job, and after he too had failed in their eyes, they had resorted to the nomination of a soldier from the ranks. The fact that both Marcus and Constantine were low-ranking soldiers is suggestive of the other trend already visible during the last years of the reign of Theodosius I 'the Great' (he received the title 'Great' for his promotion of the Catholic/Orthodox faith). It is very probable that prior to their promotion both Marcus and Constantine, just like most of the military forces in Britain, had obtained local wealthy patrons. In short, it is probable that the local magnates had hijacked the local military forces as their *bucellarii* – it should not be forgotten that many of the soldiers had also come originally from their estates, which means that there were existing bonds between the soldiers and their landlord and the families still living on the lands of the landlord. This was a revolt led by the wealthy propertied classes. The subsequent referral to the existence of several tyrants in Britain suggests that the most powerful magnates had already obtained de facto control of their respective cities with their *bucellarii* during the 390s.

The Council as such always considered itself to be representative of Roman interests and the *conciliarii* maintained this stance at least until the third consulship of Aetius in 446 when they sent their last embassy to Rome in an effort to beg help (Gildas 21–23). When this was not forthcoming, they apparently asked the Saxons to help them. In short, the setting up of usurpers by the Britons can be seen as a very strong statement against the corruption of the imperial authorities, and for the equality of the noble members of the council – much in reminiscence of the spirit of the much later *Magna Carta*. It is not a coincidence that the descendants of this people and culture were to later produce the stories of the freedom-loving Robin Hood, and among their American offspring the stories of other freedom fighters and noble bandits.

The Gallic Prefecture and the West 407: Constantine III vs. Honorius

After having been nominated as *Augustus* on the basis of his name, Constantine sought to further the association with his famous predecessor by taking the name of Flavius Claudius, thereby claiming a family connection with the former imperial family. He did not stop there. He recalled his elder son, who was a monk, from a monastery and renamed him Constans, while his younger son was renamed Julian (Iulianus). The names were meant to recall the Western emperors of the Flavian dynasty.[2] It is also possible that Constantine's intention was to seek support for his cause from both the Christians with the name of Constans and from the pagans with the name of Julian.

After having taken the throne, Constantine moved quickly to fulfil the hopes of his backers. He nominated Justinian (Iustinianus) and Nebiogastes (Neviogastes) as *magistri militum*, assembled his army – probably at Rutupia – embarked his troops on ships, and landed them at Bologne. I agree with Drinkwater (1998, 275) that Constantine must have had an effective army and navy in order to be ready to attempt such a venture, which means that the troop withdrawals from Britain undertaken by Stilicho previously at least in 401 cannot have been so drastic as to leave Britain defenceless. In fact, I would suggest that it was the transferral of troops by the British usurper Constantine that created the power vacuum on the island that the British Council and the remaining forces found so difficult to rectify. The force that Constantine took over the Channel cannot have been as small as the c. 6,000 men suggested by Drinkwater, but need not necessarily have been as large as the usual major armies of the period. It would have sufficed to possess perhaps about 20,000, men consisting of most of the remaining regulars, *foederati* and *bucellarii*, because that would have been substantial enough when there was clear readiness among the armies of Gaul to support a Western usurper, as they had always done in the fourth century (e.g. in 306, 350, 383, and 392). Nebiogastes may also have been a Frank, just like another commander of Constantine called Edobichus. The nomination of Franks to high positions would have secured the support of the Frankish *foederati* to the usurper's cause.

Constantinus III
(source: Cohen)

Constans
(source: Cohen)

The forces in Gaul and Spain declared their support for the usurper immediately after the landing (Zos. 6.2.2), with the result that the *PP* of Gaul, Petronius, withdrew the place of government either from Lugdunum (Lyon) or from Treves (Trier) to Arles, where he established a Gallic Council in imitation of the earlier Council of the Three Gauls. Drinkwater suggests that it is possible that an initial change of place of government from Trier to Lyon and the creation of the Gallic Council had already taken place before the usurper's landing in order to secure provincial loyalty for the new capital, and that the transfer of the capital from Lyon to Arles took place after the invasion. Similarly Drinkwater suggests that Constantine did not advance immediately to Arles, but left it in Honorius' hands in an effort to secure a reconciliation and that Constantine took the city of Arles in 408 only after Honorius' general had launched an attack. I find this line of argument unconvincing, mainly because Zosimus (6.2.1–2) states that Constantine won to his side all the armies up to the Alps dividing Gaul from Italy after having stayed at Bononia for only a few days.[3] If one trusts Geoffrey of Monmouth's account (6.12ff.), then there was some fighting in Armorica (see also Syvänne, *Britain in the Age of Arthur*). Consequently, it is more probable that the Gallic Council at Arles was created by the *PP* of Gaul Petronius in 407 as suggested by Chastagnol.[4] The reason would indeed have been to gain the support of the Gallic nobility against the usurper. The second argument against Drinkwater's claim is the strategy adopted by Constantine. Constantine clearly sent his *magistri militum* Justinian and Nebiogast as his vanguard to secure the southern approaches from Italy, while he himself assumed defensive positions at Lugdunum to oppose the route from the direction of Vindonissa and his British general Gerontius, together with the Frankish *foederati*, secured the north of Gaul with their headquarters at Treves. This tripartite division of responsibilities is proven by the fact that Justinian and Nebiogast faced Sarus in the south, and that the relief army under Gerontius and the Frank Edobichus came from the north. It is possible that Gerontius had been nominated as *Mag.Mil. per Gallias* while Nebiogastes and Justinian were praesental *magistri*.

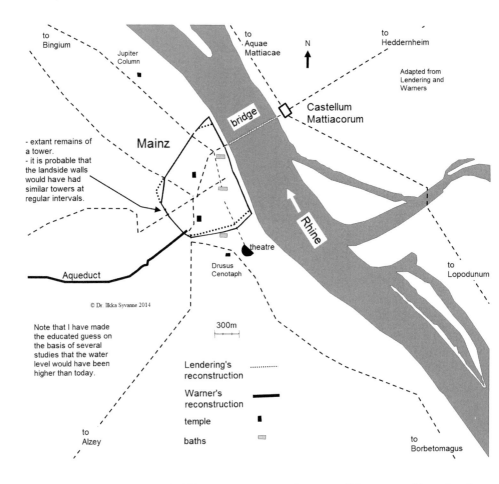

However, before he divided his army to oppose three possible routes of invasion from the West, there were other things that Constantine had to do. Firstly, he needed to secure the support of the regular armies of Gaul and the Frankish Federates, which he achieved. Secondly, he had to fight against the Vandals, Alans and other tribesmen that had been incited by Stilicho against the usurpers of Britain. These he defeated with relative ease.

The reason for this conclusion is that Zosimus (6.3.1–3) states that the Romans killed most of the Vandal, Alan and Suevi invaders of the year 406, but did not pursue and annihilate them. As a result of this, the barbarians were able to flee, recover from their defeat, and call reinforcements. The events of the year 408 prove that the invaders were pushed over the Rhine near the city of Mainz, which means that the local Alamanni [Suevi] tribes either withdrew to defensible locations within their own territory or were subdued by the newcomers. This sequence fits well with what we know of the situation. It is quite obvious that Constantine's first priority was to defeat the invaders, but since he was also in a hurry to secure Gaul against Honorius' forces, it is also equally obvious why he failed to pursue his advantage fully against the barbarians. Zosimus (6.3.3) confirms this. Constantine's next move was indeed to secure the approaches to Gaul with garrisons and to secure the Rhine frontier. This means that Stilicho's attempt to stem the usurpers of Britain with barbarians had failed.

In the meanwhile, early in 407 Stilicho was finalizing his plans to invade Illyricum in alliance with Alaric, probably in order to force Arcadius to accept his leadership or at least to occupy Illyricum. Since Alaric was in Epirus, which was part of the Eastern Empire (Zos. 5.29.1), it is clear that Alaric had invaded the East in preparation for the forthcoming war. The idea of invading East Rome in conjunction with Alaric was not new. As noted above, according to Zosimus' account (5.26.2) Stilicho had already formed an alliance with Alaric before the invasion of Radagaisus with the idea of taking Illyricum from East Rome. This must mean the treaty made after the Battle of Verona in 402. Stilicho had spent the fall of 406 and the winter of 406/7 in making the final preparations. Alaric had been promised money to support his army and had been nominated as *magister militum per Illyricum*, with Iovius *PP* of Illyricum. With this in mind, Stilicho had also established his headquarters at Ravenna and had assembled his forces in readiness in some unnamed locale (probably in Aquileia and/or Ravenna). There is no doubt that Stilicho's plan to start a civil war against Arcadius was simply idiotic in a situation in which Constantine III had invaded Gaul. Stilicho's vainglorious personal ambitions were becoming a real threat to the Roman Empire and it is not surprising that so many of his former supporters turned against him.

However, when Stilicho was about to march his forces into Illyricum, he at first received the false news that Alaric was dead, which was followed up by the very real news that the usurper Constantine had crossed from Britain to Gaul. According to Zosimus (5.29.7–8), Stilicho later claimed that the Emperor Honorius had actually forbidden him to carry out his Eastern invasion – with the implication that Stilicho would have invaded the East in the spring of 407 regardless of the threat posed by Constantine. If Zosimus' account reflects actual facts (I doubt that), then this means that Stilicho considered the forces posted in Italy (probably those with Sarus) to be sufficient to deter any operation by the usurper. Zosimus claims that the person who had turned Honorius' head against the invasion was Stilicho's wife Serena. Her intention was supposedly to end the hostilities and reconcile her brothers Honorius and Arcadius with each other. In the circumstances Stilicho could do very little and was forced to halt his march and then return to Rome to discuss the situation with the Emperor.

What is particularly noticeable about this episode is the supposed inability of Stilicho to keep his wife on a leash. Serena was the sister of the emperors and she had her own political goals. She was also quite ready to use her influence on her brother, the Emperor, contrary to the wishes of her husband, and there was nothing that Stilicho could do about that. However, there are other intrinsically likelier explanations for this (in my opinion). It is possible that Serena used her influence on her brother because she was aware of the probably secret agreement made by Honorius and Arcadius against her husband Stilicho (see below) and wanted to recall her husband to the court before they could lose their power over Honorius. It is also possible that Stilicho did not want to carry out the invasion of the East when a usurper threatened Italy and used his wife to convince Honorius to recall him. Whatever the circumstances, Stilicho could not simply disobey, because he did not have the loyalty of the army behind him. The army was loyal to Honorius and the House of Theodosius. On top of this, the Vandal origins of Stilicho made him very suspect to the natives when this was combined with his large-scale enrolment of barbarians into the army and with his repeated refusal to destroy defeated enemies. Furthermore, it is also clear that the emperors were really reconciled at this time, because Zosimus (6.8.2–3) states in no uncertain terms that the emperors had concluded an alliance with each other while Stilicho was still alive, and that as part of this deal Arcadius had promised to send

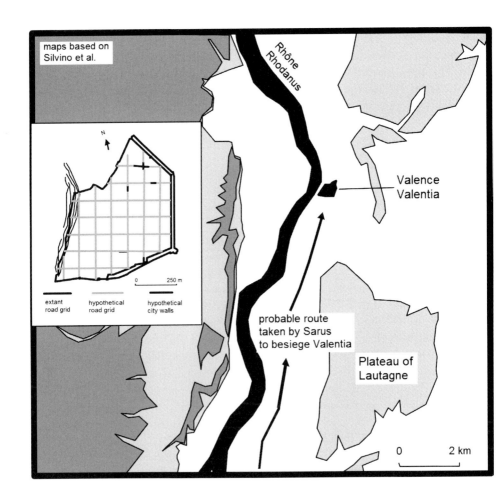

military help (six *tagmata* consisting of 40,000 men) for his brother against the usurper. This means that the Eastern and Western courts were reconciled at some point in time between the summer of 407 and early summer 408. This also means that it is possible that the brothers had concluded an alliance to get rid of Stilicho, which would not be at all surprising. However, the Eastern forces did not arrive in 408 thanks to the complications caused by Arcadius's death.

After the necessary consultation (i.e. the obtaining of the Emperor's approval), Stilicho divided his army in two. He sent the *strategos* Sarus with an army (*strateuma*, with the implication that it included regulars) against the usurper, while he stayed behind with the reserves to defend Italy. The alliance between the brothers Arcadius and Honorius must have been very unwelcome news to Stilicho.

Sarus, who undertook the campaign against the usurper, held either the rank of *MVM per Gallias* or less likely the title of *Comes* (*Foederatum?*). Sarus defeated Justinianus, killed him and most of his troops, and took a huge amount of booty, after which he advanced north against the usurper and Nebiogastes in Valentia. Constantine trusted in the impenetrability of the walls (double walls covered most of the land side of the city), but his *Magister* Nebiogastes made overtures of peace, which Sarus reciprocated. After having exchanged oaths, Nebiogastes foolishly surrendered – only to be instantly killed by Sarus. Constantine appointed the Briton Gerontius and the Frank Edobichus as the new *strategoi* (i.e. as praesental *magistri*). When their forces then approached Valentia, Sarus abandoned the siege after it had lasted only for seven days. The *magistri* gave hot pursuit and Sarus was able to save his army only with great difficulty and by giving up all his booty to the *Bacaudae* which he encountered in one of the Alpine passes leading into Italy.

The presence of the *Bacaudae*-bandits/local paramilitary rebels in the Alps is a sign of the times. The local peasants, mountaineers, members of the lesser gentry and the younger sons of the nobility were quite prepared to abandon civilization and form free groups of bandits akin to the seventeenth-century Buccaneers.[5] The rough Alpine area with its passes provided the bandits protection, as well as good opportunities for robbery and banditry. The same phenomenon is in evidence throughout the Roman Empire at this time. The civilians were quite ready either to abandon civilization and flee the tax-gatherers and corrupt military officers, or join the barbarian invaders. It was better to be free and poor than a slave of the corrupt system.

In the meanwhile, Honorius' relatives, the brothers Didymus and Verenianus, revolted against the representatives of Constantine III in Spain. I fully agree with Drinkwater's analysis (1998, 279ff.) that this revolt had resulted from the initial success of Sarus. The situation appeared favourable for the lawful regime, but then disaster struck. Honorius was eager to gain his indepence from Stilicho and this was to cost the Romans dear.

The Imperial Family 406–408

When discussing the events that led to the downfall of Stilicho we should not forget family relations. Honorius' wife Maria, Stilicho's daughter, died in very-late 407 or in early 408 (Inscr. 12, Claud. Epithal.; Jord. Get. 154, Rom. 322). This weakened Stilicho's grip on Honorius at a time when the brothers Arcadius and Honorius decided that it was time for Honorius to assert his position. Stilicho, however, had still one more card to play, but he was naturally hesistant to do that. The sexually depraved Emperor Honorius had developed an insane desire to marry Maria's underage sister Thermantia. In contrast to her husband, Stilicho's wife Serena was eager to grasp the opportunity and demanded that the marriage should take place. According to Zosimus, Serena realized that Thermantia was not old enough to marry, but still wanted to go through with the ceremony so that the bond with her brother would not break. However, in order to protect her daughter, Serena sought a woman who was able to ensure that Honorius would not be able to have sex with Thermantia. Zosimus claims that this was a success and that Thermantia died a virgin. The downside of the lack of sexual relations was naturally that Thermantia's grip on her husband was weak. It is quite possible that his sexual impotence undoubtedly caused Honorius to blame Thermantia and her parents for his condition with dire consequences for the state. However, since it was claimed that Maria had also died while still a virgin, it seems probable that in truth Serena had played no role in Honorius' impotence.

Stilicho's Changing Plans and His Downfall

After Sarus had withdrawn from Gaul, Stilicho planned to continue the campaign in person in 408. With this in mind he assembled a new army for the invasion of Gaul at Ticinum. At the same time he presumably renewed his alliance with the barbarians on the east side of the Rhine, in the same manner as Constantius II had done in 350–353, in order to divert part of the enemy force to that front. The death of Arcadius changed the plans once again.

On the basis of Zosimus' account (5.29.1ff.), it is usually thought that Alaric was angry over the fact that the invasion of the Prefecture of Illyricum had not materialized in 407, as a result of which he left Epirus (i.e. he had invaded East Roman territory) either in late-407 or early-408, marched to Emona, then 'attacked' Noricum and sent an embassy to Stilicho in Ravenna demanding 4,000 lbs of gold for both his stay in Epirus and for his 'invasion' of Italy and Noricum. The figure of 4,000 lbs of gold suggests that Alaric had about 30,000 *foederati* horsemen, who would have had a minimum of 7,500–15,000 squires/servants, in addition to which would have come their families.[6] The lowest estimate for the number of squires is based on the minimum requirement for the soldiers to possess at least 1 servant per 4 soldiers in the Roman cavalry. However, when one remembers that in the regular Roman cavalry elite units such as the *foederati* and *bucellarii* were expected to have more servants it is quite probable that there could easily have been well over 15,000 squires. The tribal traditions would actually suggest that there would have been at least one squire per knight/optimate, but I have here adopted a conservative approach, because Alaric's army consisted of the survivors of his previous disasters. In normal circumstances the *foederati* bolstered the size of their contingent with the squires (e.g. the *Strategikon* 3.6 has one rank of squires inserted into seven-man files to form an eight-man file), which would mean that the cavalry contingent under Alaric would have consisted of approximately 33,000–35,000 men so that the rest of the squires together with the elderly, young, women and children (in total perhaps 100,000 persons)[7] would have stayed behind in the camp. It is possible that there were also other Federate forces in Pannonia and Noricum that may have joined Alaric at this time, but these were already settled on land and did not need new sources of livelihood.

It is usually thought that by occupying Emona and Noricum Alaric poised his army in readiness to invade Italy in an effort to obtain payment from the Western government. I would suggest that it had indeed been Stilicho who had ordered Alaric's march to Noricum and the Julian Alps, as claimed by his enemies. The reason for such an order would have been the fact that the reinforcements promised by Arcadius had not yet arrived (Zos. 6.8.2) and Stilicho needed to place an army to Emona to protect the approaches to Italy while he invaded Gaul in person. The reason for this conclusion is that after Stilicho's downfall Alaric sought to prove his loyalty to Honorius while also attempting to protect members of Stilicho's family from killers (Zos. 5.36.1ff, esp. 5.37.3–39.1). He was clearly not an enemy of Stilicho. It should also be noted that the money supposedly extorted by Alaric was meant not only as compensation for his prolonged, futile stay in Epirus, but also for the invasion of Noricum and Italy. This suggests that the areas in question were in barbarian hands and that Stilicho had ordered Alaric to march there to protect the approaches to Italy, and this was represented by the enemies of Alaric and Stilicho as an invasion. In short, it is very probable that Alaric was operating under Stilicho's orders. Alaric's operation, however, may have been represented purposefully in such a manner as to poise a not-so-veiled threat to make it easier for Stilicho to obtain the money that he needed, which quite evidently had not been paid to Alaric by the clearly-incompetent Emperor and Senate despite the agreement Stilicho had reached with Alaric. Even though not mentioned by any source, it is very probable that the Eastern government exploited the retreat of Alaric from Epirus by re-occupying it immediately and it is also probable that they would also have moved in to fill the resulting power vacuum in the evacuated sections of Dalmatia as Alaric moved north.

Stilicho went in person to Rome to obtain approval from both the Senate and the Emperor. When the meeting of the Senate was convened at the Palace, the majority voted for war against Alaric, contrary to the wishes of Stilicho. The ugly anti-Gothic spirit was raising its head also in the West. The senators and the Emperor considered it shameful to buy peace from Alaric. John Matthews (Stilicho's era, especially 253ff.) has analyzed in detail how the senators (especially Italian and Gallic) gained influence from ca. 364 onwards and how their attitudes affected the fate of the Empire. The highly-influential senators (whose support Stilicho needed) were unwilling to contribute conscript soldiers to the army and they were also unwilling to pay subsidies to the barbarians, the latter of which they considered beneath their dignity – the fact that such payments were also taken from the senators was not unimportant either. This in turn meant that they actively promoted as a class an aggressive military solution to all problems in the old manner without realizing that this would have required them to allow a full-scale conscription on their estates and the paying of other possibly extraordinary taxes needed to support this army. Stilicho took the podium and responded that Alaric's stay in Epirus had come about as a result of an agreement with Honorius and that the invasion of Arcadius' realm would have been carried out in 407 had Honorius not sent an order to abort the mission. Stilicho showed Honorius' letter and claimed that it had been his wife Serena who had caused Honorius to send the letter. According to Stilicho, Serena preferred the maintenance of peace between Honorius and Arcadius, who were her brothers. As noted above, I would suggest that the alliance of the brothers was likely to be directed against Stilicho. Stilicho's personal interference changed the vote so that the majority of the senators voted for the granting of the money out of the fear they felt towards Stilicho.

The payment of gold to the former enemy Alaric was highly unpopular. Most importantly, the incompetent simpleton but still-always-devious Honorius appears to have felt it beneath his dignity to pay the barbarian, and he was now more than ready to plot the downfall of Stilicho. It was easy for Stilicho's enemies, led by the *Magister Scrinii* Olympius, to exploit this and bring about the downfall of Stilicho. Olympius, who was a native of the Black Sea region, had obtained his position with Stilicho's help, but was clearly not loyal to his benefactor and may have acted on behalf of the Eastern government as a sort of undercover operative/agent provocateur. The aim of the plotters was to wrest control of the army from Stilicho and his supporters by exploiting the loyalty of the troops towards the Theodosian dynasty and their Emperor. Their aim was to ensure that Honorius would go to review the regulars at Ticinum (see below). However, Serena and Stilicho tried to forestall this.

Stilicho, who had now obtained the money he needed, was preparing to return to Ravenna to finalize the deal with Alaric. It was then that Honorius informed Stilicho that he wanted to accompany Stilicho to review the army in Ravenna. Zosimus claims (5.30) that Serena had advised Honorius to abandon Rome for the safety of Ravenna when Italy was threatened by so formidable an enemy as Alaric. He also claims that Stilicho was opposed to this and claims that Stilicho organized a mutiny of the soldiers under Sarus (clearly party to the plot to kill Stilicho, possibly because Sarus was envious of Alaric's promotion over him) in Ravenna so that Honorius would abandon his goal. When Honorius still insisted on going there (I would suggest that this is a mistake for Ticinum), contrary to the wishes of Stilicho, Stilicho's adviser Justinianus guessed that the purpose was to bring about the downfall of his master. Not unnaturally Justinianus fled before this could happen. I would suggest that Stilicho and Serena were both aware that there was a plot to cause their downfall and with this in mind they decided to urge Honorius to accompany Stilicho to Ravenna, where Stilicho would be able to keep the emperor under guard and surrounded by his own loyal barbarian *bucellarii*. It is probable that the revolt in Ravenna of the Federate troops was caused by none other than Sarus with the intention of forcing Honorius to seek safety with the native Roman forces assembled at Ticinum, and that Stilicho rather attempted to dissuade Honorius from the latter course so that he could keep Honorius under his own control. However, this was not to be.

Stilicho was dispatched to Ravenna to pacify the mutiny while Honorius stayed in Bononia. The plotters had now managed to separate Honorius and Stilicho, which they undoubtedly used to their best advantage by making further whispers against Stilicho. When Stilicho reached the mutinous troops at Ravenna, he stated that the Emperor had ordered them to be punished and that on top of this the worst mutineers were to be decimated. The fearful soldiers begged for mercy and Stilicho wisely promised that he would obtain pardon from the Emperor, which was duly granted.

It was then that the news of the death of Arcadius reached the Emperor and Stilicho. Stilicho returned to Bononia, where he stated to Honorius that he wanted to travel in person to Constantinople to become guardian for Arcadius' underage son Theodosius II. Honorius in his turn informed Stilicho that he too wanted to make the journey to the

East, but according to Zosimus Stilicho dissuaded him on the grounds that Honorius' presence was needed in Italy threatened by a usurper. In addition to this, the travel costs of the Emperor were just too great. Stilicho stated that the best policy was for himself to travel to the East with Honorius' letters while Alaric attacked the usurper with the combined army of barbarians and regulars, while the Emperor stayed in Italy to protect it. Honorius claimed to agree and gave Stilicho letters for the Eastern Emperor, but then marched to Ticinum.

According to Sozomen (9.4), Stilicho took the *Labarum* (note that the Imperial *Labarum* was in the West; had Theodosius taken it there?) and intended to march to the East at the head of four *arithmoi* of soldiers (*stratiôtai*). These *arithmoi* must mean *mere/legiones* of approximately the same strength as those that later arrived from the East, each of which had probably about 5,000 footmen and 1,600 horsemen. It is quite clear that Stilicho could not have hoped to achieve anything with a mere 4,000–4,800 men, which is the usual interpretation for the strength of four *arithmoi* at this time (4 x 1,000/1,200 men = 4,000–4,800 men). Consequently, it is probable that Stilicho intended to take 20,000 regular footmen and 6,400 horsemen, in addition to which Stilicho would have had his own personal Hunnish *bucellarii* (perhaps about 10,000 men?). Even if there is no definite proof for this, there is also a very strong possibility that Stilicho had once again employed the services of Uldin, just as he had in 405. There are three reasons for this suggestion. Firstly, Uldin invaded Thrace during the summer of 408 at about the same time as Stilicho would have arrived in the East with his troops. Secondly, Uldin had previously acted as Stilicho's ally, and Uldin's Huns would have given Stilicho the required leverage against the Eastern Government. And thirdly, Stilicho was certainly not above using barbarians against a legitimate Roman government, as his cooperation with Alaric and the invaders of Gaul prove. It should be noted that had Stilicho been successful in his schemes it is probable that Alaric would have conquered Gaul in Honorius' name while Stilicho would have gained control of East Rome, but with the cost of having to fight a war against Persia. It is difficult to state with any certainty what would have been the consequences of all this. The other alternative is that we should date Uldin's invasion to coincide with the dispatch of reinforcements by the Eastern government to help Honorius in the late summer of 409, because the dating of Uldin's invasion of the Balkans is uncertain (see later).

Zosimus (5.32.1ff.) asserts that Stilicho was unaware of any ill-feeling towards him by Honorius (or by the regulars posted at Ticinum) and that it was Olympius who turned Honorius and the soldiers against Stilicho when Honorius reached Ticinum. This is unlikely to be true. It is probable that the plotters led by Olympius had already turned Honorius against Stilicho while Honorius was at Rome and it was because of this that Serena had suggested to Honorius that he should travel with Stilicho to Ravenna. However, the final straw that tilted the balance against Stilicho appears to have happened only when both were staying in Bononia. Stilicho's decisive mistake was his statement that he intended to travel to Constantinople alone. This decision sealed Stilicho's fate. It is easy to see why Honorius in these circumstances feared that Stilicho would first overthrow Theodosius II and place his own son Eucherius on the throne and after that he would overthrow Honorius himself with the help of the Eastern forces. In fact, it is not impossible that Stilicho could have considered such an option when he already aware of the plotting against him. It was because of this that Honorius travelled to Ticinum. Honorius' purpose was to instigate the regulars against Stilicho with the help of Olympius. This was easy enough to do. The regulars were not favourably disposed towards the half-Vandal who had previously defeated them in 394 and had then formed an alliance with their former enemy Alaric. It was easy for them to believe that Stilicho was planning to overthrow Theodosius and install his own son as Emperor of the East. The propagandists also appear to have claimed that Eucherius intended to restore the pagan cults, which definitely worked up the mostly Christian troops to anger. It seems probable that Stilicho had been aware of this danger even before this date, because he had overturned his previously tolerant attitude towards the pagan cults a couple of years back, but to no avail as the impact of the propaganda proves.

Zosimus (5.31.6ff.) claims that Stilicho stayed in Bononia and did not put into effect his plan to march to Constantinople when Honorius left for Ticinum. He also makes the claim that Stilicho did not send any orders for the regulars to march to Ravenna or anywhere else out of fear that these forces would meet the Emperor on the way, with the result that the soldiers would incite Honorius against him. I would rather suggest that Stilicho was fully aware of the danger that he was in and was desperately seeking a way out of it. Stilicho was certainly aware that his advisor Justinianus had already fled because Justinianus had considered Stilicho's position untenable. He could not seek help from the Federates posted at Ravenna because these were under his enemy Sarus and neither could he seek help from the Western regulars whose loyalty he had never gained. It was also clear that Stilicho knew that without the support of the Western army he would not be able to obtain any support from the East either. After all, he had fought against the Eastern government on many occasions. Stilicho did have some troops at his disposal in Bononia, because it was a major military base (see above and below), but their numbers were too few to oppose the regulars at Ticinum and probably also the Federates under Sarus at Ravenna. In these circumstances Stilicho apparently resorted to the only option left open to him and did nothing in an effort to make certain that his enemies at least would not be able to find any excuse for accusing him of treachery against the Emperor. Stilicho could still hope that the commanders he had put in charge of the army at Ticinum would be able to keep order in the army. This was not to be.

According to Zosimus, the *Magister Scrinii* Olympius incited the soldiers against Stilicho with the claim that he intended to overthrow Theodosius and crown his son Eucherius as Emperor. In addition to this, Stilicho was accused of having incited the barbarian invasion of Gaul (correctly in my opinion) and of having formed an alliance with Alaric (correctly), while Eucherius was (probably falsely) accused of having planned to reinstate the old religion. Olympius also took the trouble to visit the sick soldiers in an effort to win the hearts and minds of the rank-and-file, and this worked.

On the fourth day after the Emperor's arrival at Ticinum, the soldiers were assembled in front of the imperial palace, supposedly because Honorius intended to exhort them before their campaign against the usurper. It was then that Olympius gave the signal for his agent provocateurs and assassins to start the long-awaited operation. In a killing frenzy they attacked and killed the *PP* of Gaul Limenius, the *Mag.Eq. per Gallias* Chariobaudes, the *Mag.Eq.* Vicentius, and the *Com. Dom.* Salvius, all supporters of Stilicho. It was then that Honorius retreated inside the palace and some of the magistrates managed to follow him to safety. However, the soldiers/assassins followed after their prey. They killed all the high-ranking officials they could find and pillaged the city in the process. It was then that the Emperor, dressed only in a short tunic without any imperial regalia, came out of the palace into the middle of the city and calmed the men. This did not save the magistrates who had been captured. They were summarily executed. These included the *Mag. Off.* Naimorius, the *Comes Sacrarum Lagitionum* Patroinus, the unknown *Comes Rerum Privatarum*, and the *Quaestor* Salvius, all evidently men appointed by Stilicho. After that the Emperor withdrew to rest, supposedly because he feared that the soldiers could also harm him. The killing continued until late afternoon and included also the *PP* of Italy, Longinianus. Basically the entire upper echelon of the imperial administration was assassinated at the behest of Honorius and Olympius. This was certainly not conducive to the orderly administration of the Empire just at the time when the Empire sorely needed experienced administrators and generals.

Contrary to popular opinion regarding Honorius, I do not consider him to have been a mere marionette in the hands of Olympius. Honorius should rather be considered to have been a person with mediocre intellect who had his own strong views of what was the right policy in the circumstances – it is quite clear that he considered it beneath his imperial dignity to cooperate with the barbarians, especially with the Goths. However, since he lacked his own powerbase – his only claim to power was his birth and all the officials surrounding him were Stilicho's men – he first needed to find some low-ranking person willing to help him get rid of Stilicho and his men. Olympius performed this task ideally. It should be kept in mind, however, that even after this Honorius still lacked a true personal powerbase, as a result of which he needed to change his favourites periodically so that none of them could gain a position from which to threaten him. On the basis of this one can consider Honorius to have been a typical mediocre leader who lacked any real understanding of the policies needed in the circumstances, but who clearly knew how to play one person against another in an effort to stay in power. He was a very devious person, but not a bright one. Essentially, it was Honorius and his anti-Gothic policies that brought about the downfall of West Rome.

When the news of the uprising reached Stilicho at Bononia he assembled the leaders of the Federate forces that were present nearby to discuss the situation. According to Zosimus, the leaders were unanimous that if the mutineers had killed the Emperor then they would attack the regulars and teach them a lesson. However, if the mutineers had only killed the leaders, then only the ringleaders of the revolt were to be punished. When they learnt that the Emperor was alive, Stilicho decided not to attempt to punish the soldiers because they outnumbered his barbarian allies in Bononia (Zos. 5.33.2). I would suggest that there were well over 50,000 barbarians in or near the city and that the regular army posted at Ticinum to oppose Constantine must have been truly huge. The reason for this conclusion is that after Stilicho's downfall there were over 30,000 Federates left to join Alaric and that Sarus possessed enough Federates at Bononia to fight against the united army of 30,000 Federates and Alaric's over 30,000 Goths. We should not forget that all of these Federate contingents also included squires/servants that could be used to bolster combat strength (e.g. Str. 3.6). The more than 30,000 barbarians who later joined Alaric seem to have consisted primarily of the Sarmatians and Alans settled in or near Concordia, Altinum and Cremona (see below), and possibly also in Aquileia. The numbers available for Stilicho may even have been greater because the above estimations do not include the *bucellarii* Huns of Stilicho. However, the smallness of this army in comparison with the regulars was not the only reason for Stilicho's decision to go to Ravenna. According to Zosimus (5.33.2), the second of the reasons was the fact that Stilicho knew that he could not trust the Emperor. I would suggest that Stilicho's goal was to attempt to recruit the army posted at Ravenna to his cause. Zosimus (5.34.1) goes on to claim that Stilicho was at a loss concerning what to do because his barbarians supposedly still wanted to attack the regulars and not wait for any reinforcements. However, we should also not forget that Honorius had Stilicho's daughter as de facto hostage, which must have been partially responsible for Stilicho's indecisiveness. It is in fact possible that the overthrow of Stilicho had been planned well in advance of the event and that the marriage with the second daughter had been planned in order to obtain a hostage.

However, while Stilicho was still pondering his options, Sarus made the decision on his behalf. Sarus showed his true colours and attacked Stilicho's Huns when these were sleeping and captured Stilicho's baggage train (Zos. 5.34). The size of Sarus' force is not known with any certainty, but is unlikely to have consisted of a mere 200–300 men (Zos. 6.13.2; Soz. 9.9.3; Olymp. fr.6) at this date because after this he was still the commander of the local federate forces that were supposedly large enough to face Alaric and his allies later. I would suggest that Stilicho must have possessed truly sizable forces of Huns at his disposal that were eliminated with one surgical strike.

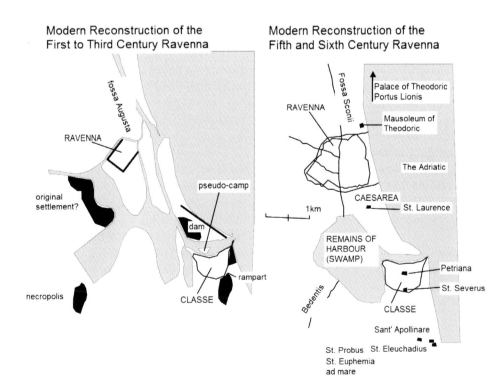

Modern Reconstruction of the First to Third Century Ravenna

Modern Reconstruction of the Fifth and Sixth Century Ravenna

Missoriorum of Theodosius I and his sons Arcadius and Honorius with their bodyguards. (*Source: Joseph Wilpert*, Die Römischen Mosaiken und Malereien Vol.2. *Freiburg im Breisgau, 1916*)

Various pieces of metalwork used to construct helmets, etc. (*With permission of Vicus Ultimus*)

Emperor Theodosius I Magnus Augustus seated on a horse. Adapted from the Column of Theodosius so that the saddle cloth is slightly changed, the sword made longer (even the short *gladius* was longer than the sword in the illustration) and horse changed. Note the probable use of the leather muscle armour (alternative interpretation would be mail or scale, but this is less probable than leather), the stoppers in the sword, and the crested Pseudo-Attican helmet. (© *Dr Ilkka Syvänne*)

Members of the Polish re-enactment group Vicus Ultimus in period equipment. (*With permission of Vicus Ultimus*)

A soldier equipped with chain mail armour, ridge-helmet and axe as depicted by Vicus Ultimus. (*With permission of Vicus Ultimus*)

Coins: Top – Coin of Arcadius.
Bottom – Coin of Honorius.

Above: Hattenroth's drawing (1884) depicting a Heerführer (above, left) and Hattenroth's drawing (1891) depicting Aetius (above, right), both of which which are based on Diptych of Stilicho. These two reconstructions give a good picture of the actual appearance of Stilicho's clothes.

Below left: Stilicho's wife Serena with son Eucherius. **Below right:** Stilicho with a shield showing the heads of Arcadius and Honorius. The intention was to demonstrate Stilicho's claim to be the guardian of both emperors.

Worms helmet as reconstructed by Vicus Ultimus. (*With permission of Vicus Ultimus*)

© Dr. Ilkka Syvänne 2013

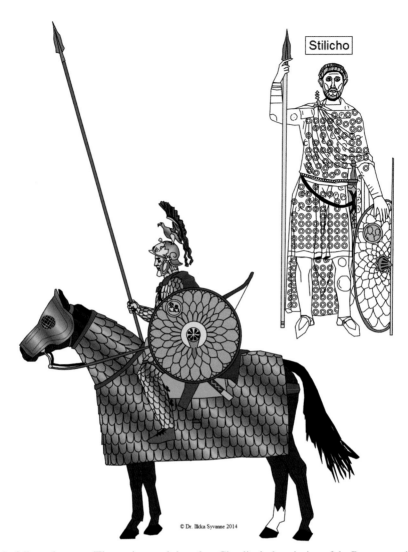

Stilicho in full-combat gear. The equipment is based on Claudian's description of the Roman cavalry forces in his *Against Rufinus* 2.353ff. (these men and horses wore steel and iron armour of pliant scales/lamina, which gives a greyish appearance) and in his *Honorius' VI Consulship* 569ff. (horsemen wearing steel and horses bronze, the latter of which gleamed like gold). The other sources are: Claudian (Gothic, 458-460; Stilicho's grey hair visible beneath the helmet, which suggests that Stilicho let his hair grow longer during military campaigns than shown in the famous diptych); Theodosius' Column; late Byzantine painting and Column of Trajan for the leg armour; Diptych of Stilicho with his family (above right). Notably, Claudian likens the cataphracted Roman horsemen and their horses to statues as was typical for the ancient sources. I have reconstructed the rider's leg armour on the basis of late Byzantine illustrations which have similar armour. Please note, however, that Claudian's referral to the use of the scale armour does not give us enough details to make any certain conclusions as to the exact type of armour worn. Since there exists no artistic period evidence for the type of armour shown here (the scale armour worn by the Sarmatians in Trajan's Column is not realistic) and the painting which I have used for the reconstruction of the leg and arm armour is late, the reconstruction should be seen hypothetical. It is possible that in combat the helmet would have had a visor to protect the face in the manner that similar helmets were used in the past. The armour worn by the rider could also be mail and/or he could wear a breastplate, and/or it could be gilded with gold if Stilicho wanted to present similar appearance as the Imperial Guard. The bow and quiver could also be placed in the back as shown in the period illustrations, but I have made the assumption that Stilicho would have followed the Alan/Hun practice because he would have liked to endear himself with his *bucellarii* guards who used a similar style of equipment. (© *Dr Ilkka Syvänne*)

Flavius Arcadius Augustus (384–408). Author's drawing based on an extant bust of Arcadius and other East Roman works of art describing emperors. (© *Dr Ilkka Syvänne*)

A Finnish re-enactor Jyrki Halme demonstrating one of the fighting stances adopted by the late Roman front rank soldiers. (© *Jyrki Halme*)

Jyrki Halme in equipment that the soldiers would have typically used when not in combat. (© *Jyrki Halme*)

Jyrki Halme as a late Roman front rank fighter as the soldier could have looked when resting during marching or other duty. (© *Jyrki Halme*)

Flavius Honorius Augustus (393–423) in 406. Diptych of Probus, Consul 406, at Aosta representing the Emperor Honorius. (*Source: Sybel 1909*)

Finnish re-enactor Jyrki Halme in period clothing worn by the soldiers when not fighting based on Piazza Armerina mosaics. (© *Jyrki Halme*)

Jyrki Halme in another type of light equipment worn at the time. (© *Jyrki Halme*)

Flavius Constantius 3 (Aug. Feb. 8–Sept. 2, 421). Left: The central figure is likely to be Constantius, and the two emperors at the top Honorius and Theodosius II. Note the equipment and dress of the Germanic prisoners (Goths?) at the bottom of the diptych. Right: I identify the central figure to be Constantius, but Sybel thinks him to be anonymous. Note the equipment and dress of the Germanic prisoners (Goths?) at the bottom of the diptych. (*Source: Sybel 1909*)

A slinger equipped with a staff sling (could be a legionary or auxiliary). Drawn partially after Phil Parker. The trousers, shirt and haircut date the soldier to the fourth to sixth centuries.
(© *Dr Ilkka Syvänne*)

A regular slinger (could be a legionary or auxiliary). Adapted from the Column of Trajan by adding trousers and Phrygian hat used during the late Roman period. (© *Dr Ilkka Syvänne*)

Top left: The super heavy cavalry *clibanarius* equipped for long and short range combat. The heavy cavalry cataphracts differed from these: horses wore only frontal armour; the men carried shields and used the less heavy Gallic version of the *contus*-spear. (© *Dr Ilkka Syvänne*)

Top right: A cavalry officer in the Column of Theodosius. (© *Dr Ilkka Syvänne*)

Centre: Note the new type of saddle, which may have been copied from the Huns. (*Source: Column of Theodosius by Menestrier*)

Bottom left: Horseman drawn after the Column of Theodosius. Note the use of leather armour and *gladius*. (© *Dr Ilkka Syvänne*)

Bottom right: A horseman belonging to the elite *Comites Alani* who served under the *Magister Equitum* in Italy. He uses a flayed skin of an enemy soldier as his saddle cloth to demonstrate his manhood and warrior qualities. The extant versions of the *Notitia Dignitatum* give two different colourings for the shield: The white version carried by the horseman and the blue version shown on the right. (© *Dr Ilkka Syvänne*)

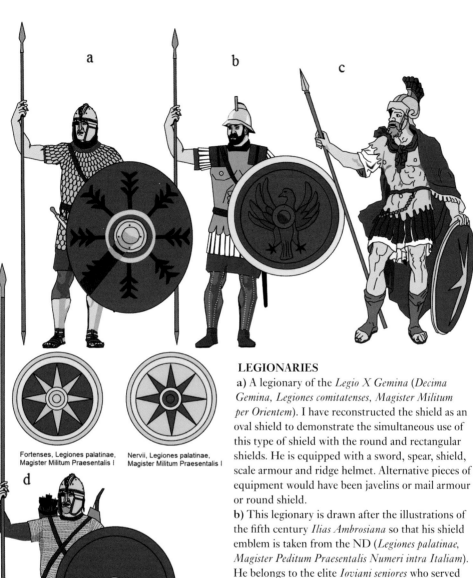

Fortenses, Legiones palatinae,
Magister Militum Praesentalis I

Nervii, Legiones palatinae,
Magister Militum Praesentalis I

LEGIONARIES

a) A legionary of the *Legio X Gemina* (*Decima Gemina, Legiones comitatenses, Magister Militum per Orientem*). I have reconstructed the shield as an oval shield to demonstrate the simultaneous use of this type of shield with the round and rectangular shields. He is equipped with a sword, spear, shield, scale armour and ridge helmet. Alternative pieces of equipment would have been javelins or mail armour or round shield.

b) This legionary is drawn after the illustrations of the fifth century *Ilias Ambrosiana* so that his shield emblem is taken from the ND (*Legiones palatinae, Magister Peditum Praesentalis Numeri intra Italiam*). He belongs to the elite *Ioviani seniores* who served under the *Magister Peditum* in Italy.

c) A footman drawn after the Column of Theodosius. On the basis of the shield (two outer rings and a star) it is likely that he belonged either to the *Fortenses* (*Notitia Dignitatum Legiones palatinae, Magister Militum Praesentalis I*) or to the *Nervii* (ND, *Legiones palatinae, Magister Militum Praesentalis I*). I have here reconstructed the shield colours according to the *Fortenses* colours. Note that the elite soldier is equipped with a shield, spear, helmet, sword (behind the man) and wears probably leather armour just like his western counterpart. I have purposefully coloured his leather armour with gold to show his elite status even if the leather could be coloured with any colour.

d) A legionary of *Prima Italica* (*Legiones pseudocomitatenses, Magister Militum per Orientem*). He is equipped with a *spatha*-sword, mail-armour, shield, composite bow, quiver of arrows, Deurne ridge helmet, and a long version of the *hasta*-spear meant for use against cavalry. In other words, he is equipped as multipurpose legionary (as described by Syrianos Magister and Vegetius) for specialized use against the Persian cavalry. (© *Dr Ilkka Syvänne*)

Fifth century infantry archers according to the illustrations of the fifth century Ilias Ambrosiana. Top Left: Foot archer in light equipment (tunica, trousers, shoes, cloak, quiver, bow) with a sword and shield added. The shield was an optional piece of equipment used by those who wanted to be better prepared for close quarters combat. Top Right: Foot archer equipped with ersatz armour (muscle cuirass of leather), helmet, sword, quiver, bow and sword. (© Dr Ilkka Syvänne)

Jyrki Halme depicting a late Roman front rank fighter of the elite units with bronze muscle armour. (© Jyrki Halme)

Jyrki Halme demonstrating one of the ways to draw the knife used by fifth century Roman soldiers. (© Jyrki Halme)

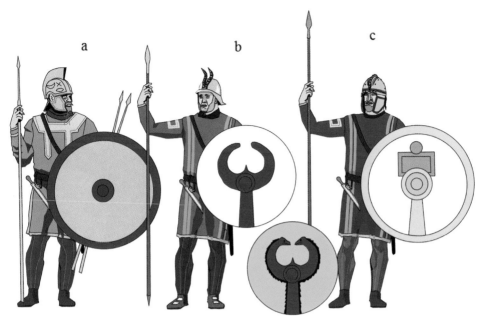

EXAMPLES OF AUXILIA PALATINA (ELITE 'MEDIUM INFANTRY') (© *Dr Ilkka Syvänne*)

a) A member of the *Heruli Seniores* equipped for use against infantry (*Auxilia Palatina, Magister Peditum Praesentalis intra Italiam,* West). He is equipped with a *spatha*-sword, crested ridge helmet, shield and three javelins.

b) A soldier of the *Cornuti*. The shield emblem carried by the man means that he belongs to the *Cornuti seniores, Auxilia Palatina, Magister Peditum Praesentalis, Numeri intra Italiam* (West). The other shield emblem shown below right belongs to the *Cornuti, Auxilia Palatina, Magister Militum Praesentalis* (East). He is equipped with a *spatha*-sword, shield, and a short version of the *hasta* or with a *lancea* meant for thrusting and throwing. Note the horned helmet, which is taken from the Arch of Constantine. This type of helmet was undoubtedly used also for head butts.

c) A member of the elite *Felices Honoriani seniores* who belonged to the *Auxilia palatina*. The shield emblem is drawn after the ND (*Felices Honoriani seniores, Auxilia palatina, Magister Militum per Orientem*). The fact that he belongs to the *Honoriani seniores* suggests that these units were originally created by Arcadius at the same time as he created his *Arcadiaci/Arcadiani*. He is equipped with a *spatha*-sword, shield, Deurne ridge helmet, and a short version of the *hasta* or with a *lancea* meant for thrusting and throwing.

Left: Typical Pictish warrior showing his tattoos and bravery. (© *Dr Ilkka Syvänne*)
Right: Typical Irish warrior in his equipment. (© *Dr Ilkka Syvänne*)

Top Left: Saxon spearman. **Top Centre:** Saxon swordsman armed with a *seax* (figure drawn after Richard Underwood). **Top Right:** Saxon foot archer armed with a wooden self-bow. The men on the left and right should be seen to be representative of the so-called young ones of their tribe who would have been led by the veteran in the middle. The more seasoned veterans would have consisted of more bulky, fully bearded men. Note the use of light equipment, which would have been the standard for most of the men on board. This, however, was not decisive in fighting. The fighting spirit and morale were the decisive factors and the Saxons were known for their pagan fury and bloodthirsty human sacrifices which frightened their less seasoned opponents senseless. Note that with the exception of the north Germans, Goths and Scandinavians most of the Germanic warriors were equipped with similarly light equipment. The armoured forces consisted usually only of the tribal elite (the retinues of the nobles) who were often also mounted. See my *Britain in the Age of Arthur* for further details.

An Anglo-Saxon elite warrior, chieftain or king in Britain according to Gamber and Alclud. Their reconstruction is based mainly on the Sutton Hoo treasure. (© *Dr Ilkka Syvänne*)

Hunnic cavalry. (© *Dr Ilkka Syvänne*). I have here made the educated guess that the Hun cavalry used leather stirrups even if this is not specifically mentioned by the extant sources. The reason for this is that the leather stirrups were known in the steppe regions occupied by the Huns at least from the second century BC onwards and because the iron stirrups make an appearance in the Roman sources only in the sixth century.

Hunnic light cavalry riding a steppe pony. He is equipped with a coat, bows, arrows and a sword. He may also carry a shield.

Hunnic heavy cavalry consisting of the tribal elite. He is equipped with a spear, sword, bow, quiver, helmet and shield and wears mail armour. His horse is equipped with felt armour.

Typical examples of Berber cavalry seated on Berber horses (height 153 cm, bad tempered kickers, a hardy breed able to carry great weights). The Berbers were justifiably famous as horse javelineers, which is the reason for their inclusion in the Roman army. The Berbers also used small numbers of mounted archers and large numbers of unarmoured light infantry equipped as spearmen, javelineers, slingers and bowmen.

Left: Regular Persian heavy foot soldier equipped with a spear, sword, helmet and a shield made out of cane and leather. **Right**: Regular Persian foot archer equipped with a bow, quiver and sword. (© *Dr Ilkka Syvänne*)

Persian *clibanarius* first half of the fifth century (a helmet, lamellar and mail armour, sword, bow, quiver and horse lamellar armour). I have made the educated guess that the Persians would have adopted the stirrups early as a result of their contacts with the Indians who were using such. There is solid evidence for their use only from the sixth century onwards. It should also be noted that period evidence does not exist for the type of lamellar shown in this illustration with the implication that this depiction of the lamellar should be seen merely as a guess of one possible type of lamellar armour in use. I have also made a guess regarding the way the sword would have been suspended from the belt.

Persian large
oceangoing dhow/
warship of the
Baghlah-class.

40m

© Dr. Ilkka Syvanne 2014

op left: Elite Daylami footman in Persian service equipped with a helmet, shield, spear, sword, dagger
d scale armour. (© *Dr. Ilkka Syvänne*) **Bottom**: The Persians adopted this type of cataphract cavalry
efore the 450s when the relief of Peroz shows him wearing this type of equipment. The likeliest date for
e change is the turn of early-fifth century when the Persians faced particularly dangerous nomadic foes
luns, Hepthalites and Kidarites) employing powerful archery shots, hence the use of shields.

An Arab multipurpose lancer (a bow, quiver, spear, mail armour, helmet, shield, and sword). The use of armour shows that the individual belonged to the wealthy section of society. Persian influence is shown by the coat and other gear worn by the trooper. The Arab cavalry lancers were excellent scouts, skirmishers and guerrilla fighters, and were particularly fearsome at close quarters fighting with swords. Even the Goths were frightened by the Arab cavalry in front of the city of Constantinople in 378. Most of the Arabs at this time were pagans, but there were also large numbers of Jewish and Christian Arabs. The Arab lancer uses a lancing style that became known as the Damascus style. The Arab cavalry typically used camels for travel and mounted their horses only for combat or training.

Finnish re-enactor Jyrki Halme as a late Roman front rank fighter wearing typical fifth century attire as used by the imperial elite units, which in this case means the muscle armour of bronze. (© *Jyrki Halme*)

Jyrki Halme as a late Roman draco-carrier. (© *Jyrki Halme*)

In the circumstances, Stilicho had no other option available to him than to flee to Ravenna. At the same time, he issued an order to all of the cities which had families of barbarians living inside to close their gates from the Federate forces because some of those (i.e. Sarus) had now turned against the Roman state. Stilicho had now lost control of the Federate forces at Bononia and his only hope was to retain the loyalty of the rest of the Federates, namely those that had families as hostages inside the cities, while also gaining control of the regulars stationed at Ravenna. However, the Emperor and Olympius (now appointed *Mag.Off.*) had already sent orders to the regulars at Ravenna to arrest Stilicho, and when Stilicho learnt of this he fled to a nearby church while his barbarians, other associates, servants and slaves armed themselves to protect their master. The soldiers managed to convince Stilicho to leave the church by stating that they had only orders for his arrest, but when Stilicho was brought out the messenger handed over another letter which ordered his execution. When Stilicho's armed men attempted to rescue him, Stilicho ordered them to stop, after which he submitted his neck to the executioner's sword on 22 August 408. The executioner of Stilicho was a man named Heraclianus, who was duly rewarded with the office of *Comes Africae* for his troubles. In the meanwhile, Eucherius fled from the city in an effort to reach Rome where his mother was staying (Zos. 5.34.5). However, it is actually possible that Eucherius was led away from the scene to Rome by the eunuchs sent by Honorius with Thermantia (Zos. 5.35.3, 5.37.3–4), or that they managed to locate Eucherius in his hiding place. In my opinion it is quite possible that Honorius had ordered the eunuchs to induce Eucherius to implicate himself and his father in a plot of some sort against Honorius to justify his actions. What is certain is that Eucherius did not flee immediately to Rome (see later), possibly because it became apparent that the city of Rome was in the hands of his enemies, but stayed somewhere in hiding until the eunuchs in question lured Eucherius to Rome.

After having discussed the circumstances in which Stilicho died, Zosimus (5.34.5ff.) presents a eulogy of him. Stilicho was supposedly the most moderate of all of those in power and did not attempt to make his son an Emperor. Zosimus also exaggerates that Stilicho never sold military office or stole the soldiers' salaries, because he notes those practices for the beginning of Stilicho's rule. On the basis of this it is usually assumed that it was at some point before this that Zosimus had changed his source to a source favourable towards Stilicho. This indeed seems to be the case. However, as noted previously it is entirely plausible that Stilicho may also have changed his policies after he had secured his position so that he had really attempted to put a stop to corruption, and this in fact this may have contributed to his downfall when there were ambitious persons who had not been able to buy their magistracies as expected.

After the death of Stilicho, Olympius and Honorius moved in to further secure their position so that the remaining friends and supporters of Stilicho were purged and replaced by Olympius' nominees. The *PSC* Deuterius, the *Primicerius Notariorum* Petrus and many others were tortured in vain to produce evidence against Stilicho, and then killed. Honorius ordered his wife Thermantia to be returned to her mother and Stilicho's son Eucherius to be hunted down and killed (Zos.5.35.3). Since the eunuchs Arsacius and Terentius were later taking both Eucherius and Thermantia to Rome, it is possible that the orders to kill Stilicho had been delivered by them or by an officer accompanying their retinue. In Rome, the *CRP* Heliocrates confiscated property from all those who had held any office under Stilicho and placed it in the treasury.

The regular soldiers who were inside the cities killed all barbarian women and children they found inside the cities and looted their property. Since this was done simultaneously in all cities, the order must have come from Honorius. This was sheer lunacy. The barbarian soldiers had actually maintained their loyalty to the Emperor by not rebelling and Sarus had even performed a service to the Emperor and his henchmen by killing Stilicho's bodyguards. Not unnaturally, when the 'barbarians' learnt of this, they unanimously assembled together to the number of over 30,000 men and decided to join Alaric (Zos. 5.35.5–6). The decision to kill the families of the barbarians is utterly incomprehensible as a policy move, because the hostages were (and are) valuable only when alive – Alaric and the Visigoths would not make the same mistake when they subsequently captured Galla Placidia. The only explanation to this imbecilic action is that Honorius and his inner circle felt an insane racist hatred towards all things barbarian and against the Goths in particular. The fact that Sarus was able to keep his army loyal to him up to the point when Honorius failed to hire him proves that the families of Sarus' barbarians had not been billeted in the cities. This in turn implies that the butchered families consisted mainly of the old Sarmatian and Alan settlers, which makes it probable that the bulk of Sarus' Goths and Alans were recent arrivals from the year 405/6.

Stilicho the Ambititious Vandal, 395–408

There is no doubt that Stilicho was a capable military commander. Most importantly, Stilicho was also an uncorruptible disciplinarian and it was thanks to this that the Roman army remained a formidable fighting force as long as he was in charge. He was also a man who managed to perform a fine balancing act when dealing with the various barbarian forces both inside and outside the Empire – this is not surprising in light of the fact that he was of Vandal origins and therefore in a position to know how to think like a barbarian and how to handle the barbarians.

When the barbarians posed a threat, Stilicho always managed to defeat the barbarian enemies piecemeal and/or divide the number of potential invaders so that he was able to play one group of barbarians against the other group of barbarians. As a result of these successes, Stilicho was able to recruit large numbers of first-class barbarian cavalry into the Roman army. There is no doubt that if he would have been able to retain his hold on power that he would have been able to maintain the cohesion of the West Roman armed forces so that none of the barbarian regulars or Federates would have deserted, as happened in 408 as a result of the racist actions of Honorius' government.

Stilicho's greatest folly was to attempt to conquer East Rome in order that he could become the Father of both emperors. One may also suspect that he may indeed have had imperial aspirations for his son as claimed almost unanimously by all ancient sources. It was this and his friendly relations with the barbarians that made him suspect to the natives – especially to the members of the senatorial class – and to the emperors and which led to his downfall. We do not know what the result of Stilicho's march to Constantinople in 408 would have been in a situation in which the two halves were at peace and when Honorius' government was threatened by Constantine III, but it would still appear probable that if Stilicho had retained his hold on power then Honorius' government would have been better off. The barbarians in Italy would not have revolted and Alaric could have been used against the usurper. However, it is very uncertain what the situation would have been in the East if Stilicho had managed to obtain the guardianship of Theodosius II. Would this have resulted in a war with Persia? Who knows. Regardless, it was irresponsible of Stilicho to attempt to make a coup in the East just for personal reasons when the West was threatened by another usurper. It is quite clear that Stilicho's personal ambitions were the principal motivator behind his own actions.

Chapter Nine

Honorius in Power:
The West Roman Collapse in 408–410

Alaric Enters the Stage

Alaric, however, still maintained his loyalty to the Empire because of his previous agreement with Stilicho. Instead of declaring a well-justified war against Honorius, Alaric sent ambassadors who stated that he would maintain the peace and take his army back to Pannonia in return for a small sum of money (which was needed for the upkeep of the soldiers). He also suggested the exchange of hostages (Gaudentius' son Aetius and Jovius' son Jason in exchange for Gothic nobles) to ensure mutual goodwill. Aetius had served as hostage during the years 405–408, but had in the meanwhile been released. The idiotic Honorius refused. As noted by Zosimus (5.36), Honorius should have either paid the small sum in return for peace or assembled his *'stratiôtôn tagmata'* (legions of soldiers) for war. He did neither. Zosimus quite rightly points out that Honorius should have appointed Sarus as *MVM* (*stratêgon tou polemou pantos*) – Zosimus 5.36.2–37.1, 1814 unknown translator p.161ff. with underlining and a comment added.

When Alaric demanded peace on those conditions, the emperor refused to grant it, although if he would have disposed of his affairs with prudence, he should have chosen one of the two alternatives... He ought either to have deferred the war, and to have obtained a peace by a small sum; or if he preferred to fight, he should have collected together as many legions as possible, and have posted them in the route of the enemy... He should likewise have appointed commander and Magister for the campaign Sarus who alone was sufficient to strike terror into the enemy because of his bravery and military experience, and who had also under him a force of Barbarians sufficient to make a good defence. [*Note that this implies that Sarus probably had more than 30,000 horsemen, possibly as much as 50,000 horsemen, because it is clear that he had to have a large army to offer good resistance against Alaric who had 30,000 foederati and his own Gothic army.*] The emperor, however, neither accepted the offers of peace, nor made Sarus his friend, and nor collected the Roman army, but placed all his hopes on Olympius, and thereby became the cause of horrible catastrophes for the state; for the command was bestowed on such persons who aroused contempt in the enemy. Turpilio was appointed Magister Equitum, Varanes as Magister Peditum and Vigilantius as Comes Domesticorum Equitum. It was because of these and other similar appointments that all persons were in despair, and they thought that the complete destruction of Italy was before their eyes. Alaric ridiculed the preparations made by Honorius and began his expedition against Rome.

The above quote from Zosimus summarizes aptly the idiotic policy of Honorius and Olympius. They were not ready to buy the services of either Alaric or Sarus. Both were considered detestable barbarians. <u>This was the key decision that led to the downfall of the West Rome!</u> Had Honorius decided to pay Alaric and use his services against Constantine III in Gaul and then against the Alans, Vandals, and Suevi none of the catastrophes that happened later would have occurred. The best evidence for this is that the Visigothic army, which consisted of Alaric's Goths and of the over 30,000 barbarians plus the army of Sarus, was easily able to crush first the usurpers Iovinus and Sebastianus under Athaulf and then later the Alans and Vandals in Spain, when led by their new king.

The new commanders nominated by Honorius and Olympius to the highest military posts were incompetent by any standards and especially so in comparison with the previous set of officers, but their job cannot have been made any easier by the fact that Honorius had removed from them almost all of the cavalry forces posted in Italy thanks to the order to kill the barbarian families and by not employing Sarus. Regardless, some of the Alan, Sarmatian and Alamannic Federates in the north of Italy presumably stayed loyal because we later find an Alan king operating in the area. Their only recommendation to the posts appears to have been their loyalty to Olympius. The fact that the new *magistri* lacked adequate cavalry forces made it difficult or next to impossible for them to conduct an active campaign of harassment. They could of course have done that with infantry forces by conducting fighting marches between major supply bases and along the coastlines using their fleets in a supporting role, but this would actually have required some sort of elementary understanding of the military situation from the *magistri*, which neither apparently possessed.

Of note is the fact that the Persian Varanes, just like Olympius, had come from the Eastern half of the Roman Empire. Since Varanes went on to hold the post of *MVM Praesentales* in the East in 409 and then held the consulship for the year 410, it is quite possible that the overthrow of Stilicho had been an undercover operation performed by secret agents sent from the East. It should be noted that the reins of power in the East were at the time held not only by the *PPO* Anthemius but also by Antiochus the Persian and that Varanes was also Persian by birth. The death of Stilicho ensured that the Persians would continue to hold on to the supreme positions in the East, which also ensured peace with Persia. The reason why such a plot could be accomplished is the fact that Honorius was intensely hostile towards the Goths and most importantly it is clear that he yearned to assume full imperial powers and it was possible to accomplish this only by killing Stilicho and all of his supporters in one blow. Since the assassination of the whole top brass at Ticinum was performed so effectively, it is possible that the Easterners could even have sent an assassination squad to perform this. Obviously, there is no concrete evidence for any of this – this is my own educated speculation based solely on the eastern origin of the principal actors and on the effectiveness of the coup.

Alaric began his military operations against Honorius by sending a request for help to his wife's brother Athaulf (Ataulfus, Ataulphus, Atavulfus, Atiulfus, Ataulf, Athaulfus) who commanded a sizable army of Huns and Goths in Upper Pannonia. This force must have been a federate force in Roman service just like the one under Alaric himself. Alaric advanced through Aquileia, Concordia, and Altinum to Cremona. Alaric presumably started his invasion in about mid-September 408. The route would also have passed through Verona (PLRE 2 Alaricus 1). We do not know whether Aquileia possessed any federate troops, but there were Sarmatian settlements at least near Concordia at Opitergium and near Altinum at Patavium, and at Verona and Cremona and all around the city of Cremona. In addition to this, there were some other settlements of Alans close by. Alaric's itinerary proves that his first order of importance was to protect the barbarian federates who had called him into Italy. It is these forces from Concordia up to the neighbourhood of Cremona that presumably consisted of more than 30,000 barbarians, the core of which must have consisted of the Sarmatian settlers (see the accompanying map drawn after Bachrach). The treatment shown by Honorius and his administration under Olympius towards these Sarmatian settlers who had now lived in their respective settlements for almost 80 years and who had always been loyal Roman subjects and soldiers is despicable and incomprehensible. Instead of loyal subjects and soldiers, they had created an enemy army within Italy that was more than eager to join Alaric – and, as noted above, Alaric could also have been an ally rather than an enemy. Honorius and Olympius forced him to become one. The desertion of the Sarmatian and Alan settlers

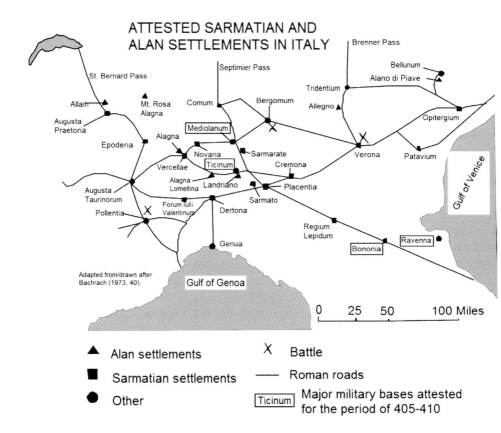

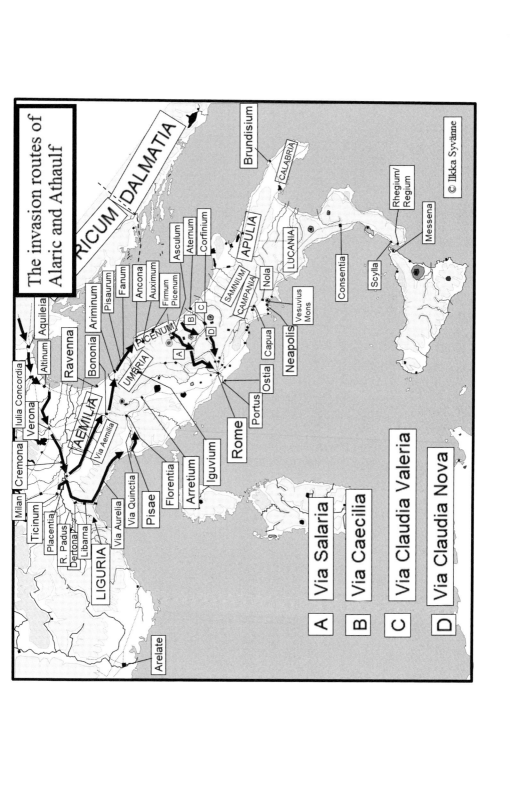

The invasion routes of Alaric and Athaulf

A Via Salaria
B Via Caecilia
C Via Claudia Valeria
D Via Claudia Nova

© Ilkka Syvänne

of Italy to Alaric does not mean that all of them deserted, but so many of them did that the Roman defences in the north of Italy were compromised. The fact that the north of Italy still has place names indicating the places where the Alans and Sarmatians were settled as well as the fact that we find Alans operating in these areas later proves that those Sarmatians and Alans who had become completely assimilated decided to stay behind despite what Honorius did.

After having collected the federate reinforcements, Alaric advanced to the military assembly point of Bononia, which was called Oecubaria (Zos. 5.37.2). This was where Sarus' forces were posted. Zosimus does not state what happened, but it is clear that Sarus now lost control of his army so that he was left with only the 200–300 personal followers (his *bucellarii*) mentioned later by the sources (Zos. 6.13.2; Soz 9.9.3; Olymp. fr.6.10ff.). The rest joined Alaric. This means that Alaric's forces had been reinforced now by more than 60,000–80,000 horsemen, so that he had a minimum of 110,000–120,000 horsemen in his army and may even have had more (especially when one adds the squires to the figure). After having reinforced his army with the *foederati* of Bononia, Alaric decided to bypass Ravenna. Honorius had by then taken refuge in the city, as he had previously been advised to do by his sister Serena. Alaric sacked Ariminum and the rest of the cities of the province of Flaminia. Then Alaric advanced to the Province of Picenum and from there to Rome[1] destroying all the cities and forts en route. This unfortunately leaves open which of the roads leading from Picenum to Rome Alaric used (see the map).

Alaric's goal was clearly not to capture Honorius in Ravenna, but to force him to grant Alaric and his forces the official status that had previously been agreed upon and probably also to save the lives of Stilicho's son and wife. It should not be forgotten that Stilicho's son was actually a member of the imperial family and was consequently eligible to become Emperor and could therefore be used either as a puppet Emperor like Attalus later and/or to put pressure on Honorius. Therefore it is unsurprising that Honorius had given the order to kill Eucherius. According to Zosimus (5.36.2ff.), Alaric would have saved Eucherius had the eunuchs Arsacius and Terentius not managed to take Eucherius back to Rome, where he was killed as ordered by Honorius. This actually implies that Honorius had managed to place his trusted henchmen into the inner circle of Eucherius, who then directed his movements according to the needs of the moment. After the eunuchs had accomplished their first task of importance, they returned Thermantia to her mother and travelled back to Ravenna. According to Zosimus, the eunuchs decided to sail to Gaul (clearly a mistake, either by Zosimus or by a copyist), since the most direct route was now blocked by Alaric's army, but ended up in Genua (clearly the intended destination) from which they travelled to Ravenna. The Emperor rewarded the eunuchs amply. Terentius was appointed *Praepositus Sacri Cubiculi* and Arsacius his adjutant *Primicerius Sacri Cubiculi*. In addition to this, Honorius removed the *Comes Africae* Bathanarius from office and replaced him with Heraclianus, the murderer of Stilicho, because Bathanarius was the husband of Stilicho's sister.

Of particular importance is once again to note the eastern connection with the persons performing the actual dirty work on behalf of Honorius. As the name implies, the eunuch Arsacius had clearly come from the East. It is also probable that as eunuch Terentius was similarly an Easterner and it is therefore not surprising that Terentius was exiled to the East after his patron Olympius fell in 409. Heraclianus, who usurped power and then failed in 413, also attempted to seek asylum in the East, but was killed before he was able to accomplish this. As noted above, the circumstantial evidence (the origin of the plotters) points to the possibility that the eastern government was an active participant in the downfall of Stilicho in favour of Honorius.

Strangely enough, some pieces of legislation resulting from the death of Stilicho are only recorded for the months of October and December: Stilicho's property was confiscated and he was declared a public enemy (25 Oct. 408 CTh 9.42.21); and the blockade Stilicho had initiated against the Eastern government was stopped (10 Dec. 408 CTh 7.16.1). This must have resulted from some oversight by the authorities or from mistakes done by some later copyists. For example, it is strange that Honorius would have been promised 40,000 soldiers to assist him against Constantine III while Stilicho's blockade prevented this, unless of course Stilicho had maintained the blockade to put pressure on the Eastern government or had reinstated the blockade against the caretaker government of Theodosius II after it had failed to deliver the reinforcements. In light of the events, the latter is in fact the likeliest alternative, because why else would Stilicho have wanted to travel to Constantinople in person except to make certain that his wishes would be followed. However, if my above-mentioned line of reasoning is correct, then the Easterners struck first. As regards the confiscation of Stilicho's property and his condemnation, I would suggest that these happened immediately, but were only recorded later in the lawbooks when someone noted the absence.

In the meantime, Constantine III had exploited the opportunity provided by Alaric's invasion of Italy. He sent his son Constans, who had already been elevated as *Caesar*, with Gerontius and the bulk of his forces to reoccupy Spain. Constantine clearly gave precedence to the crushing of Honorius' relatives in Spain in comparison with the barbarian invasion of Gaul. It actually seems probable that the barbarian invasion of Gaul was contained to the north of Gaul until their alliance with Gerontius allowed them to advance to the south of Gaul (see later). As regards what happened next in Spain, there is discrepancy in our two main sources Orosius and Zosimus.

According to Orosius, the brothers Verenianus and Didymus assembled their slaves and dependants from their estates and blocked the passes of the Pyrenees, where Constans' forces, which included the *Honoriaci* (formerly Federates, but now part of the regular army), overpowered them. The *Honoriaci* were then rewarded by giving them permission to pillage the plains of Pallantia.

According to Zosimus, Constans and Gerontius crossed into Spain, where Constans appointed Apollinaris as *PP*, someone unknown as *Mag. Off.* (there is a lacuna in the text) and various other magistrates and military officers. In truth, most of the officials and officers would have been appointed in advance of the campaign. It is usually thought (e.g. in PLRE2) that Apollinaris was appointed as *PP* of Gaul, but the circumstances clearly prove that Constans obtained a personal court with its own officials and officers that were meant for the reconquest of Spain, and the position was therefore not necessarily that of *PP* of Gaul but the Caesar's *PP*, even if it is certain that the resources of Gaul were used in the reconquest of Spain. After this, the brothers attacked Constans with their Lusitanian troops, but were defeated. This implies that the passes were either not defended or very lightly defended, and that the brothers engaged Constans in pitched battle only after he had already entered Spain. After their defeat the brothers withdrew to

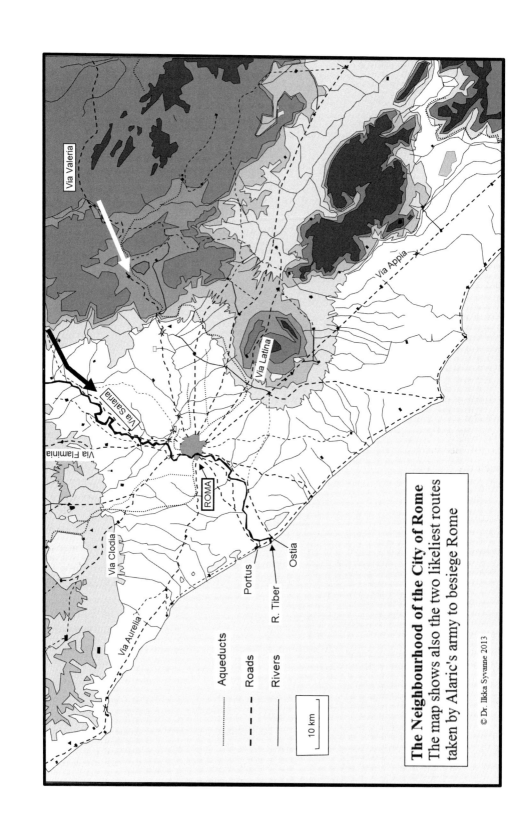

The Neighbourhood of the City of Rome
The map shows also the two likeliest routes taken by Alaric's army to besiege Rome

Via Valeria

Via Flaminia

Via Salaria

Via Latina

Via Appia

Via Clodia

Via Aurelia

ROMA

Portus

Ostia

R. Tiber

Aqueducts

Roads

Rivers

10 km

© Dr. Ilkka Syvänne 2013

their estates, where they raised a new army consisting of their own slaves, dependents and free farmers. Constans' army defeated these with equal ease and captured the brothers with their families. However, their brothers Theodosius and Lagodius managed to flee to Italy and the East respectively.

In my opinion, Zosimus' more detailed version is to be preferred in this case even if Orosius does retain details that are missing from Zosimus. The operation to crush the revolt lasted until very early 409, when Constans together with the captured brothers Verenianus and Didymus returned to Gaul where the brothers were immediately executed – to the detriment of Constantine's cause as we shall see. By then Constantine's situation was critical, because it seemed as if Alaric would become Honorius' ally.

When Alaric's forces reached the neighbourhood of Rome in the fall of 408 and began to lay siege, the Senate started to suspect that Serena had invited the Goths. Zosimus claims that Serena was innocent, which, if true, would still not mean that Serena would not have been quite eager to be rescued by Alaric. Consequently, the Senate which was also urged on by Galla Placidia, the Emperor's half-sister and Eucherius' husband, had Serena executed in the hopes that Alaric would then abandon the siege. This was foolish. If anything this only urged Alaric to further efforts. Alaric encircled the city, and posted blocking forces opposite each of the gates. Most importantly, Alaric took control of the River Tiber and thereby prevented supplies from reaching the city. Alaric also seems to have managed to capture the corn supplies, together with the bulk of the ships sent from North Africa to Portus, the port city of Rome.

The fact that Alaric was able to encircle the whole city proves that his army was truly huge. Note, for example, how Galerius had possessed too few troops to encircle the city in 307 (see Vol. 1). By assigning more than 30,000 horsemen to each side of the city, the total force would have consisted of 120,000 horsemen. Notably, Procopius in his *History of the Wars* claims that the Ostrogoths besieged Rome with 150,000 men (see the map).

The timing of the blockade was most fortunate for Alaric because the grain supplies from North Africa for the winter of 408/409 had not yet reached the city of Rome. Despite knowing this, the Romans did not surrender because they hoped that a relief army from Ravenna would arrive any day. In this context it should be noted that the pagan or pro-pagan *PVR* Gabinius Barbarus Pompeianus who was in charge of the Roman grain supply and its paramilitary forces failed to perform his duty even adequately. His first duty would have been to ensure adequate supply of food for a siege and if that was impossible then at least to make certain that any surplus population would have been removed from the city and that all available supplies from outside the city would have either been brought inside or burned so that Alaric would not be able to besiege the city. He should also have sent an order along the coast to the corn ships not to bring their supplies to the ports of Portus and Ostia. He did none of these measures. The Romans were being led to their destruction like sacrificial lambs by a pagan incompetent who only sought to counter the threat with pagan sacrifices. When this same Pompeianus then tried to satisfy the demands of Alaric (see later), he attempted to confiscate the property of the Christian Melania (engaged in charitable works) because he did not want to touch the property of the pagans (see Matthews p.290 after *Vita S. Melanie* 19). The end result was a riot in which the hungry mob killed the incompetent prefect.

When the hopes of the Romans were dashed and no relief army arrived, they at first halved their daily food ration, which was then cut down to a third, but eventually the Romans ran out of food altogether and plague, the companion of famine, arrived. The corpses could not be buried and those parts of the city where these were collected became uninhabited. Notably, the members of the upper classes did not suffer from hunger, because Zosimus (5.39.4) notes that Laeta, the widow of Gratian, and her mother Tisamena showed their compassion by sharing their food with many people. In other words, only those Romans suffered from hunger that were reliant on governmental food supplies or were not given food by those who had food. When the situation was so bad that the people were on the brink of resorting to cannibalism, the Senate sent an embassy to negotiate with Alaric. They attempted to improve their terms by claiming that the desperate people who were in arms were quite ready to die fighting if the terms were not agreeable. This was obviously a sign of desperation, but fortunately for the Romans Alaric had no intention of destroying the city of Rome because his objective was to obtain official Roman recognition and salaries for his troops. The chosen ambassadors were the governor Basilius and *Primicerius Notarium* Ioannes (Johannes). The latter was a friend of Alaric (and as *Primicerius Notarium* he can also be considered to have been a spy) and the senators hoped that he would be able to influence Alaric if he was indeed in charge of the army. According to Zosimus, the Romans were unaware of who was in command because an earlier rumour had claimed that the besieging army was commanded by one of Stilicho's friends. This proves that the counter-intelligence operations among the federate army were very effective, which is not surprising considering the fact that the Federates had previously been so treacherously treated.

According to Zosimus 5.40.3ff. (1814 unknown translator p.165ff. with comments added inside parentheses):

When the ambassadors came to him, they were ashamed of the ignorance in which the Romans had so long remained [*as they should have because this proves that the Roman intelligence operations were in a complete mess*], but delivered the message of the senate. When Alaric heard that the people were trained and ready to fight, he remarked, 'The thicker grass is more easy to mow than the thinner'. Having said this, he laughed immoderately at the ambassadors. But when they spoke of peace, he used such extreme and arrogant expressions that were excessive even for a haughty barbarian. [*A racist comment typical for the Roman upper classes.*] He declared that he would not abandon the siege on any condition but that of receiving all the gold and silver in the city, all the household goods, and the Barbarian slaves. One of the ambassadors asked that if he would take all these, what will he leave for the citizens? He replied: 'Their lives'. When the ambassadors received this answer, they desired time to communicate it to the citizens and to consult them in what manner they should act… [*In the meanwhile*] Pompeianus, the prefect of the city, accidentally met with some persons who had come to Rome from Tuscany, who related that a town called Narnia had been delivered from danger by prayers to the gods in the ancient mode of worship. Having discoursed with these men, he performed all that was in his power according to the chief priests. Recollecting, however, the opinions that were then prevalent, he resolved to proceed with greater caution, and proposed the whole affair to the bishop of the city, whose name was Innocentius. Preferring the preservation of the city to his own private opinion, he gave them permission to do privately whatever they knew to be convenient. [*Considering the source this is suspect, but not impossible.*] They declared, however, that what they were able to do would be of no utility unless the public and customary sacrifices were performed, and unless the senate ascended to the capitol, performing there, and in the different markets of the city, all that was essential. But no person daring to join in the ancient religious ordinances, they dismissed the men who had come from Tuscany and applied themselves to the endeavouring to appease the Barbarians in the best possible manner.

The Senate sent the ambassadors back and after many discussions the parties agreed that the Romans should pay 5,000 lbs of gold, 30,000 lbs of silver, 4,000 silk tunics, 3,000 scarlet skins and 3000 lbs of pepper. In addition to this, Alaric had demanded that the senators would speak on his behalf to the Emperor in order to obtain the Emperor's blessing for the treaty, which also included an alliance between Rome and Alaric.

Alaric's demands were quite reasonable in light of the fact that Alaric's army now consisted of his own men (previously promised 4,000 lbs of gold), in addition to which came more than 30,000 *foederati*, plus the forces formerly commanded by Sarus. When one compares these sums with the senatorial earnings of this period given by Olympiodorus (fr. 41.2), it becomes even clearer that the Romans were imbeciles when they did not pay Alaric the sums of money that he had demanded in return for military service on behalf of the Roman Empire. According to Olympiodorus, there were many Roman households (presumably senatorial '*oikoi*') that had yearly income of 4,000 lbs of gold, in addition to which they obtained grain, wine and other produce which had a market value of 1,320 lbs of gold for a grand total yearly income of 5,320 lbs of gold. The yearly income of the households at Rome belonging to the second class (presumably poorer senators) consisted of 1,000–1,500 lbs of gold. Upon assuming the position of praetor, the poorer and middle class members of this upper class could spend 1,200 up 2,000 lbs of gold while the wealthiest could spend up 4,000 lbs of gold during the associated festivities lasting for seven days. It is probable that Olympiodorus has included this piece of information for the purpose of criticising the stinginess of the upper class when their country needed their money. It is easy to see that even a single household could have paid the entire sum of money demanded by Alaric.

The senators were forced to pay the ransom out of their own pockets according to the census because the city of Rome at the time did not possess any public treasury. According to Zosimus, Palladius, who was put in charge of collecting the ransom, failed to collect the whole payment either because the rich had hidden part of their property or because the emperor's greed had reduced the nobles to poverty. The former was obviously the real cause because even a single rich senatorial family could have paid those from their yearly income. Furthermore, there was enough gold left to be pillaged in 410 and 411, which makes it almost certain that Palladius had been bribed. In order to make up for the difference, Palladius stripped the gold and silver decorations from some of the statues and melted some made out of gold and silver (suitably including the statue of Bravery/ Virtus, as noted by Zosimus).

After the ransom had been collected, with the approval of Alaric the Senate sent an embassy to obtain the Emperor's confirmation for the peace negotiated between the Senate and Alaric. In return for the peace and alliance, Alaric demanded not only the payment, but also some aristocratic children as hostages. Alaric's demands were clearly quite reasonable. He did not even seek revenge for the wrongs committed by the Romans against the families of his followers or against him and his followers. He just wanted a return to the state of affairs under Stilicho. Honorius agreed to peace and the ransom (or rather the salary overdue) was paid to the barbarians. After this, Alaric provided a market for the citizens for three days, granted the right of safe exit through certain gates, and allowed food to be brought from the harbour to the city. Notably, the citizens still had enough money and property to pay for the food. The barbarians then withdrew to Tuscany. The likeliest reason for the withdrawal of Alaric to Tuscany is that there were not enough supplies left to feed both his army and the city of Rome. It is also possible that Alaric expected Athaulf to bring his army along the Via Aurelia to join Alaric because this route was still unpillaged. According to Zosimus, the slaves fled from the city daily to join the barbarians, who now supposedly numbered 40,000. This has been taken as evidence that Alaric had only 40,000 followers, but this is a mistake that doesn't take into account the rest of the evidence. I do not reiterate my earlier analysis, but only note that prior to noting the fleeing of the slaves to join the barbarians, Zosimus stated that Alaric had withdrawn to somewhere in Tuscany (means the unpillaged Province of Tuscia and Umbria north of Rome, which also included Etruria), which means that the barbarians close to the city of Rome were not the main force, but some sort of guarding force left to ensure that the Romans kept their part of the bargain – which included the release of the slaves. The 40,000 must have consisted of the freed slaves and of this guarding force.[2] Some of the freed slaves attacked the Romans who were on their way to the harbour to bring up supplies. When Alaric learnt of it, he immediately put a stop to this breach of agreement. The notable point in this is the very high level of discipline among Alaric's forces. Despite all of their sufferings at the hands of the treacherous Romans, they did not pillage or break the treaty after it had been signed, and they punished the freed slaves who wanted to exact revenge.

After this, peace prevailed until the turn of the year 409. It was then that Constantine III sent some eunuchs as ambassadors to Honorius to suggest that in return for recognition and pardon, he would send an army to assist Honorius against Alaric. Constantine's goal was to prevent an alliance between Alaric and Honorius. Probably thanks to his irrational hatred of Alaric, Honorius foolishly agreed on condition that his relatives Didymus and Verenianus were returned to him, and he sent the imperial robes for Constantine III as a sign that he recognized Constantine III as Emperor. Unfortunately for Constantine, Honorius' relatives had already been killed before he had sent his embassy. The help promised by Constantine caused Honorius and Olympius to back down from the previously agreed treaty with Alaric. Not even the pleadings of Pope Innocentius I could turn Honorius' head. When Honorius had not confirmed the treaty officially by January 409, had failed to send the promised hostages, and had failed to fulfil the other terms of the agreement, the exasperated Senate sent another embassy consisting of Caecilianus (a senator and former *vicarius*), Attalus (a senator, former governor, and future puppet-Emperor of Alaric) and Maximianus (a senator) to Honorius. Zosimus claims that the embassy achieved nothing thanks to Olympius' machinations, after which it was sent back to Rome. Unfortunately for the Roman Empire, Olympius and Honorius were also still preoccupied with the hunt of Stilicho's supporters, both real and imaginary. It was probably thanks to this that Honorius had sacked Theodorus from the office of *PPI* and appointed Caecilianus as his successor by 21 January 409 (PLRE1), or alternatively because Honorius wanted to remove Olympius' supporters from office one by one (see below). The appointment of Caecilianus as *PPI* was obviously also meant as a bribe. Attalus was nominated as *CSL*. In the meantime, Olympius handed two brothers, Marcellianus and Salonius – both members of the *Schola* of *Notarii* – to the new *PPI* for interrogation on the basis of a false charge. Both were put on trial and tortured to implicate supporters of Stilicho, but with no result.

As regards the embassy of the Roman Senate to Honorius, its returning members were accompanied by five elite *tagmata* that had already been called from Dalmatia to protect the city of Rome. Their commander was the *comes* Valens. Zosimus' (5.45.1) '*ta de tagmata tauta eplêroun andres hexakischilioi*' is usually translated as 'these regiments comprised six thousand men in all', or similar.[3] There is a slight possibility that the literal translation of this sentence ('these *tagmata* comprised/contained six thousand men') should be emended with the word 'each' with the sense that each of the *tagmata* was made up of 6,000 men in all so that there were altogether 30,000 men in the '*pente stratiôtika tagmata*'. The figure of 6,000 men seems a very small figure for the defensive needs of the city, but if true (and it may quite well be) would still be representative of the typical depleted unit-sizes of the Late Roman Empire, and reminds the historian of the inherent difficulties in the interpretation of the sources – *tagma*, just like *arithmos*, can mean many different-sized units. Furthermore, we should remember that the core part of Belisarius' army was not much larger when he defended the city of Rome successfully against the Goths in the sixth century. Furthermore, the smallness of the army may have been intended to fool Alaric into the belief that there was nothing afoot. Unfortunately, one cannot make any absolute judgment in this case – however, see also below.

According to Zosimus (5.45.2), Valens was a bold man who did not think it necessary to use a route that was not guarded by the enemy, with the result that Alaric was able to assemble his whole army against him. The fact that Zosimus states that Alaric needed to assemble his whole army against Valens' army suggests that we need to amend the above-mentioned sentence with the word 'each' as suggested above, so that Valens' army comprised 30,000 men in all, but if we accept the literal sense of the sentence then we will have to interpret Zosimus' referral to the use of the whole army of Alaric as an exaggeration (a detachment of c. 30,000 men would have been more than enough to kill 6,000 men), or that Alaric performed a 'maximum overkill' by using about 120,000 men to kill a mere 6,000. He would not even have been able to deploy this massive force simultaneously against the Romans but would have been forced to rotate his men. Even though one cannot be entirely sure, the circumstantial evidence does strongly suggest that we should amend Valens' army to encompass 30,000 men. I would also suggest that Valens' plan was to march the army through Alaric's lines openly so as not to cause any suspicions that the Romans were up to something. After all, the truce between Alaric and Honorius had not yet been officially broken, even if Honorius had failed to fulfil its clauses. Alaric, however, was no fool. Consequently, when Valens's force reached the

Gothic lines, Alaric annihilated the Roman relief force so that only 100 men, including Valens and Attalus, managed to reach the safety of the city of Rome. These men were undoubtedly let through purposefully so that the Roman Senate would hear the bad news: Honorius had broken the treaty and the relief army had been annihilated. Zosimus does not hide the fact that it was actually Honorius who had broken the peace and not the barbarian Alaric.

On his arrival, Attalus sacked the *CRP* Heliocrates because he had not performed his task of confiscating the properties of Stilicho's supporters with due harshness. Heliocrates was able to save his life only by seeking asylum in a church. The Emperor and Olympius were clearly too preoccupied with the task of hunting down the former supporters of Stilicho and their efforts to fill up the treasury with this excuse, and all this took place at a time when they should have had more pressing things on their minds. Their policies can partially be excused on the grounds that they probably feared that Stilicho's former friends would side with Alaric, and also because they urgently needed money to pay the soldiers. Honorius and Olympius needed cash and lots of it. They had lost possession of Britain, Gaul and Spain to Constantine. Dalmatia, Pannonia, Noricum and Raetia had been pillaged and were not securely held by Roman forces. Significant portions of northern Italy had been pillaged in 400–402, 405–406 and now in 408–409, on top of which Alaric controlled Rome and the Province of Tuscia and Umbria, plus the Province of Campania. The only secure sources of income left to tap in full were North Africa, Sicily and the senatorial estates of south Italy. The new *Comes Africae* Heraclianus did send much-needed financial aid to Honorius (Zos. 6.10.2), but this seems to have been insufficient to meet the needs – hence the need to obtain additional resources through confiscations.

Alaric's attack against the relief army under Valens officially signalled the end of the truce, with the result that Maximilianus who was outside the city of Rome fell into barbarian hands. His father Marinianus ransomed him with 30,000 gold coins (c. 417 lbs of gold), which once again proves that the senators had previously concealed part of their property.[4] The siege must have been renewed either in late January or February, because it was in February 409 that the *PVR* Pompeianus was killed by an angry mob at a food riot in the Forum (PLRE2). Considering the level of his incompetence that had caused all the sufferings of the people, this is not surprising and may even be considered to have been a well-deserved end.

Since the city of Rome was once again put under a full siege, the senators sent another embassy led by Attalus to meet Honorius at Ravenna. At the same time as this embassy reached Honorius, the Emperor received the news that Athaulf had crossed the Julian Alps. Since it was reported that Athaulf's army was not large, the Emperor ordered all his forces, consisting of both cavalry and infantry billeted in the various cities of Italy, to intercept and destroy the enemy. He also gave 300 Huns to Olympius for the purpose of attacking Athaulf. The Huns surprised Athaulf's Goths in their encampment near the city of Pisae and killed 1,100 Goths while losing only 17 of their own men. However, when the Huns realised that the enemy army was actually much larger than reported, they fled back to Ravenna. Athaulf had clearly marched his army through a number of military outposts to reach the city of Pisae on the west coast, which suggests that the garrisons en route had been too small to oppose even his 'puny' army. My educated guess is that it was about 10,000 strong. Athaulf's intention was clearly to march along the Via Aurelia to Rome, because the western coastline of Italy was still unpillaged and therefore could support an army passing through it. Furthermore, by using this road it was possible to avoid the main Roman army posted at Ravenna.

The eunuchs were able to present the flight of the Huns as a defeat, which reinforced their accusation that the policies of Olympius had caused all the disasters the Romans were facing. Honorius was more than eager to accept this vilification because it offered him the opportunity to lay the blame of the policy failures squarely on Olympius. In fact, I would go so far as to suggest that it was actually Honorius himself who sought to absolve himself of the blame by claiming that Olympius was solely responsible for the failed policies. The fact that Honorius yearned to rule himself was not unimportant either. In order to oust Olympius and his Eastern henchmen Honorius allied himself with two other court factions, the supporters of appeasement with Alaric (Iovius, the new *PPI*: see below) and the supporters of appeasement with Constantine III (Allobichus, the *Com.Dom.Eq.*). Iovius had befriended Alaric when he was *PPIL* in 407. We do not know how Allobichus had established his contacts with Constantine, but it is probable that he was a Frank and therefore had friends and relatives serving under Constantine (see later). Olympius fled to Dalmatia. After this, Honorius started to plot the removal of Olympius' creatures from office. He could not make his move immediately because he needed to gain control of the army under the *praesental magistri*.

Honorius's first move was to appoint the pagan Generidus as *strategos* of Dalmatia, Upper Pannonia, Noricum, Raetia and all the provinces up to the Alps. This was clearly a special command, the likeliest purpose of which was to remove the troops posted in those provinces from the control of the praesental *magistri*. We do not know Generidus's title – both *magister* and *comes* are plausible, even if the former is likelier. Generidus had previously been forced to resign his military office in Rome (clearly a special command to defend the city of Rome, possibly *Comes Italiae*: see PLRE2) when Honorius had forbidden pagans from holding any military and civilian offices. He must have accompanied the embassy to Ravenna. Generidus boldly stated that he would not accept his new appointment unless Honorius repealed this law against the pagans. Honorius conceded and obtained in return a first class officer. According to Zosimus, Generidus was an old school disciplinarian who reasserted discipline into the army. Most importantly, despite the obvious pagan bias of Zosimus,[5] he also appears to have been incorruptible, as a result of which he was able to distribute the military rations to the soldiers in full, which enabled him to maintain discipline, which in turn improved the fighting spirit up to the point where he was able to regain full control of the provinces from the barbarians. The defeat suffered by the Hun Primate Uldin in Thrace in 408–409 undoubtedly contributed to the success achieved by Generidus. He need no longer send any assistance to the Huns and other Federates of Pannonia (see Chapter 12: East 408–423).

Honorius appears to have started to plot the downfall of the Eastern faction very soon after the execution of Stilicho. The fact that the Eastern *Mag.Ped.* Varanes was replaced by the *Com. Dom. Eq.* Vigilantius in either late-408 or very-early 409 (Varanes was the Eastern *MVM Praes.* in 409 and consul in 410) so that Allobichus was appointed to Vigilantius' previous post strongly suggests the probability that Honorius started to make changes in the offices very early on in order to assert his own power against his

Eastern helpers. The fact that Vigilantius was removed from the immediate vicinity of the Emperor through promotion made it possible for Honorius to use Allobichus more freely against the Eastern faction. The *Com. Dom. Ped.* Valens appears to have been loyal and therefore there was no need to remove him at the time.

The new *PPI* Iovius and the *Com. Dom. Eq.* Allobichus soon proved very worthy of the trust placed in them.[6] Both men were in charge of intelligence gathering and the implementation of justice. Even if the sources imply that Iovius took the lead in the plotting, it is still clear that the role of the *Com. Dom. Eq.* Allobichus, as commander of Honorius' personal units of bodyguards, in which capacity he also conducted intelligence operations, was undoubtedly instrumental for the overall success of the operation. Unfortunately, we do not know the composition of Honorius' *Domestici* at this time, but we may make the educated guess that it included at least the above-mentioned Huns (as *bucellarii*?) and some other units.

We do not know when Honorius dismissed Caecilianus, but we know that Iovius was in office by 1 April 409 (PLRE2). We do not know whether the downfall of Olympius happened before or after this date, but what is practically certain is that it happened in the spring, just like the downfall of the *magistri*. Honorius' appointees Iovius and Allobichus incited the soldiers to mutiny. The plot was undoubtedly modelled after the one instigated by Olympius in 408. The mutineers occupied the harbour and when Iovius arrived to ask their demands, the soldiers requested the removal of the *magistri* Turpilio and Vigilantius, together with the *PSC* Terentius and *Primicerius Sacri Cubiculi* Arsacius from office. The suitably 'frightened' Honorius assembled either his Consistory or the Senate[7] (considering the time period the latter is probably meant), where it was voted that the *magistri* were to be exiled for perpetuity. When the exiles embarked on ships, they were killed on Iovius' orders. Zosimus claims that Iovius feared that if the exiles one day learned that the mutiny had been incited by him, that the exiles would then demand that the Emperor should punish him. As stated above, I would actually claim that the whole operation was carried out with the prior approval of none other than Honorius himself. Terentius was exiled to the East, and Arsacius to Milan. Honorius appointed Eusebius as new *PSC* while Valens (the former *Com.Dom.Ped.*) was appointed as *Mag.Ped.* and Allobichus as *Mag.Eq.* (Zos. 5.48.1).

The stage was now set for a reconciliation with Alaric. The probable reason for the change of policy was that Honorius must have learnt by March/April 409 that Constantine had killed his Spanish relatives, which made Constantine's help against Alaric unwelcome in Honorius's eyes. Consequently, Iovius sent an embassy to Alaric bearing letters from both Honorius and Iovius with the request that he and Ataulf would come to Ariminum to negotiate. Alaric agreed. He demanded that the Emperor pay him and his followers a fixed sum of money and corn each year, and that his followers be allowed to live in the two Venetias (i.e. the Sarmatian and Alan settlers would be given back their lands), and in the Noricums and Dalmatia (i.e. the Goths would be granted these territories). Iovius wrote down the agreement in the presence of Alaric and sent it together with his own private letters to the Emperor in which he urged the Emperor to confirm the negotiated agreement. Iovius also urged the Emperor to appoint Alaric as *MVM* so that Alaric would be prepared to lower his demands – but all to no avail. Honorius accused Iovius of rashness. He stated that the gold and corn assignments were quite OK, but that he would never appoint Alaric or any of his relatives to any military command or position of honour. Honorius' irrational hatred of Alaric had once again intervened with otherwise sound policy decisions. When Iovius then foolishly ordered this reply to be read aloud in Alaric's tent, Alaric flew into a rage and ordered his army to march to Rome. Was this Iovius' intention all along or was he just that careless?

Iovius returned to Ravenna. In order to absolve himself of the blame of the debacle, Iovius instructed the Emperor and all the officials to swear an oath that they would never make peace with Alaric. After the oath had been taken by all, Honorius summoned 10,000 Huns to assist him. The deal was sealed with the handing of the 18-year-old *tribunus praetorianus* Aetius (the famous *Patricius*) as hostage to the Huns. The Dalmatians were ordered to provide corn, sheep and oxen to feed the allies. The regular army was ordered to assemble against Alaric and scouts were sent to observe Alaric's march on Rome.

It is probable that Olympiodorus's famous embassy (Olymp. fr. 19) to Donatus and the Huns took place at this time. According to Olympiodorus, the sea voyage (undoubtedly from Ravenna to Aquileia) was dangerous – after all, it would have been undertaken in the middle of winter. According to the fragment, Olympiodorus recalled how Donatus was at first deceived by an oath and then killed, with the result that the first of the Hunnic kings, Charaton, was enraged. The envoys, however, managed to calm him down with good excuses and plentiful gifts/bribes. This has caused plenty of speculation, because it is clear that Donatus is a Roman name. In my opinion, the fact that Donatus was Roman and was deceived by an oath to be killed makes it almost certain that Donatus was working for an enemy of Honorius and that at least some members of the embassy consisted of professional assassins sent to kill Donatus. Who was Donatus' employer? Was the employer Constantine III or Gerontius or Alaric or Athaulf or the eastern government?

In the meantime, however, Alaric had repented his decision and sent bishops as ambassadors to Honorius with the message that he was ready to lower his demands. He no longer demanded any office or honour, and was ready to settle his entire force in the Noricums alone. In addition to this, he no longer demanded a yearly payment in gold. The yearly corn rations sufficed as payment. In return for this, he promised to fight against any enemy on behalf of the Emperor. Zosimus notes that everyone marvelled at the moderation of the man. Unfortunately, the men who were in a position to decide did not. Iovius and Honorius claimed that since all had taken an oath never to make peace with Alaric it was impossible to do that. Zosimus's (5.51.2) words summarize the situation well: 'So blind were the minds of those in charge of the state at that time in the absence of the gods' care.'[8] The Roman leadership consisted of imbeciles – if the real reason for the uncompromising position was the oath, it was even more so. Alaric marched his entire army to besiege the eternal city probably in late-spring or early-summer 409.

According to Zosimus, it was then that Constantine III grasped his opportunity and sent another envoy called Iovius to Honorius for the ratification of the peace agreement. He also asked pardon for the murder of Didymus and Verenianus on the grounds that their murder had not been ordered by him. Was Constantine planning to frame Gerontius or was it really true that the murders had been committed without his prior approval? In return for the pardon and agreement, Constantine promised to come to Honorius' assistance with the Gallic, Spanish (the inclusion of the Spanish army in the list proves that the offer was made before the revolt of Gerontius) and British army against Alaric, who was besieging Rome. The timing of the offer could not have been more opportune, and, despite what Zosimus states, may actually have occurred at the same time as Alaric made his last offer to Honorius, which could then have induced Honorius to reject Alaric's peace proposal. It is in fact possible that Alaric had made his last very reasonable offer because he was already aware that Constantine was promising to come to assist Honorius.

It is now time to discuss the events that had taken place in Gaul after 408 in greater detail.

The Great Barbarian Migration of 408

As discussed above, I would suggest on the basis of Orosius (38–40), who is a period author, that the Vandals, Alans, and Suevi invaded Gaul for the second time in 408. He states that the peoples mentioned attacked the Franks across the Rhine two years before the sack of Rome at the instigation of Stilicho, which dates this event securely to the year 408. Similarly, Isidore of Seville in his *Historia de regibus Gothorum, Vandalorum et Suevorum* 71 (probably after Orosius) also states that the crossing of the Rhine by the Alans, Suevi and Vandals took place two years before the sack of Rome at the instigation of Stilicho, but he dates it wrongly to the year 406. This error is understandable, because his likely source (Orosius) states that the invasion took place at the same time as Gratian and Constantine usurped power. The authors have clearly confused or grouped together two different barbarian invasions, both instigated by Stilicho against the British usurpers, namely the one crushed by Constantine III in 407 (Zos. 6.3.2) and the later one in 408. In short, there is no doubt that the Vandals, Alans and Suevi invaded for the second time in 408 at the instigation of Stilicho. It is also easy to see why Stilicho adopted this strategy when Sarus' operation had failed, and it is also easy to see why Stilicho fell from favour.

Jerome's Letter to Ageruchia (*Epistola 123*, esp. 123.16–17) clarifies both the composition of the invasion force as well as the routes taken by the invaders and the extent of the ravages.[9] I date the letter to the year 408 on the basis of the fact that Stilicho was still alive (Jerome critized one half-barbarian for the fact that he had bought a shameful peace from Alaric) and the barbarians had not yet invaded Spain. According to Jerome, the invaders consisted of the Quadi, Vandals, Sarmatians, Alans, Gepids, Heruls, Saxons, Burgundians, Alamanni and Pannonians. It should be noted, however, that in each case some of the tribesmen remained behind. The Pannonians consisted evidently of the Roman forces posted there, which must mean primarily the Vandal Federates (Jord. Get. 115), but may also have included other units such as Alans, Sarmatians, Goths, Huns and possibly even regulars. On the basis of Jerome's list one can make the educated guess that Radagaisus' forces in 405 had probably included contingents drawn from the Quadi, Suevi-Iuthungi, Sarmatians, Alans, Pannonian Vandals (and other local forces) and possibly also from the Hasdingi and Siling Vandal tribes north of the Danube. The case for the eastern Heruls is less certain, but it is possible that a splinter group of those was also accompanying the invaders, even if it is likelier that Jerome meant western Heruls. The reason for this conclusion is that these tribes were all neighbours of each other and therefore likely to march out en masse. Since the leading group among them were the Alans (see Lebedynsky 2012, 20, 49 on the basis of Hydatius), it is clear that the Alans in question migrated with all of their sub-tribes and allies into Pannonia, where they were joined by the local federate Roman forces. The probable reason for the migration of the Alans and their subtribes and allies was the invasion of the Greuthungi/Ostrogoths under Thorismund the Amal against the Gepids on behalf of the Huns at about this time (see above with Lebedynsky 2012, 33). The Alans must have concluded an alliance with Radagaisus, clearly an enemy of the Amals, before the crossing of the Danube.

As discussed above, the invaders of 406 were defeated by Constantine's forces with the result that they were forced to retreat back across the Rhine, where they presumably obtained a place of asylum because the army included the Suevi-Iuthungi.[10] In the course of the year 407 the tribes appear to have obtained reinforcements from the east, which either consisted of the Burgundians (mercenaries or more likely most of the tribe) and/or of the rest of the Siling and Hasdingi Vandals. It is impossible to know whether the entire Vandal nation marched out in 404/5 or whether tribesmen had remained behind that could be called as reinforcements in 407. What is certain is that the invaders probably asked the Burgundians to join them at this time, because Jerome's letter can be dated to the year 408 and the final crossing of the Rhine by the Burgundians occurred only after 410/411 (see later). The Alans, Vandals, Suevi, Gepids and Quadi would have known well the Burgundian leadership, because they had been their neighbours. The negotiations cannot have been too difficult. The Burgundians faced the Huns and Ostrogoths in the East, while an alliance with the the allied tribes of Alamannia now offered them an easy escape and plenty of booty.

As regards the Saxons and western Heruls, it is not known whether they just exploited the confusion and invaded at the same time or whether they too were allied with the invaders. Similarly, we do not know which of the towns and areas in north-west Gaul were sacked and pillaged by the Saxons and Heruls and which by the allied invaders under the Alans. What is certain is that the Saxons and Heruls must have played a significant role in the pillage of those areas and in fact may have contributed to the willingness of the allied invaders to turn south towards Aquitania. It is also clear that the Saxons and other tribes invaded not only north-west Gaul, but also Britain (Zos. 6.5.2–3). If the Saxons and Heruls invaded on their own initiative, it is possible that when the armies came face-to-face that they purposefully avoided fighting each other and may even have agreed to a division of areas to be pillaged. The later accounts suggest that the Saxons conquered at least the territory between Boulogne and Rouen and may have already moved to the territory of Calvados around Bayeux in Normandy and the islands of the Loire.

There are also strong reasons to connect the success of the invasion by the Vandals, Alans and Suevi in 408 with the absence of troops from the Rhine frontier that had been caused by the counter attack of Gerontius and the Frankish *foederati* under Edobichus against the forces of Sarus in late 407, which was then followed up by the reconquest of Spain with the bulk of the usurper's forces in late 408. As noted above, it was Alaric's invasion of Italy that made it impossible for Honorius' army to invade Gaul in the autumn of 408 and spring of 409, which in turn enabled Constantine to reconquer Spain from Honorius' relatives. Constantine in his turn was unable to engage the barbarian invaders from across the Rhine, because the concentration of Honorius' forces at Ticinum forced him to keep part of his army in defensive positions in south-east Gaul. On top of that, after Constantine had dispatched his son to crush Honorius' relatives in Spain (autumn 408), he also lacked adequate numbers to engage the barbarian invaders anywhere.

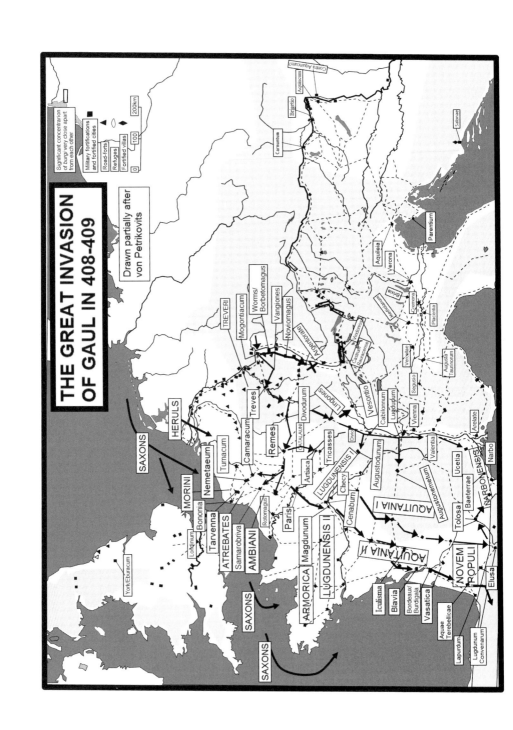

THE GREAT INVASION OF GAUL IN 408-409

Drawn partially after von Petrikovits

Significant concentration of burgi very close apart from each other

■ Military fortifications and fortified cities
◀ Road-forts
◆ Refuges
◆ Fortified villas

0   100   200km

SAXONS
HERULS
SAXONS
SAXONS
SAXONS

MORINI
MERULS
AMBIANI
ATREBATES
ARMORICA
NEMETAEUM
TREVERI
MORINI

York/Eburacum
Londinium
Bononia
Tarvenna
Samarobriva
Rotomagus
Magdunum
Paris
Turnacum
Camaracum
Treves
Remes
Mogontiacum
Worms/Borbetomagus
Vangiones
Noviomagus
Augustonetum
Divodurum
Lingones
Cenabum
Checy
Artiaca
CATALAUNI
Tricasses
Augustodunum
Vesontio
Cabilonum
Lugdunum
Castello
Vidobona
Augustonemetum
Vienna
Segusio
Valentia
Augusta Taurinorum
Vercellae
Arelate
Narbo
Uceta
Baeterrae
Tolosa
Placentia
Cremona
Mediolanum
Brixia
Verona
Aquileia
Parentium
Salonae
Brigetio
Carnuntum
Contra Aquincum?
Aquincum

ARMORICA
AQUITANIA II
AQUITANIA I
LUGDUNENSIS II
LUGDUNENSIS I
NARBONENSIS
NOVEM POPULI

Iculisma
Blavia
Bordeaux/Burdigala
Vasatica
Aquae Terebellicae
Lapurdum
Lugdunum Convenarum
Elusa

The situation was further complicated by the treaty that Alaric and the Roman Senate concluded in late 408. In this situation Constantine had to recall his son from Spain at the earliest opportunity, which came in early 409.

The fact that the Alans were the leading tribe until their almost complete annihilation by the Visigoths in 417 (see later) suggests strongly that the original size of the invading force must have been truly awesome, even if the absence of troops from the Rhine contributed to the success of the invasion. We can arrive at a rough estimate by using the known size of the Vandal contingent in 429. The Vandals and the remnants of the Alans who crossed the Straits of Gibraltar in 429 consisted of 80,000 warriors (or 80 chiliarchies) plus their families, but we have to remember that by then they had suffered a series of defeats. The Visigoths and the Suevi had both inflicted serious defeats on the Vandals/Alans and the fighting trek from the Rhine to the Straits had undoubtedly reduced the numbers too. We should not forget that the invading force included also contingents from other tribes. For example, the Burgundian force that advanced to the Rhine as allies of Rome during the reign of Valentinian I consisted of c. 80,000 warriors and it is certain that the Burgundians would not have left their homelands without defenders on that occasion. In short, the invading force crossing the Rhine over the course of several days must have consisted of a minimum of 200,000 warriors, plus their families on wagons. It is in fact likely that the invading forces encompassed more than 240,000 warriors. Sizable armies were quite necessary for the conquest of the well defended walled cities of Gaul and Spain.

We can reconstruct the rough outline of the invasion routes as well as the extent of the ravages on the basis of the above-mentioned letter of Jerome and on the basis of the references to pillaged places in the lives of Christian saints. According to Jerome, the invaders crossed the Rhine close to the city of Moguntiacum (Mainz, headquarters of the *Dux Mogontiacensis*), which they captured and pillaged evidently in 408. Thousands were killed inside the church where the people had taken refuge. The city of Vangiones fell after a long siege. After this, the invaders sacked the cities of Remes (Durocortum/modern Reims), Attrebatae/Atrebates (an ancient tribe), Morini (an ancient tribe), Turnacum/Tornae (modern Tournai), Nemetae/Nemetaeum (modern Arras, a city located in the territory of the Attrebatae), Argentorate (modern Strasbourg, headquarters of the *Comes Argentoratensis* and the *Dux Germaniae Prima*), Germaniae (the province and ducate of Germania Prima), Aquitania, Novem Populi (province), Lugdunensis (province of Lugdunum/Lyon, modern Lyonnais), and Narbonensis (the province named after Narbo). The later lives of saints and '*chansons de geste*' name the following cities, which are usually considered unreliable, but the information in them does in my opinion fit with the existing period evidence: Angoulême (Iculisma), Arcis-sur-Aube (Artiaca), Autun (Augustodunum), Beziers (Baeterrae), Bazas (Vasatica), Besançon (Vesontio), Cambrai (Camaracum), Checy, Clermond-Ferrand (Augustonemetum), Eauze (Elusa), Langres (Andematunum/Lingones), Laon (Alaudanum), Lyon (Lugdunum), Meung-sur-Loire (Magdunum near Aurelianum/Cenabum), Metz (Divodorum), Paris, Reims (Remes/Remorum/Durocortorum), Troyes (Tricasses, Augustobona), and Uzès (Ucetia).[11]

Gerontius and his Barbarians

The fragments of Renatus Profuturus Frigeridus preserved by Gregory of Tours can be used to shed light on the course of the barbarian invasions and the imperial campaigns.[12]

The following quotations (with some slight changes and additions inside parentheses) are taken from Lewis Thorpe's outstanding translation of Gregory of Tours:

> Meanwhile Goar had gone over to the Romans [*he had deserted to Constantine's side*], and Respendial, the king of the Alans, therefore withdrew his forces from the Rhine. The Vandals were hard-pressed in their war against the Franks, their king Godigisel was killed and about 20,000 of their front-line troops had been slaughtered, so that, if the army of the Alans [*i.e. those under Respendial*] had not come to their rescue in time, the entire nation of Vandals would have been wiped out. (Gregory of Tours 2.9.)

There are three plausible ways to interpret this piece of evidence. Firstly, it is possible that the event took place in the initial stages of the campaign in 408. Secondly, it is possible that it refers to the invasion of 406. Thirdly, it is possible that the event took place only after Constantine III had sent his son and generals against the invaders (see below) so that the Franks in question would have been fighting under Edobichus. I have construed the events according to the first alternative, because the place of the fragment in Gregory's text suggests this. When one interprets the sequence of the invasion on the basis of this, it appears probable that some Roman commander or diplomat serving under Constantine III had managed to stage a coup in the initial stages of the campaign by bribing Goar to change sides, with the result that the invasion almost failed. The Burgundians may also have changed sides at the same time as Goar because both are later found working together under former officers of Constantine (see later). The withdrawal of Respendial from the Rhine suggests a retreat to the east and not to Gaul, which was still held by the Franks and Romans. The Vandals who had already crossed over were almost wiped out by the remaining Frankish federates (the rest of the Frankish federates being with Constantine near Arelate after Sarus' invasion in early 408 and then in Spain under Constans and Edobichus in late 408) had not the Alans under Respendial returned to the Rhine and apparently crossed to the Roman side. The arrival of the Alans then tilted the battle in favour of the invaders who then progressed to pillage Mogontiacum and the neighbouring towns, forts and cities (e.g. Vangiones after a long siege).

After this, Gregory of Tours (2.9 tr. by Thorpe pp.123–124), commentary inside parentheses and underlining added by I.S. describing how Constantine III recalled his son from Spain:

> The tyrant Constantine summoned his son Constans, who was also a tyrant, from Spain [*i.e. most of Constantine's forces were in Spain at the time and Constantine wanted his son to return as fast as possible to face the possible spring offensive by Honorius' forces in 409; Alaric had by then concluded a treaty with the Roman Senate, which only demanded Honorius' stamp of approval and it seemed possible that Alaric would invade Gaul on behalf of Honorius; see Zosimus 6.5.2 with above and below*], so that they might confer together about affairs of state. As a result Constans left his wife and the administrative affairs of his court in Saragossa, entrusted all his interests in Spain to Gerontius and hurried to meet his father by forced marches. They duly met. Quite a few days passed, but no news arrived from Italy to disturb Constantine

[*Constantine's envoys had managed to obtain recognition from Honorius with the promise of help against Alaric; this was a diplomatic coup that broke up the possible alliance between Honorius and Alaric*]. He therefore returned to his daily round of over-drinking [*a typical vice among the Late Roman soldiers and top brass at this time and likely to cause plenty of leadership problems*] and over-eating, and told his son that he might as well go back to Spain [*i.e. the alliance between Honorius and Alaric had not materialized so Constans was free to go to Spain to remove Gerontius from office, while Edobichus would hold the front against the barbarian invaders in the north: see below*]. No sooner had Constans sent his troops on ahead, while he himself lingered a little longer with his father [*it was undoubtedly then that Constans was named Augustus*], than messengers arrived from Spain to say that Gerontius had proclaimed Maximus, one of his own dependants, as Emperor. [*The reason for Gerontius' revolt was the fact that Constantine III had decided to conclude a peace with Honorius; Constantine undoubtedly knew that the Briton Gerontius was vehemently opposed to such a course and had therefore decided to replace him with Iustus, only to be forestalled by Gerontius, while it is also possible that Gerontius feared that he would be made a culprit of the killings; see also Zosimus 6.5.2; In contrast to what Gregory states, Maximus was probably Gerontius' son, who at the time of his elevation served in the Domestici, which has led to the confusion.*] Maximus was supported by a horde of troops collected from various barbarian tribes [*i.e. mercenaries collected from the Vandals, Suevi-Alamanni, Alans etc. who had clearly negotiated a treaty with Gerontius; Gerontius marched north to join these allies and left Maximus at Tarraco*] and he was ready for any contingency. Constans and the Prefect Rusticus, one-time Master of the Offices, were very frightened by this news. They sent Edobech in advance to the people of Germania [*i.e. they sent a vanguard under Edobichus to the province of Germania Prima against one branch of the invading barbarians, possibly that which had been forced to linger in front of Vangiones and which had probably then advanced towards Argentorate; the other sources also prove that Edobichus was ordered to collect as many allies from the Franks and Alamanni as he could*] and they themselves set out for Gaul, with the Franks, the Alamanni and a whole band of soldiery, intending to return to Constantine as soon as they could [*i.e. Constans returned in haste from Spain to Arelate to take control of the campaign against Gerontius and his barbarian allies who were advancing towards Lugdunum and Arles; when Constans marched back to Arelate he seems to have left Maximus at Tarraco in possession of most of Spain, even if he probably replaced the native Spanish forces guarding the Pyrenees with the Honoriaci to block Maximus behind the Pyrenees*].

The above information can actually be used to clarify Sozomen (9.12–13) and other sources that have condensed the series of events. Firstly, since we know that Edobichus later collected reinforcements from the Franks and Alamanni across the Rhine (Soz. 9.13.2) and then advanced to relieve the besieged Constantine III at Arelate, we know that Edobichus had either achieved a success against the invaders in Germania I (Mogontiacum) or had at least managed to avoid being defeated by them. This may mean that he defeated the Vandals or that he was able to collect reinforcements thanks to this. Sozomen also claims that when Gerontius had proclaimed Maximus as Emperor, an event which is to be dated to the year 409, Constantine dispatched his son Constans to Vienne to guard it

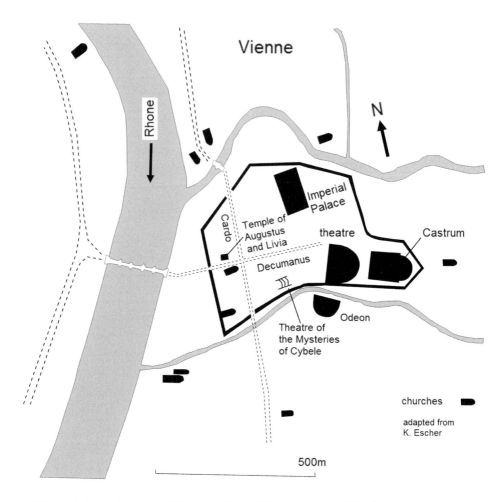

Vienne

Rhone

N

Imperial
Palace

Cardo

Temple of
Augustus
and Livia

theatre

Castrum

Decumanus

Odeon

Theatre of
the Mysteries
of Cybele

churches

adapted from
K. Escher

500m

and the neighbouring towns. The guarding of Vienne (north of Arelate) makes sense only
if Constans was dispatched against one division of the barbarian invaders that was now
allied with Gerontius while other barbarian divisions approached Spain, probably also
as allies of Gerontius (note that Maximus took refuge among these barbarians in Spain
after Gerontius had died). Gerontius had clearly marched north from Spain and joined
forces with the barbarians, because the sources state that he then defeated and killed
Constans in Vienne. This may have taken place in the palace or the church. This in turn
means that Gerontius had previously allowed Constans to advance to Spain unhindered.
Constans seems to have replaced the local units guarding the passes of the Pyrenees
with the *Honoriaci*, the units of which subsequently betrayed the passes to the barbarian
invaders, the allies of Gerontius. The passes had previously been guarded by a civilian
paramilitary *burgarii* (CTh 7.14.1: Spanish *burgarii*) who were clearly better at their job
than the so-called professionals.

   As noted above, the Briton Gerontius could not accept any reconciliation with the
Emperor against whom he had raised the flag of revolt, and neither could the inhabitants
of Britain and north-west Gaul which had been ravaged by the invading barbarians

(Zos. 6.5.2). Constantine had not only failed to protect the Britons and Gauls, but had even concluded an alliance with the hated Emperor against whom they had all risen. Consequently, in the absence of any reliable authority, the inhabitants of these areas revolted against Constantine and Roman law and reverted to their 'native customs' so that the people were ruled by the ruling classes of the cities (Zos. 6.5.2, 6.10.2). In essence these peoples formed their own paramilitary forces to bolster the existing garrisons with which they fought against the invaders. The inhabitants undoubtedly also hoped that by revolting they could obtain the support of Gerontius, who had formed an alliance with some of the invaders.

When Honorius then agreed to conclude the alliance, Constantine marched his troops to Italy in the summer of 409. His stated purpose was to attack Alaric on behalf of Honorius. However, two things then happened. Firstly, Honorius and his friends suspected, probably correctly, that Allobichus was working for Constantine, with the result that they assassinated Allobichus when he was marching ahead of the Emperor in a procession. It seems probable that Constantine indeed planned to oust Honorius with the help of Allobichus and that the campaign against Alaric was just a ruse to achieve this. What is certain is that when Constantine failed to use the Via Aurelia to march straight to Rome and continued his march first to Libarna and from there to the River Padus (Po) – clearly with the intention of marching straight to Ravenna – the already paranoid Honorius started to suspect Allobichus' intentions.

The assassination of Allobichus signalled the return of the Eastern faction to power. Olympius was recalled and appointed once again as *Mag.Off.* (Olymp. fr.8.2). The loyal Valens now became the only *MVM Praes.* Secondly, and most importantly, Gerontius had in the meanwhile marched north from Spain past Constans and had joined forces with the barbarian invaders, probably somewhere near Lugdunum (the city must have been taken by Gerontius' barbarian allies by the time Constans reached Arelate, because Constans was dispatched to defend Vienne and not Lugdunum). Constantine had no other alternative than to abandon his Italian campaign and return to Arelate on the double. Father and son reached the city at the same time (Olymp. fr. 15.2) and it was then that Constantine sent Constans to defend Vienne and Edobichus across the Rhine to collect reinforcements from among the Franks and Alamanni (Olymp. fr. 17.1–2; Soz. 9.13ff.). As noted above, Edobichus was successful in his undertaking, but Constans fared less well. Gerontius with his barbarian allies defeated and killed Constans at Vienne and then put Constantine under siege at Arelate in the late summer (or early fall) of 409.

Unsurprisingly, Olympius' recall was also accompanied by the promotion of other Easterners into positions of prominence. The most important of these was the experienced veteran general Constantius, a pure-bred Roman from the city of Naissus, the future emperor Constantius III and father of Valentinian III. There are two possibilities for the sequence of Constantius' rise to dominance in the West. Firstly, it is possible that Constantius was already nominated to the position of *Com. Dom. Eq.* in the summer of 409 (either before or after Allobichus' murder) and then to the position of *Mag.Ped.* after the *MVM* Valens had failed in his effort to find reconciliation with Alaric and Attalus in late 409, so that Ulfilas (Ulphilas) became the *Mag.Eq.* The other possibility is that Constantius arrived together with the Eastern reinforcement *tagmata* in late 409 and was straightaway promoted to the position of *Mag.Ped.* while Ulfilas became his *Mag.Eq.* and it was in this position with the support of the Eastern forces that he became the dominant person in the Western court. The latter alternative is the likelier one. The reasons for this set of conclusions are that someone had to replace the *magistri* who were no longer in office and because no *magistri* are recorded for the year 410 when Constantius and Ulfilas were clearly acting as principal commanders of Honorius's armed forces.

It was at about this time that those barbarians who had turned into north-west Gaul and then south into Aquitania reached the Pyrenees, which were protected by the *Honoriaci*. As noted above, the barbarian invaders appear to have acted as allies of Gerontius. In essence the barbarians were freeing the usurper Maximus from the blockade installed by Constans so that the route from Spain to his father's forces was opened up. The dishonourable *Honoriaci* joined the barbarians and they together with the Alans, Vandals, and Suevi entered Spain either on 28 September or 12 October 409 (Hydatius Olympiad 297; Oros. 7.40). The provinces of Spain were ruthlessly pillaged by the barbarians for three years, while the tax collectors set up by Gerontius plundered all wealth from the citizens to be consumed by the soldiers. The pillage in its turn resulted in famine and pestilence. The worst was over when finally in 411 the barbarians decided amongst themselves to carve up Spain.

North Africa, and Tripolitania and Cyrenaica 408–425

The *Chronica Gallica 452* records the killing of the *Comes Africae* Johannes (Iohannes, Ioannes) by the people for the year 408/9, but this year is difficult to reconcile with the information provided by Zosimus. He claims that Bathanarius was immediately succeeded by Heraclianus in 408/9, but as noted by the PLRE 2 it is possible that Zosimus has made a mistake. The other possibility is that the *Chronicle* has placed the event in the wrong cycle (PLRE 2), which would date the death to the year 423/4. This latter year would connect the event with the death of Honorius and the rise of John so that Bonifatius would probably be the person who had caused the death of Johannes. If the victory of Ortygius (see below) over the Austuriani took place in the same year, it is also possible that the death of Honorius had caused the Austuriani to rebel, also in 423.

Cyrenaica was not the only area troubled by the Austuriani/Laguatan/Marmaridae during the early-fifth century. The fact that the title of *Dux et Corrector Limitis Tripolitani*, attested for the year 393, had been promoted into *Comes et Dux Provinciae Tripolitanae* suggests that Tripolitania had been facing endemic warfare at the hands of the Austuriani (and/or Garamantes?). In fact, Flavius Ortygius, who held this office between 408 and 423, is recorded as having defeated one Austuriani attack during his tenure.[13] The likeliest date for this war is the period from ca. 408–412 for the reason that the Austuriani were also then active on the Cyrenaican front (see Appendix 3), but it is still possible that the war took place in 423 after the death of Honorius had dissolved the previous treaty (see above).

Alaric Sets Up the Puppet Emperor Attalus in the Summer of 409

Alaric, who had now twice been betrayed by Honorius, advanced against the city of Rome in the late spring of 409. This must have happened slightly before Constantine III marched his army into Italy, supposedly to support Honorius against Alaric. At first, Alaric put forth the reasonable demand that the citizens and Senate of Rome were to

Attalus
(Source: Cohen)

join his cause against the treacherous Honorius, but when the Senate showed signs of hesitation, Alaric once again besieged the city. While one half of his forces stayed behind to blockade the city, Alaric advanced with the rest against the city of Portus (the harbour of Rome). He besieged it for a few days and then captured it with all the supplies stored inside. Alaric threatened to distribute the supplies to his troops unless the Senate submitted to his will. The Senate saw no other way out than to give in. This probably happened in mid-to-late July. It is not certain when the Goths put to sea in the captured vessels and raided coastal areas (but miraculously not the island of Igilium, where many Romans had taken refuge) as stated by Rutilius Namatianus (325ff.). It is possible that this event took place earlier in 409. The other alternative is that it took place later, in 410 or 411, or during all of those years.

Alaric's goal was to create his own puppet Emperor and administration. Consequently, the Senate invited Alaric to Rome, and after a vote appointed the *PVR* Attalus as Emperor. Attalus in his turn appointed Alaric as *Mag.Ped.*, or according to Olympiodorus a *MVM*, Valens as *Mag.Eq.* (the *comes* or *dux* who had previously led the Dalmatian *tagmata*), Athaulf as *Com.Dom.Eq.*, Ioannes as *Mag. Off.*, Lampadius as *PPI*, and Marcianus as *PVR*. Ridley (Zos., p.228) rightly notes the fact that Attalus attempted to balance Alaric's and Athaulf's powers by appointing native Romans to the other key positions.

According to Zosimus (6.7.4), the Romans were in festive spirits after having received competent administrators and because the pagan Tertullus was given the consulship for the year 410. Most notably, Attalus was himself a pagan who was baptized by an Arian Gothic bishop only when he became Emperor. In fact, Attalus seems to have made it his policy goal to unite both halves of the Roman Empire and all religions under his rule. It is no wonder that the pagan Zosimus was ready to shower praise on the new administration, even though he still makes it quite clear that Attalus was an idiot. The only people in the city of Rome who were vehemently opposed to this development were the family of the Anicii, because until then they had had almost total control over the wealth of the city. This family clearly wanted to continue to rule the city in the background and did not want outside interference.[14]

Attalus, however, proved quite incompetent as a ruler. Alaric's sound advice was that Attalus should dispatch a suitable force against the *Comes Africae* Heraclianus so that Heraclianus would be unable to cut off the grain supply. Alaric suggested that Attalus send the *dux* Drumas with a moderate force of barbarians to depose Heraclianus. The idiot posing as a ruler claimed to know better. The seers had foretold Attalus that he did not need any military force to overthrow Heraclianus. In desperation, at a meeting of the Senate, the new *Mag.Off.* Ioannes suggested that Attalus at least forge a letter in the name of Honorius in which Heraclianus was relieved of duty, but to no avail. The headstrong believer in seers would have none of that, and this time the equally idiotic majority in the Senate agreed. They did not want to send barbarian soldiers into North Africa. Instead, Attalus sent Constans, without an army, to remove Heraclianus from office and he was to do this in Attalus' name and not with a forged document, while Attalus himself marched the army against the city of Ravenna. In contrast to Attalus, Honorius' administration acted promptly and immediately dispatched reinforcements to North Africa to secure its corn (Zos. 6.8.3).

When Alaric was near Ravenna, the desperate Honorius sent the *PPI* Iovius, *MVM* Valens, *Quaestor* Potamius, and Iulianus (the *Primicerius Notariorum*) to negotiate. He was even ready to recognize Attalus as co-emperor. Attalus refused. His only concession was that he allowed Honorius to leave unharmed to live the rest of his days on some island. The desperate Honorius had placed ships in full readiness in the harbour of Ravenna to help him flee to the East, and he was on the point of fleeing when ships bearing six *tagmata* of Eastern troops arrived in the port during the night. This must have happened in late August or early September 409. These forces had been expected when Stilicho was alive. The reasons for the delay in the sending of the troops had been the threat posed by Stilicho to the caretaker government in the East in the summer of 408 and the threat of war against Persia, as well as the invasion of Uldin (twhich ook place either in 408 or 409). Honorius was elated. He replaced the guards on the walls with these fresh Eastern troops. He feared that his Western troops could betray him. It is probable, even if unprovable, that Flavius Constantius, the future Emperor, arrived with these forces and was duly appointed as the new *Mag.Ped.* while Ulfilas (probably a Goth) became his *Mag.Eq.* After Stilicho's death, Honorius had avoided the appointment of Goths to any important post, which makes it very probable that Ulfilas had arrived from the East. In other words, the Easterners replaced the western *MVM* Valens, who had lost Honorius's confidence. It was a military coup by the Easterners with the full backing of Honorius. It was thanks to this that Honorius decided to stay in Ravenna and wait for news of what had happened in Africa. If his reinforcements had defeated Attalus' men, he would launch a full scale war against Alaric and Attalus, but if Attalus had gained possession of Africa, he would flee to the East.

It was also then that the power behind the throne in the city of Ravenna changed. The *PPI* Iovius, who shuttled between the rulers, decided to desert to Attalus, who duly rewarded him with the office of *PPI* on his staff, together with the title/honour of Patrician. The actual sequence of events suggests that Iovius was actually acting as Honorius' double agent in Attalus' inner circle, his mission to cause Alaric to abandon Attalus. The other alternative is that he was the consummate politician/turncoat, always able to change his horse mid-stride. According to fragment 14 (Bibl.Cod. 80, p.170) of Olympiodorus, after the negotiations with Attalus had failed the power passed to the chamberlain, Eusebius, who, shortly afterwards, was beaten to death with sticks thanks to the machinations of Allobichus. As is clear, the names are mistaken. Allobichus had already been killed during the summer of 409. The other fragments (5.3 and 8.2.) make it clear that Eusebius was actually Olympius and that the person who had Olympius killed was Constantius. The absence of other competitors made Olympius the power behind the throne for a short period of time, but his return to power proved to be short. Honorius no longer trusted him. It is probable that when the new *Mag.Ped.* Constantius had Olympius executed publicly in front of the Emperor it was done with Honorius' prior approval. Olympius' ears were cut off first, after which he was brutally beaten to death with clubs. The violent rise of Constantius had brought to the forefront the Eastern military faction. The Easterners showed a greater understanding of the realities. They were ready to negotiate with the Goths and other barbarians.

The size of the Eastern force appears to have been very significant. According to Zosimus (6.8.2), the six *tagmata* consisted of 40,000 men, which, as noted above, suggests the use of old legionary sizes with approximately 5,000 footmen and 1,600 horsemen.[15] The large size of this army is confirmed by the statement of Procopius (Wars 3.2.36) that the East Romans sent a fleet with a very great number of soldiers to assist Honorius. In other words, the core of Constantius' infantry force would have consisted of 30,000 footmen and the core of Ulfilas' cavalry of 10,000 horsemen. Regardless, Italy was still desperately short of recruits. The best evidence for this is the Edict (CTh 7.14.20) issued at Ravenna on 8 February 410 in which Honorius demanded that the provinces of Africa, Sardinia, Sicily and Corsica were to provide recruits. Only those diginitaries who had fled from Italy or the city of Rome were exempt from this duty. These areas were the only areas still under Honorius's control that had not been utterly devastated in the previous years. The situation was desperate indeed. Another Edict (7.15.1) issued at Ravenna on 29 April 409 proves that the situation was not good in Africa either. The barbarians who had been given land in return for guarding the borders and border fortifications had sold their properties to the civilians, with the result that entire sections of the border lay undefended. This Edict ordered the new owners either to perform the duty of guarding the border themselves or hand the land to barbarians or veterans. There was clearly a dearth of defenders everywhere.

In the meanwhile, Heraclianus had captured and killed Constans after which he had posted guards along the coastline and stopped all traffic between North Africa and Rome, with the result that the city of Rome once again started to suffer from famine. This proves that the blockade began so early in the fall of 409 that the corn shipments had not yet reached the city of Portus. When the news of the failure was brought before Alaric and Attalus, the latter convened a session of the Senate in which the situation was discussed. According to Sozomen (9.8), it was then that Alaric advised that they ought to send 500 'barbarians' against Heraclianus, but I would suggest that this was rather the piece of advice Alaric had given previously and that now a larger force was needed. However, if Alaric really did give this piece of advice now, his intention was clearly to kill Heraclianus with a bold commando operation performed by elite forces. According to Zosimus, Iovius also wanted to send barbarians to oust Heraclianus, but this was opposed by Attalus.

Alaric was desperate. Attalus had turned out to be an utter fool who had no brains and no chance of success. In this situation Alaric was ready to listen to Iovius' advice. Iovius advised Alaric to abandon the siege of Ravenna, which Alaric had intended to maintain until the city surrendered. Iovius was working for Honorius, but it cannot be said that he would not have been right about the abilities of Attalus. By abandoning the siege of Ravenna, Alaric now made it possible for him to abandon Attalus if need be. However, for the moment Alaric stayed loyal to Attalus. It was then that the loyalty of the *Mag.Eq.* Valens became suspect, with the result that he was killed. This obviously had the added benefit of making Attalus even more reliant on Alaric, and the suspicion of treason may have just been used as a suitable excuse to get rid of Valens. After this, Alaric attacked those cities in Aemilia which had not declared their support for Attalus. The only city that Alaric could not take was the city of Bononia, not even after a siege. Consequently, Alaric advanced to Liguria to force its cities to declare their support for Attalus.

Honorius Strikes Back: Constantius Assumes Command in 410

In the spring of 410 the new power behind the throne, the native Roman Flavius Constantius from Naissus, took charge of imperial policies and military operations. Since it was impossible to attack Alaric while he held Honorius' sister Galla Placidia as a hostage, it was decided either to assassinate Alaric or negotiate a peace/truce with him (see below), while the first campaign was to be directed against Gerontius and Constantine III in Gaul. Both were in a highly vulnerable position. Constantine and his son Julian were besieged by Gerontius at Arelate, while Gerontius' own position was weakened by his alliance with the barbarians, by his de facto loss of Spain to his erstwhile allies (these undoubtedly had their own objectives), and by the fact that Edobichus was collecting a relief army to assist Constantine in the north. Honorius adopted a policy designed to cause defections among the supporters of Gerontius and Constantine by dispatching letters to Britain in which he urged the cities to defend themselves against the invaders (Zos. 6.10.2). In other words, Honorius recognized the cities as representing Roman interests in the area. The cities in question must have organized themselves into some sort of provincial council which then coordinated its efforts with the regular units of the army and navy posted in their territory.

Ravenna and Constantinople also coordinated their efforts on other fronts. According to the Edict (CTh 7.16.2) issued in the name of Honorius and Theodosius on 24 April 410 at Constantinople to the *PPO* Anthemius (during the consulship of Varanes, the former *Mag. Ped.* of the West in 408 and *MVM Praes.* of the East in 409):

> All naval bases [*stationes navium*], harbours, shores, and all points of departure from the provinces, even remote places and islands, shall be encircled and guarded by the skilful regulation of Your Magnificence, so that no person may be able to infiltrate into the regions of Our Empire either by violence or by stealth, either openly or secretly … unless … he bears sacred imperial letters from my uncle [Honorius], to Me. … which has been agreed upon between Me and My Lord and uncle, Honorius in memoranda that We have exchanged with each other.[16]

The next Edict [CTh 7.16.3] from the year 420 clarifies how this was done in practice. Since each *defensor locorum* was responsible for the prevention of smuggling in his own sector, it seems probable that the local civilian paramilitary forces under their own officials coordinated their efforts with the imperial officials and officers. The aim of the above Edict was clearly to prevent any unauthorized communication between West and East because there existed the possibility that the usurper Attalus, who was Ionian by birth and therefore an Easterner, could attempt to undermine the position of the Theodosian House also in the East – for example by trying to tamper with the loyalty of the Gothic Federates in the East. The Late Roman Empire was a police state, much akin to eighteenth-century France, nineteenth-century Russia, or North Korea today.

However, it was impossible to make any move against either Gerontius or Constantine before Alaric could be neutralized somehow. By marching to Liguria, Alaric had actually placed his army between Gaul and Ravenna and one may speculate that he may even have contemplated the possibility of opening up negotiations either with Gerontius or with Constantine. Constantius and Honorius were in a difficult position, but Attalus' stupidity solved the problem for them.

When, as a result of the embargo and the profiteering of the food sellers in the city of Rome, the famine became so bad that the people were on the point of resorting to cannibalism, Attalus convened another full session of the Senate. This must have happened in the spring of 410. Unsurprisingly, the vast majority of the Senate was now quite prepared to dispatch Drumas with his Goths against Heraclianus, but this was opposed by Attalus and some small numbers of xenophobic senators who did not want to dispatch any barbarians with the Roman regulars. This was the last straw. Alaric decided to abandon Attalus and opened negotiations with Honorius. Alaric marched his army from Liguria along the Via Aemilia to Ariminum, where in full public view he then stripped from Attalus, and from all his officials, their symbols of office, before sending the imperial regalia to Honorius. Honorius in his turn pardoned them all. However, Alaric kept Attalus and his son Ampelius under protective guard, together with Honorius' sister Galla Placidia (Zos. 6.12.3).[17] Galla Placidia was used as a hostage to ensure Alaric's own safety in case Honorius was planning to double cross him again – something that he had done frequently.

The Fall of Rome on 24 August 410: Vae Victis

After this Alaric left his main army at Ariminum and together with his bodyguards advanced close to the city of Ravenna to negotiate in person with Honorius. Then the unthinkable happened. Sarus the freebooter attacked Alaric and his retinue with his 300 followers, either on his own initiative or as an ally of Honorius. The badly-shaken and enraged Alaric managed to flee. Sozomen and Philostorgius claim that Sarus had attacked on his own initiative to prevent the treaty between his personal enemy Alaric and Honorius, but it is clear from Alaric's reaction that he believed that Honorius had hired Sarus to assassinate him. We shall never know the truth for certain, but it would well have been in character for Honorius (and Constantius) to have attempted such a ploy. Furthermore, Zosimus' account (6.13.1–2, esp. 6.13.2) implies that Sarus had indeed acted on behalf of the double-crossing Honorius. Zosimus states that the condottiere Sarus who was staying in Picenum with his 300 followers was attacked by Athaulf with his entire army because Athaulf had a personal grudge against Sarus. Badly outnumbered, Sarus fled to Honorius to assist him in his war against Alaric. Even though this is an argument from silence, since Zosimus fails to mention Sarus' attack on Alaric during the negotiations near Ravenna, Sarus' attack on Alaric must have happened after Sarus had already joined Honorius.

Alaric, who was bent on exacting revenge for the attempted murder, besieged the city of Rome for the third time. According to Philostorgius (Olymp. fr. 11.2), Alaric besieged Rome and attacked the city of Portus one year after his previous attack, which dates the start of the siege to late-spring or early-summer 410 (see the Maps). The city was taken through treachery when the Goths were given passage through the Salarian gate on the night of 24 August 410 (Bury 1.183). According to Procopius (Wars 3.2.14ff.), the city was either captured by a ruse when Alaric sent 300 youths as slaves to the Roman aristocrats, who then on a pre-appointed day captured the Salarian Gate; or that it was betrayed by a noblewoman called Proba because she saw that the citizens were once again starving and had started to resort to cannibalism. The full name of Proba was Anicia Faltonia Proba and she belonged to the influential family of the Anicii. Three of her sons became consuls. The Anicii were clearly bent on taking back the control of their city with the help of Alaric. Proba, however, was afterwards forced to flee to Heraclianus, who treated her harshly. Alaric gave his troops permission to plunder and pillage the city for three days, but forbade bloodshed. In addition to this, he ordered that the soldiers were not to violate the basilicas of the holy Apostles Peter and Paul, and while the pillaging was already underway Alaric ordered some of his Goths to draw their swords and form a double line to protect a procession of nuns and other Christians who were carrying sacred vessels from the other churches to that of the Basilica of the Apostles. This procession was joined by a number of other Christians and even by pagans who then sought asylum in the basilica by pretending to be Christians. Despite all the orders and precautions, it is still clear that the attackers killed, raped and burned, but not to the extent that was typical in instances in which a besieged city had been taken. The Goths showed exceptional discipline in all of their doings – one can say with good justification that they almost always showed a greater amount of restraint and discipline than the Roman regulars. The future events detailed in this volume and in the next volumes present other such instances.

The Death of Alaric in late 410: Long Live the New King Athaulf!

On the third day the Goths left the city of their own volition. The likeliest reason for this was that the Goths wanted to leave the area in which diseases were spreading like wildfire as a result of the famine. After this, Alaric marched his army through Campania (capturing Nola and Capua, but failing to take Neapolis) to Lucania and Bruttii/Bruttium. Alaric's forces pillaged everything en route, but presumably not in Bruttii because they stayed there for a while. Alaric's plan was to ship his army via Sicily to North Africa, the breadbasket of Rome. South of Italy, Sicily and North Africa were also the only parts of West Rome hitherto unpillaged and therefore still well worth taking. When Alaric had embarked his forces on ships at Bruttium to cross to Messena in Sicily, apparently in late autumn, his fleet was wrecked by a storm with the loss of several ships. The size of the fleet carrying the Goths and their allies must have been truly imposing, even if it is uncertain whether Alaric embarked all his men. It is probable that most of these ships had been captured from the city of Portus and consisted of the three-masted grain ships designed to carry huge payloads. Unfortunately, we do not know what Alaric's plan was. It is possible that he intended to settle his entire people (Goths, Alans, Sarmatians, Huns and others) in North Africa or that he intended to leave part of his army under Athaulf in Bruttium while he conquered North Africa in person, so that he could eventually conquer the whole of Italy.

After this Alaric abandoned his attempt to cross the straits in the middle of autumn and winter and apparently started to march back north, possibly to besiege Neapolis, but he fell ill en route and died at Consentia in Bruttium. The course of the River Busentus near the city of Consentia was then dried by converting the river and Alaric (together with part of the treasure taken from Rome) was buried in the bed of the river, after which the river was converted back to its channel. The slaves (undoubtedly Romans) that had performed this onerous duty were duly killed to hide the location of the burial place of the great king of the Goths. The location of the burial place has ever since been a source of great interest to many generations of treasure hunters, but to my knowledge the treasure still lies buried with the great Gothic king at the bottom of the river. In my opinion there exist no good reasons to suspect the veracity of this tale, even if similar burial tales exist of several other kings.

Consequently, Alaric had died before his dream of finding a permanent abode for his Goths within the Roman Empire was finalized. On the basis of Claudian's account it is clear that most of Alaric's 'Goths' consisted of the Tervingi, but as I have discussed above, by now his nation at arms included vast numbers of others (Alans, Sarmatians, Greuthungi, Huns, Romans etc.) who were to become the Visigothic nation, thanks to the unifying experience of fighting together. All of these were amalgated into one entity under Alaric's inspiring leadership. In fact, the greatest of Alaric's achievements was the de facto creation of the Visigothic nation. I will henceforth call this mixed migrating army and nation the Visigoths.

None of the sources imply that any foul play took place in the death of Alaric – after all he appears to have been a man in his fifties and late autumn is known for its flus. However, it should still be taken into account that the Romans had possessed the necessary skills to murder their enemies with diseases and poisons for centuries by then (see e.g. Syvänne, 2004, 2006; Mayor). There were actually two ways in which the Romans could have killed Alaric with a disease (and not by a drug that produced symptoms resembling a disease): to spread it to the army as a whole, either through the air, food or water, and then hope that Alaric would also get the disease; or by using a similar means of delivery against Alaric alone (e.g. a slave could have administered it). The fact that the sources do not mention such is actually not a proof that a murder did not take place. If the assassination was carried out properly no-one would know that such had taken place. In fact, it is unlikely to be a coincidence that we do not know of any specific instance in which the sources state that the Romans had used diseases to eliminate their enemies for the precise reason that such operations were hush-hush. The Romans would not have put in writing instructions on how to kill enemies with diseases unless these were also used in practice. Instructions can be found in Julius Africanus' *Kestoi* and in the Late-Roman and Byzantine military treatises that borrowed material from him. Obviously, this doesn't prove that Alaric was killed with a disease or poison, but one still has to remember that his death was very opportune for the Romans.

The Visigoths chose Alaric's nephew-in-law Athaulf as his successor. Unlike the Romans, who only pretended to be a republic, the Visigoths actually followed the democratic principles of the Tervingi and other Goths who either chose judges or kings on the basis of ability. Alaric did have children, because we know that Theoderic I was his grandson, but none of these was suited to be his successor, presumably because of age or some other reason at the time of Alaric's death. According to Jordanes (Get. 159), after his elevation Athaulf sacked the city of Rome once again and then his men plundered Italy like locusts and emptied it of both private and public wealth. This statement has sometimes been considered suspect, but if this did not take place in late-410 or early-411, then it is probable that it took place when Athaulf marched his Visigoths along the western coast to southern Gaul, probably in the summer and/or fall of 411. It would have been strange if his forces did not sack the city of Rome once again when they marched past it. The Romans would have been unable to do anything because Honorius feared for the life of his sister. What is certain, however, is that Athaulf and his Visigoths pillaged and sacked Italy until Iovinus proclaimed himself emperor in Gaul in 411 (see later). It was then that Attalus suggested to Athaulf that he march his forces to Gaul to support Iovinus. As noted above, the march to Gaul along the west coast (Via Aurelia) must have taken place in the course of the summer and/or autumn of 411. It should be stressed that at this time, the Visigoths also possessed a fleet, which provided logistical support and assisted in the sieges of the coastal cities. On the basis of Olympiodorus's statement (fr. 18) that Iovinus was distressed because Athaulf had brought his army to south Gaul and blamed Attalus for having advised this, it appears very probable that Athaulf had marched his forces to support Iovinus on his own initiative, and that Iovinus was forced to come to terms with the fact (see also Bury 1.194).

The devastation caused by Alaric and Athaulf along the west coast of Italy was so severe that the former *Mag.Off.* (412) and *PVR* (summer 414) Rutilius Namatianus decided to use ships even in mid-November in 416 to travel to Gaul to inspect the damage to his estates there. According to him (37ff), the cities and bridges along the Via Aurelia and in Tuscia lay in ruins. However, the city of Rome was a special case. According to Olympiodorus (fr. 25), the city of Rome had recovered so quickly from the devastation that in the autumn of 414 the *PVR* Albinus had to petition an increase to the amount of supplies to meet the needs of the increased population. This was obviously a reflection of the devastation of the rest of Italy. Even with the tax breaks that had been granted immediately to restore economic vitality after the Visigoths had left, there were plenty of people who could not find subsistence outside the walls of Rome and who therefore migrated into the city in order to be fed at the expense of the state. The Romans had food which was shipped from North Africa.

Chapter Ten

The West Roman Counter-attack in 410–418

Constantius vs. Gerontius in 410
Constantius vs. Constantine III in 410–411

In the meantime, probably already in June 410, Constantius put into effect the first part of his military plan, which was to take Gerontius and Constantine out of the equation, which would in turn strengthen his hand vis-à-vis both Honorius and Alaric. Constantius could not attack Alaric because Alaric still had Galla Placidia as hostage. Honorius had given clear instructions for Constantius not to endanger Placidia's life, but to obtain her freedom by other means. In return for accomplishing this, Constantius was apparently very early on promised Galla Placidia's hand in marriage.

Constantius and Ulfilas led their army along the coastal road to Arelate against Gerontius, who was still besieging Constantine. The later presence of strong naval forces under Constantius as well as the location of the city of Arelate makes it probable that the navy sailed alongside Constantius' land army as it marched along the coastal road from Italy to Gaul in order to provide supplies for it and also to assist it in the siege operations along the Rhodanus. The sources unfortunately fail to mention the size of the invading army (or the navy if it was present), but we can make an educated guess on the basis of the probable battle site (see the accompanying map). When the forces of the legitimate Emperor approached, most of Gerontius' army deserted with the result that Gerontius was forced to flee with a few of his troops back to Spain. The Spanish soldiers considered Gerontius' position untenable and turned against him. The fact that the barbarians had invaded Spain on behalf of Maximus and were pillaging Spain did not endear the usurper to the soldiers either. They surrounded Gerontius' house (presumably in Spain) during the night and attacked. Gerontius along with one Alan friend and some dependants fought back by pouring arrows at the attackers. According to Olympiodorus/Sozomen, the defenders managed to kill over 300 attackers before their arrows ran out. It was then that some of the dependants escaped into the night by letting themselves down from the building. Gerontius would have also escaped but his love for his wife Nonnichia impeded this. She could not flee. When the soldiers set the house on fire, the three decided to commit suicide. Gerontius cut off the head of his Alan friend, then Nonnichia threw herself at the sword, after which Gerontius struck himself with the sword, but since this was ineffective (presumably because the sword was too long), Gerontius drew a dagger which he carried by his thigh (note that he carried the dagger in the same way as the Alans!) and plunged it into his heart.

When the news of the death of Gerontius was brought to Maximus, he had no other alternative but to seek asylum among the barbarian invaders of Spain. He had no troops of his own. It was then in 411 that the Alans, Vandals and Suevi carved up Spain so that the (Hasding?) Vandals took possession of most of Gallaecia, the Suevi-Alamanni the western part of Gallaecia on the edge of the ocean, the Siling Vandals Baetica, and the Alans the provinces of Lusitania and Carthaginiensis. The remaining Spaniards who had survived in the cities and forts surrendered and became their subjects (Hydatius Olymp. 297). The reason for the decision to carve up Spain was that the Emperor whom the barbarians had come to support had been overthrown when his father's forces deserted him. According to an extant letter dated to the period between 409 and 423 Honorius sent the Patrician Sabinianus (presumably as *MVM* of Spain) to take charge of the operations in Spain against the barbarians (PLRE2). The likeliest period for this action is the year 411, meaning that Sabinianus would have taken control of those Roman troops that had deserted Iovinus. He seems to have achieved this, but he was clearly unable to stop the barbarians. The only area left in Roman control was the Province of Tarraconensis and it too was soon taken over by the Visigoths.

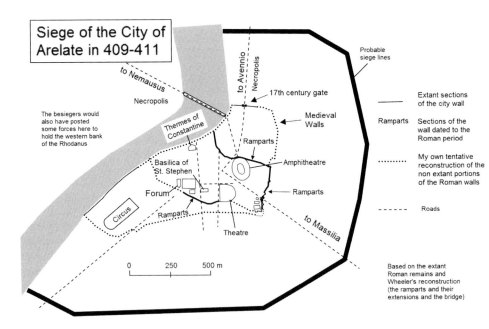

In the meanwhile, Constantius and Ulfilas had put Constantine under siege at Arelate, presumably using the siege lines already built by Gerontius. Unfortunately, we do not know whether Constantius transferred the British, Gallic and Spanish deserters to North Africa immediately after their desertion to his side or whether he did this only after the surrender of Constantine. In early 411 Constantine still refused to surrender because he had been brought the news that Edobichus was bringing a very large army of Franks and Alamanni. Constantius and Ulfilas decided to cross the Rhodanus (modern Rhone) and engage the relief army before it could reach the siege lines of Arelate. Even though Olympiodorus/Sozomen (fr. 17.2) do not mention that Constantius left any troops behind to continue the siege, it is clear that he did. Otherwise, Constantine could have sallied out of Arelate while Constantius and Ulfilas were on the other side of the river. Unfortunately, we do not know whether the besiegers left behind consisted of a detachment brought by Constantius from Italy or of the above mentioned deserters.

Constantius and Ulfilas decided to use an ambush. Constantius posted his infantry in full sight of the approaching enemy while Ulfilas placed his cavalry forces in hiding behind the expected place of the enemy battle line. It is unfortunate that Sozomen fails to give any description of the actual battle formation or of the battle site, but there is one probable location along the road leading into Arelate on the eastern side of the Rhodanus which would fit the circumstances (see the accompanying map). The probable places for the battle and ambushers are based on the fact that the enemy would have been unable to reconnoitre the spot where the ambushers would have been if deployed in this manner. The alternative locations are based on the presumption that Constantius deployed his army between the hills (rather than between the hill/town and river as in the likelier alternative) and the enemy advanced carelessly past the ambushers because they were at a distance of 10 km from the marching army. However, as stated above, the probable locations on the map are inherently likelier on the basis of the impossibility for the enemy to detect the ambushers in the spot where I have reconstructed them to be.

On the basis of the above one can make some educated guesses regarding the army sizes and the likely battle formations. The locale as well as the facts that Edobichus was dismounted and (Olympiodorus states) that Constantius commanded infantry all combine to suggest that Constantius did indeed deploy all of his forces on foot between the hill/town on the left and small river on the right. This location would also have forced the enemy to cross the river in order to attack Constantius' infantry line. It is possible that he still retained small numbers of cavalry as reserves so as not to betray that he had placed cavalry in ambush. The defensive locale would have suggested to the advancing enemy force that Constantius had purposefully adopted to use a defensive infantry array behind a river to block the advance of the enemy army. The use of the infantry line protected by terrain would also have forced the advancing enemy to use infantry formation to break through Constantius' phalanx, because the cavalry was essentially useless against the tight infantry phalanx. This would also have been a psychologically sound tactic, because the Franks and Alamanni consisted mainly of footmen and would therefore have been quite prepared to dismount their small cavalry forces so that they could add more weight to their attack.

As regards Constantius' infantry array, it is very probable that he adopted the single phalanx formation because he expected that the ambushers would attack the enemy's rear, which meant that he would not have needed to protect the rear of his infantry with a double phalanx or with 'regimental' squares of the type deployed by Theodosius previously at the battle of Poetovio in 388 (see Vol. 2), let alone adopt the use of a single square or *epikampios opisthia* for the entire army. The location and the situation pretty much rules out the use of the convex, crescent, and *epikampios emprosthia* formations. However, if Constantius for some reason wanted to protect the rear, he could have adopted any of these (i.e. double phalanx, square/squares, *epikampios opisthia*) even if the hollow oblongs would then be the likeliest alternative. The fact that the barbarian relief army was clearly deployed as a phalanx also bespeaks for the likelihood that Constantius used the single phalanx formation because the width of his formation would have induced his enemies also to deploy their army with an at-least equally-wide front, which in turn

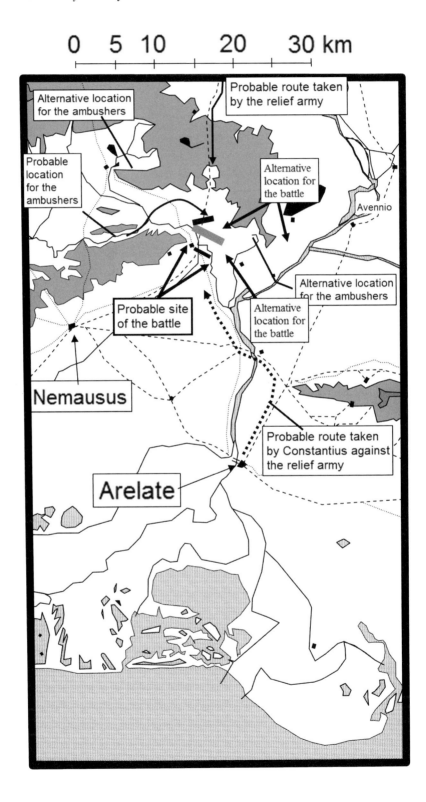

Probable route taken
by the relief army

Alternative location
for the ambushers

Alternative
location for
the battle

Probable
location
for the
ambushers

Avennio

Alternative location
for the ambushers

Probable site
of the battle

Alternative
location for
the battle

Nemausus

Probable route taken
by Constantius against
the relief army

Arelate

would have made the ambush more effective – the single phalanx usually lacked the depth to form a double phalanx and even when deployed 16 deep the men (plus LI) still had to be disciplined enough to form first a double front to face the rear and then march the rear towards the enemy to form the double phalanx. Consequently, we can use the single phalanx as the basis on which to calculate strengths of the respective armies (see the map with the captions).

When Edobichus' army had bypassed the place of ambush, had formed their battle line and had started to engage Constantius' forces, the signal was given for Ulfilas to launch his ambush. When Ulfilas' forces charged at the enemy's rear, the rout was immediate and complete because Edobichus' forces were unable to respond to the attack when locked in frontal combat. This proves that the Franks and Alamanni had deployed their infantry as a single phalanx, and it should be remembered that the bulk of the armies of both peoples consisted of infantry, which means that the relief army consisted mostly of footmen in light equipment. Some of the enemy were killed, some fled, but most simply surrendered by throwing down their weapons. This latter behaviour was encouraged by Constantius, who pardoned all those who threw down their weapons.

Edobichus mounted a horse (he had clearly dismounted to encourage the infantry phalanx to greater efforts; had he also dismounted the rest of his cavalry?) and fled to the estates owned by his friend Ecdicus. Ecdicus, however, betrayed his friend, cut off his head and took it to Constantius in the hopes of receiving a reward. Constantius thanked him publicly for the service to the state, but did not reward him in any other way and then ordered him to leave his presence. Constantius considered such an action despicable and bad for the morale of the army. Whether he was right in his judgement in this situation we do not know, but in general it would have been in the interest of the state to encourage defections from the ranks of the enemy by rewarding handsomely those who defected.

Opposite: If one makes the educated guess that Constantius had a smaller army than his opponent thanks to the fact that he had been forced to leave part of his army to continue the siege, it seems probable that he could not form as long a line as his enemy except by thinning the line.

Consequently, I have made the educated guess that the depth of Constantius' infantry phalanx was only 12 men (8 HI + 4 LI). Since the length of the phalanx with the intervals and cavalry wings was approx. 3km (one can make the educated guess that the intervals and cavalry would have occupied at least 300-500m of the line), the size of the army was about 30,000-32,000 men in the line, plus, conservatively estimating, perhaps about 4,000-6,000 men in the reserves. This is the likeliest alternative because the military treatises considered the 4 HI + 2 LI to be without depth. This is actually very close to the number of men Constantius had brought with him to Ravenna. It is improbable that Constantius could have formed his HI four deep, because it would have meant that his entire army consisted only of elite units.

It is impossible to know how many horsemen Ulfilas would have had, because he clearly did not have enough men to cover the entire length of the battle line (some enemy forces managed to flee), but about 8,000-10,000 horsemen would be a good guess because this is close to the figure of horsemen brought from the East.

Edobichus had probably more men than Constantius and we can make the educated guess that he was able to deploy his army in greater depth to effect a breakthrough so that he had probably 24 men in a file [(16 HI + 8 LI) x 2,700 metres] for a total of 65,000 footmen, plus perhaps about 6,000 men as reserves. The fact that Edobichus had to mount his horse to flee suggests that he had dismounted his men to break through Constantius' infantry phalanx.

However, considering Constantius' track record as a general, it is probable that he struck the right balance between the two different courses in this case. He knew much better how to maintain the morale of his army than us.

The Aftermath and Iovinus' Usurpation 411–412

After their victory Constantius and Ulfilas re-crossed the river to continue the siege. According to Sozomen (Olymp. fr. 17.2), when Constantine learnt the sad news of Edobichus' defeat, he put off the purple and entered a church, where he was ordained a priest. When this happened the defenders entered negotiations with the besiegers and opened the gates after Constantius had promised to spare them. Following this, Constantius put Honorius's representatives in charge of the local administration. Constantine and Julian were sent to Italy, but they were killed en route before they reached their destination.

However, there also exists an alternative version to these events. According to the fragment of Frigeridus preserved in Gregory of Tours (2.9. Tr. by Thorpe, 124, comment added inside parentheses), Constantine appears not to have donned the priest's robes immediately after the defeat of Edobichus:

> Constantine had been beleaguered for about four months when messengers arrived all of a sudden from northern Gaul to announce that Jovinus had assumed the rank of Emperor and was about to attack the besieging forces with the Burgondes, the Alamanni, the Franks, the Alani and a large army [*of regulars*]. Things then moved very quickly. The city gates were opened and Constantine came out. He was immediately packed off to Italy, but the Emperor sent a band of assassins to meet him and he was beheaded up on the River Mincio.

On the surface it would seem that Gregory or Frigeridus have confused the relief armies of Edobichus and Iovinus with each other, but the fact that the previous fragment does mention Edobichus suggests that the order of events is correct and that Constantine did not immediately surrender after the defeat of Edobichus, but awaited for the arrival of Iovinus for four months. When it was then reported that Iovinus was not coming to help him because he had usurped power, Constantine surrendered to Constantius in the hopes of receiving a pardon. The other sources state or imply that Iovinus' usurpation came only after the surrender of Constantine, but as said, I find Frigeridus' version more reliable in this case.

Regardless of the truth, what is clear is that one of Constantine's followers called Iovinus (Jovinus) was not ready accept Constantius' victory and therefore usurped power in his turn, presumably early in 411. He formed an alliance with the Burgundian king Guntiarius (also known as Gundahar, possibly the same as Gundicharius) and the Alan Goar, both of whom appear to have been allies of Constantine III from 408 onwards. In addition to this, Iovinus obtained mercenary troops from the Franks and Alamanni. The allies assembled at *Mundiacum* in *Germania Secunda* (Olymp. fr. 17), which the modern researchers have either interpreted as *Mundiaco* (modern Monzen in *Germania Secunda*: B. Bachrach, 1973) or as *Mondiacum* (modern Mainz in *Germania Prima* by the vast majority). I prefer the second alternative. When the allies joined Jovinus' forces at Mainz, he was proclaimed Emperor. It was now at the latest that the Burgundians were given possession of *Germania Prima* as Federates of Iovinus. It is possible that the Alans of Goar were also settled close by in the area around Rheims (see later).

The usurper marched south. Constantius did not offer any resistance, but withdrew his army to Italy. We do not know whether Constantius left garrisons in some of the cities (e.g. at Massilia and Arelate) which appears probable (Olymp. fr. 17.2.60ff.), but it is certain that with the probable exception of some cities most of the south of Gaul was immediately abandoned to the usurper and the Visigoths who soon marched to support Iovinus. Furthermore, the fact that Arelate soon started to mint coins in Iovinus' name means that it was also in Iovinus's hands (Drinkwater 1998, 289). Indeed the probable reason for the abandonment of at least part of the just re-conquered south of Gaul by Constantius was not the usurper's army, but the fact that Attalus had managed to convince Athaulf to march his army north to support the usurper. Constantius wanted to avoid being caught in between two powerful enemy armies.

As noted above, Iovinus had not called the Visigoths to join him, as a result of which he was forced to negotiate with Athaulf on almost equal terms when the latter's army arrived in the south of Gaul either in 411, or in 412 as claimed by Prosper Tiro. The end result of these negotiations appears to have been that Iovinus was forced to concede land to Athaulf's Visigoths and to Athaulf in person powers to veto any major policy decision. This decision Iovinus was to regret, but when faced with the prospect of having to fight against Athaulf Iovinus chose rather to make a compromise. Soon after Athaulf's march to Gaul came another fugitive in his footsteps from Italy. This man was Sarus. He was also seeking employment under Iovinus. Sarus had deserted Honorius because Honorius had started to suspect Sarus' honesty when his attendant Belleridus had been killed and Honorius gave no explanation for this and did not punish the murderer or murderers. When Sarus together with his 18 or 20 followers approached, Athaulf assembled 10,000 warriors and went to meet him. Sarus fought heroically, but in the end he was lassoed and captured alive only to be killed later.[1]

In the spring of 412 Iovinus made the mistake of appointing his own brother Sebastianus as Augustus without having consulted Athaulf. Athaulf was angry and did not accept this. The reason for the anger is not known. Perhaps it was the just the fact that Athaulf had not been consulted which angered him or alternatively that Athaulf had wanted to appoint Attalus as Iovinus' co-ruler. This rift was exploited by the *PPG* Dardanus, who managed to convince Athaulf to turn against Iovinus in early 412. Drinkwater (1998, 291ff.) has speculated that Dardanus was a private citizen at the time of his betrayal of Iovinus (and the Gallic nobility) and was only afterwards rewarded with the position of *PPG* by Honorius. His speculation does indeed seem sound because it would explain many of the problems in the sources, but ultimately one cannot know for certain thanks to the fact that there is no definite evidence. For example, it is possible that Iovinus and Athaulf had been unable to conquer the entire south of Gaul[2] with the result that Dardanus was present in south Gaul (e.g. in Marseille) and therefore in close proximity to negotiate.

The Fectio website (re-enactors and Robert Vermaat) in its timeline for the fifth century has mentioned an alternative and rather attractive theory for the above-mentioned events. According to this theory, Athaulf marched uninvited to the south of Gaul to offer his support for Iovinus in 412. However, when Athaulf's enemy Sarus also arrived to serve under Iovinus, Athaulf stopped the negotiations and killed Sarus with the result that Iovinus appointed his brother Sebastianus as Augustus.

Iovinus
(source: Cohen)

Sebastianus
(source: Cohen)

After Athaulf had decided to abandon Iovinus, he sent an embassy to Honorius in which he promised to deliver the heads of both usurpers in return for a *foedus*. The terms of this treaty appear to have been that the Roman state was required to grant lands for the Visigoths (in Aquitania?) and provide them with food supplies in return for military service and the return of Galla Placidia. Honorius agreed to the terms. At the same time as this happened, Athaulf also managed to obtain the desertion of Goar and his Alans to his side. Iovinus' policies were clearly detrimental to his own cause. Consequently, it is not surprising that Athaulf defeated and captured Sebastianus and another brother of Iovinus with ease, after which he was able to put Iovinus under siege at Valentia (Valence) or at Narbo (Narbonne). Iovinus was forced to surrender, after which Athaulf sent both Iovinus and Sebastianus to Honorius. However, both were killed in transit by Dardanus so that their heads were put on display at Ravenna on 30 August 412. This callous murder earned Dardanus a bad name among the Gallic nobility. This is not surprising in light of the fact that most of the Gallic nobility had supported the usurpers, including Iovinus. According to Hydatius's version (Olymp. 298.19), Honorius' *duces* crushed and killed Iovinus and Sebastianus in Narbo, which does suggest that the Romans had assisted Athaulf, but it is still impossible to know their exact role – perhaps they helped in the siege, because the Visigoths were known to be poor besiegers. One obvious possibility is that the *duces* included Constantius.

The parties to the *foedus*, however, faced an unforeseen problem. The Visigoths had been promised both land and subsistence. This deal was destroyed by the usurpation of Heraclianus in North Africa in 412. Honorius was now unable to deliver the provisions he had promised, because it is absolutely certain that Heraclianus stopped the grain deliveries at the same moment as he usurped power. In this case, Honorius indeed does not seem to have tried to double cross Athaulf, but Athaulf did not know that. It was then that Constantius asked Athaulf to return Galla Placidia and solemnly promised to deliver the missing provisions afterwards, but only if Galla Placidia was handed over to him first. Unsurprisingly, Athaulf had very little trust left in Roman promises and prepared to wage war against the faithless Romans. However, in order to lull the Romans into the belief that nothing was amiss, Athaulf pretended to agree. He advanced his army to Massilia (Marseille) with the intention of capturing it through treachery, but his attempt failed miserably. This actually suggests that Massilia had probably remained in Constantius' hands after 411. The other alternative would be that Athaulf had surrendered it to Constantius/Honorius immediately after his defection, but this is less likely in a situation in which the other party had not yet fulfilled their promises. The defenders fought back with determination. The heroic Bonifatius (Boniface) engaged Athaulf in combat and delivered so powerful a blow to Athaulf that he was forced to retire to his tent and abandon the assault and siege. Had they fought a single combat? This happened presumably in late summer or early autumn in 412.

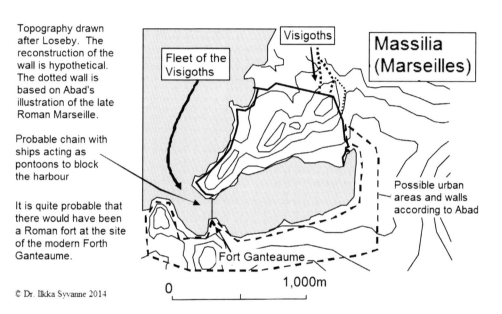

Topography drawn after Loseby. The reconstruction of the wall is hypothetical. The dotted wall is based on Abad's illustration of the late Roman Marseille.

Probable chain with ships acting as pontoons to block the harbour

It is quite probable that there would have been a Roman fort at the site of the modern Forth Ganteaume.

Visigoths

Fleet of the Visigoths

Massilia (Marseilles)

Possible urban areas and walls according to Abad

Fort Ganteaume

0   1,000m

© Dr. Ilkka Syvänne 2014

We do not know the whereabouts of Bonifatius between 412 and 416, but in 417 he served as tribune of the *foederati* in Africa (PLRE2). He seems to have distinguished himself, with the result that he was probably promoted to the post of *praepositus limitis* (PLRE2) and I would suggest that he had been promoted to the post of *Comes Africae* by 422. This was to have great historical significance later when Bonifatius remained a steadfast ally of Galla Placidia.

After this, Athaulf advanced against Narbo (Narbonne) at the time of the harvest (Hydat. Olympiad 298.19), Tolosa (Toulouse) and Burdigala (modern Bordeaux), all of which he managed to capture – probably through voluntary surrender (see the Maps at the beginning). We should not forget that it is probable that at this time the Visigoths still possessed a fleet (captured previously in Italy), which provided logistical support and supported operations against coastal cities such as Massilia and Narbo. As a result of these successes and the fleet, Athaulf was able to establish himself in Narbonensis and Aquitania. The sequence of events suggests that Athaulf nominated Attalus as his puppet Emperor immediately on his arrival at Narbo in about 412/3, at which time Attalus also nominated his own officials. These included Paulinus of Pella (Eucharistus 264ff, esp. 291ff.), who was nominated as *Comes Privatarum Largitionum*. Paulinus and his fellow nobles centred at Bordeaux in Aquitania were ready to accept Attalus' overtures because they attempted to appease the Goths. The Gallic nobility was fed up with Honorius and his corrupt minions who had failed to defend them. Consequently, the Aquitanians welcomed the Goths into their territory so that at least part of the Gothic host was billeted in the city of Bordeaux, the rest being billeted around the major population centres between Narbonne and Bordeaux.

Paulinus notes that Attalus lacked a powerbase and therefore did not possess any real power, which also meant that Paulinus had received an empty honour. However, it was probably thanks to this empty honour that Paulinus' own house at Burdigala was not ordered to house any Gothic troops – much to his own detriment, as we shall see – because unlike the Roman regulars, the Goths were in the habit of protecting their hosts. When Athaulf came to the conclusion that the re-nomination of Attalus as Emperor had been useless and had not brought about defections among the Romans, he decided to abandon him. It is possible that it was then that Athaulf decided to establish '*Gothia*' in place of '*Romania*', but in my opinion it is probable that he had already been seduced to change his position by none other than Galla Placidia, because he married her on his arrival at Narbo. It is because of this that I would suggest that she had already seduced Athaulf at Burdigala with her beauty and with her sound advice so that Athaulf wanted to marry Galla Placidia and make his Visigoths the soldiers of a new '*Romania*'. It is probable that Galla Placidia was suffering from the so-called Stockholm Syndrome (sometimes called also as Helsinki Syndrome) as a result of which she had started to identify her own interests with those of her Visigothic captors. The other alternative is that Athaulf was just too handsome for her to resist even if it is clear that there were also political reasons for Athaulf's behaviour.

When Athaulf then deposed Attalus and his officials, he ordered his troops to burn the city of Bordeaux as they started their retreat to Narbo. It was then that the Gothic guests protected the houses in which they had been billeted and looted and torched the houses which lacked Gothic guests (Paul. Euch. 280ff.). As former officials of Attalus, Paulinus and his mother were targeted in particular. They were robbed, but still allowed to depart without injury to the town of Vasatica. The nobles of Vasatica (Bazas) prepared for siege, but not all were happy with the policies followed by the Gallic nobility, because Paulinus states that the local slaves and some youths attempted to assassinate him. The assassin, however, was captured even before Paulinus reached the town and the ringleaders were killed. The fact that the local youths and slaves had formed a revolutionary resistance group ('*Bacaudae*') with the intention of killing the local nobles is very significant. This shows the general state of unhappiness of the people towards the corrupt Roman officials and local nobility/gentry, which was to have dire consequences for the Empire because it eased the transition from the Roman Empire into those of its successor states in the west. It is clear that many locals considered it preferable to live under the Visigoths.

When the united forces of Athaulf and Alans had set out for a long siege of the town of Vasatica, which lay on the route leading to Toulouse (Tolosa) and Narbonne (Narbo), Paulinus was naturally frightened. It should be stressed that even though Athaulf did not have with him his whole force, the Visigoths possessed more than enough men to take the small town of Bazas. Not unnaturally, in this situation Paulinus came up with a plan to flee from the city with the help of the king of the Alans, whom he considered to be friendly to him. Paulinus also knew that the king was unhappy at being forced to fight against the

Romans. Consequently, it is not surprising that the king, who was by now eager to desert Athaulf and rejoin the Romans, came up with a better plan. The king stated that he would be unable to protect Paulinus and his dearest outside the city. He claimed that this was possible only if he was admitted inside to join Paulinus. Paulinus and the leading citizens agreed, as long as they first received the king's wife and favourite son as hostages. The king sent both, after which he led his warriors and their families next to the city walls to form a barrier of wagons and soldiers around the city. This must mean that part of the city which lacked walls altogether. Paulinus and the leading city councellors had taken a huge gamble which had paid off handsomely. This was a great bonanza for the Romans and not only for the city of Vasatica. The king was a very powerful warlord whose services would prove to be of great value. On the basis of the size of the town surrounded, the Alan king had a maximum of 10,000 warriors with him, but we do not know whether he had also left part of his forces behind in other cities as had the Visigoths. It is sometimes suggested that the Alan king would have been Goar, but Sambida (i.e. Sangiban?) seems the likelier candidate (see later). Athaulf had no other alternative than to abandon the siege and continue the march to Narbo.

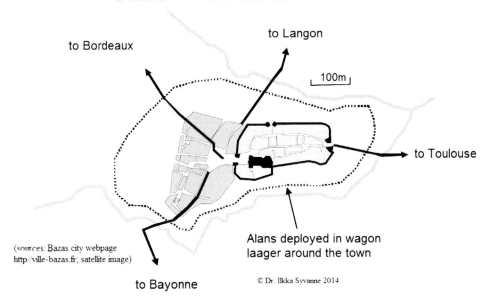

Bazas 4th-6th centuries AD

to Langon

to Bordeaux

100m

to Toulouse

Alans deployed in wagon
laager around the town

(sources: Bazas city webpage
http://ville-bazas.fr; satellite image)

to Bayonne

© Dr. Ilkka Syvänne 2014

In the meanwhile, while Athaulf was moving west, Constantius seems to have followed in his footsteps and secured with the help of the navy (see below) the control of the Rhodanus (i.e. the western portion of Narbonensis), together with north and north-west Gaul. The reason for this conclusion is the fact that Frigeridus (apud. Greg. Tours 2.9) states that the *duces* of Honorius captured and killed Decimus Rusticus (Prefect of the tyrants), Agroetius (*Primicerius Notariorum* of Iovinus) and many other Gallic noblemen at the time when the Franks sacked and burned the city of Treves for the second time. I would date these Frankish attacks in the north against Treves and other areas to the years

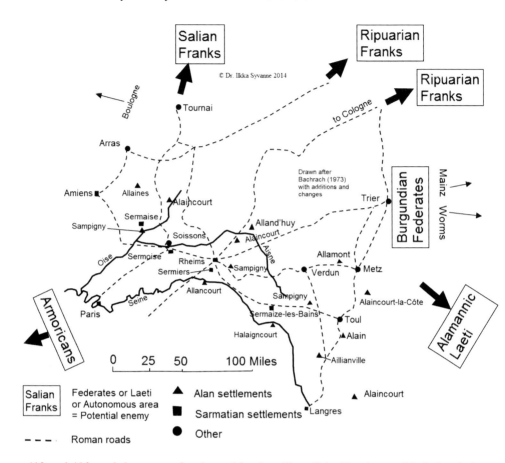

412 and 413, and the reason for the sudden hostility of the Franks would obviously have been the downfall of Iovinus.

Constantius' forces must have simultaneously started operations against the Franks because Honorius confirmed the Burgundians in possession of *Germania Prima* as Roman federates in 413 (Prosper 413; Bury, 1.200). In other words, Constantius divided the enemy forces (the Burgundians had also been allies of Iovinus) by buying off the Burgundians to his side against the Franks. It seems probable that the Alans of Goar were also given some land at the same time because Goar had previously cooperated with the Burgundians. The Alans and Burgundians would have been used to pacify the Franks and Armoricans. The area which was given to Goar is not known, but Bachrach's (1973, 59ff.) educated guess, which is based on place names and locale close to Goar's next known locale near Orleans, is the likeliest alternative (see the accompanying map). The area included old Sarmatian settlements and may also have included earlier settlements of Alans. Therefore, the location was ideal. In this position the Alans were ideally positioned to intervene against the Franks, Burgundians and Armoricans. One may also imagine that the remnants of the older Sarmatian units were now placed under Goar. The core areas of the Burgundian settlement ran from Mainz to south of Worms so that the city of Worms probably served as 'capital' of the First Burgundian Kingdom. The epitaph of Hariulf in Trier proves that some Burgundians were also stationed there (he was *Domesticus* and a member of the Burgundian royal family), but Paulinus' account of the sieges of Trier prove that their role in the defence of the city was not that significant. For a fuller analysis of the Burgundians, see Escher.

The operation of dividing the enemy forces seems to have been a success, because we soon learn that 'Exuperantius' (probably in the capacity of *Dux Tractus Armoricani et Nervicani*: see PLRE2, Rutilius Namatianus 213ff.) pacified the Bacaudae of Armorica in about 415–417. This would have been difficult to accomplish had the Franks still controlled the Rhine frontier. It is unfortunate that we do not know the name of the commander who must have defeated the Franks at this time – the obvious candidates include Constantius (this would explain why the Visigoths were able to operate relatively freely in south-west Gaul and is therefore quite plausible) and/or Ulfilas (another very probable candidate), or Sabinianus (least likely), or someone unknown. Rutilius Namatianus (401ff.) also implies that his friend Victorinus, who had been forced to flee from Tolosa in about 413/4 when it was taken by Athaulf, had before that served as *Vicarius Britanniarum*, which may imply that Victorinus had been *Vicarius* in about 412/3. Whatever the case regarding Victorinus, the fact that Britain was retaken in about 412/3 is confirmed by the fact that before the mid-fourth century the local authorities in Britain repeatedly asked for help from the continent, either for spiritual reasons or for reasons of defence against enemies. It is difficult to see this to have happened unless Britain was considered to be part of the Roman Empire. It should also be noted that the retaking of Britain implies also the pacification of the Franks and Saxons alongside the Bacaudae of Armorica. Constantius was rewarded for his great services with his first consulship for the year 414. Since Constantius was uncorrupted he did not possess enough money to celebrate his consulship and it was because of this that he received the estates of Heraclianus to cover the costs (see below). This, however, was not the end of troubles, neither with the Franks nor with the freedom-loving Armoricans as we shall see.

Ian Hughes (2012, 59–61) has also noted another very important development that took place in Gaul, which was that the hierarchial ties to the Emperor at Ravenna broke down thanks to the fact that the Gallic aristocracy had sided with the usurpers. This had meant that ever smaller numbers of Gallic aristocrats had been enrolled into the imperial administration in Italy, which meant fewer chances of promotion in the imperial administration through patronage, which in its turn meant that the members of the Gallic aristocracy started to seek advancement within the Church. The breakdown of the imperial administration resulting from the usurpations and barbarian invasions had also meant that the Gauls had become used to self-rule, and since the Church was usually the only functioning organisation it is not surprising that the locals started to see their bishops as their spokesmen towards the Emperor. The imperial administration in its turn sought to appease the Gallic aristocracy, which had become used to self-rule, by appointing the Prefects of Gaul from their ranks and not from the ranks of Italian senators as previously.

The Usurpation of Heraclianus in 412–413

As noted above, the *Comes Africae* Heraclianus was nominated as consul for the year 413 but instead of showing gratitude for this he revolted, apparently in the spring of 412 while the Visigoths and Alans under Athaulf had abandoned the south of Italy and marched to the south of Gaul. The evacuation of Italy by the Visigoths opened the route for Heraclianus to invade. Heraclianus married his daughter to his second-in-command, his *Domesticus* Sabinus in order to secure his loyalty.

According to Orosius (7.42.12–13), Heraclianus had amassed for the invasion of Italy the largest fleet known to Orosius' day. It was claimed to have consisted of 3,700 ships (!), which if true does indeed support Orosius' amazement. This suggests that Heraclianus had been preparing for the revolt for a long time – in fact he seems to have used most of his property to build up the resources necessary for the usurpation because afterwards it was found out that Heraclianus' property was barely worth 2,000 lbs of gold (PLRE2) – and he was a man known to take bribes! Heraclianus' timing was also impeccable and undoubtedly the result of careful planning. In other words, even though Heraclianus was also a hopeless drunkard like most of the high-ranking military men of his age, he had not gambled away his future as a result of some drunken fit. Honorius' gifted commander Constantius and most of the field army and imperial fleet had been sent to Gaul and Spain, so Italy lay open for invasion. The timing of the invasion to late-412 or early-413 must also have been a great surprise, because naval operations were usually not undertaken during the winter season. In addition to this, for a *Comes Africae* Heraclianus possessed an exceptionally strong army, because Honorius had previously in 409 reinforced his army with the forces assembled at Ravenna (see above) and with the Gallic troops of Gerontius and Maximus in 411 (Oros. 7.42.5). Orosius claims that the Gallic troops were then recalled ('*reuocati sunt*') to Italy, but one can perhaps venture to see in this an attempt by the central government to transfer the troops back to Italy when they started to harbour suspicions regarding Heraclianus, a move which failed thanks to the fact that the latter revolted immediately – at least that is my educated guess. It seems improbable that Heraclianus would have surrendered the forces in question when given the order to send them to Italy if he planned to usurp power as he did.

Heraclianus took command of the invasion in person and disembarked his forces with the aim of taking the city of Rome. According to Hydatius (a.413) and Orosius (7.42.14), Heraclianus was defeated at Utriculum (probably Ocriculum just north of Rome en route to Ravenna) by the *Comes* Marinus, which resulted in the slaughter of 50,000 soldiers, most of whom must have belonged to Heraclianus. On the basis of this it is clear that Constantius's forces were in north-west Italy and south-east Gaul, where they secured the important cities against Athaulf, while Generidus or his successor secured the Alps and Illyricum. We do not know the details of the battle, but since we do know that Heraclianus' army was essentially wiped out, it seems probable that Marinus managed to surround the enemy and/or to force it against an obstacle. The location, Ocriculum, suggests two alternatives: Marinus could have deployed his main forces on the other side of the river to block the advance of Heraclianus' force while placing some ambushers on the hills behind the enemy line for the battle to become such a slaughter; or, even more likely, Marinus could have deployed his forces on the higher ground behind Ocriculum and let the enemy cross the river, after which he would have outflanked the enemy from his advantageous position (he may also have posted some forces in ambuscades) and then forced them against the river which blocked their route of retreat (see the accompanying map into which I have reconstructed the latter alternative). The death of 50,000 mostly-native soldiers at this date was a horrible disaster for the Roman Empire.

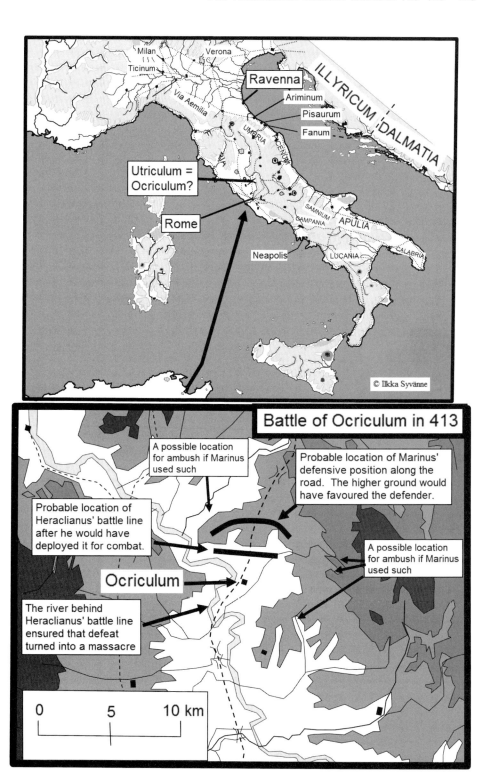

The defeated Heraclianus embarked on a ship and fled to Carthage, where a group of soldiers/assassins sent by Honorius killed him on 7 March 413. This seems to have happened even before the arrival of Marinus, who pursued the defeated foe to Carthage. Heraclianus' son-in-law Sabinus fled to Constantinople, but was then returned to the West and punished with exile. Sabinus clearly thought that the Eastern government would be hostile enough to protect the son-in-law of a usurper, but in this he was clearly mistaken. Whether he had any other reason (for example knowledge of negotiations between Heraclianus and the Eastern government prior to the revolt) for his belief in the general hostility between the different halves of the Empire, we do not know. Marinus, who had proved himself a capable military commander, proved himself too violent and strict in exacting reprisals against Heraclianus' followers and supposed followers (see the sources mentioned with the PLRE2).

At the same time as this operation was going on Honorius sought to force a new unity on the Church of Africa. The task was entrusted to the *tribunus et notarius* Marcellinus, who had prior to this served in the same capacity under Heraclianus. Marinus, however, had him and his brother killed at Carthage, either because he suspected that Marcellinus had sided with Heraclianus or because he had been bribed with gold to do so (see PLRE2). The sources suggest that Marcellinus was innocent. As a result of this incident Marinus was recalled from Africa and dismissed from service. Thereby the Roman Empire lost another able commander (and a native one!). His services would have been needed amidst all the troubles.

The Edict (CTh 7.18.16) issued to the *Comes et Magister* Gaiso at Ravenna on 12 June 413 is illustrative of the desperation felt by the imperial authorities at the time.[3] By then the manpower shortages were so bad that soldiers who had spent a year without any leave of absence were to be demoted only ten ranks, those who had spent two years were to be demoted 20 ranks, those who had spent three years were to be demoted 30 ranks, and it was only after four years of absence that the soldier was to be removed from the official registers and punished with the full force of the law. The punishments were lowered in a desperate attempt to lure the deserters back into ranks.

Athaulf's Moves and Constantius' Counter-Moves in 414–415

In January 414 Athaulf (Athaulfus) married Galla Placidia, the half-sister of Honorius and Arcadius, at Narbonne (Narbo). According to Olympiodorus (fr.24), Athaulf's marriage was the result of advice and encouragement given by Candidianus. It is very unfortunate that we do not know who this person was. The PLRE 2 suggests that he was a mere advisor to Athaulf, but I would not preclude the possibility that he was one of the *magistri* with the name Candidianus (in PLRE 1–2), all of whom by the way may be one and the same person. The marriage was celebrated in the Roman manner in the house of Ingenuus, one of the leading citizens of Narbonne (Narbo). The nuptial hymns were sung by Attalus (the former Emperor), Rusticius and Phoebadius.

The marriage signified that Athaulf intended to unite the Goths and Romans under the rule of his own dynasty, which combined the House of the Balthi with the House of Theodosius. According to Orosius (Tr. by Raymond p.396, parentheses added), who based his account on an eyewitness account of a native of Narbo:

It seems that at first he [*Athaulf*] ardently desired to blot out the Roman name and to make all the Roman territory a Gothic empire in fact as well as in name, so that, to use the popular expressions, *Gothia* should take place of *Romania* [*this is the first known instance of the use of this name for the Roman Empire*], and he, Athaulf, should become all that Caesar Augustus had been. Having discovered from long experience that the Goths, because of their unbridled barbarism, were utterly incapable of obeying laws [*i.e. this was the expression of their freedom, which so lured the Romans too*], and yet believing that the state ought not to be deprived of laws without which a state is not a state, he chose to seek for himself at least the glory of restoring and increasing the renown of the Roman name by the power of the Goths, … He was helped especially by his wife, Placidia, who was a woman of the keenest intelligence and of exceptional piety; by her persuasion and advice he was guided in all measures leading to good government.

The marriage into the imperial family made Athaulf theoretically eligible to be a legitimate Emperor of the Romans. This was not as far fetched as it may seem today, because the Eastern Empire was at the time ruled by a 'half-barbarian' Theodosius II. In other words, this marriage was a policy decision, which signified an attempt to unite the Roman Empire with the Gothic Empire. In short, he aimed to breathe new life into the Roman Empire with his Gothic army. However, this was not to be, because the gifted *Comes et Magister* Constantius, headquartered at the city of Arelate, used a combination of military action (details unknown but may have included the fighting of battles and at least one naval battle, since he was rewarded with the title of *Patricius*, which is attested for him for the first time in 415) and a naval blockade to overcome the Visigoths. Constantius' goal was not to destroy the Visigoths, but to force them to evacuate Gaul and move into Spain where they would be confronted by the other barbarians, the Vandals, Alans and Suevi, so that eventually they would be forced to hand over Galla Placidia and make a peace agreement. It is very unfortunate that we do not know how Constantius forced the Visigoths to move on and how he cut off the grain supply to them when the Visigoths also possessed a fleet. The obvious answer is that Constantius' own fleet must have inflicted a decisive defeat on the Visigothic fleet which the sources just group into one of several victories achieved by Constantius. It is otherwise very difficult to see how Constantius could have blockaded the Visigoths.

According to Orosius, the Visigoths had already moved from Narbonne into Spain in 414, but modern research (e.g. Wolfram) suggests that the Visigoths evacuated Narbonne only in 415. I prefer the former, because it was in Barcelona (Barcino) that Galla Placidia bore Athaulf a son. Naturally, en route to Spain the Visigoths pillaged everything they could lay their hands on. Constantius' ultimate goal was to force the Visigoths to release Galla Placidia and become *foederati* so that these could be used as his forces. Whether this was a wise decision is another question, but it may have seemed like the best policy at the time it was made.

Regardless of this, as noted above for a while it seemed as if Athaulf's imperial dreams could come true, for Galla Placidia gave birth to a son who was named Theodosius, but he died soon after the birth. Had he lived, he would have had as good claims on the throne as Theodosius II had in the East. Theodosius II was also a half-barbarian, because his

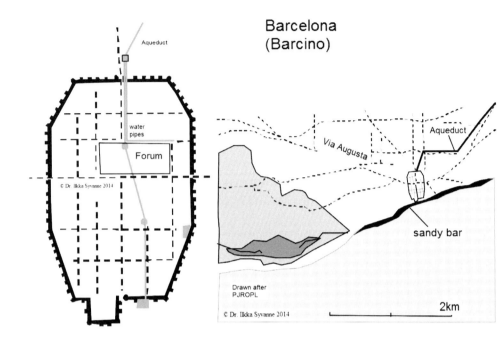

Barcelona (Barcino)

mother was a Frank. This seems like such a lucky strike for the Romans that one wonders whether the death was caused by foul play. The fifth-century Romans were certainly not above assassinating their enemies. The birth of the son had made Athaulf even friendlier towards the Romans, but unsurprisingly this was vehemently opposed by Constantius, who had been promised Galla's hand in marriage (Olymp. fr.26.1–2). Consequently, there was little chance for peace as long as the situation persisted.

Fortunately for Constantius and Honorius, Athaulf had made the mistake of keeping one of Sarus' servants, called Dubius, in his stables, together with Sarus' brother in the ranks of his followers. Dubius avenged the death of his first master by murdering his second master (Bury 1.190). It is probable that this was done at the instigation of Sarus' brother Sigeric (Singeric/Sigiricus/ Singerichus/ Segerichus), who duly usurped power, which suggests a premeditated operation. One wonders whether some Roman undercover operatives/agent provocateurs/double agents had contributed to the situation. Athaulf's death was announced at Constantinople on 24 Sept. 415 (Chron. Pasch. 415).

Sigeric attempted to secure his own position by killing Athaulf's children from his first marriage and by treating Galla Placidia harshly. She was forced to walk on foot for 12 miles among the captives, and she was once again made a hostage. Sigeric's rule, however, proved short. He was murdered after only seven days, following which he was succeeded by Vallia (Valia/Wallia). This time the succession was legitimate, because Vallia was elected by the Visigothic nobility (senate).

While the above events were taking place there appears to have been a change in the defensive structures in the Balkans in that the Western Government transferred Dalmatia to the jurisdiction of East Rome, presumably because Ravenna lacked resources to defend the area. The proof that Dalmatia was under East Roman administration in about 414/5 consists of two inscriptions in Salona which name only Eastern consuls, one of whom was not recognized by Honorius (MacGeorge, 39). It is possible that this administrative change or occupation of the area took place as a preparatory move in 408/9, before the dispatch of help to Honorius.

The Foedus of 416

In 415 Vallia was elected with the task of continuing the war. However, contrary to the wishes of the majority of the Visigoths, Vallia sought to avoid direct confrontation with Constantius and rather tried to transport his entire people from Spain to Africa, but a violent storm at a distance of 12 miles from the Straits of Gibraltar (Strait of Gades) prevented this. This probably means that the Visigoths had either managed to convince the Alans of Carthaginiensis and Silings of Baetica to allow them a free passage, or alternatively that they had forced their way through. Vallia probably attempted the dangerous crossing in mid-winter 415/6 because it is probable that the Roman fleet would have been withdrawn to their harbours. As a result of this disastrous attempt Vallia was able to convince his followers that the wisest policy was to agree to a peace with the Romans. Had the Visigoths not agreed, they would have starved to death because on the one side they were subjected to a naval blockade by Constantius' fleet and on the other side the Vandals prevented them from obtaining supplies except through the payment of exorbitant sums of money. All this makes it quite clear that the Visigothic fleet was too weak to challenge Constantius' fleet. According to Olympiodorus, the Vandals called the Goths *Truli*, because the Goths were forced to buy grain from the Vandals at one *solidus* (gold coin) per *trula*, which was 48 times the normal rate (Blockley, p.218).

By the spring of 416 Vallia had no alternative but to open up negotiations and the Romans sent the *agens in rebus* Euplutius to negotiate the treaty (Olymp. fr. 30). Vallia agreed to hand over Galla Placidia together with hostages and promised to serve loyally as *foederatus* against other barbarians in return for food (*annona*). Attalus had either already been abandoned to his own devices in 415, or had fled before this only to be captured by Constantius's forces, or was now handed over to Honorius (the sources have different versions, see e.g. PLRE), after which he was publicly mutilated in the presence of Honorius and then exiled to the Lipari Islands – which can be seen as an act of kindness in light of the period practices.

This time the Romans delivered the grain (600,000 measures of it) and Vallia duly handed Galla Placidia to Euplutius so that he could deliver her to Honorius. Constantius must have been in triumphant mood. He had not only triumphed over the Visigoths, but could finally marry the Emperor's sister Galla Placidia. Galla Placidia, however, was unwilling to marry Constantius. Consequently, Honorius forced her to go through with the ceremony on the same day as Constantius obtained his second consulship on 1 January 417. The marriage was consummated and a daughter called Iusta Grata Honoria was born in 417/8, while a second child, the future emperor Valentinian III (Placidus Valentinianus), was born on 2 July 419. Constantius could look forward to a bright future.

In the meanwhile, however, the Visigoths had started the agreed operations against the four barbarian peoples that had divided Spain amongst themselves. Vallia conducted the military campaign against the barbarians with ruthless efficiency. It is possible to restore

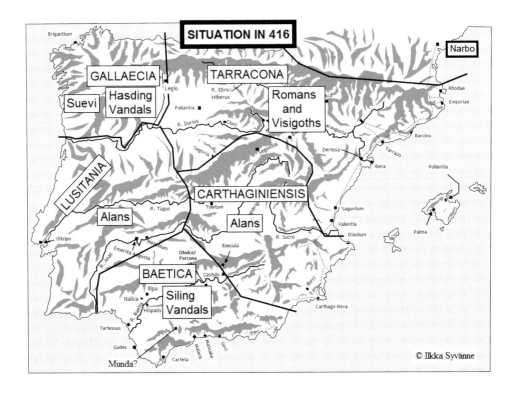

the sequence of events when one combines Hydatius' Chronicle (23–24/Olymp. 299) with the geography. The Visigoths crushed first the barbarians in Carthaginiensis in 417 (Hydat. 23), which I take to mean the combined armies of Alans and Vandals, after which Vallia advanced against the Siling Vandals in Baetica (24). Hydatius states that all of the Silings were killed, but this is an overstatement even if it reflects the maginitude of the defeat accurately. Following this, the Visigoths marched to Lusitania, where they inflicted a crushing defeat on the Alans and killed their king Addax in battle. The remnants of the Alan army were forced to seek protection from King Gunderic of the Hasdingi Vandals in Gallaecia. Before their crushing defeat the Alans had been the overlords of the Vandals and Suevi, but now they became a subtribe of the Vandal nation and as such partook in the conquest of North Africa. According to Orosius (7.43.14ff.), the kings of the Alans, Vandals and Suevi had already sent ambassadors to Honorius to beg for a peace and *foedus* when Vallia was fighting against them. It was then that Constantius unwisely called off the attack, quite evidently because Honorius had agreed to the terms proposed. By 420 the Romans and Vandals were already at each other's throats.

It would be interesting to know whether Honorius had agreed to sign treaties with the Vandals and Suevi at the instigation of Constantius, or whether he had acted on his own (obviously after having discussed the matter at his Sacred Consistory). The facts that the Visigoths were recalled by Constantius and that he re-negotiated the *foedus* with the Visigoths (Hydat. 24 Olymp. 299; Prosper a.419) are not conclusive because he could have been ordered to do so. On the other hand, it would be entirely in keeping with Constantius' strong position at this time that he was behind the order. I would suggest that Constantius was indeed behind this decision and policy as implied by the sources – Honorius was not known for his readiness to make any concessions to the Goths. The purpose of the decision was not to allow the Visigoths to defeat and incorporate the remaining Vandal and Alan forces into their own, which would have made the Visigoths ever more dangerous, but to force the Vandals and Suevi to become *foederati* as well so that they would counterbalance each other. Since the fighting stopped for two years, it seemed as if this goal was achieved, but all the same this decision proved to be a grave mistake. The Romans had now lost their best, and in practice their last, chance of defeating the Vandals and Suevi, but in Constantius' defence one must say that he cannot have foreseen this. After all, Constantius had been able to defeat the Visigoths through manoeuvring and he could expect to be able to do that with equal ease against the weaker Vandals and Suevi. However, that would have required able leadership, which was conspicuously lacking after Constantius' death – after his death there followed a succession of bad or mediocre field commanders, the sole exception being Aetius – which naturally ensured the downfall of West Rome. The second part of Constantius' treaty was the settlement of the Visigoths in Aquitania II. This was also initially a success, but once again in the absence of able Roman military and political leadership it too turned into an unmitigated disaster.

When Constantius had prevented the Visigoths from carrying out the wholesale destruction of the Vandals, Alans and Suevi, he obviously had to placate them somehow with the approval of Honorius. Constantius chose to reward Vallia and the Visigoths with land in *Aquitania II*, with small batches of land also in *Novempopulana* and *Narbonensis* in return for their service as *foederati*. Despite the previous devastation caused by the Visigoths in this area, it still economically viable enough to support the whole Visigothic nation. The idea was clearly to protect the western passes of the Pyrenees with the Visigoths if the Vandals and Suevi failed to live up to their promises, while the eastern passes would be protected by new settlements of Alan *foederati*. The plan may also have been to isolate the rebellious Armoricans in their own territory. The placing of the Visigoths in Aquitania II also removed from them the fleet with which they had terrorized the coasts of Italy and which had enabled them to take the coastal cities of Spain. This in fact must have been the most important part of the plan. The forcing of the Vandals, Alans and Suevi away from the Mediterranean coast must have been part of the same plan. The Romans clearly considered the Atlantic coast to be of secondary importance, and that it could therefore be left partially in barbarian hands.

The Foedus of 418: Gothia is Born

Vallia, however, did not live to see the fruits of his *foedus*. It was left for his successor Theoderic I (418–451) to settle the Visigoths in their new and permanent homes. Theoderic's succession to the throne was smooth because he was either the son of Alaric I or was married to Alaric's daughter. The reason for this conclusion is that his son Theoderic II was grandson of Alaric I. The strength of the Visigothic position is evident from the fact that in contrast to the usual rules of *hospitalitas*, the Visigoths took two-thirds of the property of their Roman hosts for their own use and left only one-third to the natives. The norm was that the soldier(s) were entitled to receive only a third, but there was little that the Romans could do when the Visigothic horde arrived in their new homes.

The creation of the Visigothic Kingdom of Federates in Aquitania was accompanied by additional important security measures on the part of Honorius's government. He set up a new Gallic Council under the *PPG* at Arelate, consisting of the governors of the seven provinces, of the highest class of decurions, and of the representatives of the landed gentry. According to Wolfram's (2005, 147) calculation, the first session of the Council took place before the granting of Aquitania to the Visigoths, with the implication that the Council was convened for the first time with the purpose of making the granting of land acceptable to the Gallic nobility. In fact, Wolfram even suggests that the purpose of giving land to the Visigoths in Gaul was to use the Visigoths against the internal enemies threatening the existing social order. If this indeed was the primary purpose, it proved to be a grave mistake.

The concept for the Council was not new as provincial councils had existed until the third century and new ones had been created in Africa and possibly in Spain during the fourth century, and the *PPG* Petronius had also created one in 407 (Bury 1.207). However, the circumstances in which this council was created were entirely new. There were now two barbarian kingdoms, the Visigoths and the Burgundians, not to mention the other *foederati* and *Bacaudae* within Gaul that offered for the disaffected a chance of fleeing the imperial oppression. The intention of the new council was to tie the upper classes more tightly into the imperial system by giving them a voice in the imperial administration. The councillors could now debate public questions, make complaints against corrupt officials and make suggestions to the *PPG*. This solution failed to address the grievances of the population at large, who voted with their feet.

The second of the security measures adopted by Constantius appears to have been to settle the Alans, who had deserted the Visigoths, in the area around the Visigothic settlements, and between their settlements and the city of Narbonne, to protect this vitally important corridor between Gaul and Spain against possible Visigothic revolt. The same Alans could be used to protect the route from Spain to Gaul. Two detachments of Alans

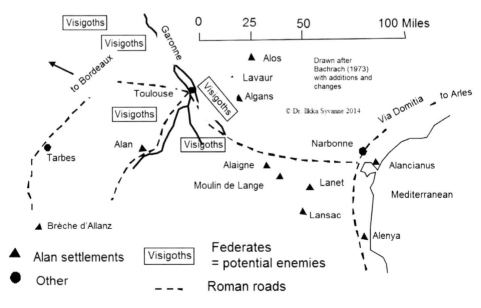

also appear to have been placed to protect the road from Toulouse to Spain. Bachrach has reconstructed the likely locations on the basis of the place names (see the map).

It seems probable that we should also see the Edict ordering the expulsion of the Jews from Imperial service and armed forces, issued on 10 March 418 by Honorius to the *PPI* Palladius, as a security measure (CTh 16.8.24). According to this Edict, the Jewish *agentes in rebus* and *palatini* (note that either the Jews had been able to make their way back into the *agentes* after the Edict in 404 had expelled them, or that it had not been put into effect in practice by those in charge) were to be allowed to complete their service, but no new ones were to be admitted. However, all those who had joined the armed services were to be removed from office immediately. The fact that the Jews were allowed to complete their service in the 'Secret Service' and in the court does suggest that their loyalty was not really suspect. Why else would they had been left in their posts? This begs the question of why this Edict was issued. It cannot have improved morale among those who were left to fulfil their service. Had there been some instances in which the Jews had cooperated with the barbarian invaders, for example in Spain, that had made them suspect? It is unfortunate that the Edict doesn't state why it was issued. Perhaps the likeliest reason was simply that the loyalty of the Jews was considered suspect in general terms by the bigoted Catholics and the state considered their presence in the military to be particularly dangerous. It is indeed very difficult to see any reason for this policy in the West.

Paulinus' *Eucharisticus* (496ff.) offers us a very good view into the mindset of the Gallic youth. Two of his sons (presumably the younger sons), who belonged to the upper class and cannot therefore be considered to have been destitute, decided to seek their fortunes among the Gothic settlers because they yearned for freedom. The Visigoths did not oppress their subjects like the Roman authorities with heavy taxes and illegal corrupt practices. On top of it all, the Visigoths actually protected their hosts from depredations, unlike the regular Roman army which was known to abuse their hosts when billeted in cities. Paulinus' text (571ff.) also makes it clear that despite their quite apparent military might the Visigoths were prepared to follow legal procedures, because he states that a Goth bought his property in Massilia. In other words, even the rich and powerful preferred the freedom promised by the Goths over the straightjacket of the Roman Empire. The imperial administration was just too oppressive and corrupt for many citizens to bear. This had had three consequences. The members of the upper class had formed councils at least in Britain and Gaul. Honorius co-opted these councils by making them legal and thereby gained the support of the nobles, but this obviously failed to satisfy those who craved real freedom. The nobles in their turn oppressed the poor as city councillors and imperial officials. The slaves, peasants and some members of the upper-classes (mainly the younger sons who had to seek their fortunes) formed groups of bandits and revolutionaries who purposefully lived like barbarian bandits outside the law. The imperial administration was usually able to suppress these groups thanks to the fact that they possessed better military organization, but they were unable to do this when the discontented sought a place of refuge among the barbarian settlers, especially among the Visigoths. The Visigoths proved too powerful for the imperial authorities to crush.

I would go so far as to claim that the principal reason for the collapse of West Rome was not the military problems caused by the creation of barbarian kingdoms within the

Empire, but rather the general disaffection of the people against the representatives of the imperial administration. The presence of the barbarian kingdoms within the Empire offered for all the disaffected a chance to escape imperial oppression, or alternatively the chance to betray their cities to these newcomers at the first opportunity. This yearning for freedom proved just too strong for the imperial authorities to contain effectively.[4] The situation in the East was entirely different, but had clear parallels. The East was fortunate in that it faced on its eastern frontier only nations that were equally or even more oppressive than the Roman authorities. The Sassanian Empire was a particularly unattractive alternative for the locals with its oppressive religious police. It was known to be oppressive and to persecute Christians with extreme harshness. Not a nice prospect for the mostly Christian population of the East. However, when the Huns made an appearance in the East as happened in 395, there were locals who were not afraid of them, but rather joined them for the sake of freedom (see above). Consequently, the East Romans were fortunate in that they faced the Huns only in the Balkans. In fact, as we shall see later in the context of Priscus' account, the Hunnic Kingdom of Attila contained some Roman turncoats who preferred to live in freedom among the Huns, but their numbers remained small largely because the Huns were just too barbarian in their lifestyle. One may actually suspect that the relative ease with which the Huns (and later the Ostrogoths) took cities in the Balkans resulted at least partially from the disaffection of the local populace against the corrupt imperial authorities. In short, I would suggest that the principal cause for the survival of the East and collapse of the West lay in the relative preponderance of such barbarian enemies among the latter that provided real freedom for its subjects. The Sassanians invited only scorn, hatred and fear and the Huns were just too uncivilized.[5]

Chapter Eleven

The West 418–423

Turmoil in Spain 419–424

The peace which was achieved in 418 proved ephemereal. The fighting started as a tribal conflict between the Vandals and Suevi in 419 and it resulted from a personal quarrel between Gunderic the King of the Vandals and Hermeric the King of the Suevi. The Vandals blockaded the Suevi in the Erbasian Mountains (*Nerbasis montibus*) with the result that the *Comes Hispaniorum* Asterius had to intervene in 420. He forced the Vandals to abandon their siege and to flee to Baetica. Asterius was duly rewarded for his services with the title of *Patricius* in 420/421. According to the Gallic Chronicle 452 (p.656), Maximus usurped power in Spain in about 420. I would connect this with the above so that the Vandals had probably raised the former usurper Maximus ("domestic" of Gerontius) as their figurehead ruler and it was this that had made it necessary for Asterius to intervene. The reason for the promotion of Asterius as Patrician would have been the defeat he had inflicted on the Vandals and especially against the usurper. On the basis of the fact that the usurper was executed only in about 422 (CGall. 452, p.656; Marc. a.421/2; Ann. Rav. a.422), the operation to catch him and his military commander Jovinus probably lasted until 421 or 422 after which he was sent to Ravenna. The fact that the imprisoned Maximus and Jovinus arrived at Ravenna in 422 may suggest that they were only captured during that year by the next commander of Spanish operations, Castinus (*MVM* after 422). However, Spain was by no means pacified.

In Baetica, the Vandals had access to the markets of the Mediterranean world, which made it necessary for the courts of Ravenna and Constantinople to coordinate their efforts against the barbarians. According to the Edict (CTh 7.16.3) issued in the name of Honorius and Theodosius to the *PPO* Eustathius at Constantinople on 18 Sept. 420, each *defensor locorum* was to ensure that the masters of the ships and merchants made accurate customs declarations in the presence of an imperial bodyguard or member of the ducal office (*ducianus*) to prevent the Vandals from smuggling contraband (weapons, metals ect.) to the barbarian nations.

The war against the Franks also restarted soon enough, because Frigeridus (apud Greg. 2.9) states that at about the same time as Asterius was made Patrician in 420/421, the *Com. Dom.* Castinus was sent to Gaul to fight a campaign against the Franks. This campaign was apparently a success.

In the meanwhile, Constantius had returned to court to take his place beside his spouse. Constantius' predominant position was once again acknowledged with the Consulship for the third time in 420, but this was not enough either for him or for his wife. After Galla Placidia had given birth to Valentinian, the Empire had a potential successor to the throne. In this situation Constantius felt that he would be entitled to become recognized as ruler also in name and not only in fact. Consequently, he forced Honorius to nominate him as his *co-Augustus* and Galla Placidia as *Augusta*. The ceremony took place on 8 February 421. At the same time as this happened, Honorius conferred the title of *Nobilissimus* on Valentinian.

According to Olympiodorus (fr. 37), Constantius was an experienced soldier from Naissus who had taken part in many campaigns from the reign of Theodosius I onwards. He was supposedly free from greed until he married Galla Placidia in 417, which suggest that the soldiers under his command were better motivated than the other Roman soldiers at the time. However, the same fragment goes on to state that after his marriage Constantius stole property from all sides, with the result that after his death legal suits came from all sides to reclaim their lost property. It is impossible to know whether he or his wife did resort to illegal practices to obtain money or whether this was a claim put forward by their enemies. If there is any truth behind them, one can perhaps conclude that Galla Placidia had taken the lead in the effort to amass as much money as possible by any means available, because the text implies that this was not in character for Constantius. Fragment 36 also makes it clear that Galla Placidia was a strong-willed wife who was quite prepared to force Constantius to follow her wishes. According to the fragment in question, an Asian magician called Libanius arrived at Ravenna in 421 and achieved great fame in a short period of time, with the result that Galla Placidia learnt of this. The staunchly Catholic Galla Placidia threatened her husband with a divorce unless he executed the wizard. Since Constantius' official standing was entirely dependent on his relationship with the imperial house, he had to concede. What is notable about this episode is that the equally staunchly Catholic Constantius was quite prepared to tolerate dissents and pagans while his wife was not.

The elevation of Constantius, however, created an unforeseen problem. When Constantius' images were sent to the East to obtain Theodosius II's confirmation for the proclamation, Pulcheria and Theodosius II surprisingly refused to recognize him. This has unsurprisingly caused plenty of speculation among the modern historians, because such a decision in the midst of the Persian War of 421–422 seems simply idiotic. The possible reasons for this lunacy include: 1) Pulcheria and Theodosius II had never forgiven Galla Placidia's marriage with Athaulf; or 2) they may have hoped to reunite the Empire after the childless Honorius died.[1] I would add to this two other possibilities. Firstly, it is possible that Honorius, who had been unwilling to nominate Constantius and Placidia in the first place, sent a message to the Eastern court to the effect that they were not to accept the elevation so that he could launch one of his plots against Constantius. The subsequent events also make it clear that Honorius had developed an insane incestuous lust towards his sister. In light of this it would not be impossible to imagine that Honorius planned to have Constantius murdered or killed in combat with Eastern forces. It should be noted that Honorius seems to have had incestuous lusts all along, because the daughters of Stilicho were also his relatives. It is also possible that on the basis of the initial successes of the campaign against Persia, Pulcheria's government made the terrible mistake of believing that it could soon transfer its forces west to face Constantius III. The second possibility is that the leading members of the Theodosian family just thought that it was their sole God-given right to rule the Roman Empire, which naturally precluded husbands.

Constantius had no other alternative than to prepare for war against the East. The whole situation was insane. East Rome was fighting against Persia and the Vandals were still roaming free in Baetica, but in the circumstances Constantius had no other alternative. If he would have waited and settled unfinished business in the West, he would have only given time for the Eastern government to conclude a peace with Persia. On top of this, Constantius had himself started to have second thoughts about the elevation. Constantius considered the throne to be a gilded cage – a sentiment many modern commoners who have married into royal families would share. He no longer had any freedom; he could no longer come and go as he pleased; and he could not enjoy the pastimes he had enjoyed. He was a man who liked to spend the evenings at banquets and parties (quite evidently in the company of his officers and men) in which he was cheerful and affable – he even competed with the clowns in the merrymaking. Constantius' soldiers undoubtedly loved him as a good companion and comrade-in-arms. In contrast, on public processions and occasions Constantius was always unhappy and morose, which clearly reflects his personality traits. It is therefore not surprising that he felt unhappy in his gilded gage.

In light of the above, it is not surprising that according to the official version Constantius soon fell ill and died of pleurisy on 2 September 421. He had ruled for six months.[2] I would suggest that the official version was just a cover up for a poisoning performed by Honorius' assassins. Indeed, Theophanes (AM 5913) states plainly that Constantius was murdered and there is no doubt that he is right. He is also the only author to preserve the exact date of death. It is quite clear that Honorius had once again struck and killed an able military commander, probably the best he had ever had. It is difficult to know whether this was a blessing or a curse. The death of Constantius restored the state of peace between the two realms, which was certainly a blessing in the short term. On the other hand, it is possible that had Constantius lived and forced the Eastern government to accept the inevitable (if he had marched his army to the Balkans, the Eastern government would have been forced to negotiate) that the Western realm would have been ruled with greater acumen.

Constantius the Comes et Magister, Patricius and Augustus 410–421

It is justified to say that Constantius saved the Western Realm in 410–416 from usurpers, Visigoths, Alans, Vandals and Suevi. It is quite clear that without his contribution West Rome would have succumbed under these multiple pressures. Honorius and his staff had already proved themselves utter failures. The usurpers had also shown themselves unsuited to govern any part of the realm, which is proven by the numerous revolts against them. In light of this, it is clear that Constantius had temporarily breathed new life into the corpse. As we shall see, his murder led to a new set of problems, as the command of the armies was given to incompetents. The situation was complicated even further by the fact that the competing marshals started to vie for power after 425, with dire consequences for the West.

My drawing of a coin struck in the name of Augustus Constantius III in 421, the man who saved the West from collapse in 410-418.

The Power Struggle between Honorius and Galla Placidia 421–423

According to Olympiodorus (fr. 38, Tr. by Blockley 201–202 with one change):

> The affection of Honorius towards his sister grew so great after the death of her husband Constantius that their immoderate pleasure in each other and their constant kissing on the mouth caused many people to entertain shameful suspicions about them. But as a result of the efforts of Spadusa and of Placidia's nurse, Elpidia … and through the co-operation of Lentius, her Curator, this affection was replaced by such a degree of hatred, that fighting often broke out in Ravenna and blows were delivered by both sides.

On the basis of this fragment it is difficult to be certain whether Galla Placidia reciprocated the incestuous feelings of her brother, but what is certain is that the depraved Honorius certainly had sexual desires towards her. The fact that the hatred became so deep suggests that Galla Placidia must have had some sort of loving feelings towards Honorius, because love often turns into deep hatred, but the love that she may have felt could easily have been simply a sisterly love towards her brother, in which case the hatred could have been caused by Honorius' sexual desires. The probable reason for the breakup between the brother and sister was that Galla's friends had brought to light incriminating evidence against Honorius regarding the circumstances of Constantius' death. According to the fragment in question, Placidia's barbarian retainers, whom she had inherited from Athaulf and Constantius, literally fought against Honorius's forces in the streets, but in the end Honorius proved stronger and exiled both Placidia and her children to Constantinople in 423. According to Cassiodorus (a.423/1205, p.155), Honorius exiled Placidia and Valentinian because it was suspected that Placidia had invited enemies to come to her assistance. This must mean the Visigoths, and it also places the desertion of the Visigoths in Spain in its correct light (see below).

The fact that the struggle between Honorius and Galla had lasted for over a year and also involved military officers such as the *Comes Africae* Bonifatius, who stayed loyal to Placidia even after her downfall, proves that the battle had not been an easy one. In fact, Bonifatius sent her money and promised his assistance for whatever purpose. At a later date, Bonifatius assisted Placidia to regain the throne. Bonifatius controlled the grain supply of Rome and Italy, and his support for Placidia was therefore of the greatest importance. Bonifatius had been one of Constantius' officers (Bonifatius was native of Thrace and had therefore probably come to the West with Constantius) and was clearly quite eager to support Constantius' widow against Honorius. Bonifatius was known for his personal bravery and honesty, so much so that Procopius later called him and Aetius the last Romans. According to Olympiodorus (fr. 40), Bonifatius defeated the Berbers often, regardless of whether he had few (i.e. guerrilla warfare) or many (i.e. battles) men, and he always emerged victorious from his single combats. In short, he employed every means available to him to defeat the Berbers. He was also known for personal exploits that could have been borrowed from the Arabian Tales. For example, when a peasant's wife was having an extramarital affair with a barbarian *foederatus*, Bonifatius rode alone into the night, found the pair, cut off the barbarian's head and brought the head to the peasant. These kinds of exploits made the reputation of the man.

On the other side were the opponents of Constantius who belonged to Honorius' inner circle. These included the *Com. Dom.* Castinus, who had fought successfully against the Franks in about 420. The fact that he was promoted to the position of *MVM* in 422 proves that he owed his rise to the fall of Constantius. It is probable that as *Com. Dom.* he had participated in the murder of Constantius. In 422 he was sent to replace the Patrician Asterius in Spain, who appears to have been Constantius' nominee. Just before he was supposed to sail to Spain or when both had reached Spain, Castinus quarrelled with Bonifatius, who duly fled back to Africa where he effectively became an independent entity who supported Placidia. It seems probable that he managed to gain control of the unfortified city of Carthage very soon after his return. What is certain is that he had gained control of North Africa and Carthage by the time he was appointed *Comes Africae* by the Eastern Government in 423. This quarrel between Castinus and Bonifatius becomes understandable if we assume that Castinus had indeed been one of the men who had contributed to the death of Constantius and who was opposed to Placidia and her party.

Castinus continued the unfinished campaign against the Vandals in Baetica in 422. His forces consisted of a large army, the numbers of which had been bolstered by Gothic auxiliaries (Hyd. Olymp. 300, 28). At first his efforts met with success and he was able to reduce the enemy to starvation with a siege, which must have included the use of the above-mentioned trade embargo. It is possible or even probable that it was Castinus who captured the usurper Maximus and dispatched him to Ravenna in 422. However, when the Vandals were on the point of surrender, the foolish commander decided to engage the desperate enemy in pitched battle. Hydatius claims that Castinus' defeat was caused by the Visigoths, who betrayed him. If there is any basis of truth to this claim, then the Visigoths either did not want to destroy the Vandals or rather they wanted to destroy Castinus, the enemy of Galla Placidia. What is certain is that Asterius did not have similar difficulties with the Visigoths as Castinus. It is quite probable that the desertion of the Visigoths would have kindled the above-mentioned suspicions against Placidia.

Honorius did not have long to live after his victory over Constantius and Galla Placidia. According to the official version he died of dropsy on 15 August 423. In this case it is in fact quite probable that Honorius died of natural causes because there was no well-planned takeover of the government immediately after his death. The other alternative is that some patriotic person finally found enough courage to poison Honorius in order to get rid of the imbecile pervert who played the role of the Emperor. However, as just said, the circumstantial evidence would still suggest natural causes.

Honorius the Impotent 395–423

There is no doubt about the fact that Honorius was the man who contributed most to the eventual downfall of West Rome. He was a man equipped with mediocre intellect, which was combined with a devious character, sexual depravity (an incestuous paedophile who at least periodically suffered from impotence, which was lucky to those would have otherwise suffered from his sick desires), a love of relatives, and an insane racist hatred of Goths and other barbarians. If there was one constant in Honorius' policies, it was his attempt to hold on to the reins of power by any means possible – the actual well-being of his subjects and the defensive needs of the Empire were of secondary importance to him. What mattered were Honorius and his relatives.

Honorius' love towards his relatives dominated his policy decisions. Honorius was for a while ready to support Stilicho and Serena in return for their daughters (Honorius' relatives), but when Honorius had developed an urge to take full control of the Empire and there was a danger that Stilicho could bring the East under his rule, Honorius acted quickly to wrest full control of the Empire from Stilicho and his minions. Honorius was ready to conclude a peace with the usurper Constantine III in return for his Spanish relatives, but when he learnt that they had been killed, he changed his course once again, only to revise it yet again for political reasons. Honorius had also clearly ordered his commanders not to engage Alaric and Athaulf in decisive action because they had his sister Galla Placidia as hostage. It can be said that Honorius' sole military goal between 412 and 416 was to obtain Galla Placidia back from the Visigoths. In the end Honorius even developed an insane incestuous lust towards his half-sister Galla Placidia, which undoubtedly influenced Honorius' decision to murder her husband. However, in this case the mere fact that Constantius' position was too strong would have sufficed.

Honorius' whole career as Emperor after 408 was marked by devious plotting, murders and assassinations to keep him in power. This was combined with horribly bad policy decisions. He killed the best military commanders he had (Stilicho and his supporters, Constantius) or sacked them, as he did to Marinus. Honorius' insane racist hatred towards the Goths and other barbarians led him to betray Alaric and Sarus and to murder the families of the Sarmato-Alan settlers in Italy with the result that Italy, Gaul and Spain were ravaged by hordes of barbarians. If he had concluded a treaty either with Alaric or Sarus none of that would have happened. This series of bad decisions in 408 was the principal reason for the eventual downfall of the Roman Empire.

Honorius' sole achievement as Emperor was to outlive all the usurpers and die in bed of natural causes, to the detriment of the Roman Empire.

Honorius
(source:
Cohen)

Constantius III
(source: Cohen)

Maximus
(source: Cohen)

Chapter Twelve

The East 408–423

Anthemius 408–414

When Arcadius died on 1 May 408 he was only 31 years old, but had still been prudent enough to create the conditions in which it was possible for his seven-year-old son Theodosius to retain his life and power. Theodosius was not only underage but was also a quarter- or half-barbarian.[1] Consequently extraordinary safety measures had already been taken prior to 402. As noted before, the most important of these was the fact that Arcadius had asked the Persian *Shahanshah* Yazdgerd I to act as guardian for his son. Thanks to the very good relations between the House of Theodosius and the House of Sasan resulting from the peace and alliance granted by Theodosius I after his victories over the Persians, Yazdgerd had agreed to Arcadius' suggestion, regardless of the opposition of the nobles and magi. It had been a truly bold move for Arcadius to ask the former arch-enemy to act as a guardian for his son. The end result of this policy was peace for the Eastern frontier as long as nobody made any move against Theodosius II.

The very first thing Yazdgerd did after Arcadius' death was to threaten the Romans with war if anyone so much as attempted to oust Theodosius. He acted as expected. The peace was confirmed for 100 years and the empires sealed it with a new trade treaty which stipulated that henceforth trade between the two states was to be restricted to the cities of Nisibis, Callinicum and Artaxata (CJ 4.63.4 dated to 23 March 409; Blockley 1992, 54). This was presumably a good solution from the Persian point of view because henceforth Roman merchants would be unable to conduct spying operations in the Persian interior and also because it made it easier for the Persians to intervene against such potential Christian deserters as might attempt to use some other route to flee from Persia disguised as merchants. The very good neighbourly relations between the empires, first under Arcadius and then under the caretaker government led by Anthemius, improved the position of the Christians in Persia. Yazdgerd I even showed personal interest in the religion and allowed it to flourish in his realm. Some Christian sources even go so far as to claim that Yazdgerd was Christian or about to become one himself, but this is demonstrably false.

The renewal of the treaty also confirmed the eunuch Antiochus the Persian as Yazdgerd's representative in the Eastern court. Anthemius also continued to exercise executive power as some sort of regent, with the official title of *PPO* and *Patricius*. He was advised by the equally-talented pagan sophist Troilus and naturally by Antiochus. What is notable about this administrative structure is that it is entirely different from the official structure. The *PPO* was de facto ruler of the entire Empire including all its civil servants and military. The late Roman bureaucracy had clearly retained enough flexibility for it to be able to adapt to the new circumstances.

The death of the Emperor had made any previous treaties void, so that all treaty relations had to be renewed with each tribe. Sozomen's statement 9.4 that Uldin refused to conclude a *foedus* in 408 with the Romans should be interpreted to refer to the treaty-less condition between the states after the death of Arcadius. This meant that the East Romans also faced potential troubles with the Huns in the Balkans at a time when they were forced to transfer troops to the eastern frontier. As noted by Maenchen-Helfen (63–4), there exists two pieces of legislation which prove that the Romans were well aware of the potential Hunnic attack. The Edict (CTh 11.17.4) given at Constantinople on 11 April 408 by the emperors Honorius and Theodosius to the *PPIL* Herculius is a good indication of this. The Edict required all persons, regardless of their privileges, from the richest to the poorest, to contribute to the construction of walls and to the purchase and transport of supplies in Illyricum. Since we know that Arcadius died on 1 May, it is clear that either the names of the emperors or the date are wrong. The other alternative is that Arcadius had already handed over power before his death, but there is no indication of this. I would suggest that the Edict was given immediately after Arcadius' death, because the caretaker administration of Anthemius was fully aware of the Hunnic threat and also of the potential threat posed by Stilicho. There also exists another Edict (CTh 15.1.49) issued at Constantinople by the same *Augusti* to Herculius dated to 9 April 412. It included the same requirements. It is not known with certainty whether this Edict should also be re-dated, but it too shows that the situation was considered so grave that all persons were required to contribute to the defence of Illyricum.

According to Maenchen-Helfen's reconstruction, the Hunnic invasion materialized in summer 408.[2] If his dating of 408 (or alternatively the winter of 408/9) is correct, then the Romans would have transferred forces to their eastern border as a result of Yazdgerd's threat, but we do not know this for certain. I would suggest that there is also an alternative explanation for the absence of troops in the Balkans, because we do not know the date of Uldin's invasion with any certainty.[3] Another possibility is a pact of cooperation between Uldin and Stilicho so that the latter could become a guardian of the East as well. It is also possible that Uldin's invasion was timed to the late summer/fall of 409, if Uldin exploited the transferral of East Roman forces to Ravenna. The former date receives support from the fact that the treaty between the Huns and East Rome would have already become void in 408 or from a pact between Uldin and Stilicho, but none of the sources refer to any transferral of troops to the East at this time. In contrast, there is definite evidence for the transferral of large numbers of men to Ravenna for the year 409. Unfortunately, it is impossible to be certain, both dates are possible, but I am still inclined to accept Maenchen-Helfen's dating of summer 408.

According to Sozomen (9.5) and the Theodosian Code (6.5.3), Uldin's army was huge and consisted of the Huns and the Sciri and of some unnamed barbarous tribes who dwelled near the Danube. It is usually (e.g. Maenchen-Helfen, 66) assumed that the Germanic Sciri consisted mostly of infantry, and in light of the fact that the Sciri were unable to flee with the same ease as the other tribes this may be true, but we should not make the mistake of assuming that the Sciri would not have possessed cavalry. It is certain that they did, because they had lived right next to various nomads for centuries and it is possible that they did indeed fight as cavalry because the evidence is far from conclusive.

Uldin's first target was the city of Castra Martis which he conquered. After this, he appears to have marched to Naissus and from there to Serdica and then via the Succi Pass to Thrace. The Romans appear not to have attempted to face the invaders on the battlefield, because they were heavily outnumbered. This situation was to persist throughout the existence of the East Roman Empire. Whenever the East Romans faced a military threat in the East (whether in the form of Persians or later Muslims), they usually lacked adequate forces to engage any larger confederacy of tribes in the Balkans – and at the height of their power the Huns possessed a minimum of 60,000 horsemen and a maximum of about 150,000 horsemen or even more, which meant that the East Romans were in trouble even if they managed to combine the Army of Illyricum, the Army of Thrace and the two Praesental armies. It was actually improbable that the Romans could achieve such an assembly of forces, because they usually seem to have lacked any advance warning of the Hunnic invasions or their armies were fighting against other enemies. Furthermore, it is probable that the Huns followed the same practice as the Persians (see Vol. 1) and sent fast-moving, roving units of horsemen deep into Roman territory to force the Romans to seek shelter within fortifications, which prevented the assembly of forces. As stated above, it is probable that the Romans had transferred most of their troops to the Persian border because Yazdgerd I threatened the Romans with war.

We hear nothing about any action by any *Comes* or *Magister Illyricum*. However, Sozomen does mention that the *hyparchon tôn Thrakiôn strateumatôn* made repeated propositions of peace to Uldin. The title of the Roman commander would literally mean the Prefect of the Army of Thrace, which would mean that Anthemius took charge of the defence in person, but it is still likelier that we should translate the *hyparchon* as *strategos/magister* so that the army was under some professional soldier. According to Sozomen, Uldin pointed to the sun and stated that it would be easy for him to conquer any place under the sun, so that if the Romans really wanted peace they would henceforth have to pay tribute to the Huns. It seems probable that the Roman peace proposals were just a ruse because soon after this we learn that the Roman *hyparchon* had managed to bribe some of Uldin's *oikeioi* (presumably members of Uldin's own household/retinue or tribe) and *lochagoi* (tribal leaders) to desert him. This was a text book example of what to do when one faced Huns or other nomads, and was included as such in the sixth-century *Strategikon*.[4] When the Roman commander faced Huns, he was always instructed to attempt to bribe the enemy leaders. The opportunity for this came with the visit of the Roman envoy. This breakup of the confederation was only the last stage of the collapse of Uldin's Empire. The Alans and some of the Goths and Vandals had already broken free in 404–406. The Huns were not good masters.

After the desertion of very important sections of Uldin's army, it was easy for the Romans to defeat the remaining forces. Uldin managed to flee back across the Danube only with great difficulty. Many of Uldin's own troops were killed, together with warriors of the other tribes. The sources make it quite clear that the bulk of the casualties and captured consisted of the Sciri. According to Sozomen, the Sciri attempted to flee, but were overtaken by pursuers and then cut to pieces so that large numbers of them were taken in chains to Constantinople. It should be noted that the fact that the Sciri were overtaken by pursuers does not prove definitely that the Sciri consisted mainly of infantry, but it does make it more likely.

There is no doubt that the war ended in a great victory by early 409. The Edict (CTh 5.6.2) issued to the *PPO* Anthemius (note that it is probable that Anthemius was himself behind this piece of legislation) at Constantinople on 23 March 409 refers to the plunder taken from the barbarians. The Edict (CTh 6.5.3) given to Anthemius at Constantinople on 12 April 409 asserts that the Sciri, who had been captured as a result of a victory over a multitude of Huns and Sciri, were to be distributed to farms as workers (with the status of *colonus*) in overseas provinces so that the Sciri could not return to Thrace or Illyricum under any circumstances. This proves that the Romans captured so many Sciri that these had to be distributed overseas so that they would not pose any threat to Thrace in the future. As noted by Blockley (1992, 53), the Romans had learnt from their previous mistakes.

Maenchen-Helfen (70–72) has noted that the dissolution of Uldin's tribal confederacy in Thrace in 408–409 may have contributed to the success of Generidus in Raetia and Dalmatia in 409, achieved against the returning Uldin unless Zosimus has exaggerated the successes of the pagan commander. In my opinion, however, it is unlikely that Generidus would have fought against Uldin himself, but against the Federates consisting of the remaining Goths, Huns and Alans in Pannonia (see also MHLR vols. 4–5).

It was largely thanks to the foresight of Arcadius and his advisors that, in great contrast to the turmoil of the West, after Arcadius' death East Rome could concentrate on the re-establishment of good governance and on the securing of its borders. As noted above, the Eastern government was ready to conclude peace with the West during the lifetime of Stilicho, and Anthemius was quite prepared to continue to follow this same policy. It was actually the only prudent course to adopt. It would have been contrary to Eastern interests if the West would have fallen into the hands of a usurper or Alaric. Consequently, when the Huns had been defeated and peace with Persia had been secured Anthemius dispatched a fleet with 40,000 men to Ravenna in 409. It was a sound policy decision and proved decisive. Without this Eastern help Honorius would have been ousted.

Anthemius' government concentrated on the improvement of the administration, economy and defences and it did not exclude barbarians from military offices. A good example of these enlighted policies is the securing of Constantinople's food supply in 408/409. When Constantinople in 408 was suffering from food shortages resulting from the lack of adequate numbers of transport ships permanently based at Alexandria, in 409 Anthemius, with the approval of the Senate, reorganized the entire logistical network between Alexandria and Constantinople so that this would not happen again. It is possible that the billeting of troops inside Constantinople when the Huns had raided Thrace contributed to the food shortage. Similarly, it is probable that adverse weather patterns and/or climate changes, and the resulting problems with the Berbers and Arabs contributed to this (See Appendix 3). The island of Carpathus (Synesius praises the sailors of this island to the heavens) was made a half-way station between Constantinople and Alexandria, and the *PVC*, the Prefect of Egypt, and the *praeses insularum* (governor of the Islands along the coast of Asia Minor) were to organize the logistics together so that each had responsibility for his own section of the route. In 412 the Illyrian towns also received help so that their economies could be rebuilt.[5]

Even though the building of the so-called Theodosian Walls for the city of Constantinople formed the core of Anthemius' fortification programme in the Balkans, he did not neglect the frontier defences. As noted above, the defences of the entire Prefecture of Illyricum were strengthened with extraordinary measures – even the privileged classes were made to pay for the defence. Anthemius also sought to improve the defensive and offensive capabilities of the Danube frontier armies against the Huns by rebuilding the frontier fleets in 412. The Edict (CTh 17) issued to the *MVM per Thracias* Constans at Constantinople on 28 January 412 was meant to secure the Danube frontier. According to this Edict, the *dux* and his staff along the Moesian border were to build 90 new *lusoriae* (river patrol craft) and repair 10 old craft, and each year after that for a period of seven years they were to repair 4 *iudiciariae* (reconnaissance patrol craft) and 10 *agrarienses* (inshore patrol craft), which means that by 419, after a period of seven years, there were to be 100 *lusoriae*, 28 *iudiciariae* and 70 *agrarienses*. The *dux* of Scythia was to build 110 new *lusoriae* and repair 15 old ones immediately, and after that each year for a period of seven years he was to repair 5 old *iudiciariae* and 12 *agrarienses* so that by 419 there were to be 125 *lusoriae*, 40 *iudiciariae* and 84 *agrarienses*. The *duces* and their staff were to make reports on progress each year to the *MVM* and any neglect was to result in heavy fines.

The same Edict also specifies how the craft were to be used and deployed. The craft were meant for war and were to be distributed to their fortified bases with an eye to spying/reconnoitring missions as well as for the purpose of opportune military expeditions. The new vessels were not to be used as transport vessels for military supplies. This duty was reserved only for the old repaired vessels. In short, the East Romans foresaw three missions for their river fleets: 1) observation and spying; 2) opportunistic piratical raids against enemy coasts and shipping; and 3) transport of supplies.

The so-called Theodosian Walls were also finally completed during this period, in 413.[6] These walls made all potential attacks against the city of Constantinople futile as long as the Eastern Emperor possessed a fleet in the city capable of protecting the sea lanes. Holum (1982, 89) is certainly correct in suggesting that the wall was not only meant against foreign enemies, but also against domestic ones. It secured the civilian government against generals like Gainas. The construction of these walls changed the strategic configuration of the area for the next 1,000 years. The city which had previously fallen several times now fell only to usurpers and twice to foreign enemies in 1204 and 1453.

The Theodosian Walls of Constantinople[7]

The land portion of the Theodosian Walls consisted of a water-filled ditch, an outer terrace *parateichion* with a crenellated parapet, an outer wall, an inner terrace *peribolos*, and of the inner wall. The Blachernae portion of the land wall consisted of a single wall. The length of the land walls was 5,650 metres. The minimum requirement to man the land walls during a siege was about 10,000 men, but, in addition to this, a proper defence of the walls would have required the rotation of troops and the placing of reserves behind the walls so that the real requirement was much greater, and we should not forget that other parts of the city (especially the sea wall) also required defenders. Fortunately, Constantinople was a megapolis, which possessed reserves of paramilitary civilian forces, the most important of which were the circus factions.

The sea wall consisted of a single wall, but these were less formidable than the land walls because the Romans did not expect to face any serious threats from the sea. The problems in the dating of the various sections of the wall are such that Foss and Winfield (70ff.) concentrated their discussion only to those sections that could be dated. The Chronicon Paschale (a. 439) states that Theodosius ordered the construction of the walls for the entire length of the seaward side of the city in 439, which has sometimes been taken to mean that it was the *PPO* Cyrus (439–441) who built the sea walls, but this is probably a mistake. It is clear that the sea walls were built simultaneously with the land walls because it would have otherwise been too easy for the enemy to bypass the ends of the land walls during night-time simply by swimming. It is also quite clear that Cyrus merely reconstructed the sea walls because these had been brought down by an earthquake (see Marc. a. 446/7), and/or new walls were added to protect the harbours better.

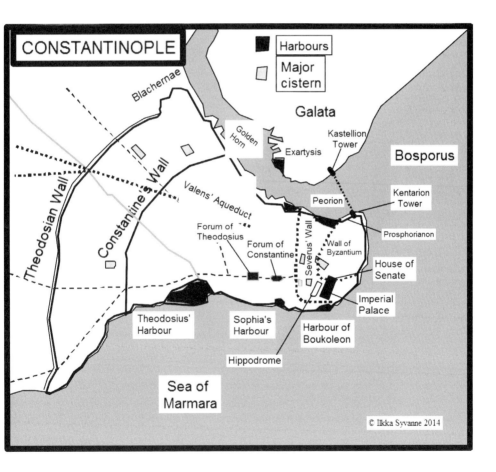

Foss and Winfield (p.43) state well the purpose of the land walls when they note that the fortifications provided two essential elements for defence: an obstacle to the enemy and protection for the defenders. The broad, deep ditch which was protected by a crenellated balustrade and by the low outer wall, kept the attackers at a distance so that they could be subjected to fire from the main defence provided by the high inner wall. The aim was to subject the approaching enemy to a bombardment of artillery fire, archery and slinging during the approach and then to force them to stop before the moat for additional punishment. The purpose was to destroy the siege engines before these could be brought against the defences and to prevent attempts to fill up the ditch. The depth of the defences from the moat to the inner wall was more than 65 metres and it rose more than 35 metres to the top of the towers of the inner wall.

The moat was filled with water for most of its length. The different contours of the terrain were taken into account by placing dams in the moat to keep the water where it was desired. Behind the moat stood the outer terrace which was called *parateichion* or *proteichisma*, which was a forward-placed defensive embankment protected with a crenellated stone wall the height of a man. The crenellation protected the archers posted behind it. The *parateichion* could also be used as an assembly area for soldiers meant either to serve as an additional bulwark for the city, or for assaults against the besiegers.

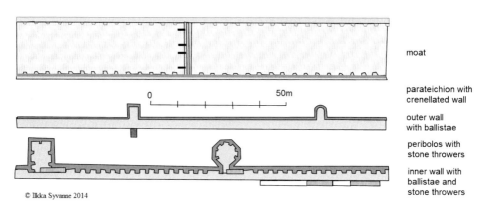

moat

parateichion with crenellated wall

outer wall with ballistae

peribolos with stone throwers

inner wall with ballistae and stone throwers

© Ilkka Syvänne 2014

The outer circuit wall rose eight metres above the terrace and was faced with small limestone blocks separated by bands of bricks. The lower half of this wall was covered by a solid mass of infill all the way up to the inner wall, which formed the inner terrace called *peribolos*. The land fill made the outer wall practically impossible to break with battering rams and very difficult to undermine as well. The outer wall rose four metres above the inner terrace and consisted of two levels of defence. The lower half consisted of 2,500 casemates that were suitable for the mounting of small ballistae and for use by archers. The original openings were apparently too large and were later made narrower. The upper level of the outer wall consisted of crenellated battlements that were manned by archers and slingers. The outer wall had projecting alternating semi-circular and rectangular towers to provide additional defence and forward and flanking fire for the structure. The towers of the outer wall had two levels, the lower level chambers with loopholes suited to archers (three in the square towers and four in the circular), and the upper level crenellated platform suited to small ballistae. The square towers had postern gates on the right side that could be used for sallies in order that the soldiers would be covered by their shields when they went out.

The inner terrace, the *peribolos*, had a depth of 20 metres (excepting where there were towers) and was used for the placing of stone-throwing catapults behind the cover of the outer wall and as an assembly area for the men intended for sallies. The men placed in this area could also be used to pepper the attackers with arrows and stones.

The inner wall rested on bedrock and was on average almost five meters thick and 12 meters high. The outer facing, the shell, consisted of squared limestone blocks and the filling of mortared rubble. The bands of bricks bonded the core and stonework. The lower part of the wall did not have any loopholes and was smooth because the outer wall covered it. On the top lay the walk, which was protected by crenellated battlements behind which stood the defenders (archers, slingers etc.). The wall between the Sea of Marmara and the Golden Horn had a minimum of 96 towers (20 metres high), but the exact number is not known because the walls close to the Golden Horn were later rebuilt. Most of the towers are square in shape, but there are 20 polygonal towers. In the southern section, the square and polygonal towers alternate; then follows a section which has only square towers, after which there are polygonal towers at irregular intervals. The stonework of the towers resembled the walls but was structurally different to accommodate the chambers. The lower chambers were lighted by small loopholes and some of them had postern gates to the inner terrace. It should be noted that it is possible that the small loopholes were larger at the time of the construction so that the Romans could employ the larger ballistae at an angle of 45 degrees to shoot stones in the manner suggested by Philo (see Introduction) and that the holes were later filled up when the use of this type of ballista was abandoned.

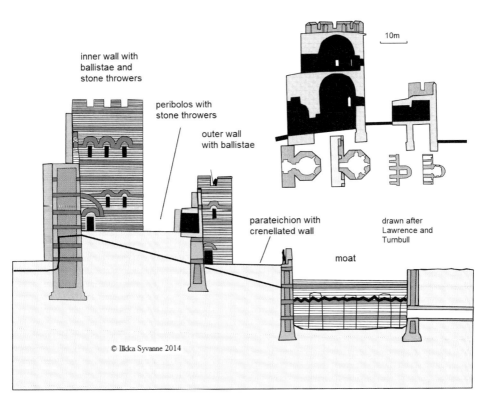

inner wall with
ballistae and
stone throwers

peribolos with
stone throwers

outer wall
with ballistae

10m

parateichion with
crenellated wall

drawn after
Lawrence and
Turnbull

moat

© Ilkka Syvänne 2014

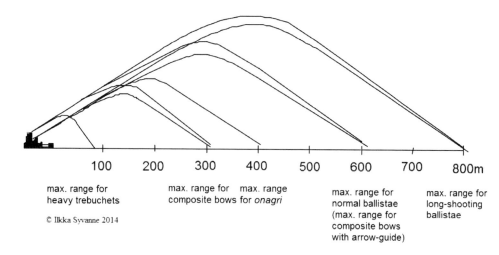

| 100 | 200 | 300 | 400 | 500 | 600 | 700 | 800m |

max. range for
heavy trebuchets

max. range for   max. range
composite bows for *onagri*

max. range for
normal ballistae
(max. range for
composite bows
with arrow-guide)

max. range for
long-shooting
ballistae

© Ilkka Syvänne 2014

However, this is a mere suggestion on my part and would require the actual tearing up of the existing parts of the wall to see whether there are signs of later filling of the windows. The lower chambers, open to the inside, were used as living quarters or as storage space by the local civilians and/or by the soldiers in transit or posted to protect the walls. The upper chambers could be reached only by stairways placed at irregular intervals against the inner face of the wall. These chambers had loopholes (2 in front, 3 each side) that could be used by small- to medium-sized ballistae or by archers. At the top of each tower stood the crenellated platforms where the Romans mounted the larger ballistae, *onagri* or trebuchets/mangonels.

The regular ballistae were able to shoot darts to a distance of about 600 metres and the long-shooting version up to 800 metres, the *onagri* could shoot stones weighing about 30 kg to a distance of 400 metres and the traction trebuchets (the pullers would have been on the *peribolos*) could shoot rocks weighing about 120–180kg up to a distance of about 75–150 metres. This means that any enemy attempting to approach the Theodosian Walls was subjected to a murderous fire by hundreds of artillery pieces which could pierce both shield and armour up to distances of 300–400 metres or more. Naturally, the top of the towers could also be used by archers, slingers and others to defend the walls. The defenders of the inner wall could subject any attacker that managed to reach the outer wall to a bombardment from above and from the sides (from the towers that projected 10.5 metres from the inner wall), while the Romans posted on the towers of the outer wall could also bombard them from the sides, in addition to which the enemies that had reached the *peribolos* could be caught between two phalanxes by troops that could sally from the postern gates of the inner wall. As long as the Romans had a plentiful supply of manpower that could be rotated between rest and duty or used as reserves, it was not easy to breach such defences, and we should not forget that the city/metropolis also had a plentiful supply of civilian paramilitary forces that could be used very effectively on the walls.

We do not know with certainty whether the fourth- and fifth-century Romans were using trebuchets, but these were certainly introduced at the latest by the late-sixth. The references to the sizes of rocks thrown by Roman artillery[8] does support the probability that they were already using mangonels (it was essentially a large counterweight crane that had been in use for a very long time, and the concept was familiar to every Roman engineer/architect from Archimedes' works), but the problem with this is that the largest ballistae-stone throwers of antiquity were also able to launch such rocks. As a result of this, it is impossible to be absolutely certain about the date of the introduction of the trebuchets. However, the fact that the Romans started to use prow-towers at this time does lend some credence to this conclusion. In sum, the weight of the evidence supports the probability that the Romans had started to use mangonels already in the fourth century. The trebuchet was easier to build than the large ballista and it is therefore possible that at least the Persians could have copied it from the Romans. (See Syvänne (2004) with the Chapter 'Persian War 421–422'.)

Anthemius' Anticorruption Policies

Under Anthemius' rule, starting with the reign of Arcadius, the state started to curb corruption among the military officers with greater intensity than before (e.g. CTh 7.1.27–32, 7.11.1), but at the same time Anthemius also recognized that it would be impossible to prevent certain forms of corruption that had become usual. For example, he accepted that the soldiers could commute their *annonae* for money (e.g. CTh 7.4.30). Despite the good intentions, this resulted in a new form of corruption: the soldiers sought to overvalue the produce due to them so that the taxpayers would be forced to pay the soldiers more than their fair share. The government responded by legislating against this (CTh 7.4.30), but further Edicts issued by Anthemius' successors (i.e. CTh 7.4.35–6 in 423–4) prove that the abuses persisted. The same policy of allowing the commutation of the subsistence allowance into money was also followed in the West (CTh 7.4.34 on 19 Nov, 414). The imperial authorities were forced to accept that the soldiers wanted to be paid with cash that they could use as they wished. It is clear that the Roman government could not stop military corruption altogether (new legislation followed immediately; e.g. in 415 the Edicts 7.7.4–5 against unlawful pasturage on civilian lands), but it is still clear that it must have had some positive effect because the Eastern forces clearly outperformed their Western colleagues during the fifth century.

The state also intervened against the rampant corruption of the *curiosi* (inspectors of the Imperial Post with special duties as investigators/special operatives). The Edict given at Constantinople on 9 Nov. 412 (CTh 6.29.10) stated that the previous imperial constitution had been repealed because it had turned out that imperial supplics had been stolen, and competent (i.e. uncorrupted and presumably new) *curiosi* would be sent to the various regions, provinces, coastal districts, ports and other places to ensure that this would not happen again. The Western government followed this two years later with a measure that was even more drastic. The Edict issued at Ravenna on 3 March 414 (CTh 6.29.11) ordered that the *PPI* Hadrianus was to remove all *curiosi* from office and provide aid to decurions, shipmasters, and all guilds to compensate for the thefts committed by the *curiosi*. The Ravenna government repeated the same order for Dalmatia in the following year on 8 Jan. 415 (CTh 6.29.12) because some *curiosi* had usurped the same office and had caused terrible economic damage to the coasts and islands of Dalmatia with their illegal demands. The *PPI* was instructed to make certain that absolutely all *curiosi* were removed from Dalmatia and that if anyone was caught usurping the office he would be punished severely. These instances show well how the corrupt special inspectors could misuse their powers to the detriment of the state. The removal of these men from office was a wise policy to adopt because the Roman state needed to compete for the hearts and minds of the subjects more than ever when its borders had been penetrated by the barbarians. Unsurprisingly, the lead in this was taken by the East and Honorius' incompetent government simply followed their example.

It should be stressed that even though Anthemius' government acted strongly against some forms of corruption, it did not do that in other fields. Synesius' Letter 73 refers to the selling of governorships under Anthemius and Troilus. In other words, Anthemius and Troilus continued the practice of selling civilian offices (governor, vicar and proconsul) to the highest bidder. Synesius' Letter also makes it clear that when Anthemius had nominated the highest bidder, Andronicus of Berenice, as governor of Cyrenaica, he had violated the ancient principle of not nominating natives as governors of their native land. The reason for this was that a native governor was in a position to act against his local personal enemies. He could bring fraudulent charges against them and act as a judge and loot their property. In short, Synesius did not actually criticize the practice of selling governorships but the selling of such offices to the locals.

In other words, the Romans and the Roman government accepted that the governors who had bought their offices would tax the inhabitants heavily so that they could cover their costs and obtain some profit. What was not acceptable was that the military men would also get their hands on the profits. This dual standard certainly made it more likely that the officers would also follow the example set by the civilian administrators, even if it incurred penalties. As far as the financial situation is concerned the corrupt policy of auctioning off the governorships seems to have been a success, because at the end of Anthemius' rule the state coffers were full.

The Massive Onslaught of the Berbers and Arabs

The fact that Anthemius concentrated most of his attention on the good governance of the Empire did not prevent the occurrence of further problems. The Berbers had ravaged the Libyas and Egypt from the early 390s onwards and their ravages culminated in 410 in a massive invasion which threatened the whole Middle East. On top of that, the Arabs also appear to have started raiding Roman territory at the same time as the Berbers. Anthemius appears to have solved the problem by dispatching reinforcements to the area, which finally pacified the region for almost 40 years. The problems caused by the Berbers and Arabs from ca. 409 until 411/412 definitely hindered the ability of the Eastern government to conduct military campaigns in other theatres and should always be kept in mind when analysing the situation (see Appendix 3).

The Downfall of Anthemius

Despite the troubles facing the Libyas, Egypt, Palestine, Phoenicia and Syria in 410, Anthemius was at the height of his powers in that year. While he served as *PPO*, his son Flavius Anthemius Isidorus (PLRE2 Isidorus 9) served as *PVC*, which meant that the two highest offices of the Empire were now in the hands of the same family. This had happened only once before, when Tatianus was *PPO* and his son Proculus *PVC* in 388–392, and it had not ended well for the two. At about the same time as this happened, Anthemius married his daughter to Procopius (who later served as military commander during the Persian War in 422), who was a descendant of the usurper Procopius and therefore a member of the former imperial family. Holum (1977, 160) has noted that in this situation the rivals of Anthemius must have become frightened that Anthemius' next move would be to marry his grandson Flavius Anthemius Isidorus Theophilus with the Emperor's sister Pulcheria in order to secure his position even further. In order to forestall this, the young Pulcheria (born 19 Jan. 399) famously decided to devote herself to virginity in about 412–413. In order to make this decision secure she also convinced her younger sisters to do the same. Most importantly, Pulcheria made certain that this decision could not be overruled later by making her and her sisters' devotion to virginity a public event in the Great Church of Constantinople in 412–413. At the same time as this happened, Pulcheria further managed to convince her brother Theodosius II to abandon his advisor the *cubicularius* Antiochus. Henceforth, it would be Pulcheria who would guide Theodosius' education and policies. Pulcheria appears to have been more mature than her years, but it is still probable that she had some older persons as her advisors because politically this was a very prudent move. These advisors undoubtedly included priests and possibly some politicians like the former *PPO* Aurelianus.[9]

The rise of Pulcheria meant the downfall of Anthemius. The first to go was Anthemius' son Isidorus, who finished his term as *PVC* (between 28 Oct. 412 and 21 March 413) at about the same time as Pulcheria publicly devoted herself to celibacy. The next to go was Antiochus. Theophanes (AM 5905) dates the fall of Antiochus to the year 412/3 (Greatrex p. 179 in Greatrex and Bardill). We do not know whether Anthemius died in office or was sacked, but the latter is likelier. Regardless, he ended his tenure in office gloriously. The Emperor (or rather Anthemius) issued an Edict on 9 April 414 which remitted all the fiscal arrears for a period of 40 years in the provinces of Oriens. This if anything proves how well Anthemius and his friend Troilus had ruled the Empire. Anthemius had had enough money for all the expensive building projects that he had undertaken to protect the Empire and still enough money left to forgive all the unpaid taxes. It is therefore quite clear that the Christian Chronicler Socrates (7.1; tr. Bohn's Library, 334–5) has expressed the views of most when he stated that:

> The management of public affairs was therefore entrusted to Anthemius the Praetorian Prefect, … By his directions the imperial city was surrounded by high walls. He was justly esteemed the most prudent man of his time, and seldom did anything unadvisedly, but consulted with the most judicious of his friends respecting all practical matters; Troilus the sophist was more especially his counsellor, who while excelling in philosophical attainments, was not inferior to Anthemius himself in political wisdom. Almost all things were therefore done with the concurrence of Troilus.

The fact that the sophist Troilus (probably officially Christian despite being 'Hellene') receives such praise from the Christian Chronicler makes it absolutely certain that

Anthemius had ruled the Eastern Empire really well and ended his term in office in such a manner that it was remembered long after him.

Kenneth G. Holum has noted in his ground-breaking monograph *Theodosian Empresses* (p.82) that the Neoplatonist Damascius' Life of Isidore suggests a possibility that Lucius, who was a pagan and *MVM Praesentalis*, attempted to murder Theodosius II in his palace. According to the story told by Damascius, one day Lucius went into the imperial apartments with the intention of killing the Emperor, but the attempt failed because Lucius was unable to draw his sword from its scabbard despite attempting to do that three times. After this he fled. The reason for this was that Lucius supposedly saw a giant and a burly woman standing behind the Emperor with her protective arms around him. As noted by Holum, the woman undoubtedly represented the Fortune/Tyche of the Emperor, who prevented the killing. Holum is undoubtedly also correct that in truth there would have been some other more concrete form of defence, for example in the form of bodyguards or eunuchs, preventing the drawing of the sword. It is of course possible that there could also have been some woman holding Theodosius in her arms, the most likely candidate being Theodosius' sister Pulcheria. If Pulcheria had protected the Emperor with her own body while the giant (the bodyguard) blocked Lucius' attempts, this would obviously explain why she was able to become the sole ruler of the Empire in 414.

Holum (p.82, n.17) also notes that this Lucius (a Roman pagan) was just the type of person whom one would expect to have held a military command under Anthemius and that it is possible that he was the otherwise unknown Lucius who held the consulship in 413. It was typical for the *MVM Praes.* to hold the consulship in the same year as he was promoted to the position. The PLRE2 registers three Lucii, but it is actually probable that the above-mentioned Lucius is the same *tribunus* of the *Scholae* who was ordered by the *Magister Officiorum* (Helion?) to drive off Chrysostom's supporters from the Baths of Constantine in the Easter of 404 (Holum, 1982, p.82. n.17). It is easy to see that Anthemius would have promoted the career of this loyal officer so that he would have reached the position of *MVM Praes.* by 413. It would also be possible to equate the *MVM* Lucius with the Flavius Lucius who was *CSL* on 27 Jan. 408, but the case for this is not as strong as for the tribune. Taken together, it is possible that the *MVM* Lucius resented the rise of Pulcheria and the downfall of his patron Anthemius and therefore wanted to kill the Emperor, either in 413 or 414. Whether he did this on his own initiative or at the instigation of Anthemius or his friends is not known, but since none of the sources mention the execution of Anthemius, it is probable that Anthemius was not implicated in the plot – if there was a plot and not only an intention to kill which was not carried through. On the other hand, we do not know what happened to Anthemius after his downfall. As regards Lucius' fate, it is clear that he was probably executed if his intention became so public as to find its way to a biography. Since it is also clear that he would have suffered *damnatio memoriae*, it is probable that the sources have failed to record the deeds that he had committed to reach the position of *MVM Praes.* In my opinion, it is likely that this Lucius was the unknown *MVM per Thracias* who crushed the Huns of Uldin in 408/9.

Lydus and the Caucasian Passes

Lydus' account 3.52–3 of the history of the Roman and Persian dealings over the Caspian Gates[10] (Derbend/Darbend Pass) includes interesting evidence regarding the diplomacy between the empires. According to Lydus, the Persians initiated discussions of the defence of the Caspian Gates after Jovian had handed over the territories in the East during the prefecture of Salutius (PLRE 1 Saturninus Secundius Salutius 3, *PPO* in 361–365, 365–367). It is possible that this happened during the reign of Jovian rather than during the reign of Valens, because the relationship between the two superpowers had worsened to the point of war (Valens was about to start operations against Persia when Procopius usurped power, see Vol. 2). According to Lydus, the Persians next initiated negotiations during the reign of Yazdgerd, which leaves open which Yazdgerd was meant, but Yazdgerd I appears to be the likeliest candidate. The Persians suggested that they build a fort at Derbend and set up a garrison jointly against their mutual enemy, the Huns. Lydus states laconically that while the Romans were under pressure in the West and North, the Persians were in the meanwhile forced to build fortifications in the area because the barbarians threatened them.

Lydus' statement can be seen to mean that the Romans did not conclude any treaties with the Sassanids, but the matter is more complicated than that. The eastern sources make it clear that the Romans had definitely 'loaned' their gold-miners before 420 (these could have also been used in construction work), that their architects were active in the East and that they also loaned military contingents after 440 (see Vol. 4 with Syvänne and Maksymiuk 2019). Blockley has also noted that the 1,000 lbs of silver paid by Arcadius to Yazdgerd can mean that the Romans had agreed to contribute money to the defence of the Caspian Gates on a yearly basis. It is indeed possible that the deal made between Arcadius and Yazdgerd in about 402 included such a clause, which the Romans later chose to forget so that they would not have appeared to have paid tribute to the Persians.[11] I would suggest that there is also another possibility, which is that the persons who were responsible for the loaning of gold-miners and architects were Anthemius and Antiochus and that it was this that contributed to their downfall. It is quite possible that the Persian representatives (which included Antiochus) in Constantinople would have witnessed the building of the Theodosian Walls and their completion in 413, with the result that they demanded that the Romans would help them to build similar walls at Derbend. There is obviously no concrete evidence for this, but it is easy to see that their enemies could have claimed that they had made East Rome tributary to Persia if they had handed over the workers and engineers to the Persians for the construction projects in question, and there is definite evidence for the presence of Roman gold-miners and architects in Persian territory.

Pulcheria and Theodosius II 414–422

Pulcheria's choice as the successor of Anthemius was Monaxius, who may have held the office simultaneously with the elderly Aurelian/Aurelianus (probably c. 75 yrs.) who was nominated as *Patricius*.[12] It is unfortunate that we do not know the details behind his nomination. On 4 July 414 Pulcheria was nominated as Augusta. After this, for some unknown reason Monaxius was relieved of his office so that Aurelian became the sole

PPO. On 30 December Aurelian dedicated the portrait of Pulcheria in the Senate House, along with her fellow Augusti Honorius and Theodosius. This meant that Pulcheria's position was considered equal to the emperors. Aurelian had probably proved a better flatterer than Monaxius and was therefore either promoted to the office or kept his office after Monaxius ended his term. It seems probable that Aurelian followed his previous policies regarding barbarians, but he was replaced by Monaxius before August 416. We do not know the reason for this change of policy – perhaps Aurelian had just retired because of his age – but it was after Aurelian's downfall that we have the first extant evidence for the rise of the Germans back into the highest military offices (see PLRE2). On the basis of this, it is possible to speculate that those who entertained a more conciliatory attitude towards the barbarians had gained Pulcheria's ear, quite probably because she considered the barbarian commanders to be a lesser threat to the House of Theodosius. However, it is possible that this results merely from the poor survival of evidence for the period.

It comes as no great surprise that the devout Christian Pulcheria changed the policies of her predecessor Anthemius. She made the Imperial Palace effectively a closed cloister in which she, her sisters and the Emperor devoted their time to fasting, the singing of hymns and the observance of canonical hours. Pulcheria was now in total charge of Theodosius' education and his imperial policies. According to Sozomen (9.9), Pulcheria ensured that Theodosius received a complete education so that he was taught the military skills expected of an Emperor (how to ride and use arms) together with literature, science and imperial etiquette, and, most importantly, she made certain that Theodosius became a devout Christian. The seclusion of Theodosius within the confines of the palace together with the attention devoted to all things Christian ensured that Theodosius II would be susceptible to hear only Pulcheria's advice. Pulcheria's own devotion to asceticism and celibacy in its turn made her susceptible to the advice given by priests, monks and holy men. It is possible that this was merely a charade and that Pulcheria kept lovers.[13]

Pulcheria's regime was markedly harsher towards the Jews and Hellenes than Anthemius' administration had been, which is not surprising when one remembers the hatred Pulcheria felt towards Anthemius and his pagan friends. Pulcheria issued harsh legislation against the Jews and excluded from administrative posts all those that were suspected to be sympathetic towards Hellenism (i.e. paganism) or Hellenic culture. Not unnaturally Pulcheria's attitude towards the Jews, Hellenes and heretics encouraged the worst behaviour among Christian fanatics. The foremost of these fanatics was the Patriarch of Alexandria, Cyril, who had succeeded Theophilus in 412. The imperial government had proved incapable of preventing the appointment of Cyril to the See. The conflict between Cyril and the Prefect reached a boiling point in 414/5. Egypt was not the only place where the Jews faced trouble, but it should be noted that the behaviour of the most fanatic of the Jews was the principal cause for their troubles (see also Appendix 3). In one instance near Antioch, a group of drunken Jews killed a boy with the result that the Christians attacked the Jews. The contest between the Jews and Christians appears to have been relatively equal, even though the latter undoubtedly had a numerical advantage. When this was reported to the Emperor, he ordered the local governor to find out the culprits and punish them. It was his responsibility to do that. This action seems to have pacified the situation. What is notable about this is that the religious tension between the Jews and Christians was so bad that a crime committed by a small group of bad apples (present in any group of population) was enough to incite the powder keg.[14]

The Road to War 417–421

After Pulcheria became de facto ruler of the East, the relationship between East Rome and Persia started to deteriorate. Her religious views intervened with the demands of *realpolitik*. The fire worshippers were no longer under imperial protection. Most importantly, Holum has proved that the old Roman doctrine of Imperial Victory and Victory of Christ became mixed in the imagination of the deeply religious Pulcheria so that she started to consider both to be identical. This meant that Pulcheria thought that it would be necessary for the Emperor to fight crusades in the name of Christ to prove his right to the throne.

Notably the new government took a strong stance against corruption (the so-called pickles) among the officer cadre. According to the Edict (CTh 7.11.2) issued at Constantinople to the *PPO* Monaxius on 28 July 417, the tribunes and *comites* had illegally demanded bathing from the provincials, while the *duces* of the Euphrates frontier had exacted a *tremis* (one third of a *solidus*) per day for wood and baths during the past three years. The officers were ordered to return the money they had extorted twofold, and the Edict ordered that the same punishment was to be exacted also in the future from any officers that extorted money from their hosts. In the same year on 27 September 417 (CTh 15.11.2), the government intervened on behalf of the *Praeses* (governor) of *Euphratensis*. The frontier dukes and their staffs were ordered to send the wild beasts intended for the imperial court in such a manner that the beasts were not to be retained in any municipality for a period longer than seven days on pain of being fined 5 lbs of gold each. This suggests that Pulcheria's government took very seriously the problem of corruption among the top brass. This was beneficial both for the fighting spirit of the army and for the morale of the civilian population. However, as we shall see, unlawful exactions from the civilians were by no means the only form of corruption the Roman military was practising in the East.

It is unfortunate that we do not know whether the above-mentioned legislation should be connected with the revolt that took place in the Province of Palestine at some point in time between 1 Sept. 417 and 31 Aug. 418 (Marc. a.418.1), which was crushed by the newly appointed Gothic *Comes* Plintha. The fact that the revolt took place in Palestine suggests that the rebels consisted of the Saracen Federates. The likeliest reason for the revolt of the Saracens was the corruption of imperial officials/officers who could have stolen the provisions/payments meant for the Saracens. The *Novella* 24 (NTh 24)

Plinta on a plate

of Theodosius II which is dated to the year 443 addresses this problem.[15] According to this *Novella*, the *duces* were not to extort subsistence allowances of the Saracen *foederati* or other *gentes*. Religious reason for the revolt is less likely because Pulcheria and the Arabs were both Orthodox Christians. The location also suggests that the revolt was instigated by the Salihids, which further explains why their position as a leading tribe was subsequently taken over by Aspebetus and his followers.[16] The revolt must have been very significant because Plintha was rewarded with the position of *MVM Praes.* and the consulship in 419.

Maenchen-Helfen (p.75) has also noted a key piece of legislation (CTh 9.40.24 dated 24 Sept. 419) which proves that the East Romans also faced some barbarian pirates on the waters of the Black Sea in the late 410s. The Edict states (tr. by Pharr, p.258):

> The same Augustuses to Monaxius, Praetorian Prefect. Those persons who have betrayed to the barbarians the art of building ships, that was hitherto unknown to them, shall be freed from imminent punishment and imprisonment because of the petition of the Most Revered Asclepiades, Bishop of the City of Chersonesus, but We degree that capital punishment shall be inflicted both upon these men and upon any others if they should perpetrate anything similar in the future. [See also my *Britain in the Age of Arthur*.]

As noted by Maenchen-Helfen, the only candidates as pirates in the Crimean waters were the Huns and Goths, but the former were the likelier perpetrators. The same piece of legislation also proves several other things. Firstly, the city of Chersonesus was clearly in Roman hands. Secondly, the Romans clearly still possessed naval supremacy in the waters despite the fact that some persons had taught the barbarians the art of building ships because the government was prepared to pardon the culprits. Thirdly, the Romans possessed such an effective security apparatus in the area that they had become aware of the crime and had accordingly imprisoned the guilty persons. Fourthly, the Edict proves that there were barbarian pirates on the Black Sea, which required anti-piracy operations by the Roman naval detachments posted in the area of which we know next to nothing. The same conclusion can obviously be reached from the fact that the Roman government had taken care to rebuild the Danubian fleets in conjunction with the rebuilding and reinforcing of the existing fortifications along the Danube, in the Balkans, and along the Black Sea coast. The nomadic Huns, however, never became a real naval threat to the Romans because they remained landlubbers by heart. This in its turn made it impossible for the Huns to ever conquer the city of Constantinople. The same was true of the city of Chersonesus, which was also located on the coast. As long as the Huns lacked credible naval forces they could not do much against this city either because it was fortified well enough (see the accompanying map).[17]

When Pulcheria's government assumed a harsher stance towards the 'heretics', Jews and Zoroastrians, Yazdgerd took note of the worrisome development and attempted to defuse the time bomb by sending the Persian *Catholicos* Yablaha as his envoy to Constantinople, either in 418 or 419. The Roman religious authorities subjected him to an examination of faith, which he passed, but as noted by Blockley (1992, 56) this was a very insensitive thing for the Romans to do. The Romans in their turn sent Acacius of

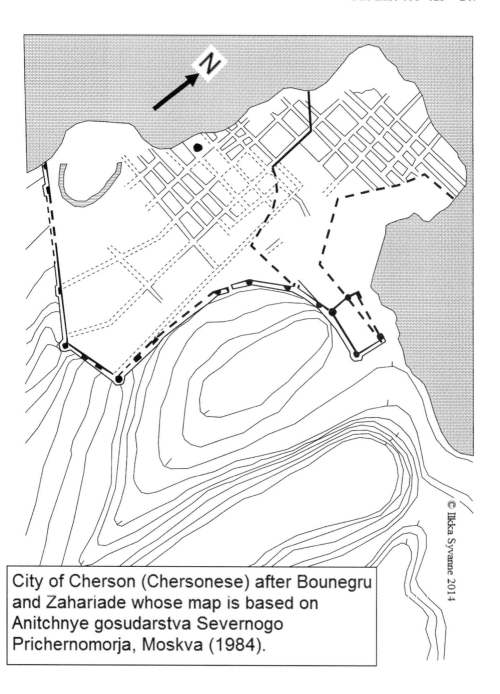

City of Cherson (Chersonese) after Bounegru
and Zahariade whose map is based on
Anitchnye gosudarstva Severnogo
Prichernomorja, Moskva (1984).

Amida to Persia to take part in the Synod of 420 which was organized by Yablaha. Neither
side was willing to break the relationship, but then the Christians of Persia committed
an outrage. The Christians had already started to act in a more aggressive manner before
this, presumably in 419, which had caused Yazdgerd to adopt harsher measures to contain
Christian bigotry. Yablaha and Isaac, the *Catholicos* of Armenia, had managed to restrain

the *Shahanshah*, but now the Bishop Abdaa destroyed a fire-altar in Khuzestan and refused to restore it. This was too much. Yazdgerd was forced to instigate a persecution of Christians in order to pacify the angry Persian nobility, magi, and populace, either in late 419 or in early 420. The nobles and magi were already angry with the ruler because of his centralizing tendencies and because of his habit of forcing a feudal relationship on the nobility. It is probable that the advice to attempt to pacify the angry nobility and magi had come from the Prime Minister, Mihr-Narseh, who is known to have been a devout Zoroastrian of the sect of Zurvan.

According to Cyril of Scythopolis (*Vit. Euthym.* 10, partial tr. in REF2, p.37), when Yazdgerd I launched the persecution of the Christians, the magi stationed the Saracen phylarchs at all points to prevent the flight of Christians to Roman territory. One of the Arab phylarchs called Aspebetus considered the persecution inhuman and instead of preventing the flight actually helped Christians across the border. When Aspebetus' enemies accused him before Yazdgerd, Aspebetus took his family and wealth and fled to Roman territory, where he was received by the *magister militum per Orientem* Anatolius. He was duly appointed as phylarch of the Federate Saracens in Arabia. As noted by Shahid, Aspebetus was a very high-ranking defector from the Persian side. The name Aspebetus in all probability means the office of *Aspet*.[18] The fact that Anatolius immediately nominated Aspebetus as phylarch in Arabia also suggests that he had been a very high-ranking person before his defection. The Phylarchate of Arabia definitely includes the *Provincia Arabia* (probably with all tribes of the Province) and possibly Palestine (because his son held the phylarchate in that Province), which makes it probable that Aspebetus was made phylarch of most of the Federate Saracen tribes, including the Salihids. The revolt of the Salihids in 419 would have made their position untenable. The fact that Aspebetus was made phylarch of the Federate tribes was clearly resented, because later, in 460, his son (the phylarch of Palestine) was imprisoned in Arabia as a result of a plot of a fellow phylarch.[19]

In the midst of all this, the Persian *Shahanshah* Yazdgerd I died in 420. He was probably assassinated, which means that his measures failed to satisfy the most ardent fire-worshippers among the nobility and magi. According to the official story, a white horse kicked and killed Yazdgerd and then disappeared. This happened in Gurgan/Hyrcania or at Tus, the latter of which was the traditional fiefdom of the Kanarangiyan family. Ferdowsi and Dinawari give a list of noblemen who had formed an alliance against Yazdgerd and his offspring. These included the Great Houses of the Mihran, the Karin, and Kanarangiyan. Pourshariati considers the list anachronistic, but I am inclined to take the information at face value like Christensen because the information does fit the circumstances.[20] However, it should still be noted that the other noble houses probably joined them after the assassination, because Tabari's information suggests that the Surens and Isbahbudhans supported the new ruler against Bahram (see below).

The conspirators decided that they would not accept Yazdgerd's offspring as his successor, and decided to nominate a member of the collateral line of the Arsacids/Sasanians called Khusrov as their next *Shahanshah*.[21] Consequently, when Shapur, the eldest son of Yazdgerd and the *Marzban* of Armenia, arrived to assert his right to rule, the nobility killed him (see below). When Bahram received the news of the death of his father and of the elevation of Khosrov, he asked for help from his tutor al-Mundhir.

He assembled all the Arab sheiks under his rule for a meeting with Bahram. The Arabs decided to back Bahram's claim. However, since al-Mundhir was well-aware that he did not possess enough soldiers to challenge the Persian Empire in a regular war, he decided to resort to the use of a guerrilla campaign. He assembled and equipped 10,000 horsemen under his son Numan and sent those against the two royal cities Ctesiphon and Bih-Ardashir (Veh-Ardashir/Seleucia), which lay on the opposite sides of the Euphrates.

The Arabs pitched an encampment near the cities and started to send raiding/reconnaissance forces to pillage the area with orders to take captives but not to shed blood. If the Persians sent soldiers against Numan, his father ordered him to engage them (presumably with skirmishes while retreating into the desert). The aim was to force the nobility to negotiate.[22] This ploy worked. The nobility did not like to see their estates pillaged and they forced the new ruler, whose position was still weak, to do something. The 'great men of the state' and the nobles dispatched Yazdgird's former head of the Chancery Juwani to negotiate. When Bahram and al-Mundhir asserted the former's right to rule, Juwani suggested face-to-face negotiations with the magnates because he lacked the powers to conclude any treaty. They sent Juwani back to organize a meeting, after which al-Mundhir and Bahram led 30,000 horsemen towards the twin cities so that the Arab forces supporting Bahram's claim near Ctesiphon now consisted of 40,000 horsemen altogether. Unlike most modern historians, I see no reason to doubt the size of this force. The figure is entirely in keeping with the sizes recorded for the earlier and later Arabic forces (e.g. Palmyra, the Muslims).

The nobility demanded that Bahram not follow the policies of his father, which also entailed the lowering of taxes, an increase in the army's pay, and greater offices for the nobility. The lowering of taxes and the increase in the army's pay meant the lowering of the feudal 'taxes', because the nobility were required to pay a certain amount of money to the treasury from which was deducted the amount of money needed for the upkeep of the feudal army.[23] Bahram promised to do all these. According to Tabari, it was then that the nobility stated that they could not break their oaths to Khosrov and suggested as a compromise that the imperial regalia were to be placed before two lions so that the man (either Bahram or Khosrov) who would be able to snatch these would be the new ruler. Once again, this story is an entirely plausible compromise for men who were used to the showing of personal bravery and bravado both in hunting and on the battlefield. Bahram accepted the challenge. According to Tabari (i.861), the Chief *Mobadh/Mobad*, who had the responsibility of crowning each new ruler, placed the imperial regalia and crown on the ground, after which Bistam the *Isbahbad* brought two hungry lions with their cubs to the site. This suggests two things. Firstly, since it is known that the Surens crowned the rulers, it is clear that we should identify the Chief *Mobadh* with the *Hazarbed* (Prime Minister) Mihr-Narseh. Secondly, Bistam the Isbabadh should be identified as Bistahm of the Isbahbudhan family, which would make him the hereditary commander of the cavalry forces.[24] This means that the other noble houses had joined ranks with the conspirators after the assassination of Yazdgerd. This unity of the nobility weakened the independence of the ruler with far reaching consequences.

Bahram offered to give the first opportunity to Khosrov, but he declined so that Bahram would have to try his chances first. The aim of the nobility and Khosrov was to cause the death of Bahram with this ploy, but to their great surprise Bahram managed to kill both lions with a mace and take the regalia (especially the case if Bahram was only 15–16 years of age). The nobility and Khosrov had no other choice than to accept the result. The bravery and martial skill shown by Bahram at the very beginning of his rule were to become his trademarks, which were to cause changes in the military methods employed by the Persian army at large. The first to have a taste of this were the Romans.

The relative weakness of Bahram vis-à-vis the nobility and the *Hazarbed* and Chief *Mobadh* Mihr-Narseh meant that he had to continue the persecution of Christians that had begun under his father, with the result that ever more Christians crossed the border into the safety of the Roman Empire. The fact that Bahram's rise to power was followed by the revolt of Persarmenia against the Persians also resulted in the flight of still more Christians over the border. Pulcheria could not overlook such actions against her fellow Christians, but Bahram was in no position to compromise. The stage was set for a confrontation.[25]

Pulcheria's government seems to have made the decision to protect the Christian fugitives and to invade Persarmenia and Persia early on, because it issued an Edict (CJ 8.10.10, tr. in REF2 36–7) on 5 May 420 which permitted all those who desired the right to surround their lands and premises with a wall in the provinces of Mesopotamia, Oshroene, Euphratensis (established by Constantius II), Syria Secunda, Phoenice Libanensis, Cilicia Secunda, both Armenias, both Cappadocias, Pontus Polemoniacus, and Helenopontus, which were in greatest need of fortifications, but also in addition to these in other provinces. That part of Armenia, *Armenia Interior,* which had been ceded to the Romans in 387, had not yet been fully incorporated into the provincial structure but remained a sort of feudal territory (n.28 p.257 in REF2). It is clear that the intention was to improve the defences for the forthcoming war, but modern researchers have not reached any consensus regarding other possible implications of this law. I am inclined to believe that Holum (1977, 162) is correct in suspecting that the imperial authorities adopted this dangerous practice of allowing the civilians to build their own fortifications because the intention was to use all available manpower for the offensive.[26]

It seems likely that we should connect the lack of military action for the year 420 with the mutiny of soldiers mentioned by Marcellinus Comes (420.2).[27] According to him, the soldiers revolted and killed their general (*ductor*) Maximinus. It is unfortunate that we do not know who this Maximinus was and what was the cause of the revolt. PLRE2 (Maximinus 2) assumes that the title *ductor* means the *magister militum per Orientem*, and in light of the inaction on the eastern front this seems probable. The likeliest reason for the mutiny is the one mentioned by the editors of the REF2 (p.257, n.27), namely that the general in question was corrupt. When the soldiers were in such a state of tumult that the high command could suspect their combat readiness, it comes as no great surprise that the Roman government postponed the invasion to the following year. The morale of the army clearly needed a boost and Pulcheria provided that.

Indeed, I would suggest that it was not only Pulcheria's own religious convictions that resulted in the presenting of the forthcoming war as a Crusade against the infidels, but also the very real need to improve the morale of the mutinous army. According to Holum, the mint of Constantinople started to issue a strikingly new victory type, the Long-Cross Solidi, at the instigation of Pulcheria in 420. The soldiers were to be paid with money that promised victory in the name of the Cross. At about the same time, Holum noted that Pulcheria instructed her brother Theodosius II to give a plentiful donation for the poor to the Archbishop of Jerusalem, together with a golden cross studded with precious stones to be erected at Golgotha. In return for these gifts, the Archbishop sent relics consisting of the right arm of St. Stephen Protomartyr. Just like Constantine the Great before her, Pulcheria was duly instructed in a dream what to do with these. A new church devoted to St. Stephen was to be built in the imperial palace and the relics were to be deposited there. With this gesture Pulcheria identified her and her brother with the 'first athlete of Christ'. The placing of the golden cross at Golgatha signified Christ's victory over death and symbolically the victory of the emperor over his infidel enemies. The long-cross was to be the symbol of the emperor and his Christian army. Holum has correctly noted that for the Christian authors the cross was the *vexillum* or *tropaion* which symbolized Christ's victory over death, and that the *Labarum* (symbol of Christ) of Constantine the Great had become the instrument of his victory. Pulcheria's religious symbolism went even further than the above. Pulcheria presented the vows of virginity that she and her sisters had taken as them having devoted/sacrificed themselves to God and that this self-sacrifice would bring victory to the emperor.[28] In short, whereas the pagans could devote themselves to gods by sacrificing themselves in combat, these Christian virgins would bring about victory through their devotion to Christ and God (which also included other symbolic sacrifices).

© Ilkka Syvänne 2014

Rough Word-art sketch of
Solidus of Pulcheria minted in
Constantinople ca. 420-22.

A bronze (or gold) *fibula*
= a brooch worn on the
right shoulder by Roman
officials and soldiers.

This same line of reasoning can be developed even further when one remembers that the original *Labarum* of Constantine had been taken to the West by Theodosius I and had apparently remained there because in 408 Stilicho had intended to use it as his standard during his march to Constantinople. On the basis of this, it is clear that the Easterners needed their own battle standard of Christ, and Pulcheria gave it to them. It is quite probable that, even if the sources fail to mention this, the new imperial battle standard was the Long Cross, just as it had previously been the *Labarum*. It is in fact possible or even probable that Pulcheria converted the portable large golden cross which was studded with gems known as 'the Cross of St. Constantine the Great' for this purpose. According to Constantine Porphyrogenitus (*De Cer.*), it was used in coronations and in the veneration of the faithful, and it was carried in procession together with the *labara* (these were copies of the original, which was now in the West) and other military standards (Holum,

1977, 166). The new imperial standard was also propagated to the troops through coinage just as the *Labarum* had been previously. The use of such a miracle-working talisman to encourage the troops as the *Labarum* or the Long-Cross would not be the last such instance in the history of Rome. In the sixth century and after the East Romans often paraded the 'Image of Christ Not Made by Human Hand'. 'Miracle-working' icons were also used for a similar purpose. Holum (1977, 155.157) has dismissed the claims of the African bishop Quodvultdeus that the soldiers wore bronze crosses (the *fibulae*) on their cloaks as talismans of victory as Quodvultdeus' later (he wrote in about 450) purposeful falsification to prove that the promises of God would work out. It is possible that Holum is correct, but it is also possible that the imperial authorities could have given to the *fibulae* a religious significance purposefully on this occasion to encourage the men. As we shall see, Pulcheria's Crusade and religious propaganda did lift the morale of the army. It performed remarkably well against the Persians.

The Persian War 421–422

The three main sources for the Persian War of 421–422 are Socrates (who neglects Armenian events), Moses Khorenatsi (who neglects the Roman role), and the Georgian Chronicles (neglected until now because the evidence has been previously misdated by 100 years), but valuable information can also be found from other sources like Theodoret, all usefully collected in the REF2. The following analysis of the events is based on these and on the valuable modern analyses of Greatrex (1993, 1996, 2008), Holum (1977, 1982), Schrier, Blockley (1992), Shahid, and my old analyses (book, articles and lecture) of the strategy and tactics (2004, 2010–2011, Vol. 2) used by the Romans during this war. I will deal with the different pieces of evidence separately and then combine these into a narrative.

Socrates
According to Socrates (7.18), Bahram V Gur launched a very oppressive persecution of Christians with the result that these fled to Roman territory. The Patriarch of Constantinople Atticus (405–425) gave them a place of refuge and asked the emperor to place them under his protection. At the same time as this happened, there also arose other causes of disagreement. Bahram refused to send back Roman gold-miners who had been working in Persian territory and the Persians also confiscated/robbed the goods of Roman merchants. The Romans obviously complained about this while the Persian King demanded the return of the Christian fugitives. The stage was set for war and according to Socrates the Roman Emperor forestalled the Persians by attacking first.

Wall Building Projects in Persia
Even if the likeliest reason for the presence of Roman gold-miners is that they were used to mine gold in Persarmenia, their presence in Persian territory still raises another interesting possibility, which is that they were used to build fortifications against the northern nomads. The reason for this is that the gold-miners were in all probability Isaurians who were not only used in this capacity, but also as construction workers, engineers and siege specialists. The PIPLA (598ff.) notes that at the time of his death

Yazdgerd I was said to have been at Gorgan/Gurgan.[29] Of note is also the fact that Yazdgerd established an important mint there in the 410s – the production of this mint peaked during the reign of Yazdgerd II. This suggests the possibility that the construction work of the Great Wall of Gurgan may have already started during the reign of Yazdgerd I, even if the PIPLA suggests that the building of the walls spanned several reigns so that most of the walls would have been completed during the reigns of Yazdgerd II and Peroz.

My own educated guess is that the construction of the great Gurgan Walls was indeed started with Roman assistance during the reign of Yazdgerd I, but that the walls were not completed during his reign. It seems probable that the inspiration for the use of walls against the Huns came from the Romans because it is unlikely that the construction of the Theodosian Walls would have passed unnoticed. The gold-miners would not have been the only Roman construction workers in Persia at the time. According to Tabari (i.850–1), Yazdgerd I built a palace called al-Khawarnaq with the help of a Roman architect for his son Bahram in the city of Hira. The Persians clearly needed Roman assistance for their most important construction projects. It seems probable that the work on the Gurgan Walls was halted during the reign of Bahram V, but was then restarted during the reign of Yazdgerd II. The reason for this conclusion is that as part of his terms of peace in 440 (see later) Yazdgerd clearly demanded that the Romans send a detachment to assist him against the northern nomads, and the production of the mint of Gurgan peaked in his reign.

I would also suggest that the Romans assisted the Persians in the building of the Derbend Wall during the reign of Yazdgerd I. The evidence for this can be gathered from the confused account of John Lydus when it is combined with other extant evidence. According to Lydus, after Yazdgerd had failed to make the Romans share the expenses of building and garrisoning the Pass, the Persians built it anyway. After this, the Persians used the building of the Walls as an excuse to extort money from the Romans by claiming that the Romans had wronged them by not paying their share and invaded the Syrias and Cappadocias 'little by little' (implies war). As a result of this, the elder Theodosius (a mistake for Theodosius II) sent the first Sporacius ('*Sporakion ton prôton*') to negotiate with the Persians. The principal reason for not dating the war to the years 421–422 is that we know that the Romans had loaned gold-miners and architects to the Persians, which rather suggests that the Romans had made a contribution to the upkeep/building of the walls. Then there is also the problem that the only certain early dating for the construction of the walls is the reign of Yazdgerd II, but once again this is not conclusive because Kettenhofen (Derbend 2011) has noted that the archaeologists have failed to consider the possibility that Yazdgerd II's wall could have actually been a reconstruction of earlier damaged walls. Consequently, it is actually possible to date the earliest Sassanian phase of construction to the reign of Yazdgerd I, which means that there are two possible dates for the negotiations led by Sporacius: under Bahram V Gur in 422 and under Yazdgerd II in 440 or 441. The latter of these is inherently likelier because the latter war would better fit the circumstances in which Sporacius was negotiating. Furthermore, the first Sporacius would have been Flavius Sporacius (Sporacius 3 in the PLRE2) who was *Comes* in 448 and *Comes Domesticorum Peditum* in 450–451 and not the *PVC* Sporacius (PLRE2 Sporacius 1) of the years 474/491.

In sum, I would suggest that the likeliest date for the first building phase of the Derbend Walls was the reign of Yazdgerd I after the year 412, that the situation was then confirmed in the peace negotiations in 422 and thereafter in the periodical negotiations some of which included the demonstration of Persian military might as happened in 441. It is quite clear that both Empires sought to counter the nomadic threat with walls.

Moses Khorenatsi

According to Moses (326ff.), when Yazdgerd I died, his son Shapur/Shapuh, the *Marzban* of Armenia, marched to Ctesiphon, but was immediately assassinated by the nobility. The Armenians exploited the situation by revolting against the Persians. The general (*Sparapet?*) Nerses Chichrakatsi collected the Armenian princes together with their feudal retinues and gave battle to the Persian army. The Persians were defeated and according to Moses their general was killed by Aprsam Spanduni, after which they scattered leaderless into the mountains and Armenia remained in anarchy for three years (420–423). This must mean that it was actually the Armenian general who had lost his life at the battle thanks to the treachery of Aprsam Spanduni. Moses (p.326) then goes on to claim that the new ruler Bahram V Gur (420–438/9) made peace with the 'Greeks' and did not approach their sector but sought vengeance against the Persarmenians. This is clearly inaccurate, for we know full well that Rome and Persia were at war in 421–422 and that Armenians fought on both sides. However, it is still clear that Bahram concluded peace with the Romans in 422 before he concluded peace with Armenia. Both Moses and Vardan (p.169) state that the Patriarch Sahak together with his grandson Vardan Mamikonean and Saint Mesrop fled to the Roman sector of Armenia, which clearly implies that the Persians had invaded Armenia and had defeated the Armenian army in 420. Since Rome and Persia were still at peace, the *MVM per Orientem* Anatolius did not welcome Sahak with due cordiality. Consequently, Sahak sent a letter to the *MVM per Orientem* Anatolius[30] in which he thanked him for the place of refuge and asked his permission for the sending of an embassy, consisting of the 'Saint' Mesrop and his grandson Vardan Mamikonean (the title of *Sparapet* was hereditary in the family), to the emperor Theodosius II and the Patriarch of Constantinople Atticus (405–425). Sahak begged the emperor to assist the Armenian rebels against the Persians. It was very wise for Sahak to include Atticus in the negotiations, because Atticus could use his authority to influence the religiously motivated Pulcheria.

Theodosius, or rather his sister Pulcheria, was quite ready to interfere and appointed Vardan as *stratelates* and Mesrop as 'head teacher/doctor' (*ecclesiasticos/eklesiktikos*), and then sent them back with money and orders to establish Christian schools. He also sent instructions to the *strategos* Anatolius in the Roman sector of Armenia to help the Armenians and to build a city (Theodosiopolis, mod. Erzerum/Erzurum; the other Theodosiopolis at Rhesaina was built by Theodosius I[31]) in Armenia to serve as a base for the Roman armies in the region. I would suggest that Pulcheria sent the order to build the city because Anatolius had suggested this. In my opinion, it is not a coincidence that it was Anatolius who fortified Theodosiopolis – he had already fortified Smyrna. He was clearly an expert in fortification work.

On the basis of this it is clear that Theodosius II promised Roman help and money, and it is possible that this served as the actual *casus belli* between the superpowers.

For what it is worth, Quodvultdeus claimed that Theodosius started the war against the Persians because he wanted to protect the Armenian refugees. As regards the title *stratelates* (general), its usual meaning is *magister militum* and it is therefore possible that Theodosius appointed Vardan as a Roman general, but it is inherently likelier that he nominated Vardan as *Sparapet* of Armenia.

Many of the Armenian princes then assembled their forces and fled to the Roman sector to serve under the new *Sparapet*, with the result (according to Moses, pp 330–331) that Bahram proposed a peace treaty through Smbat the *Aspet* because Bahram knew that he would not be able to hold the country without the support of the Armenian princes. As a result, Sahak left Mesrop in charge of Roman Armenia, together with the brothers of Vardan Hmayeak and Hamazaspean, and entered the province of Ayararat where he assembled all the nobility. In the meanwhile Mesrop had been given the task of rooting out the Borborite heretics in the western sector, possibly because they were considered disloyal. Sahak then sent Smbat the *Aspet* and Vardan the *stratelates* (i.e. *Sparapet*) to negotiate a treaty. The King of Kings signed the treaty and gave an edict of amnesty for the rebels in 423,, and appointed a new Arsacid king for Armenia called Artashes/Ardashir. This proves that Bahram urgently needed to pacify Persarmenia, because nomads threatened the eastern frontiers.

This series of events suggests that the new *Sparapet* Vardan together with the *Aspet* Smbat had pushed the Persians away from Persarmenia in 421 with the result that Bahram suggested peace negotiations either in late 422 or in 423, probably because he also faced problems in the east. We do not know what role the *MVM per Orientem* Anatolius played in these events, but it is very probable that he had actually initially taken charge of the operations and had re-conquered Persarmenia for the Armenians (the Armenian sources are in the habit of forgetting the role played by the Romans in their wars), after which he would have left Persarmenia – either immediately after having accomplished this or at latest when peace was concluded in 422. The reasons for this conclusion are: 1) Anatolius had been ordered to assist the Armenians and he possessed an intact army in readiness on the border, unlike the Armenian rebels who were only assembled there afterwards; and 2) it is probable that the re-conquest of Persarmenia took place immediately after the bloody battle with the Persians near the city of Theodosiopolis/Erzurum/Karin mentioned by the Georgian Chronicles, which probably took place at about the same time as the offensive (possibly diversionary) campaign launched by the *MVM Praes.* Ardaburius from Amida to Arzanene (see later).

As is clear the Armenian sources have left out all the main events of the war between Rome and Persia and the problems facing Bahram in the east which were the real reasons for the readiness of Bahram to conclude a peace with the Armenian rebels. It was not only the desertion of many of the Armenian princes, but most of all the series of defeats suffered by the Persian armies at Roman hands.

The Building of the Fortress City of Theodosiopolis (Erzurum/Karin) in 421[32]

The building of Theodosiopolis close to the Armenian border was very important for several reasons. Firstly, it served as a defensive bulwark against attacks from Persarmenia. Secondly, it served as an advanced base and assembly point for invasions into Persarmenia. The previous staging point for invasions, the city of Satala, lay on the former border (before the division of Armenia) and therefore there was a clear need to push the assembly point closer to the new border. The supply line, however, would still have exploited the sea lanes to the city of Trebzon, from which supplies would have been transported to Theodosiopolis and Satala.

It seems probable that the reorganization of the military commands attested later in Edict (CJ 12.59.10, Krueger's ed. p.1097 has a false number, in truth 12.60.10), namely the creation of the *Dux Utriusque Ponti* and *Dux Utriusque Armeniae*, should be dated to the period just before the war of 421 or to the period immediately after it (see also the Introduction).[33] If the former is the case, then the emperor reorganized the commands at the suggestion of Anatolius to improve cooperation between the different military units just before the war so that there were separate defences to defend the supply lines (Ponti), and Armenian and Iberian fronts, but if the latter is true then the reorganization would have resulted from an analysis of what could be improved after the war. It is not known whether the forces of the *Dux Armeniae* were divided to form these new commands or whether new units were formed for the purpose. My own educated guess is that the Romans used a combination of both, so that the *Dux Armeniae* was forced to give part of his troops (those posted in Pontus) to the *Dux Utriusque Ponti*, but was at the same time compensated with the addition of Armenian feudal units to his force.

The fortifications built at the new city, which was naturally named Theodosiopolis, were very advanced and showed the way to the future. The most advanced feature of the fortifications was the use of the so-called pentagonal prow–towers, which resembled the later bastions. The angled shape of these towers made them very resistant against stones and rocks thrown by the heaviest stone throwers. The shape of the towers was not new. The principle had been known ever since Hellenistic times (Philon of Byzantium, *Mechanike Syntaxis* 5.A.3: hexagonal, pentagonal and tetragonal towers), but the fact that the *MVM per Orientem* Anatolius decided to bring these principles back into use suggests that the Romans had changed their defensive priorities. The fourth-century towers were either square, round, u–shaped or fan-shaped, or octagonal with a flat side facing the enemy, which suggests that in the fourth century the Romans did not have to fear that the enemy would be able to breach the walls with stone throwers – rather it was more likely that the Roman ballistae and stone throwers placed in the towers would make short work of the enemy artillery (see Vols. 1–2). The adoption of the prow–towers on the eastern front at this time suggests that the effectiveness of the Persian artillery had improved. The idea was clearly to negate the effect of enemy stones with angled defences.

The following description by Moses 3.59 (tr. by Thomson, 331–2) gives a good idea of the defensive solutions adopted by Anatolius when the city was built:

> After the general Anatolius, on receiving the royal command, had come to our country and travelled through many of our provinces, he decided to build a city in the province of Karin, … He judged the site to be the centre of the country, not very distant from the places where the sources of part of the Euphrates gush forth … At the very floor of the pretty mountain he found many small crystal-clear springs flowing forth, and at that spot he founded the city. Surrounding it with a deep ditch, he set the foundations of the wall at a great depth [*1st wall*]; above it he built very high and fearsome towers, the first of which he named Theodosius in

honour of Theodosius. Beyond this he built jutting towers like ships' prows [*2nd wall*] and passages with hollow compartments facing the mountain. He did the same on the northern side facing the plain; but to the east and west he erected circular towers. In the centre of the city on an elevated spot, he built numerous storehouses and named them Augusteum in honour of Augustus. And he brought in additional water to many places through underground conduits [*that were safe from an enemy unless someone betrayed where these were located*]. He filled the city with arms and a garrison and named it Theodosiopolis ... And over the warm springs he constructed buildings of dressed stone.

Modern archaeological research has shown that very little of the original Theodosian defences remain intact, but the extant evidence still suggest that the medieval fortifications were built on the ancient foundations. For a full analysis of these, see Thomas Alexander Sinclair's survey of Eastern Turkey.[34] It should be noted, however, that Sinclair, together with most archaeologists, considers the prow-towers to date from a later medieval or Byzantine period, but in my opinion this is a mistake. Moses Khorenatsi's text clearly states that Anatolius built prow-towers and in this case his statement should be accepted at face value, even if it is possible that Moses' account could have been coloured by the fact that he is a sixth-century author who could therefore have witnessed the later sixth-century walls and assumed that those would date from the reign of Theodosius II. There are four reasons for this conclusion: 1) Moses was using an older source that referred to the building of the city; 2) As noted above, the prow-tower was not a new invention and any architect (or even the emperor Theodosius II himself, who was known for his bookish learning) with access to a library that had a copy of Philon of Byzantium's *Mechanike Syntaxis* could have used his text as a source of inspiration; 3) There exists a number of prow-towers from this period, the earliest of which are Valentinian I's prow-towers at Alta Ripa and which could have served as sources of inspiration (Foss and Winfield, 30); and 4) The reason why the number of examples of prow-towers multiply in the sixth century is that the latter half of the fifth century saw relatively little building activity in the form of new fortifications thanks to the treaty with Persia which forbade the construction of new fortifications – the reconstruction work on the old destroyed/decayed fortifications tended to follow the original designs.

Tournefort's description of the town also gives a good summary of the probable state of affairs during the late-Roman period (English tr. 1718, Vol. 2, p.195; I have added comments inside parentheses):[35]

The Town of Erzeron is better than that of Trebizond: the Inclosure of this first is of double Walls, defended by square or pentagonal Towers [*it is therefore quite clear that the round towers of the Roman walls were later rebuilt as square ones*]; but the Ditches are neither deep nor well kept [*the ditches of the Roman period would have been well-kept*]. The Begler-bey or Bassa of the Province lives in an old Seraglio very ill built. The Janizary-Aga dwells in a kind of Fort [*i.e. in the reconstructed East Roman citadel*], in the highest part of the Town. ... there are eighteen thousand Turks in Erzeron, six thousand Armenians, and four hundred Greeks [*i.e. a total of*

24,400]. The Turks who are in Erzeron are almost all of them Janizaries; they reckon about twelve thousand there, and above fifty thousand in the rest of the Province.

Procopius (Buildings 3.5.1–12) claims that Theodosius II built only the fortress on the hill and that the walls surrounding the city were later added by Anastasius. Anastasius's walls were supposedly thick enough, but not high enough (only 30 ft high). In addition to this, his walls lacked outworks (*proteichisma*) and a moat, and had one high hill too close to the wall. Consequently, Kavadh's forces had been able to take the city easily by assault in 502. According to Procopius, Justinian added the outworks and a deep moat/ditch, and added one storey like a gallery (with narrow embrasures suited for shooting) on top of the pre-existing wall. The top of the hill, that was overtopping the walls, was levelled. The towers were also strengthened to make them individual fortresses.

As is obvious, Procopius's account needs closer analysis. It is clear that Procopius has made a mistake regarding the date of the building of the walls of the city. The fact that the Persians assaulted the walls in 502 makes it almost certain that the walls had been built during the reign of Theodosius II because the re-fortification of the eastern border began only after the 502–506 war. It would in fact be incredible if the Persians had demanded the addition of the clause which forbade the building of new forts close to the border after the war 421–422 if Theodosius had only built the very small fortress on the hill, as claimed by Procopius. This fort would have been too small to act as a forward-posted assembly point for an army such as it was meant to serve. This means that Anastasius merely repaired the pre-existing walls after the 502–506 war. However, it is possible that Procopius is correct in stating that the city lacked a *proteichisma* before the reign of Justinian, and it is very probable that he is correct in stating that the wall was heightened by Justinian and that the nearby hill was partially levelled by him. The case for the moat is less certain because it is possible that the original could have been built in 421 but left unrepaired after 422. The strengthening of the towers could be taken to refer to a rebuilding of those as prow-towers, but as noted the prow-towers were already well-known before the sixth century, and I would suggest that we should accept Moses' statement regarding those. Consequently, I would suggest that Justinian actually rebuilt the round towers into square ones that were still visible in the eighteenth century. This would be the best explanation for Procopius's statement when one remembers Moses' statement that Theodosius's towers consisted of prow- and round-towers.

Tournefort's account makes it clear that even as late as in the early-eighteenth century the bulk of the inhabitants of Erzurum still consisted of soldiers, in this case of Janissaries. On the basis of this and on the basis of the fact that the East Roman Armenian Field Army posted at Satala in 530 consisted of 20,000 horsemen plus infantry (see Syvänne, 2013), one may make the educated guess that the approximate size of the garrison of Theodosiopolis was about 20,000 horsemen during times of defensive war and perhaps about 12,000 in times of peace. When the intention was to initiate a major invasion of Persarmenia, the city could also serve as a forward-based assembly area so that the troops posted in the city and outside (in fortified marching camps) just prior to invasion would be considerably greater. Most of these soldiers would have consisted of the Armenian feudal cavalry under the *Dux* of Armenia. Despite the fact that the Janissaries were footmen, one may still hazard a guess that the Armenian feudal cavalry in the three Roman Armenias would also have reached the figure of perhaps 40,000–50,000 horsemen,[36] even if most of these would have been spread out to defend the various feudal domains and castles.

The illustrations (Tournefort's drawing 1717; my sketch map) intend to show the strength of the defences as well as to provide the reader with some sense of what type of fortification the Romans built and in what kind of terrain. The accompanying map is my own tentative reconstruction of the city defences based on Tournefort's illustration, Moses' text and satellite street map of the modern city of Erzurum.

ERZERON

Veüe d'Erzeron Capitale d'Armenie.

to Trebizont

Prow-towers

Tentative reconstruction of the
Walls of Theodosiopolis (Erzurum)

© Ilkka Syvänne 2014

N

Moat

Round-towers

200m

Extant walls both
medieval and
modern built on top
of Roman walls

I have emended here
one octagonal tower

to Satala?

Round-towers

to Persarmenia

There should probably
be one prow-tower on
this spot even though
Tournefort's illustration
lacks one

Prow-towers

to Manzikert

The Georgian Chronicles

The next important sources to analyze are the Georgian Chronicles (216ff.) and the events of the reign of Vaxtang. As I have already proven in the second volume, Toumanoff and others have misdated the reign of Vaxtang by about 100 years.[37] Vaxtang was the grandson of Mirian (lived during the reign of Constantine the Great) and cannot have lived at the turn of the sixth century. When one peels away the layers of legendary material and the inaccurate references to the reigns of Roman emperors, one is left with a core story that can be used to reconstruct the events of the early fifth century. The Georgian Chronicles make it clear that the good diplomatic relationship that had prevailed between Rome, Persia and Iberia after the year 384 had been further cemented by a marriage contract between the Iberian King Vaxtang and the Romans. The Chronicles (pp.216–218, 222–224) claim that Vaxtang married Elene (Helena), the daughter of the Emperor, and that the Emperor gave part of the territory close to the Iberian border as a dowry to the King. This is obviously only partially true. The fact that the children were still minors in 421 makes it certain that Helena cannot have been the daughter of Theodosius II but the daughter of some other nobleman. The later events, however, make it probable that the Romans did grant some territories as a dowry, but in all probability in such a manner that the areas were to be considered Roman territory even if the feudal territories were simultaneously also considered part of the Iberian realm.

The Chronicles state that at a time when Xuasro (Yazdgerd I) died and was followed by his son Xuasro (Bahram), the new ruler sent a message to Vaxtang in which he demanded Vaxtang's daughter in marriage (from the first marriage with a Persian lady) and that Vaxtang take part in the invasion of Greece (East Rome). When Vaxtang received the envoy, he was engaged in the building of the city of Tpilisi (Tiflis) and had just laid the foundations (p.218–9). In addition to this, Vaxtang had also fortified several other places, in particular in the province of Ujarma. This was truly an era of large-scale fortification projects throughout the East and Vaxtang was clearly following the same principles. This was also to prove useful in the war that was to follow. Vaxtang was about 60 years old but still quite prepared to don a suit of armour. He categorically refused to accept the demands set by the Persian King and sent orders via heralds to the people to abandon all unfortified villages and cities and to flee to the Caucasus or to Kaxeti, which was forested and considered impenetrable for the Persians. Vaxtang sent messengers to inform the emperor; sent his eldest son King Dachi to Kaxeti in the Valley of Lopoti; left his wife and children in the Valley of Ujarma; left Demetre, Nerse and Biwritian at Mcxeta; and went in person to the forward-based citadel at Darpaka in Kaxeti.

The Persian King Xuasro (Bahram) advanced into Iberia, and destroyed the city of Kambechoan, the fortress of Cherem, and Velis-cixe. When this is combined with the information that the Persians had clearly occupied most of Armenia after they had killed the *Sparapet* in battle, it becomes clear that Bahram continued his campaign immediately from Armenia into Iberia. If the information regarding the plans of Bahram to invade East-Roman territory in conjunction with the Iberians is correct, then the subsequent Roman invasion of Persarmenia and Persia can be considered to have been a pre-emptive strike while Bahram was still fighting against the Iberians, and there is actually no reason to suspect this because the Persians had clearly undertaken a series of hostile measures prior to the Roman invasion.

When the Persians reached a place called Iori in Kaxeti their progress was halted by the presence of Vaxtang's army at Darpaka. The armies fought inconclusively for three days, after which Vaxtang summoned the *Catholicos* Peter and stated the Persians did not fight to impose tribute but to force the Iberians to abandon Christianity. It is quite easy to connect this with the policy followed by Bahram V Gur at this time. It was then that Vaxtang dispatched the *Catholicos* to the safety of Ujarma, because he considered the cities of Ujarma safe from Persians thanks to the fortification programme that he had initiated.

After that Vaxtang resorted to a desperate stratagem to force the invaders out because he was fighting against great odds. According to the Chronicles, the Iberian army consisted of 240,000 men and the Persian army of 740,000 men. If one takes off one zero from the end, the figures are about right (see Vol. 1). Vaxtang divided his army into three divisions: he arrayed the infantry by the cliffs and sent to one side the *pitiaxsh* (vitaxa) Bakur and the *spaspet* Juansher, while he himself with 100,000 men (i.e. with 10,000 men) intended to make a night attack against the Persian camp. The intention was clearly to fool the enemy into the belief that the Iberian army was where the footmen and cavalry stood so that Vaxtang could attack unobserved from another direction. The plan was a success. Vaxtang attacked at dawn and managed to advance as far as the royal tent. The King was supposedly too fast and managed to flee on horseback so that Vaxtang was able to kill only Bartam (Bahram), the son of the King. It is easy to see how the confusion regarding the names of the Persian kings has arisen in this case. It is quite clear that in truth this Bartam/Bahram was not the son of the King but the Persian King himself, who had managed to mount a horse and flee. The Chronicle claims that the Iberians slew 130,000 (= 13,000) Persians while the Persians killed 28,000 (= 2,800) Iberians, but the victory was not complete because the Persians possessed so large an army. The Persians regrouped their army at Rustavi. On top of this, the Iberians suffered a terrible disaster in the midst of their victory. A Persian had shot an arrow at Vaxtang's breast and it had penetrated his lung. The mortally wounded Vaxtang went to Ujarma and ordered the generals to stay in their posts.

When the Persians learnt of the wound, they destroyed Tpilisi and Armazi and advanced against Mcxeta, but were unable to take it. Consequently, they ravaged all the areas around it. It was then, according to the Chronicle (pp.221–2), that the King of the Greeks died and was succeeded by Zeno (474–491). This is a good example of the placing of the events in the wrong era by the unknown chronicler and can be discarded. However, it is possible that the Zeno whose name has caused the confusion was Zeno (Zenon 6 in the PLRE2) who is attested as being the *MVM per Orientem* in 447–451. The Georgian Chronicle claims that Zeno came to Sper with the intention of entering Iberia to assist Vaxtang against the Persians, but when he learnt that Vaxtang was mortally wounded he halted at Kanu-kalaki. Xuasro advanced there and the armies fought an inconclusive but very bloody encounter at Karnipora (Thomson's note p.222: possibly to be identified with Karin), after which the Persians withdrew to Iberia and from thence back to Persia. According to the Armenian version, 'Zeno' came to Sper to assist the Iberians, but then returned to Karin (Theodosiopolis/Erzurum) when he learnt that Vaxtang was mortally wounded. It was then that the Persian King ravaged Tpilisi and Armazi, and the surroundings of Mcxeta, after which he advanced against the Greeks

(=Romans). The battle ended in stalemate and the Persian king withdrew to Iberia and thence to his own land.

When one combines the accounts with the other pieces of evidence it is easy to build an overall picture of the events that took place in Iberia and Armenia. Firstly, it is clear that the name Zeno hides behind it the name of the *MVM per Orientem* Anatolius who may have been assisted by the Isaurian general Zeno (Zenon 6 of PLRE2). The campaign plan of Anatolius was clearly to bring supplies *via* the city of Trebizont to Theodosiopolis and to assemble the Roman army first at Satala (in Sper) whence he marched it to Theodosiopolis (Karin). There it was united with the Armenian forces with the aim of marching to Iberia through Persarmenia along the road from Theodosiopolis *via* Artaxata to Mcxeta in order to assist Vaxtang against the Persians. When Anatolius then learnt that Vaxtang was mortally wounded, he retreated to his forward base located at Theodosiopolis to await for further developments, which was the arrival of the Persian army under Bahram V Gur. The probable route used by the Persian army would have taken them from the neighbourhood of Mcxeta to Artaxata in Armenia and from there to the city of Theodosiopolis along the road leading into Roman territory. It is quite probable that the Persian aim in attacking the Romans near the city of Theodosiopolis was firstly to protect Persarmenia and secondly to put a stop to the building project.

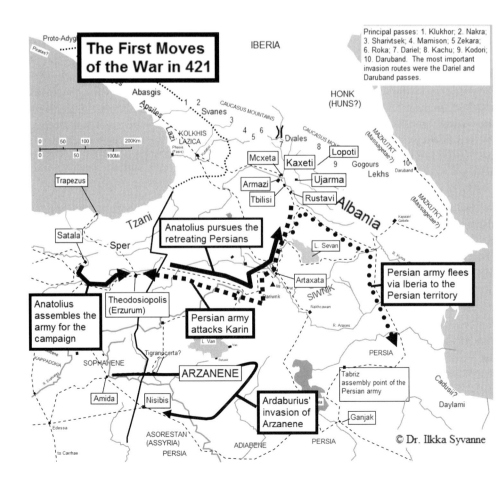

One can make a rough estimate of the size of the Roman army located at Karin on the basis of the figures given by the chronicler regarding the Persian army. Since at the beginning of the campaign the Persian army probably consisted of about 74,000 men, of whom Vaxtang had killed 13,000, the total force left would have been about 56,000 men, if one assumes that the Persians would have suffered about 5,000 casualties in the other operations. In order for the Romans to be able to oppose this force, they must have had at least about 40,000 troops. It would have been relatively easy for Anatolius to assemble this force because the approximate paper strength of the Army of the East and Frontier Army of Armenia consisted of 11,776 cavalry (*equites* and *alae* calculated as 512) and 31,800 infantry (*Aux. Pal.* as 1,000 men, *Comitatenses* LGs as 1,000; frontier LGs as 3,000 and cohorts as 480).[38] When one adds to these figures the Armenian feudal forces on Roman territory and the remnants of the Persarmenian army, it is quite possible that Anatolius' army may even have outnumbered the Persians quite considerably. One would of course need to add to the figures the servants, engineers etc. so that the real overall figures would have been far greater.

The claim that the battle would have been a bloody stalemate is misleading if not utterly false because the Chronicle states that after the battle the Persians withdrew all the way to Iberia and did not attempt to defend Persarmenia. If the battle had really been a draw, the Persians would have stayed in Persarmenia. This means that Anatolius had effectively defeated the Persians by not losing the encounter. One may in fact make the educated guess that the Roman army may have once again been deployed as a 'city' (i.e. as a hollow square) as it had been on several occasions during the previous war in Armenia during the reign of Valens (see Vol. 2) because that would explain the claim that the battle had ended in bloody 'stalemate'. In other words, that the Persians repeatedly attacked the hollow square in vain while detachments of Roman and Armenian cavalry skirmished outside the square and then withdrew inside whenever threatened by the Persians. Obviously, there is no concrete evidence for this, even if the referral to the stalemate would make the use of this tactical formation by the Romans quite probable. It is entirely plausible that even a cavalry battle could have ended in a stalemate.

The Persian withdrawal to Iberia meant that Anatolius had liberated Persarmenia and the fact that the Persians subsequently evacuated Iberia too means that the Romans had also liberated Iberia. The evacuation of Iberia was absolutely necessary for the Persians, because Bahram's forces were in really deep trouble. Firstly, Vaxtang's successor, his son Dachi, still possessed an army which meant that the Iberians could threaten the Persians from the north while the Roman army under Anatolius threatened it from the south. In addition to this, Ardaburius' operations in Arzanene threatened the Persian lines of supply, because if Ardaburius penetrated deeper into Persia he could have cut off the route of retreat for the Persian army away from Iberia. The only routes open for the Persians were to flee via Iberia to Albania or to Tabriz in Persian territory. The fact that the Persians were unable to use the two more direct routes (Artaxata to Ganjak; the road south of L. Sevan) back to Persia must have resulted from two reasons: Ardaburius' invasion of Arzanene had cut off the route leading to Ganjak; Anatolius and the Armenian nobles must have pressed the pursuit really hard so that the route south of L. Sevan was also cut off.

Socrates[39]

As noted above, according to Socrates' version the Romans launched a pre-emptive strike before the Persians could act. The Emperor placed Ardaburius in charge of the campaign. He invaded Persian Arzanene through Armenia. In other words, he probably assembled the army at Amida and then advanced via the most direct route which bypassed the city of Tigranocerta into Arzanene. As noted above, it is possible that Ardaburius' purpose was to cut off the route of retreat for the Persian army posted in Armenia. The Persian general Narses placed his army squarely on the invasion route to stop the Romans but was defeated in a battle. Narses retreated with the remnants of his army while Ardaburius advanced into Arzanene. After this Narses attempted a diversionary invasion of Roman Mesopotamia, but this attempt was forestalled by Ardaburius who marched his army there after having ravaged Arzanene at great speed. Despite fielding a large force, Narses felt unable to fight another pitched battle against Ardaburius and therefore retreated behind the walls of Nisibis. When Ardaburius reached the neighbourhood of the city, Narses suggested that they meet in combat on a predetermined day. Ardaburius' answer was that the Romans fought not when the Persians wanted but when they judged it to be in their own interest. Narses informed the *Shahanshah* of the developments and the King of Kings started to assemble a large army against Ardaburius with the intention of leading it in person. According to the intelligence received by the Romans, Bahram intended to deploy all his available forces against Ardaburius, which implies that Bahram had ordered the eastern armies to be transferred west, with dire consequences for the defence of the East as we shall see. When the emperor received the intelligence report, he ordered the transferral of reinforcements from the Balkans to the East. If Ardaburius had previously had only his own division of the Praesental Army, it was now reinforced with the other Praesental Army and other forces from the Balkans.

Socrates describes well how war could affect population and soldiers when there was dearth of news from the front. He states that the Constantinopolitans were very nervous until 'some persons from Bithynia', who were travelling to the city of Constantinople 'on their own affairs', reassured the inhabitants that a vision of angels had reassured them that the Romans would win – all they needed to do was to pray to God and victory would be assured. This message then comforted not only the inhabitants but also the soldiers. It is quite obvious that the East Roman government had organized this propaganda stunt to calm the populace and to improve the fighting spirit of the Army of the Balkans en route to the eastern front.

Socrates' account (7.18–19) also includes very valuable evidence for the speed of messages between the eastern front and the Imperial Palace and of the quality of military intelligence available to the court. Firstly, it is clear that the quality of information was pretty good, because the Romans were well aware that the Persians were assembling an army under Bahram for use against Ardaburius which enabled the emperor to dispatch reinforcements from the Balkans in a timely fashion to meet the emergency. Socrates also notes the exploits of a remarkable military courier called Palladius and it is worthwhile to quote Socrates' own description of the exploits of this man (tr. in Bohn Library, p.354):

> The emperor received intelligence of what was done in an incredibly short space of time. For he had the good fortune to possess among his subjects a man endowed with extraordinary energy in both body and mind, named Palladius;

who so vigorously managed the public conveyances, that he would reach the frontiers of the Roman and Persian dominions in three days, and again return to Constantinople in as many more. The same individual traversed other parts of the world on missions from the emperor with equal celerity; so that one man once said, not inaptly, 'This man by his speed seems to contract the vast expanse of the Roman territories.' The king of the Persians himself was astonished at the expeditious feats which were related to him of this courier; but we must not stay to give further details concerning him.

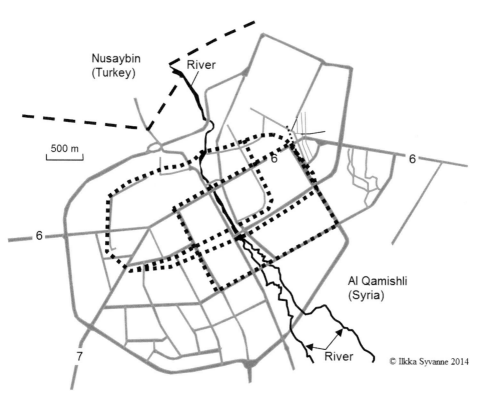

The City of Nisibis (modern Al Qamishli in Syria)

I have added to the map several alternative hypothetical reconstructions of the wall system of the ancient city of Nisibis (shown with dotted lines) based on the existing road network. The likeliest variants of the alternatives are shown with bold lines, because Nisibis was a fortress city and not a metropolis and because in this alternative the river has only one outlet at each end of the wall. It should be noted, however, that we do not know the exact course of the river in antiquity. This would mean that the city would have occupied about 225 or 275ha with the implication that it had a population of about 112,500 – 137,500 inhabitants (if the pop. density was about the same as in a Roman marching camp, the larger figure being more appropriate for a city) and more if it had a population density resembling a metropolis. The placing of the lines is also approximate – the walls could have been either on top of the roads or on the 'inner' side. The reader should be aware that these reconstructions are hypothetical because there exist no visible traces of the walls and because the area has not been subjected to a thorough archaeological survey. The situation is likely to remain the same for the foreseeable future because the ongoing Syrian civil war will prevent all archaeological work in the area as long as it lasts. The fact that the area is located on the border between Turkey and Syria will also pose its own problems.

This account proves that the Palladius in question was not only a man of great vigour but also a man whom the emperor trusted to bring and deliver important messages. He was a man whose loyalty and judgement were above suspicion. It is possible that he was the *agens in rebus* Palladius 5 of the PLRE2, as suggested by the entry. The fact that his exploits became known to Bahram also proves that the Persians had their own informants among the Romans or that the Romans bragged about his exploits to the king, for example when this Palladius accompanied Roman envoys sent to meet the king.

In sum, Socrates' account makes it very clear that the Romans possessed good intelligence apparatus that was able to report in a timely fashion what the Persians were planning. In addition to this, the account also proves that the Romans rather trusted one very able courier to deliver the most important messages rather than used a relay of couriers one after another to deliver a sealed letter.

After Ardaburius had disregarded the Persian suggestion, he placed the city of Nisibis under proper siege, and built wooden siege towers that the Romans moved against the walls by employing machines (ropes and pulleys so that the pullers were well behind the wheeled towers?). According to Socrates, the Romans were able to kill large numbers of defenders with the help of these towers (see the Map on previous page). The success of the Roman operations caused added anxiety among the Persians who speeded up their preparations to bring relief for the defenders.

The swiftness of the Roman operation suggests that Ardaburius had used cavalry for the invasion of Arzanene, while the subsequent siege operations suggest the use of a mixed army of infantry and cavalry. Thanks to the fact that Socrates fails to give any troop compositions and army strengths it is impossible to know for certain. It is possible that the infantry with the siege train was marched to besiege the city of Nisibis from its base (e.g. the city of Theodosiopolis/Resaina or Edessa or Amida) only after Nisibis had already been blockaded by a cavalry army. What is certain is that the Roman army under Ardaburius was an exceptionally large and capable force which was able to defeat the Persian field army posted in Mesopotamia with relative ease. Consequently, it comes as no great surprise that the Persians also assembled a huge army against them, in fact so large that when the Emperor learnt of the preparations made by the Persians he dispatched additional reinforcements from the Balkans.

The implication is that the Roman field armies consisted of two major armies: one under Anatolius consisting of the Eastern Field Army, the Armenian Frontier Army, Armenian feudal forces and Persarmenian rebels; and the other under Ardaburius consisting of the forces grouped around the core of his own Praesental Army (a minimum of 6,656 cavalry and 24,000 infantry). In addition to this, Ardaburius would have commanded at least the frontier armies of Oshroene, Syria and Mesopotamia, which gave him an additional military potential of 21,380 cavalry and 21,840 infantry, but it is probable that the strengths of the frontier armies were below their establishment figures so that one can perhaps suggest that Ardaburius had at his disposal only half of these (about 10,000 cav. and 10,000 inf.). The rest of the soldiers would have either been left to guard the forts and cities, or would have existed only on paper.[40] This would give him a total of 16,656 cavalry and 34,000 infantry.

However, this was not the entire strength committed by the Romans. We know that the Federates were united under a commander called the *Comes Foederatum*, the existence of which is for the first time attested for this conflict, in addition to which came the many *bucellarii* units serving under the different commanders. The minimum figure for the Federates serving under the Gothic *Comes Foederatum* Areobindus would have been about 30,000 horsemen,[41] so that with these Areobindus would have had a minimum of 46,656 cavalry and 34,000 infantry and an unknown number of *bucellarii* but which must have numbered in the thousands. In addition to this, it is possible that Areobindus may have reinforced his army with about 5,000 Federate Arabs, but this is uncertain because he seems to have marched from Amida to Armenian territory and may therefore have felt no need for these.

It is also possible (but not certain) that the second Praesental Army was also dispatched at the beginning of the war because the purpose was to launch a major invasion of Persian lands so that the additional reinforcements that Theodosius sent in late 421 would have consisted of the Field Army of Thrace (3,584 cav. and 20,000 inf.) and reinforcements from the other regular armies of the Balkans (the future emperor Marcian was dispatched from Greece) and possibly of additional Federate forces from the Balkans. It is probable that these reinforcements were placed under the newly-appointed *MVM per Orientem* Procopius (see later). If the second Praesental Army had already been dispatched at the beginning of the war, Areobindus could have easily put together an army of about 51,800 cavalry and 57,000 infantry plus the thousands of *bucellarii*, and after the arrival of the Army of Thrace 56,384 cavalry and 77,000 infantry plus the other probable reinforcements. We should not forget that if desired Ardaburius could also have drawn cavalry detachments from the frontier armies of Phoenice, Arabia, and Palestine. This was a huge army, which makes it understandable why Bahram assembled a similarly huge army, which also included detachments from the East which in turn left a power vacuum in the area that the Hephthalite Huns filled by invading (see later).

According to Socrates, even after he had collected reinforcements from far and wide Bahram still feared Roman valour and therefore asked Alamundaras (al-Mundhir) to aid him. Al-Mundhir was pleased to help his protégé and stated that the King should fear nothing. He promised to deliver Antioch into his hands. Socrates fails to describe the route taken by al-Mundhir or the strategic objective of this move, but I agree with Shahid that the goal must have been to create a strategic diversion while Bahram moved his main army to Nisibis. I also agree with Shahid that it is probable that al-Mundhir followed the same approximate route as his namesake in the sixth century, namely the route along the Euphrates which bypasses Sura and Callinicum. The exact route is pure guesswork, but my own educated guess is that al-Mundhir marched on the eastern side of the river with the intention of crossing the main branch of the Euphrates opposite the city of Barbalissus. Socrates states that it was near the Euphrates River that God put into the minds of the Saracens an irrational panic that the Roman army was about to attack them, with the result that the armed Saracens plunged into the Euphrates River where about 100,000 of them perished.[42] It is clear that the number of drowned cannot have reached the figure of 100,000 because Areobindus sent a general to pursue the defeated Saracens (see below), but contrary to the commonly prevailing view among modern historians this figure is probably only slightly exaggerated if it referred to the size of the entire army under al-Mundhir. The fact that al-Mundhir was the head of the largest Arabic confederacy of the era, which had possessed enough men (40,000 men according to Tabari) to force the Persian magnates to negotiate, makes it clear that, if Bahram had given al-Mundhir reinforcements, the size of his army could easily have approached the figure of perhaps 50,000–60,000 horsemen plus non-combatants. Theophanes (AM 5918) has confused two battles, the one against al-Mundhir and Procopius' battle against the Persians (see below), but his account seems to confirm the large size of the Arabic contingent because he states that it consisted of myriads of men.

After this Socrates states that when the Romans, who were besieging Nisibis, learnt that Bahram was approaching with a multitude of elephants, they became frightened, burned all their siege engines and retreated to Roman territory (see also 'The Persian War of 440/441' in Vol.4). I take this to mean that when Ardaburius learnt that Bahram was approaching and that the Saracens had invaded, he burned his siege engines and marched on the double (presumably with his cavalry to surprise al-Mundhir while the infantry was deployed inside Theodosiopolis/Resaina and/or Edessa) against the Saracens, whom he surprised from behind when the Saracens were approaching the crossing near Barbalissus. The likeliest reason for the panic among the Saracens is that the Romans had cut off their route of retreat by suddenly appearing behind their army. These events must have taken place either in the late-autumn of 421 or very early in 422 because the news of Ardaburius' victory over the Persians (i.e. that which had taken place before the siege of Nisibis) had reached Constantinople on 6 September 421.

After this, Socrates summarizes the events so heavily that one can learn only the gist of what happened (tr. in Bohn Library p.353):

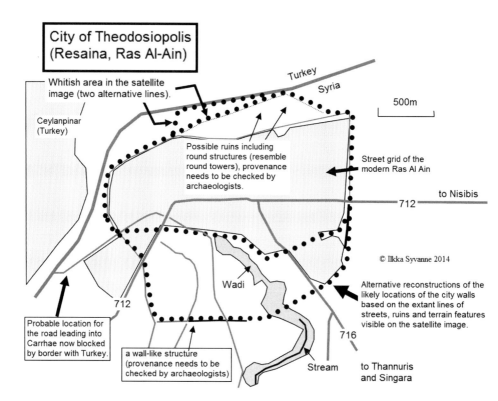

City of Theodosiopolis (Resaina, Ras Al-Ain)

Whitish area in the satellite image (two alternative lines).

Ceylanpinar (Turkey)

Turkey / Syria

500m

Possible ruins including round structures (resemble round towers), provenance needs to be checked by archaeologists.

Street grid of the modern Ras Al Ain

to Nisibis

712

© Ilkka Syvänne 2014

Wadi

Alternative reconstructions of the likely locations of the city walls based on the extant lines of streets, ruins and terrain features visible on the satellite image.

712

Probable location for the road leading into Carrhae now blocked by border with Turkey.

a wall-like structure (provenance needs to be checked by archaeologists)

716

Stream

to Thannuris and Singara

What engagements took place, and how Areobindus, another Roman general, killed the bravest of the Persians in single combat, and by what means Ardaburius destroyed seven Persian commanders in an ambuscade, and Vitianus, another Roman general, vanquished the remainder of the Saracens, I believe I ought to pass by, lest I should digress too far from my subject.

Fortunately, we can put more flesh on the bones from other sources and by making some educated guesses. Since Vitianus seems to have lived at Seleucia in Isauria (PLRE2), he was either the local *Comes* or a *Comes* of the field army that had been billeted at Seleucia, which means that it is probable that Ardaburius left the pursuit of the Saracens to Vitianus, who performed his duties well. We may make the educated guess that Vitianus would have been given at least 15,000–20,000 horsemen to perform the pursuit if the Romans managed to kill at least half of the enemy force in the ambush. This means that now Ardaburius would have had too few horsemen left to engage Bahram in pitched battle, hence his resorting to the use of guerrilla warfare.

Theodoret's account makes it clear that when Ardaburius abandoned Nisibis, Bahram marched against Theodosiopolis, which must mean the city of Resaiana/Theodosiopolis (see the map). My tentative reconstruction of the city walls (several different alternatives are given in dotted lines) is entirely based on my educated guess of the likely places of the ancient walls on the basis of the satellite image of the street grid and visible remains, and is therefore to be considered conjectural until archaeological work is done on the site. Bahram besieged the city for 30 days, during which he used 'thousands' of siege engines

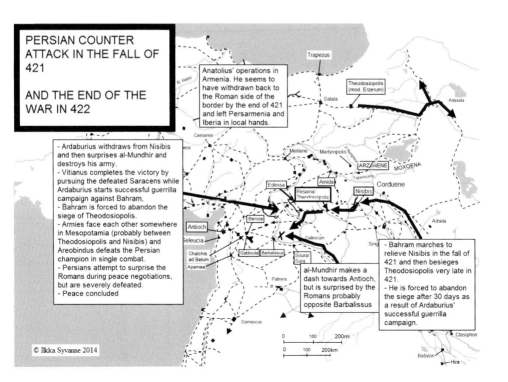

together with numerous siege towers against the city. The Roman generals did not dare to bring any help to the city so that it was left for Bishop Eunomius to destroy the strength of the enemy engines. He ordered that a stone thrower, which was named after the Apostle Thomas, be placed on the battlements and ordered a huge stone to be loaded. After this, he ordered the artillerymen to shoot at one of the enemy kings who had blasphemed the Lord, with the result that the stone landed on his foul mouth and scattered his brains on the ground. When Bahram witnessed this, he supposedly assembled his army, withdrew and made peace. Socrates' account makes it clear that the inaction of the generals is exaggerated. The best explanation for the ambush prepared by Ardaburius in which seven Persian generals died is that Ardaburius ambushed and destroyed the Persian shielding force and that it was as a result of this that Bahram withdrew to face Ardaburius' army. Socrates' account also makes it clear that the Persians were suffering from hunger, which must have resulted from two things: the guerrilla campaign conducted by Ardaburius (i.e. the many engagements of Ardaburius) and from the winter season. This probably means that Bahram had by now lost so many men that it was possible for Ardaburius to engage his army in pitched battle.

I would suggest that the single combat between the *Comes Foederatum* Areobindus and the Persian champion took place immediately after Bahram had withdrawn from Resaina/Theodosiopolis in very early 422. This same event is described by both Socrates and Malalas, which makes it probable that such an event really took place. Malalas claims that the battle took place only after the new *MVM per Orientem* Procopius arrived (see below), but Socrates' account implies that it took place before that and I am here following Socrates. According to the more detailed version of Malalas, the Persian king sent a message to the Romans when the armies were about to fight that if the Roman champion would defeat the Persian champion in single combat he would agree to conclude a 50-year peace and pay tribute. The Roman commander accepted the challenge and sent the *Comes Foederatum* Areobindus forward while the Persians sent Ardazanes from the division of the Immortals. It is quite probable that the *Comes et Magister Officiorum* Helion (see below) had arrived just prior to this event with instructions to seek peace with Persia and with the information that the new *MVM per Orientem* Procopius would arrive shortly. It seems probable that the Huns had launched their invasion of the Balkans during the winter of 421/422 immediately after they had detected the withdrawal of the Roman forces from the Balkans to the Eastern Front, and that the emperor now sought to obtain peace at almost any cost so that the reinforcements sent under Procopius could be recalled. When the champions then approached each other on horseback, Areobindus decided to employ a lasso while the Persian used a lance so that when the latter was nearing Areobindus, he dodged the spear by bending down to his right while lassoing his foe, with the result that the Persian was brought down and then killed by Areobindus. According to Malalas, Bahram then concluded peace, but he has left out one important battle which is described by Socrates.

The accounts of the single combat between Areobindus and Ardazanes are also important because these allow one to make an educated guess regarding the Roman battle array. The Strategikon divided the cavalry formation into two cavalry lines so that the commander of the first line (as *hypostrategos*) was the *Comes Foederatum*, and when we remember that Ardaburius is the first attested *Comes Foederatum*, it is quite possible that the practice of making the *Comes Foederatum* commander of the first cavalry line dates from this period, so that Ardaburius would himself have commanded the second support line as *strategos*. This in turn can mean that Ardaburius used a cavalry army consisting of about 31,000–49,000 horsemen, such as is described by the diagram in the Strategikon. Given that Ardaburius had probably dispatched 15,000–20,000 Federate horsemen with Vitianus, it seems probable that he had no more than about 31,000–35,000 men in the ranks. Obviously there is no definite proof for this, but in light of the extant evidence there is a strong possibility for this to be the case (see the Introductions to Vols. 1–3).

Meanwhile, however, other very important events had taken place in Constantinople. Pulcheria's administration had foolishly refused to recognize Constantius III as Augustus, with the result that the latter had prepared an army with the intention of invading the East. The probable reasons for Pulcheria's foolish decision were firstly that she did not accept a person who did not belong to the House of Theodosius as emperor (she had herself refused to marry), secondly she may have hoped to unite the two halves of the Empire under Theodosius after Honorius died, and thirdly that she knew that Honorius had accepted the situation only under duress. This meant that the East Romans faced the prospect of having to fight two major wars simultaneously. The East Romans appear to have sent assassins to the West, who must have received assistance from Honorius because it is clear that Constantius was murdered (see above). The news of the success of the assassination must have reached Constantinople in mid-to-late September because Constantius died on 2 September 421. It was after this that the Eastern court could start to plan the sending of reinforcements to the East, which were placed under the above-mentioned Procopius.

The Marriage of Athenais/Eudocia with Theodosius II on 7 July 421

Another and even more momentuous event had taken place in Constantinople during the summer of 421. According to the legend, the twenty-year-old Theodosius had informed his sister Pulcheria that he wanted to marry a beautiful maiden and that low birth would not be a hindrance. Both Pulcheria and Theodosius' friend Paulinus began to search for such a lady. It was then that a beautiful young maiden called Athenais, the daughter of the Athenian sophist Leontius, arrived at Constantinople to make a complaint against her brothers regarding her father's will. Her father's sister arranged an audience with Pulcheria and when Pulcheria saw how beautiful and eloquent Athenais was she decided to make further inquiries. When Pulcheria learnt that Athenais was still a virgin and had received a classical education from her father, she went to meet her brother, the emperor. Theodosius' interest was aroused. He instructed that the girl should be brought to his apartments so that he and his friend Paulinus could examine her unobserved. Theodosius' passions were inflamed and his friend Paulinus agreed that she was a true beauty. Athenais was duly converted to Christianity and named Eudocia so that the emperor could marry her on 7 July 421. When her brothers learnt that Eudocia/Athenais had become empress, they fled, but Eudocia recalled them so that Theodosius could reward them. Gesius was promoted immediately to the position of Praetorian Prefect of Illyricum in 421, while the other brother Valerius became *CRP* in 425, Consul in 432 and then *Magister Officiorum* in 435.

The marriage of Eudocia with Theodosius was a very momentous event because Eudocia was able to influence the emperor by using her womanly wiles, but one may also suspect that Theodosius had himself started to wonder whether the policies of Pulcheria had been wise – in the summer of 421 East Rome faced the prospect of having to fight the army of Constantius III while it was fighting against the Persians. The subsequent events make it quite clear that when Theodosius had taken control of his administration he always sought to avoid the need of having to fight two major wars simultaneously.

The incontestable fact that Eudocia was able to change the internal and external policies has caused Kenneth G. Holum (1977; 1982, 112ff.) to suspect the above legendary account on the grounds that it is too good (a rags-to-riches/Cinderella tale) to be true. He also suspects that it is unlikely that Pulcheria could have brought about the marriage because Athenais was a pagan and supported Anthemius's policies. I see no reason to adopt this line of thinking. Romantic events do happen and it is entirely plausible that Pulcheria could have made such a mistake by thinking that her own influence over her brother would be ensured if she picked the wife – being a virgin she would not necessarily have known the importance of sex and that sisterly-love just could not compete with that. However, I am inclined to believe that Holum is correct in stating that the likeliest person behind the rise of Eudocia/Athenais was Theodosius' friend Paulinus, who could easily have arranged the meeting between Pulcheria and Athenais on behalf of those who supported the policies of Anthemius.

The marriage resulted almost immediately in the restoration of the friends and family of the late Anthemius. Of particular importance is the fact that this group favoured peace with Persia. Anthemius' own son Isidorus became Praetorian Prefect of Illyricum in 424, *PPO* in 435–436 and consul in 436. Anthemius' son-in-law Procopius was nominated to succeed Anatolius as *MVM per Orientem* in the autumn of 421. He and his army (presumably consisting of the reinforcements from the Balkans and the Army of the East) reached the front just in time to take part in the last and decisive battle very early in 422. Eudocia's maternal uncle Asclepiodotus was nominated as *CSL* by April 422 and then as consul and *PPO* in 423. His rise to *PPO* signified a marked change in the religious policies followed by Theodosius (see below). And finally and most importantly, Eudocia was herself nominated as Augusta on 2 January 423. The rise of the Anthemians also meant the restoration of Antiochus to a position of influence. Antiochus is attested to have reached (or been reappointed as) *Praepositus Sacri Cubiculi* at some point in time between 423–430 or 432–439 (Bardill in Greatrex and Bardill; Greatrex 2008). It is possible that the restoration of Antiochus' fortunes should also be connected with the promotion of the *praepositi sacri cubiculi* to the grade of the *illustres* in 422 (mentioned by Bardill p.188) in preparation for the appointment or reappointment of Antiochus to this position in 423. In my opinion this is not surprising in light of the fact that the fortunes of Antiochus and the 'party' of Anthemius were interlinked. It is perhaps not a coincidence that the next downfall of Antiochus, which Bardill dates close to the year 439, was followed by yet another Persian War in 441.

Peace to last for '100 Years'!

According to Socrates' version, when Helion reached Mesopotamia he found that the Romans had built a trench for their own protection (i.e. the Romans had built a fortified camp). As noted above, it is probable that this took place just before the single combat between the champions because that would explain why Ardaburius had accepted the challenge – he would not have had the right to conclude a peace as a result of a single combat without prior permission from the emperor, but the situation would have changed after the Roman Prime/Foreign Minister *Magister Officiorum* Helion arrived with instructions to conclude a peace.

In order to assess what happened next it is best to quote Socrates 7.20 (tr. Bohn Library pp.354–356 with some changes and comments added in parentheses):

He [*Helion*] sent … as his deputy Maximinus, an eloquent man who was the assessor of Ardaburius, the commander-in-chief of the army [*strategos*], to make preliminary arrangements concerning the terms of peace. Maximinus, on coming into the presence of the Persian king, said he had been sent to him on this matter, not by the Roman emperor, who was ignorant of the state of things, and thoroughly condemned the war, but by his generals [*clearly a face-saving lie*]. And when the sovereign of Persia would have gladly received the embassy, because his troops were suffering from want of provisions [*resulting from the time of the year and the Roman guerrilla campaign*]; the corps among them which is distinguished by the name of the Immortals [*Athanatoi*], numbering about 10,000 of his bravest men, counselled the king not to listen to any overtures of peace, until they should have made an attack upon the Romans, who, they said, were now off-guard. The king, approving their advice [*he may have learnt of the Hunnic invasion of Thrace, see below*], ordered the ambassador to be imprisoned and a guard set over him; and permitted the Immortals to put their design upon the Romans into execution. They therefore, on arriving at the place appointed, divided themselves into two divisions [*tagmata*],[43] with a view to surround some section of the Roman army. The Romans, observing but one body of Persians approaching them [*a single line of cavalry hid behind the Immortals on both flanks*], prepared themselves to receive it [*i.e. Ardaburius deployed a single cavalry line which was probably slightly longer than the Persian line, but his purpose was merely to fool the Persians as we shall see*], not having seen the other division because they had attacked suddenly. But just as the battle was about to start, Divine Providence so ordered it, that a Roman army [*stratos*] under the general [*stratelates*] Procopius appeared on the heights. He perceiving that his comrades were in danger, attacked the Persians in the rear. Thus were they, who but a little before had surrounded the Romans, themselves surrounded [*i.e. the Romans had used one of their standard cavalry tactics to fool the enemy into surrounding their only visible cavalry line so that the enemy outflankers could then be ambushed by the second Roman cavalry line which had been hidden behind a hill*], and in a short time utterly destroyed; and those who broke forth from their ambuscade [*ek tês enedras*], being next attacked by the Romans, were in like manner every one of them slain with darts [*kai toutous sympantas katêkontisan*] [*This is actually a doublet of the former sentence and should rather be interpreted that the Romans followed up their success by outflanking the main Persian line after they had destroyed the outflankers; it seems probable that Socrates has misunderstood his source*]. In this way it became known to the Persians that the Immortals were mortals; Christ having executed this vengeance upon that people, because of their having shed the blood of so many of his pious worshippers. The king of the Persians, on being informed of this defeat [*i.e. he had remained behind either in a fortified camp with infantry and some cavalry, or at Nisibis*], pretended to be ignorant of what had been done; ordering the embassy to be admitted he thus addressed Maximinus; 'I agree to the peace, not as yielding to the Romans, but to gratify you …'. Thus was that war concluded which had been undertaken on account of the suffering Christians in Persia …; and with it terminated the persecution which had been excited in Persia against the Christians.

In sum, the Persians attempted to surprise the Romans by attacking them when they expected that the Persians would fulfil their part of the bargain. The Persian plan was based on the use of two ruses: 1) attack during peace negotiations; and 2) the hiding of the second line. It is improbable that the Romans would have been unaware of the presence of the ambushers as suggested by Socrates, because the posting of the support line behind a hill in hiding was one of the standard Roman tactical ploys. The Persians in their turn hid the ambushers/second line by posting it directly behind the first in the same manner as one of the standard tactical ploys of the Romans, but appear not to have taken into account the fact that their presence was visible to the Romans posted on the hill from which Procopius' forces descended onto the plain. This the likeliest alternative, but it is of course possible that the Persian ruse could have been betrayed by a spy/ deserter or that Ardaburius guessed what the Persians were planning possibly because of some Persian mistake (for example the standards of the Immortals could have been in the wrong place or missing). The Persians in their turn appear not to have known that a second Roman army under Procopius had arrived on the scene with the result that they did not expect to be ambushed as they saw all enemy forces of which they were aware in front of them. As I have stated previously (2010, 2011), it is theoretically possible that the first Roman line could have been an infantry line because the line to be surrounded need not have been cavalry, but that would not have been the standard Roman tactical practice, whereas the use of two separate cavalry lines was, hence the conclusion that the Romans used two cavalry lines. Socrates' account proves that the Roman ploy worked like a dream and the Persians were soundly defeated. Socrates' account and the tactics adopted mean that the Persian army was completely surrounded and annihilated. Theophanes' confused account (AM 5918) confirms this. He states that the Romans encircled the Persians and killed them all including the 10,000 Immortals together with their generals. The different stages of the battle are described below.

As to the sizes of the different contingents involved, we know only that the Immortals possessed 10,000 men, which means that the first Persian line hiding them must have included more men than that, perhaps as many as 30,000–40,000 men. Tabari (i.868) includes a legendary account of the exploits of Mihr-Narseh which may be connected with this battle. According to Tabari, Bahram sent Mihr-Narseh against the Romans at the head of 40,000 and ordered him to discuss the terms of peace with the Romans. Mihr-Narseh then supposedly entered Constantinople at the head of these troops and the emperor agreed to fulfil all that Mihr-Narseh desired. It is probable that this account has confused two separate wars, the 421–422 and 441 wars, so that the successes of the latter have been projected to occur in the former (see Vol.4). However, since we know that Bahram did not command the army at the decisive battle, it is quite possible that the commander of the army was Mihr-Narseh and that he had 40,000 cavalry with him, the Immortals included. This would have given him approximate parity with the likely numbers possessed by Ardaburius, but not with the combined army of Ardaburius and Procopius.

As regards the Roman cavalry force present at the battle, we can make the educated guess that after the division of the army following victory over the Saracens, Ardaburius was left with a minimum of 31,000-horsemen, which would have been arrayed in the first line. Procopius' army would have consisted at least of the armies of Thrace, the East and of the cavalry of the Armenian army, and probably also reinforcements from the other armies (*Limitanei, Bucellarii, Foederati*) deployed in the Balkans (Marcian came from Greece, which belonged to the *MVM* of Illyricum). We also know for certain that Procopius deployed only cavalry because otherwise it would have been impossible to achieve contact with the cavalry Immortals and then pursue and surround them, and he also needed to possess enough horsemen to be able to achieve this. In light of this it is probable that he had done the following in order to reach the scene of operations as fast as possible: 1) left some forces of infantry (together with the Armenian feudal cavalry) behind in Roman Armenia to protect these areas if the Persarmenians were defeated; and 2) left the 'Balkan' infantry behind with the order to follow, or that he had already dispatched the 'Balkan' infantry back to the Balkans. The approximate paper strengths of the regular cavalry forces of the armies of Thrace (3,584), the East (5,120) and Armenia (5,824) would have given Procopius the theoretical potential of 14,528 horsemen. It is probable that at least the latter two had suffered casualties and it is also probable that the Army of Thrace had suffered some injuries during the march, which means that these armies probably could not contribute more than 10,000–12,000 horsemen. This would have been sufficient to destroy the 10,000 Immortals from ambush, but it is still probable that we should add to these figures additional

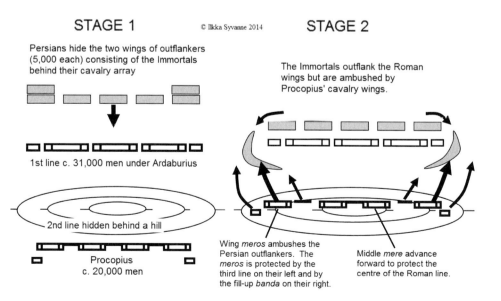

STAGE 1   © Ilkka Syvänne 2014   STAGE 2

Persians hide the two wings of outflankers (5,000 each) consisting of the Immortals behind their cavalry array

1st line c. 31,000 men under Ardaburius

2nd line hidden behind a hill

Procopius
c. 20,000 men

The Immortals outflank the Roman wings but are ambushed by Procopius' cavalry wings.

Wing *meros* ambushes the Persian outflankers. The *meros* is protected by the third line on their left and by the fill-up *banda* on their right.

Middle *mere* advance forward to protect the centre of the Roman line.

reinforcements from the other armies of the Balkans so that Procopius probably possessed about 15,000–20,000 horsemen.

The accompanying diagrams present the main stages of the battle.

Aftermath

As noted above, the defeat made Bahram ready to accept the peace negotiations. It is also probable that he faced another problem in the east (see my article available online at Historia-i-Swiat and academia.edu), namely the Hephthalite invasion, the result of the collection of forces from every corner of his Empire to defeat Ardaburius' army in Nisibis. The Romans were also eager to conclude peace so that they could transfer their armies back to the Balkans against the Huns. It seems probable that Procopius (Wars 1.2.11ff.; REF2 42–3) describes the next stage of negotiations when he mentions a meeting between Anatolius and Bahram. He claims that before the negotiations Bahram had invaded Roman territory with a mighty army, but had achieved nothing because he was confronted by Anatolius who had been dispatched by Theodosius II. Procopius has probably confused the two different occasions in which Anatolius negotiated by summarising the events, but it is clear that the description of what followed after this occurred in 422 as claimed by the REF2. According to Procopius, when Anatolius approached the Persian army alone, he leapt down from his horse and advanced on foot towards Bahram. When Bahram witnessed the great respect demonstrated by Anatolius towards him, he wheeled his horse about and then led his army to Persian territory, where he received Anatolius with equal respect and accepted the peace terms presented by Anatolius, but with the additional clause that neither party was to build any new fortifications in his own territory near the mutual border. This clause was clearly added because of the fortification of the city of Theodosiopolis/Erzurum/Karin.

The terms of peace included at least the following (Holum 1977, 170; Blockley 1992, 57–8):

1) Each side agreed not to receive any Saracen deserters from the other side.
2) Each side agreed not to construct new fortifications near the border.
3) The Persians agreed to stop persecuting Christians and the Romans agreed to stop persecuting the fire worshippers. In other words, both sides promised to protect religious minorities.

I do not agree with the suggestion of Holum and Blockley that the Romans would have agreed to renew or continue payments to the Persians in return for their defence of the Derbend Pass. This agreement was made after the War of 440, for which see Volume 4. In addition to this, the Armenian sources imply in no uncertain terms that the Romans were in possession of the city of Nisibis in 440 (see Vol.4), which may mean that one of the terms for peace included the handing over of this city to the Romans or that Ardaburius had captured it (despite what Socrates stated). If the Armenian sources are correct, then the war ended in truly great success, despite the simultaneous war in the Balkans. The Georgian sources also make it clear that the peace treaty resulted in another change in the geopolitical makeup of the region, which was that Iberia now belonged firmly in the Roman camp. In contrast, the Romans appear to have agreed to leave Persarmenia within the Persians' sphere of influence but that the Armenians would retain political and religious autonomy under their own ruler (see the events of 428 with Moses p.331, 339–340 and PLRE 2 Dionysius 13). Regardless of this, it is still clear that the terms of peace were such that both sides could accept. The generous action of the Bishop of Amida Acacius (Soc. 7.21) secured goodwill. He ransomed the 7,000 Persian prisoners that the Romans had captured in Arzanene and then sent them back to Bahram. The king was very impressed by this and sent a request that the emperor grant him the permission to meet this man. Theodosius agreed and sent Acacius to meet the Persian ruler. This stands as another instance of the wise use of Bishops and clemency to create an atmosphere of trust between the two superpowers – this may be another instance of the influence wielded by Antiochus, who had engaged in similar policies before.

As noted above, the war had brought about a change in the geopolitical position of Iberia. Before the war Iberia was on friendly terms with both superpowers but as a result of the war Iberia became a Roman client state. In addition to this, the death of Vaxtang had created a situation in which the country would ultimately become divided into western and eastern halves because when Vaxtang died he divided his realm so that the Western side was entrusted to three *eristavis* who looked after the widow Helena and her children and in particular after her two sons Leon and Mirdat, while the eastern half of the realm was given to his eldest son Dachi (by his Persian wife) who was also nominated as the King of Iberia. However, when Leon died, Dachi exchanged territories with Mirdat so that he took the South-West border regions while Mirdat was given the western territory up to the Black Sea. At a later date, the descendants of Dachi became subjects of Persia while the descendants of Mirdat became subjects of Rome, but this was still years off in 422 (see later). Vaxtang had also given his son the mission to finish the fortification and building projects that his own death had left unfinished. The most important of these was the completion of the building of the city of Tpilisi which now became the capital of Iberia/Georgia, a position which it has retained ever since (see Appendix 2 for a description of the city).

In contrast to Iberia, the Romans accepted that the Persarmenian rebels would have to accept some form of Persian dominance, the exact terms of which they would have to negotiate with the Persians but within the confines of the peace agreed between Rome and Persia. These peace terms appear had included some sort of agreement that granted the subject Armenians some form of autonomy under the Persians. The Persians were also quite prepared to make concessions in order to pacify Armenia. As Moses (p.330–331) states, Bahram knew that he could not hope to hold the country without the support of the Armenian princes. The other reason for the readiness to make concessions was that the Hephthalites had invaded Khurasan and Bahram urgently needed to pacify Persarmania before he could hope to face the nomadic invaders. It is also probable that Bahram wanted to obtain the services of the famed Armenian lancers against the massive forces wielded by the Hephthalites. Bahram granted a general amnesty to all rebels, together with religious freedom, and gave to the Armenians a new Arsacid king who took the name of Artashir. Consequently, Persarmenia remained in the Persian sphere of influence, which was to prove a valuable asset for them in the future.

The Edict issued to the *PPO* Theodorus at Constantinople on 7 March 423 (CTh 7.15.2) proves that the war had revealed another problematic form of corruption that was practised in the East. This Edict orders that, if any other person than a garrison soldier was in possession of lands belonging to the border fortresses, they were to immediately abandon such property on pain of death and confiscation of property. This makes it clear that some sections of the border had probably been undermanned and the soldiers inadequately equipped because the properties assigned to support them were not in their hands. This brings forth the question: who were the persons that had sold the lands belonging to the *Limitanei*? Were they the soldiers themselves or was it their officers? If the latter, then this would have represented a new form of corruption on the part of the officer cadre on top of their previous practices (confiscation of salary, positions not filled, bribes in return for exemptions from duty, protection rackets etc.). The government, however, seems to have taken the problem very seriously as the harsh punishments imply.

I would suggest that the *Dux Augustae Euphratensis*, which is attested for the first time for the year 466 or 472 (CJ 12.60.10) was also created now by dividing the command of the *Dux Syriae* in half, a result of analysis of the events that took place during the war of 421–422 rather than before it or as a result of the war of 441. The reason for this is that the Persian War of 421–422 had demonstrated to the Romans that there could be the simultaneous need for a frontier army behind the Frontier Army of Oshroene (Bahram had marched against Theodosiopolis/Resaina) and also in Syria proper against threats coming from the Euphrates River or the desert (al-Mundhir had advanced against Antioch). It is less likely that such a division of duties would already have been created before the hostilities. It is not known with certainty whether the *Dux Syriae* gave part of his forces to the *Dux Augustae Euphratensis*, or whether new forces were raised for the new command, or whether the Romans used a combination of both alternatives.[44]

Chapter Thirteen

The Usurper John (423–425) Sets the Stage for the Rise of Aetius and Bonifatius, the 'Last Romans'

John usurps Power

Aﬁter the death of Honorius on 15 Aug. 423, the Western court was for a while without a ruler because there was no obvious successor at hand after Galla Placidia and Valentinian had been exiled. When none of the mighty and powerful volunteered for the position, the *Primicerius Notariorum* John (Ioannes) usurped power on 20 Nov. 423 with the support of the *MVM* Castinus: or rather the other way around; Castinus raised John to the throne so that he could rule through him. Castinus and the other enemies of Placidia were undoubtedly eager to secure the throne for their own man. What is notable about the situation is that the choice fell on John, who belonged to the notaries who among their other duties also served as intelligence officers – had John performed such services at the behest of Castinus against his enemies? The *notarii* and the bodyguards clearly made suitable candidates for high positions to those who needed to set up emperors whom they expected to control. According to a late source (Nicephorus Callistus 14.7), John was a Goth, while Theophanes (AM 5938) calls him a Vandal. By nature he was moderate and gentle (Procopius Wars 3.3.6–7), but if the previous sources are correct and John was a barbarian by birth it is no wonder that his rule was not well received by the East Roman government. It should be noted, however, that even if John had been a Roman by birth, it is still unlikely that the Theodosian House would have accepted anyone else but their own member as a ruler of the West.

John (Ioannes, Johannes)
Augustus 423-425
(source: Cohen)

After having gained the throne, John moved to secure his position by rewarding his supporters and by attempting to obtain recognition from the Eastern government. The most notable supporters of John were Castinus, who was appointed *Mag.Ped.* and consul for the year 424, and Flavius Aetius, who according to Gregory of Tours (2.8) was *cura palatii* (Governor of the Palace) or according to Philostorgius (12.14) a '*hypostrategos Iôannou tou Tyrannou*' (second-in-command/under/lieutenant general of John the Tyrant). Crispinus may have continued in his office as *Mag.Eq.* We do not know who John's *PPI* was, but his *PPG* was Exsuperantius. The last mentioned was a native of Gaul and John's purpose was to gather support for his rule from among the upper classes of Gaul.

John's position was by no means strong. Bonifatius had not accepted his rule and continued to support Galla Placidia. The consequent lack of corn for the city of Rome made it necessary for the usurper to prepare a fleet against Bonifatius, which sailed under Sigisvultus according to the Gallic Chronicle 452 in 424. Hodgkin has suggested that it was Castinus who sailed against Bonifatius because we hear nothing of his exploits during the subsequent fighting in Italy – hardly a plausible scenario had Castinus been present in Italy – and because Prosper places Sigisvultus' campaign to the year 427. I am inclined to accept Hodgkin's view. Consequently, when the eventual attack from the East came, John lacked both a navy and an army to engage them (Prosper a. 424). In addition to this, the soldiers in Gaul mutinied and killed the PPG Exsuperantius 'Pictavus' at Arles at some point in time during the year 424 (Prosper a.424) and it is probable that the killing of the *Mag.Eq.* per Gallias Gaudentius, who was the father of Fl. Aetius, by the soldiers took place at the same time in 424 rather than in 425, as claimed by the Gallic Chronicle. This conclusion is quite certain because the Gallic Chronicle places the building of the walls of Carthage in the year 425, which is hardly plausible when one takes into account the fact that when the Easterners invaded John's forces were at the same time fighting against Bonifatius (Prosper a. 424). It is quite clear that Bonifatius must have built the walls before the Western forces arrived (see later).

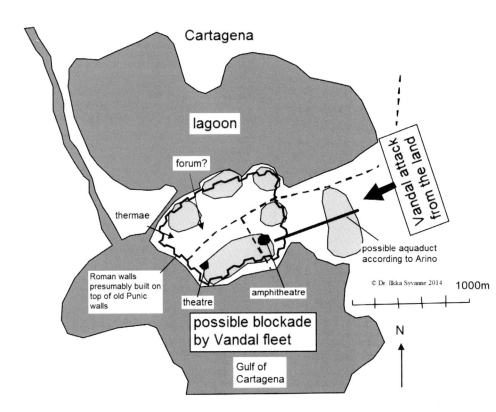

The death of Honorius had also made all previous treaties with the Germanic Federates void, on top of which the Visigoths were effectively in a state of revolt against the state after their betrayal of Castinus in Spain. There was certainly no chance of any peace treaty between these and Castinus. The defeat of Castinus in Spain had also meant that the country remained at the mercy of the Vandals. According to Hydatius (a.425), the Vandals had by now obtained ships from the local harbours and had pillaged the Balearic Islands and had invaded Mauretania. The Vandal piratical raids against Mauretania were undoubtedly facilitated by the ongoing war between John's forces and the forces of Bonifatius (see later). It is possible, even if none of the sources mention this, that Bonifatius had already established contact with the Vandals and that their raids in Mauretania were directed against the forces sent to destroy Bonifatius. The Vandals also sacked the cities of Carthago Spartaria (Cartagena) and Hispalis (Sevilla), and pillaged Spain far and wide. It is not known whether the Vandals had obtained ships prior to their conquest of Cartagena or only after it, but the former seems likelier because the Vandals could have obtained ships more easily from other less-defended towns and villages of the coast which could then have been used to place Cartagena under siege from the sea. In addition, later events make it clear that at least some of the Franks had revolted and captured territory in the north of Gaul. There was no hope that John could obtain any help from Britain, Gaul or Spain.

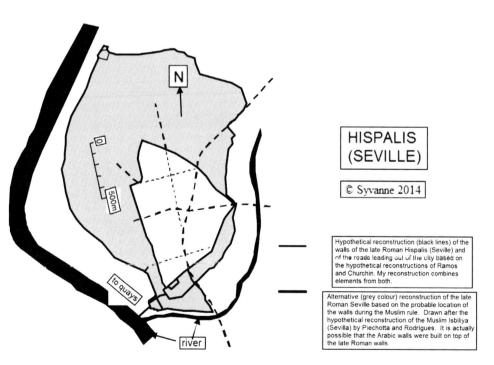

HISPALIS (SEVILLE)

© Syvanne 2014

Hypothetical reconstruction (black lines) of the walls of the late Roman Hispalis (Seville) and of the roads leading out of the city based on the hypothetical reconstructions of Ramos and Churchin. My reconstruction combines elements from both.

Alternative (grey colour) reconstruction of the late Roman Seville based on the probable location of the walls during the Muslim rule. Drawn after the hypothetical reconstruction of the Muslim Isbiliya (Sevilla) by Piechotta and Rodrigues. It is actually possible that the Arabic walls were built on top of the late Roman walls.

The East Roman Invasion 424–425[1]

In these circumstances the Eastern government had three basic options available to it: firstly, it was possible to recognize John, but this would have meant the abolition of

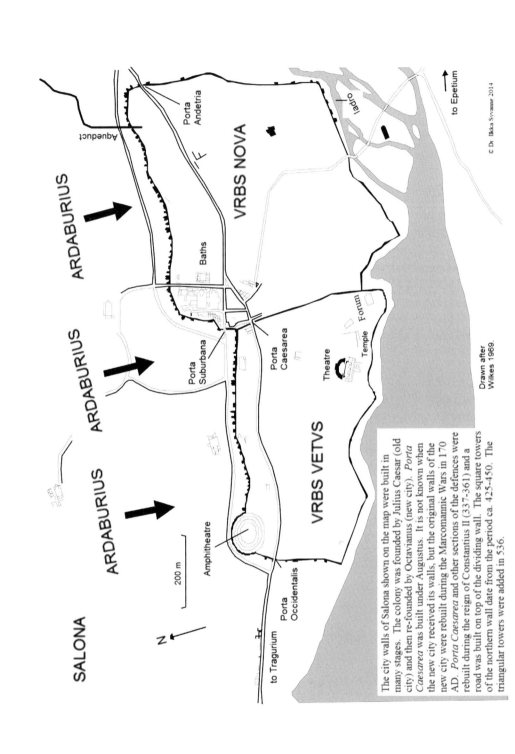

SALONA

ARDABURIUS

ARDABURIUS

ARDABURIUS

N

200 m

Porta
Occidentalis

to Tragurium

Amphitheatre

Porta
Suburbana

Baths

Aqueduct

Porta
Andetria

VRBS NOVA

Iadro

to Epetium

VRBS VETVS

Porta
Caesarea

Theatre

Temple

Forum

© Dr. Ilkka Syvänne 2014

The city walls of Salona shown on the map were built in
many stages. The colony was founded by Julius Caesar (old
city) and then re-founded by Octavianus (new city). *Porta
Caesarea* was built under Augustus. It is not known when
the new city received its walls, but the original walls of the
new city were rebuilt during the Marcomannic Wars in 170
AD. *Porta Caesarea* and other sections of the defences were
rebuilt during the reign of Constantius II (337-361) and a
road was built on top of the dividing wall. The square towers
of the northern wall date from the period ca. 425-450. The
triangular towers were added in 536.

Drawn after
Wilkes 1969.

the principle that the emperor would come from the House of Theodosius; secondly, it was possible to conquer the West and make Theodosius II the sole ruler; and thirdly, it was possible to support Galla Placidia and Valentinian in return for some territorial concessions.[2] Theodosius and Pulcheria adopted the third course and thereby decided to support the existing division of the Empire in two halves. In return for their support they demanded that the West was to hand over either the whole of Western Illyricum (Dalmatia, Pannonia II, Valeria, Savia, Noricum) or at least part of it (Pannonia II, Valeria and part of Dalmatia) to the Eastern government, an agreement which was to be officially sealed when Valentinian and Eudoxia were married in 437 (Cass. Var. 11.1.9; Jord. Rom. 329). Placidia had no other alternative than to agree. The Eastern forces were dispatched to occupy Salona, which was to act as a staging post for the forthcoming invasion after which John's ambassadors were imprisoned (see below).

Pulcheria and Theodosius sent Placidia and Valentinian to Thessalonica, where Valentinian was named Caesar on 23 Oct. 424 by the *Mag. Off.* Helion, who placed the imperial robes on the five-year-old Valentinian. It is probable that Valentinian's bethrothal with Theodosius II's daughter Licinia Eudoxia took place at the same time, because this event is also dated to the year 424. This marriage contract would have sealed the alliance, but the marriage itself was postponed to a later date when Eudoxia and Valentinian both reached maturity. At the same as this happened the Eastern government recognized Constantius III posthumously as Augustus in order to make Valentian III as his legitimate successor, and recognized Galla Placidia as Augusta to make her the legitimate regent of the West as long as Valentinian III was underage.

According to Olympiodorus (fr. 43.1–2), Theodosius had assembled a large army which was put under the command of the *MVM Praes.* Ardaburius and his son the *strategos* (*MVM?*) Aspar and (*MVM?*) Candidianus, and it was the duty of these two to escort Placidia and Valentian back to Italy. The retinue crossed Pannonia and Illyricum and then stormed and took Salona, which belonged to the Western Empire. After that the commanders divided the army so that Aspar and Candidianus (accompanied by Placidia and Valentinian) led the cavalry to Aquileia while Ardaburius embarked the infantry on ships. The marching route through Thessalonica, Pannonia and Illyricum to Aquileia given by Philostorgius suggests the probability that the army marched from Thessalonica via Naissus and Singidunum to Sirmium or Cibalae. The purpose of this route would have been to secure the main highways in the Balkans as well as the main route on land to Italy. On the basis of road network Sirmium or Cibalae would actually have been natural places to divide the army so that Aspar could have marched his cavalry either via Siscia or Poetovio straight into Aquileia while his father marched his infantry to Salona where he would have embarked the men on ships.

In fact, Socrates (7.23) has preserved a different version of the events. According to him, Pulcheria and Theodosius purposefully concealed the death of Honorius as long as they could and sent in great secrecy an army to occupy Salona. After this, they imprisoned John's ambassadors and dispatched Ardaburius to Salona, from where he set sail for Aquileia. This version suggests that Salona had already been captured before the arrival of Aspar, which makes it possible that Ardaburius actually had already divided his army at Sirmium or Cibalae as suggested by the road network. However, since neither of the sources state this, it seems safest to assume that father and son both marched to Salona with the intention of taking their armies side-by-side to Aquileia (this route bypassed the potentially risky area near the Huns) so that the navy protected the left flank and carried the infantry and supplies while the cavalry protected the right flank, coast and places of mooring from possible surprise attacks from land. The fleet would probably have been assembled at Thessalonica as well, and then sailed around Greece to Salona to transport the infantry and supplies. The obvious aim for the use of the fleet side-by-side with the cavalry army was that it enabled the supplying of the cavalry army until such time as it could be launched in a surprise lightning attack on Aquileia.

It is probable that Socrates has misplaced the timing of Aspar's attack against Salona. It is inherently likelier that Aspar took Salona by surprise before the emperor imprisoned the ambassadors. Ardaburius' plan was clearly to surprise the enemy through several ruses: 1) John's ambassadors were kept busy; 2) Salona was taken by surprise; 3) the invasion was timed to occur in the middle of winter; 4) the cavalry was used to surprise the city of Aquileia before the news of the capture of Salona could reach it; and 5) the invasion was timed to coincide with the absence of the Italian fleets and Praesental armies, which were fighting against Bonifatius.

It is possible that Ardaburius initiated the restoration of the walls of the northern section of Salona immediately after having taken the city, because the city faced potential enemy invasion from the north (Aetius was busy collecting an army of Huns), but it is equally possible that the full-scale restoration was initiated only after about 434. Wilkes (1969, 418) supports the former view and Lawrence (184) the latter.

When John learnt of the actions taken by the Eastern court (presumably it would have been the capture of Salona that alerted him), he dispatched his trusted aide Aetius to the Huns in Pannonia to obtain their help against the Easterners. Aetius was the best man for the job, because he had formerly served as hostage among the Huns and therefore knew the Hunnic Khagan Ruga in person. Aetius' instructions were to attack the Easterners from behind after they had reached Italy while John's armies engaged them from the front (Greg. 2.8).

When the Eastern forces were en route to Aquileia disaster struck. The fleet was scattered in a storm so typical for the winter season and Ardaburius with two of his triremes were driven ashore near Ravenna and captured by John's soldiers. The fact that Philostorgius states that the enemy was able to capture only two triremes suggests that the vast majority of the ships eventually managed to make their way to Aquileia. In the meanwhile, however, Aspar had marched his mounted army so quickly that he had outstripped the enemy's intelligence with the result that he was able to capture Aquileia without a strike. John treated Ardaburius with great respect because his aim was to achieve a peace treaty with Theodosius through Ardaburius. Consequently, John gave Ardaburius complete freedom of movement within the city of Ravenna, which was to lead to his own downfall. Ardaburius managed to obtain the support of some recently-retired generals and organize a plot to overthrow the usurper. In the meanwhile, Candidianus had not remained idle because he captured many cities and 'won great fame', which in turn lifted the morale which had suffered a blow as a result of the loss of the commander Ardaburius. I would suggest that while Candidianus was conducting his campaign of conquest mainly with infantry, Aspar stayed behind at Aquileia to secure the gateway to Italy. He was undoubtedly aware of the Hunnic threat. It is quite

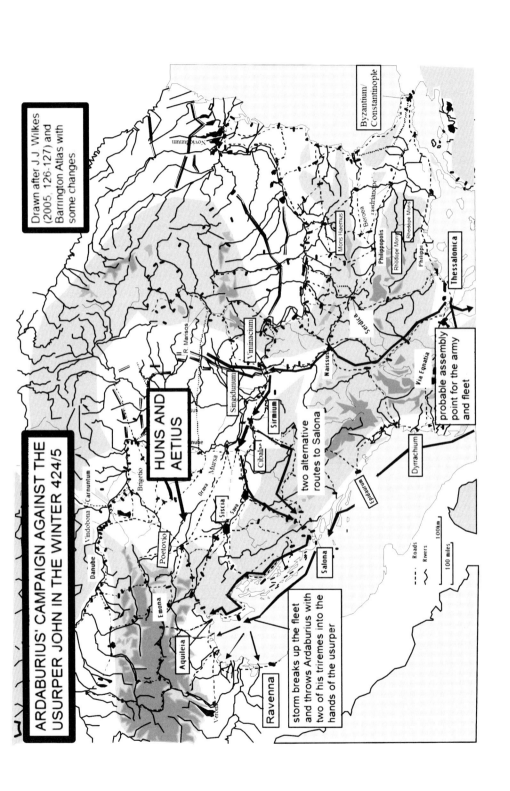

ARDABURIUS' CAMPAIGN AGAINST THE USURPER JOHN IN THE WINTER 424/5

Drawn after J J Wilkes (2005, 126-127) and Barrington Atlas with some changes

HUNS AND AETIUS

two alternative routes to Salona

probable assembly point for the army and fleet

storm breaks up the fleet and throws Ardaburius with two of his triremes into the hands of the usurper

Ravenna

Byzantium/ Constantinople

Thessalonica

Mons Haemus
Beroea
Hadrianopolis
Philippopolis
Rhodope Mons
Philippi

Serdica

Naissus

Via Egnatia

Dyrrachium

Epidaurum

Salona

Siscia

Poetovio

Emona

Aquileia

Verona

Vindobona
Carnuntum
Brigetio

Danube

Drava
Mursa
Sava

Cibalae

Sirmium

Singidunum

Viminacium

R. Marisos

Novae

Carnuntum

Roads
Rivers
100 miles
100 km

probable that the successes achieved by Candidianus contributed to the willigness of the disaffected soldiers to desert John.

When Ardaburius was satisfied with the results of his plotting, he sent a message to his son Aspar to come with the cavalry to the city of Ravenna. When Aspar arrived, he was guided through the swamp, and then let into the city. The usurper was captured after a short struggle by Aspar's forces and was then dispatched to Aquileia. Galla Placidia had John mutilated and humiliated in public, after which he was executed. After this, Valentinian was taken to Rome for two reasons. Firstly, he was to be declared emperor in the presence of the Senate, and secondly, he was transferred away from Ravenna to a more secure area because Aetius was fast approaching. Aetius with 60,000 Huns reached the city of Aquileia only three days after John had been killed.[3] Aspar engaged his army, which resulted in heavy casualties on both sides, and which convinced Aetius to begin negotiations with the government of Valentinian III. Aetius obtained pardon from the emperor in return for convincing the Huns to return to Pannonia. He achieved this by paying them in gold. It is possible that Aetius may have paid the entire sum out of his own pocket, because he came from a wealthy senatorial family known to have had yearly incomes of 1,000–4,000 lbs (or even more) of gold. Since we know that in 434 the Eastern government was able to keep Rua satisfied with a mere 350 lbs of gold per annum, it is possible that Aetius would not even have needed to use his entire yearly income to achieve this aim. In return for his surrender Aetius appears to have been given the title *MVM*

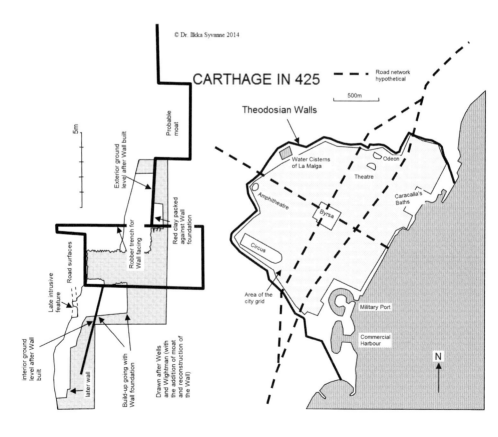

per Gallias. In other words, he became the successor of his late father Gaudentius, who had also occupied the position of *Magister Equitum per Gallias.* This appointment was a poisoned-chalice because Aetius' father had apparently been killed in a mutiny just prior to this, but this was the best result that Aetius could hope for in the circumstances. Aetius therefore needed to take control of the troops that had just killed his father. It is also clear that Aetius would not have sent all of the Huns back to their homes because he needed some troops for his own protection and also for the impending campaign against the Visigoths.

I would suggest that even though none of the sources mention what happened to the forces John had sent to North Africa, they surrendered only after the usurper had died and Aetius had obtained a pardon. The likeliest reason for the fact that Castinus was only punished with exile and not executed was that he was at the time at the head of

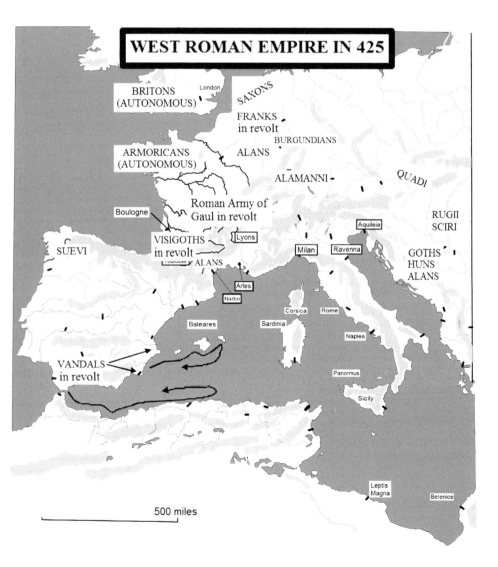

his undefeated troops, which must have been the army John had previously sent against Bonifatius. It is probable that while Aspar's forces had been fighting in Italy, Castinus' forces had besieged Bonifatius behind the recently-built walls which have received the name Theodosian Walls from modern researchers. By East Roman standards these walls were unimpressive, but adequate for the job. The West Roman army was kept at bay, just like the Vandals later (see the map). In short, my educated guess is that Castinus surrendered his army and navy in return for being punished only with exile. It is possible that when Castinus surrendered Bonifatius 'confiscated' part of his army and fleet for his own use and dispatched only those parts of these that he did not need back to Ravenna. Regardless, it is still clear that the bulk of Castinus' forces were returned to their garrisons and bases. Bonifatius was rewarded with the office of *Comes Domesticorum et Africae*.

Galla Placidia
(source: Cohen)

Valentinianus III   Eudoxia
(source: Cohen)   (source: Cohen)

Chapter Fourteen

The Roman Empire in 425

It would be easy to think with twenty-twenty hindsight that the Roman Empire was tottering on the brink of extinction, but this situation was not as grave as it might seem. The military successes of the East Romans against the Persians, Huns and West Romans prove that they had successfully rebuilt their military might after the disasters of the turn of the fifth century. East Rome possessed a strong economy, a large army and a powerful navy, and its Gothic Federates had proved their loyalty after the Gainas affair. In short, the East Romans could expect to be able to weather any storms that the future held in store for them if their military leadership just lived up to its task, and even when things turned out badly the East Romans could hope to weather any storm thanks to the stone walls of Constantinople and the wooden walls of its impressive navy.

The situation was not as bright for the West Romans, but even they could hope to be able to overcome their misfortunes. It is clear that the reign of Honorius had been a massive disaster for the Romans, especially after the murder of Stilicho. It is true that the barbarian Federates, the Visigoths and the Vandals were in revolt in 425. It is also possible that the Franks had already revolted by 425, even if their revolt is only mentioned for the first time in 428 (see Vol.4). It is similarly true that the Roman Army of Gaul was in revolt. But the situation was still not irreversible. The Roman Army of Gaul was in revolt only against the usurper so it proved easy for the new government to obtain its support.

The barbarian federate forces inside the Empire posed a far greater threat to the Romans. The Visigoths and their allies must have possessed at least 100,000–150,000 warriors, the Vandals 80,000 warriors and the rebel Franks at least the same number. Even though this represented a truly massive numerical threat, the barbarians were not united and could therefore be dealt with separately, but it would be misleading to think that the principal threat posed by the barbarians would have been military. The subsequent events prove that the barbarians posed a far greater threat for the authorities in the hearts and minds of the populace. The contrast between the barbarian rulers and the corrupt imperial authorities made the former appear quite benevolent. The only thing that prevented the Roman populace going en masse to the barbarian side was that the Visigoths were Arians and the Franks pagans.

The very successful military campaigns of Constantius III prove that the West Roman Empire still possessed adequate military resources to save it from disaster if these forces were united under a single capable military leader who had the same leadership capabilities as Constantius III or Probus or Aurelianus, but this was not to be. The latter were warrior emperors and could therefore allocate the resources in the best possible way to achieve the desired outcome, but most of the fourth century emperors were not warriors. At the time of his military successes Constantius III had been a general who had adequate resources for the job, but the situation was more complex after 425 when there were three leading military commanders vying for pride of place in the West. It is therefore not surprising that the result was a disastrous civil war at a time when the Romans should have shown unity against the barbarians. Most of the Romans were naturally quite unaware that they were marching straight into disaster, but it is understandable why they were unaware of this – in the past there had always been some skilled commander or Emperor who had saved them and it seemed to them that the Roman Empire would be eternal. Would Aetius and Bonifatius, the last Romans, live up to this expectation? Volumes Four and Five will give you the definitive answer to that and many other questions, the most important of which is: Why did West Rome fall when East Rome survived for another 1,000 years?

Theodosius II
(source: beger 1696)

Appendix I

Tournefort (1717, 1718 p. 374ff.): 'SMYRNA is the finest Port at which one can enter into the Levant, built at the bottom of a Bay, capable of holding the biggest Navy in the World. ... Smyrna is one of the largest and richest Cities of the Levant: The Goodness of Port, so necessary for Trade has preserv'd it, caus'd it to be rebuilt several times, after it had been destroy'd by Earth-quakes. Tis as it were the Rendevous of Merchants from the four Parts of the World, and the Magazine of the Merchandize they produce. They reckon fifteen thousand Turks in this City, ten thousand Greeks, eighteen hundred Jews, two hundred Armenians, as many Franks [for a total of 27,200]. ... There is no Bassa in Smyrna, but only one Sadar, who commands two thousand Janizaries, lodg'd in and about the City. ... we went to take a walk by the side of the Castle which stands on the shore ... is a square Fort, whose Sides are about a hundred paces long, flank'd with four mean Bastions, and defended by a square Tower which stands in the middle [the fort protecting the entry to the bay, date unknown but original structure may date from the fifth century]: ... Of the ancient Buildings of these Baths, ... there remains nothing at present but one little Cellar, in which is the Reservoir into which two Pipes empty themselves, one of hot Water, the other of cold. These Baths are to the South-East of Smyrna, ... Clazomene, which they take to be the Village of Vourla [the islands] ... Clazomene formerly kept Smyrna and all the Country about the Bay in so much awe, that Tzachas, a famous Mahometan Corsair, was obliged to get possession of it, when he fix'd himself at Smyrna under Alexis Comnenus. ... Pausanias says ... that the Ionians forty'd it, ... Some days after, we went to the old Castle of Smyrna [the citadel], situate on a Hill which commands the City. The Turks have quite demolish'd one of the finest marble Theatres in Asia. which stood upon the Brow of this Mountain, on the side which looks to the Road where the Ships lie. ... The ancient Castle, built by John Ducas, is upon the top of this Hill; its circumference is irregular, and savours of the Times of the later Greek Emperors, under whom they used the finest Marbles in the building of the Walls of Cities. ... The place where the Castle now stands, was taken up, in the flourishing time of Greece, by a Citadel under the protection of Jupiter Acraeus, ... Pausanias assures us, that the top of the Mountain of Smyrna, call'd Coryphus, gave the Name of Coryphaeus to Jupiter, who had a Temple there. ... M. Spon writes, that this ancient Smyrna was between the Castle on the shore and the present City; there remain still some of its Ruins upon the Water-side. ... THE 25th of January we went from Smyrna for Ephesus, ... At going out of the City, we enter'd upon a Military Way, which is still pav'd with large Pieces of Stone, cut almost like Lozenges. ... We arriv'd ... at Tchericui, a poor Village in a great uncultivated Plain, where we saw the Remains of a great old Wall of Stone, which has been an Aqueduct, according to the People of the Country, to carry Water to Smyrna.' Comments added in parentheses. For the potential population levels of Smyrna during the 18th century and later, see also Olnon and Georgelin.

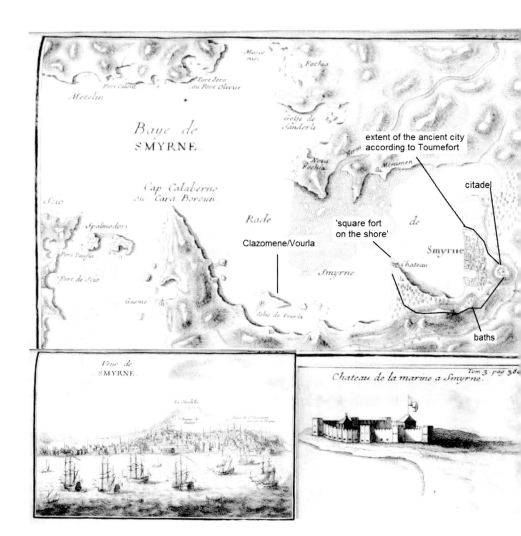

Appendix II

The following description by Tournefort gives a good description of the city of Tpilisi (Tiflis, Teflis, Tbilisi) in 1717 (then in Persian hands) and when one takes into account the fact that the city and its walls were in perfect condition during the reign of Dachi and his successors it becomes quite obvious that the fortifications provided a good deal of security for the Christian people of Tpilisi against Persian invaders (comments added inside parentheses):

> Teflis is a pretty large Town, and very populous; the Houses are low, dark, and for the most part built of Mud and Bricks; …where they are very far now-a-days from keeping up to the Description given us of them by Strabo: *'Most parts of Iberia, says he, is well inhabited; it contains large Towns, and Houses cover'd with Bricks; their Architecture is good, as is also that of the publick Edifices and Squares* [this also held true during the fifth century, which has to be taken into account when making estimations of the strength of the city at the time]. *At present* [i.e. those were higher and in better condition before] *the Walls of Tiflis are hardly higher than those of our Gardens, and the Streets are ill pav'd. The Citadel is in the highest part of the Town, upon a fine Situation, but the Inclosure is almost ruinated, and defended by very sorry towers. The whole Garison consist in a few wretched Mahometan Trades-people, who are paid to for keeping Guard of it* [this would not have been the case under Dachi when the location would have been guarded by Iberian knightly elite troops]. …

The City stretches from South to North. The Citadel is in the middle. It might be made a considerable Place [as it had undoubtedly been]*; for the side of the Mountain on which it is situated is very steep, and the River Kur, which runs along it, is not fordable. The Circuit of the Town takes up the side of this Mountain, and makes a kind of Square, the sides whereof descend to the very bottom of the Valley; but half the Walls are ruin'd. … The Prince's Palace, which is below the Citadel, is very ancient, and tolerably well laid out, … 'Tis believed there are about twenty thousand Souls in the City'* [the figure would have been higher during the fifth century]

Libya and Egyptian frontier from ca. 390 until 460

The Limes in Cyrenaica/Libya[1]

I will present a somewhat longer analysis of Cyrenaica than other areas here, because the events described took place over several years and because these events are not easy to include in the main narrative. During the early Empire Cyrenaica ranked as a senatorial province, but since it was exposed to barbarian attacks it also appears to have possessed its own garrison. We do not know the garrison's size, but it was clearly inadequate to deal with the Jewish uprising on AD 115, as a result of which it may have been strengthened. Regardless, the Romans seem to have relied mainly on the combination of a small but mobile force stationed at strategic locations in small square fortifications, as well as on fortified farms, fortified cities and alliances with tribes both inside and outside the provinces. The events of the third century prove that the Roman defences were quite inadequate to deal with the major invasion of a large tribe or a tribal confederacy. Around 269-270, the Marmaric tribes (i.e. the confederation later known as the Laguatan/Austuriani) invaded and even conquered the city of Cyrene, with the result that the then-governor of Egypt Tenagino Probus had to march to the scene. As noted, he must have been in a hurry to crush the Egyptian refugees. Probus duly re-founded the city as Claudiopolis after the emperor Claudius II, but the city never recovered its former wealth. The Marmaridae had proved to be a powerful foe. In fact, the need to provide additional protection for the Libyas was later recognized by Diocletian, who united the commands of Egypt and the Libyas under the *Dux Aegypti Thebaidos utrarumque Libyarum* (see Vol. 1).

According to Roques, this system was modified in 398 as a result of the fall of Gildo. The *MVM per Orientem* Simplikios/Simplicius visited Libya and created a new office, the *dux Libyarum* for both Libyas, at the behest of the Central Government and thereby separated the military administration of the two Libyas from Egypt. The other possibility is that he created two *duces*, one *dux* per province, but the case for this is less certain. He also seems to have transferred the *Comitatenses* to Pentapolis to bolster its defences against a possible attack by Gildo's Berber supporters. Roques has shown that the likeliest date for the creation of two *duces* for the Libyas is the period after ca. 443 but before 472. It should be noted, however, that this is not absolutely certain because Synesius' account does not deal with the events that took place in *Libya Inferioris*, and his account could also be used to support the creation of two *duces*.

Roques has proven that at the turn of the fifth century the military forces of the two Libyas consisted of the *Comitatenses* (*xenoi*/strangers of Synesios) billeted in the cities, *Limitanei* (*epichôrioi*/local soldiers) stationed in the forts, Federates (*symmachoi*/allies), and of the paramilitary citizen militias (*lochoi*/units under *lochagoi*) consisting of the youth (*ebhebes*), rustics, tribesmen and urban dwellers. The command structure of the Libyan army (both cavalry and infantry) in Synesius consisted of: the *stratêgos* (*dux Libyarum*/general), *hypostratêgos* (*vicarius*/vicar/second-in-command), *taxiarchoi* (*tribuni*/tribunes), *dimoiritês* (leaders of double files?), and common soldiers. The citizen militias served under *defensores civitatis* or under some other local magistrate, magnate or member of the clergy (city administrators or wealthy decurions, deacons and bishops).

The evidence for the units and army strength is very sparse and consists of three early inscriptions, the information provided by Synesius in his letters, and the Edict of the Emperor Anastasius. The inscriptions at Cyrene attest the presence of a cohort of Macedonians for the years 209/211 and a cohort of *Macedonica Gordiana Equitata* for the years 238-244. It is likely that both refer to the same unit. The third inscription from Ptolemais attests the presence of a cavalry *vexillatio* of *Legio III Augusta* for the late-third or early-fourth centuries. The later whereabouts of these units is unknown. Synesius' letters attest the presence of the following units in Pentapolis at the turn of the fifth century:

Synesius	Roques	My Interpretation (add to the figures recruits and supernumeraries)
Dalmates	1 *vex.* of *comitatenses* (500 men) at Ptolemais	Can mean either *comitatenses* or *limitanei*
Arabs	1 *ala* of *limitanei* (500 men)	*equites Saraceni* (*limitanei*) (512 men)
Thraces	1 *ala* of *limitanei* (500 men)	*thorakoforoi* = *equites clibanarii* or *catafractarii* (512), can mean either *comitatenses* or *limitanei*
Marcomanni	1 *ala* of *limitanei* (500 men)	*equites Marcomanni* (*limitanei*) (512 men)
Hunnigardae	1 *vex.* of palatine forces (*comitatenses*) (40 men)	Can mean *comitatenses*, *limitanei*, *foederati*, or *bucellarii*
Balagritai	*equites sagittarii indigenae* (*limitanei*) (500 men) at Cyrene	Can mean either *limitanei* or *foederati* (512 men)

The reason for my reluctance to make firm conclusions regarding the type of forces meant is that the evidence is by no means as certain as Roques thinks. There was plenty of variation. The best examples of this are the Hunnigardae. The Romans certainly recruited Huns into their regular forces, but they also used them as Federates and *bucellarii*. It is therefore impossible to be certain what type of troops the 40 Huns were. In my opinion it is also possible that the *Balagritai* were actually federates who were integrated into the defensive system, because the title of their commander was Phylarch.

The paper strength of the above units would add up to about 2,540 men in addition to which one should also include the other garrisons posted in the forts and cities. There is unfortunately no way of knowing what Synesius has left out. We also know that the troops were not at their paper strength thanks to the massive corruption. The officers kept dead soldiers in their roster books and allowed their soldiers to take leaves of absence in exchange for bribes. Discipline was poor and the soldiers had no actual combat experience thanks to the long period of peace. Just like the army protecting the provinces of Egypt, the Libyan army had become a glorified police force unable to fight any real war and which only oppressed the population.[2] In my opinion, thanks to the massive corruption, the best way to estimate the actual size of the force defending the Libyas is the Edict of Anastasios. According to this text, each of the five *arithmoi* (*numeri*) posted in the five cities of Pentapolis had 200 men, which would probably be closer to the real strength of the units also at the turn of the fifth century than the paper strengths of 512 men for each cavalry unit. The text also gives us the strength of each of the garrisons in the *'fossata'*, which were to consist of 100 men per *kastra/castra*. This would mean that the cities had about 1,000 horsemen to act as reserves while the forts had a minimum of about 2,500, but may have had as many as 4,000 men. The latter may still have included the units posted in the area during the third- and fourth-centuries. Thanks to the fact that the army was spread out, poorly motivated, and lacked combat experience, the soldiers were quite ill-equipped to face the storm that approached. It is therefore not surprising that the authorities subsequently dispatched reinforcements, which included units from the Comitatenses, Federates and even Phycuntian (Fykountioi) oarsmen/marines.

Goodchild's studies of the defences of the two Libyas still stand as the standard works on the subject. According to him, the positioning and types of defensive structures prove that the principal threats to the Roman frontiers in Cyrenaica, prior to the creation of

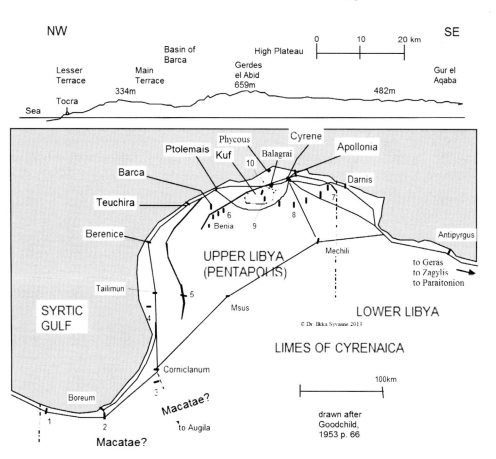

the Marmaric Confederation, were tribal bandits and outlaws, and only secondarily the Berber tribes. The defences facing the tribes of the south-west were quite formidable in light of the extant literary record, which only proves that there are significant holes in our knowledge of Berber activities. The lack of similar defences on the eastern side facing 'Dry Libya' suggests that the threat was not considered as significant, but this may result from lack of archaeological work. Regardless, the situation changed with the birth of the Marmaric Confederacy in the mid 260s.

The Roman defences aimed at protecting the agricultural lands of Cyrenaica as well as its five cities (i.e. the Pentepolis) consisting of Berenice (Benghazi), Tauchira, Ptolemais, Cyrene, and Apollonia. The great number of fortified farms proves that bandits and outlaws formed a very significant problem for the locals, but despite the endemic nature of this threat it did not threaten the existence of the whole province. It was the large-scale invasions of the Berber tribes and their ability to cut the Cyrenaica Limes in two by occupying the so-called Kuf that was the real problem. The Romans set about countering this by creating several layers of defences that included the fortification of all of the interior as well as the fortification of crossroads, strategic hills and oases.

The eastern-most defences were placed along the coastal road of the Syrtic Gulf and consisted of small square fortresses placed at Bir Umm el-Garanigh (Site 1: 35 by 32 metres), and Boreum (Site 2). Just before the next fortress in line at Corniculanum there was a guard tower (Site 3) the purpose of which was undoubtedly to act as a forward warning post for the fort. The fort of Corniculanum (garrisoned during the first century by Syrian troops) was placed at the strategic crossroads which protected the coastal Syrtic route as well as the caravan track to the oases of Aquila.

Between Corniculanum and Berenice (Benghazi) there were scattered fortified farms on both sides of the caravan route, some of which were roughly-built amidst native tribal villages. The latter appear to have been local friendly Libyan tribesmen. In the middle of this zone lay a defensive line of four forts, from the square fort of Gasr Haddumah (Site 4: walls 20 by 20 metres with a 7-metre-broad ditch) to Tailimum (38 by 44 metres) to Esh-Sheleidima (Site 5; not smaller than Tailimum) to Msus (a watchtower 7.5 by 6 metres and enclosure 19.5 by 19.5 metres). The apparent purpose of this line of forts was to protect the coastal route while also preventing a right hook by the enemy via the desert behind these defences. This same line of fortifications (like the other Roman defences) was also subsequently occupied by colonial Italy. North of this line of forts, almost to the gates of Berenice, were other smaller fortifications of inferior construction and of uncertain dating.

On the coast between Berenice and Ptolemais were still more forts that appear to date from the fifth- or sixth-centuries, which would suggest that the coastal areas (including civilian farmsteads) also received fortifications in the fifth century to make certain that the ravages of the early-fifth century would not be repeated. Similarly, the southern and western approaches of the coastal plain were protected by still more forts and fortified farms. The most important of these was the fortress of Gast el-Geballa at el-Benia (Site 6), which occupied a dominant hill at the junction of several valleys and thereby controlled the surrounding countryside. At a later date, the outer edges of this area also possessed a number of well-fortified farms along the edges of the cultivated zone. The dating is uncertain, but Goodchild (1953, 68-69) has speculated that these would be later (sixth century?) and would probably belong to the so-called *limitanei*.

The outer defences of the Cyrene plateau consisted of a half-moon of forts (15 km or less apart) from Kuf to Darnis. Some of these forts may have been built during the Late Roman period to complete the defensive perimeter. The weak point of the defences was the Kuf region, which consisted of very broken country with deep ravines and occasional heavy forests. The roughness of the terrain and the too-few forts in the region enabled the Austuriani to occupy this area in about 390-395, or soon thereafter, but definitely by 401.

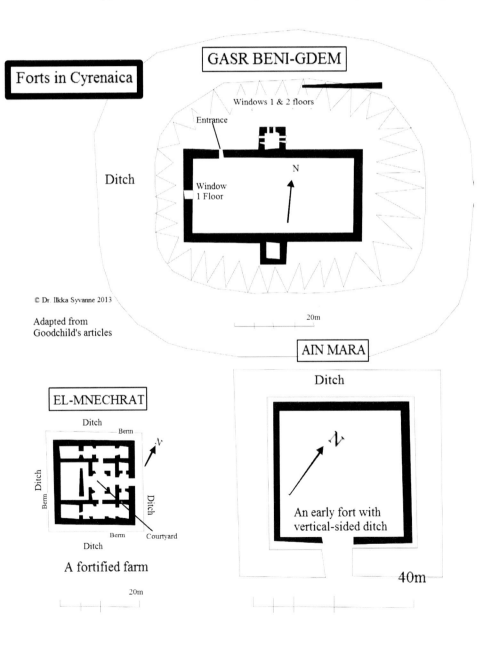

Forts in Cyrenaica

GASR BENI-GDEM

Windows 1 & 2 floors

Entrance

Window 1 Floor

N

Ditch

© Dr. Ilkka Syvänne 2013

Adapted from
Goodchild's articles

20m

AIN MARA

Ditch

EL-MNECHRAT

Ditch

Berm

Berm

Ditch

Ditch

Berm   Courtyard

Ditch

A fortified farm

20m

An early fort with
vertical-sided ditch

40m

The Romans had built some forts in the area before this, but this disaster brought home to the Romans the need to build additional fortifications in the area. The Romans actually built so many castles in this area in the course of the fifth- and sixth-centuries that the colonial Italians called it the triangle of the castles. The most important of these being the great Roman fortress of Gasr Beni-Gdem (Site 10; 44 by 23 metres) with large windows for ballistae. According to Goodchild (1953, 71), the sole purpose of this massive fort was to dominate the most dangerous areas of the Kuf, because it bore no relationship to the main Roman lines of communication. The two southernmost and oldest of the forts were situated 5 km from each other at a distance of 35 km south of the city of Cyrene. These were the Fort of Gasr er-Remtait (Site 8; 33 by 33 metres) and Gasr el-Maragh (a watch tower 15 by 15 metres). The easternmost fort of the crescent at Ain Mara (Site 7; 34 by 34) protected a group of springs. Synesius' texts prove that the last-mentioned had been broken to rubble by an earthquake by AD 400, which must have created a hole in the regional defences but fortunately for the Roman on the less-threatened side.[3]

The actual coastal plateau of Cyrenaica was also heavily fortified from the inland to the coast. The cities themselves were obviously fortified, but so were the villages and farms around it. Most of the latter, however, appear to have been built after the reign of Constantine I on the basis of the fortified churches and most likely after the disasters of 360s, 390-412 and 450. These churches doubled as forts with ditches for the villages surrounding them. The five cities had already received their circuit walls during Hellenistic or early-Roman times, but after the disasters of the early-fifth century, a period of retrenchment followed, at least in the cities of Cyrene and Ptolemais. Walls were no longer repaired nor manned, and new defensive structures were built inside the cities. Many of the walls were rebuilt or received new walls during the reign of Justinian,

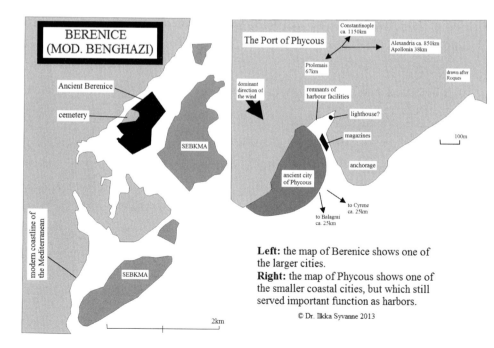

Left: the map of Berenice shows one of the larger cities.
Right: the map of Phycous shows one of the smaller coastal cities, but which still served important function as harbors.

© Dr. Ilkka Syvänne 2013

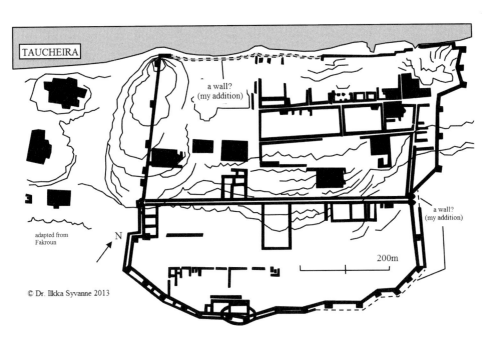

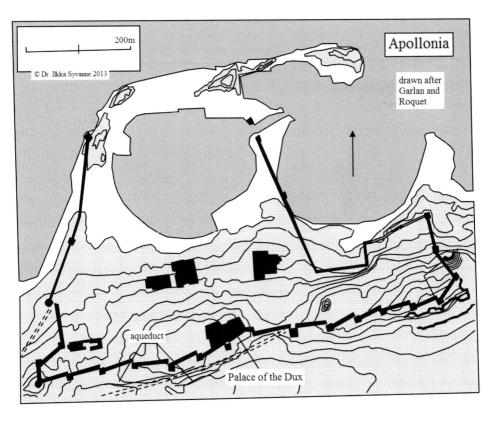

but we do not know whether these coincided with the ancient walls. As is obvious, the five cities that made up Pentapolis (Berenice, Taucheira, Ptolemais, Cyrene, Apollonia) and the other cities in *Libya Inferioris* (Darnis, Antipyrgos, Geras, Zagylis, Paraitonion) and the smaller towns/villages (e.g. Boreum, Corniclanum, Barca, Balagrai, Phycous etc.; the accompanying maps do not include all of these) were by far the best-defended and were usually able to defend themselves against the Berbers. This was particularly true of the coastal cities which could be supplied via the sea. The accompanying illustrations show some of the cities of this area. The Berbers were so inept as besiegers that even the smaller forts and the fortified villages, manors and churches could usually expect to be able to defend themselves unless subjected to a long blockade. It should be noted, however, that this was usually good enough for the Berbers, who could loot the countryside at their will when the populace hid inside the fortifications.

On the basis of the current state of archaeological knowledge, the eastern approaches to the Pentapolis were less well defended, possibly because the Marmaric tribes were considered a lesser threat to the well-being of the Pentapolis area and because the area south of the cities of the Lesser Libya was just desert. On the basis of the fall of Cyrenaica to the Marmaric tribes in the third century and because Justinian subsequently fortified and garrisoned the ancient Antipyrgus (Tobruk), it is quite possible or even probable that this is a mirage created simply by a lack of archaeological excavations. For example, on the basis of our current knowledge, Mekili, the watering-point, track centre and eastern counterpart for Msus, appears not to have had a Roman fort. However, since there is an early Islamic fort on the site, it is quite possible that the Roman fort has been buried under it. Similarly, it is possible that Antipyrgus would also have had fortifications and a garrison before Justinian's reign, making the defences approximately symmetrical on both sides of Cyrenaica. In short, in light of the third-century events (the Marmaric attacks and the amalgamation of the military commands of Egypt and Libyas by Diocletian) and lack of adequate archaeological work, I would consider it more than likely that there were also some small forts on the eastern side of the Pentapolis prior to Justinian, even if on a lesser scale than on the western side.

Of note is the fact that, just like many of the tribes of North Africa, the Marmaric tribes were actually inside Roman-held territory and therefore technically Romans. In practice this was not so. Only the tribal elite was partially Romanized. They could simultaneously hold Roman office and still be tribal chieftains or nobles: they never entirely abandoned their tribal origins. Some of the tribesmen also settled in cities or towns or became farmers. The vast majority of the population, however, remained semi-nomads and retained their tribal heritage, which also means that despite the granting of Roman citizenship to all free Romans they were left out and treated as barbarians.

In sum, the main goal of the defensive structures of the two Libyas was the protection of the Pentepolis and its surrounding agricultural regions. At the core of this defensive system were the alliances and treaties made with the tribes of the interior (including the areas under other governors), which enabled the Romans to defend the area with very small numbers of soldiers protected by fortifications. Most of the armed forces consisted of highly-mobile cavalry troops, which acted as a police force against bandits, robbers and raiders. At the turn of the fifth century these included Arabian cavalry, *Dalmatae*, *Marcomanni*, Thracian *clibanarii* cavalry, *Unnigardae* (Huns), and possibly also the units present in the area in the third and fourth centuries. The permanent defensive structures consisted of several layers of forts at strategic sites as well as of the local forts, fortified farms and by city walls of the coastal plateau. When the delicate balancing act between the different tribes failed and they formed a confederacy or one tribe achieved supremacy, the Romans were in trouble, as the events of 270, the 360s, 390-410, 449-450, and 512-513 prove. Regardless, in the end, after the Romans had brought reinforcements, they were always able to stabilize the situation. The tribes of North Africa simply did not possess adequate siege skills to be able to exploit their periodic dominance of the open terrain, with the result that the Romans could always expect to possess bases from which to launch counter attacks.

The Cyrenaican Wars ca. 390-450

As noted in the text, in 1983 Denis Roques noted an important and until then overlooked phenomenon of the late-390s: the eastward migration of the Austuriani and Mazikes (in a manner reminiscent of the eastward advance of the Fatimids) which caused a series of problems for both Cyrene and Egypt. This conclusion, however, required the addition of the role of the Arabs in these events, which was noted by Irfan Shahid in her BAFOC. The key texts are Synesius' letters and other writings, saints' lives describing events in Egypt, and finally Jerome's letter 126 (in PL 22 col. 1086) and his Preface to the Commentary of Ezekiel (Book 3 PL 25 col. 75). I have dated Synesius' letters according to the reconstruction of Jona Lendering (2007). Therefore, my reconstruction of the events differs considerably from the one presented by Roques.

The fact that the Arabs raided Palestine, Phoenicia and Syria at about the same time as the Berbers raided Cyrenaica/Pentapolis and Egypt suggests some sort of temporary climate change, such as a prolonged drought or alternatively a spread of locusts after many good crops had caused them to multiply over the desert zone from Africa to Mesopotamia.

The first signs of trouble came from Tripolitania. We know of this only because we possess the titles of two officers who served in the area. The title of Silvanus (Silvanus 5 PLRE1), *Dux et Corrector Limitis Tripolitanae* recorded for 27 March 393, and the title of his successor Flavius Macedonius (Macedonius 8 PLRE1), *Comes et Dux Tripolitanae* with the honour *Patricius*, strongly suggests that these special titles had been given to the men in question in response to some crisis. The honour of Patricius is particularly relevant in this context. It implies that Macedonius had fought against great odds and had achieved a significant victory over the Berbers. One may actually speculate that it was thanks to the overwhelming victory achieved by Macedonius over the Austuriani, probably in the mid- to late-390s that the latter decided to turn their attention towards the East. Philostorgius' account (11.8) proves that in about 395-399[4] the Mazices and Austuriani had at first directed their attention equally between both East and West, because he states that the Berbers devastated Libya and a significant portion of Egypt and had also attacked the Africans (presumably Tripolitania) to their west. It is clear that the Mazices and Austuriani had already caused significant damage to the Cyrenaican economy during the period 395-396, because Synesius had been deputed to ask for tax relief for his native city of Cyrene when he gave the 'Crown Money' to Arcadius in 397.

The Roman decision in 398 to divide the command *Comes et Dux Aegypti Utramque Libyarum* created by Diocletian into two separate commands, *Comes et Dux Aegypti* and *Dux Libyarum*, made it easier for the barbarians to penetrate into Cyrenaica because the Cyrenaicans could no longer automatically expect help from Egypt (Roques, 1983, 669–670). It should be noted that at the time the West had no interest in coordinating its war efforts with the East because the two halves of the Roman Empire were essentially at war with each other.

The Berbers renewed their raids against Cyrenaica in about 399/400 because in his letter numbered 120 (dated to 400) the worried Synesius asked his brother to send him news of the events that had taken place over there, and in the later letter 104 (dated to 401) Synesius describes military operations in which he had personally taken part near the city of Cyrene in 401. In other words, Synesius had returned home to defend his fatherland immediately after he had received confirmation of the bad news.

According to Synesius (Letter 104 to his brother[5]), in 401 the Romans at Cyrene were well aware of the impending approach of enemy forces because they had been warned by scouts. The phylarch (*fylarchos*) of the *Balagritae* led his forces out of the city of Cyrene to the plain (Wadi) and deployed his cavalry for combat (as we shall see the *Balagritae* were mounted) and waited for the approach of the enemy. The use of the phylarch in this context implies the presence of some tribal unit (Berber or Arabs, see for example Letter 4, where Synesius praises the fighting spirit of the Arab horsemen). In the meantime, the cowardly commander (probably *tribunus*) Ioannes, a native of Phrygia, was nowhere to

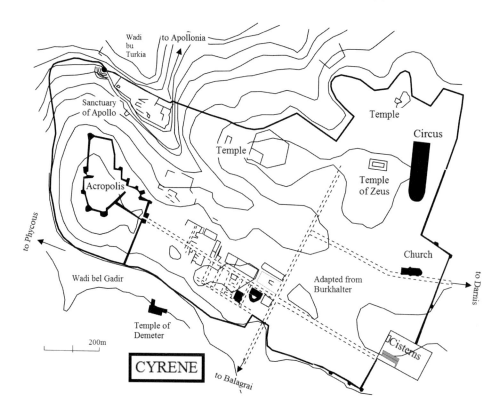

be found. Synesius quite rightly noted that Ioannes and his friends were very brave and bold in peacetime, but when there was any real danger looming on the horizon they were the greatest cowards of all. When the enemy did not appear, the Romans withdrew inside the city. What is notable about this is that this Roman cavalry force not only included regulars, but also local nobility like Synesius, which indicates that at least those locals who possessed horses and could presumably hire *bucellarii* participated in the military action.

The Romans repeated their action for five days, but the enemy stayed in the frontier regions, devastating and pillaging at will. It was then that Ioannes became convinced that it would be safe to come out, only to be the cause of confusion. Ioannes pretended to be a real military man and shouted to the soldiers a series of military commands without really understanding their meaning (in Synesius' opinion), and then led the whole force forward. The Roman army descended from the mountains on to the plain where they were met by fleeing and terrified peasants, but before the peasants could warn the Romans of the approaching enemy, the enemy was there right in front of them. The enemy were mounted, suffering from hunger, desperate and therefore quite prepared to fight the Romans. Before the Berbers reached the distance of a javelin throw, they jumped off their horses and formed a battle line, as was their habit. Synesius was of the opinion that the Romans should also dismount because the terrain was unsuited to cavalry manoeuvres, but Ioannes demanded that the Romans perform a cavalry charge. However, when the time came to perform the charge, Ioannes turned his horse and fled at full gallop, giving full rein while shouting and applying spear and whip on his horse to speed it up and down hill and out of sight, and with him went part of the army. The rest of the Romans halted and formed a battle line to receive the enemy attack. The Romans no longer had the courage to take the initiative, but the enemy was also not eager to advance. As a result of this, the Berbers marched slowly to the left while the Romans marched slowly to the right until both had reached safety. It was then that the Romans went after Ioannes in an effort to find out where he was. They found him in the caves of Bombaea (unknown, it cannot be Bombaea in Egypt[6]), which were a true labyrinth.

On the basis of Letter 40, dated to the year 403, the Romans achieved a crushing victory over the Berbers under the leadership of Uranius who probably (this is not specified) held the special office of *Comes Pentapoleos*.[7] This must have happened in 402 because in that year Synesius was still constantly guarded by soldiers (Letter 101). Synesius also refers to the existence of the office of the *Comes Pentapoleos* in his Letter 146, which is dated to the year 402 by Jona Lendering. This office must have been created as a response to the crisis that had resulted from the mishandling of the situation by the previous leadership (i.e. Ioannes and his superior the *Dux Libyarum*, who did not leave his headquarters at Ptolemais to assume leadership of the defence but left it to his officers). Uranius was presumably appointed to this office and given reinforcements with which to solve the situation. On the basis of Synesius' referral to victory, Uranius performed his duty admirably.[8]

However, his successor Cerealis, who must have been appointed to the office in 403 (Letter 40: Uranius celebrating his Libyan victory in 403) by the *MVM* Simplicius was corrupt to the bone (Letters 130, 131/2, 132/3). Cerealis moved the field army (evidently brought to Libya by Uranius) from one city to another, not for any military purpose but

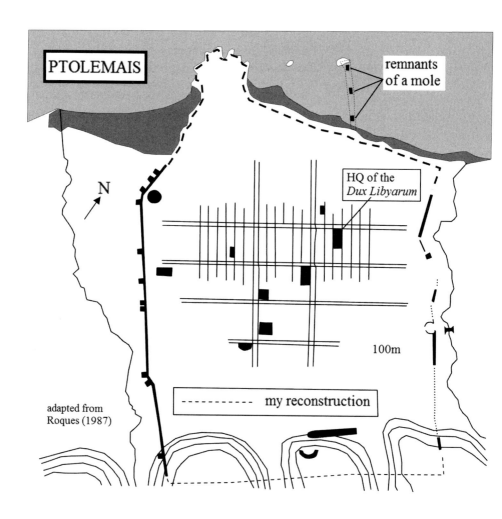

PTOLEMAIS

remnants of a mole

HQ of the *Dux Libyarum*

N

100m

adapted from Roques (1987)

- - - - - - - - - my reconstruction

for the purpose of extorting gold from the cities in return for not billeting his field army there (Letter 130). Cerealis granted exemption from service and furloughs in return for payments in gold and possessions (Letter 130). In addition to this (Letter 131 or 132 depending on the edition), Cerealis sold the horses of the *Balagritae* and caused the *hippotoxotai* (mounted archers) to become *toxotai* (archers). When the Macatae (Maketai/ Makatoutai who are probably to be identified as Mazices) Berbers noted the poor state of the Roman defences, they came in countless hordes like leaves and flowers in the spring. In this situation Synesius, who seems to have spent the previous two years in Egypt, returned in haste to assume leadership of the defence of his own city.

Synesius' Letters 18-19, dated to 404, contain important information regarding the way in which the regular army in Cyrenaica was paid. These letters suggest that Synesius' elder brother Euoptius was in charge of some regular unit(s) of the Roman army in Cyrenaica, as according to Synesius the Alexandrians sent money for Euoptius to pay his troops. This implies that the Roman government had made the Alexandrian Senate responsible not only for the upkeep of the army in Egypt but also in the Libyas.

This solution had undoubtedly been adopted when Diocletian had placed both areas under the *Comes Aegypti*, and had not been abolished when the command was divided in 398. During the time that the Libyan armies were under the command of Cerealis, all the money and effort put to the maintenance of the army were wasted.

When the Macatae then invaded in 405, Cerealis loaded all his ill-gotten loot (the gold) on double-sailed merchantmen, before he himself embarked on one of the ships and abandoned Cyrenaica to its own devices (Letter 130). However, before he left, this 'brave' man sent instructions to the commanders and leading citizens of the cities on how they were to conduct the defence. Cerealis instructed the men to stay within the walls, not attempt to make any sallies out of the cities, and not attempt to fight pitched battles. Cerealis had also scattered the forces into different walled towns, which ensured that this would be the case (*Catastasis* 2). It was now impossible for the Romans to assemble in such numbers as to be able to fight a pitched battle. Cerealis also instructed the citizens to guard the walls in four watches during the night. Synesius is quite right in ridiculing these instructions, because he and the others were already doing the precise things this 'general' was instructing them to do. Unsurprisingly, Synesius sent a letter of complaint (130) to the *MVM* Simplicius, whom he knew, regarding the conduct of Cerealis. We do not know whether this produced any results. I would suggest that the elderly Innocentius, who was suffering from ill health, was Cerealis' successor, because the governor (*Catastasis* preface) who served at the same time as Innocentius was Gennadius the Syrian who was clearly succeeded by Andronicus of Berenice (Letter 23).

Since the *Comes* Cerealis had abandoned Cyrenaica and had instructed the *strategoi* (Synesius' Letter 132/3 calls them cowards) to stay within the walls, it comes as no great surprise that the barbarians achieved great successes from the very start of their invasion. When the soldiers hid inside the cities it was easy for the barbarians to capture the stocks of cattle, dromedaries, and horses that were on the pasture and to torch all the crops (Letter 130). This time the invaders did not spare any little boys, who were usually taken alive to be sold as slaves, because the barbarians got so many captives that they simply did not possess the manpower to guard them all. Consequently, they could be picky and chose only women to be sold as slaves. In addition to this, they captured Battia (unknown) and Aprosylis (unknown). When the soldiers hid inside the forts and cities, the civilians like Synesius took the lead in the defence. He and presumably the other leading citizens of Cyrene had made preparations to defend the city. These included the building of stone-throwing machines that could throw large stones for long distances from the towers. The defenders had at their disposal bows and arrows, but the latter had been made in Egypt and were of inferior quality (they would not fly straight). Consequently, Synesius asked his Syrian friend Olympius to send him Syrian arrows of superior quality. It was easy to buy new bows from the market and to repair old ones so there was no need for Synesius to ask his friend to send those (Letter 132/3). Synesius also had at his disposal a small body of *stratiotai* (soldiers) drawn from the *Tagma* of *Balagritai* that had become foot archers thanks to the robbery by Cerealis (Letter 131/2). Regardless of this, Synesius considered their services very valuable for the defence of the wells of the city of Cyrene, and of the river, because the city could hold its own only if it had access to these water sources. In addition to this, the defenders included Phycuntian (Fykountioi) oarsmen, but Synesius considered them as useful as soldiers as his gardeners. The presence of the

Phycuntian marines/oarsmen in the city suggests that the Roman military authorities may have dispatched them to Cyrene to operate the stone-throwers and other siege engines. The marines appear to have been specialists in these fields of service and were deployed wherever sieges were expected.

Synesius, however, was not willing to stay inside the walls, because he realized that the active defence of the city was better than hiding inside, especially as the water supply for Cyrene was vulnerable to outside attack. Consequently, Synesius enrolled *lochoi* (alternatively units of unspecified size, or files) under *lochagoi* (either commanders of units or files) out of his own pockets. In other words, he had bought the services of some mercenary *bucellarii*. In addition to this, he collected his own peasants and armed them, and attached to their numbers a large force of *Asousamanti/Asusamas* (presumably some local tribe). He had also sent orders for the *Dioestae/Dêôstai/Disithitai/Soestai* (presumably another local tribe) to meet him at Cleopatra (unknown locale). Synesius was also hoping that his forces would be reinforced by others who would follow his lead once his army started its march.

Synesius states that the enemy was not willing to hold their ground against a determined opponent, which implies that the enemy was unwilling to fight a pitched battle against the civilian militia he had gathered. The barbarians only attacked and slaughtered the timid. Synesius in person scouted the area as far out as possible in an effort to locate the bandits, and during the night he and small numbers of young men patrolled a hill near the city so that the women could sleep in safety (Letter 131/2). It is unfortunate that Synesius fails to tell us how this stage of the war ended. He only states (Letters 119 and 134 dated to 406) that the *praeses* (governor) Tryphon saved the city of Cyrene, presumably in 406. This suggests that eventually the civilian governor took charge of the defence of the province and led the civilian militia and regulars at his disposal in Ptolemais against the invaders, forcing them to leave the immediate vicinity of Cyrene. On the basis of Synesius' letters (118, 119, 131, 134), his cousin Diogenes (either a *tribunus* or a *dux*) performed well during the war, but as a result had incurred the envy of some, which in turn had caused an informer to extort money from him. Synesius states that Diogenes was an honest man and refused to pay, with the result that the informer took the matter to the courts – where the informer lost his case. After this, the informer decided to turn the case from a civil suit into a criminal charge (presumably a charge of treason). When this happened, Diogenes had to go in person to Constantinople to defend himself and Synesius did all he could on his behalf.

The above is very typical for the wars that took place after the year 365 (see Vol. 2) and what happened during the great barbarian migrations in the West. The utterly corrupt *Comes Pentapoleos* Cerealis looted the province and soldiers, and then fled when difficulties beckoned. It was left for the civilians to take the matter of their defence into their own hands when the poorly motivated soldiers hid inside the walls, just as happened in Gaul and Britain, where the city councils and *bacaudae* also took over defensive duties in the absence of any real military authority.

The war, however, did not stop when the governor Tryphon relieved Cyrene, for we know that it continued unabated at least until 412. Synesius' Letter 108 to his brother from the year 407 shows him once again taking the lead in organizing the local defence. Synesius had already obtained 300 short thrust-and-throw spears (*logchai*) and 300 single-edged curved sabres (*kopides*), in addition to which he had 10 two-edged swords (*xifē*). He had also prepared clubs made out of olive trees and hatchets. The problem was that Cyrenaica did not produce any iron weapons and it was because of this that Synesius was proposing to start to manufacture arms for the citizen militia. However, Synesius' brother Euoptius forbade this. Synesius agreed, but complained that the government was clearly against those who wanted to defend themselves while there were no soldiers to be seen.

The barbarians and local militia had agreed to meet in a battle when the mounted scouts sent by Synesius had met the barbarians and held a discussion. When this had been agreed Synesius had sent the above-mentioned letter, together with his children to his brother so that he could look after them. Synesius doesn't specifically state what happened, but then goes on to relate a battle which had taken place between the barbarians and the local militia which had been led by priests of Axomis. Since Synesius doesn't claim to have taken any part in the latter, it is perhaps fair to guess that he referred to two different battles. It seems probable that the battle fought by Synesius' men did not end in victory, because he would have otherwise made more of it. However, the peasant militia led by the priests did achieve considerable success. The priests placed their militia in Myrtle Valley, which was a long deep ravine covered with forests. The barbarians charged into the defile only to be met by a deacon called Faustus who had advanced before the rest. The unarmed deacon took a stone and hit the first to approach him on the temple, stripped off his armour and then killed piles of barbarians on top of the first. It is quite clear that Faustus had either received some sort of military training in his youth or had a martial arts background (e.g. as a *pankration*, wrestling, or boxing).

At the time, Synesius had only fifteen men serving under him. Consequently, he was able to conduct only foraging expeditions and raids and not fight any mass battles (Letter 122). This does suggest that Synesius had lost his militia of over 300 men. He may also have been forced to leave the city of Cyrene, because he appears to have lost a power struggle in the local Senate with Julius over the hiring of foreigners into the army (Letter 95). The hiring of foreigners had been recommended by the corrupt officers (tribunes?) Helladius and Theodorus, who benefited financially from the hiring of non-Romans. These officers then used their mercenaries to take control of the city, its Senate and its army. Before this, Synesius had also made a motion in the local Senate in which he had demanded that the office of the *Comes* was to be abolished and that the cities were to return to the old form of government in which they were all under the Prefect of Egypt. His idea was clearly to obtain direct support from Egypt, but this motion had also been overruled and undoubtedly opposed by the local officers. It was probably because of this that Synesius had been forced to find a place of refuge somewhere in the southern extremity of Cyrenaica (Letter 148 dated to the year 408) and I would connect this with the six month exile before Synesius accepted the bishopric (Letter 96).

Synesius' *Catastasis* makes it clear that the new *strategos* (*Comes*) Innocentius remained inactive (possibly because of his ill health), presumably inside the city of Ptolemais, while the Austuriani ravaged the countryside. In 407 or 408 Synesius sent a letter (24) to the *MVM* Simplicius in which he clearly reprimanded him for not doing enough on behalf of Cyrenaica, which proves that the war continued unabated. Regardless of this, or because of some action taken by Simplicius, some sort of stability was apparently achieved because the governor Gennadius had managed to fill the state coffers by 408. It was only in 410 that things got out of hand.

In 408 or 409 Synesius sent a letter (73; I have re-dated the letter, see below) to Troilus, his fellow philosopher and advisor to the *PPO* Anthemius. Synesius pleaded that Troilus ask Anthemius to act on behalf of Cyrenaica. According to Synesius, Pentapolis would be doomed to perish if the war and famine was allowed to continue. Most importantly, Synesius stated that Anthemius should not allow Cyrenaica to be ruled by another Cyrenaican, by which he meant his personal enemy Andronicus of Berenice. Synesius stated that the government should follow the stated principle that it was not acceptable for a native to be a governor. The reason for this principle was that as governor the native was in a position to exact vengeance on his personal enemies. It must also have been common knowledge that Andronicus had been loaned money with which he had bought the office. This mean that he had to collect money by whatever means possible from a war-devastated country to pay his debts. As a native Andronicus knew who had money to be robbed. Synesius also pleaded on behalf of the former governor Gennadius the Syrian. Gennadius had been accused of embezzling money, but Synesius considered him a good governor who had brought more money to the state coffers than his predecessors, and all that without any illegal actions.

On the grounds that Synesius claims that the defence of Cyrenaica collapsed after Anysius left (Letter 59), it is probably preferable to re-date the letters referring to the actions of Anysius and Andronicus to the year 409 on the grounds that Jerome's texts suggest that the defence of Cyrenaica and Egypt collapsed in 410. This also means that I re-date the start of Synesius' bishopric to the year 409.

Synesius' letters along with his *Catastasis* and *Constitutio* allow one to make a rough reconstruction of what took place in Cyrenaica in 409-410. The year 409 appears to have started with heavy-handed tax gathering by Andronicus of Berenice, who employed torture to get his hands on any piece of valuable property. In practice Andronicus targeted his political enemies. As noted above, Andronicus obtained his governorship at the same time as Synesius became Bishop of Ptolemais (the locals had requested that he assume this position) and this brought their mutual antagonism to a boiling point because Synesius attempted to protect those who sought asylum in his church, but to no avail as Andronicus' henchmen dragged the unfortunate victims out. Most notably, Andronicus found willing collaborators among Synesius' enemies. Soon after this, Thoas/Thomas (not included in the PLRE2 but possibly an *agens in rebus*) came from Constantinople with a list of persons – presumably prepared by Anthemius himself – who were to be subjected to interrogation on the grounds of some suspicion (had they cooperated with Gennadius?). It is possible that the *PPI* suspected that the persons named had planned something sinister because the list named two men who were to be executed. The harbours were closed so that the persons in the list could not escape. The list included associates and friends of Synesius (see Letter 79). After this, Andronicus and those who backed his policies targeted some of Synesius' relatives, with the result that Synesius was eventually abandoned by all his friends, and even his brother stopped communicating with him (letters 8, 10, and 46).[9] Synesius' answer was to excommunicate Andronicus which was actually a very powerful tool at his disposal and which did cause plenty of trouble for the governor. It is clear that the upper class of the Province of Cyrenaica were divided into two parties. This was certainly unhelpful when the province faced formidable enemies, as it did at the turn of the fifth century.

In 409 the Austuriani launched their attack through the vulnerable region between Cyrene and Kuf, because Synesius at Ptolemais received a message from Cyrene that the Austuriani were approaching (Letter 94). He immediately dispatched a messenger to the *strategos* Anysius at Taucheira, but the envoy returned bearing the news that the *strategos* had already learnt of the invasion and had led his *Unnigardae/Ounigardai* (clearly Huns) to the higher ground. According to Synesius (*Constitutio*), Anysius had plenty of infantry and cavalry but only trusted the 200 *Unnigardae*. According to Synesius, Anysius used these *Unnigardae* in a manner that resembles Belisarius' use of mounted archers to conduct guerrilla warfare against the besiegers of Rome, but with the difference that Anysius usually led the *Unnigardae* in person while Belisarius in most cases left the command to his subordinates. Anysius used his *Unnigardae* very efficiently in mobile, quickly moving warfare in which he hit the enemy forces here and there and thereby broke their attack in a series of fast encounters. At some point in time during this campaign Anysius led 40 *Unnigardae* in person to defend the city of Ptolemais against 1,000 enemy horsemen. We do not know why he chose to take only 40 Huns with him and left the remaining 160 horsemen somewhere else. Perhaps he divided his force under different commanders after the enemy force had been broken into smaller pieces so that each of his five subordinates led a force of about 40 horsemen (5 x 40 = 200). Synesius was awestruck (as is this historian) by the combat performance of the 40 Huns under Anysius. The Huns defeated the 1,000 Austuriani in two to three sharp encounters so that less than 200 of the enemy survived the encounter. It is no wonder that Synesius considered the Huns to have been the best soldiers ever to grace the soil of Pentapolis. In his opinion a mere 400 Huns would have sufficed to protect the entire Pentapolis from enemy attack (*Catastasis* 3). Regardless, Synesius was not blind to the fact that the Huns alone could not defeat the enemy. In order to do that he suggested that the Huns would need an infantry phalanx to support them which would then strike the second blow. He acknowledged that the army under Anysius had been too small to finish the war. When Anysius' term of service ended, the enemy returned with a vengeance (Letter 59). I date this to the year 410 on the grounds of Jerome's texts (see below).

It should be noted that it is quite possible that Anysius was not a *comes* or *dux*, but a garrison commander with the title of *tribunus* because Ptolemais, not Taucheira, was the regional HQ of the *comes/dux*. This may mean that the *comes/dux* in 409-410 was still the feeble Innocentius. On the other hand, it is possible that the *comes/dux* had simply marched away from his permanent residence – after all Anysius was exceptionally energetic and mobile in his actions. On balance it is likelier that Anysius was the *comes* or *dux* in 409.

The key texts for the events of 410 are Jerome's Letter 126 (in PL 22 col. 1086) and his Preface to '*the Commentary of Ezekiel*' (Book 3 PL 25 col. 75). Jerome states in the letter that the barbarians attacked Egypt, Palestine, Phoenicia and Syria like a torrent in 410 and in his commentary he notes the devastation of the whole of Oriens, Egypt and Africa and the capture of Bethlehem. In this context he refers to the *Barcaei* of Vergilius and to the Ishmael of the Holy Scriptures. On the basis of this, Roques has drawn the conclusion that the *Barcaei* must refer to the Berbers of Barca in Cyrenaica so that, when one takes into account the other evidence suggesting that the Austuriani were ravaging Cyrenaica and Egypt at the same time, the invaders of Palestine, Phoenicia and Syria must also have included the migrating Austuriani. However, this analysis fails to take into account the referral to Ishmael. In contrast, Irfan Shahid (BAFC 22-23) claims on the basis of the referral to Ishmael that the Arabs were responsible for all the devastation, but in turn she has failed to take into account the referrals to the Barcaei and Africa.

When one places the locations that were invaded on the map, it becomes apparent that it would have been quite possible that the Austuriani could have raided all the places mentioned by marching through the north of Egypt and then along the coast all the way to Syria, but this does not preclude a simultaneous invasion by the Ishmaelites (i.e. Arabs), who must have been responsible for some or most of the devastation, and they may even have coordinated their actions with the Berbers. What is notable about the list of places taken is that the invaders did not devastate the provinces of *Arabia* and *Augusta Libanensis*, both of which had sizable concentrations of Arab *foederati*. This would mean that the Arabs who revolted were stationed either in Palestine (i.e. Sinai), or in Syria, or in the neighbouring deserts to the east. Considering the areas of devastation, it is possible that only the Arabs of Palestine/Sinai revolted because they could have easily attacked both Egypt (which was already in a state of emergency thanks to the problems caused by the Austuriani) and could also have marched along the coast up to Syria. As noted, it is even possible that the Arabs of Sinai and the Austuriani joined forces and did the ravaging together. It is very unfortunate that we do not possess any details of what happened, mainly thanks to the fact that all of the extant sources are interested in describing the fall of Rome in 410, but what is certain is that the Romans mounted some sort of effective counter-attack that pushed the invaders either out of the country or forced them to submit.

As noted above, the Austuriani intensified their operations immediately after Anysius had left. However, Anysius had not taken the *Unnigardae* with him, but had left forty men behind to protect the city of Ptolemais. These were obviously not sufficient to deter the tens of thousands Berbers descending on Cyrenaica in 410. It should be noted that the forty *Unnigardae* were by no means the only troops that were garrisoned at Ptolemais, because Synesius refers also to Dalmatians. However, we can take for granted that there were even more troops than this stationed in the provincial HQ of the *Comes* and *Praeses*. When Anysius had already departed or was departing, the forty Huns left at Ptolemais made a request through Synesius to Anysius that they were not to be incorporated into the regular Roman army because, if they were not allowed to fight as a separate unit and continue to receive the special imperial largesse promised to them together with relays of their native horses and equipment, they would become useless to the emperor. Synesius added his own request to this, which was that Anysius was to ask the emperor to dispatch 160 additional Huns so that there would have been 200 Huns under Anysius' personal command (Letter 78). I take this to mean that Synesius requested that Anysius stay. He also appears to have sent the same general request to the imperial authorities in a form of panegyric of Anysius, because in his *Constitutio* (also known as *In Praise of Anysius*) Synesius demands openly that Anysius should take the lead of the 200 Huns in person. Anysius would not stay and as far as we know no new units of *Unnigardae* were dispatched to Cyrenaica.

Thanks to the fact that the Roman forces were scattered in the many towns and none of the Roman commanders used guerrilla warfare against the invaders as Anysius had done, the Austuriani were once again free to roam at will. As noted above, it is quite possible that the ineffectual Innocentius was still in charge and was partially to blame for the disaster that ensued. The Austuriani proceeded to besiege both the smaller fortified villages and even the cities. The plain of Barca was filled with fresh graves and the churches of the district of Ampelus (presumably somewhere near Barca and Ptolemais) were burned. The walls of the villages were torn down, but the fate of the larger cities is uncertain. The referral that Synesius could no longer go to his native city of Cyrene (Catastasis 7) has usually been taken to mean that the Austuriani had captured Cyrene, but it is possible that this referred merely to the fact that Synesius' political enemies had taken control of the city or that the Berbers blocked the route. However, on balance, since Synesius also refers to the siege of cities, it is safest to assume that Cyrene had indeed fallen. It was not easy to protect and supply this city, because it was located inland and its only water sources were vulnerable to outside attack.

Synesius also states that the Ausurians (i.e. Austuriani) had equipped their horses with the breastplates of the Thracian cavalry and had taken the shields of the Marcomanni. He claims that the Austuriani would not have had any need for these, but that their only intention was to mock Roman uniforms. This is utter rubbish. It is clear that the Austuriani had equipped their horses with armour and had taken the stronger Roman shields precisely because they had learnt to respect the power of the Hunnish bow. In other words, they had added armour and shields to their equipment to withstand the Hun archery. Regardless, Synesius asserts that a mere 400 Huns would have sufficed to defend Pentapolis, but at the same time he states that these men would have been needed before the Romans had been completely routed and the resources of the enemy had not increased to such massive proportions. He also maintains that in the final struggle even women joined the fighting. Is this a referral to the final stages of the fall of Cyrene or to some pitched battle? The former seems likelier. It is probable that the Austuriani advanced to Egypt after they had pillaged Cyrenaica. Roques (p.670-1) lists the instances in which the Berbers are mentioned to have raided Egypt and its monasteries and the Great Oasis between 407 and 409, all of which point to the fact that the Austuriani were moving eastwards. One of these was the sacking of the Monastery of Skete in 408. In fact, as noted by Roques, Synesius even refers to the fact that the city of Alexandria was not safe from the camel-mounted Austuriani hoplites. It was probably because of this that the Alexandrians prevented their *strategos* (*Comes Aegypti*) from attempting to bring relief to Cyrenaica.[10]

The information in Jerome suggests that at least Egypt was subjected to the unwelcome visit by the marauding Austuriani and it is possible that they advanced even further east and north-east, all the way up to Syria. As noted above the Arabs of Sinai may also have joined them, but I would still suggest that it is likelier that the Berbers did not travel further than Sinai and that the rest of the attacks in the East were conducted by the Arabs. From Letter 62 of Synesius we know that the Romans under the '*hêgemon*' Marcellinus (who had the dignity of *clarissimus*) inflicted a crushing defeat on the Berbers in Cyrenaica in a battle that lasted a single day. Jona Lendering and the PLRE 2 date the letter to the year 413 so that the event would have taken place in 412. In my opinion, this is quite possible, but one should not discount the possibility that the event took place in 411. The reason for this is that it is possible or even probable that the successful counter-offensive to drive the barbarians out of Syria, Phoenicia, Palestine and Egypt would have taken place in 410-411 and would have been immediately followed by further campaigning in Cyrenaica to crush the enemy force once and for all. It is not certain whether Marcellinus was involved in the operations from Syria down to Egypt, or whether he was merely in charge of the operations in Cyrenaica in 411-412. The fact that Marcellinus was able to crush the enemy in a single battle suggests a very significant effort by the Romans, with the implication that they had dispatched a sizable army (at least 20,000-30,000 men) to crush the Berbers.

Consequently, one can say that the tribes of Tripolitania were in an almost constant state of revolt from the early 390s onwards and since the problem then spread east in the form of migration, it is probable that the cause of the revolt and migration was drought and/or the emergence of locusts after good years, or flooding, or a combination of these that had caused the tribes to attempt to seek a livelihood elsewhere. The freezing of the Straits of Bosporus and the famine among the Vandals and Berbers suggest that the troubles were caused by a climate change, which can be seen as a minor Ice Age. For the Romans this obviously meant that the trade contacts with Central Africa were cut off and that their own agricultural areas outside the fortified cities were pillaged and burned.

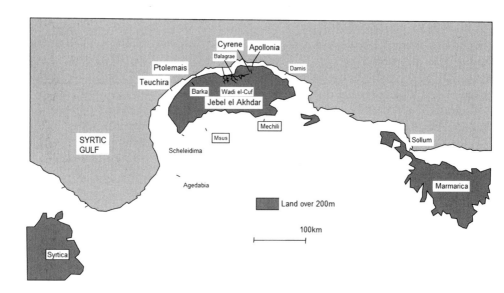

Egypt, Nubia, Aksum, Arabia, India

The principal problems facing Egypt were urban unrest caused by different religious groups and the peoples of the south which consisted principally of the Blemmyes and Nobatae. The previous two centuries had also shown that the Arabs of Sinai, the Aksumites of Ethiopia and the Berbers of Libya could also cause periodic troubles. The last-mentioned problem resurfaced during this period, stronger than ever before.

Egypt, and especially the city of Alexandria, were in an almost constant state of religious turmoil during this period. The principal reasons for this were the many Patriarchs who reasserted their religious standing and their favourite doctrine through violence, which was not only directed against their co-religionists that they considered heretics, but also against Jews, pagans and the imperial authorities. The Patriarch Theophilus gathered a loyal following of religious fanatics which he used to pursue his goals. This did cause some problems, but the real problems started only after his death. In 412 he was succeeded by his nephew Cyril, despite the best efforts of the *comes Aegypti* Abundantius who supported Timothy (Soc. 7.7). The partisans of Theophilus who were now supporting his nephew Cyril proved too powerful for even for the military to handle. We do not know the details of the affair, but we do know that Abundantius gave up. This was unfortunate because Cyril was a bigot of the first order.

The problems resurfaced in 414-415 after the religious Pulcheria had ousted Anthemius. She resented everything the Egyptian Anthemius had represented. Consequently, it is not surprising that Cyril felt emboldened to challenge the *praefectus augustalis* of Egypt, Orestes. Cyril considered the governor Orestes detestable because Orestes was friendly with the famed female pagan philosopher/mathematician Hypatia, because Orestes held Hellenic culture in high esteem, and because he protected the Jews from persecution. The things came to a boiling point when on one occasion some Jews, who were spending their time in a theatre on the Sabbath, voiced their resentment to Orestes (he was there to publicize an edict dealing with theatrical performances) that Cyril had placed one of his spies, Hierax, in the audience to spy on Orestes and to provoke trouble. Orestes, who resented the growing power of Cyril, used this opportunity to arrest Hierax, after which he subjected him to a public torture in the theatre. This was a very grave mistake – a provocation against Cyril and his supporters. In response, Cyril threatened the leading Jews with dire consequences if they continued to molest Christians, which only provoked the Jewish fanatics amongst their ranks. These Zealots formed a plot to attack Christians. They all wore a ring made of bark so that they would be able to recognize each other and then on a certain night started to run about in the streets yelling that Alexander's Church was on fire. When people gathered to save the church, the Jews attacked and killed them. The retribution came in the morning. Cyril gathered great mass of people, with which he went to the synagogue and drove all the Jews out of the city while allowing his followers to loot all their possessions. Orestes was angry that the city had lost so many of its inhabitants. The fact that the Jews were important for the functioning of the economy was undoubtedly at the top of his concerns.

Orestes sent a report to the emperor in which he complained about Cyril, while Cyril sent his own letter to the emperor in which he explained his reasons for the expulsion of the Jews. Orestes was adamant that the Jews should be allowed back into the city, with the result that Cyril called the 500 monks of Nitria that his uncle had armed into the city. When these 500 monks met the prefect in his chariot, they started to insult him as an idolater and pagan. Orestes protested that he was a Christian who had been baptized by the Bishop of Constantinople, but to no avail. One of the monks, called Ammonius, threw a stone at Orestes, which hit him in the head. As a result of this most of Orestes' frightened guards fled, but the populace rushed in to support the prefect and forced the monks to flee. They also apprehended Ammonius and handed him over to the prefect.

The prefect had him tortured in public with the result that Ammonius died. After this Orestes sent a report to the emperor while Cyril sent his own letter. Cyril deposited Ammonius' body in a church and declared him a martyr. This did not gain the support of the majority of the Christians, because they knew that Ammonius had committed a crime and died as a result.

After this, the *parabalani* (lay brethren who were fanatical supporters of Cyril), led by Peter, decided to kill Hypatia because she was in their eyes guilty of spreading pagan views and most of all because they considered her to be the reason behind Orestes' hostility towards Cyril. They ambushed her when she was returning in her carriage to her home and dragged her to the Church of Caesareum, where they stripped her and cut her into pieces with shells. This was so reprehensible an outrage that it hurt Cyril's cause more than anything. Pulcheria sent a special commissioner, Aedesius, to investigate the affair. The results of this inquiry are unknown, but on 29 September 416 the government reduced the numbers of the *parabalani*, forbade their presence at public gatherings, and placed them under the Prefect. This suggests that the inquiry supported Orestes' version of events and recognized the danger posed by the *parabalani* to public order. The Jews were presumably allowed back into the city at the same time. However, this situation did not last. The deeply-religious Pulcheria restored the *parabalani* to the Patriarch and raised their number from 500 to 600 on 3 Feb. 418.[11] Consequently, Cyril had at his disposal two paramilitary groups of religious fanatics (500 armed monks and 600 *parabalani*) with which to challenge any decision put forth by the authorities. The soldiers attached to the Prefect's staff to protect him and to maintain public order and to gather taxes were just too few to challenge them. Consequently, if the Prefect faced conflict with the Patriarch, he needed military assistance from the *Comes Aegypti*, and as we have seen this could also be insufficient to restore order if the Patriarch had inflamed the passions of his partisans among the populace.

The troubles with the Blemmyes had begun during the reign of Theodosius I. In around 392-394 the Blemmyes under their king Tamal upset the strategic balance in the Nile Valley by conquering five cities (Phoinikon, Khiris (location unknown), Thapis, Talmis, and Prima) in Lower Nubia. This area corresponds roughly with the Dodekachoinos. The city of Kalabsha and its temple dedicated to the god Mandulis became the principal religious centre of this area, because the cult centre of Isis on the island of Philae was in Roman hands. The temple inscription names five Blemmye kings: Tamal, Isemne, Degou and Phonen. The last of these was recorded as the *phylarch* Phonoin and was therefore no longer an independent king.[12] The Romans appear not to have intervened directly, but used their Nobatian allies for this as their treaty stipulated. As noted above, the Blemmyes were not the only peoples troubling Egypt at this time. The Austuriani were also causing plenty of troubles between 405-412.

At some unknown point in time before the years 410-420 (it is assumed that King Kharamadoye was buried at Ballana between these dates) the Nobatae King Kharamadoye re-conquered the area from the Blemmye king Isemne. However, we know that by 423 the area was back in Blemmye hands – perhaps because the Romans could not provide any support for the Nobatae during their Persian War of 421-422. On top of that, the Romans appear to have concluded a treaty with the Blemmyes at some point in time after 392 because an inscription on the walls of the Mandulis temple records the arrival of a

letter from the Roman *Comes*. It is also probable that Olympiodorus' visit in 423 to the area controlled by the Blemmyes was not a mere curiosity trip made because he had been invited by the Blemmyes, but a diplomatic mission on behalf of the Roman Empire.[13]

Despite the fact that the Romans had negotiated a treaty with the Blemmyes they appear not to have abandoned their treaty with the Nobatae. We do not know whether the Romans made any attempts to reconcile the Blemmyes and Nobatae, but even if they did the peace between the two did not last long. At some point in time before c. 450 the Nobatae King Silko, 'the King of the Noubades and all the Aithiopians', described in inscription his three campaigns against the Blemmyes. He defeated the Blemmyes twice and on the third occasion he conquered their cities. This marked the end of Blemmye rule in Lower Nubia and the last of the Blemmye rulers in the area, Phonoin/Phonen, became Silko's *phylarch*. The fact that Silko called himself *Basiliskos* (kinglet) in his Greek inscription proves that he considered himself a client king (*foederatus*) of the Eastern *Augustus/Basileus*.[14]

The letter of Phonen to Silko's successor Abourni in c. 450 (tr. in Burstein 126-8) shows that Silko's victory over the Blemmyes had essentially consisted of the forcible eviction of the Blemmyes from the cities, which he had used to extort a payment of sheep, cattle and camels from Phonen. In return Silko had promised to give the lands back, but after he had received the gifts he failed to fulfil his promise. After Silko's death Phonen conquered one city but was once again defeated, this time by Abourni. Phonen had then sent his brother as an ambassador to sue for peace, but Abourni had killed him. Despite this breach of a truce, Phonen was prepared to accept peace if Abourni retreated from the cities. It is unfortunate that we do not know what happened next, but it is certain that Abourni won and annexed the Blemmyes because we do know that Phonen was the last Blemmye king mentioned in the inscription. It was this united force of Nobatae and Blemmyes that the Romans faced next.

Indeed the annexation of the Blemmyes made the Nobatae too powerful for their own good. This was even more so because the Kingdom of Silko and Abourni did not consist solely of the northern branch of the Nobatae (Nobatia) and Blemmyes, but also of the other Nobatae (later known as the kingdoms of Makuria and Alwa). This is proven by the fact that Silko had also (tr. of the inscription in Burstein, 123-5) subdued the 'other Nobatai' in the 'upper countries' (= Upper Nubia), together with rulers of other peoples, so that he could call himself the 'King of all Aithiopians'. It is in fact possible that he may even have subdued the kingdom of Aksum, because its ruler was called *Basiliskos Mikros* (minor kinglet) by a Roman traveller at this time, with the implication that the King of Aksum held a lesser rank as the *basiliskos* of the Nobatae (see below).

The Leiden Papyrus, which is a petition from the Bishop of Syene and Contra Syene Appion to the emperors Theodosius II and Valentinian III, complains about the raids made by the Blemmyes and the Anoubades (i.e. the Nobatae) and asks for military assistance against them. It is unfortunate that the Papyrus cannot be dated more accurately than to the general period of c. 425-450, but on the basis that the King Silko was a Roman client king and that the Roman military response came in 452/3, one can perhaps speculate that the petition took place in about 447-450. In this context the information provided by Evagrius (chapters 1.7 and 2.5), Priscus (frgs. 4.4, 26-27.2) and Jordanes (Rom. 333) are of the greatest value for the dating of these events. These sources suggest that the Austuriani, Mazices, Blemmyes and Nobatae ravaged Libya and Egypt in the late-440s and early-450s, which once again suggests that the Sahara and the deserts of Nubia were suffering from drought, or of a devastation caused by locusts after years of good harvests, or of floods that would have resulted in the loss of harvests and spread of diseases. The fact that the famous Marib dam was burst open in Yemen in about 449 suggests the latter, as the likeliest reason for the destruction of the dam is that it was broken by masses of water (see later).

Priscus fr. 26 states that the *strategos* Maximinus went to the East in 453 to meet Ardabur I at Damascus (he was fighting against the Arabs, who may also have been affected by the same weather phenomenon) and from there he marched to the Thebaid in Egypt, where he appears to have inflicted a heavy defeat on the Nobatae and Blemmyes. The Blemmyes and Nobatae sued for peace. Maximinus negotiated a peace for 100 years. The barbarians promised to hand over their prisoners, plunder, pay war damages, and give as hostages children of the nobility. In return for this, the Romans promised free access for pilgrims to the Temple of Isis at Philae and promised that the cult statue would once again start to make annual voyages on a barge to Lower Nubia. The death of Maximinus soon after this made the treaty void in the eyes of the barbarians. They were forced to release their hostages by force, which implies some sort of daring commando operation. After this, they resumed their raids. It was presumably then that the *Alexandrinae urbis procurator* Florus took the matters into his own hands by assuming command of the troops with which he defeated the Blemmyes and Nobadae invaders and expelled them from Egypt. It was probably thanks to this that Florus was then nominated as *Comes Aegypti et Praefectus Augustalis* in 452 or 453. The combining of the commands was timely because at the time Egypt was simultaneously threatened by civil disorder and military crisis.[15]

While Florus had been in Thebais dealing with the Blemmyes and Nobadae, the Synod of Alexandria had exiled the popular Patriarch Discorus and appointed Proterius as his successor. The church and populace were divided in their opinions and when the new Patriarch arrived riots ensued. It is probable that the historian Priscus and Florus both reached the city of Alexandria at about this time only to witness the chaos. Florus sent soldiers to stop the riot, but to no avail. The rioters threw rocks at the soldiers and forced them to flee to the former temple of Isis. The rioters besieged the place and then burned the soldiers alive. Florus' only reaction was to dispatch a report of the incident to the emperor Marcian. On the basis of this it is clear that Florus had too few men available to pacify the city, which means that he had left most of his forces in the Thebaid to keep the Blemmyes and Nobatae in order. The emperor immediately dispatched 2,000 recently-enrolled troops, that arrived at Antioch on the sixth day thanks to the favourable winds. The soldiers proceeded to rape wives and daughters and did many other things that were 'far worse'. The arrival of the reinforcements enabled Florus to pacify the city of Alexandria swiftly in either 453 or 454. He stopped the distribution of corn to the populace, and closed the public baths and all other places of entertainment. The combination of hunger and lack of entertainments brought the population to its knees so that the populace assembled in the Hippodrome and begged Florus to restore their bread and circuses. Florus agreed and the riots ended. A more detailed discussion of the events can be found in Volume Four.[16]

The extant circumstantial evidence from the fifth century suggests that the Aksumite Empire broke up into pieces at some point in time between 390 and 440. Firstly, the above suggests that the Aksumites had lost their nominal control over the Blemmyes and Nobatae together with the land route to Egypt because the wars between the Romans and the Blemmyes and Nobatae could not have taken place if the Aksumites had retained control over the land trade routes. Secondly, the Sabaeo-Himyarite kingdom was ruled by Abakarib Asad during the first third of the fifth century (I would date his reign to the period after c. 432) and he is considered by Arabian tradition to have been the greatest ruler of south Arabia. He extended his kingdom into Central Arabia and according to the tradition he was converted to Judaism at Medina. The conversion is a clear indication that he had broken relations with the Aksumites and it may also have meant a break with the Romans who had previously sponsored the conversion of the Himyarite kings into the Christian faith. I would suggest that we should connect the rise of Abakarib Asad with the Persian invasion under Bahram V Gur in about 431-434 so that Bahram would have invaded Yemen to oust the Aksumites, after which he installed Abakarib as his client king in the area. However, it is possible that Bahram actually acted as a Roman ally in this case while the Romans marched another army to Mecca. There also exists a letter by Bishop of Helenopolis Palladius (lived between 368-431) which describes a journey by a *scholastikos* of Thebes to India to study under the Brahmins and which contains important pieces of information. According to this letter, the *scholastikos* made a stop at Adulis, where he waited until he was able to catch an 'Indian ship' for his travel to India. Even when one takes into account the normal Roman racial prejudices, the title *Basiliskos Mikros* that the *scholastikos* uses for the king of Aksum in this letter leaves little room but to conclude that at that time the king of Aksum was no different from the kinglets of Nubia.[17]

On the basis of the above, I would suggest that the Aksumites lost control of the Blemmyes and Nobatae in the early 390s, because the Romans under Theodosius I and Arcadius no longer considered it necessary to bolster the Aksumite Kingdom because they were allied with Persia, and that the Aksumites lost control of Yemen and the Horn of Africa as a result of Bahram's invasion. If Bahram and the Romans conducted a joint campaign in Arabia, Ethiopia and Africa, then it is clear that the Aksumites would have turned against the Romans before this date (probably because they had not received any help from the Romans against the Blemmyes and Nobatae), which would mean that the aim of the superpowers was to restore the previous status quo in the area. What appears to be certain, however is that the kingdom of Aksum was a client kingdom of Rome in about 437. It is not known whether we should connect this with the inscription of the King Silko, which states that he was ruler of all Ethiopians, because his campaigns in the area cannot be dated securely. It is possible that he campaigned on behalf of Rome against Aksum at the same time as Bahram invaded Yemen and the Horn of Africa, but it is also possible that he exploited the weakened state of Aksum and only invaded the area after the Persians had left, but I would still consider the former to be likelier.

In short, the Aksumite rulers had probably lost their grip on the Blemmyes and the Nobatae probably in the 390s. The likeliest reason for this would have been that the Romans would not have considered it necessary to prop up the position of their Aksumite ally when they themselves were allied with Persia. This would certainly have been the case after Arcadius made Yazdgerd I guardian of his son and the latter had sent the eunuch Antiochos to act as guardian for the young Theodosius II. The final nail to the empire-status of Aksum was the invasion of Yemen, the Horn of Africa and East Africa by Bahram in about 431-434. It is in fact probable that in the aftermath of these disasters the Aksumites were temporarily subdued to tribute-paying status by King Silko, as suggested by his inscription. The maritime trade via the port of Adulis continued as before, but it is still probable that thanks to the peace, the Persian merchants were able to offer their wares and services at more affordable prices than before, which undoubtedly increased their market share at the cost of the Roman, Aksumite and Himyarite merchants.

As with everything in life, this situation did not last. The Book of the Himyarites states that at some point in time in the fifth century the Aksumites under Hiuna conquered Himyar. Munro-Hay notes that the name Hiuna bears close resemblance to the Greek name of one Aksumite ruler who was called Eon. On top of this, the title used by this King Eon can be interpreted to mean *Basileus Habasinon* (King of Habaschat), which was one of the titles used by the rulers of South Arabia. In addition to this, his coins have been found in South Arabia and so have those of his successors until the reign of Kaleb (ruled during the first half of the sixth century). Munro-Hay notes that stylistically the coins of Eon probably belong to the early fifth century and therefore the identification is uncertain. On the other hand, since the dating of coins on the basis of their appearance is an uncertain art, we can perhaps make the assumption that the coins of Eon are later and are to be dated to the 450s. It was then that the Jewish Kingdom of Himyar began its downfall. In about 449 or 455 a large section of the economically-vital Marib dam collapsed. These damages were repaired, but in 450 or 456, the dam suffered even greater damage and 20,000 men were detailed to repair it. This happened during the reign of Shurahbiil Yafur, the son of the great Abukarib Asad. It is impossible to know whether this contributed to the events that followed, but despite the fact that the dam was apparently repaired again, it is still clear that the damage to the economy would have been significant just before the Aksumites invaded. According to the Arab-Islamic tradition, Shurahbiil's successor Abdkulal converted to Christianity.[18] I take this to mean that it was then (probably in the late-450s) that the Aksumite King Eon/Hiuna re-conquered Himyar. We do not know whether the Aksumites were allies of Rome when this happened, but it is still probable, even though ultimately unprovable, that the invisible hand of Roman diplomacy was behind these events. The reason for this conclusion is that the next time that we have any information regarding the relationship between Rome and Ethiopia, these were clearly amicable. In spite of the fact that both superpowers preferred to maintain peace (there were only short outbreaks of hostilities in 440 and in Leo's reign), the Romans no longer felt it necessary to respect the Persian position, especially after c. 447. It was in the Roman interest to prop up the position of their allies and to improve the relative position of their own merchants and allies in the Arabia Sea and Indian Ocean.

Bibliography

Primary Sources on the Web:

Most of the primary sources (e.g. Claudian, Jerome, Eunapius, Olympiodorus, Priscus, Malchus, Zosimus, Zonaras, Philostrogius, Rufinus, Socrates, Sozomen, Theodoret, Vegetius, various Armenian sources etc.) are now available on the web either as old editions and translations or as html documents. Good places to start seeking those are Robert Bedrosian's Armenian Resources, the Internet Archive, Google Books, and the Tertullian Project. Whenever possible I have used Loeb or Budé editions and translations, excepting when I have been writing in such locations where I have had not access to my books or library. The following list (Select Primary Sources) refers only to those modern editions/translations that I have cited in the text or notes.

Select Primary Sources and Translations
Blockley R.C. (tr. and com.), *The Fragmentary Classicising Historians of the Later Roman Empire: Eunapius, Olympiodorus, Priscus and Malchus.* 2 Vols. Liverpool 1983. A very useful collection of sources with comments.
Candidus, see Blockley.
Claudian (Claudius Claudianus), two vols. tr. M. Platnauer (Loeb ed. 1922).
Claudian (Claudianus, Claudius), two vols. tr. M. Platnauer (Loeb ed. 1922); *The Works of Claudian in Two Volumes*, ed. and tr. by A. Hawkins, London (1817).
Codex Justinianus, ed. P. Krueger, Berlin 1877.
CTh = Theodosian Code, Latin text available on the web, English tr. C. Pharr, *The Theodosian Code and Novels and the Sirmondian Constitutions.* Princeton 1952.
Eunapius, see Blockley
Georgian Chronicles, *Rewriting Caucasian History. The Medieval Armenian Adaptation of the Georgian Chronicles. The Original Georgian Texts and The Armenian Adaptation*, tr. R.W. Thomson. Oxford 1996.
Gordon C.D., *The Age of Attila.* New York (1960). A very useful collection of translated sources (Candidus, Olympiodorus, Priscus, Malchus, Ioannes Antiochenus/John of Antioch) with commentary.
Gregory of Tours, *The History of the Franks*, tr. Lewis Thorpe. London 1974.
Hydatius, *The Chronicle of Hydatius and the Consularia Constantinopolitana*, ed. and tr. R.W. Burgess. Oxford (1993).
The Irish Annals = Annals of the Kingdom by the Four Masters from the Earliest Period to the Year 1616. Vol.1, Dublin 1856.
Julius Africanus, Kestoi, *Les 'Cestes' de Julius Africanus*, ed. and tr. J.-R. Vieillefond. Paris (1970).
Lydus, John, *De magistratibus, Ioannes Lydus On Powers or The Magistracies of the Roman State*, ed. and tr. A.C. Bandy. Philadelphia (1983).
Malchus, see Blockley.
Moses Khorenatsi, *History of the Armenians*, tr. R.W. Thomson. Cambridge and London (1978).
Olympiodorus, see Blockley
Philon, Mechanike Syntaxis 5, in Y. Garlan (1974) *Recherches de poliorcétique grecque.* Paris., pp.279–327 (with French tr. by Garlan), commentary etc. pp.328ff.
Philostorgius, *Church History*, tr. P.R. Amidon. Atlanta (2007).

Priscus, see Blockley.

REF2 = *The Roman Eastern Frontier and the Persian Wars. Part II AD 363–630*. Eds. G. Greatrex and S.N.C. Lieu. London and New York (2002). A useful collection of sources.

Rufinus, *The Church History of Rufinus of Aquileia*, tr. P.R. Amidon. New York, Oxford (1997).

Strategikon, *Das Strategikon des Maurikios*, ed. G.T. Dennis, German tr. E. Gamillscheg. Vienna 1981; *Maurice's Strategikon*, tr. G.T. Dennis. Philadelphia (1984).

Synesius, Opera; a very useful collection and commentary of translated texts of Synesius is to be found on the web at livius.org. maintained by Jona Lendering. When dating the letters I have used a combination of his and Alan Cameron's dating schemes.

Tabari, *The History of al-Tabari. Vol. V. The Sasanids, the Byzantines, the Lakhmids, and Yemen*. tr. C.E. Bosworth. New York (1999).

Tafrij, Muslim Manual of War being Tafrij al-Kurub fi Tadbir al-Hurub by Umar ibn Ibrahim al-Awasial-Ansari, ed. and tr. George T. Scanlon, Cairo (1961).

Vardan Arewelci, 'The Historical Compilation of Vardan Arewelci', tr. R.W. Thomson in *DOP* 43 (1989), 125–226.

Vegetius, *Flavius Vegetius Renatus, Epitoma Rei Militaris*, ed. and tr. Leo F. Stelten. New York 1990.

Zosimus, *Zosimus. New History*. (1990), tr. R.T. Ridley. Melbourne; *Nea Historia*, tr. and ed. Paschoud. Budé Paris. 4 Vols. (older English tr. available from the web).

Zosimus, *Zosimus. New History*. (1990), tr. R.T. Ridley. Melbourne; *Nea Historia*, tr. and ed. Paschoud. Budé Paris. 4 Vols.; A dated English translation by unknown hand (possibly J. Davis) *The History of Count Zosimus Sometime Advocate and Chancellor of the Roman Empire*, (London 1814).

Select Secondary Sources

Ariño B. D., 'Las murallas romanas de Cartagena en la segunda mitad del siglo I a.e.', (available from academia.edu).

Ayvazyan, personal communication via email.

Bachrach B. (1973), *A History of the Alans in the West*. Minneapolis.

Barrington Atlas of the Greek and Roman World (2000). Ed. R.J.A. Talbert. Princeton.

Bishop M.C. and Coulston J.C.N (2006 2nd ed.), *Roman Military Equipment From the Punic Wars to the Fall of Rome*. Oxford.

Blockley R.C. (tr. and com.), (1983), *The Fragmentary Classicising Historians of the Later Roman Empire: Eunapius, Olympiodorus, Priscus and Malchus*. 2 Vols. Liverpool.

Blockley R.C. (1992), *East Roman Foreign Policy. Formation and Conduct from Diocletian to Anastasius*. Leeds.

Bury J.B., (1923, Dover ed. 1958), *History of the Later Roman Empire*. 2 vols. Dover.

—— (1911), *The Imperial Administrative System In the Ninth Century: With A Revised Text of Kletorologion of Philotheos*. London.

Cameron, A. (1993), *Barbarians and Politics at the Court of Arcadius*. Berkeley, Los Angeles, Oxford.

—— (1970), *Poetry and Propaganda at the Court of Honorius*. Oxford.

Campbell D.B. (2006), *Besieged*. Oxford.

Cascarino G. and Sansilvestri C. (2009/2010), *L'esercito Romano. Armamento e organizzazione. Vol. II: Dal III secolo alla fine dell'impero d'occidente*. il Cerchio Città di Castello.

Chandler D.G. (1966), *The Campaigns of Napoleon*. New York.

Coello T. (1996), *Unit Sizes in the Late Roman Army*. Bar. Int. Ser. 645. Oxford.

Coulston J.C.N. (2002), 'Arms and Armour of the Late Roman Army', in D. Nicolle ed., *A Companion to Medieval Arms and Armour*. Woolbridge, pp. 3–24.

Croke B. (1977), 'Evidence for the Hun Invasion of Thrace in A.D. 422', in *GRBS* 18.4, pp. 347–367.

Crumlin-Pedersen O. (1997), 'Large and Small Warships of the North', in *Military Aspects of Scandinavian Society in a European Perspective, AD 1–1300*, ed. A. Nørgård Jørgensen and B.L. Clausen. Kopenhagen, pp. 184–194.

Daszewski W.A. and Michaelides D. (1988), *Guide to the Paphos Mosaics*. Bank of Cyprus Cultural Foundation.

Delmaire R. (1995), *Les institutions de bas-empire romain de Constantin à Justinien*. Paris.

Drinkwater J.F. (2007), *The Alamanni and Rome 213–496*. Oxford.

—— (1998), 'The Usurpers Constantine III (407–411) and Jovinus (411–413)', *Britannia* 29, pp. 269–298.

Elting J.R. (1988), *Swords Around a Throne*. New York and London.

Escher K. *Les Burgondes Ier-Vie siècles apr. J.-C.* Paris.

Fields, Nick (2008), *The Walls of Rome*. Oxford.

Filippo R. de, 'Nouvelle définition de l'enceinte romaine de Toulouse', *Gallia* 50, pp. 181–204.

Georgelin H. (2012), 'Armenian Inter-Community Relations in Late Ottoman Smyrna', in *Armenian Smyrna/Izmir*, ed. R.G. Hovanissian. Costa Mesa, pp. 177–190.

Goodchild R.C. (1952), 'Mapping Roman Libya', *The Geographical Journal* 118.2, pp. 142–152.

—— (1953), 'The Roman and Byzantine Limes in Cyrenaica', *JRS* 43, pp. 65–76.

Greatrex G. (2008), 'Deux notes sur Thédose II et les perses', *An Tard* 16, pp. 85–91.

—— (2007), 'Dukes of the Eastern Frontier', *Wolf Liebeschuetz Reflected*, in eds. J. Drinkwater and B. Salway. London, 87–98.

—— (1993), 'The Two Fifth-Century Wars Between Rome and Persia', *Florilegium* 12, 1–14.

Greatrex G. and Greatrex M. (1999), 'The Hunnic Invasion of the East of 395 and the Fortress of Ziatha', *Byzantion* 69, pp. 65–75.

Greatrex G. and Bardill J. (1996), 'Antiochus the Praepositus: A Persian Eunuch at the Court of Theodosius II', in *DOP* 50, pp. 171–197.

Grenier M. A. (1955), 'Essai de topographie narbonnaise', *Comptes rendus des séances de l'Academie des Inscriptions et Belles-Lettress* 99, pp. 352–362.

Haldon J. (2008), 'Structures and Administration', in *The Oxford Handbook of Byzantine Studies*, eds. E. Jeffreys, J. Haldon, and R. Cormack, pp. 539–553.

Hendy M.F. (1985), *Studies in the Byzantine Monetary Economy c.300–1450*. Cambridge.

Hodgkin T. (1892), *Italy and Her Invaders* (2 Vols.). Oxford.

Holum K.G. (1977), 'Pulcheria's Crusade A.D. 421–22 and the Ideology of Imperial Victory', *GRBS* 18, pp. 153–172.

—— (1982/1989), *Theodosian Empresses. Women and Imperial Dominion in Late Antiquity*. Berkeley, Los Angeles, London.

Hughes I. (2010), *Stilicho: The Vandal Who Saved Rome*. Barnsley.

—— (2012), *Aetius: Attila's Nemesis*. Barnsley.

Jones A.H.M. (1964/1986), *The Later Roman Empire 284–602*. Oxford.

Kettenhofen E. (1994/2011), 'Darband', in *Iranicaonline/Encyclopedia Iranica*.

Laroche D., 'La refondation de la cité', in *d'Izmir à Smyrne*. Louvre, pp. 40ff.

Lebedynsky I. (2012), *La grande invasion des Gaules 407–409*. Paris.

Lendering, Jona, website livius.org.

Liebeschuetz J.H.W.G. (1990), *Barbarians and Bishops*. Oxford.

MacGeorge P. (2002), *Late Roman Warlords*. Oxford.

Maenchen-Helfen O.J. (1973), *The World of the Huns*. Berkeley.

Marsden, E.W. (1969–1971), *Greek and Roman Artillery*. (2 Vols.) Oxford.

Matthews J. (1975/1990/2001), *Western Aristocracies and Imperial Court AD 364–425*. Oxford.

Mattingly D.J. (1995), *Tripolitania*. London.

Mayor A. (2003), *Greek Fire, Poison Arrows & Scorpion Bombs*. Woodstock, London, New York.

Miller M. (1975), 'Stilicho's Pictish War', *Britannia* 6, pp. 141–145.

Milne J.G. (1913), *A History of Egypt Under Roman Rule*. London.

Morrison J.S. with contributions by J.F. Coates, (1996), *Greek and Roman Warships 399–30 B.C.* Oxford.

Munro-Hay S. (1991), *Aksum. An African Civilization of Late Antiquity*. Edinburgh.

Nafziger G.F. (1988), *Napoleon's Invasion of Russia*. New York.

Nossov K. (2005), *Ancient and Medieval Siege Weapons*. Guilford.

O'Flynn J.M (1983), *Generalissimos of the Western Roman Empire*. Edmonton.

Paulinus, *see* web.

Petrikovits von H. (1971), 'Fortifications in the North-Western Roman Empire from the Third to the Fifth Centuries AD', *JRS 61*, pp. 178–218.

Pharr, *see* Th/Theodosian Code.

PIPLA = *Persia's Imperial Power in Late Antiquity. The Great Wall of Gorgan and Frontier Lanscapes of Sasanian Iran*. Eds. E.W. Sauer, H.O. Rekavandi, T.J. Wilkinson and J. Nokandeh. Oxford and Oakville (2013).

Pitassi M. (2011), *Roman Warships*. Woodbridge and Rochester.

—— (2009), *The Navies of Rome*. Woodbridge and Rochester.

PJROPL = Palet J.M, Julia R., Riera S., Orengo H.A., Picornell L., Llergo Y, 'The role of the Montjuïc promontory (Barcelona) in Landscape Change: Human Impact During Roman Times', in *Variabilités environnementales*. Antibes 2012, p. 323ff.

PLRE1, (1971/2006), *The Prosopography of the Later Roman Empire*, A.H.M. Jones, J.R. Martindale & J. Morris. Volume 1 A.D. 260–395. Cambridge.

PLRE2, (1980/2011), *The Prosopography of the Later Roman Empire*, J.R. Martindale. Volume 2 A.D. 395–527. Cambridge.

Pourshariati P. (2008), *Decline and Fall of the Sasanian Empire*. London and New York.

Rihll T. (2007), *The Catapult. A History*. Yardley.

Roques D. (1983), 'Synésios de Cyrène et les migrations berbers vers l'Orient (398–413)', in *Comptes-rendus des séances de l'Academie des Inscriptions et Belles-Lettres* 127.4, pp. 660–677.

—— (1987), *Synésios de Cyrène et la Cyrenaïque du Bas-Empire*. Paris.

Rotherberg G. (1999/2001), *The Napoleonic Wars*. London.

Salway P. (2001), *A History of Roman Britain*. Oxford.

Samson R (1991), *The Residences of Potentiores in Gaul and Germania in the Fifth to Mid-Tenth Centuries*, PhD Thesis, University of Glasgow.

Scanlon, *see* Tafrij.

Schippmann K. (2001), *Ancient South Arabia*. Princeton.

Schrier O.J. (1992), 'Syriac evidence for the Romano-Persian War of 421–2', *GRBS* 33, pp. 75–86.

Shahid I. *BAFOC*, (1984), *Byzantium and the Arabs in the Fourth Century*. Washington.

—— *BAFOC*, (1989, 2006), *Byzantium and the Arabs in the Fifth Century*. Washington.

Silvino T., Maza G., Faure P., Tran N., Argant T., (2011), 'Les origines de la colonie romaine de Valence (Drôme)', *Gallia* 68–2, 109–154.

Syvanne (Syvänne/Syvaenne) I. ASMEA 2014–2015 presentations due to be published.

—— See *MHLR* Vols. 1–2 with academia.edu for the other sources.

—— (2004), *The Age of Hippotoxotai*. Tampere.

—— 2015a, "The Reign of Bahram V Gur: The Revitalization of the Empire through Mounted Archery", in Historia i Świat 4, 2015. Written with the generous support of the ASMEA Research Grant.

—— A list of some of the publications after the year 2015 can be found from Pen & Sword Books website and from academia.edu

Tarraco, Archaeological Visual Guide (available e.g. from academia.edu).

Torres C. (1992), 'Povoamento antigo no baixo alentejo de Mertola', *Arquelogia Medieval* 1, pp. 189–202.

Trombley F.R. and Watt J.W. (2000), *The Chronicle of Pseudo-Joshua the Stylite*. Liverpool.

Warners E. (2007), 'Some remarks on the topography of Franconafurd', in *Post-Roman Towns, Trade and Settlement in Europe and Byzantium*, ed. J. Henning. Berlin and New York, pp. 341ff.

Wells C.M. and Wigthman E.M. (1980), 'Canadian Excavations at Carthage, 1976 and 1978: the Theodosian Wall, Northern Sector', *JFA* 7.1, pp. 43–63.

Welsby D.A. (2002). *The Medieval Kingdoms of Nubia*. British Museum, London.

Wilkes J.J. (2005), 'The Roman Danube: An Archaeological Survey', *JRS* 95, pp. 124–225.

—— (1969), *Dalmatia*. London.

Wolfram H., (1990), *History of the Goths*. Berkeley, Los Angeles, London.

—— (2005), *The Roman Empire and Its Germanic Peoples*. Berkeley, Los Angeles, London.

Notes

Chapter 1

1. The author acknowledges the generous support of the Research Grant awarded by the ASMEA in 2015 for the writing of the study of the Late-Roman and Persian intelligence systems. The writing of the study in question would have been impossible without this. The diagram and information regarding the intelligence systems is based on this study.
2. For additional details, see also Vols. 1–2.
3. For Napoleonic matters mentioned, see e.g. Rothenberg, 25ff., 160ff.; Nafziger; Chandler, 739ff.; Elting, 553ff. (corruption of the logistical services). There exists vast literature on French Revolutionary and Napoleonic wars so this is only a small sample.
4. For Late Roman equipment in general, see Bishop and Coulston, Bishop's academia.edu website, Coulston, and the MHLR Volumes 2–4.
5. See the narrative.
6. The following are of relevance when discussing the *foederati* and *bucellari*: the Romans started to consider the Federates part of the regular army and natives started to be enrolled into the Federates; Oros. 7.40ff., esp. 7.40.7 during the reign of Honorius; Feds very lucrative for the natives Oros. 7.41.7; natives join the *bucellarii* and *foederati* Olymp. frg. 7.4; Syvänne, MHLR Vol.2; Syvänne, *foederati*, 2015.
7. For the *foederati*, see MHLR Vol.2 with the previous endnote and the text.
8. See the next note with MHLR Vols. 1–2 and the narrative.
9. For a fuller discussion of siege equipment, see Vol. 1 with Syvänne (2004), Marsden, Rihll, Nossov and Campbell. The last four include long analyses and very nice illustrations and are all highly recommended. In addition to this, I recommend the reading of the analysis of Chevedden regarding the dating of the introduction of at least one variant of the counterweight trebuchet by Alexios Komnenos.
10. Foss and Winfield, 30; Lawrence, 177ff., Narrative.
11. For a modern attempt by archaeologists to find traces of Roman buildings, see the articles available online at academia.edu. The results are very incomplete and Montalbani's illustration remains the most complete reconstruction in existence that I know of. One can only hope that further research will get funding.

Chapter 2

1. Syvänne MHLR Vol.2.
2. Excluding the illustrations of Hun cavalry and some minor changes, this chapter has been borrowed from Vol.2 in its entirety.

Chapter 3

1. The principal sources for the years 395–408 (the era of Stilicho) are: Zosimus, Claudian, Synesius, Jordanes, Eunapius, Olympiodorus, Priscus, Jerome, Philostorgius, Theoderet, Sozomen, Socrates, Theophanes, the Chronicle of Paschal, Prosper, Gallic Chronicle, and the Chronicle of Edessa. I refer to a specific source only if there is a particular need to argue something (e.g. when my account differs from the commonly-accepted version). I have also found very useful the following secondary sources (see the referrals and endnotes): Maenchen-

Helfen; Alan Cameron (1970, 1993); O'Flynn; Liebeschuetz (1990); Hughes (2010); PLRE 1–2. The chronology of events between 395 and 415 in this and following chapters is based mostly on Alan Cameron's two reconstructions (1970, 1993), but I still depart from these in some places.

2. E.g. by Ian Hughes (2010, 38ff.), John Matthews (253ff.), and Alan Cameron (161ff.). See in particular Matthews for an analysis of the rising influence of the senators during the regime of Stilicho and Honorius.

3. For the religious policies of Stilicho, see Hughes contra the PLRE1 (Stilicho, pp.857–8 based mainly on Symmachus' letters), further sources therein.

4. The reconstruction of the events of the year 395 is mainly based on Claudian *Ruf.* 2.1ff. and Zosimus 5.1ff. The other sources are mentioned in the text.

5. Claudian's referrals to the pillaging of Macedonia, Thessaly, Pelion, Corinth, Athens, the Peloponnese, Arcadia, and Sparta in various places are allusions to future events and not to the events that took place before the death of Rufinus. The sequence of places refers to the route taken by Alaric's Gothic forces while other Goths marched from Pannonia to Illyricum/ Dalmatia.

6. The evidence for the birth of the Visigothic nation (nation or an army?) is conveniently collected by Hernández (280ff.). My view is that we are dealing with a large Gothic nation (much larger than admitted by any other modern researcher) which incorporated others scattered throughout this text. My view is based solely on the evidence provided by the period narrative sources, which clearly refer to a large Gothic nation.

7. Wilkes, 1969, 419.

8. This is actually quite easy for a Finn to recognize because twentieth-century Finnish history has several examples of similar behaviour. Firstly, it is claimed by some historians that during the late-1930s Marshal Mannerheim (later President) used the Germans (Mannerheim actually despised the Nazis, but was quite prepared to use them) whom he provoked through his friends to oust the then Finnish Foreign Minister Holsti so that he would be replaced by a new Foreign Minister who would adopt Mannerheim's pro-Scandinavian policy. President Kekkonen is also famously suspected of having used the Soviets from the late-1950s until the 1970s against his political opponents in Finland. The most famous of these is the crisis of 1961, just before the presidential elections, which he was likely to lose. He is suspected (but not proven without a doubt) to have ordered from the Russians an ultimatum, which he then solved by travelling in person to the Soviet Union to meet its leaders face-to-face. As a result of this Kekkonen seemed indispensable to the populace and to his opponents so that henceforth Kekkonen's position in Finland was basically unchallenged. In the early 1970s on one occasion Kekkonen is also suspected of having used the Soviets to oust his remaining opponents, which the Soviets then misinterpreted as Finland being ripe for revolution, but with the result that Kekkonen put a stop to all such foolishness. It is claimed that as a result of this the Soviets actually sought to oust Kekkonen and replace him with a more malleable person called Ahti Karjalainen, but with little success. Kekkonen's position could not really be challenged before his health finally collapsed quite visibly in 1981. It is actually claimed by some that at least one of his successors was a Soviet spy. There are similar examples even closer to the time of writing, both in Finland and in Europe (e.g. in Germany), but it is not always certain whether the Russians just want to back their favourite politicians by creating fake crises to solve or whether the crises have been ordered from them. I have included this here only to demonstrate that similar suspicions have been presented also in modern circumstances and the story in which Rufinus would have first instigated Alaric's revolt and then diffused it in person by meeting Alaric face-to-face is not as farfetched as assumed by classicists.

9. This chapter is based mainly on Claudian (*In Ruf.* 2 books), Zosimus (5.1ff.), and Jordanes (*Getica* 146ff.).

10. Based on Zosimus 5.8.1ff. and Claudian *Eutrop.* 1. (esp. 1.151ff.).

11. Based on Zosimus 5.8.1ff. and Claudian *Eutrop.* 1. (esp. 1.151ff.) and Eunapius frg. 64.3ff.
12. When in office Aurelianus apparently moved to initiate the programme that he and his fellow conspirators had devised. The most important part of it was the dilution of the existing barbarian units with native Romans so that these could be made loyal to the Empire. Synesius refers to this in his texts, and even more importantly it is probable that Orosius (7.40ff., esp 7.40.7, 7.41.7) and Olympiodorus (frg 7.4) refer to the same. In addition to this, Aurelianus recalled Eutropius from exile and had him executed. See PLRE 1 for a summary of his career
13. The above and following reconstruction of the administrative posts and policies in the East is based on the outstanding studies of Synesius by Cameron and Long, and by Liebeschuetz (1990). I agree with Cameron and Long that Eutychianus was not a pagan but a staunch Christian and that Eutychianus was not really pro-German, but rather a career administrator and a realist/pragmatist who followed the policy best suited to the circumstances. However, I disagree with Cameron and Long in that I believe that there was indeed an anti-Gothic party led by none other than Aurelianus and that Synesius tried to attract the attention of this party with his orations (held behind closed doors) against the barbarians.
14. This chapter builds upon the conclusions reached by Maenchen-Helfen (pp.51–59) and Greatrex and Greatrex, both of which are highly recommended. References, translations and quotes to the sources mentioned here can be found in both. I have chosen here to follow Greatrex and Greatrex, Alan Cameron and others that there was another Hun invasion in 397 or 398, which the eunuch Eutropius crushed probably in 398. However, despite being indebted to the analyses mentioned, I have still interpreted the information provided by the sources differently. For example, my interpretation is that there were more divisions than three (i.e. there were four) and naturally I also interpret the routes taken by the separate Hun divisions differently.
15. On the basis of Claudian's referral (*In Ruf.* 2.28) to the use of the Caspian Gates ('Caspia claustra') it is usually suggested that the Huns used the Darial Pass. However, it is actually possible that he meant the Darbend Pass, because it lies next to the Caspian Sea while the Darial Pass is in the middle of the Caucasus. However, since Theodoret refers to the invasion of the Iberian lands and because Claudian states that they used a newly discovered pass I have still opted to accept that the Huns used the Darial Pass in this occasion.
16. The information is in Pseudo-Dionysius, but it is usually assumed that he used the sixth-century John of Ephesus as his source.

Chapter 4

1. This chapter is based mainly on Zosimus (5.5.1ff.) and Claudian (*IV Hon.* 459ff.). Other sources are conveniently listed in the PLRE2, Alaricus1.
2. Hughes (2010, 98–99).
3. Refortification of Sparta in Lawrence (p.180).
4. It is of course possible that Stilicho tightened the guarding of the coasts only later to the point stated in the Edict of 408, but the fact that no amount of guards have ever been able to stop smugglers, together with Eunapius' lack of credible information of the political situation in the West, all suggest that Stilicho put in place the entire set of regulations in 397 or 398.
5. The principal sources for this chapter are Orosius, Claudian (esp. *Gildo, Eutr.* 1.371ff. and *Stilicho* 1.244ff.) and Zosimus (esp. 5.11.1ff.).
6. In spite of the fact that none of the sources mentions this, Ian Hughes adds to the list of places visited during the journey a visit to Sicily on the grounds that it would not have been possible to sail directly from Sardinia to Carthage. This is false. The Roman ships were entirely capable of even longer distances and the trip to Sicily would actually have been longer than to Carthage
7. PLRE2 Iovius 2 (possibly the same as PP Iovius 3):
8. Roques (1987, 217ff.) with Appendix 3. The various theories can be found in Roques' excellent analysis.

9. This same pattern can be detected in Europe also in the Middle Ages and Early Modern period. When the climate was warmer, the Vikings inhabited even Greenland, but when it became colder the populations declined. The sixteenth century was warm and a period of population growth while the seventeenth century saw a minor Ice Age, as it is sometimes called, and was a period of stagnation for many countries, but not for Sweden which actually benefited from it.
10. For the existence of Gothia at the turn of the fifth century, see Vasiliev (e.g. 23, 32ff.). He proves on the basis of John Chrysostom's texts that there existed Gothia in the Taman Peninsula of the Crimea, which consisted of the Tetraxitae, Eudosians and Marsian Goths. John even ordained a bishop called Unila for the Goths of Crimea in around 400.

Chapter 5
1. Based mostly on Zosimus (5.11.1ff.) and Claudian *Eutropius* 2.
2. Zos. 5.11.11ff.; Claudian *Eutr.* 2.
3. Cameron and Long, 4, 227–9.
4. Greatrex and Bardill p. 172: the embassy was possibly led by the *Comes Sacrarum Largitionum* Athemius.
5. Greatrex and Greatrex 67–68; Greatrex and Bardill p. 172; REF2. 31–2; Blockley 1992, 48–49.
6. Zosimus 5.19.4 states later that more than 7,000 Goths met their end at the Arian Church. Considering that there were 7 *Scholae* in the East (ND *Or.* 11), it is possible that Zosimus may have mistaken the 7,000 men to refer to the number of Goths who died at the Church. Liebeschuetz (1990, 112) has actually mistakenly read Zosimus' text so that there were 7,000 men inside the city that formed a fifth of Gainas' entire army (Syn. *De Prov.* 2.2). Considering the fact that it is indeed possible that each of the *Scholae* units had about 1,000 men at this time, this is actually quite plausible and would lend support to the claims of Sozomen and Socrates that Gainas' troops intended to attack the Imperial Palace immediately after the *Scholae* had left the city. Gainas' purpose would indeed have been to replace the 7 *Scholae* units with his 7,000 Goths. If this line of reasoning is correct, then Gainas would have 35,000 men at his disposal. I have here adopted this view despite the uncertainties.
7. I have here followed the account given by Sozomen (8.4) and Socrates (6.6) which are inherently more plausible than Zosimus' account, which claims that Gainas attempted to conquer Constantinople only after he had left the city.
8. Liebeschuetz, 1990, 122ff.
9. Tr. Bohn Library, p. 310.
10. Date in Cameron and Long.
11. The quote is from the translation of Eunapius by Blockley, p.111. This same accusation was made earlier by Hannibal's cavalry commander of Hannibal after the victory of Cannae.
12. Zosimus 5.21; Eunapius frg. 69.1–4.
13. Cameron and Long, 245ff.
14. E.g. in 1903 the city had a population of 300,000 (Georgelin, 179–180).
15. See the perceptive comments of Hughes (2010, 114ff.) regarding Stilicho's situation. Note, however, that I do not agree with all of his suggestions

Chapter 6
1. Bury 1.160; O'Flynn, 37–38.
2. These figures are comparable to the number of Helvetii who were migrating to Gaul in 58 (Caesar, Gallic War 1.29 based on tribal records kept in Greek: 368,000 Helvetii of whom about 92,000 were able to bear arms) and with the other migrating masses mentioned by the various ancient sources, and since these figures are comparable with later figures of tribes (see e.g. Syvänne, 2004) it is clear that the standard size of a migrating tribal confederacy was ca. 350,000 persons of whom about 80,000–100,000 were able to bear arms. There is no reason to doubt Caesar's

figures, even if these were meant for propaganda purposes. It would have been too dangerous for him to lie about this when his army included large numbers of political enemies.

3. Translation by O'Flynn, 215.

4. Vol 1: At the same time the Romans transferred altogether 300,000 Sarmatian fugitives into Thrace, Scythia, Macedonia and Italy according to Origo (1.6.31). The Alans together with the Goths and other Federates settled in the East rose to prominence when one of their members, the Alan Aspar, became the de facto ruler of the East. See also Vol. 2 with the PLRE 1–2.

5. Claudian *Gothic*, 560–563, 580–597; Orosius 7.37; Paulus Diaconus/Paul the Deacon, *Historia Romana* 12.13; Jerome, *Contra Ruf.* 3.21.

6. Information regarding the Roman wall is based on Fields.

7. Claudian *Gothic* 267ff., the revolt of already-pacified Raetia and Noricum as a result of the Gothic invasion of Italy (363ff.). Claudian's text clearly states that Stilicho was present at Milan just before the arrival of the Goths in the winter of 400/401.

8. The following is mainly based on: Zosimus, Orosius, Augustinus (*Civ. Dei*), *Chron. Gall 452*, Olymp., Marc. Com., Jord. *Get.*, Prosper Tiro, *Ann. Rav.*, etc. For additional details regarding the sources, see the PLRE1-2, which usefully collects the references to the sources for each individual. It should be noted that my interpretation of the course of the campaign differs completely from the previous reconstructions. For alternative reconstructions of the events, policies, campaign etc. I refer the reader to the works of O'Flynn, Liebeschuetz, Cameron (1970), Lebedynsky (2012), Bury, Hughes (Stilicho).

9. Ridley has amended the figure of 40,000 into 4,000 on the grounds that 'it must have been a mistake', but in my opinion this is actually a modern mistake caused by a false perception that the Late Romans (and the barbarians) were unable to field forces of the size that the very same historians are readier to accept for the earlier period or for the modern pre-industrial period. This is a great fallacy caused by the unfounded rationalizations of Delbruck, which actually sometimes smack of racist/nationalistic viewpoints. His arguments regarding the small sizes of the Germanic armies is a case in point. One only has to remember the complexity of the logistical network that the Romans needed to support their cities of hundreds of thousands of men on top of the other cities, towns, garrisons and forts. If they were able to support cities of over 500,000 men, then they were certainly capable of supporting armies of lesser size close to rivers and coasts. In contrast to the above, Pachoud has retained the original 40,000 (Bude ed.) and not amended it to fit modern prejudiced ideas. It should also be noted that in this case the *arithmos* of Zosimus cannot have consisted of about 1,000 to 1,200 men, because thirty *numeri* would have meant only an army of about 30,000–36,000 men and it is difficult to imagine that Stilicho could have considered his federate army of at least 60,000 men to be too small to face the regulars posted at Ticinum in 408. It is improbable that the size of the army of Ticinum in 408 would have been significantly larger than the whole assembled army at Ticinum in 406 because then Stilicho still possessed the armies of Gaul to bolster his military strength while in 408 the Army of Gaul sided with Constantine III (see later).

10. Florentia (Florence) was founded in 59 BC as a Roman colony with the purpose of guarding the ford across the river Arno, which remained its main purpose until the sixth century. The fort was a quadrangular *castrum* (450m per side) with two main roads crossing it so that there were four main gates. A wooden bridge on stone foundations was built (Vecchio) across the Arno at the end of the second century AD and later rebuilt with stone. The town continued to grow so that sizable suburbs were already located outside the walls along the Via Cassia (east of the fort) by the end of the first century AD. The growth was halted by the Gothic invasion of Radagaisus. Before his invasion the population had reached the figure of at least 10,000 persons. The city survived Radagaisus' siege in reduced form, but was later utterly ruined during the Romano-Gothic war of the sixth century.

11. In other words, each of the enemy divisions could have halted their own migrating mass and formed a vast wagon laager or laagers to serve as defensive bases while the cavalry forces were sent to the assistance of the threatened division.

Chapter 7

1. See e.g. the quote in Bury 1.142–147 (esp. 147) with Holum (1982/89, 54–56.

2. The dating of this key decision to the years 401–403 was suggested by Geoffrey Greatrex and Jonathan Bardill in an important article in 1996. The following discussion of the guardianship and Antiochus' position is based on: Greatrex and Bardill (the relevant Part 1 written by Greatrex); Greatrex 2008, 85–87; and REF2 32ff.

3. As regards the dating of al-Mundhir's reign, I follow here Tabari (i.850–63) who clearly states that Yazdgerd placed his son Bahram in the care of al-Numan, the king of Hira, who ruled 15 years under Jazdgerd I (i.e. from 404/5 until 420) and 14 years under Bahram (i.e. from 420 until 434), after which he renounced the world to serve the God. This al-Numan (i.850–4) is clearly to be equated with the al-Mundhir (i.854–63) who raised Bahram and then helped him to gain the throne in 420. In other words, I do not accept Shahid's dating 418–462 for the reign of al-Mundhir – Tabari's al-Numan and al-Mundhir are one and the same man. However, there also exists another possibility which is that Tabari has confused al-Mundhir with his son al-Numan (e.g. because al-Mundhir's name appears to have been al-Mundhir al-Numan) and that the Numan, who was on friendly terms with Christians and converted to Christianity in 410s had he not lived on Persian territory, was al-Mundhir's son. Sources for the friendly pro-Christian Numan collected in REF2 35–6.

4. See BAFIC.

5. For a full commentary and analysis of the sources, see BAFIC. However, contrary to Shahid I believe that the Salihids were probably given control over most of the tribes in the area in a manner reminiscent of what had happened during Imru al-Qays' rule, and if they were not given control over the entire front facing both Persia and Arabia, they were certainly given control of the front facing Arabia as suggested by Shahid.

6. Cameron & Long, 246–250.

7. Cameron & Long, 249–250; Maenchen-Helfen, 67.

8. Jordanes's referral (*Get.* 280–281) to the location and alliance between the Suevi and Alamanni prove that the former were formerly known as the Iuthungi.

9. In this instance it is important to understand that the building of defences should not be compared with the twentieth-century so-called Maginot mentality. In Roman context the walls proved very effective as long as the defenders were willing to defend them, whereas in the case of the Maginot line the defenders failed to take into account the latest trends in warfare which had made the walls redundant.

Chapter 8

1. As regards this and following chapters, if you want an alternative but plausible reconstruction of the events taking place in the Gallic Prefecture between 406 and 418, I recommend Matthews' excellent study of the western aristocracy (1975/1990, pp. 306–328 with scattered references to the same era thereafter). It should always be kept in mind that the evidence for the period is so poor that it allows several different interpretations.

2. Drinkwater 1998, 272 (partially after Seeck).

3. If Drinkwater could for some reason be correct, then one may speculate that it was actually Stilicho and Honorius who had created the situation in which the local councils and senates consisting of the nobles had assumed greater powers than at any time before. In support of this one can claim that Stilicho had created such when he had left the defence of Britain in local hands in about 401. However, the extant evidence rather suggest that if Stilicho created such a council for Britain that similar councils were not created elsewhere at the same time and that the creation of such for Gaul was a desperate countermeasure by Honorius' government to divide the Gallic nobles.

4. The various alternatives given by Drinkwater 1998.

5. Notably, the same phenomenon can be detected also in Finland during the Swedish rule from the sixteenth until the seventeenth centuries. Peasants simply abandoned their farms in order to avoid taxes and moved into the forests to restart their lives. It is no wonder that so many Finns from Savo/Savolax were ready to move first into Sweden and then to North America.

6. The calculation is based on the figures of Hendy. According to him, the period *solidus* weighed 1/72 of pound of gold, which means that when the cavalryman's *annona* (equalled 5 *solidi*) and *capitus* (equalled 4 *solidi*) were compensated in gold he was to receive 9 *solidi* per year for his own expenses which included the equipment, horses, servants and family. The 4,000 lbs equals 288,000 *solidi* which in turn would equal 32,000 horsemen which I have lowered to 30,000 horsemen to take into account the salaries of the higher ranking men.

7. Wolfram (2005, 97) estimates that 4,000 lbs of gold would have allowed about 90,000 persons to live comfortably for one year, which in his opinion tallies nicely with the estimate of 100,000 persons for the entire tribe. I have accepted this overall figure here.

Chapter 9

1. The provinces may in fact have been united as the Province of Flaminia and Picenum. However, Zosimus' text can also be used as evidence for the separation of the provinces at the time of Alaric's invasion or at the time when Zosimus wrote.

2. The same thing has also been noted by Paschoud in his translation and commentary of Zosimus (3.1, pp.285–6).

3. This translation is by Ridley p.122.

4. As noted by John Matthews (292), this proves that at least his father had managed to safeguard his money when Palladius confiscated property. Matthews thinks that the father's name was Marcianus, but this is likely to be a mistake. I prefer the Marinianus of the PLRE1.

5. Zosimus essentially claims that all pagan officeholders were incorruptible while the Christians were corrupt to the bone. Regardless of this, it appears probable that Generidus was indeed incorruptible as claimed.

6. It should be noted that the removal of the *magistri* could even be discussed in the Sacred Consistory because the *magistri* were not permanent members of the Sacred Consistory.

7. Zosimus 5.47.2 fails to state which state organ voted. Honorius's purpose was clearly to tie other important men behind his decision. For the increased role of the Senate during this era, see John Matthews' magisterial study of the rise of the importance of the senators under Stilicho and Honorius (esp. 253ff.). The fall of Stilicho forced the senators to assume an even greater role in the governance of the Empire.

8. Tr. by Ridley p.125. See also John Matthew's very perceptive comments of this situation (300–301). The Roman government was in no situation to refuse and it still did so thanks to a mistaken sense of patriotism.

9. For a complete and valuable analysis of the sources and the various invaders, see esp. Lebedynsky, 2012. Note, however, that my interpretation and analysis of the sequence of events and of the campaign differs from his. Regardless, his analysis is still highly recommended, because I base some of my conclusions on those reached by him. Furthermore, his analysis and reconstruction of the events is also valuable for the reason that it offers an alternative view, which is plausible even if I disagree.

10. It is less probable that they would have subdued the tribal allies of the Suevi.

11. For the pillaged cities or cities and forts otherwise mentioned in the context of the Vandal invasion included in the Christian hagiographies, martyrologies saints' lives etc., see Lebedynsky 2012 and Jacobsen. The list of sacked cities is based on their studies.

12. P. Wynn has used this same fragment of Frigeridus in a similar manner as a basis of his reconstruction of the events that took place between 406 and 411. His important article was kindly brought to my attention by Robert Vermaat. I recommend this article highly for its superb analysis of the sources and secondary sources. However, my actual reconstruction of

the events differs fundamentally mainly because my interpretation of the other evidence causes me to interpret Frigeridus' text in a different light. E.g. despite Wynn's very valuable analysis of the textual tradition of the fragment and its editions, I do not agree with his interpretation that Respendial would have been *rex Alamannorum*. On the basis of the internal evidence of the fragment together with the fragment of Olympiodorus, it is quite clear that Rependial was *rex Alanorum*. This is confirmed by the existence of the Greek inscription (a person with the name of *Rhespendialos*) in Olbia from the so-called Sarmatian period. This was clearly an Alan-Sarmatian name because it dates from an area under their control before the arrival of the Goths in the third century.

13. Mattingly, 1995, 177–8.
14. In fact, despite the many consulships they had held in 310, 322, 325, 331, 341, 350, 371, 379, 395 (both consulships), 406, 408 (after this only in 431), the only emperor that hailed from this ancient family was Anicius Olybrius in 472. See Ridley (Zos., p.228).
15. Note, however that Sozomen's text which is thought to have come from Olympiodorus (fr. 10) states that '…*adokêtos en hex arithmois amfi tetrakischilioi stratiôtai* …' which is usually interpreted to mean that the six *tagmata* encompassed four thousand men in total. I prefer Zosimus' version on the grounds that 4,000 men would have been far too small a force to have made any difference except as a commando strike force, which it was not. This is also confirmed by Procopius' referral (Wars 3.2.36) to the size of the Eastern army helping Honorius as a very great number of men. In fact, I would go so far as to claim that we may need to translate Sozomen's *amfi* in this case that all *tagmata* consisted of 4,000 men so that the total envisaged by Sozomen would have been 24,000, which I would take to refer to the footmen in addition to which would have come the cavalry, but as stated Zosimus' figure of 40,000 men in total is the figure I trust.
16. Tr. by Pharr in CTh p.174 with parentheses added.
17. Note that e.g. Orosius claims that Placidia was only captured from the city of Rome after its fall on 24 August 410. However, in my opinion Zosimus' account is to be preferred in this case. Alaric certainly had the opportunity to capture Galla Placidia before that in 409 and it would have been an unbelievable oversight on his part if he had not used Placidia as a hostage from 409 onwards.

Chapter 10
1. Sources for this chapter and following can easily be found in the PLRE and PLRE2.
2. Soz./Olymp. (fr.17.2.61ff.) claims that from 411 onwards the people around Arelate were Honorius' subjects even if it is certain that Arelate itself surrendered to Iovinus (the minting of coins in his name makes this certain).
3. It is usually thought that the date of this Edict is incorrect on the assumption that Gaiso is known to have been *CSL* in 409 and then *Comes et Mag.Off.* in 410, but is not known to have been *Comes et Mag. Mil.* in 413. See e.g. PLRE 2. In my opinion this is not conclusive. We simply do not know the names, titles and dates for all the office-holders for those years. However, if we assume that the series of assumptions in the PLRE 2 is correct, then the Edict/Law in question would have been equally in place for the year 410 because the situation must have been even worse then. Regardless, it is likelier that the date is correct. Gaiso's name is Germanic, which suggests that his rise coincided with the rise of the Easterners and Constantius.
4. This section was aptly written on 6 December 2013, the Independence Day of Finland.
5. Discussed at greater length in the research papers presented at ASMEA 2014–2015.

Chapter 11
1. Bury 1.209.
2. Olymp. frgs 23, 33–34, 37. Other sources in PLRE 2.

Chapter 12

1. Arcadius' wife Aelia Eudoxia was the daughter of Bauto the Frank. Theodosius was therefore either a half-barbarian if Bauto's wife was barbarian or quarter-barbarian if Bauto's wife was Roman.
2. The sources are usefully collected and discussed by Maenchen-Helfen, 63–67.
3. Maenchen-Helfen dated the invasion on the grounds that Jerome refers to the death of Stilicho in the preface to Book XI in his Commentary on Isaiah (which mentioned the Hunnic invasion). He states that the allusion must have occurred almost immediately after Jerome learnt of the execution of Stilicho in September or October 408, but this is not necessarily so. He could also have made the allusion later than that.
4. For further details, see Syvänne, 2004.
5. Bury 1.213 with Appendix 3.
6. It should be noted that researchers have not reached an agreement regarding the start of the building project. Some place it to the year 405, others to 408 and still others to 412 or 413. However, it is usually thought that the project was finished in 413, but there is no agreement regarding the dating of the sections of the wall. Some researchers think that the outer wall was built later after the inner wall while others think that the outer wall was built before the inner and that the inner wall was added only in about 447. I agree with Foss and Winfield that both walls were built at the same time, because the structure of the inner wall suggests that the outer wall (it protected the lower portion of the inner wall) was built at the same time. We know that the outer wall was built at this time because it houses on the lower level the storage and living quarters that are attested in the Theodosian Code for the year 422 (see later). Foss and Winfield suggest that the crenelation to the outermost section beside the moat was added later possibly as an emergency measure, but I would suggest that this piece of work was also done at the same time – the building of these crenallations could equally well have been the first stage of the process as it could have produced additional protection for the city for example when the Huns threatened Constantinople in 408. There is also no agreement regarding the date when the sea walls between the Theodosian and Constantinian walls were built, because some researchers suggest that the sea walls were built in 447, but other dates have also been suggested. In my opinion it is quite obvious that the sea walls were also added to cover the exposed area between the walls at the same time as the Theodosian Land Walls were completed. The section known as the Blachernae was completed later to protect the so-called Palace of Blachernae, but there are traces of some walls possibly meant for the fourteenth region of the city. Unfortunately, there are so few traces of these left that it is impossible to reconstruct their structure. My own suggestion is that the Palace of Blachernae was already protected by the Theodosian Wall but that the protruding part built under Manuel Comnenus was an addition made by him. However, since it is still possible that even this wall was built on top of previous structures I have left the line of the wall intact in the accompanying illustration (as all reconstructions of the walls have). In general for the walls and for the various views, see: Foss and Winfield; Lawrence; Turnbull.
7. This discussion of the walls is based on the excellent accounts of Foss and Winfield, and Turnbull, but I have added my own views and comments here and there.
8. See Syvänne, 2004.
9. Holum 1977,158–161; 1982, 93ff.
10. The sources often confuse the Darial Pass and Derbend Pass with each other so that the term Caspian Gates could mean either of these. However, in this case it is clear that the Derbend Pass is meant.
11. See the later chapters together with Blockley 1992, 50–53.
12. See Holum 1977 with 1982, p.96–7.
13. Holum, 1977, 161–162. It should be noted that Nestorius later accused Pulcheria of hypocrisy because she supposedly had had several male lovers.

14. Soc. 7.16; Holum, 1977, 161–2. It should be noted that the situation is not that different even today. It is easy to imagine that if a group of people belonging to some minority group were to kill a small boy brutally that it could result in rioting in many countries that are usually considered tolerant.

15. Full analysis of the Novella in BAFIC, 49–50.

16. I.e., I do not agree with Shahid's analysis that the Salihids would have been the principal Arab *foederati* also after ca. 421.

17. The strategic importance of the city and Crimea for the security of the Black Sea cannot be stressed enough. It comes as no great surprise that the Russians have secured the area in early March of 2014 (written on 4 March 2014). However, it should be noted that the strategic configuration for the area was entirely different in the fifth century.

18. Could it be possible that the sources have confused several different Numans with each other so that Aspebetus would have been the pro-Christian Numan who frequently held discussions with the Romans? As noted by Shahid, the name Aspebetus refers to a Persian title/office. Shahid (BAFIC, 43) thinks that the name referred to the office of *spahbed*, but in my opinion the office must be that of *Aspet/Asbedh* (cavalry commander). Therefore the title Aspebetus can hide behind it the name Numan. Another possibility is that the name Aspebetus hides the name Zokomos, but the details of his family (Zokomos was childless before he received help from a priest while Aspebetus had a lame son who was healed by St. Euthymius) do not correspond with the details given of Aspebetus' family.

19. Full analysis of the sources for Aspebetus in BAFIC, esp. 40–49. Note, however, that my interpretation differs slightly from Shahid's. E.g. Shahid considers it improbable that Aspebetus ruled over the Salihids.

20. Pourshariati, 66–69.

21. The following is based on Tabari i.854ff.

22. The Muslims were to adopt a somewhat similar approach before the Battle of Al-Qadisiyah c. 634–6 (for the problems of dating the battle, see Pourshariati). Yazdgerd III's (632–651) position was still weak and the pillaging of the lands belonging to the nobles forced him to commit his army against the Muslims on their own chosen battlefield. For a fuller analysis, see my article in the DF (at the time of writing still forthcoming).

23. For a discussion of the circumstances, see Pourshariati, 67–70.

24. Bosworth (p.91) identified the Isbabahd with the Spahbed who according to him was the supreme commander of the army (i.e. the Iran-Spahbed). I have here preferred to identify 'Isbabahd' with the family name.

25. In light of recent events in Europe one may of course question whether these were mere excuses.

26. However, see also REF2 (p. 257 n.29).

27. An old man called Cyriacus attempted to murder the *PVC* Aetius in 419 (PC a. 419), but the circumstances behind the assassination attempt are not known. Aetius survived to become *PPO* in 425.

28. Holum 1977; 1982, 103ff.

29. The other location mentioned in the context of Yazdgerd's death, the city of Tus, was also located in an area which was to receive new fortifications against the northern nomads in the fifth century.

30. I.e. I agree with Greatrex (1993; 2008, 87ff.) that Anatolius was *MVM per Orientem* at the time.

31. See the excellent analysis of the evidence in Greatrex, 1993, 2008.

32. In other words, I agree with Greatrex's analyses (1993; 2008, 87ff.) that this city was built by Anatolius in 420/1.

33. It is of course possible that one should date the reform to the immediate aftermath of the Persian War of 440/441, but that was not a major war which rather suggests a connection with the Persian War of 421–422.

34. Sinclair, 185ff with e-mail sent to the author.
35. Armen Ayvazyan, who is a specialist of eighteenth-century Armenia, kindly pointed me to this source.
36. Most of Armenian forces consisted of cavalry. See Chapter 2 in Vol.1.
37. See Vols. 1–2. The mix-up has resulted from the fact that some unknown Georgian author has misplaced the reign of Vaxtang to the wrong period, probably because he has mixed the Roman general Leo with the Emperor Leo and the reigns of the two Theodosii. From all this it is quite clear that the Georgian Chronicles are based on oral traditions which the Georgian author has superimposed on written histories, but in such a manner that he or his oral source has combined several different individuals into one composite individual or have created duplicate characters (e.g. Persian, Armenian and Georgian kings grouped as one composite Georgian king; see Vols 1–2) or have confused different similarly named persons with each other (which are also sometimes placed in the wrong time period) or have added legendary clearly untrue material to extol the achievements of their heroes in the same manner as e.g. Firdausi, al-Tabari and other similar sources that are based on oral traditions. In sum, the information in the GC has to be treated with great scepticism.
38. This is only a very rough estimation because the *Auxilia Palatina* units could consist of fewer men, the frontier legions of either less or more men, and the *Comitatenses* legions could be considerably larger if originally formed during the reign of Diocletian as I noted in Volumes 1–2.
39. Most of the evidence mentioned hereafter has been usefully collected in REF2.
40. Cavalry units estimated as 512 men, *Aux. Pal.* as 1,000 men, *Comitatenses* LGs as 1,000 men, *Limitanei* LGs as 3,000 men and cohorts as 480 men. As noted before, the *Comitatenses* LG may have been larger and the *Aux.Pal.* Smaller, in addition to which the frontier forces were likely to have had less men than their paper strengths, but even then it is possible that with the addition of recruits (these were supernumerary) the units could still achieve their full combat compliment. However, the legislation that was issued immediately after the war suggests that the frontier armies were below their paper strengths (see later).
41. There were so many Federate settlements of Goths and Huns around the East Roman Empire that this is a minimum.
42. I.e. I agree with Greatrex (1993, p.2) that the Saracens had attempted to manoeuvre southwest of the main Roman army and had been defeated by the Romans. I disagree strongly with Shahid's conjecture (BAFIC 30) that the defeat of the Lakhmids could have resulted from the defection of the Christian element in al-Mundhir's army to the Roman side. On the contrary, there would have been a real danger that the Arab Federates in Roman service could have cooperated with the invader because it is clear that the Sheik whose position was secured by a contingent of Tanukhids could expect to have willing collaborators among the Federate Tanukhids posted precisely in the area through which his march took him. Since we hear nothing of such suggests two alternatives: the Tanukhids in Roman service stayed loyal; or, some of them cooperated but were surprised alongside with others because Areobindus' sudden movement took them all by surprise. He had brought his army from Amida to the scene of operations and it is quite possible that his army did not include any Arabs that could have betrayed him but rather Armenians whose knowledge of the area of operations was naturally better suited to the circumstances.
43. In one of my previous studies I interpreted this to mean that the Immortals divided themselves into two lines, the first and the ambushers, but I now consider this to be improbable on the grounds of the situation – the Persian aim was to win the war and not fight an inconclusive battle with a mere 10,000 horsemen. The first line would have consisted of most of the Persian horsemen while the Immortals would have been deployed behind these as two separate divisions on both flanks to outflank the Romans. The Persian plan was to fool the Romans into the belief that the Persians had deployed only a single cavalry line so that the Romans would

also deploy only a single cavalry line, which would probably be longer than the Persian line so that the Romans would think that their array would outflank the Persians on contact.
44. For an analysis of the *duces* of the eastern frontier from the fifth to the sixth century, see Greatrex (2007). He dates the change to the period before the year 450 and suggests that the creation of the *Dux* of Euphratesia (centred on Barbalissus) was done in response to Saracen raids.

Chapter 13

1. This chapter is based on the sources mentioned in the text, the PLRE (referrals to sources under each name) and notes. The main sources, however, are Olympiodorus and Sokrates.
2. These are noted by Bury.
3. Contrary to the consensus opinion among modern historians there is nothing incredible in the figure of 60,000 horsemen. For example, in the sixth century, in a somewhat similar situation, the East Romans bought the services of 60,000 Avars against the Slavs, and in the latter case the figure can be considered to be definitely accurate because the East Romans shipped the Avars across and could calculate the numbers of men and horses that they took across the river. See Syvänne (2004). In short, it is entirely plausible that 60,000 Hunnic horsemen came to assist John.

Appendix III

1. The following discussion of the defences of Cyrenaica is mostly based on Goodchild's articles, Vol. 1 and Roques (1987, 217–295). Contrary to the usual practice, the discussion also includes earlier and later elements in order to make it easier for the reader to get an overall picture of the situation in this area so that he or she can then consult this chapter later if needed. Note also that I have accepted the theories regarding the forming of the Marmaric/Austurian/Laguatan Confederacy, which Roques does not.
2. See esp. Roques (1987, 253ff.).
3. Obviously, the arrival of the Muslims from the east would change that.
4. He dates the invasions to the time period when the Huns invaded Asia in 395 and Tribigild began his revolt in 399.
5. PLRE 2 (Ioannes 2) dates this letter to the period 404/411, but I have here followed Jona Lendering's dating.
6. Note, however, that according to the letters 50 (dated to 404) and 123 (dated to 404) Synesius lived for two years in Egypt. If one were to assume that the dating of the letters is incorrect, then it is possible that Synesius fled to Egypt after the failed attack. However, according to the dating given by Jona Lendering, Synesius continued to perform curial functions in 402 (Letter 100) and it was only after that that he was able to devote his time to philosophy and other pursuits. Considering the situation mentioned above with Synesius' bravery, it seems very likely that Jona Lendering's dating is correct.
7. The PLRE 2 dates the victory to the period 404/412 and speculates that he was either *Dux Libyarum* or private landholder.
8. Synesius apparently withdrew from public service in 402 and lived as a 'philosopher' in Egypt during the years 403–404. The letters prove that he did not stop working for the benefit of his dearly beloved fatherland, but continued to send pleas to his friends in Constantinople in an effort to obtain tax relief or the sacking of some corrupt magistrates from office during the years 402–405. In addition to this, Synesius wrote several letters of recommendation on behalf of his friends in an effort to further their careers.
9. Synesius died in 413 as a broken man not because of the troubles he had faced (which were bad enough) but because he had lost his three sons.
10. See Catastasis.
11. Bury 1.218–9.

12. Welsby 2002, 16–17.
13. Welsby 2002, 17–19.
14. Welsby 2002, 17.
15. Jordanes *Rom*. 333/Priscus fr. 27.2 with comments of Blockley p.392; Milne, 100–101.
16. Priscus fr. 28.1–2; Milne 100–101; Welsby 2002, 19.
17. Based on information provided by Munro-Hay (Chapter 4.6) and Schipmann (64), but the conclusions drawn from their information are mine. It should also be noted that Schipmann considers the evidence for the conversion of Abakarib into Judaism to be uncertain.
18. Munro-Hay Chapter 4.6; Schippmann 64–65.

Index